Yamaha TDM850, TRX850 & XTZ750
Service and Repair Manual

by Matthew Coombs

Models covered
TDM850. 849 cc. 1991 to 1999
TRX850. 849 cc. 1996 to 1999
XTZ750. 749 cc. 1989 to 1995

(3540-288-11Y1)

© J H Haynes & Co. Ltd. 2000

A book in the **Haynes** Service and Repair Manual Series

ISBN 978 1 78521 011 2

Library of Congress Catalog Card Number 98-75325

British Library Cataloguing in Publication Data
A catalogue record for this book is available from the British Library.

J H Haynes & Co. Ltd.
Haynes North America, Inc

www.haynes.com

Contents

LIVING WITH YOUR YAMAHA

Introduction

Daily (pre-ride) checks

MAINTENANCE

Routine maintenance and servicing

Contents

REPAIRS AND OVERHAUL

Engine, transmission and associated systems

Chassis and bodywork components

Electrical system

Wiring diagrams

REFERENCE

Index

Yamaha
Musical instruments to Motorcycles

The Yamaha Motor Company

The Yamaha name can be traced back to 1889, when Torakusu Yamaha founded the Yamaha Organ Manufacturing Company. Such was the success of the company, that in 1897 it became Nippon Gakki Limited and manufactured a wide range of reed organs and pianos.

During World War II, Nippon Gakki's manufacturing base was utilised by the Japanese authorities to produce propellers and fuel tanks for their aviation industry. The end of the war brought about a huge public demand for low cost transport and many firms decided to utilise their obsolete aircraft tooling for the production of motorcycles. Nippon Gakki's first motorcycle went on sale in February 1955 and was named the 125 YA-1 Red Dragonfly. This machine was a copy of the German DKW RT125 motorcycle, featuring a single cylinder two-stroke engine with a four-speed gearbox. Due to the outstanding success of this model the motorcycle operation was separated from Nippon Gakki in July 1955 and the Yamaha Motor Company was formed.

The YA-1 also received acclaim by winning two of Japan's biggest road races, the Mt. Fuji Climbing race and the Asama Volcano race. The high level of public demand for the YA-1 led to the development of a whole series of two-stroke singles and twins.

Having made a large impact on their home market, Yamahas were exported to the USA in 1958 and to the UK in 1962. In the UK the signing of an Anglo-Japanese trade agreement during 1962 enabled the sale of Japanese lightweight motorcycles and scooters in Britain. At that time, competition between the many motorcycle producers in Japan had reduced numbers significantly and by the end of the sixties, only the big-four which are familiar with today remained.

Yamaha Europe was founded in 1968 and based in Holland. Although originally set up to market marine products, the Dutch base is now the official European Headquarters and distribution centre. Yamaha motorcycles are built at factories in Holland, Denmark, Norway, Italy, France, Spain and Portugal. Yamahas are imported into the UK by Yamaha Motor UK Ltd, formerly Mitsui Machinery Sales (UK) Ltd. Mitsui and Co. were originally a trading house, handling the shipping, distribution and marketing of Japanese products into western countries. Ultimately Mitsui Machinery Sales was formed to handle Yamaha motorcycles and outboard motors.

Based on the technology derived from its motorcycle operation, Yamaha have produced many other products, such as automobile and lightweight aircraft engines, marine engines and boats, generators, pumps, ATVs, snowmobiles, golf cars, industrial robots, lawnmowers, swimming pools and archery equipment.

The FS1-E - first bike of many sixteen year olds in the UK

Two-strokes first

Part of Yamaha's success was a whole string of innovations in the two-stroke world. Autolube engine lubrication, pressed steel monocoque frame, electric starting, torque induction, multi-ported engines, reed valves and power valves kept their two-strokes at the forefront of technology.

In the 1960s and 70s the two-stroke engined YAS3 125, YDS1 to YDS7 250 and YR5 350 formed the core of Yamaha's range. By the mid-70s they had been superseded by the RD (Race-Developed) 125, 250, and 350 range of two-stroke twins, featuring improved 7 port engines with reed valve induction. Braking was improved by the use of an hydraulic brake on the front wheel of DX models, instead of the drum arrangement used previously, and cast alloy wheels were available as an option on later RD models. The RD350 was replaced by the RD400 in 1976.

Running parallel with the RD twins was a range of single-cylinder two-strokes. Used in a variety of chassis types, the engine was used in the popular 50 cc FS1-E moped, the V50 to 90 step-thrus, RS100 and 125, YB100 and the DT trail range.

The air-cooled single and twin cylinder RD models were eventually replaced by the LC series in 1980, featuring liquid-cooled engines, radical new styling, spiral pattern cast wheels and cantilever rear suspension (Yamaha's Monoshock). Of all the LC models, the RD350LC, or RD350R as it was later known, has made the most impact in the market. Later models had YPVS (Yamaha Power Valve System) engines, another first for Yamaha - this was essentially a valve located in the exhaust ports which was electronically operated to alter port timing to achieve maximum power output. The RD500LC was the largest two-stroke made by Yamaha and differed from the other LCs by the use of its vee-four cylinder engine.

With the exception of the RD350R, now manufactured in Brazil, the LC range has been discontinued. Two-stroke engined models have given way to environmental pressure, and thus with a few exceptions, such as the TZR125 and TZR250, are used only in scooters and small capacity bikes.

The Four-strokes

Yamaha concentrated solely on two-stroke models until 1970 when the XS1 was produced, their first four-stroke motorcycle. It was perhaps Yamaha's success with two-strokes that postponed an earlier move into the four-stroke motorcycle market, although their work with Toyota during the

The distinctive paintwork and trim of the RD models

1960s had given them a sound base in four-stroke technology.

The XS1 had a 650 cc twin-cylinder SOHC engine and was later to become known as the XS650, appearing also in the popular SE custom form. Yamaha introduced a three cylinder 750 cc engine in 1976, fitted in a sport-tourer frame and called the XS750, TX750 in the USA. The XS750 established itself well in the sport tourer class and remained in production with very few changes until uprated to 850 cc in 1980.

Other four-strokes followed in 1976, with the introduction of the XS250/360/400 series twins. The XS range was strengthened in 1978 by the four-cylinder XS1100.

The 1980s saw a new family of four-strokes, the XJ550, 650, 750 and 900 Fours. Improvements over the XS range amounted to a slimmer DOHC engine unit due to the relocation of the alternator behind the cylinders, electronic ignition and uprated braking and suspension systems. Models were available mainly in standard trim, although custom-styled Maxims were produced especially for the US market. The XJ650T was the first model from Yamaha to have a turbo-charged engine. Although these early XJ models have now been discontinued, their roots live on in the XJ600S and XJ900S Diversion (Seca II) models.

The FZR prefix encompasses the pure sports Yamaha models. With the exception of the 16-valve FZR400 and FZR600 models, the FZ/FZR750 and FZR1000 used 20-valve engines, two exhaust valves and three inlet valves per cylinder. This concept was called Genesis and gave improved gas flow to the combustion chambers. Other features of the new engine were the use of down-draught carburetors and the engine's inclined angle in the frame, plus the change to liquid-cooling. Lightweight Deltabox design aluminium frames and uprated suspension improved the bikes's handling. The Genesis engine lives on in the YZF750 and 1000 models.

The vee-twin engine has been the mainstay of the XV Virago range. Since 1981 XVs have

The XS650 led the way for Yamaha's four-stroke range

Yamaha's XS750 was produced from 1976 to 1982 and then uprated to 850 cc

been produced in 535, 700, 750, 920, 1000 and 1100 engine sizes, all using the same basic air-cooled sohc vee-twin engine. Other uses of vee engines have been in the XZ550 of the early 1980s, the XVZ12 Venture and the mighty VMX-12 V-Max.

Anti-lock braking, engine management, catalytic converters and hub center steering are all features found on present-day models, ensuring that Yamaha remain at the forefront of technology.

The new parallel twins

Yamaha's four-stroke parallel twins date back to 1970 when the 653 cc XS1 was introduced. There followed a long line of the XS style twins during the 1970s, then after a few year's break from producing parallel twins, Yamaha released a revolutionary new twin cylinder engine.

The XTZ750 Super Ténéré was the first model to use Yamaha's five valve parallel twin engine. This new engine used the cylinder head technology developed from the FZR Genesis, and was inclined forward in the frame to allow the use of two downdraught carburettors. Engine height was reduced by using dry sump lubrication which does away

A new family of four-strokes was released in 1980 with the introduction of the XJ range

with the need for an oil reservoir at the bottom of the engine, and the engine was shortened by positioning the gearbox shafts one on top of the other rather than alongside each other. The engine was liquid-cooled and the vibration inherent in a parallel twin engine smoothed out with two balancer shafts.

Using suspension derived from Yamaha's YZ motocross bikes, a Deltabox swingarm and lightweight steel frame, plus twin pot brake calipers, the XTZ shared much with the works Yamahas used for the African rallies. Rider comfort was however not compromised, and the bike's large capacity fuel tank, dual front headlights and good instrumentation make it equally good for on-road use.

In 1991 Yamaha introduced a new class of motorcycle, the TDM, a cross between a dual-purpose bike and a sportsbike. It had the height and upright riding position of the Super Ténéré, but the frame, performance and comforts of a sport bike. To describe the TDM as 'standard' would be too bland – it's a definite do-everything all-rounder bike.

The TDM used the XTZ's five valve parallel twin engine but with revised bore and stroke to give it a 849 cc engine capacity. The engine was used as a stressed member in the Deltabox aluminium frame and unlike the XTZ's rear suspension linkage, the TDM's rear shock was mounted directly to the swingarm.

The TDM remained mainly unchanged until 1996 when significant mechanical and styling changes were made. To increase engine

The 1991 to 1995 style TDM

torque and produce an off-beat note, the 360° crank engine used previously was replaced by a 270° version, and a throttle position sensor was fitted to the carburettors for improved fuel and ignition control. The engine oil tank, previously sited on the frame below the seat, was incorporated in a separate compartment on top of the upper crankcase. A carburettor warmer system was fitted which routed engine coolant around the carburettor bodies.

Handling was improved by modifications to the Deltabox frame and larger diameter front forks. A curvaceous style new fairing completed the new look TDM. Since then the only significant changes to the TDM have

been an electric fuel pump instead of the vacuum type originally fitted, an electronic speedometer incorporating a digital clock/odometer, a fuel gauge and hazard turn signals.

Developed originally for the Japanese home market, the TRX850 went on sale in Europe in 1996 following a launch at the Paris show. The TRX used the 270° crank engine from the 1996 TDM fitted in a lightweight steel trellis frame which had a hint of Italian influence in its design. Although its engine, fuel and ignition systems are shared with the TDM, the distinctive frame, half fairing and split level seat give the TRX a true sportbike image.

Acknowledgements

Our thanks are due to Paul Branson Motorcycles of Yeovil, GT Motorcycles of Yeovil and Mr Searle of Weston-Super-Mare who supplied the machines featured in the illustrations throughout this manual.

We would also like to thank Mitsui Machinery Sales (UK) Ltd for permission to reproduce certain illustrations used in this manual, NGK Spark Plugs (UK) Ltd for supplying the colour spark plug condition photos and the Avon Rubber Company for supplying information on tyre fitting. Thanks are also due to Kel Edge for supplying the photograph of the XTZ750 on the rear cover.

About this Manual

The aim of this manual is to help you get the best value from your motorcycle. It can do so in several ways. It can help you decide what work must be done, even if you choose to have it done by a dealer; it provides information and procedures for routine maintenance and servicing; and it offers diagnostic and repair procedures to follow when trouble occurs.

We hope you use the manual to tackle the work yourself. For many simpler jobs, doing it yourself may be quicker than arranging an appointment to get the motorcycle into a dealer and making the trips to leave it and pick it up. More importantly, a lot of money can be saved by avoiding the expense the

shop must pass on to you to cover its labour and overhead costs. An added benefit is the sense of satisfaction and accomplishment that you feel after doing the job yourself.

References to the left or right side of the motorcycle assume you are sitting on the seat, facing forward.

We take great pride in the accuracy of information given in this manual, but motorcycle manufacturers make alterations and design changes during the production run of a particular motorcycle of which they do not inform us. No liability can be accepted by the authors or publishers for loss, damage or injury caused by any errors in, or omissions from, the information given.

Professional mechanics are trained in safe working procedures. However enthusiastic you may be about getting on with the job at hand, take the time to ensure that your safety is not put at risk. A moment's lack of attention can result in an accident, as can failure to observe simple precautions.

There will always be new ways of having accidents, and the following is not a comprehensive list of all dangers; it is intended rather to make you aware of the risks and to encourage a safe approach to all work you carry out on your bike.

Asbestos

● Certain friction, insulating, sealing and other products - such as brake pads, clutch linings, gaskets, etc. - contain asbestos. Extreme care must be taken to avoid inhalation of dust from such products since it is hazardous to health. If in doubt, assume that they do contain asbestos.

Fire

● Remember at all times that petrol is highly flammable. Never smoke or have any kind of naked flame around, when working on the vehicle. But the risk does not end there - a spark caused by an electrical short-circuit, by two metal surfaces contacting each other, by careless use of tools, or even by static electricity built up in your body under certain conditions, can ignite petrol vapour, which in a confined space is highly explosive. Never use petrol as a cleaning solvent. Use an approved safety solvent.

● Always disconnect the battery earth terminal before working on any part of the fuel or electrical system, and never risk spilling fuel on to a hot engine or exhaust.

● It is recommended that a fire extinguisher of a type suitable for fuel and electrical fires is kept handy in the garage or workplace at all times. Never try to extinguish a fuel or electrical fire with water.

Fumes

● Certain fumes are highly toxic and can quickly cause unconsciousness and even death if inhaled to any extent. Petrol vapour comes into this category, as do the vapours from certain solvents such as trichloro-ethylene. Any draining or pouring of such volatile fluids should be done in a well ventilated area.

● When using cleaning fluids and solvents, read the instructions carefully. Never use materials from unmarked containers - they may give off poisonous vapours.

● Never run the engine of a motor vehicle in an enclosed space such as a garage. Exhaust fumes contain carbon monoxide which is extremely poisonous; if you need to run the engine, always do so in the open air or at least have the rear of the vehicle outside the workplace.

The battery

● Never cause a spark, or allow a naked light near the vehicle's battery. It will normally be giving off a certain amount of hydrogen gas, which is highly explosive.

● Always disconnect the battery ground (earth) terminal before working on the fuel or electrical systems (except where noted).

● If possible, loosen the filler plugs or cover when charging the battery from an external source. Do not charge at an excessive rate or the battery may burst.

● Take care when topping up, cleaning or carrying the battery. The acid electrolyte, even when diluted, is very corrosive and should not be allowed to contact the eyes or skin. Always wear rubber gloves and goggles or a face shield. If you ever need to prepare electrolyte yourself, always add the acid slowly to the water; never add the water to the acid.

Electricity

● When using an electric power tool, inspection light etc., always ensure that the appliance is correctly connected to its plug and that, where necessary, it is properly grounded (earthed). Do not use such appliances in damp conditions and, again, beware of creating a spark or applying excessive heat in the vicinity of fuel or fuel vapour. Also ensure that the appliances meet national safety standards.

● A severe electric shock can result from touching certain parts of the electrical system, such as the spark plug wires (HT leads), when the engine is running or being cranked, particularly if components are damp or the insulation is defective. Where an electronic ignition system is used, the secondary (HT) voltage is much higher and could prove fatal.

Remember...

✗ **Don't** start the engine without first ascertaining that the transmission is in neutral.

✗ **Don't** suddenly remove the pressure cap from a hot cooling system - cover it with a cloth and release the pressure gradually first, or you may get scalded by escaping coolant.

✗ **Don't** attempt to drain oil until you are sure it has cooled sufficiently to avoid scalding you.

✗ **Don't** grasp any part of the engine or exhaust system without first ascertaining that it is cool enough not to burn you.

✗ **Don't** allow brake fluid or antifreeze to contact the machine's paintwork or plastic components.

✗ **Don't** siphon toxic liquids such as fuel, hydraulic fluid or antifreeze by mouth, or allow them to remain on your skin.

✗ **Don't** inhale dust - it may be injurious to health (see Asbestos heading).

✗ **Don't** allow any spilled oil or grease to remain on the floor - wipe it up right away, before someone slips on it.

✗ **Don't** use ill-fitting spanners or other tools which may slip and cause injury.

✗ **Don't** lift a heavy component which may be beyond your capability - get assistance.

✗ **Don't** rush to finish a job or take unverified short cuts.

✗ **Don't** allow children or animals in or around an unattended vehicle.

✗ **Don't** inflate a tyre above the recommended pressure. Apart from overstressing the carcass, in extreme cases the tyre may blow off forcibly.

✔ **Do** ensure that the machine is supported securely at all times. This is especially important when the machine is blocked up to aid wheel or fork removal.

✔ **Do** take care when attempting to loosen a stubborn nut or bolt. It is generally better to pull on a spanner, rather than push, so that if you slip, you fall away from the machine rather than onto it.

✔ **Do** wear eye protection when using power tools such as drill, sander, bench grinder etc.

✔ **Do** use a barrier cream on your hands prior to undertaking dirty jobs - it will protect your skin from infection as well as making the dirt easier to remove afterwards; but make sure your hands aren't left slippery. Note that long-term contact with used engine oil can be a health hazard.

✔ **Do** keep loose clothing (cuffs, ties etc. and long hair) well out of the way of moving mechanical parts.

✔ **Do** remove rings, wristwatch etc., before working on the vehicle - especially the electrical system.

✔ **Do** keep your work area tidy - it is only too easy to fall over articles left lying around.

✔ **Do** exercise caution when compressing springs for removal or installation. Ensure that the tension is applied and released in a controlled manner, using suitable tools which preclude the possibility of the spring escaping violently.

✔ **Do** ensure that any lifting tackle used has a safe working load rating adequate for the job.

✔ **Do** get someone to check periodically that all is well, when working alone on the vehicle.

✔ **Do** carry out work in a logical sequence and check that everything is correctly assembled and tightened afterwards.

✔ **Do** remember that your vehicle's safety affects that of yourself and others. If in doubt on any point, get professional advice.

● If in spite of following these precautions, you are unfortunate enough to injure yourself, seek medical attention as soon as possible.

Frame and engine numbers

The frame serial number is stamped into the right side of the steering head. The engine number is stamped into the top of the crankcase on the right-hand side of the engine. Both of these numbers should be recorded and kept in a safe place so they can be furnished to law enforcement officials in the event of a theft. There is also a carburettor identification number on the intake side of each carburettor body, and a colour code label on the top of the rear fender under the passenger seat. The colour code label may also contain the bike's production year and model code.

The frame serial number, engine serial number, carburettor identification number and colour code should also be kept in a handy place (such as with your driver's licence) so they are always available when purchasing or ordering parts for your machine.

The procedures in this manual identify the bikes by model type (eg TDM) and if necessary by production year. Note that the production year does not necessarily correspond with the year of sale or registration.

The model code number is very useful when ordering parts for your bike and is linked to the production year as shown in the accompanying table. There should be a sticker on the bike's rear frame section (usually visible once the seat is lifted) which gives the model code number (eg 4TX4, meaning a 1999 TDM), the Yamaha production code number, and a letter indicating the colour code. The frame and engine numbers can also be used to establish the production year and model code, although these are not available for post-1995 models. The accompanying table gives model identification data for models available in the UK market.

Buying spare parts

Once you have found all the identification numbers, record them for reference when buying parts. Since the manufacturers change specifications, parts and vendors (companies that manufacture various components on the machine), providing the ID numbers is the only way to be reasonably sure that you are buying the correct parts.

Whenever possible, take the worn part to the dealer so direct comparison with the new component can be made. Along the trail from the manufacturer to the parts shelf, there are numerous places that the part can end up with the wrong number or be listed incorrectly.

The two places to purchase new parts for your motorcycle - the accessory store and the franchised dealer - differ in the type of parts they carry. While dealers can obtain virtually every part for your motorcycle, the accessory dealer is usually limited to normal high wear items such as shock absorbers, tune-up parts, various engine gaskets, cables, chains,

Model type	Prod Yr	Model code	Frame No.	Engine No.
TDM850	1991	3VD1	000101 on	000101 on
	1992	3VD4	022101 on	022101 on
	1993	3VD5	040101 on	040101 on
	1994	3VD7	060101 on	060101 on
	1995	3VD9	079101 on	079101 on
	1996	4TX1	not available	
	1997	4TX2	not available	
	1998	4TX3	not available	
	1999	4TX4	not available	
TRX850	1996	4UN1	000101 on	000101 on
	1997	4UN3	not available	
	1998/9	4UN4	not available	
XTZ750	1989	3LD1	000101 on	000101 on
	1990	3LD3	032101 on	032101 on
	1991	3LD4	048101 on	048101 on
	1992	3LD5	063101 on	063101 on
	1993	3LD6	079101 on	079101 on
	1994	3LD7	092101 on	092101 on
	1995	3LD8	100101 on	100101 on

The engine number is stamped into the top of the crankcase on the right-hand side of the engine.

The frame number is stamped on the right-hand side of the steering head

brake parts, etc. Rarely will an accessory outlet have major suspension components, cylinders, transmission gears, or cases.

Used parts can be obtained for roughly half the price of new ones, but you can't always be sure of what you're getting. Once again, take your worn part to the breaker's yard for direct comparison.

Whether buying new, used or rebuilt parts, the best course is to deal directly with someone who specialises in parts for your particular make.

Note: *The daily (pre-ride) checks outlined in the owner's manual covers those items which should be inspected on a daily basis.*

1 Engine/transmission oil level check

Level check procedure

✔ Position the bike upright (not on its sidestand) on a level surface.
✔ On 1991 to 1995 TDM models, remove the seat (see Chapter 8). On XTZ models, remove the right-hand side cover (see Chapter 8).
✔ Check the oil level as shown in the appropriate photo sequence and top up if necessary.
✔ Now start the engine and warm it up to normal operating temperature.
Caution: Do not run the engine in an enclosed space such as a garage or workshop.
✔ With the bike still in an upright position, let it idle for a further 10 seconds then stop the engine.
✔ Taking care to avoid scalding your hands, recheck the oil level and top up if necessary.

The correct oil

● Modern, high-revving engines place great demands on their oil. It is very important that the correct oil for your bike is used.
● Always top up with a good quality oil of the specified type and viscosity and do not overfill the oil tank.

Caution: Yamaha advise against using chemical oil additives, or oils with a grade of SH/CD or higher, or oils labelled ENERGY CONSERVING II. Such additives or oils could cause clutch slip.

Oil type	API grade SE, SF or SG
Oil viscosity	SAE 10W30 or 10W40

Bike care:

● If you have to add oil frequently, you should check whether you have any oil leaks. If there is no sign of oil leakage from the joints and gaskets the engine could be burning oil (see *Fault Finding*).

TDM850 (1991 to 1995) and XTZ750 models

1 On TDM models, remove the seat (see Chapter 8) to access the oil filler cap (arrowed).

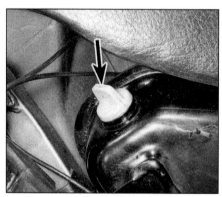

2 On XTZ models, remove the right-hand side cover (see Chapter 8) to access the oil filler cap (arrowed).

3 Unscrew the oil filler cap from the oil tank. The dipstick is integral with the oil filler cap, and is used to check the engine oil level. Check the condition of the cap O-ring and renew it if damaged or deteriorated.

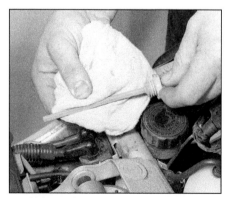

4 Using a clean rag or paper towel, wipe all oil from the dipstick. Insert the clean dipstick back into the tank, but do not screw it in.

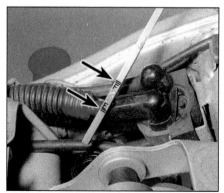

5 Remove the dipstick and observe the level of the oil, which should be somewhere in between the F (full) and E (empty) level lines (arrowed).

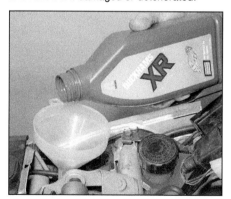

6 If the level is below the E line, top the oil tank up with the recommended grade and type of oil, to bring the level up to the F line on the dipstick. Do not overfill.

TDM850 (1996-on) and TRX models

7 Wipe the oil level window (arrowed) in the oil tank so that it is clean.

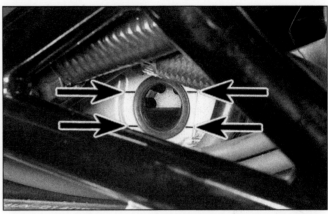

8 With the motorcycle held vertical, the oil level should lie between the upper and lower level lines marked on the oil tank (arrowed).

9 If the level is below the lower line, remove the filler cap (arrowed) from the top of the oil tank.

10 Top the tank up with the recommended grade and type of oil, to bring the level up to the upper line on the window.

2 Brake fluid level checks

Warning: Brake hydraulic fluid can harm your eyes and damage painted surfaces, so use extreme caution when handling and pouring it and cover surrounding surfaces with rag. Do not use fluid that has been standing open for some time, as it absorbs moisture from the air which can cause a dangerous loss of braking effectiveness.

Before you start:

✔ Support the motorcycle in an upright position, using an auxiliary stand if required.

✔ When checking the front brake fluid level turn the handlebars until the top of the master cylinder is as level as possible.

✔ On XTZ models remove the right-hand side cover to view the rear brake fluid level (see Chapter 8).

✔ Make sure you have the correct hydraulic fluid. DOT 4 is recommended.

✔ Wrap a rag around the reservoir being worked on to ensure that any spillage does not come into contact with painted surfaces.

Bike care:

● The fluid in the front and rear brake master cylinder reservoirs will drop slightly as the brake pads wear down.

● If any fluid reservoir requires repeated topping-up this is an indication of an hydraulic leak somewhere in the system, which should be investigated immediately.

● Check for signs of fluid leakage from the hydraulic hoses and components - if found, rectify immediately.

● Check the operation of both brakes before taking the machine on the road; if there is evidence of air in the system (spongy feel to lever or pedal), it must be bled as described in Chapter 7.

Front brake fluid level

1 On TDM and XTZ models, the front brake fluid level is visible through the window in the reservoir body - it must be above the LOWER level line (arrowed).

2 On TRX models, the front brake fluid level is visible through the reservoir body - it must be between the UPPER and LOWER level lines (arrowed).

3 On TDM and XTZ models, if the level is below the LOWER level line, remove the two reservoir cover screws and remove the cover and the diaphragm.

4 On TRX models, if the level is below the LOWER level line, remove the reservoir cap clamp screw (arrowed), then unscrew the cap and remove the diaphragm plate and the diaphragm.

5 Top up with new clean hydraulic fluid of the recommended type, until the level is above the LOWER level line. Take care to avoid spills (see **Warning** above).

6 Ensure that the diaphragm is correctly seated before installing the plate (TRX models) and cover or cap.

Rear brake fluid level

7 On TDM models, the rear brake fluid level is visible by looking up under the seat from the left-hand side of the rear wheel - it must be above LOWER level line (arrowed).

8 On TRX models, the rear brake fluid level is visible through the reservoir body - it must be above LOWER level line (arrowed).

9 On XTZ models, remove the right-hand side cover (see Chapter 8) - the rear brake fluid level is visible through the reservoir body - it must be above LOWER level line (arrowed).

10 If topping up is required, on TDM models remove the seat and on TRX models remove the side covers (see Chapter 8). On TRX and XTZ models, remove the cap clamp, then on TRX models support the reservoir or refit the screw. Unscrew the reservoir cap (arrowed) and remove the plate and diaphragm.

11 Top up with new clean hydraulic fluid of the recommended type, until the level is above the lower mark. Take care to avoid spills (see **Warning** above).

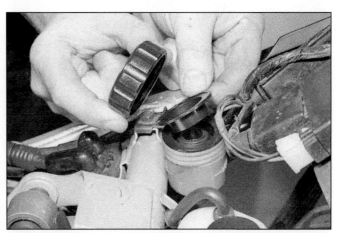

12 Ensure that the diaphragm is correctly seated before installing the plate and cap. Tighten the cap securely. On TRX and XTZ models, fit the cap clamp.

3 Coolant level check

> ⚠️ **Warning: DO NOT remove the radiator pressure cap to add coolant. Topping up is done via the coolant reservoir tank filler. DO NOT leave open containers of coolant about, as it is poisonous.**

Before you start:

✔ Make sure you have a supply of coolant available - a mixture of 50% distilled water and 50% corrosion inhibited ethylene glycol anti-freeze is needed. **Note:** *Yamaha specify that soft tap water can be used, but NOT hard water. If in doubt, boil the water first or use only distilled water.*

✔ Always check the coolant level when the engine is cold.

✔ Support the motorcycle in an upright position, using an auxiliary stand if required, whilst checking the level. Make sure the motorcycle is on level ground.

Bike care:

● Use only the specified coolant mixture. It is important that anti-freeze is used in the system all year round, and not just in the winter. Do not top the system up using only water, as the system will become too diluted.

● Do not overfill the reservoir tank. If the coolant is significantly above the UPPER level line at any time, the surplus should be siphoned or drained off to prevent the possibility of it being expelled out of the breather hose.

● If the coolant level falls steadily, check the system for leaks (see Chapter 1). If no leaks are found and the level continues to fall, it is recommended that the machine is taken to a Yamaha dealer for a pressure test.

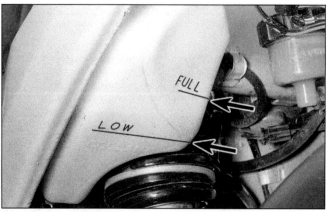

1 On TDM models, the coolant reservoir FULL and LOW level lines are visible by looking up under the seat from the left-hand side of the rear wheel. The coolant level lines (arrowed) are marked on the reservoir.

2 On TRX models, remove the seat (see Chapter 8). The coolant FULL and LOW level lines (arrowed) are marked on the inside of the reservoir.

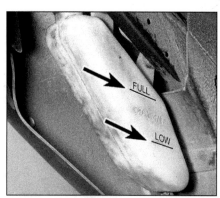

3 On XTZ models, the coolant reservoir FULL and LOW level lines are visible by looking up under the mudguard from the right-hand side of the rear wheel. The coolant level lines (arrowed) are marked on the reservoir.

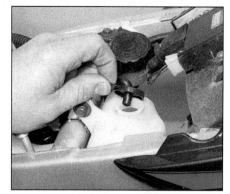

4 If the coolant level is not between the UPPER and LOWER markings, on TDM models remove the seat and on XTZ models the left-hand side cover (see Chapter 8). Remove the reservoir filler cap.

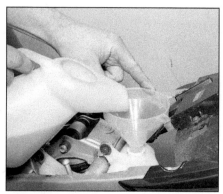

5 Top the coolant level up with the recommended coolant mixture. Fit the cap securely, then install the seat, and on XTZ models the side cover (see Chapter 8).

4 Tyre checks

The correct pressures:
● The tyres must be checked when **cold**, not immediately after riding. Note that low tyre pressures may cause the tyre to slip on the rim or come off. High tyre pressures will cause abnormal tread wear and unsafe handling.
● Use an accurate pressure gauge.
● Proper air pressure will increase tyre life and provide maximum stability and ride comfort.

Tyre care:
● Check the tyres carefully for cuts, tears, embedded nails or other sharp objects and excessive wear. Operation of the motorcycle with excessively worn tyres is extremely hazardous, as traction and handling are directly affected.
● Check the condition of the tyre valve and ensure the dust cap is in place.
● Pick out any stones or nails which may have become embedded in the tyre tread. If left, they will eventually penetrate through the casing and cause a puncture.
● If tyre damage is apparent, or unexplained loss of pressure is experienced, seek the advice of a tyre fitting specialist without delay.

Loading/speed	Front	Rear
1991 to 1995 TDM models Rider only Rider and passenger, or high speed	28 psi (2.0 Bar) 28 psi (2.0 Bar)	33 psi (2.25 Bar) 36 psi (2.50 Bar)
1996-on TDM models All loads/speeds	33 psi (2.25 Bar)	40 psi (2.75 Bar)
TRX models Rider only Rider and passenger, or high speed	33 psi (2.25 Bar) 36 psi (2.50 Bar)	36 psi (2.50 Bar) 41 psi (2.80 Bar)
XTZ models Rider only Rider and passenger, or high speed	33 psi (2.25 Bar) 33 psi (2.25 Bar)	33 psi (2.25 Bar) 36 psi (2.50 Bar)

Tyre tread depth:
● At the time of writing UK law requires that tread depth must be at least 1 mm over 3/4 of the tread breadth all the way around the tyre, with no bald patches. Many riders, however, consider a minimum of 2 mm tread depth to be a safer limit. Yamaha recommend a minimum of 1.5 mm on the front and 2 mm on the rear.

● Many tyres now incorporate wear indicators in the tread. Identify the triangular pointer on the tyre sidewall to locate the indicator bar and replace the tyre if the tread has worn down to the bar.

1 Check the tyre pressures when the tyres are cold and keep them properly inflated.

2 Measure tread depth at the centre of the tyre using a tread depth gauge.

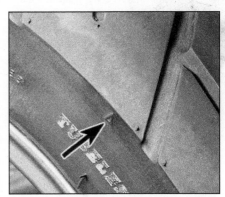

3 Tyre tread wear indicator bar location marking (usually either an arrow, a triangle or the letters TWI) on the sidewall (arrowed).

5 Suspension, steering and final drive check

Suspension and steering:
● Check that the front and rear suspension operates smoothly without binding.
● Check that the rear suspension is adjusted as required.
● Check that the steering moves smoothly from lock-to-lock.

Final drive:
● Check that the drive chain slack isn't excessive, and adjust if necessary (see Chapter 1).
● If the chain looks dry, lubricate it (see Chapter 1).

6 Legal and safety checks

Lighting and signalling:
● Take a minute to check that the headlight, auxiliary light, tail light, brake light, instrument lights and turn signals all work correctly.
● Check that the horn sounds when the switch is operated.
● A working speedometer graduated in mph is a statutory requirement in the UK.

Safety:
● Check that the throttle grip rotates smoothly and snaps shut when released, in all steering positions. Also check for the correct amount of freeplay (see Chapter 1).
● Check that the engine shuts off when the kill switch is operated.
● Check that sidestand return spring holds the stand securely up when retracted.

Fuel:
● This may seem obvious, but check that you have enough fuel to complete your journey. If you notice signs of fuel leakage - rectify the cause immediately.
● Ensure you use the correct grade fuel - unleaded, minimum 91 RON (Research Octane Number) is recommended.

Chapter 1
Routine maintenance and Servicing

Contents

Degrees of difficulty

Easy, suitable for novice with little experience	**Fairly easy,** suitable for beginner with some experience	**Fairly difficult,** suitable for competent DIY mechanic	**Difficult,** suitable for experienced DIY mechanic	**Very difficult,** suitable for expert DIY or professional 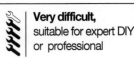

Specifications

Engine

Cylinder identification	No. 1 (left-hand), no. 2 (right-hand)
Spark plugs	
Type	NGK DPR8EA-9 or Nippondenso X24EPR-U9
Electrode gap	0.8 to 0.9 mm
Engine idle speed	
TDM 1991 to 1995 models	1000 to 1200 rpm
TDM 1996-on models and all TRX models	1050 to 1250 rpm
XTZ models	1100 to 1200 rpm
Carburettor synchronisation – intake vacuum	
TDM 1991 to 1995 models	250 to 270 mm Hg
TDM 1996-on models	270 to 290 mm Hg
TRX and XTZ models	240 to 260 mm Hg
Carburettor synchronisation – max. difference between carburettors	
TDM 1991 to 1995 models and all XTZ models	10 mm Hg
TDM 1996-on models and all TRX models	5 mm Hg
Valve clearances (COLD engine)	
Inlet valves	0.15 to 0.20 mm
Exhaust valves	0.25 to 0.30 mm
Cylinder compression	
TDM 1991 to 1995 models	
Standard	152 psi (10.5 Bar)
Maximum	158 psi (10.9 Bar)
Minimum	146 psi (10.1 Bar)
Max. difference between cylinders	14.5 psi (1.0 Bar)
TDM 1996-on models and all TRX models	
Standard	175 psi (12.0 Bar)
Maximum	182 psi (12.5 Bar)
Minimum	145 psi (10.0 Bar)
Maximum difference between cylinders	14.5 psi (1.0 Bar)
XTZ models	
Standard	138 psi (9.5 Bar)
Maximum	144 psi (9.9 Bar)
Minimum	132 psi (9.1 Bar)
Maximum difference between cylinders	14.5 psi (1.0 Bar)

Cycle parts

Drive chain slack	
TDM models	40 to 50 mm
TRX models	20 to 30 mm
XTZ models	25 to 35 mm
Front brake lever freeplay (XTZ models)	2 to 5 mm
Rear brake pedal height (see text)	
TDM 1991 to 1995 models	17 to 41 mm
TDM 1996-on models	29 mm
TRX models	57 mm
XTZ models	5 to 25 mm
Brake pad friction material wear limit	
TDM and TRX models	0.5 mm
XTZ models	1.5 mm
Clutch cable freeplay	
TDM 1991 to 1995 models	8 to 12 mm
All other models	10 to 15 mm
Throttle cable freeplay	
TRX models	3 to 7 mm
All other models	3 to 5 mm
Tyre pressures (cold) and minimum tread depth	see Daily (pre-ride) checks
Swingarm – XTZ models	
Side clearance	0.4 to 0.7 mm
Bearing spacer length (right-hand)	90.95 to 91.10 mm
Bearing spacer length (left-hand)	80.95 to 81.10 mm
Washer thickness	1.9 to 2.0 mm

Recommended lubricants and fluids

Engine/transmission oil type . . . . API grade SE, SF or SG motor oil*
Engine/transmission oil viscosity . . . . SAE 10W30 or 10W40
Engine/transmission oil capacity
   TDM 1991 to 1995 models and all XTZ models
      Oil change . . . . 3.8 litres
      Oil and filter change . . . . 3.9 litres
      Following engine overhaul – dry engine, new filter . . . . 4.2 litres
   TDM 1996-on models and all TRX models
      Oil change . . . . 3.5 litres
      Oil and filter change . . . . 3.6 litres
      Following engine overhaul – dry engine, new filter . . . . 4.2 litres
Coolant type . . . . 50% distilled water, 50% corrosion-inhibited ethylene glycol anti-freeze. **Note:** *Yamaha specify that soft tap water can be used, but NOT hard water. If in doubt, boil the water first or use only distilled water.*
Coolant capacity
   Radiator and engine . . . . 1.7 litres
   Reservoir
      XTZ models . . . . 0.45 litre
      All other models . . . . 0.3 litre
Brake fluid . . . . DOT 4
Front fork oil type, capacity and level . . . . see Chapter 6 Specifications
Drive chain . . . . SAE 30 to 50W engine oil or chain lubricant suitable for O-ring chains
Steering head bearings . . . . Lithium-based multi-purpose grease
Swingarm pivot bearings – TDM and TRX models . . . . Molybdenum disulphide grease
Swingarm pivot bearings – XTZ models . . . . Lithium-based multi-purpose grease
Suspension linkage bearings – TRX models . . . . Molybdenum disulphide grease
Suspension linkage bearings – XTZ models . . . . Lithium-based multi-purpose grease
Wheel bearings and grease seal lips . . . . Lithium-based multi-purpose grease
Gearchange lever/clutch lever/front brake lever/rear brake
pedal/sidestand pivots . . . . 10W30 motor oil
Cables . . . . 10W30 motor oil
Throttle grip . . . . Multi-purpose grease or dry film lubricant

*Yamaha advise against using chemical oil additives, or oils with a grade of SH/CD or higher, or oils labelled ENERGY CONSERVING II. Such additives or oils could cause clutch slip.

Torque settings

Rear axle nut
   TDM 1991 to 1995 models . . . . 105 Nm
   TDM 1996-on models . . . . 107 Nm
   TRX models . . . . 117 Nm
   XTZ models . . . . 90 Nm
Rear brake caliper bracket bolt (TDM models) . . . . 35 Nm
Crankcase oil drain plug . . . . 35 Nm
Oil filter housing drain plug . . . . 30 Nm
Oil filter cover bolts . . . . 10 Nm
Steering head bearing adjuster nut (using service tool)
   1991 to 1995 TDM models
      Initial setting . . . . 52 Nm
      Final setting . . . . 3 Nm
   1996-on TDM models and all TRX models
      Initial setting . . . . 48 Nm
      Final setting . . . . 16 Nm
   XTZ models
      Initial setting . . . . 38 Nm
      Final setting . . . . 6 Nm
Steering stem nut
   1991 to 1995 TDM models . . . . 110 Nm
   1996-on TDM models . . . . 108 Nm
   TRX models . . . . 110 Nm
Steering stem bolt (XTZ models) . . . . 80 Nm
Fork clamp bolts (top yoke) . . . . 23 Nm
Cooling system drain plugs . . . . 10 Nm
Oil gallery bolt . . . . 10 Nm

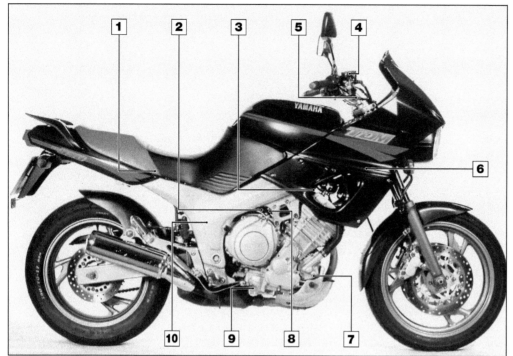

TDM

1 Rear brake fluid reservoir
2 Oil level window (1996-on)
3 Oil filler cap (1996-on)
4 Front brake fluid reservoir
5 Throttle cable upper adjuster
6 Radiator pressure cap
7 Coolant drain plug on water pump
8 Clutch cable lower adjuster
9 Oil filter and filter housing drain plug
10 Battery (1996-on)

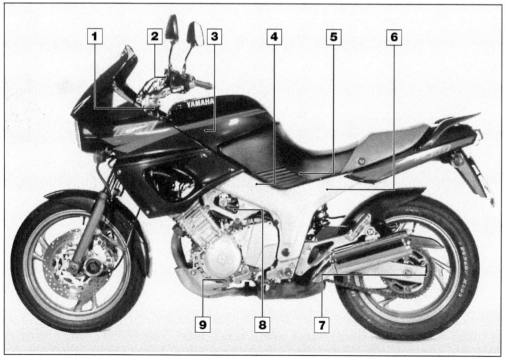

TDM

1 Steering head bearings
2 Clutch cable upper adjuster
3 Air filter
4 Battery (1991 to 1995)
5 Oil filler cap/dipstick (1991 to 1995)
6 Coolant reservoir
7 Drive chain adjuster
8 Idle speed adjuster
9 Oil drain plug

TRX

1 Coolant reservoir
2 Rear brake fluid reservoir
3 Oil level window
4 Oil filler cap
5 Front brake fluid reservoir
6 Throttle cable upper adjuster
7 Radiator pressure cap
8 Coolant drain plug on water pump
9 Clutch cable lower adjuster
10 Oil filter and filter housing drain plug

TRX

1 Clutch cable upper adjuster
2 Steering head bearing adjuster
3 Air filter
4 Idle speed adjuster
5 Battery
6 Drive chain adjuster
7 Oil drain plug

XTZ

1 Rear brake fluid reservoir
2 Oil filler cap/dipstick
3 Throttle cable upper adjuster
4 Front brake fluid reservoir
5 Steering head bearing adjuster
6 Coolant drain plug on water pump
7 Clutch cable lower adjuster
8 Oil filter and filter housing drain plug

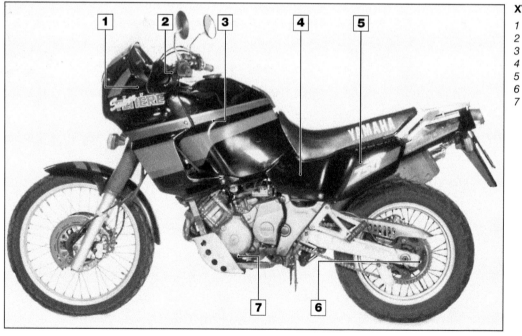

XTZ

1 Radiator pressure cap
2 Clutch cable upper adjuster
3 Air filter
4 Battery
5 Coolant reservoir
6 Drive chain adjuster
7 Oil drain plug

Note: *The daily (pre-ride) checks outlined in the owner's manual covers those items which should be inspected on a daily basis. Always perform the pre-ride inspection at every maintenance interval (in addition to the procedures listed). The intervals listed below are the intervals recommended by the manufacturer for each particular operation during the model years covered in this manual. Your owner's manual may have different intervals for your model.*

Daily (pre-ride)

☐ See *'Daily (pre-ride) checks'* at the beginning of this manual.

After the initial 600 miles (1000 km)

Note: *This check is usually performed by a Yamaha dealer after the first 600 miles (1000 km) from new. Thereafter, maintenance is carried out according to the following intervals of the schedule.*

Every 300 miles (500 km)

☐ Check, adjust and lubricate the drive chain (Section 1)

Every 4000 miles (6000 km) or 6 months (whichever comes sooner)

☐ Check the spark plug gaps and plug condition (Section 2)
☐ Check and adjust the idle speed (Section 3)
☐ Check/adjust the carburettor synchronisation (Section 4)
☐ Clean and check the air filter element (Section 5)
☐ Check the fuel system and hoses (Section 6)
☐ Change the engine oil (Section 7)
☐ Check the brake pads (Section 8)
☐ Check the brake system and brake light switch operation (Section 9)
☐ Check and adjust the clutch (Section 10)
☐ Check the battery (Section 11)
☐ Check the condition of the wheels and tyres (Section 12)
☐ Check the wheel bearings (Section 13)
☐ Check the sidestand (Section 14)
☐ Check the tightness of all nuts, bolts and fasteners (Section 15)
☐ Check the cooling system (Section 16)
☐ Check and adjust the throttle and choke cables (Section 17)
☐ Lubricate the clutch/gearshift/brake lever/brake pedal/sidestand pivots and the throttle/choke/clutch cables (Section 18)

Every 4000 miles (6000 km) or 6 months (whichever comes sooner) (continued)

☐ Re-grease the swingarm and suspension linkage bearings (XTZ models) (Section 19).
☐ Check the suspension (Section 20)
☐ Check and adjust the steering head bearings (Section 21)

Every 8000 miles (12,000 km) or 12 months (whichever comes sooner)

Carry out all the items under the 4000 mile (6000 km) check, plus the following:
☐ Change the engine oil and filter (Section 22)
☐ Renew the fuel filter (1999 TDM models) (Section 23)

Every 16,000 miles (24,000 km) or two years (whichever comes sooner)

Carry out all the items under the 8000 mile (12,000 km) check, plus the following:
☐ Re-grease the swingarm and suspension linkage bearings (TDM and TRX models) (Section 24).
☐ Re-grease the steering head bearings (Section 25).
☐ Change the brake fluid and renew the brake master cylinder and caliper seals (see Section 26)
☐ Renew the coolant (Section 27)

Every 28,000 miles (42,000 km)

Carry out all the items under the 4000 mile (6000 km) check, plus the following:
☐ Check and adjust the valve clearances (Section 28)

Every four years

☐ Renew the brake hoses (Section 29)

Non-scheduled maintenance

☐ Check and adjust the headlight aim (Section 30)
☐ Check the cylinder compression (Section 31)
☐ Check the engine oil pressure (see Section 32)
☐ Renew the fuel hoses (Section 33)
☐ Change the front fork oil (Section 34)

1 This Chapter is designed to help the home mechanic maintain his/her motorcycle for safety, economy, long life and peak performance.

2 Deciding where to start or plug into the routine maintenance schedule depends on several factors. If the warranty period on your motorcycle has just expired, and if it has been maintained according to the warranty standards, you may want to pick up routine maintenance as it coincides with the next mileage or calendar interval. If you have owned the machine for some time but have never performed any maintenance on it, then you may want to start at the nearest interval and include some additional procedures to ensure that nothing important is overlooked. If you have just had a major engine overhaul, then you may want to start the maintenance routine from the beginning. If you have a used machine and have no knowledge of its history or maintenance record, you may desire to combine all the checks into one large service initially and then settle into the maintenance schedule prescribed.

3 Before beginning any maintenance or repair, the machine should be cleaned thoroughly, especially around the oil filter, spark plugs, valve cover, side panels, carburettors, etc. Cleaning will help ensure that dirt does not contaminate the engine and will allow you to detect wear and damage that could otherwise easily go unnoticed.

4 Certain maintenance information is sometimes printed on decals attached to the motorcycle. If the information on the decals differs from that included here, use the information on the decal.

Every 300 miles (500 km)

1   Drive chain and sprockets – check, adjustment and lubrication

Check

1 A neglected drive chain won't last long and can quickly damage the sprockets. Routine chain adjustment and lubrication isn't difficult and will ensure maximum chain and sprocket life.

2 To check the chain, place the bike on its sidestand and shift the transmission into neutral.

3 Push up on the bottom run of the chain and measure the slack midway between the two sprockets, then compare your measurement to that listed in this Chapter's Specifications **(see illustration)**. As the chain stretches with wear, adjustment will periodically be necessary (see below). Since the chain will rarely wear evenly, roll the bike forwards so that another section of chain can be checked; do this several times to check the entire length of chain and position the tightest spot midway between the sprockets on the bottom run of the chain.

4 In some cases where lubrication has been neglected, corrosion and galling may cause the links to bind and kink, which effectively shortens the chain's length. Such links should be thoroughly cleaned and worked free. If the chain is tight between the sprockets, rusty or kinked, it's time to renew it. If you find a tight area, mark it with felt pen or paint, and repeat the measurement after the bike has been ridden. If the chain's still tight in the same area, it may be damaged or worn. Because a tight or kinked chain can damage the transmission countershaft bearing, it's a good idea to renew it.

5 Check the entire length of the chain for damaged rollers, loose links and pins, and missing O-rings and renew it if damage is found. **Note:** *Never install a new chain on old sprockets, and never use the old chain if you install new sprockets – renew the chain and sprockets as a set.*

6 If you suspect that the chain may be worn out, you can measure a 10-link length and compare it with the wear limit. This requires the chain to be removed from the bike and first cleaned (see Chapter 6).

7 Remove the front sprocket cover (see Chapter 6). Check the teeth on the engine sprocket and the rear wheel sprocket for wear **(see illustration)**.

8 Inspect the drive chain slider on the swingarm for excessive wear and renew it if worn (see Chapter 6).

Adjustment

9 Rotate the rear wheel until the chain is positioned with the tightest point at the centre of its bottom run, then place the machine on its sidestand. On TDM models, slacken the brake caliper bracket bolt on the top of the swingarm **(see illustration)**.

10 Where fitted, remove the split pin from the rear axle nut. Slacken the nut **(see illustrations)**.

1.3 Push up on the chain and measure the slack

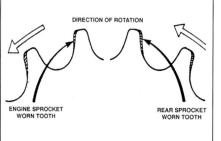

1.7 Check the sprockets in the areas indicated to see if they are worn excessively

1.9 On TDM models, slacken the bolt (arrowed)

1.10a Rear axle nut (arrowed) – TDM models

1.10b Rear axle nut (arrowed) – TRX models

1.11a On TDM and XTZ models, slacken the locknut (arrowed) . . .

1.11b . . . and turn the adjuster as required

1.11c On TRX models, slacken the locknut (A) and turn the adjuster (B) as required

11 Slacken the adjuster locknut on each side of the swingarm, then turn the adjusters evenly until the amount of freeplay specified at the beginning of the Chapter is obtained at the centre of the bottom run of the chain **(see illustrations)**. Following chain adjustment, check that each chain adjustment marker is in the same position in relation to the marks on the swingarm **(see illustrations)**. It is important each adjuster aligns with the same notch; if not, the rear wheel will be out of alignment with the front. **Note:** *If you need to check wheel alignment refer to Chapter 7.*

12 If there is a discrepancy in the chain adjuster positions, adjust one of them so that its position is exactly the same as the other. Check the chain freeplay as described above and readjust if necessary.

13 Tighten the axle nut to the torque setting specified at the beginning of the Chapter, then tighten the adjuster locknuts securely **(see illustration)**. Where removed, fit a new split pin onto the axle nut **(see illustration)**. On TDM models, tighten the brake caliper bracket bolt to the specified torque **(see illustration 1.9)**.
Caution: On models with a split pin securing the axle nut, if the groove in the nut does not align with the hole in the axle after the specified torque has been reached, tighten the nut to align it – DO NOT loosen it.

Lubrication

14 If required, wash the chain in paraffin

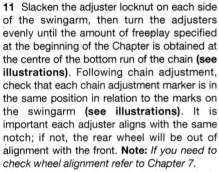
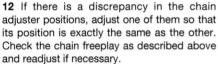
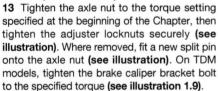

1.11d On TDM and XTZ models, check the relative position of the marker (A) and the notches (B) on each side

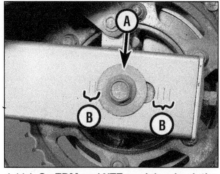

1.11e On TRX models, check the relative position of the notches on the marker (A) and the notches in the swingarm (B) on each side

(kerosene), then wipe it off and allow it to dry, using compressed air if available. If the chain is excessively dirty it should be removed from the machine and allowed to soak in the paraffin (see Chapter 6).
Caution: Don't use petrol, solvent or other cleaning fluids which might damage the internal sealing properties of the chain. Don't use high-pressure water. The entire process shouldn't take longer than ten minutes – if it does, the O-rings in the chain rollers could be damaged.

15 For routine lubrication, the best time to lubricate the chain is after the motorcycle has been ridden. When the chain is warm, the lubricant will penetrate the joints between the

side plates better than when cold. **Note:** *Yamaha specifies SAE 30 to 50W engine oil; you can use an aerosol chain lube, but make sure that it is suitable for O-ring chains.* Apply the oil to the area where the side plates overlap – not the middle of the rollers **(see illustration)**.

> **HAYNES HINT** *Apply the oil to the top of the lower chain run, so centrifugal force will work the oil into the chain when the bike is moving. After applying the lubricant, let it soak in a few minutes before wiping off any excess.*

1.13a Tighten the axle nut to the specified torque

1.13b Use a new split pin, where appropriate

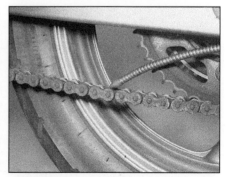

1.15 Apply the oil to the overlap in the side plates

Every 4000 miles (6000 km) or 6 months

2 Spark plugs – check and adjustment

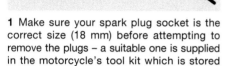

1 Make sure your spark plug socket is the correct size (18 mm) before attempting to remove the plugs – a suitable one is supplied in the motorcycle's tool kit which is stored under the seat.

2 On XTZ models, remove the fuel tank and the air filter housing (see Chapter 4).

3 Using compressed air if available, clean the area around the base of the spark plugs to prevent any dirt falling into the engine when the plugs are removed.

4 Check that the cylinder location is marked on each plug lead, then pull the spark plug cap off each spark plug (see illustration). Using either the plug tool supplied in the bike's toolkit or a deep socket type wrench, unscrew the plugs from the cylinder head (see illustration). Lay each plug out in relation to its cylinder; if either plug shows up a problem it will then be easy to identify the troublesome cylinder.

5 Inspect the electrodes for wear. Both the centre and side electrodes should have square edges and the side electrodes should be of uniform thickness. Look for excessive deposits and evidence of a cracked or chipped insulator around the centre electrode. Compare your spark plugs to the colour spark plug reading chart at the end of this manual. Check the threads, the washer and the ceramic insulator body for cracks and other damage.

6 If the electrodes are not excessively worn, and if the deposits can be easily removed with a wire brush, the plugs can be re-gapped and re-used (if no cracks or chips are visible in the insulator). If in doubt concerning the condition of the plugs, renew them, as the expense is minimal. Yamaha do not specify a renewal interval, but leave it to the discretion of the owner.

7 Cleaning spark plugs by sandblasting is permitted, provided you clean the plugs with a high flash-point solvent afterwards.

8 Before installing the plugs, make sure they are the correct type and heat range and check the gap between the electrodes (see illustrations). Compare the gap to that specified and adjust as necessary. If the gap must be adjusted, bend the side electrode only and be very careful not to chip or crack the insulator nose (see illustration). Make sure the washer is in place on the plug before installing it.

9 Since the cylinder head is made of aluminium, which is soft and easily damaged, thread the plugs into the heads turning the tool by hand (see illustration). Once the plugs are finger-tight, the job can be finished with a spanner on the tool supplied or a socket drive (see illustration 1.4b). If a torque wrench can be applied, tighten the spark plugs to the specified torque setting. Otherwise tighten them by 1/4 to 1/2 turn after they have been fully hand-tightened and have seated. Do not over-tighten them.

 HAYNES HiNT *As the plugs are quite recessed, you can slip a short length of hose over the end of the plug to use as a tool to thread it into place. The hose will grip the plug well enough to turn it, but will start to slip if the plug begins to cross-thread in the hole – this will prevent damaged threads.*

10 Reconnect the spark plug caps, making sure they are securely connected to the correct cylinder. Install all other components previously removed.

 HAYNES HiNT *Stripped plug threads in the cylinder head can be repaired with a Heli-Coil insert – see 'Tools and Workshop Tips' in the Reference section.*

2.4a Remove the spark plug cap . . .

2.4b . . . then unscrew the spark plug

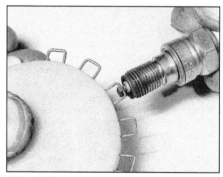

2.8a Using a wire type gauge to measure the spark plug electrode gap

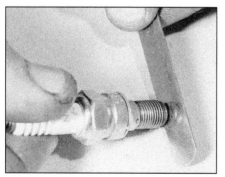

2.8b Using a feeler gauge to measure the spark plug electrode gap

2.8c Adjust the electrode gap by bending the side electrode only

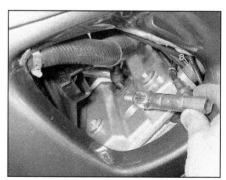

2.9 Thread the plug in as far as possible by turning the tool by hand

3.3a Idle speed adjuster screw (arrowed) – TDM models

3.3b Idle speed adjuster screw (arrowed) – TRX models

3 Idle speed – check and adjustment

1 The idle speed should be checked and adjusted before and after the carburettors are synchronised (balanced) and when it is obviously too high or too low. Before adjusting the idle speed, make sure the valve clearances and spark plug gaps are correct. Also, turn the handlebars back-and-forth and see if the idle speed changes as this is done. If it does, the throttle cable may not be adjusted or routed correctly, or may be worn out. This is a dangerous condition that can cause loss of control of the bike. Be sure to correct this problem before proceeding.
2 The engine should be at normal operating temperature, which is usually reached after 10 to 15 minutes of stop-and-go riding. Make sure the transmission is in neutral, and place the motorcycle on its sidestand.
3 On TDM and TRX models, the idle speed adjuster is located on the left-hand side **(see illustrations)**. On XTZ models, the adjuster is located at the back of the carburettors between the float chambers. With the engine idling, adjust the idle speed by turning the adjuster screw until the idle speed listed in this Chapter's Specifications is obtained. Turn the screw clockwise to increase idle speed, and anti-clockwise to decrease it.

4 Snap the throttle open and shut a few times, then recheck the idle speed. If necessary, repeat the adjustment procedure.
5 If a smooth, steady idle can't be achieved, the fuel/air mixture may be incorrect (check the pilot screw settings – see Chapter 4) or the carburettors may need synchronising (see Section 4). Also check the inlet manifold rubbers for cracks which will cause an air leak, resulting in a weak mixture.

4 Carburettors – synchronisation

⚠️ **Warning: Petrol (gasoline) is extremely flammable, so take extra precautions when you work on any part of the fuel system. Don't smoke or allow open flames or bare light bulbs near the work area, and don't work in a garage where a natural gas-type appliance is present. If you spill any fuel on your skin, rinse it off immediately with soap and water. When you perform any kind of work on the fuel system, wear safety glasses and have a fire extinguisher suitable for a Class B type fire (flammable liquids) on hand.**

⚠️ **Warning: Take great care not to burn your hand on the hot engine unit when accessing the**

gauge take-off points on the intake manifolds. Do not allow exhaust gases to build up in the work area; either perform the check outside or use an exhaust gas extraction system.

1 Carburettor synchronisation is simply the process of adjusting the carburettors so they pass the same amount of fuel/air mixture to each cylinder. This is done by measuring the vacuum produced in each cylinder. Carburettors that are out of synchronisation will result in decreased fuel mileage, increased engine temperature, less than ideal throttle response and higher vibration levels. Before synchronising the carburettors, make sure the valve clearances and idle speed are properly set.
2 To properly synchronise the carburettors you will need a pair of vacuum gauges or a manometer; these instruments measure engine vacuum and can be obtained from motorcycle dealers or mail order parts suppliers. If you don't have access to either of these instruments entrust the work to a dealer.
3 Start the engine and let it run until it reaches normal operating temperature, then shut it off.
4 Remove the fuel tank (see Chapter 4).
5 On 1991 to 1998 TDM models, release the clamp securing the No. 1 cylinder vacuum hose to the fuel pump and detach the hose, then pull the blanking plug out of the end of the No. 2 cylinder vacuum hose **(see illustrations)**. If in doubt, trace each hose from the take-off stub on the top of each inlet manifold between the carburettor and the cylinder head to make sure you have the correct one. On 1999 TDM models, pull the blanking plug out of both vacuum hoses situated down the right-hand side of the engine; if in doubt about their location, trace the hoses from their take-off stubs on the inlet manifolds.
6 On TRX models, release the clamp securing the No. 2 cylinder hose to the fuel pump and detach the hose **(see illustration)**. The No. 1 cylinder vacuum hose has already been detached from the fuel tap when removing the fuel tank. If in doubt, trace each hose from the take-off stub on the top of each intake

4.5a On TDM models, detach the No. 1 vacuum hose (arrowed) from the fuel pump . . .

4.5b . . . and remove the blanking plug (arrowed) from the No. 2 hose

4.6 On TRX models, detach the No. 2 vacuum hose (arrowed) from the fuel pump

4.7a On XTZ models, detach the vacuum hose (arrowed) . . .

4.7b . . . and remove the blanking plug (arrowed)

4.12 Carburettor synchronisation screw (arrowed) – air filter housing removed for clarity

manifold between the carburettor and the cylinder head to make sure you have the correct one. If access is not too restricted, the hoses can be detached from the intake manifolds themselves.

7 On XTZ models, release the clamps securing the vacuum hose and the blanking plug to the take-off stubs on the inlet manifolds between the carburettor and the cylinder head and detach the hose and plug **(see illustrations)**.

8 On TDM and TRX models, connect the gauges to the vacuum hose ends. On XTZ models, connect the gauge hoses to the take-off stubs on the inlet manifolds. Make sure there are no air leaks as false readings will result.

9 Arrange a temporary fuel supply, either by using a small temporary tank or by using extra long fuel pipes to the now remote fuel tank. Alternatively, position the tank on a suitable base on the motorcycle, taking care not to scratch any paintwork, and making sure that the tank is safely and securely supported. If using the main tank, switch the tap to ON or RES on TDM and XTZ models, and to PRI on TRX models.

10 Start the engine and let it idle. If the gauges are fitted with damping adjustment, set this so that the needle flutter is just eliminated but so that they can still respond to small changes in pressure.

11 The vacuum readings for both cylinders should be the same. If the vacuum readings differ, proceed as follows.

12 The carburettors are adjusted by turning the synchronising screw situated in-between the carburettors, in the throttle linkage **(see illustration)**. **Note:** *Do not press down on the screw whilst adjusting it, otherwise a false reading will be obtained.* When the carburettors are synchronised, open and close the throttle quickly a few times to settle

the linkage, and recheck the gauge readings, readjusting if necessary.

13 When the adjustment is complete, recheck the vacuum readings, then adjust the idle speed (see Section 3) until the speed listed in this Chapter's Specifications is obtained. Detach the temporary fuel supply, then remove the gauges. Refit the vacuum hoses and/or blanking plugs as required by your model (see Steps 9, 10 and 11).

14 Install the fuel tank (see Chapter 4).

5 Air filter – cleaning

1 Remove the fuel tank (see Chapter 4). On XTZ models, also remove the air filter housing (see Chapter 4); it is possible to remove the covers and elements with the housing in situ but access to the screws is restricted and the screws are easily dropped.

2 On TDM and TRX models remove the screws securing the air filter cover to the filter housing, then remove the cover and withdraw the filter element from the housing **(see illustrations)**.

3 On XTZ models, there are two filter elements, each fitted integral with its cover on the front of the housing **(see illustrations)**.

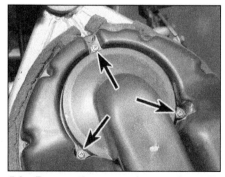

5.2a Remove the screws (arrowed) and lift off the cover . . .

5.2b . . . then withdraw the element (TDM shown)

5.3a Remove the screws (arrowed) . . .

5.3b ... and remove the cover and element together

5.4 Clean the element using compressed air if available

5.6 Make sure the element is correctly seated

4 Tap the element on a hard surface to dislodge any large particles of dirt, then if compressed air is available, use it to clean the element, directing the air from the inside out **(see illustration)**.

5 Check the element for signs of damage. If the element is torn or cannot be cleaned, or is obviously beyond further use, renew it.

6 Install the filter element, making sure it is properly seated, and install the fuel tank (see Chapter 4).

Caution: If the machine is ridden in dusty conditions, the filter should be cleaned more frequently.

6 Fuel system – check

⚠ *Warning: Petrol (gasoline) is extremely flammable, so take extra precautions when you work on any part of the fuel system. Don't smoke or allow open flames or bare light bulbs near the work area, and don't work in a garage where a natural gas-type appliance is present. If you spill any fuel on your skin, rinse it off immediately with soap and water. When you perform any kind of work on the fuel system, wear safety glasses and have a fire extinguisher suitable for a Class B type fire (flammable liquids) on hand.*

Check

1 Remove the fuel tank (see Chapter 4) and check the tank, the fuel tap, the fuel pump and the fuel and vacuum hoses for signs of leakage, deterioration or damage; in particular check that there is no leakage from the fuel hoses. Renew any hoses which are cracked or deteriorated.

2 If the fuel tap is leaking, tighten the assembly screws (see Chapter 4). If leakage persists remove the screws and disassemble the tap, noting how the components fit. Inspect all components and renew any that are worn or damaged. Some components are available individually, though it may be necessary to renew the whole tap, depending on your model.

3 If the carburettor gaskets are leaking, the carburettors should be disassembled and rebuilt using new gaskets and seals (see Chapter 4).

Filter cleaning

4 Cleaning or renewal of the fuel filter is advised after a particularly high mileage has been covered. It is also necessary if fuel starvation is suspected.

5 On TRX, XTZ and 1991 to 1998 TDM models, the fuel filters are mounted in the tank. On TDM models, the filters are integral with the fuel outlet assembly from the tank. On TRX and XTZ models, the filters are integral with the fuel tap. On XTZ models, each fuel tap has its own filter. Remove the

fuel tank and the fuel tap(s) (see Chapter 4). Clean the gauze filter to remove all traces of dirt and fuel sediment. Check the gauze for holes. If any are found, a new filter should be fitted (check for availability – it may be necessary to renew the whole tap). Check the condition of the O-ring and renew it if it is in any way damaged or deteriorated.

6 On 1999 TDM models and in-line fuel filter is fitted between the fuel tap and fuel pump. Refer to Section 23 for details.

7 Engine – oil change

⚠ *Warning: Be careful when draining the oil, as the exhaust pipes, the engine, and the oil itself can cause severe burns.*

1 Consistent routine oil and filter changes are the single most important maintenance procedure you can perform on a motorcycle. The oil not only lubricates the internal parts of the engine, transmission and clutch, but it also acts as a coolant, a cleaner, a sealant, and a protectant. Because of these demands, the oil takes a terrific amount of abuse and should be changed often with new oil of the recommended grade and type. Saving a little money on the difference in cost between a good oil and a cheap oil won't pay off if the engine is damaged. The oil filter should be changed with every second oil change.

2 Before changing the oil, warm up the engine so the oil will drain easily.

3 Put the motorcycle on its sidestand, and position a clean drain tray below the engine. On 1991 to 1995 TDM models remove the seat, and on XTZ models remove the right-hand side cover (see Chapter 8). Unscrew the oil filler cap from the oil tank to vent it and to act as a reminder that there is no oil in the engine (see *Daily (pre-ride) checks*).

4 First unscrew the oil drain plug from the crankcase and allow the oil to flow into the drain tray **(see illustrations)**. Next unscrew the oil drain plug from the oil filter housing and

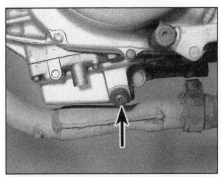

7.4a Unscrew the crankcase oil drain plug (arrowed) ...

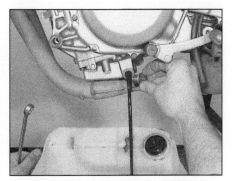

7.4b ... and allow the oil to drain

7.4c Unscrew the oil filter housing drain plug (arrowed) . . .

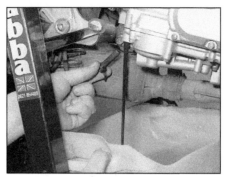

7.4d . . . and allow the oil to drain

allow the oil to flow into the drain tray **(see illustrations)**. Check the condition of the sealing washers on the drain plugs and discard them if they are in any way damaged or worn. On 1996-on TDM and TRX models, Yamaha specify using new ones as a matter of course.

5 When the oil has completely drained, fit the plugs to the crankcase and oil filter housing, using new sealing washers if required, and tighten them to the torque settings specified at the beginning of the Chapter. Avoid overtightening, as damage to the crankcase will result.

6 Refill the oil tank to the proper level using the recommended type and amount of oil (see *Daily (pre-ride) checks* and this chapter's specifications). With the motorcycle vertical, the oil level should lie between the maximum and minimum level lines on the dipstick or inspection window (according to model) (see *Daily (pre-ride) checks)*. Install the filler cap. Start the engine and let it run for two or three minutes. It is advisable to perform an oil pressure check (see Section 32). Stop the engine, wait a few minutes, then check the oil level. If necessary, add more oil to bring the level up to the maximum level line on the dipstick or window. Check around the drain plugs for leaks.

7 The old oil drained from the engine cannot be re-used and should be disposed of properly. Check with your local refuse disposal company, disposal facility or environmental agency to see whether they will accept the used oil for recycling. Don't pour used oil into drains or onto the ground.

 Check the old oil carefully – if it is very metallic coloured, then the engine is experiencing wear from break-in (new engine) or from insufficient lubrication. If there are flakes or chips of metal in the oil, then something is drastically wrong internally and the engine will have to be disassembled for inspection and repair. If there are pieces of fibre-like material in the oil, the clutch is experiencing excessive wear and should be checked.

Note: It is antisocial and illegal to dump oil down the drain. To find the location of your local oil recycling bank, call this number free.

0800 66 33 66

8 Brake pads – wear check

1 Each brake pad has wear indicators that can be viewed without removing the pads from the caliper.

2 On TDM and TRX models, the turned-in corners of the brake pad backing material form the wear indicators – when they are almost contacting the disc itself the pads must be renewed. The indicators are visible by looking at the bottom corner of the pads **(see illustration)**.
Caution: Do not allow the pads to wear to the extent that the indicators contact the disc itself as the disc will be damaged.

3 On XTZ models, the indicators are in the form of grooves in the brake pad friction material – when the pads are worn so that the grooves are only just visible the pads must be renewed **(see illustration)**.

4 If the pads are worn to or beyond the indicators, they must be renewed. If the pads are dirty or if you are in doubt as to the amount of friction material remaining, remove them and measure the amount of friction material (see Chapter 7). **Note:** *Some after-market pads may use different indicators to those on the original equipment as shown.*

5 Refer to Chapter 7 for details of pad renewal.

6 Bikes used in the UK and anywhere where salt is used on the roads are referred to Chapter 7, Section 2, Step 9 for details of brake pad and caliper lubrication to prevent corrosion.

9 Brake system – check

1 A routine general check of the brake system will ensure that any problems are discovered and remedied before the rider's safety is jeopardised.

8.2 Brake pad wear indicator (arrowed) – TDM and TRX models (TRX shown)

8.3 Brake pad wear indicator groove (arrowed) – XTZ models

9.3 Flex the brake hoses and check for cracks, bulges and leaking fluid

9.5a Rear brake light switch – TDM models

9.5b Rear brake light switch – TRX models

2 Check the brake lever and pedal for loose connections, improper or rough action, excessive play, bends, and other damage. Renew any damaged parts (see Chapter 7). Clean and lubricate the lever and pedal pivots if their action is stiff or rough (see Section 18).

3 Make sure all brake fasteners are tight. Check the brake pads for wear (see Section 8) and make sure the fluid level in the reservoirs is correct (see *Daily (pre-ride) checks*). Look for leaks at the hose and pipe connections and check for cracks in the hoses and pipes themselves **(see illustration)**. If the lever or pedal is spongy when applied, bleed the brakes (see Chapter 7).

4 Make sure the brake light operates when the front brake lever is pulled in. The front brake light switch, mounted on the underside of the master cylinder, is not adjustable. If it fails to operate properly, check it (see Chapter 9).

5 Make sure the brake light is activated just before the rear brake takes effect. If adjustment is necessary, hold the switch and turn the adjuster ring on the switch body until the brake light is activated when required **(see illustrations)**. If the brake light comes on too late, turn the ring clockwise. If the brake light comes on too soon or is permanently on, turn the ring anti-clockwise. If the switch doesn't operate the brake light, check it (see Chapter 9).

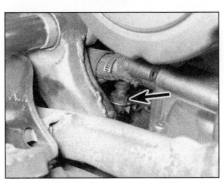

9.5c Rear brake light switch – XTZ models

6 On TDM and TRX models, the front brake lever has a span adjuster which alters the distance of the lever from the handlebar **(see illustrations)**. Each setting is identified by a number on the adjuster which aligns with the arrow on the lever bracket. Pull the lever away from the handlebar and turn the adjuster ring until the setting which best suits the rider is obtained. There are four settings.

7 On XTZ models, the front brake lever has a freeplay adjuster which alters the amount of play in the lever before the brake takes effect. Check the amount of freeplay by measuring the distance the ball end of the

9.6a Front brake lever span adjuster – TDM models

lever travels before the brake comes on and compare it to the amount specified at the beginning of the Chapter. To adjust the freeplay, slacken the adjuster locknut and turn the adjuster as required until the specified amount of freeplay is achieved **(see illustration)**. Turn the adjuster clockwise to decrease freeplay and anti-clockwise to increase it.

Caution: Make sure that the correct amount of freeplay is set. Insufficient freeplay could cause the brakes to bind and excessive freeplay may not allow them to operate to their full potential.

9.6b Front brake lever span adjuster – TRX models

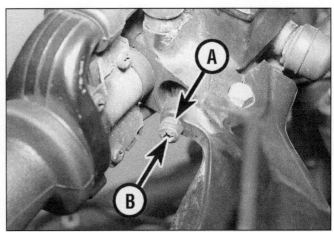

9.7 Front brake lever freeplay adjuster locknut (A) and adjuster (B) – XTZ models

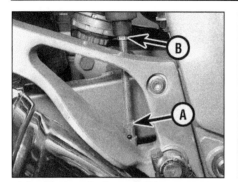

9.8a Slacken the locknut (A) and turn the pushrod using the hex (B) . . .

8 Check the position of the brake pedal. Yamaha recommend the distance between the top of the end of the brake pedal and the top of the rider's footrest should be as specified at the beginning of the Chapter. If the pedal height is incorrect, or if the rider's preference is different, slacken the clevis locknut on the master cylinder pushrod, then turn the pushrod using a spanner on the hex at the top of the rod until the pedal is at the correct or desired height **(see illustration)**. After adjustment check that the pushrod end is visible in the hole in the clevis (TDM and TRX models) **(see illustration)** or below the clevis nut (XTZ models). On completion tighten the locknut securely. Adjust the rear brake light switch after adjusting the pedal height (see Step 5).

9.8b . . . making sure the rod end is still visible in the hole (arrowed) (TDM and TRX models)

10 Clutch – check and adjustment

1 Check that the clutch cable operates smoothly and easily.
2 If the clutch lever operation is heavy or stiff, remove the cable (see Chapter 2) and lubricate it (see Section 18). If the cable is still stiff, renew it. Install the lubricated or new cable (see Chapter 2).
3 With the cable operating smoothly, check that the clutch lever is correctly adjusted. Periodic adjustment is necessary to compensate for wear in the clutch plates and stretch of the cable. Check that the amount of

freeplay at the clutch lever end is within the specifications listed at the beginning of the Chapter **(see illustration)**.
4 If adjustment is required, loosen the adjuster lockring at the top of the cable and turn the adjuster in or out until the required amount of freeplay is obtained **(see illustration)**. To increase freeplay, turn the adjuster clockwise. To reduce freeplay, turn the adjuster anti-clockwise. Tighten the locking ring securely.
5 On TRX, XTZ and 1996-on TDM models, if all the adjustment has been taken up at the lever, reset the adjuster to give a large amount of freeplay, then set the correct amount of freeplay using the adjuster nuts on each end of the threaded section in the cable bracket on the right-hand side of the engine. On TRX models, first remove the adjuster cover **(see illustration)**. To reduce freeplay, slacken the rear nut and tighten the front nut until the freeplay is as specified, then tighten the rear nut **(see illustrations)**. Subsequent adjustments can now be made using the lever adjuster only.
6 On 1991 to 1995 TDM models, if all the adjustment has been taken up at the lever, set the correct amount of freeplay using the adjuster in the cable – the adjuster is positioned a short way down the cable from the lever **(see illustration)**. Slacken the locknut and turn the adjuster as required until the correct amount of freeplay is obtained.

11 Battery – check

1 TDM and TRX models are fitted with a sealed (maintenance-free) battery, and therefore require no maintenance. **Note:** *Do not attempt to remove the battery caps to check the electrolyte level or battery specific gravity. Removal will damage the caps, resulting in electrolyte leakage and battery damage.* All that should be done is to check that its terminals are clean and tight and that the casing is not damaged or leaking. See Chapter 9 for further details.

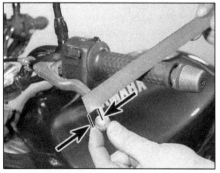

10.3 Measuring clutch cable freeplay

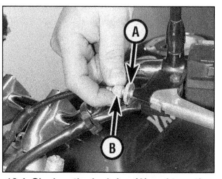

10.4 Slacken the lockring (A) and turn the adjuster (B) as required

10.5a On TRX models, remove the cover and adjust the cable as described using the nuts (arrowed)

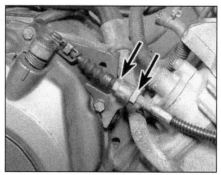

10.5b Cable adjuster nuts (arrowed) – XTZ models

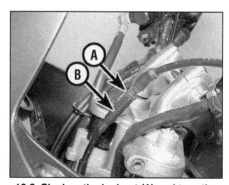

10.6 Slacken the locknut (A) and turn the adjuster (B) as required

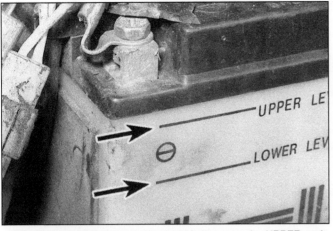

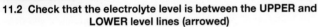

11.2 Check that the electrolyte level is between the UPPER and LOWER level lines (arrowed)

13.2 Checking for play in the wheel bearings

2 XTZ models are fitted with a standard battery which requires regular checks of the electrolyte level. Remove the left-hand side cover for access to the battery (see Chapter 8). The electrolyte level is visible through the translucent battery case – it should be between the UPPER and LOWER level marks **(see illustration)**. If the electrolyte is low, remove the battery (see Chapter 9), then remove the cell caps and fill each cell to the upper level mark with distilled water. Do not use tap water (except in an emergency), and do not overfill. The cell holes are quite small, so it may help to use a clean plastic squeeze bottle with a small spout to add the water. Install the battery cell caps, tightening them securely, then install the battery.
Caution: Be extremely careful when handling or working around the battery. The electrolyte is very caustic and an explosive gas (hydrogen) is given off when the battery is charging.
3 If the machine is not in regular use, disconnect the battery and give it a refresher charge every month to six weeks (see Chapter 9).

12 Wheels and tyres – general check

Cast alloy wheels

1 The cast alloy wheels fitted to TDM and TRX models are virtually maintenance free, but they should be kept clean and checked periodically for cracks and other damage. Also check the wheel runout and alignment (see Chapter 7). Never attempt to repair damaged cast wheels; they must be renewed. Check the valve rubber for signs of damage or deterioration and have it renewed by a motorcycle tyre specialist if necessary. Also, make sure the valve stem cap is in place and tight.

Spoked wheels

2 On XTZ models, visually check the spokes for damage, breakage or corrosion. A broken or bent spoke must be renewed immediately because the load taken by it will be transferred to adjacent spokes which may in turn fail.
3 If you suspect that any of the spokes are incorrectly tensioned, tap each one lightly with a screwdriver and note the sound produced. Properly tensioned spokes will make a sharp pinging sound, loose ones will produce a lower pitch and overtightened ones will be higher pitched. A spoke wrench will be needed if any of the spokes require adjustment. Unevenly tensioned spokes will promote rim misalignment – check the wheel runout and alignment (see Chapter 7) and seek the help of a wheel building expert if this is suspected.

Tyres

4 Check the tyre condition and tread depth thoroughly – see *Daily (pre-ride) checks*.

13 Wheel bearings – check

1 Wheel bearings will wear over a period of time and result in handling problems.
2 Support the motorcycle upright using an auxiliary stand so that the wheel being checked is off the ground. Check for any play in the bearings by pushing and pulling the wheel against the hub **(see illustration)**. Also rotate the wheel and check that it rotates smoothly.
3 If any play is detected in the hub, or if the wheel does not rotate smoothly (and this is not due to brake or transmission drag), the wheel must be removed for closer inspection of its bearings (see Chapter 7).

14 Sidestand and cut-off switches – check

Sidestand

1 The sidestand return spring must be capable of retracting the stand fully and holding the stand retracted when the motorcycle is in use. If the spring is sagged or broken it must be renewed.
2 Lubricate the sidestand pivot regularly (see Section 18).

Cut-off switches

3 The clutch and sidestand are fitted with cut-off switches to prevent the bike being started in gear unless the clutch lever is pulled in, and to prevent the bike being ridden with the sidestand down.
4 Your bike's owners handbook contains a checking procedure for the sidestand and clutch switches. To test, turn the ignition ON and make sure the engine stop switch (kill switch) is in the RUN position. Sit on the bike and retract the sidestand, then shift the transmission into gear. Pull in the clutch lever and press the starter button – the engine should start, indicating that the clutch switch is in good order. With the engine idling and the clutch lever still held in, lower the sidestand – the engine should stop; if it doesn't, the sidestand switch should be checked out. Refer to Chapter 9 for clutch switch and sidestand switch tests.

15 Nuts and bolts – tightness check

1 Since vibration of the machine tends to loosen fasteners, all nuts, bolts, screws, etc. should be periodically checked for proper tightness.

2 Pay particular attention to the following:
Spark plugs
Engine oil drain plugs
Gearchange lever, brake and clutch lever, and brake pedal bolts
Footrest and stand bolts
Engine mounting bolts
Shock absorber and suspension linkage bolts and swingarm pivot bolts
Handlebar clamp bolts
Front axle bolt and axle clamp bolts
Front fork clamp bolts (top and bottom yoke)
Rear axle nut
Brake caliper mounting bolts
Brake hose banjo bolts and caliper bleed valves
Brake disc bolts
Exhaust system bolts/nuts

3 If a torque wrench is available, use it along with the torque specifications at the beginning of this and other Chapters.

16 Cooling system – check

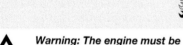
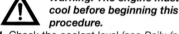

⚠️ **Warning: The engine must be cool before beginning this procedure.**

1 Check the coolant level (see *Daily (pre-ride) checks*).
2 The entire cooling system should be checked for evidence of leakage. Examine each rubber coolant hose along its entire length. Look for cracks, abrasions and other damage. Squeeze each hose at various points. They should feel firm, yet pliable, and return to their original shape when released. If they are dried out or hard, renew them.
3 Check for evidence of leaks at each cooling system joint. Tighten the hose clips carefully to prevent future leaks.
4 Check the radiator for leaks and other damage. Leaks in the radiator leave tell-tale scale deposits or coolant stains on the outside of the core below the leak. If leaks are noted, remove the radiator (see Chapter 3) and have it repaired or renew it.
Caution: Do not use a liquid leak stopping compound to try to repair leaks.
5 Check the radiator fins for mud, dirt and insects, which may impede the flow of air through the radiator. If the fins are dirty, remove the radiator (see Chapter 3) and clean it using water or low pressure compressed air directed through the fins from the rear side. If the fins are bent or distorted, straighten them carefully with a screwdriver. If the air flow is restricted by bent or damaged fins over more than 30% of the radiator's surface area, renew the radiator.
6 To access the radiator pressure cap and filler, on TDM models, remove the right-hand fairing side panel, on TRX models remove the fairing, and on XTZ models remove the left-hand fairing side panel (see Chapter 8). On TRX models, remove the security bolt holding the radiator cap **(see illustration)**. Remove the pressure cap from the radiator filler neck by turning it anti-clockwise until it reaches a stop **(see illustrations)**. If you hear a hissing sound (indicating there is still pressure in the system), wait until it stops. Now press down on the cap and continue turning the cap until it can be removed. Check the condition of the coolant in the system. If it is rust-coloured or if accumulations of scale are visible, drain, flush and refill the system with new coolant (See Section 23). Check the cap seal for cracks and other damage. If in doubt about the pressure cap's condition, have it tested by a Yamaha dealer or renew it. Install the cap by turning it clockwise until it reaches the first stop then push down on the cap and continue turning until it can turn further.
7 Check the antifreeze content of the coolant with an antifreeze hydrometer. Sometimes coolant looks like it's in good condition, but might be too weak to offer adequate protection. If the hydrometer indicates a weak mixture, drain, flush and refill the system (see Section 23).
8 Start the engine and let it reach normal operating temperature, then check for leaks again. As the coolant temperature increases beyond normal, the fan should come on automatically and the temperature should begin to drop. If it does not, refer to Chapter 3 and check the fan switch, fan motor and fan circuit carefully.
9 If the coolant level is consistently low, and no evidence of leaks can be found, have the entire system pressure checked by a Yamaha dealer.

17 Throttle and choke cables – check

Throttle cables

1 Make sure the throttle grip rotates easily from fully closed to fully open with the front wheel turned at various angles. The grip should return automatically from fully open to fully closed when released.
2 If the throttle sticks, this is probably due to a cable fault. Remove the cables (see Chapter 4) and lubricate them (see Section 18). Install the cables, making sure they are correctly routed. If this fails to improve the operation of the throttle, the cables must be renewed. Note that in very rare cases the fault could lie in the carburettors rather than the cables, necessitating the removal of the carburettors and inspection of the throttle linkage (see Chapter 4).
3 With the throttle operating smoothly, check for a small amount of freeplay in the cable assembly, measured in terms of the amount of twistgrip rotation before the throttle opens and the pull of the cable is felt; compare this amount to that listed in this Chapter's Specifications **(see illustration)**. If it's incorrect, adjust the cable assembly to correct it.

16.6a On TRX models, remove the pressure cap security bolt (arrowed)

16.6b Pressure cap (arrowed) – TDM models

16.6c Pressure cap (arrowed) – XTZ models

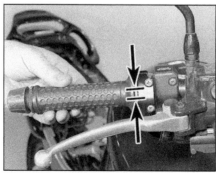
17.3 Measure the amount of freeplay at the throttle grip flange

4 Freeplay adjustments can be made at the upper end of the accelerator cable. Loosen the locknut on the adjuster **(see illustration)**. Turn the adjuster until the specified amount of freeplay is obtained, then retighten the locknut. Turn the adjuster clockwise to increase freeplay and anti-clockwise to reduce it.

5 If the adjuster has reached its limit of adjustment, reset it so that the freeplay is at a maximum, then remove the fuel tank and air filter housing (see Chapter 4) and adjust the accelerator cable at the carburettor end. Slacken the adjuster locknut, then screw the adjuster in or out until the specified amount of freeplay is obtained, then tighten the locknut **(see illustration)**. Further adjustments can now be made at the cable's upper end. If the cable cannot be adjusted as specified, renew the accelerator and decelerator cables (see Chapter 4).

 Warning: Turn the handlebars all the way through their travel with the engine idling. Idle speed should not change. If it does, the cable may be routed incorrectly. Correct this condition before riding the bike.

6 Check that the throttle twistgrip operates smoothly and snaps shut quickly when released.

Choke cable

7 If the choke does not operate smoothly this is probably due to a cable fault. Remove the cable (see Chapter 4) and lubricate it (see Section 18). Install the cable, routing it so it takes the smoothest route possible.

8 If this fails to improve the operation of the choke, the cable must be renewed. Note that in very rare cases the fault could lie in the carburettors rather than the cable, necessitating the removal of the carburettors and inspection of the choke plungers (see Chapter 4). Make sure there is a small amount of freeplay in the cable before the plungers move. If there isn't, check that the cable is seating correctly at the carburettor end. If it is, then slacken the choke outer cable bracket screw on the carburettor and slide the cable further into the bracket, creating some freeplay. Otherwise, renew the cable.

18.3a Lubricating a cable with a cable oiler clamp

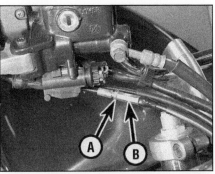
17.4 Slacken the locknut (A) and turn the adjuster (B) as required

18 Stand, lever pivots and cables – lubrication

Pivot points

1 Since the controls, cables and various other components of a motorcycle are exposed to the elements, they should be lubricated periodically to ensure safe and trouble-free operation.

2 The footrests, clutch and brake levers, brake pedal, gearshift lever linkage and sidestand pivots should be lubricated frequently. In order for the lubricant to be applied where it will do the most good, the component should be disassembled. However, if chain and cable lubricant is being used, it can be applied to the pivot joint gaps and will usually work its way into the areas where friction occurs. If motor oil or light grease is being used, apply it sparingly as it

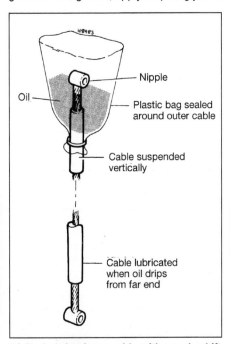
18.3b Lubricating a cable with a makeshift funnel and motor oil

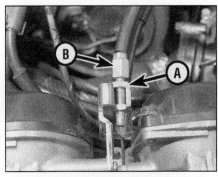
17.5 Slacken the locknut (A) and turn the adjuster (B) as required

may attract dirt (which could cause the controls to bind or wear at an accelerated rate). **Note:** *One of the best lubricants for the control lever pivots is a dry-film lubricant (available from many sources by different names).*

Cables

3 To lubricate the cables, disconnect the relevant cable at its upper end, then lubricate the cable with a cable oiler clamp, or if one is not available, using the set-up shown **(see illustrations)**. See Chapter 4 for the choke and throttle cable removal procedures and Chapter 2 for the clutch cable procedure.

4 The speedometer cable should be removed (see Chapter 9) and the inner cable withdrawn from the outer cable and lubricated with motor oil or cable lubricant. Do not lubricate the upper few inches of the cable as the lubricant may travel up into the instrument head. Note that the speedometer on 1999 TDM models is electronically operated, and thus does not have a cable.

19 Swingarm and suspension bearings (XTZ models) – re-greasing

1 The swingarm and suspension linkage components are equipped with grease nipples **(see illustration)**. Clean off the nipples using a rag, then apply some lithium-based grease to the nipples using a grease gun.

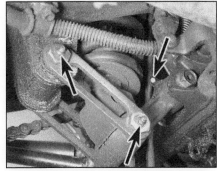
19.1 Apply grease to the nipples on the suspension linkage (arrowed) and to the nipple on the swingarm pivot

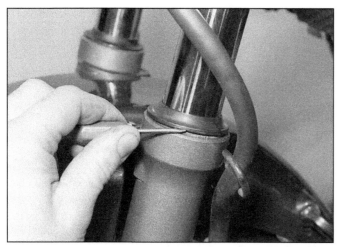

20.3 Check above and below the dust seal for signs of fluid leakage

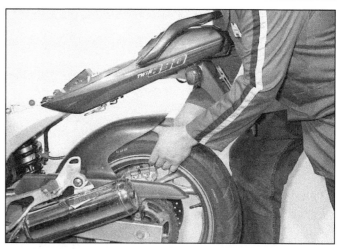

20.7 Checking for play in the rear shock mountings and suspension linkage bearings (TRX and XTZ models)

20 Suspension – check

1 The suspension components must be maintained in top operating condition to ensure rider safety. Loose, worn or damaged suspension parts decrease the motorcycle's stability and control.

Front suspension

2 While standing alongside the motorcycle, apply the front brake and push on the handlebars to compress the forks several times. Check that they move up-and-down smoothly without binding. If binding is felt, the forks should be disassembled and inspected (see Chapter 6).
3 Inspect the area around the dust seal for signs of oil leakage, then carefully lever up the dust seal using a flat-bladed screwdriver and inspect the area around the fork seal **(see illustration)**. If leakage is evident, the seals must be renewed (see Chapter 6). Check the fork tubes for scratches, corrosion and pitting as these will cause premature seal failure. If the damage is excessive the tubes should be renewed (see Chapter 6).
4 Check the tightness of all suspension nuts and bolts to be sure none have worked loose, referring to the torque settings specified at the beginning of Chapter 6.

Rear suspension

5 Inspect the rear shock for fluid leakage and tightness of its mountings. If leakage is found, the shock should be renewed or taken to a suspension specialist for overhaul (see Chapter 6).
6 With the aid of an assistant to support the bike, compress the rear suspension several times. It should move up and down freely without binding. If any binding is felt, the worn or faulty component must be identified and renewed. The problem could be due to either

the shock absorber, the suspension linkage components (TRX and XTZ models) or the swingarm components.
7 Support the motorcycle using an auxiliary stand so that the rear wheel is off the ground. Grab the swingarm and rock it from side to side – there should be no discernible movement at the rear. If there's a little movement or a slight clicking can be heard, inspect the tightness of all the rear suspension mounting bolts and nuts, referring to the torque settings specified at the beginning of Chapter 6, and re-check for movement. Next, grasp the top of the rear wheel and pull it upwards – there should be no discernible freeplay before the shock absorber begins to compress **(see illustration)**. Any freeplay felt in either check indicates worn bearings in the suspension linkage (TRX and XTZ models) or swingarm, or worn shock absorber mountings. The worn components must be renewed (see Chapter 6).
8 To make an accurate assessment of the swingarm bearings, remove the rear wheel (see Chapter 7) and the bolt securing the shock absorber (TDM models) or suspension linkage assembly (TRX and XTZ models) to the swingarm (see Chapter 6). Grasp the rear of the swingarm with one hand and place your other hand at the junction of the swingarm and the frame. Try to move the rear of the swingarm from side-to-side. Any wear (play) in the bearings should be felt as movement between the swingarm and the frame at the front. If there is any play the swingarm will be felt to move forward and backward at the front (not from side-to-side). Yamaha specify a maximum lateral movement of 1 mm measured at the rear ends of the swingarm. Next, move the swingarm up and down through its full travel. It should move freely, without any binding or rough spots. If any play in the swingarm is noted or if the swingarm does not move freely, the bearings must be removed for inspection or renewal (see Chapter 6).

9 On XTZ models, the swingarm sideplay should be measured. Push the swingarm to one side of the frame, then slip a feeler gauge between the frame and the swingarm cap on the side from which the swingarm was pushed and measure the clearance. If it is greater than specified, remove the swingarm (see Chapter 6) and follow the procedure in Section 14 of that Chapter to calculate the shims required to restore sideplay to the correct amount.

21 Steering head bearings – freeplay check and adjustment

1 Steering head bearings can become dented, rough or loose during normal use of the machine. In extreme cases, worn or loose steering head bearings can cause steering wobble – a condition that is potentially dangerous.

Check

2 Support the motorcycle on an auxiliary stand so that the front wheel is off the ground.
3 Point the front wheel straight-ahead and slowly move the handlebars from side-to-side. Any dents or roughness in the bearing races will be felt and the bars will not move smoothly and freely.
4 Next, grasp the fork sliders and try to pull and push them forward and backward. Any looseness in the steering head bearings will be felt as front-to-rear movement of the forks. If play is felt in the bearings, adjust the steering head as follows.

 HAYNES HiNT *Freeplay in the fork due to worn fork bushes can be misinterpreted for steering head bearing play – do not confuse the two.*

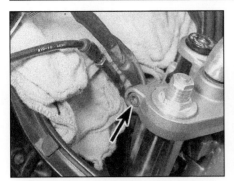

21.6a Slacken the fork clamp bolts (arrowed) . . .

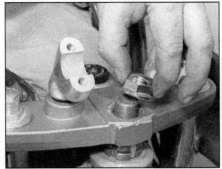

21.6b . . . and unscrew the steering stem nut

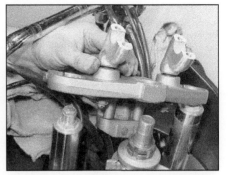

21.7 Ease the top yoke up off the steering stem and forks

Adjustment

TDM and TRX models

5 Displace the handlebars from the top yoke (see Chapter 6). On 1996-on TDM models, unscrew the bolts securing the choke knob and the cable guide to the top yoke.

6 Slacken the fork clamp bolts in the top yoke **(see illustration)**. Unscrew the steering stem nut and remove it along with its washer, where fitted **(see illustration)**.

7 Gently ease the top yoke upwards off the fork tubes and position it clear, using a rag to protect the tank or other components **(see illustration)**. Make sure no strain is placed on the ignition switch wiring. On TRX models the yoke should be supported so that the master cylinder reservoir remains upright and so that no strain is placed on the hydraulic hose.

8 Remove the tabbed lockwasher, noting how it fits, then unscrew and remove the locknut using either a C-spanner, a peg spanner or a drift located in one of the notches **(see illustrations)**. Remove the washer.

9 To adjust the bearings as specified by Yamaha, a special service tool (part No. 90890-01403) and a torque wrench are required. If the tool is available, first slacken the adjuster nut, then tighten it to the initial torque setting specified at the beginning of the Chapter, making sure the torque wrench handle is at right angles (90°) to the centreline between the adjuster nut and the wrench socket in the special tool **(see illustration)**. Now slacken the nut one turn, then tighten it to the final torque setting specified. Check that the steering is still able to move freely from side to side, but that all freeplay is eliminated.

10 If the Yamaha tool is not available, using either a C-spanner, a peg spanner or a drift located in one of the notches, slacken the adjuster nut slightly until pressure is just released, then tighten it until all freeplay is removed, then tighten it a little more. This pre-loads the bearings. Now slacken the nut, then tighten it again, setting it so that all freeplay is just removed yet the steering is able to move

freely from side to side. To do this tighten the nut only a little at a time, and after each tightening repeat the checks outlined above (Steps 3 and 4) until the bearings are correctly set. The object is to set the adjuster nut so that the bearings are under a very light loading, just enough to remove any freeplay.

Caution: Take great care not to apply excessive pressure because this will cause premature failure of the bearings.

11 With the bearings correctly adjusted, install the washer and the locknut **(see illustration 22.8b)**. On 1991 to 1995 TDM models the tapered side of the locknut must

21.8a Remove the tabbed lockwasher . . .

face down. Tighten the locknut finger-tight, then tighten it further until its notches align with those in the adjuster nut. If necessary, counter-hold the adjuster nut and tighten the locknut using a C-spanner or drift until the notches align, but make sure the adjuster nut does not turn as well. Install the tabbed lockwasher so that the tabs fit into the notches in both the locknut and adjuster nut **(see illustration 22.8a)**.

12 Fit the top yoke onto the steering stem **(see illustration 22.7)**, then install the washer (where fitted) and steering stem nut; tighten the nut to the torque setting specified at the beginning of the Chapter **(see**

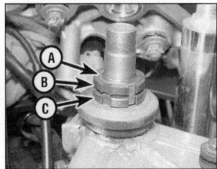

21.8b . . . then unscrew the locknut (A), remove the washer (B), and adjust the bearings as described using the adjuster nut (C)

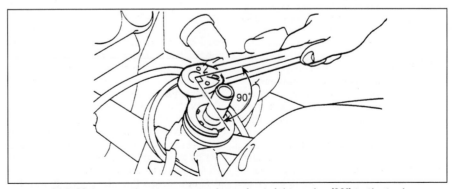

21.9 Make sure the torque wrench arm is at right angles (90°) to the tool

illustration). Now tighten both the fork clamp bolts to the specified torque setting **(see illustration)**.

13 Re-check the bearing adjustment as described above and re-adjust if necessary.

14 Install the handlebars (see Chapter 6).

XTZ models

15 Displace the handlebars from the top yoke (see Chapter 6).

16 Slacken the fork clamp bolts in the top yoke, then slacken the steering stem bolt **(see illustration)**. There is no need to remove the top yoke.

17 To adjust the bearings as specified by Yamaha, a special service tool (part No. 90890-01268) and a torque wrench are required. If the tool is available, first slacken the adjuster nut **(see illustration 22.18)**, then tighten it to the initial torque setting specified at the beginning of the Chapter, making sure the torque wrench handle is at right angles (90°) to the line between the adjuster nut and the wrench socket in the special tool **(see illustration 22.9)**. Now slacken the nut one turn, then tighten it to the final torque setting specified. Check that the steering is still able to move freely from side to side, but that all freeplay is eliminated.

18 If the Yamaha tool is not available, using either a C-spanner or drift located in one of the notches, slacken the adjuster nut slightly until pressure is just released, then tighten it until all freeplay is removed, then tighten it a little more **(see illustration)**. This pre-loads the bearings. Now slacken the nut, then tighten it again, setting it so that all freeplay is just removed yet the steering is able to move freely from side to side. To do this tighten the nut only a little at a time, and after each tightening repeat the checks outlined above

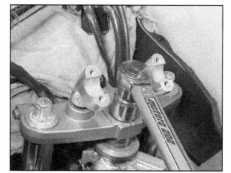
21.12a Tighten the steering stem nut . . .

21.12b . . . and the fork clamp bolts to the specified torque

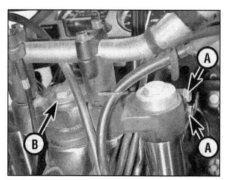
21.16 Slacken the fork clamp bolts (A) and the steering stem bolt (B)

21.18 Steering head bearing adjuster nut (arrowed)

(Steps 3 and 4) until the bearings are correctly set. The object is to set the adjuster nut so that the bearings are under a very light loading, just enough to remove any freeplay.
Caution: Take great care not to apply excessive pressure because this will cause premature failure of the bearings.

19 With the bearings correctly adjusted, tighten the steering stem bolt and both the fork clamp bolts to the torque settings specified at the beginning of the Chapter **(see illustration 22.16)**.

20 Re-check the bearing adjustment as described above and re-adjust if necessary.

21 Install the handlebars (see Chapter 6).

Every 8000 miles (12,000 km) or 12 months

Carry out all the items under the 4000 mile (6000 km) check, plus the following:

22 Engine – oil and filter change

 Warning: Be careful when draining the oil, as the exhaust pipes, the engine, and the oil itself can cause severe burns.

1 Consistent routine oil and filter changes are the single most important maintenance procedure you can perform on a motorcycle. The oil not only lubricates the internal parts of the engine, transmission and clutch, but it also acts as a coolant, a cleaner, a sealant, and a protectant. Because of these demands, the oil takes a terrific amount of abuse and should be changed often with new oil of the recommended grade and type. Saving a little

money on the difference in cost between a good oil and a cheap oil won't pay off if the engine is damaged. The oil filter should be changed with every second oil change.

2 Before changing the oil, warm up the engine so the oil will drain easily. On 1991 to 1995 TDM models and XTZ models, remove the engine bashplate (see Chapter 8).

3 Put the motorcycle on its sidestand, and position a clean drain tray below the engine. On 1991 to 1995 TDM models remove the seat, and on XTZ models remove the right-hand side cover (see Chapter 8). Unscrew the oil filler cap from the oil tank to vent it and to act as a reminder that there is no oil in the engine (see *Daily (pre-ride) checks*).

4 First unscrew the oil drain plug from the crankcase and allow the oil to flow into the drain tray **(see illustrations 7.4a and b)**. Next

unscrew the oil drain plug from the oil filter housing and allow the oil to flow into the drain tray **(see illustrations 7.4c and d)**. Check the condition of the sealing washers on the drain plugs and discard them if they are in any way damaged or worn. On 1996-on TDM and TRX models, Yamaha specify using new ones as a matter of course.

5 When the oil has completely drained, fit the plugs to the sump and oil filter housing, using new sealing washers if required, and tighten them to the torque settings specified at the beginning of the Chapter. Avoid overtightening, as damage to the crankcase will result.

6 With the drain tray still under the engine to catch any residue oil, unscrew the bolts securing the oil filter cover to the crankcase and remove the cover along with the filter,

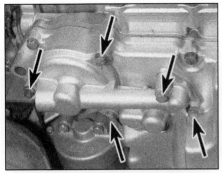

22.6a Unscrew the filter cover bolts (arrowed) . . .

22.6b . . . and remove the cover and filter

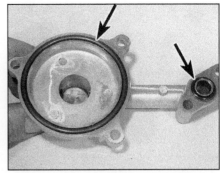

22.7a Fit the new O-rings (arrowed) . . .

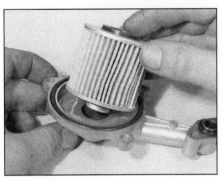

22.7b . . . then install the filter with the projection fitting into the cover . . .

22.7c . . . and fit the cover onto the engine

noting which way up it fits **(see illustrations)**. Discard the filter. Discard the O-rings as new ones must be used.

7 Fit new O-rings into the cover, making sure they fit properly in the groove and around the collar **(see illustrations)**. Fit the filter into the cover with the projection on the filter facing into the cover **(see illustration)**. Fit the cover onto the sump, then apply a suitable non-permanent thread locking compound to the bolts and tighten them to the torque setting specified at the beginning of the Chapter **(see illustration)**.

8 Refill the oil tank to the proper level using the recommended type and amount of oil (see *Daily (pre-ride) checks* and this Chapter's *Specifications*). With the motorcycle vertical, the oil level should lie between the maximum and minimum level lines on the dipstick or inspection window (according to model) (see *Daily (pre-ride) checks*). Install the filler cap. Start the engine and let it run for two or three minutes. It is advisable to perform an oil pressure check (see Section 32). Stop the engine, wait a few minutes, then check the oil level. If necessary, add more oil to bring the

level up to the maximum level line on the dipstick or window. Check around the drain plugs for leaks.

9 The old oil drained from the engine cannot be re-used and should be disposed of properly. Check with your local refuse disposal company, disposal facility or environmental agency to see whether they will accept the used oil for recycling. Don't pour used oil into drains or onto the ground – see Haynes Hint and UK's safe oil disposal contact in Section 7.

23 Fuel filter – renewal (1999 TDM models)

1 The fuel filter should be renewed periodically. To do so, loosen the hose clamps and slide them down the hoses, away from the filter. Pry the hoses off each end of the filter and connect a new filter in its place **(see illustration 15.12 in Chapter 4)**; fuel filters usually have an arrow on their body indicating the direction of fuel flow.

2 Check that there is no sign of leakage from the fuel pump. Check that the fuel pump hose connections are secure.

Every 16,000 miles (24,000 km) or two years

Carry out all the items under the 8000 mile (12,000 km) check:

24 Swingarm and suspension bearings (TDM and TRX models) – re-greasing

1 Over a period of time the grease will harden or dirt will penetrate the bearings due to failed dust seals. Unlike the XTZ, these models are not equipped with grease nipples

2 Remove the swingarm as described in Chapter 6 for greasing of the bearings.

3 On TRX models, the suspension linkage is

not equipped with grease models. Remove the linkage as described in Chapter 6 for greasing of the bearings.

25 Steering head bearings – lubrication

1 Over a period of time the grease will harden or may be washed out of the bearings by incorrect use of jet washes.

2 Disassemble the steering head for re-greasing of the bearings. Refer to Chapter 6 for details.

26 Brakes – fluid change and seal renewal

1 The brake fluid should be changed every two years or whenever a master cylinder or caliper overhaul is carried out. Refer to the

27.2a Unscrew the water pump drain plug (arrowed) . . .

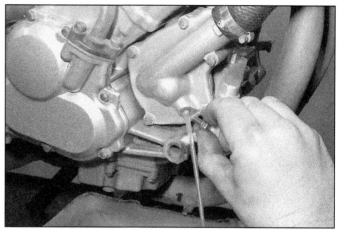

27.2b . . . and allow the coolant to drain

brake bleeding section in Chapter 7, noting that all old fluid must be pumped from the fluid reservoir and hydraulic line before filling with new fluid.

 HAYNES HiNT *Old brake fluid is invariably much darker in colour than new fluid, making it easy to see when all old fluid has been expelled from the system.*

2 Brake caliper and master cylinder seals will deteriorate over a period of time and lose their effectiveness, leading to sticking operation or fluid loss, or allowing the ingress of air and dirt. Refer to Chapter 7 and dismantle the components for seal renewal every two years.

27 Cooling system – draining, flushing and refilling

⚠ *Warning: Allow the engine to cool completely before performing this maintenance operation. Also, don't allow antifreeze to come into contact with your skin or the*

painted surfaces of the motorcycle. Rinse off spills immediately with plenty of water. Antifreeze is highly toxic if ingested. Never leave antifreeze lying around in an open container or in puddles on the floor; children and pets are attracted by its sweet smell and may drink it. Check with local authorities (councils) about disposing of antifreeze. Many communities have collection centres which will see that antifreeze is disposed of safely. Antifreeze is also combustible, so don't store it near open flames.

Draining

1 On all models remove the seat, on TDM models the right-hand fairing side panel, on TRX models the fairing, and on XTZ models the left-hand fairing side panel (see Chapter 8). On 1991 to 1995 TDM models and XTZ models, remove the engine bashplate (see Chapter 8). On TRX models, remove the security bolt holding the radiator cap **(see illustration 16.6a)**. Remove the radiator pressure cap by turning it anti-clockwise until it reaches a stop **(see illustrations 16.6b and c)**. If you hear a hissing sound (indicating there is still pressure in the system), wait until it stops. Now press down on the cap and continue turning the cap until it can be removed.

2 Position a suitable container beneath the water pump. Remove the coolant drain plug from the water pump and allow the coolant to drain completely from the system **(see illustrations)**. Retain the old sealing washer for use during flushing.
3 Position the container beneath the cylinders, then remove the drain plug from the cylinder block and allow the coolant to drain completely from the engine **(see illustrations)**. Retain the old sealing washer for use during flushing.
4 Position the container beneath the coolant reservoir and remove the filler cap. Release the clamp and detach the hose from the bottom of the reservoir and allow the coolant to completely drain **(see illustration)**. Fit the hose back onto the reservoir and secure it with the clamp.

Flushing

5 Flush the system with clean tap water by inserting a garden hose in the radiator filler neck. Allow the water to run through the system until it is clear and flows cleanly out of the drain holes. If the radiator is extremely corroded, remove it (see Chapter 3) and have it cleaned professionally.
6 Clean the drain holes then install the drain plugs using the old sealing washers.

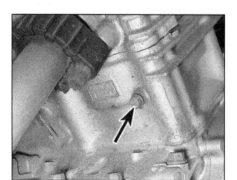

27.3a Unscrew the cylinder drain plug (arrowed) . . .

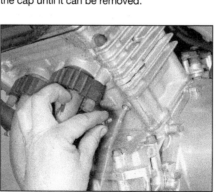

27.3b . . . and allow the coolant to drain

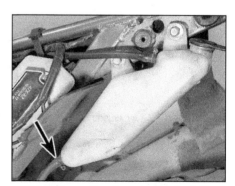

27.4 Release the clamp and detach the hose (arrowed) – XTZ shown

7 Fill the cooling system with clean water mixed with a flushing compound. Make sure the flushing compound is compatible with aluminium components, and follow the manufacturer's instructions carefully.

8 Start the engine and allow it to reach normal operating temperature. Let it run for about ten minutes.

9 Stop the engine. Let it cool for a while, then cover the pressure cap with a heavy rag and turn it anti-clockwise to the first stop, releasing any pressure that may be present in the system. Once the hissing stops, push down on the cap and remove it completely.

10 Drain the system once again.

11 Fill the system with clean water and repeat the procedure in Steps 7 to 9.

Refilling

12 Fit a new sealing washer to each drain plug and tighten them to the torque setting specified at the beginning of the Chapter.

13 Fill the system with the proper coolant mixture (see this Chapter's Specifications) **(see illustration)**. Note: *Pour the coolant in slowly to minimise the amount of air entering the system.* When the radiator appears full, pull the bike upright off its stand and shake it slightly to dissipate the coolant, then place the bike back on the stand and top the radiator up.

27.13 Use only the specified coolant mixture to fill the system . . .

14 When the system is full (all the way up to the top of the radiator filler neck), install the pressure cap **(see illustration)**. Now fill the coolant reservoir to the UPPER level mark (see *Daily (pre-ride) checks*).

15 Start the engine and allow it to idle for 2 to 3 minutes. Flick the throttle twistgrip part open 3 or 4 times, so that the engine speed rises to approximately 4000 – 5000 rpm, then stop the engine. Any air trapped in the system should have bled back to the radiator filler neck.

16 Let the engine cool then remove the pressure cap as described in Step 1. Check that the coolant level is still up to the radiator

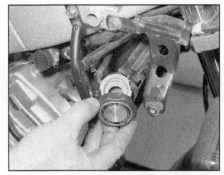

27.14 . . . then fit the pressure cap

filler neck. If it's low, add the specified mixture until it reaches the top of the filler neck. Refit the cap, then on TRX models fit the security bolt.

17 Check the coolant level in the reservoir and top up if necessary.

18 Check the system for leaks.

19 Do not dispose of the old coolant by pouring it down the drain. Instead pour it into a heavy plastic container, cap it tightly and take it into an authorised disposal site or garage – see **Warning** at the beginning of this Section.

20 Install the seat and body panels as required (see Chapter 8).

Every 28,000 miles (42,000 km)

Carry out all the items under the 4000 mile (6000 km) check, plus the following

28 Valve clearances – check and adjustment

1 The engine must be completely cool for this maintenance procedure, so let the machine sit overnight before beginning.

2 Remove the fuel tank and the air filter housing (see Chapter 4), the radiator (see Chapter 3), the spark plugs (see Section 2), and the valve cover (see Chapter 2). Each

cylinder is referred to by a number: no. 1 cylinder is the left cylinder and no. 2 cylinder is the right.

3 Make a chart or sketch of all valve positions so that a note of each clearance can be made against the relevant valve. There are two exhaust valves and three inlet valves per cylinder.

4 Unscrew the timing inspection plug and the centre plug from the alternator cover on the left-hand side of the engine **(see illustration)**. Discard the plug O-rings as new ones should

be used. The engine can be turned using a 19 mm socket on the alternator rotor bolt and turning it in an anti-clockwise direction only **(see illustration)**. Alternatively, place the motorcycle on an auxiliary stand so that the rear wheel is off the ground, select a high gear and rotate the rear wheel by hand in its normal direction of rotation.

5 Turn the engine until the 'I' mark on the rotor aligns with the static timing mark on the alternator cover (a notch in the timing inspection hole) **(see illustration)**, and the

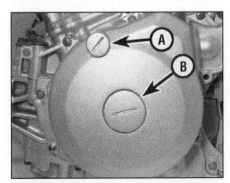

28.4a Unscrew the timing inspection plug (A) and the centre plug (B)

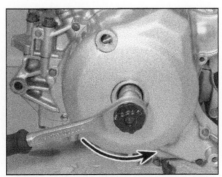

28.4b Turn the engine using a socket on the alternator bolt

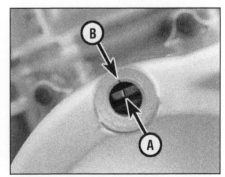

28.5a Turn the engine until the mark on the rotor (A) aligns with the static mark on the cover (B)

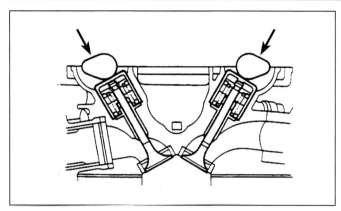

28.5b Note the position of the cam lobes (arrowed)

With the cylinder at TDC on the compression stroke the lobes should not be depressing the valves and should be facing away from each other

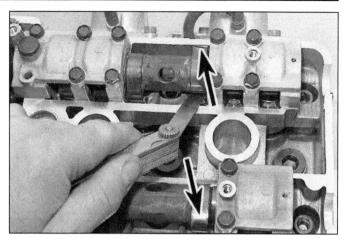

28.6 Make sure the cam lobes (arrowed) face away from each other, then check the valve clearances as shown

camshaft lobes for the No. 1 (left-hand) cylinder are facing away from each other **(see illustration)**. **Note:** *Do not confuse the 'I' mark on the rotor (which indicates TDC) with the 'H' mark which will appear first and which indicates the firing point of the ignition system.* If the cam lobes are facing towards each other, rotate the engine anti-clockwise 360° (one full turn) so that the 'I' mark again aligns with the static timing mark. The camshaft lobes will now be facing away from each other and the No. 1 cylinder is at TDC (top dead centre) on the compression stroke.

6 With No. 1 cylinder at TDC on the compression stroke, check the clearances on

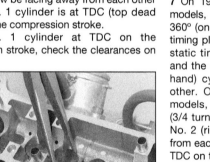

28.10a Lift out the follower . . .

the No. 1 cylinder inlet and exhaust valves. Insert a feeler gauge of the same thickness as the correct valve clearance (see Specifications) between the camshaft lobe and follower of each valve and check that it is a firm sliding fit – you should feel a slight drag when the you pull the gauge out **(see illustration)**. If not, use the feeler gauges to obtain the exact clearance. Record the measured clearance on the chart.

7 On 1991 to 1995 TDM models and XTZ models, now turn the engine anti-clockwise 360° (one full turn) so that the I mark on the timing plate again once again aligns with the static timing mark on the crankcase cover, and the camshaft lobes for the No. 2 (right-hand) cylinder are facing away from each other. On 1996-on TDM models and TRX models, turn the engine anti-clockwise 270° (3/4 turn) so that the camshaft lobes for the No. 2 (right-hand) cylinder are facing away from each other. The No. 2 cylinder is now at TDC on the compression stroke. Measure the clearances of the No. 2 cylinder valves using the method described in Step 6.

8 When all clearances have been measured and charted, identify whether the clearance on any valve falls outside that specified. If it does, the shim between the cam follower and the valve must be swapped with one of a

thickness which will restore the correct clearance.

9 Shim replacement requires removal of the camshafts (see Chapter 2). There is no need to remove both camshafts if shims from only one side of the engine need replacing. Place rags over the spark plug holes and the cam chain tunnel to prevent a shim from dropping into the engine on removal.

10 With the camshaft removed, remove the cam follower of the valve in question, then either retrieve the shim from the inside of the follower or pick it out of the top of the valve using either a magnet, a small screwdriver with a dab of grease on it (the shim will stick to the grease), or a screwdriver and a pair of pliers **(see illustrations)**. Do not allow the shim to fall into the engine.

11 A size mark should be stamped on the upper face of the shim – a shim marked 175 is 1.75 mm thick. If the mark is not visible the shim thickness will have to be measured. It is recommended that the shim is measured anyway to check that it has not worn **(see illustration)**.

12 Using the appropriate shim selection chart (either inlet or exhaust), find where the measured valve clearance and existing shim thickness values intersect and read off the shim size required **(see illustrations)**. **Note:** *If*

28.10b . . . and remove the shim either from inside the follower . . .

28.10c . . . or from the top of the valve

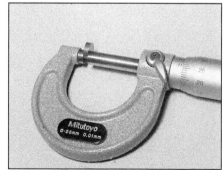

28.11 Measure the shim using a micrometer

MEASURED CLEARANCE	120	125	130	135	140	145	150	155	160	165	**170**	175	180	185	190	195	200	205	210	215	220	225	230	235	240
													INSTALLED SHIM SIZE												
0.00 ~ 0.04				120	125	130	135	140	145	150	**155**	160	165	170	175	180	185	190	195	200	205	210	215	220	225
0.05 ~ 0.09			120	125	130	135	140	145	150	155	**160**	165	170	175	180	185	190	195	200	205	210	215	220	225	230
0.10 ~ 0.14		120	125	130	135	140	145	150	155	160	**165**	170	175	180	185	190	195	200	205	210	215	220	225	230	235
0.15 ~ 0.20	RECOMMENDED CLEARANCE																								
0.21 ~ 0.25	125	130	135	140	145	150	155	160	165	170	**175**	180	185	190	195	200	205	210	215	220	225	230	235	240	
0.26 ~ 0.30	**130**	**135**	**140**	**145**	**150**	**155**	**160**	**165**	**170**	**175**	**180**	**185**	**190**	**195**	**200**	**205**	**210**	**215**	**220**	**225**	**230**	**235**	**240**		
0.31 ~ 0.35	135	140	145	150	155	160	165	170	175	180	185	190	195	200	205	210	215	220	225	230	235	240			
0.36 ~ 0.40	140	145	150	155	160	165	170	175	180	185	190	195	200	205	210	215	220	225	230	235	240				
0.41 ~ 0.45	145	150	155	160	165	170	175	180	185	190	195	200	205	210	215	220	225	230	235	240					
0.46 ~ 0.50	150	155	160	165	170	175	180	185	190	195	200	205	210	215	220	225	230	235	240						
0.51 ~ 0.55	155	160	165	170	175	180	185	190	195	200	205	210	215	220	225	230	235	240							
0.56 ~ 0.60	160	165	170	175	180	185	190	195	200	205	210	215	220	225	230	235	240								
0.61 ~ 0.65	165	170	175	180	185	190	195	200	205	210	215	220	225	230	235	240									
0.66 ~ 0.70	170	175	180	185	190	195	200	205	210	215	220	225	230	235	240										
0.71 ~ 0.75	175	180	185	190	195	200	205	210	215	220	225	230	235	240											
0.76 ~ 0.80	180	185	190	195	200	205	210	215	220	225	230	235	240												
0.81 ~ 0.85	185	190	195	200	205	210	215	220	225	230	235	240													
0.86 ~ 0.90	190	195	200	205	210	215	220	225	230	235	240														
0.91 ~ 0.95	195	200	205	210	215	220	225	230	235	240															
0.96 ~ 1.00	200	205	210	215	220	225	230	235	240																
1.01 ~ 1.05	205	210	215	220	225	230	235	240																	
1.06 ~ 1.10	210	215	220	225	230	235	240																		
1.11 ~ 1.15	215	220	225	230	235	240																			
1.16 ~ 1.20	220	225	230	235	240																				
1.21 ~ 1.25	225	230	235	240																					
1.26 ~ 1.30	230	235	240																						
1.31 ~ 1.35	235	240																							
1.36 ~ 1.40	240																								

28.12a Shim selection chart – inlet valves

[B] MEASURED CLEARANCE	120	125	130	135	140	145	150	155	160	165	170	**175**	180	185	190	195	200	205	210	215	220	225	230	235	240
													INSTALLED SHIM SIZE												
0.00 ~ 0.04						120	125	130	135	140	145	**150**	155	160	165	170	175	180	185	190	195	200	205	210	215
0.05 ~ 0.09					120	125	130	135	140	145	150	**155**	160	165	170	175	180	185	190	195	200	205	210	215	220
0.10 ~ 0.14				120	125	130	135	140	145	150	155	**160**	165	170	175	180	185	190	195	200	205	210	215	220	225
0.15 ~ 0.19			120	125	130	135	140	145	150	155	160	**165**	170	175	180	185	190	195	200	205	210	215	220	225	230
0.20 ~ 0.24		120	125	130	135	140	145	150	155	160	165	**170**	175	180	185	190	195	200	205	210	215	220	225	230	235
0.25 ~ 0.30	RECOMMENDED CLEARANCE																								
0.31 ~ 0.35	125	130	135	140	145	150	155	160	165	170	175	**180**	185	190	195	200	205	210	215	220	225	230	235	240	
0.36 ~ 0.40	**130**	**135**	**140**	**145**	**150**	**155**	**160**	**165**	**170**	**175**	**180**	**185**	**190**	**195**	**200**	**205**	**210**	**215**	**220**	**225**	**230**	**235**	**240**		
0.41 ~ 0.45	135	140	145	150	155	160	165	170	175	180	185	190	195	200	205	210	215	220	225	230	235	240			
0.46 ~ 0.50	140	145	150	155	160	165	170	175	180	185	190	195	200	205	210	215	220	225	230	235	240				
0.51 ~ 0.55	145	150	155	160	165	170	175	180	185	190	195	200	205	210	215	220	225	230	235	240					
0.56 ~ 0.60	150	155	160	165	170	175	180	185	190	195	200	205	210	215	220	225	230	235	240						
0.61 ~ 0.65	155	160	165	170	175	180	185	190	195	200	205	210	215	220	225	230	235	240							
0.66 ~ 0.70	160	165	170	175	180	185	190	195	200	205	210	215	220	225	230	235	240								
0.71 ~ 0.75	165	170	175	180	185	190	195	200	205	210	215	220	225	230	235	240									
0.76 ~ 0.80	170	175	180	185	190	195	200	205	210	215	220	225	230	235	240										
0.81 ~ 0.85	175	180	185	190	195	200	205	210	215	220	225	230	235	240											
0.86 ~ 0.90	180	185	190	195	200	205	210	215	220	225	230	235	240												
0.91 ~ 0.95	185	190	195	200	205	210	215	220	225	230	235	240													
0.96 ~ 1.00	190	195	200	205	210	215	220	225	230	235	240														
1.01 ~ 1.05	195	200	205	210	215	220	225	230	235	240															
1.06 ~ 1.10	200	205	210	215	220	225	230	235	240																
1.11 ~ 1.15	205	210	215	220	225	230	235	240																	
1.16 ~ 1.20	210	215	220	225	230	235	240																		
1.21 ~ 1.25	215	220	225	230	235	240																			
1.26 ~ 1.30	220	225	230	235	240																				
1.31 ~ 1.35	225	230	235	240																					
1.36 ~ 1.40	230	235	240																						
1.41 ~ 1.45	235	240																							
1.46 ~ 1.50	240																								

28.12b Shim selection chart – exhaust valves

28.13 Fit the follower onto the valve

28.15 Use new O-rings on the plugs

the existing shim is marked with a number not ending in 0 or 5, round it up or down as appropriate to the nearest number ending in 0 or 5 so that the chart can be used. Shims are available in 0.05 mm increments from 1.20 mm to 2.40 mm. **Note:** *If the required*

replacement shim is greater than 2.40 mm (the largest available), the valve is probably not seating correctly due to a build-up of carbon deposits and should be checked and cleaned or resurfaced as required (see Chapter 2).

13 Obtain the replacement shim, then lubricate it with molybdenum disulphide oil (a 50/50 mixture of molybdenum disulphide grease and engine oil) and fit it into its recess in the top of the valve, with the size marking on each shim facing up **(see illustration 28.10c)**. Check that the shim is correctly seated, then lubricate the follower with molybdenum disulphide oil and install it onto the valve **(see illustration)**. Repeat the process for any other valves until the clearances are correct, then install the camshafts (see Chapter 2).

14 Rotate the crankshaft several turns to seat the new shim(s), then check the clearances again.

15 Install all disturbed components in a reverse of the removal sequence. Use new O-rings on the timing inspection plug and centre plug and tighten the plugs securely **(see illustration)**.

Every four years

29 Brake hoses – renewal

1 The hoses will in time deteriorate with age and should be renewed every four years regardless of their apparent condition.

2 Refer to Chapter 7 and disconnect the brake hoses from the master cylinders and calipers. Always renew the banjo union sealing washers.

Non-scheduled maintenance

30 Headlight aim –
check and adjustment

Note: *An improperly adjusted headlight may cause problems for oncoming traffic or provide poor, unsafe illumination of the road ahead. Before adjusting the headlight aim, be sure to consult with local traffic laws and regulations – for UK models refer to MOT Test Checks in the Reference section.*

1 The headlight beam can adjusted both

horizontally and vertically. Before making any adjustment, check that the tyre pressures are correct and the suspension is adjusted as required. Make any adjustments to the headlight aim with the machine on level ground, with the fuel tank half full and with an assistant sitting on the seat. If the bike is usually ridden with a passenger on the back, have a second assistant to do this.

2 On 1991 to 1995 TDM models and XTZ models, vertical adjustment is made by turning the adjuster screw on the top outer corner of each headlight unit **(see illustration)**. Turn it clockwise to raise the beam, and anti-clockwise to lower it.

Horizontal adjustment is made by turning the adjuster screw on the bottom inner corner of each headlight unit. For the left-hand beam, turn it clockwise to move the beam to the right, and anti-clockwise to move it to the left. For the right-hand beam, turn it clockwise to move the beam to the left, and anti-clockwise to move it to the right.

3 On 1996-on TDM models, vertical adjustment is made by turning the adjuster screw on the bottom outer corner of each headlight unit **(see illustration)**. Turn it anti-clockwise to raise the beam, and clockwise to lower it. Horizontal adjustment is made by turning the adjuster screw on the top outer

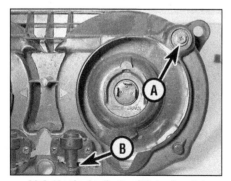

30.2 Vertical adjuster (A), horizontal adjuster (B) – 1991 to 1995 TDM models and XTZ models

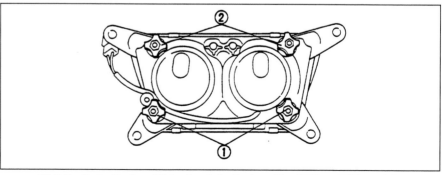

30.3 Vertical adjusters (1), horizontal adjusters (2) – 1996-on TDM models

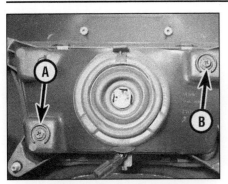

30.4 Vertical adjuster (A), horizontal adjuster (B) – TRX models

corner of each headlight unit. For the left-hand beam, turn it clockwise to move the beam to the left, and anti-clockwise to move it to the right. For the right-hand beam, turn it clockwise to move the beam to the right, and anti-clockwise to move it to the left.

4 On TRX models, vertical adjustment is made by turning the adjuster screw on the bottom left corner of the headlight unit **(see illustration)**. Turn it clockwise to raise the beam, and anti -clockwise to lower it. Horizontal adjustment is made by turning the adjuster screw on the top right corner of the headlight unit. Turn it clockwise to move the beam to the left, and anti-clockwise to move it to the right.

31 Cylinder compression – check

1 Among other things, poor engine performance may be caused by leaking valves, incorrect valve clearances, a leaking head gasket, or worn pistons, rings and/or cylinder walls. A cylinder compression check will help pinpoint these conditions and can also indicate the presence of excessive carbon deposits in the cylinder heads.

2 The only tools required are a compression gauge and a spark plug wrench. A compression gauge with a threaded end for the spark plug 12 mm diameter hole is preferable to the type which requires hand pressure to maintain a tight seal. Depending on the outcome of the initial test, a squirt-type oil can may also be needed.

3 Make sure the valve clearances are correctly set (see Section 28) and that the cylinder head fasteners are tightened to the correct torque setting (see Chapter 2).

4 Refer to *Fault Finding Equipment* in the Reference section for details of the compression test. Refer to the specifications at the beginning of the Chapter for compression figures.

32 Engine – oil pressure check

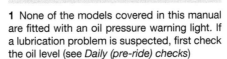

1 None of the models covered in this manual are fitted with an oil pressure warning light. If a lubrication problem is suspected, first check the oil level (see *Daily (pre-ride) checks*)

2 If the oil level is correct, an oil pressure check must be carried out.

3 To check the oil pressure, slacken the oil gallery bolt in the left-hand side of the cylinder head – there is no need to remove it **(see illustration)**.

4 Start the engine and allow it to idle. After a short while oil should begin to seep out from the oil gallery plug **(see illustration)**. If no oil has appeared after one minute, stop the engine immediately.

5 If the oil does not appear after one minute, either the pressure regulator is stuck open, the oil pump is faulty, the oil strainer or filter is blocked, or there is other engine damage. Begin diagnosis by checking the oil filter (Section 22 of this Chapter), strainer and regulator, then the oil pump (see Chapter 2). If those items check out okay, chances are the

bearing oil clearances are excessive and the engine needs to be overhauled.

6 If the oil appears very quickly and spurts out, the pressure may be too high, meaning either an oil passage is clogged, the regulator is stuck closed or the wrong grade of oil is being used.

7 Refer to Chapter 2 and rectify any problems before running the engine again.

8 Tighten the oil gallery bolt to the torque setting specified at the beginning of the Chapter.

33 Fuel hoses – renewal

> ⚠ **Warning: Petrol (gasoline) is extremely flammable, so take extra precautions when you work on any part of the fuel system. Don't smoke or allow open flames or bare light bulbs near the work area, and don't work in a garage where a natural gas-type appliance is present. If you spill any fuel on your skin, rinse it off immediately with soap and water. When you perform any kind of work on the fuel system, wear safety glasses and have a fire extinguisher suitable for a Class B type fire (flammable liquids) on hand.**

1 The fuel delivery and vacuum hoses should be renewed after a few years regardless of their condition.

2 Remove the fuel tank (see Chapter 4). Disconnect the fuel hoses from the fuel tap, fuel pump and from the carburettors, noting the routing of each hose and where it connects (see Chapter 4 if required). It is advisable to make a sketch of the various hoses before removing them to ensure they are correctly installed.

3 Secure each new hose to its unions using new clamps. Run the engine and check that there are no fuel leaks before taking the machine out on the road.

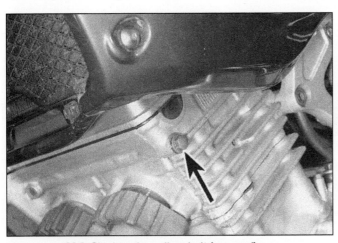

32.3 Slacken the gallery bolt (arrowed) . . .

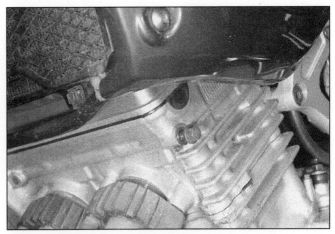

32.4 . . . then start the engine and check that the oil dribbles out within a minute

34 Front forks – oil change

TDM, TRX and 1995 XTZ models

1 Fork oil degrades over a period of time and loses its damping qualities. The forks do not have drain screws so it is necessary to remove them from the fork yokes (see Chapter 6, Section 6) and remove their top bolts, spacer and spring assembly so that they can be turned upside down and pumped to expel the fork oil.

2 Once the forks have been removed from the yokes, refer to the appropriate part of Section 7, Chapter 6, to unscrew the fork top bolt and withdraw the spacer and spring assembly. Note that there is no need to slacken the damper rod bolt as advised in the early part of this procedure because this relates to fork overhaul. Turn the fork upside down and pump the inner tube and slider to expel as much oil as possible.

3 Refill each fork with the specified amount and type of fork oil (see Chapter 6 Specifications) and install the fork spring, spacer and top bolt. Take careful note of how the oil level is measured and the importance of the level being identical in each fork. Refer to the final part of the relevant reassembly procedure in Chapter 6, Section 7 for details.

1989 to 1994 XTZ models

4 Fork oil degrades over a period of time and loses its damping qualities. These models are equipped with drain screws in the fork sliders **(see illustration 7.59 in Chapter 6)** and therefore changing the fork oil is a relatively straightforward task.

5 Position the bike on an auxiliary stand and support it under the engine so that the front wheel is off the ground. Unscrew the fork top bolt from the top of each fork tube.

 Warning: The fork spring is pressing on the fork top bolt (via the spacer) with considerable pressure. Unscrew the bolt very carefully, keeping a downward pressure on it and release it slowly as it is likely to spring clear. It is advisable to wear some form of eye and face protection when carrying out this operation.

6 Hold a piece of thick card to act as a chute beneath the fork drain screw on one fork slider, then remove the drain screw and allow the oil to drain. Pump the fork to expel all of the oil. Now do the same on the other fork leg.

7 Slide the fork tube down into the slider and withdraw the spacer, spring seat and the spring from the tube. Note which way up the spring is fitted.

8 Check the condition of the sealing washers on the drain screws and screw them back into the fork sliders.

9 Slowly pour in the specified quantity of the specified grade of fork oil (see Chapter 6

Specifications) and pump the fork at least ten times to distribute it evenly; the oil level should also be measured and adjustment made by adding or subtracting oil. Fully compress the fork tube into the slider and measure the fork oil level from the top of the tube **(see illustration 7.26b in Chapter 6)**. Add or subtract fork oil until it is at the level specified at the beginning of the Chapter. Note that bike must be upright when the oil level is measured and the oil level must be the same in each fork.

10 Extend the fork tube and slider fully, then install the spring, the spring seat, with its shouldered side fitting down into the top of the spring, and the spacer.

11 Apply a smear of grease to the top bolt O-ring and thread the bolt into the top of the fork tube.

 Warning: It will be necessary to compress the spring by pressing it down using the top bolt to engage the threads of the top bolt with the fork tube. This is a potentially dangerous operation and should be performed with care, using an assistant if necessary. Wipe off any excess oil before starting to prevent the possibility of slipping.

Keep the fork tube fully extended whilst pressing on the spring. Screw the top bolt carefully into the fork tube making sure it is not cross-threaded and tighten it to the specified torque setting (see Chapter 6 Specifications).

Chapter 2
Engine, clutch and transmission

Contents

Degrees of difficulty

Easy, suitable for novice with little experience 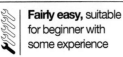	**Fairly easy,** suitable for beginner with some experience	**Fairly difficult,** suitable for competent DIY mechanic 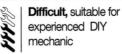	**Difficult,** suitable for experienced DIY mechanic	**Very difficult,** suitable for expert DIY or professional

Specifications

General

Type	Four-stroke parallel twin
Capacity	
TDM and TRX models	849 cc
XTZ models	749 cc
Bore	
TDM and TRX models	89.5 mm
XTZ models	87.0 mm
Stroke	
TDM and TRX models	67.5 mm
XTZ models	63 mm
Compression ratio	
1991 to 1995 TDM models	9.2 to 1
1996-on TDM models and TRX models . . .	10.5 to 1
XTZ models	9.5 to 1
Cylinder numbering	No. 1 (left-hand), No. 2 (right-hand)
Cooling system	Liquid cooled
Clutch	Wet multi-plate
Transmission	Five-speed constant mesh
Final drive	Chain

Camshafts

Inlet lobe height
  1991 to 1995 TDM models and XTZ models
    Standard . . . .   35.7 to 35.8 mm
    Service limit (min) . . . .   35.6 mm
  1996-on TDM models and TRX models
    Standard . . . .   35.95 to 36.05 mm
    Service limit (min) . . . .   35.85 mm
Exhaust lobe height – all models
    Standard . . . .   35.95 to 36.05 mm
    Service limit (min) . . . .   35.85 mm
Journal diameter . . . .   24.967 to 24.980 mm
Journal holder diameter . . . .   25.000 to 25.021 mm
Journal oil clearance . . . .   0.020 to 0.054 mm
Runout (max) . . . .   0.03 mm

Cylinder head

Warpage (max) . . . .   0.03 mm

Valves, guides and springs

Valve clearances . . . .   see Chapter 1
Inlet valve
  Stem diameter
    Standard . . . .   5.475 to 5.490 mm
    Service limit (min) . . . .   5.445 mm
  Guide bore diameter
    Standard . . . .   5.500 to 5.512 mm
    Service limit (max) . . . .   5.55 mm
  Stem-to-guide clearance
    Standard . . . .   0.010 to 0.037 mm
    Service limit (max) . . . .   0.08 mm
  Head diameter . . . .   25.9 to 26.1 mm
  Face width . . . .   2.06 to 2.46 mm
  Seat width . . . .   0.9 to 1.1 mm
  Margin thickness . . . .   0.8 to 1.2 mm
Exhaust valve
  Stem diameter
    Standard . . . .   5.460 to 5.475 mm
    Service limit (min) . . . .   5.43 mm
  Guide bore diameter
    Standard . . . .   5.500 to 5.512 mm
    Service limit (max) . . . .   5.55 mm
  Stem-to-guide clearance
    Standard . . . .   0.025 to 0.052 mm
    Service limit (max) . . . .   0.10 mm
  Head diameter . . . .   27.9 to 28.1 mm
  Face width . . . .   2.06 to 2.46 mm
  Seat width . . . .   0.9 to 1.1 mm
  Margin thickness . . . .   0.8 to 1.2 mm
Valve stem runout (max) . . . .   0.01 mm
Valve springs free length (inlet and exhaust)
    Standard . . . .   37.29 mm
    Service limit (min) . . . .   35.2 mm
Valve spring bend (max) . . . .   1.7 mm

Cylinder block

Bore
  TDM and TRX models
    Standard . . . .   89.500 to 89.505 mm
    Service limit (max) . . . .   89.6 mm
  XTZ models
    Standard . . . .   87.000 to 87.005 mm
    Service limit (max) . . . .   87.1 mm
Warpage (max) . . . .   0.03 mm
Ovality (out-of-round) (max) . . . .   0.03 mm
Taper (max) . . . .   0.05 mm
Cylinder compression . . . .   see Chapter 1

Pistons

Piston diameter (measured 4.5 mm (TDM and TRX models) or
4.7 mm (XTZ models) up from skirt, at 90° to piston pin axis)

	Standard	Service Limit
TDM and TRX models	89.420 to 89.435 mm	
XTZ models	86.920 to 86.935 mm	
Piston-to-bore clearance	0.065 to 0.085 mm	0.15 mm
Piston pin diameter	19.991 to 20.000 mm	19.975 mm
Piston pin bore diameter in piston	20.002 to 20.013 mm	20.043 mm (max)
Piston pin-to-piston pin bore clearance	0.002 to 0.022 mm	0.07 mm

Piston rings

Top ring

TDM and TRX models

Ring width . . . . 3.5 mm

Ring thickness . . . . 1.0 mm

Ring end gap (installed)

Standard . . . . 0.30 to 0.45 mm

Service limit (max) . . . . 0.70 mm

Piston ring-to-groove clearance

Standard . . . . 0.035 to 0.070 mm

Service limit (max) . . . . 0.12 mm

XTZ models

Ring width . . . . 3.3 mm

Ring thickness . . . . 1.0 mm

Ring end gap (installed)

Standard . . . . 0.30 to 0.50 mm

Service limit (max) . . . . 0.70 mm

Piston ring-to-groove clearance

Standard . . . . 0.03 to 0.07 mm

Service limit (max) . . . . 0.12 mm

2nd (middle) ring

1991 to 1995 TDM models

Ring width . . . . 3.5 mm

Ring thickness . . . . 1.0 mm

Ring end gap (installed)

Standard . . . . 0.30 to 0.45 mm

Service limit (max) . . . . 0.70 mm

Piston ring-to-groove clearance

Standard . . . . 0.02 to 0.055 mm

Service limit (max) . . . . 0.12 mm

1996-on TDM models and TRX models

Ring width . . . . 3.5 mm

Ring thickness . . . . 1.0 mm

Ring end gap (installed)

Standard . . . . 0.30 to 0.45 mm

Service limit (max) . . . . 0.70 mm

Piston ring-to-groove clearance

Standard . . . . 0.035 to 0.070 mm

Service limit (max) . . . . 0.12 mm

XTZ models

Ring width . . . . 3.3 mm

Ring thickness . . . . 1.0 mm

Ring end gap (installed)

Standard . . . . 0.30 to 0.50 mm

Service limit (max) . . . . 0.70 mm

Piston ring-to-groove clearance

Standard . . . . 0.02 to 0.06 mm

Service limit (max) . . . . 0.12 mm

Oil ring

TDM and TRX models

Ring width . . . . 2.85 mm

Ring thickness . . . . 2.0 mm

Side-rail end gap (installed) . . . . 0.20 to 0.70 mm

XTZ models

Ring width . . . . 2.80 mm

Ring thickness . . . . 2.0 mm

Side-rail end gap (installed) . . . . 0.20 to 0.70 mm

Clutch

Friction plate thickness – all models
    Standard . . . . 2.9 to 3.1 mm
    Service limit (min) . . . . 2.8 mm
Plain plates
    1991 to 1995 TDM models and all XTZ models
        Thickness (special 'slick' plate) . . . . 2.2 to 2.4 mm
        Thickness (all other plates) . . . . 1.9 to 2.1 mm
        Warpage (max) . . . . 0.1 mm
    1996-on TDM models and all TRX models
        Thickness . . . . 1.9 to 2.1 mm
        Warpage (max) . . . . 0.1 mm
Clutch springs
    Spring free length
        1991 to 1998 TDM and all TRX models
            Standard . . . . 55 mm
            Service limit (min) . . . . 53 mm
        1999 TDM models
            Standard . . . . 50 mm
            Service limit (min) . . . . 48 mm
        XTZ models
            Standard . . . . 51.8 mm
            Service limit (min) . . . . 50 mm

Oil pump

Inner rotor tip-to-outer rotor clearance
    Standard . . . . 0.0 to 0.12 mm
    Service limit (max) . . . . 0.17 mm
Outer rotor-to-body clearance
    Standard . . . . 0.03 to 0.08 mm
    Service limit (max) . . . . 0.15 mm
Rotor end-float . . . . 0.03 to 0.08 mm

Connecting rods

Big-end side clearance
    Standard . . . . 0.160 to 0.272 mm
    Service limit (max) . . . . 0.5 mm
Big-end oil clearance
    Standard . . . . 0.026 to 0.050 mm
    Service limit (max) . . . . 0.09 mm

Crankshaft and bearings

Main bearing oil clearance
    Standard . . . . 0.020 to 0.038 mm
    Service limit (max) . . . . 0.1 mm
Runout (max)
    1991 to 1995 TDM models and all XTZ models . . . . 0.02 mm
    1996-on TDM models and all TRX models . . . . 0.035 mm

Transmission

Gear ratios (no. of teeth)
    1991 to 1995 TDM models
        Primary reduction . . . . 1.718 to 1 (67/39T)
        Final reduction . . . . 2.750 to 1 (44/16T)
        1st gear . . . . 2.846 to 1 (37/13T)
        2nd gear . . . . 1.850 to 1 (37/20T)
        3rd gear . . . . 1.318 to 1 (29/22T)
        4th gear . . . . 1.074 to 1 (29/27T)
        5th gear . . . . 0.900 to 1 (27/30T)
    1996 to 1998 TDM models
        Primary reduction . . . . 1.718 to 1 (67/39T)
        Final reduction . . . . 2.471 to 1 (42/17T)
        1st gear . . . . 2.846 to 1 (37/13T)
        2nd gear . . . . 1.850 to 1 (37/20T)
        3rd gear . . . . 1.429 to 1 (30/21T)
        4th gear . . . . 1.174 to 1 (27/23T)
        5th gear . . . . 1.037 to 1 (28/27T)

1999 TDM models
    Primary reduction .... 1.718 to 1 (67/39T)
    Final reduction .... 2.688 to 1 (43/16T)
    1st gear .... 2.643 to 1 (37/14T)
    2nd gear .... 1.947 to 1 (37/19T)
    3rd gear .... 1.500 to 1 (30/20T)
    4th gear .... 1.174 to 1 (27/23T)
    5th gear .... 0.964 to 1 (27/28T)
TRX models
    Primary reduction .... 1.718 to 1 (67/39T)
    Final reduction .... 2.294 to 1 (39/17T)
    1st gear .... 2.571 to 1 (36/14T)
    2nd gear .... 1.850 to 1 (37/20T)
    3rd gear .... 1.429 to 1 (30/21T)
    4th gear .... 1.174 to 1 (27/23T)
    5th gear .... 1.037 to 1 (28/27T)
XTZ models
    Primary reduction .... 1.718 to 1 (67/39T)
    Final reduction .... 2.875 to 1 (46/16T)
    1st gear .... 2.846 to 1 (37/13T)
    2nd gear .... 1.850 to 1 (37/20T)
    3rd gear .... 1.429 to 1 (30/21T)
    4th gear .... 1.174 to 1 (27/23T)
    5th gear .... 1.037 to 1 (28/27T)
Shaft runout (max) .... 0.08 mm
Selector fork shaft runout (max) .... 0.03 mm

Torque settings

Engine mounting bolts
  TDM models
    Small triangular engine bracket bolts to engine .... 30 Nm
    Engine bracket bolts to underside of engine at back .... 30 Nm
    Lower rear mounting bolt .... 64 Nm
    Upper rear mounting bolt nut .... 89 Nm
    Engine bracket to engine bolts .... 60 Nm
    Engine bracket to frame bolts .... 30 Nm
  TRX models
    Lower rear mounting bolt nut .... 75 Nm
    Upper rear mounting bolt nut .... 75 Nm
    Upper front mounting bolts .... 55 Nm
    Engine bracket to engine bolts (left-hand side) .... 30 Nm
    Engine bracket to frame bolt (left-hand side) .... 55 Nm
    Engine bracket to engine bolt (with collar) (right-hand side) ...... 55 Nm
    Engine bracket to frame bolts (right-hand side) .... 30 Nm
  XTZ models
    Swingarm pivot bolt nut .... 90 Nm
    Lower rear mounting bolt nut .... 58 Nm
    Upper rear mounting bolt nut .... 58 Nm
    Frame downtube bolts/nuts .... 32 Nm
    Lower front mounting bolt nut .... 58 Nm
Valve cover bolts .... 10 Nm
Camshaft holder bolts .... 10 Nm
Camshaft sprocket bolts .... 24 Nm
Cam chain tensioner mounting bolts .... 10 Nm
Cam chain tensioner cap bolt .... 20 Nm
Cylinder head nuts .... 40 Nm
Cylinder head bolts .... 10 Nm
Oil pipe banjo bolt to cylinder head .... 21 Nm
Coolant hose union bolts (cylinder block) .... 10 Nm
Clutch nut .... 70 Nm
Clutch spring bolts .... 8 Nm
Clutch cover bolts .... 10 Nm
Starter clutch bolts .... 10 Nm
Selector drum retainer plate bolts .... 12 Nm
Stopper arm bolt
  1991 to 1995 TDM models and XTZ models .... 12 Nm
  1996-on TDM models and TRX models .... 10 Nm
Gearchange linkage arm pinch bolt .... 12 Nm

Torque settings (continued)

Outer sprocket cover bolts	5 Nm
Oil pump mounting screws	6 Nm
Oil pump assembly screw	6 Nm
Oil pump cover bolts	10 Nm
Oil pipe to oil pump cover bolts	10 Nm
Oil pipe banjo bolts to crankcase cover/oil tank and cylinder head	21 Nm
Oil pipe to oil tank bolts	10 Nm
Oil pressure relief valve holder bolt	10 Nm
Oil strainer cover screws	7 Nm
Oil sump bolts	10 Nm
Oil hose union to crankcase bolts	10 Nm
Balancer shaft holder bolts	10 Nm
Balancer shaft retainer plate Torx bolt	12 Nm
Oil strainer holder bolts	10 Nm
Crankcase top cover bolts (1991 to 1995 TDM models and all XTZ models)	10 Nm
Crankcase 6 mm bolts	12 Nm
Crankcase 8 mm bolts	24 Nm
Crankcase 10 mm bolts	40 Nm
Connecting rod cap nuts	
Initial setting	
1991 to 1995 TDM models and all XTZ models	46 Nm
1996-on TDM models and all TRX models	35 Nm
Final setting (all models)	48 Nm
Transmission output shaft retainer plate bolts (left-hand side)	10 Nm
Transmission input shaft bearing retainer Torx screws	12 Nm
Oil gallery bolt	10 Nm

1 General information

The engine/transmission unit is a liquid-cooled parallel twin with five valves per cylinder (three inlet and two exhaust). The valves are operated by double overhead camshafts which are chain driven off the crankshaft. The engine/transmission assembly is constructed from aluminium alloy. The crankcase is divided horizontally.

The crankcase incorporates a dry sump, pressure-fed lubrication system which uses two gear-driven oil pumps, one a feed pump to lubricate the engine, the other a scavenge pump to return oil to the tank, both driven off the crankshaft. The sump houses the oil filter, by-pass valve assembly and relief valve. The oil tank is mounted behind the engine on 1991 to 1995 TDM models and all XTZ models, and on the engine behind the cylinders on later TDM models and all TRX models. The oil pumps are gear driven off the crankshaft.

The crankshaft also drives two balancer shafts which eliminate the vibration inherent in parallel twin engines

The alternator and starter clutch are on the left-hand end of the crankshaft.

Power from the crankshaft is routed to the transmission via the clutch. The clutch is of the wet, multi-plate type and is gear-driven off the crankshaft. The transmission is a five-speed constant-mesh unit. Final drive to the rear wheel is by chain and sprockets.

2 Operations possible with the engine in the frame

The components and assemblies listed below can be removed without having to remove the engine/transmission assembly from the frame. If however, a number of areas require attention at the same time, removal of the engine is recommended.

Valve cover
Camshafts
Cylinder head
Cylinder block, pistons and piston rings
Pick-up coil assembly
Clutch
Gearchange mechanism (external components)
Alternator
Starter clutch
Oil filter
Oil pumps, oil strainer, oil pressure relief valve and by-pass valve
Starter motor
Water pump
Balancer shafts (1991 to 1995 TDM and all XTZ models)
Cam chain

3 Operations requiring engine removal

It is necessary to remove the engine/transmission assembly from the frame to gain access to the following components.

Transmission shafts
Selector drum and forks
Connecting rods and bearings
Crankshaft and bearings
Balancer shafts (1996-on TDM models and all TRX models)

4 Major engine repair – general note

1 It is not always easy to determine when or if an engine should be completely overhauled, as a number of factors must be considered.
2 High mileage is not necessarily an indication that an overhaul is needed, while low mileage, on the other hand, does not preclude the need for an overhaul. Frequency of servicing is probably the single most important consideration. An engine that has regular and frequent oil and filter changes, as well as other required maintenance, will most likely give many miles of reliable service.

Conversely, a neglected engine, or one which has not been run in properly, may require an overhaul very early in its life.

3 Exhaust smoke and excessive oil consumption are both indications that piston rings and/or valve guides are in need of attention, although make sure that the fault is not due to oil leakage.

4 If the engine is making obvious knocking or rumbling noises, the connecting rods and/or main bearings are probably at fault.

5 Loss of power, rough running, excessive valve train noise and high fuel consumption rates may also point to the need for an overhaul, especially if they are all present at the same time. If a complete tune-up does not remedy the situation, major mechanical work is the only solution.

6 An engine overhaul generally involves restoring the internal parts to the specifications of a new engine. The piston rings and main and connecting rod bearings are usually renewed and the cylinder walls honed or, if necessary, re-bored during a major overhaul. Generally the valve seats are re-ground, since they are usually in less than perfect condition at this point. The end result should be a like new engine that will give as many trouble-free miles as the original.

7 Before beginning the engine overhaul, read through the related procedures to familiarise yourself with the scope and requirements of the job. Overhauling an engine is not all that difficult, but it is time consuming. Plan on the motorcycle being tied up for a minimum of two weeks. Check on the availability of parts and make sure that any necessary special tools, equipment and supplies are obtained in advance.

8 Most work can be done with typical workshop hand tools, although a number of precision measuring tools are required for inspecting parts to determine if they must be renewed. Often a dealer will handle the inspection of parts and offer advice concerning reconditioning and renewal. As a

general rule, time is the primary cost of an overhaul so it does not pay to install worn or substandard parts.

9 As a final note, to ensure maximum life and minimum trouble from a rebuilt engine, everything must be assembled with care in a spotlessly clean environment.

5 Engine – removal and installation

Caution: The engine is very heavy. Engine removal and installation should be carried out with the aid of at least one assistant; personal injury or damage could occur if the engine falls or is dropped. An hydraulic or mechanical floor jack should be used to support and lower or raise the engine if possible.

Removal

1 Support the bike securely in an upright position using an auxiliary stand. Work can be made easier by raising the machine to a suitable working height on an hydraulic ramp or a suitable platform. Make sure the motorcycle is secure and will not topple over (see *Tools and Workshop Tips* in the Reference section). When disconnecting any wiring, cables and hoses, it is advisable to mark or tag them as a reminder to where they connect.

2 If the engine is dirty, particularly around its mountings, wash it thoroughly before starting any major dismantling work. This will make work much easier and rule out the possibility of caked on lumps of dirt falling into some vital component.

3 Remove the seat, side covers, fairing side panels (TDM and XTZ models), fairing, and engine bashplate (1991 to 1995 TDM models and XTZ models) (see Chapter 8). On 1996-on TDM models and XTZ models, the fairing can be left in situ, though it is advisable to remove

it to avoid the possibility of damaging it while removing the engine.

4 Remove the fuel tank (see Chapter 4).

5 Drain the engine oil and the coolant (see Chapter 1).

6 Disconnect the negative (-ve) lead from the battery, then disconnect the positive (+ve) lead (see Chapter 9). On 1991 to 1995 TDM models, remove the battery and the battery box (see Chapter 9).

7 Remove the radiator (see Chapter 3).

8 Remove the exhaust system (see Chapter 4).

9 Remove the carburettors (see Chapter 4). Detach the vacuum hose(s) from the inlet manifolds. On 1991 to 1995 TDM models, unscrew the bolts securing the choke knob to the left-hand engine mounting bracket and position it clear. Plug the engine inlet manifolds with clean rag. On 1999 TDM remove the fuel pump and fuel filter as a unit complete with their mounting bracket (see Chapter 4).

10 On TDM and TRX models, remove the thermostat housing (see Chapter 3). When removing the housing, remove it along with the pipe that bolts onto the valve cover, rather than separating the hose from the pipe. The pipe is secured by a bolt – make sure the pipe O-ring does not fall into the engine when easing out the pipe **(see illustration 7.2)**. Discard the O-ring as a new one must be used.

11 On XTZ models, unscrew the bolt securing the coolant pipe to the valve cover and ease the pipe out, making sure the O-ring does not fall into the engine. Discard the O-ring as a new one must be used.

12 Trace the alternator, ignition pick-up coil and neutral switch wiring from the top of the alternator cover and disconnect it at the connectors **(see illustrations)**. Release the wiring from any clips or ties, noting its routing, and coil it so that it does not impede engine removal.

13 Disconnect the spark plug caps from the spark plugs and secure them clear of the engine.

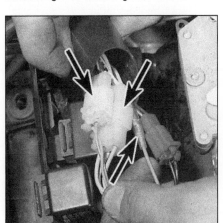

5.12a Alternator/pick-up coil/neutral switch wiring connectors (arrowed) – TDM models

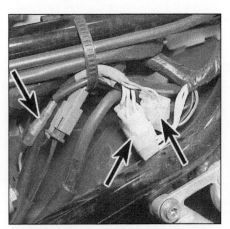

5.12b Alternator/pick-up coil/neutral switch wiring connectors (arrowed) – TRX models

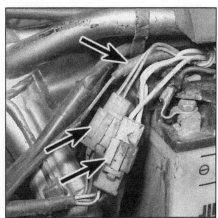

5.12c Alternator/pick-up coil/neutral switch wiring connectors (arrowed) – XTZ models

5.14 Unscrew the nut and detach the starter motor lead from the starter relay

5.16 Unscrew the bolt (arrowed) and detach the cable and hose clip

14 Disconnect the starter motor lead from the starter relay **(see illustration)**.

15 Disconnect the earth wiring connector from the main wiring loom.

16 On 1991 to 1995 TDM models and all XTZ models, the battery's main earth cable can remain attached to the engine. On 1996-on TDM models and all TRX models, unscrew the bolt securing the cable to the back of the engine and detach it along with the clip securing the hoses **(see illustration)**.

17 Detach the clutch cable from the release lever on the clutch cover (see Section 17).

18 Remove the front sprocket (see Chapter 6). On TDM and XTZ models, also remove the gearchange lever (see Chapter 6).

19 On 1991 to 1995 TDM models and all XTZ models, disconnect the crankcase breather hose from the crankcase **(see illustration)**. Also slacken the clamp and detach the hose from its union on the oil filter housing **(see illustration)**. Now unscrew the bolts and detach the oil pipe from the oil pump cover

(see illustration). Discard the O-ring as a new one must be used.

20 At this point, position an hydraulic or mechanical jack under the engine with a block of wood between the jack head and crankcase **(see illustration)**. Make sure the jack is centrally positioned so the engine will not topple in any direction when the last mounting bolt is removed. Take the weight of the engine on the jack. It is also advisable to place a block of wood between the rear wheel and the ground, or under the swingarm, to prevent the bike tilting back onto the rear wheel when the engine is removed. Check around the engine and frame to make sure that all wiring, cables and hoses that need to be disconnected have been disconnected, and that any remaining connected to the engine are not retained by any clips, guides or brackets. Check that any protruding mounting brackets will not get in the way and remove them if necessary.

21 On TDM models, unscrew the bolts securing the engine bracket to the frame and the engine on each side and remove the brackets **(see illustrations)**. Note which bolt fits where as they are of different lengths. Make sure the engine is properly supported on the jack, and have an assistant support it

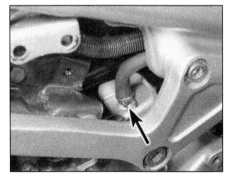

5.19a Release the clamp and detach the breather hose (arrowed)

5.19b Slacken the clamp screw (arrowed) and detach the hose

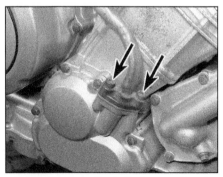

5.19c Unscrew the bolts (arrowed) and detach the pipe

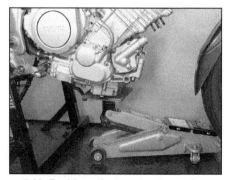

5.20 Position a jack under the engine

5.21a Unscrew the bolts (arrowed) and remove the left-hand . . .

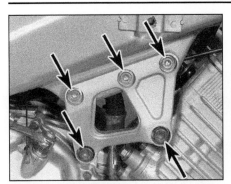

5.21b . . . and right-hand engine brackets

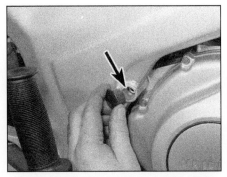

5.21c Upper rear engine mounting bolt (arrowed)

5.21d Lower rear engine mounting bolt (arrowed)

5.21e Remove the triangular bracket (arrowed) . . .

5.21f . . . and the bottom bracket (arrowed)

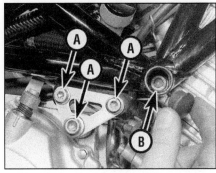

5.22a Engine bracket bolts (A) and upper front mounting bolt (B) – right-hand side

as well. Remove the cap from each end of the upper rear mounting bolt, then unscrew the nut and withdraw the bolt **(see illustration)**. Finally unscrew and remove the lower rear mounting bolt **(see illustration)**. If required, after the engine has been removed, unscrew the bolts securing the small triangular mounting bracket to the left-hand side of the engine and the bolts securing the bracket to

the underside of the engine at the back and remove the brackets **(see illustrations)**.
22 On TRX models, unscrew the bolts securing the engine bracket to the frame and the engine on each side and remove the brackets, along with the collar fitted with the right-hand bracket **(see illustrations)**. Note which bolt fits where as they are of different lengths. Remove the caps from the upper

front mounting bolts, then unscrew the bolts. Make sure the engine is properly supported on the jack, and have an assistant support it as well. Unscrew the nut from the upper rear mounting bolt and withdraw the bolt **(see illustration)**. Finally unscrew the nut on the lower rear mounting bolt and remove the bolt.
23 On XTZ models, unscrew the nut from the lower front mounting bolt and remove the bolt

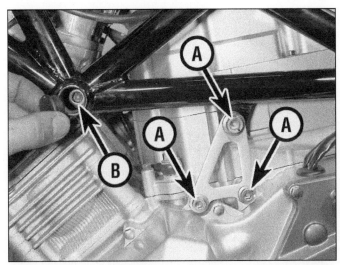

5.22b Engine bracket bolts (A) and upper front mounting bolt (B) – left-hand side

5.22c Upper and lower rear mounting bolts (arrowed)

5.23a Lower front mounting bolt (arrowed)

5.23b Downtube upper bolts (arrowed)

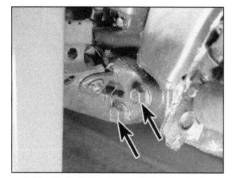

5.23c Downtube lower bolts (arrowed)

5.23d Upper and lower rear mounting bolts (arrowed)

(see illustration). Unscrew the four bolts securing each of the frame downtubes and remove the downtubes **(see illustrations)**. Remove the cap from each end of the upper rear mounting bolt, then unscrew the nut and withdraw the bolt **(see illustration)**. Unscrew the nut on the lower rear mounting bolt and remove the bolt. Remove the cap from each end of the swingarm pivot bolt, then unscrew the nut on its right-hand end. The swingarm pivot bolt also acts as the middle rear engine mounting bolt, so it must be removed. To prevent the swingarm/rear wheel assembly from becoming unstable, partially withdraw the pivot bolt from the left-hand side and slide into its place from the right-hand side a suitable bolt that will support the swingarm, making sure that it does not go into the engine mount. Withdraw the pivot bolt further until the engine is free, but leave it partially inserted so that it still supports the left-hand side of the swingarm.

24 The engine can now be removed from the frame. Check that all wiring, cables and hoses are well clear, then carefully lower the engine and manoeuvre it forward and out of the side of the frame (see *Caution* above).

Installation

25 Installation is the reverse of removal, noting the following points:
  a) Make sure no wires, cables or hoses become trapped between the engine and the frame when installing the engine.
  b) Many of the engine mounting bolts are of different size and length. Make sure the

correct bolt is installed in its correct location, with its washer if fitted. Install all of the bolts and nuts finger-tight until they are all located, then tighten them in the order given in the relevant Step below to their torque settings as specified at the beginning of the Chapter.
  c) On TDM models, if removed, and before the engine is mounted, fit the small triangular mounting bracket onto the left-hand side of the engine and the bracket to the underside of the engine at the back and tighten their bolts to the specified torque setting **(see illustration 5.21e and f)**. Locate all the mounting bolts, not forgetting the washers with the engine bracket-to-engine mounting bolts, and tighten them finger-tight. Now tighten the lower rear mounting bolt first, then the upper rear mounting bolt nut, then the engine bracket-to-engine bolts, and finally the engine bracket-to-frame bolts, tightening them all to their specified torque. Fit the caps into each end of the upper rear bolt.
  d) On TRX models, locate all the mounting bolts, not forgetting the washers with the upper and lower rear bolts (they locate under the bolt head, not the nut), and the collar between the right-hand engine bracket and the engine, and tighten them finger-tight. Now tighten the lower rear mounting bolt nut first, then the upper rear mounting bolt nut, then the upper front mounting bolts (left-hand side first), then the engine bracket-to-engine and frame

frame bolts (left-hand side), and finally the engine bracket-to-engine and frame bolts (right-hand side), tightening them all to their specified torque. Fit the caps into the upper front bolts.
  e) On XTZ models, locate the swingarm pivot bolt first, followed by the lower and upper and rear mounting bolts, then fit the frame downtubes, and finally locate the lower front bolt, not forgetting the washers with the swingarm bolt nut and the lower rear bolt nut, and tighten them finger-tight. Now tighten them in the same order to the specified torque settings. Fit the caps into each end of the swingarm pivot and the upper rear bolt.
  f) On 1991 to 1995 TDM models and all XTZ models, use a new O-ring on the oil pipe to oil pump cover union and tighten the bolts to the specified torque setting.
  g) Use new gaskets on the exhaust pipe connections.
  h) Make sure all wires, cables and hoses are correctly routed and connected, and secured by any clips or ties.
  i) Refill the engine with oil and coolant (see Chapter 1).
  j) Adjust the throttle and clutch cable freeplay and engine idle speed (see Chapter 1).
  k) Adjust the drive chain slack (see Chapter 1).
  l) Start the engine and check that there are no oil or coolant leaks before installing the body panels.

6 Engine disassembly and reassembly – general information

Disassembly

1 Before disassembling the engine, the external surfaces of the unit should be thoroughly cleaned and degreased. This will prevent contamination of the engine internals, and will also make working a lot easier and cleaner. A high flash-point solvent, such as paraffin (kerosene) can be used, or better still, a proprietary engine degreaser. Use old paintbrushes and toothbrushes to work the solvent into the various recesses of the engine casings. Take care to exclude solvent or water from the electrical components and inlet and exhaust ports.

 Warning: The use of petrol (gasoline) as a cleaning agent should be avoided because of the risk of fire.

2 When clean and dry, arrange the unit on the workbench, leaving suitable clear area for working. Gather a selection of small containers and plastic bags so that parts can be grouped together in an easily identifiable manner. Some paper and a pen should be on hand so that notes can be made and labels attached where necessary. A supply of clean rag is also required.

3 Before commencing work, read through the appropriate section so that some idea of the necessary procedure can be gained. When removing components it should be noted that great force is seldom required, unless specified. In many cases, a component's reluctance to be removed is indicative of an incorrect approach or removal method – if in any doubt, re-check with the text.

4 An engine support stand made from short lengths of 2 x 4 inch wood bolted together into a rectangle will help support the engine **(see illustration)**. The perimeter of the mount should be just big enough to accommodate the sump within it so that the engine rests on its crankcase.

5 When disassembling the engine, keep 'mated' parts together (including gears, cylinders, pistons, connecting rods, valves, etc. that have been in contact with each other during engine operation). These 'mated' parts must be reused or renewed as an assembly.

6 A complete engine/transmission disassembly should be done in the following general order with reference to the appropriate Sections of this Chapter.

Remove the valve cover
Remove the camshafts
Remove the cylinder head
Remove the cylinder block
Remove the pistons
Remove the clutch
Remove the alternator/pick-up coil
 assembly (see Chapter 9)
Remove the starter motor (see Chapter 9)
Remove the gearchange mechanism
 external components
Remove the oil pumps
Remove the oil sump
Separate the crankcase halves
Remove the crankshaft
Remove the transmission shafts
Remove the selector drum and forks
Remove the balancer shafts

Reassembly

7 Reassembly is accomplished by reversing the general disassembly sequence.

6.4 An engine support made from pieces of 2 x 4 inch wood

7 Valve cover –
removal and installation

Note: *The valve covers can be removed with the engine in the frame. If the engine has been removed, ignore the steps which do not apply.*

Removal

1 Remove the fuel tank, the air filter housing and the carburettors (see Chapter 4). Drain the coolant (see Chapter 1).

2 On TDM and TRX models, remove the thermostat housing (see Chapter 3). When removing the housing, remove it along with the pipe that bolts onto the valve cover, rather than separating the hose from the pipe. The pipe is secured by a bolt – make sure the pipe O-ring does not fall into the engine when easing out the pipe **(see illustration)**. Discard the O-ring as a new one must be used.

3 On XTZ models, unscrew the bolt securing the coolant pipe to the valve cover and ease the pipe out, making sure the O-ring does not fall into the engine **(see illustration 7.2)**. Discard the O-ring as a new one must be used.

4 If required, release the clamp securing the breather hose to the valve cover and detach the hose **(see illustration)**.

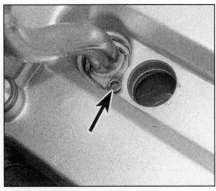

7.2 Unscrew the bolt (arrowed) and detach the pipe from the cover

5 Pull the spark plug caps off the plugs and secure them clear of the engine, noting which fits where.

6 Unscrew the bolts securing the valve cover then lift the cover off the cylinder head **(see illustration)**. On 1996-on TDM models and all TRX models, note which bolt fits where as some are of different length. If the cover is stuck, do not try to lever it off with a screwdriver. Tap it gently around the sides with a rubber hammer or block of wood to dislodge it. Also remove the gasket. Note the rubber spark plug hole gaskets fitted inside the cover and remove them if they are loose.

Installation

7 Examine the valve cover gasket and the spark plug hole gaskets for signs of damage or deterioration and renew them if necessary. Similarly check the rubber grommets on the cover bolts **(see illustration 7.10b)**.

8 Clean the mating surfaces of the cylinder head and the valve cover with lacquer thinner, acetone or brake system cleaner.

9 Install the gasket onto the valve cover, making sure it fits correctly into the groove **(see illustration)**. Also fit the spark plug hole gaskets. Use a few dabs of grease to keep the gaskets in place while the cover is fitted.

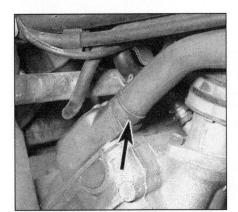

7.4 Release the clamp and detach the breather hose (arrowed)

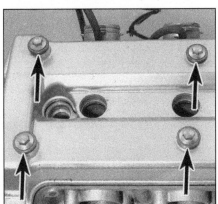

7.6 Unscrew the valve cover bolts (arrowed) and remove the cover – early TDM and XTZ type cover shown

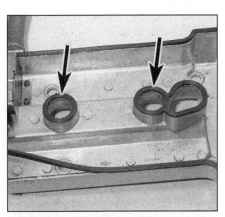

7.9 Fit the main gasket and the spark plug hole gaskets (arrowed) into their grooves

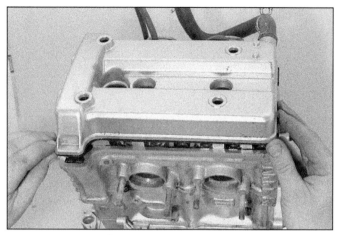

7.10a Install the valve cover . . .

7.10b . . . and tighten the bolts

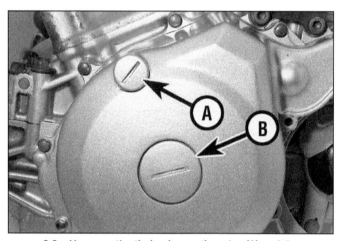

8.2a Unscrew the timing inspection plug (A) and the centre plug (B)

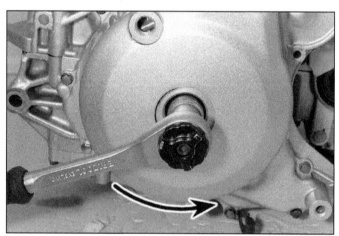

8.2b Turn the engine using a socket on the alternator bolt

10 Position the valve cover on the cylinder head, making sure the gaskets stay in place **(see illustration)**. Install the cover bolts and tighten them to the torque setting specified at the beginning of the Chapter **(see illustration)**.
11 Install the remaining components in the reverse order of removal.

8 Camshafts and followers – removal, inspection and installation

Note: *The camshafts can be removed with the engine in the frame. Place rags over the spark plug holes and the camchain tunnel to prevent any component from dropping into the engine on removal.*

Removal

1 Remove the valve cover (see Section 7).
2 Unscrew the timing inspection plug and the centre plug from the alternator cover on the left-hand side of the engine **(see illustration)**.

Discard the plug O-rings as new ones should be used. The engine can be turned using a 19 mm socket on the alternator rotor bolt and turning it in an anti-clockwise direction only **(see illustration)**. Alternatively, place the motorcycle on an auxiliary stand so that the rear wheel is off the ground, select a high gear and rotate the rear wheel by hand in its normal direction of rotation.
3 Turn the engine until the 'I' mark on the rotor aligns with the static timing mark on the alternator cover (a notch in the timing inspection hole), and the camshaft lobes for the No. 1 (left-hand) cylinder are facing away from each other **(see illustration)**. **Note:** *Do not confuse the 'I' mark on the rotor (which indicates TDC) with the 'H' mark which will appear first and which indicates the firing point of the ignition system.* If the cam lobes are facing towards each other, rotate the engine anti-clockwise 360° (one full turn) so that the 'I' mark again aligns with the static timing mark. The camshaft lobes will now be facing away from each other and the No. 1 cylinder is at TDC (top dead centre) on the

compression stroke. Before disturbing the camshafts, make a note of the timing markings on the sprockets and how they align with the cylinder head. With the No. 1 cylinder at TDC, The 'E' mark on the exhaust camshaft sprocket is parallel with the cylinder head top

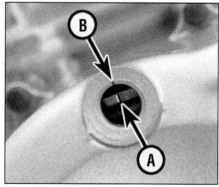

8.3a Turn the engine until the mark on the rotor (A) aligns with the static mark on the cover (B)

8.3b Note the alignment of the timing mark letters on the sprockets with the cylinder head . . .

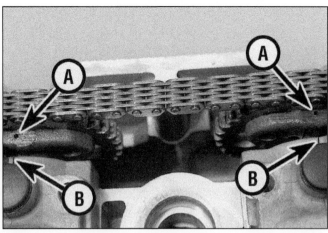

8.3c . . . and of the punch marks (A) on the ends of the camshafts with the lines (B) on the camshaft holders

surface and faces back, while the 'I' mark on the inlet camshaft sprocket is parallel with the cylinder head top surface and faces forward **(see illustration)**. Also the punch mark on each camshaft sprocket holder faces up and aligns with the mark on the top of the camshaft holder **(see illustration)**. If you are in any doubt as to the alignment of the markings, or if they are not visible, make your own alignment marks between all components, and also between a tooth on each sprocket and its corresponding link on the chain, before disturbing them. These markings ensure that the valve timing can be correctly set up on assembly without difficulty. As it is easy to be a tooth out on installation, marking between a tooth on each sprocket and its link in the chain is especially useful.

4 Unscrew the bolts securing the cam chain top guide and remove the guide, noting how it fits **(see illustration)**.

5 Slacken, but do not remove, the camshaft sprocket bolts **(see illustration)**. If the sprockets turn, counter-hold them by

inserting a screwdriver or bar through the hole in the centre of the camshaft **(see illustration 8.29a)**, or by counter-holding the alternator rotor.

6 Remove the cam chain tensioner (see Section 9).

7 Make a mark on each sprocket to denote whether it fits with the exhaust or inlet camshaft (the appropriate existing letter can be highlighted). Remove the sprocket bolts, then draw each sprocket off the end of its camshaft and slip it out of the chain **(see illustration)**. If required, also lift the cam chain front guide out of the front of the cam chain tunnel, noting how and which way round it fits (see Section 24). While the camshaft sprockets are off, don't allow the cam chain to go slack and do not rotate the crankshaft – the chain may drop down and bind between the crankshaft and case, which could damage these components. Wire the chain to another component or secure it using a rod of some sort to prevent it from dropping.

8 Before removing the camshaft holders, make a note of which fits where. All the

holders are marked with a letter and number to denote their location – I 1 is the inlet camshaft holder on the No. 1 cylinder (left-hand) side, E 1 is the exhaust camshaft holder on the No. 1 cylinder, and so on. Also each holder is marked with an arrow which points towards the cam chain. Otherwise their

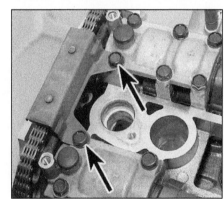

8.4 Unscrew the bolts (arrowed) and remove the guide

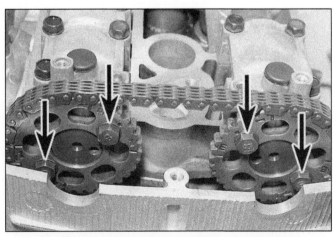

8.5 Slacken the camshaft sprocket bolts (arrowed)

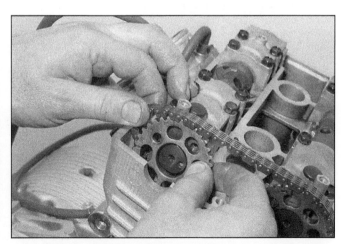

8.7 Slide the sprockets off the camshafts and out of the chain

8.9 Unscrew and remove the camshaft holder bolts (arrowed)

8.10a Lift out the follower . . .

8.10b . . . and remove the shim either from inside the follower . . .

8.10c . . . or from the top of the valve

locations are readily identifiable by the differing number or location of bolts which secures each one.

9 Before slackening the camshaft holder bolts, check whether any of the cam lobes are directly depressing the valves and if so, rotate the camshaft slightly to release the pressure; this will prevent distortion or undue strain on the holders as the bolts are slackened. Unscrew the camshaft holder bolts for the camshaft being worked on, evenly and a little at a time in a criss-cross pattern, until they are all loose **(see illustration)**.

Caution: If the bolts aren't loosened evenly, the camshaft may bind.

Remove the bolts, then lift off the camshaft holders, noting how they fit, and remove the camshafts **(see illustrations 8.26a and 8.25)**. Retrieve the dowels from either the holder or the cylinder head if they are loose. Keep all mated parts together.

10 Obtain a container which is divided into ten compartments, and label each compartment with the location of its corresponding valve in the cylinder head and whether it belongs with an inlet or an exhaust valve. If a container is not available, use labelled plastic bags. Using a pair of pliers or a magnet if necessary, lift each follower out of the cylinder head and store it in its corresponding compartment in the container **(see illustration)**. The shim is likely to stick to the inside of the follower so take great care not to lose it when removing the follower **(see illustration)**. Retrieve the shim from either the inside of the follower or pick it out of the top of the valve using a magnet, a small screwdriver with a dab of grease on it (the shim will stick to the grease), or a screwdriver and a pair of pliers **(see illustration)**. Do not allow the shim to fall into the engine.

Inspection

11 Inspect the bearing surfaces of the camshaft holders and the corresponding journals on the camshaft. Look for score marks, deep scratches and evidence of spalling (a pitted appearance) **(see illustration)**.

12 Check the camshaft lobes for heat discoloration (blue appearance), score marks, chipped areas, flat spots and spalling **(see illustration)**. Measure the height of each lobe

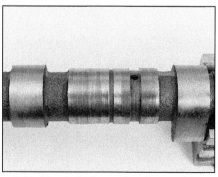

8.11 Check the journal surfaces of the camshaft for scratches or wear

8.12a Check the lobes of the camshaft for wear – here's an example of damage requiring camshaft repair or renewal

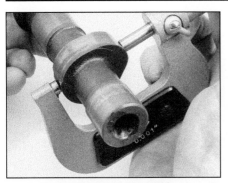

8.12b Measure the height of the camshaft lobes with a micrometer

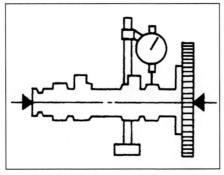

8.13 Measuring camshaft runout

8.15 Lay a strip of Plastigauge across each bearing journal, parallel with the camshaft centreline

with a micrometer **(see illustration)** and compare the results to the minimum lobe height listed in this Chapter's Specifications. If damage is noted or wear is excessive, the camshaft must be renewed. Also, be sure to check the condition of the followers.

13 Check the amount of camshaft runout by supporting each end of the camshaft on V-blocks, and measuring any runout using a dial gauge **(see illustration)**. If the runout exceeds the specified limit the camshaft must be renewed.

 HAYNES HINT *Refer to Tools and Workshop Tips in the Reference section for details of how to read a micrometer and dial gauge.*

14 Next, check the camshaft bearing oil clearances. Check each camshaft in turn rather than at the same time. Clean the camshaft, the bearing surfaces in the cylinder head and camshaft holders with a clean lint-free cloth, then lay the camshaft in place in the cylinder head.

15 Cut some strips of Plastigauge and lay one piece on each bearing journal, parallel with the camshaft centreline **(see**

illustration). Make sure the camshaft holder dowels are installed. Lay the holders in their correct place in the cylinder head (see Step 8) **(see illustration 8.26a)**. Make sure the arrow on each camshaft holder points towards the cam chain. Tighten the bolts evenly and a little at a time in a criss-cross pattern, working from the centre of the camshaft outwards, to the torque setting specified at the beginning of the Chapter **(see illustration 8.26b)**. Whilst tightening the bolts, make sure the holders are being pulled squarely down and are not binding on the dowels. While doing this, don't let the camshafts rotate.

16 Now unscrew the bolts a evenly and a little at a time in a criss-cross pattern, and carefully lift off the camshaft holders.

17 To determine the oil clearance, compare the crushed Plastigauge (at its widest point) on each journal to the scale printed on the Plastigauge container **(see illustration)**. Compare the results to this Chapter's Specifications. If the oil clearance is greater than specified, measure the diameter of the cam bearing journal with a micrometer **(see illustration)**. If the journal diameter is less than the specified limit, renew the camshaft and recheck the clearance. If the clearance is still too great, renew the cylinder head and holders.

HAYNES HINT *Before renewing camshafts or the holders because of damage, check with local machine shops specialising in motorcycle engine work. In the case of the camshafts, it may be possible for cam lobes to be welded, reground and hardened, at a cost far lower than that of a new camshaft. If the bearing surfaces in the holders are damaged, it may be possible for them to be bored out to accept bearing inserts. Due to the cost of new components it is recommended that all options be explored before condemning them as trash!*

18 Except in cases of oil starvation, the cam chain wears very little. If the chain has stretched excessively, which makes it difficult to maintain proper tension, or if it is stiff or the links are binding or kinking, renew it. Refer to Section 24 for the procedure.

19 Check the sprockets for wear, cracks and other damage. If the sprockets are worn, the cam chain is also worn, and so is the sprocket on the crankshaft. If severe wear is apparent, the entire engine should be disassembled for inspection.

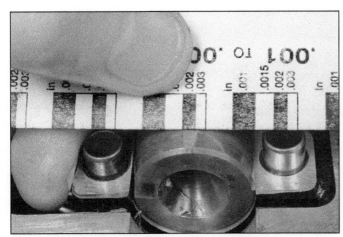

8.17a Compare the width of the crushed Plastigauge to the scale printed on the Plastigauge container

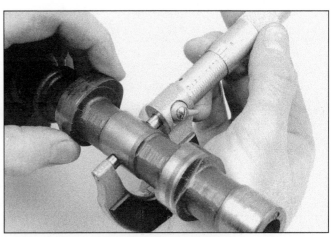

8.17b Measure the cam bearing journals with a micrometer

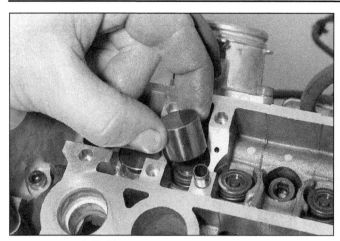

8.22 Fit the followers onto the valves

8.25 Install the camshafts as shown, with the No. 1 cylinder lobes (A) facing away from each other and the punch mark (B) on each sprocket holder facing up

20 Inspect the cam chain guide blade (see Section 24).

21 Inspect the outer surfaces of the cam followers for evidence of scoring or other damage. If a follower is in poor condition, it is probable that the bore in which it works is also damaged. Check for clearance between the followers and their bores. Whilst no specifications are given, if slack is excessive, renew the followers. If the bores are seriously out-of-round or tapered, the cylinder head and the followers must be renewed.

Installation

22 Lubricate each shim and its follower with molybdenum disulphide oil (a 50/50 mixture of molybdenum disulphide grease and engine oil) and fit each shim into its recess in the top of the valve, with the size marking on each shim facing up **(see illustration 8.10c)**. Make sure each shim is correctly seated in the top of the valve assembly, then install each follower, making sure it fits squarely in its bore **(see illustration)**. **Note:** *It is most important that the shims and followers are returned to*

their original valves otherwise the valve clearances will be inaccurate.

23 If removed, fit the cam chain front guide into the front of the cam chain tunnel, making sure it is the correct way round with the lugs properly located in the cutouts in the top of the cylinder head (see Section 24).

24 Make sure the bearing surfaces on the camshafts and in the holders are clean, then apply molybdenum disulphide oil (a 50/50 mixture of molybdenum disulphide grease and engine oil) to each of them. Also apply it to the camshaft lobes.

25 Verify that the 'I' mark on the timing rotor is still aligned with the notch (see Step 3) **(see illustration 8.3a)**. Lay the inlet camshaft (with six lobes) onto the back of the head, making sure the No. 1 (left-hand) cylinder lobes are facing backwards and the punch mark on the sprocket holder is facing up. Now lay the exhaust camshaft (with four lobes) onto the front of the head, making sure the No. 1 cylinder lobes are facing forward and the punch mark on the sprocket holder is facing up **(see illustration)**.

26 Make sure the camshaft holder dowels are installed. Lay the holders in their correct place in the cylinder head (see Step 8) **(see illustration)**. Make sure the arrow on each camshaft holder points towards the cam chain. Tighten the bolts evenly and a little at a time in a criss-cross pattern, working from the centre of the camshaft outwards, to the torque setting specified at the beginning of the Chapter **(see illustration)**. Whilst tightening the bolts, make sure the holders are being pulled squarely down and are not binding on the dowels. *Caution: The holders are likely to break if they are not tightened down evenly and squarely.*

27 When installing the camshaft sprockets, align the 'E' marks (for the exhaust camshaft) and the 'I' marks (for the inlet camshaft) on the camshaft sprockets exactly with the cylinder head surface, with the letters that are the correct way up facing each other **(see illustration 8.3b)**. Check that the punch mark on each sprocket holder is aligned with the mark on the camshaft holders **(see illustration 8.3c)**. If the camshafts need to be

8.26a Fit the holders onto the dowels . . .

8.26b . . . and tighten the bolts as described to the specified torque setting

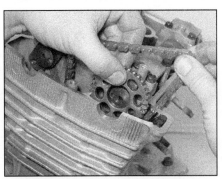

8.28a Fit the exhaust sprocket into the chain and onto the camshaft . . .

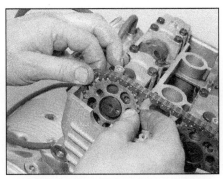

8.28b . . . then fit the inlet sprocket

8.29a Install the sprocket bolts and counter-hold the camshafts as shown . . .

8.29b . . . then tighten the bolts to the specified torque

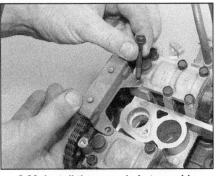

8.30 Install the cam chain top guide

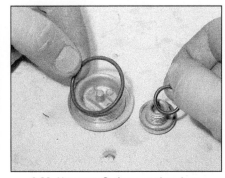

8.33 Use new O-rings on the plugs

turned slightly, use a screwdriver or bar through the hole in the middle of the camshaft to turn them.

28 Fit the cam chain around the exhaust sprocket, aligning the marks between sprocket tooth and link if made. When fitting the chain, pull up on the front run to remove all slack from it **(see illustration)**. Now fit the sprocket onto the end of the camshaft, aligning the bolt holes. Next fit the inlet sprocket into the chain and onto the inlet camshaft, making sure there is no slack in the chain between the camshafts, and aligning the bolt holes **(see illustration)**. At this point check that all the timing marks are still in **exact** alignment as described in Step 3. Note that it is easy to be slightly out (one tooth on the sprocket) without the marks appearing drastically out of alignment. If all marks align correctly, install the sprocket bolts and tighten them finger-tight. If the marks are out, verify which sprocket is misaligned and slide it off the camshaft, then disengage it from the chain and move it round as required, then fit it back into the chain and onto the sprocket, and check the marks again.

Caution: If the marks are not aligned exactly as described, the valve timing will be incorrect and the valves may strike the pistons, causing extensive damage to the engine.

29 With everything correctly aligned, tighten the sprocket bolts to the torque setting specified at the beginning of the Chapter,

using a screwdriver or bar inserted through the hole in each camshaft to prevent them turning, or by counter-holding the alternator rotor **(see illustrations)**.

30 Install the cam chain top guide and tighten the bolts to the same torque setting as the other camshaft holder bolts **(see illustration)**.

31 Install the cam chain tensioner (see Section 9). Turn the engine anti-clockwise through two full turns and check again that all the timing marks still align (see Step 3).

32 Check the valve clearances and adjust them if necessary (see Chapter 1). **Note:** *A valve clearance check is essential if you have installed any new valve components or a new camshaft.*

33 Use new O-rings on the timing inspection plug and centre plug and tighten the plugs securely **(see illustration)**.

34 Install the valve cover (see Section 7).

---

9 Cam chain tensioner – removal, inspection and installation

Note: *This procedure can be performed with the engine in the frame.*

Caution: Once you start to remove the tensioner bolts, you must remove the tensioner all the way and reset it before tightening the bolts. The tensioner extends

itself and locks in place, so if you loosen the bolts partway and then retighten them, the tensioner or cam chain will be damaged.

Removal

1 Unscrew the tensioner spring cap bolt and withdraw the springs from the tensioner body **(see illustration)**.

2 Unscrew the two tensioner mounting bolts and withdraw the tensioner from the back of the cylinder block, noting which way up it fits **(see illustration 9.1)**.

3 Discard the tensioner body gasket as a new one must be used.

Inspection

4 Examine the tensioner components for signs of wear or damage.

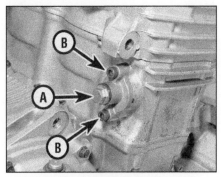

9.1 Tensioner cap bolt (A), tensioner mounting bolts (B)

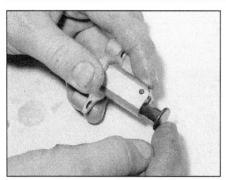

9.5 Release the ratchet and press the plunger in

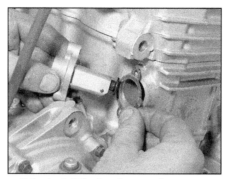

9.8a Install the tensioner using a new gasket . . .

9.8b . . . and tighten the mounting bolts to the specified torque

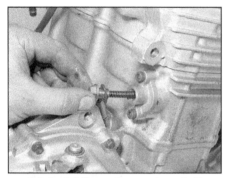

9.9 Install the springs and cap bolt

5 Release the ratchet mechanism from the tensioner plunger and check that the plunger moves freely in and out of the tensioner body **(see illustration)**.

6 If the tensioner or any of its components are worn or damaged, or if the plunger is seized in the body, the tensioner must be renewed – individual components are not available.

Installation

7 Release the ratchet mechanism and press the tensioner plunger all the way into the tensioner body **(see illustration 9.5)**.

8 Fit a new gasket onto the tensioner body, then install the tensioner in the engine and tighten the bolts to the torque setting

specified at the beginning of the Chapter **(see illustrations)**.

9 Install the springs and cap bolt, with its washer, and tighten the bolt to the specified torque setting **(see illustration)**.

10 Remove the alternator cover centre plug and turn the crankshaft anti-clockwise through two full turns using a socket on the rotor bolt **(see illustrations 8.2a and b)**. This will allow the tensioner to set itself properly. Use a new O-ring on the centre plug.

11 It is advisable to remove the valve cover (see Section 7) and check that the cam chain is tensioned and all the timing marks are in alignment (see Section 8). If the chain is slack, the tensioner plunger did not release when the spring and cap bolt were installed. Remove the tensioner again and re-check it. Again check the timing marks (see Section 8), then install the valve cover (see Section 7).

10 Cylinder head –
removal and installation

Caution: *The engine must be completely cool before beginning this procedure or the cylinder head may become warped.*

Note 1: *The cylinder head can be removed with the engine in the frame. If the engine has been removed, ignore the steps which don't apply.*

Note 2: *If no work is being carried out on the valves, the cylinder head can be removed with the camshafts in place. Holes in the camshafts and in the right-hand camshaft holders allow access to the cylinder head nuts. The camshaft sprockets must be removed.*

Removal

1 Remove the valve cover (see Section 7), the camshaft sprockets (see Section 8), and if required the camshafts (see Note 2 above). If the camshafts are being left in place, remove the blanking cap from the top of each right-hand camshaft holder, then turn the camshafts using a screwdriver or rod through the hole in the middle of the camshaft until the access holes in the shafts align with the cylinder head nuts **(see illustration)**. If the camshafts are left in place, the nuts and washers cannot be removed after they have been loosened as the camshafts will be in the way.

2 Remove the exhaust system (see Chapter 4).

3 If not already done, remove the cam chain front guide (see Section 24).

4 If required, release the clamp(s) securing the vacuum hose(s) to the inlet manifold(s) and detach the hose(s).

5 Unscrew the oil pipe banjo bolt from the cylinder head and detach the pipe from the cylinder head **(see illustration)**. Discard the banjo bolt sealing washers as new ones must be used.

10.1 Remove the blanking caps (A) from the holes in the holders. Turn the shafts using the centre holes (B) until the access holes in each camshaft align with the nuts

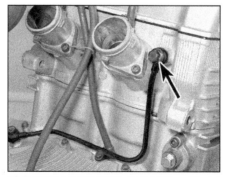

10.5 Unscrew the banjo bolt (arrowed) and detach the oil pipe

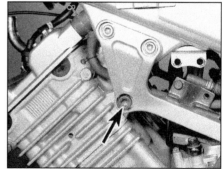

10.6a On TDM models, remove the cylinder head-to-bracket bolt (arrowed) on each side

10.6b On TRX models, remove the blanking cap, then remove the frame-to-cylinder head bolt (arrowed) on each side

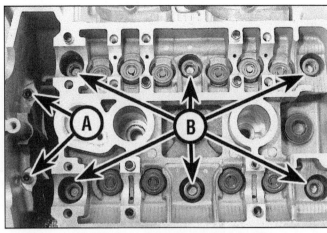

10.7 Cylinder head bolts (A) and nuts (B)

6 On TDM and TRX models, unscrew the engine mounting bolts which thread into the cylinder head on each side **(see illustrations)**. On TRX models, first remove the caps.

7 Each cylinder head is secured by two bolts, located in the cam chain tunnel, and six nuts **(see illustration)**. First unscrew and remove the bolts **(see illustration 10.16)**. Now slacken the nuts evenly and a little at a time in a criss-cross pattern until they are all slack, then remove the nuts and their washers **(see illustration 10.15)**.

8 Pull the cylinder head up off the block **(see illustration)**. If it is stuck, tap around the joint faces of the cylinder head with a soft-faced mallet to free the head. Do not attempt to free the head by inserting a screwdriver between the head and cylinder block – you'll damage the sealing surfaces. Remove the old cylinder head gasket and discard it as a new one must be used.

9 If they are loose, remove the dowels from the cylinder block. If they appear to be missing they are probably stuck in the underside of the cylinder head.

10 Check the cylinder head gasket and the mating surfaces on the cylinder head and block for signs of leakage, which could indicate warpage. Refer to Section 12 and check the flatness of the cylinder head.

Installation

11 Clean all traces of old gasket material from the cylinder head and block. If a scraper is used, take care not to scratch or gouge the soft aluminium. Be careful not to let any of the gasket material fall into the crankcase, the cylinder bores or the oil passages.

> **HAYNES HiNT** Refer to Tools and Workshop Tips in the Reference section for details of gasket removal methods.

12 If removed, install the dowels into the cylinder block **(see illustration 10.13)**. Lubricate the cylinder bores with engine oil.

13 Ensure both cylinder head and block mating surfaces are clean, then lay the new head gasket in place on the cylinder block, making sure all the holes are correctly aligned **(see illustration)**. Never re-use the old gasket.

14 Carefully fit the cylinder head onto the block, making sure it locates correctly onto the dowels **(see illustration 10.8)**.

15 Lubricate the threads of the cylinder head nuts with clean engine oil (if the camshafts are in place, one or two drops of oil can be squirted around the nuts into the stud holes). Install the nuts with their washers and tighten

them finger-tight **(see illustration)**. Now tighten the nuts evenly and a little at a time in a criss-cross pattern to the torque setting specified at the beginning of the Chapter.

16 Install the two cylinder head bolts and tighten them to the specified torque setting **(see illustration)**.

17 On TDM and TRX models, install the engine mounting bolts and tighten them to the specified torque setting **(see illustrations 10.6a and b)**. On TRX models, fit the caps into the bolt heads.

18 Install the oil pipe onto the cylinder head, using new sealing washers on each side of

10.8 Carefully lift the head up off the block

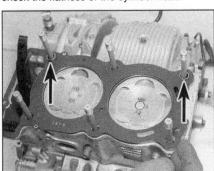

10.13 Lay a new head gasket over the dowels (arrowed) and onto the head

10.15 Install the nuts with their washers and tighten them as described to the specified torque

10.16 Install the bolts and tighten them to the specified torque

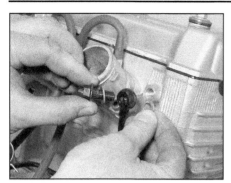

10.18a Use new sealing washers on each side of the union . . .

10.18b . . . and tighten the banjo bolt to the specified torque

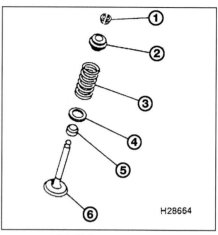

12.3 Valve components

1	Collets	5	Valve stem oil
2	Spring retainer		seal
3	Valve spring	6	Valve
4	Spring seat		

the union, and tighten the banjo bolt to the specified torque **(see illustrations)**.
19 If removed, fit the vacuum hose(s) onto the inlet manifold(s) and fit the clamp(s).
20 Install the remaining components in a reverse of their removal sequence, referring to the relevant Sections or Chapters (see Steps 1, 2 and 3).

11 Valves/valve seats/valve guides – overhaul

1 Because of the complex nature of this job and the special tools and equipment required, most owners leave servicing of the valves, valve seats and valve guides to a professional.
2 The home mechanic can, however, remove the valves from the cylinder head, clean and check the components for wear and assess the extent of the work needed, and, unless a valve overhaul is required, grind in the valves (see Section 12).
3 The engineer will renew the valves, guides and springs, recut the valve seats, clean and polish the valve ports and reassemble the valve components.
4 After the valve overhaul has been performed, the head will be in like-new condition. When the head is returned, be sure to clean it again very thoroughly before installation on the engine to remove any metal particles or abrasive grit that may still be present from the valve service operations.

Use compressed air, if available, to blow out all the holes and passages.

12 Cylinder head and valves – disassembly, inspection and reassembly

1 As mentioned in the previous section, valve overhaul should be left to an engineer. However, disassembly, cleaning and inspection of the valves and related components can be done (if the necessary special tools are available) by the home mechanic. This way no expense is incurred if the inspection reveals that overhaul is not required at this time.
2 To disassemble the valve components without the risk of damaging them, a valve spring compressor is absolutely essential. Make sure that it is suitable for motorcycle work.

Disassembly

3 Before proceeding, arrange to label and store the valves along with their related components in such a way that they can be returned to their original locations without getting mixed up **(see illustration)**. A good way to do this is to use the same container as the shims are stored in (see Section 8), or to obtain a separate container which is divided into ten compartments, and to label each compartment with the identity of the valve which will be stored in it (ie number of cylinder, inlet or exhaust side, inner, middle or outer valve). Alternatively, labelled plastic bags will do just as well.

4 Clean all traces of old gasket material from the cylinder head. If a scraper is used, take care not to scratch or gouge the soft aluminium.

 Refer to Tools and Workshop Tips in the Reference section for details of gasket removal methods.

5 Compress the valve spring on the first valve with the spring compressor, making sure it is correctly located onto each end of the valve assembly **(see illustration)**. Do not compress the spring any more than is absolutely necessary. Remove the collets, using either needle-nose pliers, tweezers, a magnet or a screwdriver with a dab of grease on it **(see illustration)**. Carefully release the valve spring compressor and remove the spring retainer, noting which way up it fits, the spring, the spring seat, and the valve, from the head **(see illustration 12.3)**. If the valve binds in the guide (won't pull through), push it back into the head and deburr the area around the collet groove with a very fine file or whetstone **(see illustration)**.

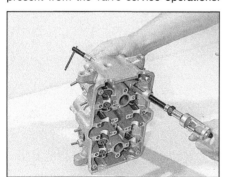

12.5a Compressing the valve springs using a valve spring compressor

12.5b Remove the collets with needle-nose pliers, tweezers, a magnet or a screwdriver with a dab of grease on it

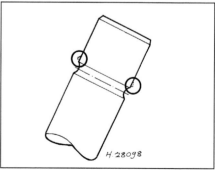

12.5c If the valve stem won't pull through the guide, deburr the area above the collet groove

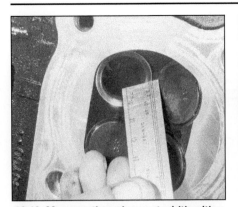

12.13 Measure the valve seat width with a ruler (or for greater precision use a vernier caliper)

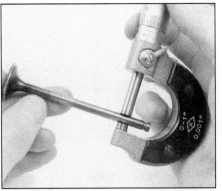

12.14a Measure the valve stem diameter with a micrometer

12.14b Insert a small-hole gauge into the valve guide and expand it so there's a slight drag when it's pulled out

6 Repeat the procedure for the remaining valves. Remember to keep the parts for each valve together and in order so they can be reinstalled in the same location.

7 Once the valves have been removed and labelled, pull the valve stem seals off the top of the valve guides with pliers and discard them (the old seals should never be reused).

8 Next, clean the cylinder head with solvent and dry it thoroughly. Compressed air will speed the drying process and ensure that all holes and recessed areas are clean.

9 Clean all of the valve springs, collets, retainers and spring seats with solvent and dry them thoroughly. Do the parts from one valve at a time so that no mixing of parts between valves occurs.

10 Scrape off any deposits that may have formed on the valve, then use a motorised wire brush to remove deposits from the valve heads and stems. Again, make sure the valves do not get mixed up.

Inspection

11 Inspect the head very carefully for cracks and other damage. If cracks are found, a new head will be required. Check the cam bearing surfaces for wear and evidence of seizure. Check the camshafts for wear as well (see Section 8).

12 Using a precision straight-edge and a feeler gauge set to the warpage limit listed in the specifications at the beginning of the Chapter, check the head gasket mating surface for warpage. Refer to *Tools and Workshop Tips* in the Reference section for details of how to use the straight-edge.

13 Examine the valve seats in the combustion chamber. If they are pitted, cracked or burned, the head will require work beyond the scope of the home mechanic. Measure the valve seat width and compare it to this Chapter's Specifications **(see illustration)**. If it exceeds the service limit, or if it varies around its circumference, valve overhaul is required. If available, use Prussian blue to determine the extent of valve seat wear. Uniformly coat the seat with the Prussian blue, then install the valve and rotate it back and forth using a lapping tool. Remove the valve and check whether the ring of blue on the valve is uniform and continuous around the valve, and of the correct width as specified.

14 Measure the valve stem diameter **(see illustration)**. Clean the valve guides to remove any carbon build-up, then measure the inside diameters of the guides (at both ends and the centre of the guide) with a small-hole gauge and micrometer **(see**

illustrations). The guides are measured at the ends and at the centre to determine if they are worn in a bell-mouth pattern (more wear at the ends). Subtract the stem diameter from the valve guide diameter to obtain the valve stem-to-guide clearance. If the stem-to-guide clearance is greater than listed in this Chapter's Specifications, the guides and valves will have to be renewed. If the valve stem or guide is worn beyond its limit, or if the guide is worn unevenly, it must be renewed.

15 Carefully inspect each valve face for cracks, pits and burned spots. Check the valve stem and the collet groove area for cracks **(see illustration)**. Rotate the valve and check for any obvious indication that it is bent. Using V-blocks and a dial gauge if available, measure the valve stem runout and compare the results to the specifications **(see illustration)**. If the measurement exceeds the service limit specified, the valve must be renewed. Check the end of the stem for pitting and excessive wear. The presence of any of the above conditions indicates the need for valve servicing. The stem end can be ground down, provided that the amount of stem above the collet groove after grinding is sufficient.

16 Measure the valve margin thickness and compare it to the specifications **(see**

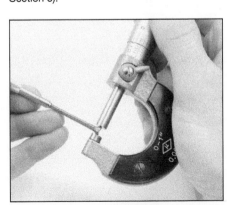

12.14c Measure the small-hole gauge with a micrometer

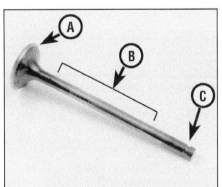

12.15a Check the valve face (A), stem (B) and collet groove (C) for signs of wear and damage

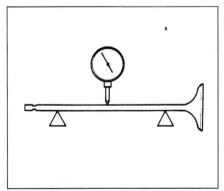

12.15b Check the valve stem for runout using V-blocks and a dial gauge

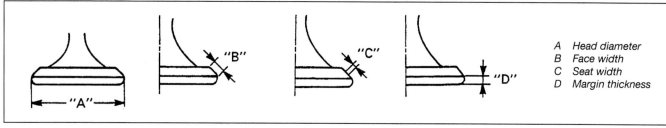

A Head diameter
B Face width
C Seat width
D Margin thickness

12.16 Valve head measurement points

illustration). If it is thinner than specified, renew the valve. The margin is the portion of the valve head which is below the valve seat.

17 Check the end of each valve spring for wear and pitting. Measure the spring free length and compare it to that listed in the specifications **(see illustration)**. If any spring is shorter than specified it has sagged and must be renewed. Also place the spring upright on a flat surface and check it for bend by placing a ruler against it **(see illustration)**. If the bend in any spring is excessive, it must be renewed.

18 Check the spring retainers and collets for obvious wear and cracks. Any questionable parts should not be reused, as extensive damage will occur in the event of failure during engine operation.

19 If the inspection indicates that no overhaul work is required, the valve components can be reinstalled in the head.

Reassembly

20 Unless a valve service has been performed, before installing the valves in the head they should be ground in (lapped) to ensure a positive seal between the valves and seats. This procedure requires coarse and fine valve grinding compound and a valve grinding tool. If a grinding tool is not available, a piece of rubber or plastic hose can be slipped over the valve stem (after the valve has been installed in the guide) and used to turn the valve.

21 Apply a small amount of coarse grinding compound to the valve face, then slip the valve into the guide **(see illustration)**. **Note:** *Make sure each valve is installed in its correct guide and be careful not to get any grinding compound on the valve stem.*

22 Attach the grinding tool (or hose) to the valve and rotate the tool between the palms of

your hands. Use a back-and-forth motion (as though rubbing your hands together) rather than a circular motion (ie so that the valve rotates alternately clockwise and anti-clockwise rather than in one direction only) **(see illustration)**. Lift the valve off the seat and turn it at regular intervals to distribute the grinding compound properly. Continue the grinding procedure until the valve face and seat contact area is of uniform width and unbroken around the entire circumference of the valve face and seat **(see illustrations)**.

23 Carefully remove the valve from the guide and wipe off all traces of grinding compound. Use solvent to clean the valve and wipe the seat area thoroughly with a solvent soaked cloth.

24 Repeat the procedure with fine valve grinding compound, then repeat the entire procedure for the remaining valves.

25 Lay the spring seat for each valve in place

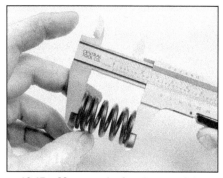

12.17a Measure the free length of the valve springs

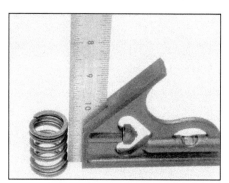

12.17b Check the valve springs for squareness

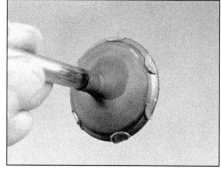

12.21 Apply the lapping compound very sparingly, in small dabs, to the valve face only

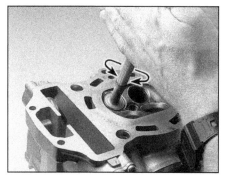

12.22a Rotate the valve grinding tool back and forth between the palms of your hands

12.22b The valve face and seat should show a uniform unbroken ring . . .

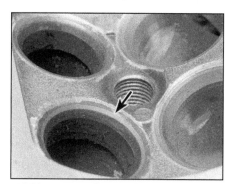

12.22c . . . and the seat (arrowed) should be the specified width all the way round

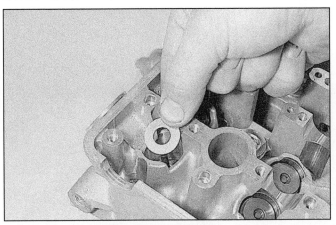

12.25a Fit the spring seat . . .

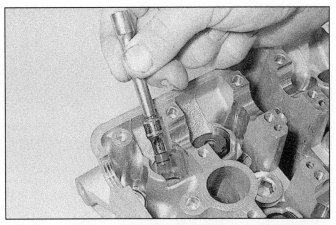

12.25b . . . then press the valve stem seal into position using a suitable deep socket

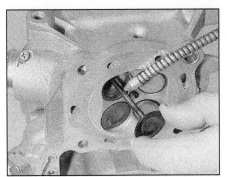

12.26a Lubricate the stem and slide the valve into its correct location

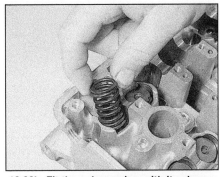

12.26b Fit the valve spring with its closer-wound coils facing down. . .

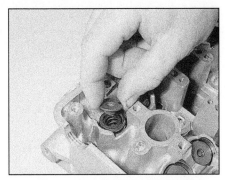

14.26c . . . then fit the spring retainer

in the cylinder head, with its shouldered side up so that the spring fits into it, then install new valve stem seals on each of the guides **(see illustrations)**. Use an appropriate size deep socket to push the seals over the end of the valve guide until they are felt to clip into place. Don't twist or cock them, or they will not seal properly against the valve stems. Also, don't remove them again or they will be damaged.

26 Coat the valve stems with molybdenum disulphide grease, then install one of them into its guide, rotating it slowly to avoid damaging the seal **(see illustration)**. Check

that the valve moves up and down freely in the guide. Next, install the spring, with its closer-wound coils facing down into the cylinder head, followed by the spring retainer, with its shouldered side facing down so that it fits into the top of the spring **(see illustrations)**.

27 Apply a small amount of grease to the collets to help hold them in place as the pressure is released from the springs **(see illustration)**. Compress the springs with the valve spring compressor and install the collets **(see illustration)**. When compressing the spring, depress them only as far as is

absolutely necessary to slip the collets into place. Make certain that the collets are securely locked in their retaining grooves.

28 Support the cylinder head on blocks so the valves can't contact the workbench top, then very gently tap each of the valve stems with a soft-faced hammer. This will help seat the collets in their grooves.

> **HAYNES HINT** *Check for proper sealing of the valves by pouring a small amount of solvent into each of the valve ports. If the solvent leaks past any valve into the combustion chamber area the valve grinding operation on that valve should be repeated.*

12.27a A small dab of grease will help to keep the collets in place on the valve while the spring is released

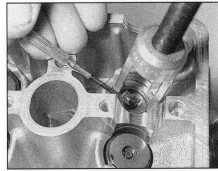

12.27b Compress the spring and install the collets, making sure they locate in the groove

13 Cylinder block – removal, inspection and installation

Note: *The cylinder block can be removed with the engine in the frame.*

Removal

1 Remove the cylinder head (see Section 10).
2 Unscrew the bolts securing the coolant hose union to the front of the block and

13.2 Unscrew the two bolts (arrowed) and remove the union

13.3 Lift the block up off the crankcase

13.4 Pick out the O-rings and discard them

remove the union **(see illustration)**. The joint pipe between the union and the water pump housing may come with the union, otherwise leave it in place in the housing. Discard the O-rings as new ones must be used.

3 Hold the cam chain up and lift the cylinder block up, then pass the cam chain down through the tunnel **(see illustration)**. Do not let the chain fall into the crankcase – secure it with a piece of wire or metal bar to prevent it from doing so. If the block is stuck, tap around the joint faces of the block with a soft-faced mallet to free it from the crankcase. Don't attempt to free the block by inserting a screwdriver between it and the crankcase – you'll damage the sealing surfaces. When the block is removed, stuff clean rags around the pistons to prevent anything falling into the crankcase. Remove the dowels from the mating surface of the crankcase or the underside of the block if they are loose. Be careful not to drop them into the engine.

4 Remove the O-ring from around each cylinder liner and discard them as new ones must be used **(see illustration)**.

5 Remove the gasket and clean all traces of old gasket material from the cylinder block and crankcase mating surfaces. If a scraper is used, take care not to scratch or gouge the soft aluminium. Be careful not to let any of the gasket material fall into the crankcase or the oil passages.

Inspection

Caution: Do not attempt to separate the liners from the cylinder block.

6 Check the cylinder walls carefully for scratches and score marks. A rebore will be necessary to remove any deep scores.

7 Using telescoping gauges and a micrometer (see *Tools and Workshop Tips* in the Reference section), check the dimensions of each cylinder to assess the amount of wear, taper and ovality. Measure near the top (but below the level of the top piston ring at TDC – about 10 mm below the top of the cylinder), centre and bottom (but above the level of the oil ring at BDC – about 20 mm above the bottom of the cylinder) of the bore both parallel to and across the crankshaft axis **(see illustration)**. Calculate any differences

between the measurements taken to determine any taper and ovality in the bore. Compare the results to the specifications at the beginning of the Chapter. If the cylinders are tapered, oval, or worn beyond the service limits, or badly scratched, scuffed or scored, have them rebored and honed by a Yamaha dealer or engineer. If the cylinders are rebored, they will require oversize pistons and rings.

8 If the precision measuring tools are not available, take the block and pistons to a Yamaha dealer or engineer for assessment and advice.

9 If the block and cylinders are in good condition and the piston-to-bore clearance is within specifications (see Section 14), the cylinders should be honed (de-glazed). To perform this operation you will need the proper size flexible hone with fine stones (see *Tools and Workshop Tips* in the Reference section), or a bottle-brush type hone, plenty of light oil or honing oil, some clean rags and an electric drill motor.

10 Hold the block sideways (so that the bores are horizontal rather than vertical) in a vice with soft jaws or cushioned with wooden blocks. Mount the hone in the drill motor, compress the stones and insert the hone into the cylinder. Thoroughly lubricate the cylinder, then turn on the drill and move the hone up and down in the cylinder at a pace which produces a fine cross-hatch pattern on the cylinder wall with the lines intersecting at an angle of approximately 60°. Be sure to use

plenty of lubricant and do not take off any more material than is necessary to produce the desired effect. Do not withdraw the hone from the cylinder while it is still turning. Switch off the drill and continue to move it up and down in the cylinder until it has stopped turning, then compress the stones and withdraw the hone. Wipe the oil from the cylinder and repeat the procedure on the other cylinder. Remember, do not take too much material from the cylinder wall.

11 Wash the cylinders thoroughly with warm soapy water to remove all traces of the abrasive grit produced during the honing operation. Be sure to run a brush through the bolt holes and flush them with running water. After rinsing, dry the cylinders thoroughly and apply a thin coat of light, rust-preventative oil to all machined surfaces.

12 If you do not have the equipment or desire to perform the honing operation, take the block to a Yamaha dealer or engineer.

Installation

13 Check that the mating surfaces of the cylinder block and crankcase are free from oil or pieces of old gasket. If removed, fit the dowels into the crankcase **(see illustration 13.15)**.

14 Fit a new O-ring into the groove around the base of each cylinder liner and press it into the groove between the liner and the cylinder block, taking care not to damage it **(see illustration)**.

15 Remove the rags from around the pistons.

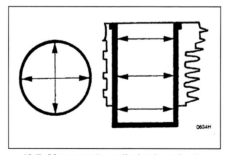

13.7 Measure the cylinder bore in the directions shown with a telescoping gauge, then measure the gauge with a micrometer

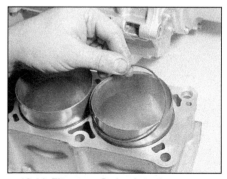

13.14 Fit a new O-ring into the groove around the liner base

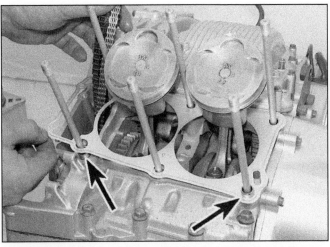

13.15 Lay the new gasket over the dowels (arrowed) and onto the crankcase

13.17 Carefully lower the block onto the pistons

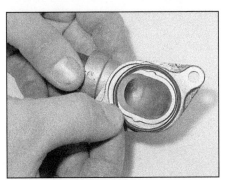

13.20a Fit a new O-ring onto the union . . .

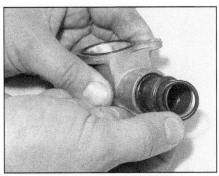

13.20b . . . and the joint pipe . . .

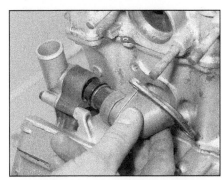

13.20c . . . then install the union

Lay the new base gasket in place on the crankcase, making sure all the holes are correctly aligned **(see illustration)**. Never re-use the old gasket.

16 If required, install piston ring clamps onto the pistons to ease their entry into the bores as the block is lowered. This is not essential as each cylinder has a good lead-in enabling the piston rings to be hand-fed into the bore. If possible, have an assistant to support the block while this is done.

17 Lubricate the cylinder bores, pistons and piston rings, and the connecting rod big- and small-ends, with clean engine oil, then install the block down over the studs until the piston crowns fit into the bores **(see illustration)**. At this stage feed the cam chain up through the block and secure it in place with a piece of wire to prevent it from falling back down.

18 Gently push down on the cylinder block, making sure the pistons enter the bore squarely and do not get cocked sideways. If piston ring clamps are not being used, carefully compress and feed each ring into the bore as the block is lowered. If necessary, use a soft mallet to gently tap the block down, but do not use force if the block appears to be stuck as the pistons and/or rings will be

damaged. If clamps are used, remove them once the pistons are in the bore.

19 When the pistons are correctly installed in the cylinders, press the block down onto the base gasket, making sure it locates correctly onto the dowels.

20 Fit a new O-ring into the groove in the coolant union face and around the pipe joint **(see illustrations)**. Fit the coolant hose union onto the front of the block and the joint pipe, or fit the joint pipe into the water pump housing if it came away with the union **(see illustration)**. Tighten the bolts to the torque setting specified at the beginning of the Chapter.

21 Install the cylinder head (see Section 10).

14 Pistons – removal, inspection and installation

Note: *The pistons can be removed with the engine in the frame.*

Removal

1 Remove the cylinder block (see Section 13).
2 Before removing the piston from the connecting rod, use a sharp scriber or felt

marker pen to write the cylinder identity on the crown of each piston (or on the inside of the skirt if the piston is dirty and going to be cleaned) as it must be installed in its original cylinder. Each piston should also have an arrow mark on its crown which should face the exhaust side of the bore **(see illustration)**. If this is not visible, mark the piston accordingly so that it can be installed the correct way round.

3 Carefully prise out the circlip on one side of the piston using needle-nose pliers or a small

14.2 Note the arrow mark on the piston which must point forwards

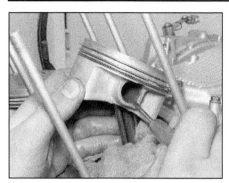

14.3a Prise out the circlip . . .

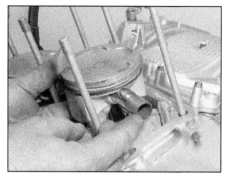

14.3b . . . then push out the pin and remove the piston

14.5 Removing the piston rings using a ring removal and installation tool

flat-bladed screwdriver inserted into the notch **(see illustration)**. Push the piston pin out from the other side to free the piston from the connecting rod **(see illustration)**. If required, remove the other circlip. Discard the removed circlip(s) as new ones must be used. When the piston has been removed, install its pin back into its bore so that related parts do not get mixed up.

 HAYNES HiNT *To prevent the circlip from pinging away, pass a rod or screwdriver, whose diameter is greater than the gap between the circlip ends, through the piston pin. This will trap the circlip if it springs out.*

HAYNES HiNT *If a piston pin is a tight fit in the piston bosses, soak a rag in boiling water then wring it out and wrap it around the piston – this will expand the alloy piston sufficiently to release its grip on the pin. If the piston pin is particularly stubborn, extract it using a drawbolt tool, but be careful to protect the piston's working surfaces.*

Inspection

4 Before the inspection process can be carried out, the pistons must be cleaned and the old piston rings removed. Note that if the cylinders are being rebored, piston inspection can be overlooked as new ones will be fitted.

5 Using your thumbs or a piston ring removal and installation tool, carefully remove the rings from the pistons **(see illustration)**. Do not nick or gouge the pistons in the process. Carefully note which way up each ring fits and in which groove as they must be installed in their original positions if being re-used. The upper surface of each ring has a manufacturer's mark or letter at one end.

6 Scrape all traces of carbon from the tops of the pistons. A hand-held wire brush or a piece of fine emery cloth can be used once most of

the deposits have been scraped away. Do not, under any circumstances, use a wire brush mounted in a drill motor to remove deposits from the pistons; the piston material is soft and will be eroded away by the wire brush.

7 Use a piston ring groove cleaning tool to remove any carbon deposits from the ring grooves. If a tool is not available, a piece broken off an old ring will do the job. Be very careful to remove only the carbon deposits. Do not remove any metal and do not nick or gouge the sides of the ring grooves.

8 Once the deposits have been removed, clean the pistons with solvent and dry them thoroughly. If the identification previously marked on the piston is cleaned off, be sure to re-mark it with the correct identity. Make sure the oil return holes below the oil ring groove are clear.

9 Carefully inspect each piston for cracks around the skirt, at the pin bosses and at the ring lands. Normal piston wear appears as even, vertical wear on the thrust surfaces of the piston and slight looseness of the top ring in its groove. If the skirt is scored or scuffed, the engine may have been suffering from overheating and/or abnormal combustion, which caused excessively high operating temperatures. The oil pump should be checked thoroughly. Also check that the circlip grooves are not damaged.

10 A hole in the piston crown, an extreme to

be sure, is an indication that abnormal combustion (pre-ignition) was occurring. Burned areas at the edge of the piston crown are usually evidence of spark knock (detonation). If any of the above problems exist, the causes must be corrected or the damage will occur again.

11 Measure the piston ring-to-groove clearance by laying each piston ring in its groove and slipping a feeler gauge in beside it **(see illustration)**. Make sure you have the correct ring for the groove (see Step 5). Check the clearance at three or four locations around the groove. If the clearance is greater than specified, renew both the piston and rings as a set. If new rings are being used, measure the clearance using the new rings. If the clearance is greater than that specified, the piston is worn and must be renewed.

12 Check the piston-to-bore clearance by measuring the bore (see Section 13) and the piston diameter. Make sure each piston is matched to its correct cylinder. Measure the piston 4.5 mm (1991 to 1995 TDM models), 4.7 mm (XTZ models), or 5.5 mm (1996-on TDM and all TRX models) up from the bottom of the skirt and at 90° to the piston pin axis **(see illustration)**. Subtract the piston diameter from the bore diameter to obtain the clearance. If it is greater than the specified figure, the piston must be renewed (assuming the bore itself is within limits, otherwise a rebore is necessary).

14.11 Measure the piston ring-to-groove clearance with a feeler gauge

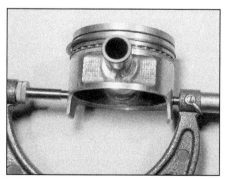

14.12 Measure the piston diameter with a micrometer at the specified distance from the bottom of the skirt

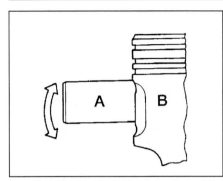

14.13a Slip the pin (A) into the piston (B) and try to rock it back and forth. If it's loose, renew the piston and pin

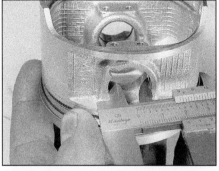

14.13b Measuring the internal diameter of the bore in the piston

14.16a Align the piston with the connecting rod small-end and insert the pin

13 Apply clean engine oil to the piston pin, insert it into the piston and check for any freeplay between the two (see illustration). Measure the pin external diameter (see illustration 28.6b), and the pin bore in the piston (see illustration). Calculate the difference to obtain the piston pin-to-piston pin bore clearance. Compare the result to the specifications at the beginning of the Chapter. If the clearance is greater than specified, renew the components that are worn beyond their specified limits.

Installation

14 Inspect and install the piston rings (see Section 15).
15 Lubricate the piston pin, the piston pin bore and the connecting rod small-end bore with clean engine oil.
16 When installing the pistons onto the connecting rods, make sure that the arrow points towards the exhaust side of the engine (see illustration 14.2). If both circlips were removed, install a new circlip in one side of the piston (do not re-use old circlips). Line up the piston on its correct connecting rod, and insert the piston pin from the other side (see illustration). Secure the pin with the other new circlip. When installing the circlips, compress them only just enough to fit them in the piston, and make sure they are properly seated in their grooves with the open end

away from the removal notch (see illustration).
17 Install the cylinder block (see Section 13).

15 Piston rings –
inspection and installation

1 It is good practice to renew the piston rings when an engine is being overhauled. Before installing the new piston rings, the ring end gaps must be checked with the rings installed in the cylinder.
2 Lay out each piston with its new ring sets so the rings will be matched with the same piston and cylinder during the end gap measurement procedure and engine assembly.
3 To measure the installed ring end gap, insert the top ring into the top of the first cylinder and square it up with the cylinder walls by pushing it in with the top of the piston. The ring should be about 20 mm below the top edge of the cylinder. To measure the end gap, slip a feeler gauge between the ends of the ring and compare the measurement to the specifications at the beginning of the Chapter (see illustration).
4 If the gap is larger or smaller than specified, double check to make sure that you have the correct rings before proceeding.

5 If the gap is too small, it must be enlarged or the ring ends may come in contact with each other during engine operation, which can cause serious damage. The end gap can be increased by filing the ring ends very carefully with a fine file. When performing this operation, file only from the outside in (see illustration).
6 Excess end gap is not critical unless it exceeds the service limit. Again, double-check to make sure you have the correct rings for your engine and check that the bore is not worn.
7 Repeat the procedure for each ring that will be installed in the cylinders. When checking the oil ring, only the side-rails can be checked as the ends of the expander ring should contact each other. Remember to keep the rings, pistons and cylinders matched up.
8 Once the ring end gaps have been checked/corrected, the rings can be installed on the pistons.
9 The oil control ring (lowest on the piston) is installed first. It is composed of three separate components, namely the expander and the upper and lower side rails. Slip the expander into the groove, then install the upper side rail. Do not use a piston ring installation tool on the oil ring side rails as they may be damaged. Instead, place one end of the side rail into the groove between the expander and the ring land. Hold it firmly in place and slide a finger

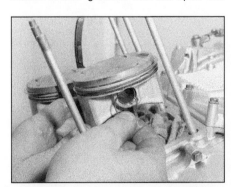

14.16b Do not over-compress the circlip when fitting it into the piston

15.3 Measuring piston ring installed end gap

15.5 Ring end gap can be enlarged by clamping a file in a vice and filing the ring ends

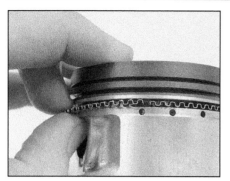

15.9a Install the oil ring expander in its groove . . .

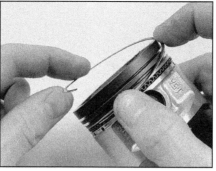

15.9b . . . and fit the side rails each side of it. The oil ring must be installed by hand

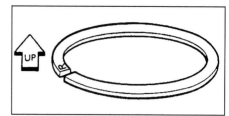

15.11 Compression ring top surface is marked by a letter

around the piston while pushing the rail into the groove. Next, install the lower side rail in the same manner **(see illustrations)**. Make sure the ends of the expander do not overlap.
10 After the three oil ring components have been installed, check to make sure that both the upper and lower side rails can be turned smoothly in the ring groove.
11 The upper surface of each compression ring is marked with a mark or letter at one end **(see illustration)**. Make sure that the identification mark or letter near the end gap is facing up when installed.
12 Fit the second ring into the middle groove in the piston. Make sure the identification letter near the end gap is facing up. Do not expand the ring any more than is necessary to slide it into place. To avoid breaking the ring, use a piston ring installation tool.
13 Finally, install the top ring in the same manner into the top groove in the piston. Make sure the identification letter near the end gap is facing up.
14 Once the rings are correctly installed, check they move freely without snagging and stagger their end gaps as shown **(see illustration)**.

16 Clutch – removal, inspection and installation

Note: *The clutch can be removed with the engine in the frame. If the engine has been removed, ignore the steps which don't apply.*

Removal

1 Drain the engine oil (see Chapter 1).
2 Detach the clutch cable from the operating lever on the clutch cover (see Section 17).
3 Working evenly in a criss-cross pattern, unscrew the clutch cover bolts **(see illustration)**. Lift the cover away from the engine, being prepared to catch any residual oil which may be released as the cover is removed.
4 Remove the gasket and discard it. Note the positions of the two locating dowels fitted to the crankcase and remove them for safe-keeping if they are loose.
5 Working in a criss-cross pattern, gradually slacken the clutch pressure plate bolts

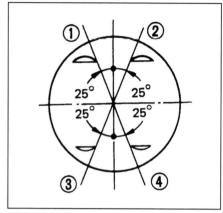

15.14 Stagger the ring end gaps as shown

1   *Top ring*
2   *Oil ring lower rail*
3   *Oil ring upper rail*
4   *Second (middle) ring*

until spring pressure is released **(see illustration)**. Counter-hold the clutch housing to prevent it turning. Remove the bolts and springs, then lift out the clutch pressure plate complete with its pull rod, thrust bearing and plate washer **(see illustrations 16.30b and a)**.
6 Grasp the complete set of clutch plates and

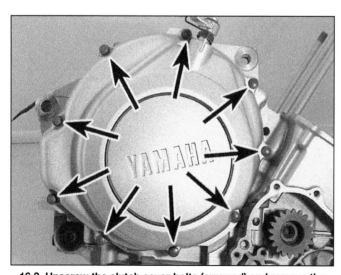

16.3 Unscrew the clutch cover bolts (arrowed) and remove the cover

16.5 Clutch pressure plate bolts (arrowed)

16.6 Remove the clutch plates as a pack

16.7a Bend back the lockwasher tabs

16.7b Slackening the clutch nut using the holding tool described

remove them as a pack **(see illustration)**. Unless the plates are being renewed, keep them in their original order. On 1991 to 1995 TDM models and 1990-on XTZ models, note the inner plate fitted in the clutch centre – if you remove it, keep it separate as it must be installed first **(see illustration 16.27)**.

7 Bend back the tabs on the clutch nut lockwasher **(see illustration)**. To remove the clutch nut the transmission input shaft must be locked. This can be done in several ways. If the engine is in the frame, engage 1st gear and have an assistant hold the rear brake on hard with the rear tyre in firm contact with the ground. Alternatively, the Yamaha service tool (pt. no. 90890-04086), or a similar home-made tool made from two strips of steel bent at the ends and bolted together in the middle (see **Tool tip**), can be used to hold the clutch centre whilst the nut is slackened **(see illustration)**. Unscrew the nut and remove the

lockwasher from the mainshaft, noting how it fits. Discard the lockwasher as a new one must be used on installation.

8 Remove the clutch centre and the outer thrust plate from the shaft **(see illustrations 16.26a and 16.25)**.

9 Support the clutch housing and remove the large sleeve from its centre **(see illustration)**. To get a grip on the sleeve, grasp the housing and wiggle it out and in – it should draw the sleeve out far enough to grip it. If difficulty is experienced, screw a 6 mm bolt (a clutch cover bolt is the correct size) into one or both of the threaded holes and pull the sleeve from the housing.

10 Remove the caged needle roller bearing from the housing if it didn't come away with the sleeve, and then remove the housing from the engine **(see illustrations 16. 24a and 16.23)**.

11 Remove the inner thrust plate **(see illustration 16.22b)** and, with the

exception of 1989 to 1991 XTZ models, the thrust washer from the shaft **(see illustration 16.22a)**.

12 On 1989 XTZ models, the clutch centre anti-judder assembly can be left intact unless the clutch has been chattering (juddering) excessively. If it is necessary to remove it, remove the wire retainer ring, plain plate, anti-judder spring and spring seat.

Inspection

13 After an extended period of service the clutch friction plates will wear and promote clutch slip. Measure the thickness of each friction plate using a vernier caliper **(see illustration)**. If any plate has worn to or beyond the service limit given in the

16.9 Remove the inner sleeve as described

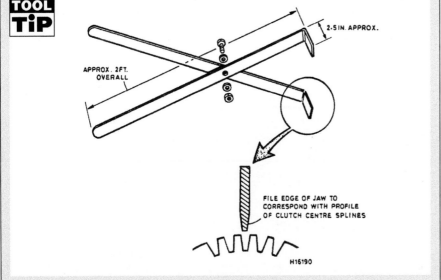

TOOL TiP

2·5 IN. APPROX.

APPROX. 2FT. OVERALL

FILE EDGE OF JAW TO CORRESPOND WITH PROFILE OF CLUTCH CENTRE SPLINES

H16190

A clutch centre holding tool can easily be made using two strips of steel with the ends bent over, and bolted together in the middle

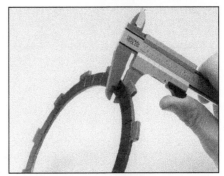

16.13 Measuring clutch friction plate thickness

16.14 Check the plain plates for warpage

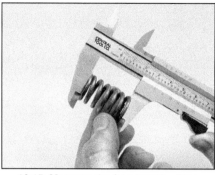

16.15 Measure the free length of the springs as shown

Specifications at the beginning of the Chapter, the friction plates must be renewed as a set. Also, if any of the plates smell burnt or are glazed, they must be renewed as a set.

14 The plain plates should not show any signs of excess heating (bluing). Check for warpage using a flat surface and feeler gauges **(see illustration)**. If any plate exceeds the maximum permissible amount of warpage, or shows signs of bluing, all plain plates must be renewed as a set.

15 Measure the free length of each clutch spring using a vernier caliper **(see illustration)**. If any spring is below the service limit specified, renew all the springs as a set.

16 Inspect the clutch assembly for burrs and

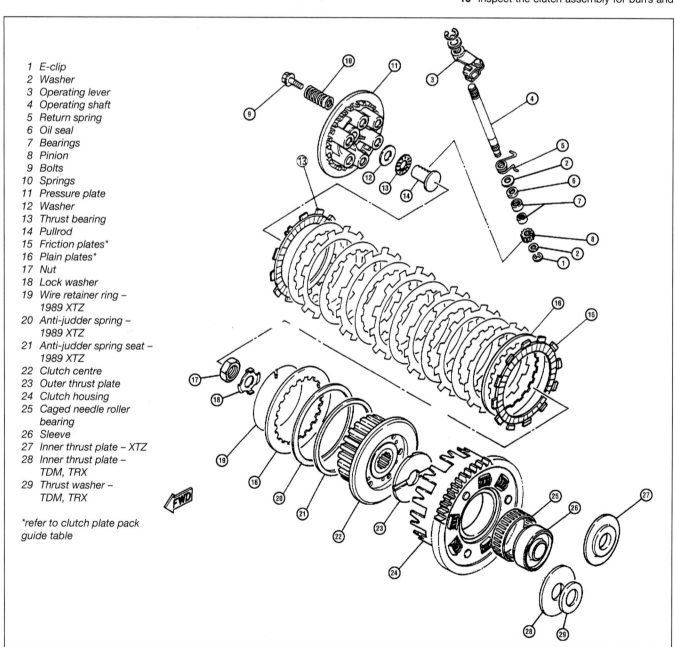

1 E-clip
2 Washer
3 Operating lever
4 Operating shaft
5 Return spring
6 Oil seal
7 Bearings
8 Pinion
9 Bolts
10 Springs
11 Pressure plate
12 Washer
13 Thrust bearing
14 Pullrod
15 Friction plates*
16 Plain plates*
17 Nut
18 Lock washer
19 Wire retainer ring –
   1989 XTZ
20 Anti-judder spring –
   1989 XTZ
21 Anti-judder spring seat –
   1989 XTZ
22 Clutch centre
23 Outer thrust plate
24 Clutch housing
25 Caged needle roller
   bearing
26 Sleeve
27 Inner thrust plate – XTZ
28 Inner thrust plate –
   TDM, TRX
29 Thrust washer –
   TDM, TRX

*refer to clutch plate pack
guide table

16.20 Clutch assembly

Clutch plate pack guide		
Model	**No. of plates**	**Order of fitting to clutch centre**
1991-93 TDM	8 friction, 8 plain	start with the special 'slick' plain plate, then alternate friction and plain plates until ending with special friction plate which has a slot in one of its tabs.
1994-95 TDM	8 friction, 8 plain	start with the special 'slick' plain plate, then alternate friction and plain plates.
1996-98 TDM and all TRX	9 friction, 8 plain	start with friction plate, then alternate plates until ending with a friction plate.
1999 TDM	9 friction, 8 plain	start with a special friction plate (black), then alternate plain and friction plates until ending with a special friction plate (black).
1989 XTZ	8 friction, 8 plain	special plain plate fitted as part of anti-judder assembly, then alternate friction and plain plates, until ending with special friction plate which has a slot in one of its tabs.
1990-94 XTZ	8 friction, 8 plain	start with the special 'slick' plain plate, then alternate friction and plain plates until ending with special friction plate which has a slot in one of its tabs.
1995 XTZ	8 friction, 8 plain	start with the special 'slick' plain plate, then alternate friction and plain plates.

indentations on the edges of the protruding tangs of the friction plates and/or slots in the edge of the housing with which they engage. Similarly check for wear between the inner tongues of the plain plates and the slots in the clutch centre. Wear of this nature will cause clutch drag and slow disengagement during gear changes, since the plates will snag when the pressure plate is lifted. With care a small amount of wear can be corrected by dressing with a fine file, but if this is excessive the worn components should be renewed.

17 Inspect the sleeve and caged needle roller bearing in conjunction with the clutch housing's internal bearing surface. If there are any signs of wear, pitting or other damage the affected parts must be renewed.

18 Check the pressure plate, thrust bearing and plate washer for signs of roughness, wear or damage, and renew any parts as necessary.

19 On 1989 XTZ models, if removed, check the clutch centre anti-judder assembly components (consisting of the wire retainer ring, plain plate, anti-judder spring and spring seat) for wear or damage, and renew any parts as necessary.

20 Check the clutch operating mechanism in the clutch cover for smooth operation. Check the pinion and pullrod teeth for signs of damage. If necessary, prise off the E-clip securing the pinion to the actuating shaft, and withdraw the shaft from the cover **(see illustration)**. Check the two needle roller bearings for roughness, wear or damage. If they need to be renewed, heat the cover in very hot water to ease removal and drift them out. If the shaft is removed, lever out the oil seal and renew it. Clean all components and lubricate the seal and bearings with grease.

Installation

21 Remove all traces of old gasket from the crankcase and clutch cover surfaces. On 1989 XTZ models, if disassembled, reassemble the clutch centre anti-judder assembly components, fitting the spring seat, the anti-judder spring, the plain plate and the wire retainer ring in that order.

22 On all except 1989 to 1991 XTZ models, fit the thrust washer and the inner thrust plate onto the shaft **(see illustrations)**. On 1989 to 1991 XTZ models, fit the inner thrust plate onto the shaft with its shouldered side inwards.

23 Lubricate the needle roller bearing and sleeve with clean engine oil. Install the clutch housing, without its needle roller bearing and sleeve, and support it in position, making sure it is engaged correctly with the primary drive gear on the crankshaft **(see illustration)**.

24 Install the needle bearing and the sleeve into the middle of the clutch housing **(see illustrations)**.

25 Lubricate the outer thrust plate with clean

16.22a Fit the thrust washer . . .

16.22b . . . and inner thrust plate onto the shaft

16.23 Slide the housing into place so that it engages the primary drive gear . . .

16.24a . . . then fit the needle bearing . . .

16.24b . . . and the sleeve into the middle of the housing

16.25 Fit the outer thrust plate . . .

16.26a . . . then slide the clutch centre onto the splines

16.26b Install the lockwasher, fitting the smaller bent tabs into the slots in the centre

16.26c Fit the nut . . .

16.26d . . . and tighten it to the specified torque, counter-holding the clutch centre

16.26e Bend up the lockwasher tabs to secure the nut

16.27 On the stated models, fit the inner plate

engine oil and fit it onto the shaft **(see illustration)**.

26 Install the clutch centre onto the shaft splines, then install the new lockwasher, engaging its tabs with the slots **(see illustrations)**. Install the clutch nut and, using the method employed on dismantling to lock the input shaft, tighten the nut to the torque setting specified at the beginning of the Chapter **(see illustrations)**. **Note:** *Check that the clutch centre rotates freely after tightening.* Bend up the tabs of the lockwasher to secure the nut **(see illustration)**.

27 On 1991 to 1995 TDM models and 1990-on XTZ models, fit the inner plain plate

on the clutch centre – if it has become muddled with the rest, it is distinguishable by its slick surface **(see illustration)**.

28 Build up the clutch plates, starting with a friction plate, then a plain plate and alternating friction and plain plates until all are installed **(see illustrations)**. Coat each plate with engine oil prior to installation. On 1991 to 1993 TDM models and 1989 to 1994 XTZ models, make sure the friction plate with the slot in one of its tabs is fitted last, and align the slot with the embossed marks on the outside of the clutch housing. **Note:** *Refer to the table accompanying illustration 16.20 for plate fitting details per model.*

16.28a Start with a friction plate . . .

16.28b . . . then fit a plain plate

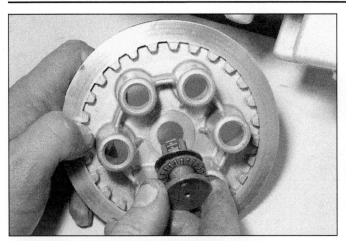

16.29 Fit the pullrod assembly in the back of the pressure plate

16.30a Install the pressure plate, aligning the punch marks (arrowed) . . .

29 Lubricate the thrust bearing and washer with molybdenum disulphide oil (a 50/50 mixture of molybdenum disulphide grease and engine oil). Install the thrust bearing and plate washer onto the pullrod, then install the pullrod assembly in through the back of the clutch pressure plate **(see illustration)**.
30 Install the pressure plate onto the clutch, aligning the punch mark on the plate with that on the clutch centre **(see illustration)**. Install the springs and the bolts with their washers, and tighten the bolts evenly in a criss-cross sequence to the specified torque setting **(see illustration)**. Counter-hold the clutch housing to prevent it turning. Check that the pullrod rotates freely.
31 If disassembled, install the clutch operating mechanism in the clutch cover. Align the shaft so that the operating lever is facing back but angled out slightly.
32 Insert the dowels in the crankcase, then set the pullrod so that its teeth point towards the rear. Install the clutch cover using a new

16.30b . . . then fit the springs, washers and bolts, and tighten them as described

gasket and tighten its bolts evenly in a criss-cross sequence to the specified torque setting **(see illustrations)**.
33 Push the clutch operating lever forward or in (according to model) until all the freeplay in the operating mechanism has been taken up. At this point the mark on the lever should align with the mark on the cover **(see illustration)**.

16.32a Fit the gasket onto the dowels (arrowed) . . .

If the marks do not align, remove the E-clip and the lever, noting how the spring fits, and move the lever around on the splines of the shaft until they do. Make sure the spring is correctly set on the lever and install the E-clip.
34 Install the clutch cable onto the lever (see Section 17).
35 Refill the engine with oil (see Chapter 1).

16.32b . . . then fit the cover

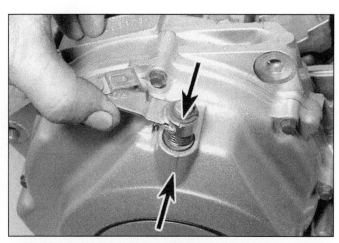

16.33 With the freeplay taken up the marks (arrowed) should align – TDM shown

17.1a Unscrew the two bolts (arrowed) and displace the tap

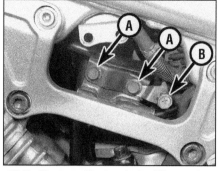

17.1b Unscrew the two bolts (A) securing the cable bracket, noting the idle speed adjuster (B)

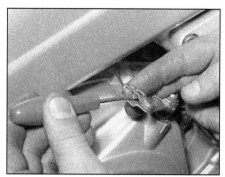

17.1c Bend back the retaining tab . . .

17 Clutch cable –
removed and installation

1 On TDM models, unscrew the two bolts securing the fuel tap and displace the tap (see illustration). Now unscrew the two bolts securing the cable bracket to the left-hand engine mounting bracket and detach the bracket, noting how the rear bolt also secures the idle speed adjuster (see illustration). Bend back the retaining tab securing the cable end in the clutch operating mechanism lever and disconnect the cable, noting how it

fits (see illustrations).
2 On TRX and XTZ models, fully slacken the adjuster nuts on the threaded section in the cable bracket on the right-hand side of the engine and slip the adjuster out of the bracket (see illustration). On TRX models, first remove the adjuster cover (see illustration). Disconnect the cable end from the clutch operating mechanism lever, noting how it fits (see illustrations 17.1c and d).
3 On all models fully slacken the lockring on the adjuster at the handlebar end of the cable then screw the adjuster fully in (see illustration). This resets it to the beginning of its adjustment span.
4 Align the slots in the adjuster and lockwheel

with that in the lever bracket, then pull the outer cable end from the socket in the adjuster and release the inner cable from the lever (see illustrations). Remove the cable from the machine, noting its routing and any guides or clips.

HAYNES HiNT *Before removing the cable from the bike, tape the lower end of the new cable to the upper end of the old cable. Slowly pull the lower end of the old cable out, guiding the new cable down into position. Using this method will ensure the cable is routed correctly.*

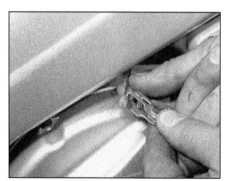

17.1d . . . and detach the cable

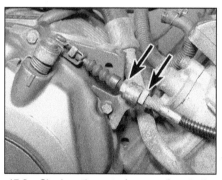

17.2a Slacken the nuts (arrowed) and slip the cable out of the bracket

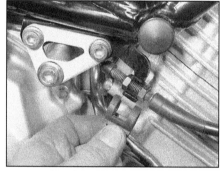

17.2b On TRX models, first remove the cover

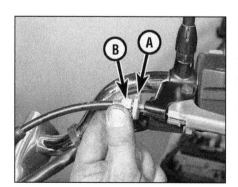

17.3 Slacken the lockring (A) and thread the adjuster (B) in

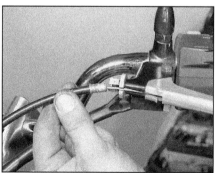

17.4a Align the slots and slip the cable out of the bracket . . .

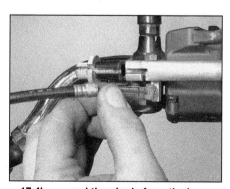

17.4b . . . and the nipple from the lever

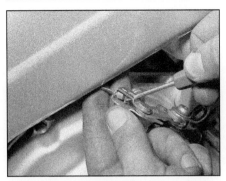

17.5 Bend the tab to secure the cable in the lever

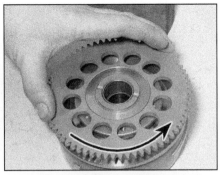

18.2 The gear should rotate freely in the direction shown

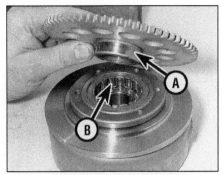

18.4 Check the surface of the hub (A) and the sprags (B) as described

5 Installation is the reverse of removal. Apply grease to the cable ends. Make sure the cable is correctly routed. Secure the cable end in the operating lever by bending the tab against it **(see illustration)**. Adjust the amount of clutch lever freeplay (see Chapter 1).

18 Starter clutch and idle/reduction gear – removal, inspection and installation

Removal

1 Remove the alternator rotor (see Chapter 9). The starter driven gear should come away with the rotor. If it doesn't, remove it from the crankshaft. The starter clutch is secured to the back of the rotor by three Allen bolts on the inside of the rotor.

Inspection

2 Install the starter driven gear into the starter clutch (if removed) and, with the rotor face down on a workbench, check that the gear rotates freely in an anti-clockwise direction and locks against the rotor in a clockwise direction **(see illustration)**. If it doesn't, renew the starter clutch – no replacement parts are available.
3 Withdraw the starter driven gear from the

starter clutch **(see illustration 18.4)**. If it appears stuck, rotate it anti-clockwise as you withdraw it to free it from the starter clutch. Note the thrust washer fitted inside the starter clutch and remove it for safekeeping **(see illustration 18.7)**.
4 Check the bearing surface of the starter driven gear hub and the condition of the sprags inside the clutch body **(see illustration)**. If the bearing surface shows signs of excessive wear or the sprags are damaged, marked or flattened at any point, the starter clutch should be renewed.
5 Examine the teeth of the starter idle/reduction gear and the corresponding teeth of the starter driven gear and starter motor shaft. Renew the gears and/or starter motor if worn or chipped teeth are discovered.
6 To renew the starter clutch sprag assembly, hold the alternator rotor in a rotor holder then undo the three bolts securing the clutch to the rotor. Remove the clutch from the back of the rotor and install the new one back onto the rotor. Tighten the bolts to the torque setting specified at the beginning of the Chapter, using the rotor holder to hold the rotor. Lubricate the starter clutch sprags with new engine oil.

Installation

7 Install the thrust washer in the starter clutch **(see illustration)**. Lubricate the hub of the

starter driven gear with clean engine oil, then install it into the clutch, rotating it clockwise as you do so to spread the rollers and allow the hub of the gear to enter **(see illustration 18.4)**.
8 Install the alternator rotor (see Chapter 9).

19 Gearchange mechanism external components – removal, inspection and installation

Note: *The gearchange mechanism (external components) can be removed with the engine in the frame. If the engine has been removed, ignore the steps which don't apply.*

Removal

1 Make sure the transmission is in neutral.
2 Remove the alternator cover (see Chapter 9). If required, disconnect the alternator and pick-up coil wiring connectors, otherwise ignore those Steps and lay the cover down so as not to strain the wiring.
3 Remove the clutch (see Section 16).
4 Remove the E-clip securing the left-hand end of the gearchange shaft in the crankcase, and slide the washer off the shaft **(see illustrations)**.
5 Note how the gearchange shaft centralising spring ends fit on each side of the locating pin in the casing, and how the pawls on the

18.7 Do not omit the thrust washer

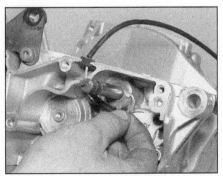

19.4a Remove the E-clip . . .

19.4b . . . and slide off the washer

19.5 Draw the gearchange shaft and selector arm assembly off the selector drum and out of the casing

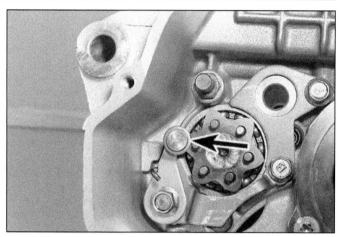

19.6a Note how the roller locates in the neutral detent (arrow), then unscrew the bolt and remove the stopper arm

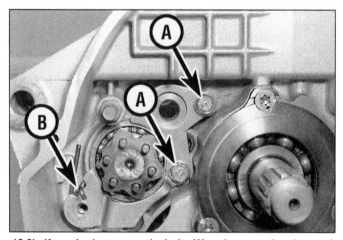

19.6b If required, unscrew the bolts (A) and remove the plate and the spring (B)

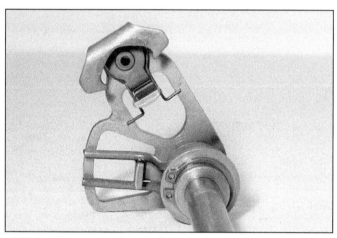

19.8 Gearchange shaft centralising spring can be removed after releasing circlip and washer from shaft

selector arm locate onto the pins on the end of the selector drum **(see illustration 19.12)**. Grasp the end of the shaft and withdraw the shaft/arm assembly **(see illustration)**.

6 Note how the stopper arm spring ends locate and how the roller on the arm locates in the neutral detent on the selector drum (gearbox in neutral), then unscrew the stopper arm bolt and remove the arm, and on 1996-on TDM models and all TRX models, the spacer **(see illustration)**. To remove the spring, unscrew the two remaining bolts securing the selector drum retainer plate and remove the plate – the spring sits behind the plate **(see illustration)**.

Inspection

7 Check the selector arm for cracks, distortion and wear of its pawls, and check for any corresponding wear on the selector pins in the selector drum. Also check the stopper arm roller and the detents in the selector drum for any wear or damage, and make sure the roller turns freely. Renew any components that are worn or damaged.

8 Inspect the shaft centralising spring **(see illustration)** and the stopper arm return spring for fatigue, wear or damage; renew them if necessary. The centralising spring is retained on the shaft by a circlip and washer – a new circlip should be used if removed. The stopper arm spring is secured by the retainer plate (see Step 6). Also check that the centralising spring locating pin in the crankcase is securely tightened. If it is loose,

19.9a Check the shaft oil seal (arrowed)

remove it and apply a non-permanent thread locking compound to its threads, then tighten it securely.

9 Check the gearchange shaft for straightness and damage to the splines. If the shaft is bent you can attempt to straighten it, but if the splines are damaged the shaft must be renewed. Also check the condition of the shaft oil seal in the left-hand side of the crankcase **(see illustration)**. If it is damaged,

19.9b If required, lever out the old seal . . .

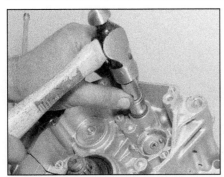

19.9c . . . and press or drive a new one in

19.10a Locate the stopper arm spring . . .

19.10b . . . then fit the retainer plate

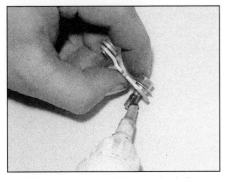

19.11a Apply thread lock to the bolt . . .

19.11b . . . then fit the stopper arm into the neutral detent on the selector drum and make sure the spring ends locate correctly

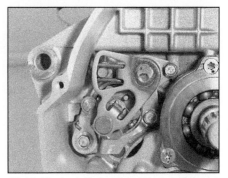

19.12 The installed assembly should be as shown

deteriorated or shows signs of leakage it must be renewed. Lever out the old seal and drive the new one squarely into place, with its lip facing inward, using a seal driver or suitable socket (see illustrations).

Installation

10 If removed, locate the stopper arm spring, then install the selector drum retainer plate **(see illustrations)**. Apply a suitable non-permanent thread locking compound to the two front bolts and tighten them to the torque setting specified at the beginning of the Chapter **(see illustration 19.6b)**.

11 Apply a suitable non-permanent thread locking compound to the stopper arm bolt **(see illustration)**. Install the stopper arm, and on 1996-on TDM models and all TRX models, the spacer, making sure the spring ends are positioned correctly **(see illustration)**. Locate the arm onto the neutral detent on the selector drum, then tighten the bolt to the specified torque setting **(see illustration 19.6a)**.

12 Slide the gearchange shaft into place and push it all the way through the case until the splined end comes out the other side **(see illustration 19.5)**. Locate the selector arm pawls onto the pins on the selector drum. Make sure the centralising spring ends locate correctly on each side of the locating pin **(see illustration)**.

13 Slide the washer onto the left-hand end of the shaft, then fit the E-clip into its groove,

making sure it is secure **(see illustrations 19.4b and a)**.

14 Install the clutch (see Section 16).

15 Install the alternator cover (see Chapter 9). Connect the alternator and pick-up coil wiring connectors, if disconnected.

20 Oil pumps – removal, inspection and installation

Note: *The oil pumps can be removed with the engine in the frame. If the engine has been removed, ignore the steps which don't apply.*

Removal

1 Two oil pumps are fitted, a feed pump to

lubricate the engine and a scavenge pump to return oil to the tank. As you look at the engine from the right-hand side, the feed pump is the left-hand pump and the scavenge pump is the right-hand pump **(see illustration 20.6)**.

2 Drain the engine oil (see Chapter 1). On XTZ models, remove the engine bashplate (see Chapter 8) and the exhaust system (see Chapter 4).

3 Unscrew the two bolts securing the oil pipe to the oil pump cover on the right-hand side of the engine **(see illustration)**. Detach the pipe and discard the O-ring as a new one must be used.

4 Unscrew the bolts securing the oil pump cover and remove the cover, being prepared to catch any residue oil **(see illustration)**.

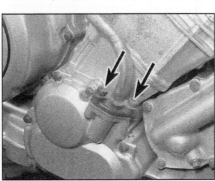

20.3 Unscrew the two bolts (arrowed) and detach the pipe

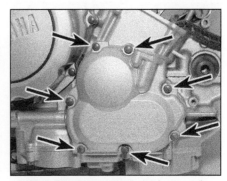

20.4 Oil pump cover bolts (arrowed)

20.5a Remove the circlip . . .

20.5b . . . and slide off the gear

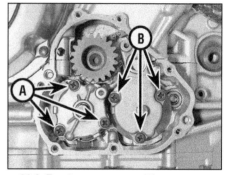

20.6 Feed pump screws (A), scavenge pump screws (B)

20.7a Remove the screw (arrowed) . . .

20.7b . . . and separate the housing

20.7c Draw out the shaft and remove the rotors

Discard the gasket as a new one must be used. Remove the dowels from either the cover or the crankcase if they are loose. Also note the oil passage collar located in the orifice in the scavenge pump cover. Discard the O-ring as a new one must be used, and remove the collar if required **(see illustration 20.18)**.

5 Remove the circlip securing the oil pump driven gear to the feed pump shaft and remove the gear **(see illustrations)**. Discard the circlip as a new one should be used. Do the same to free the driven gear from the scavenge pump.

6 Each pump is secured by three screws **(see illustration)**. Remove the screws and remove the pump, noting how it fits. Discard the gasket as a new one must be used. Note the dowel locating the scavenge pump and remove it if it is loose.

Inspection

7 If required, the pumps can be disassembled for cleaning. Remove the single assembly screw and separate the pump housing, on the feed pump noting how the cam chain guide fits **(see illustrations)**. Remove the housing locating pins if they are loose. Draw the inner rotor with the

driveshaft out of the pump housing, then remove the outer rotor **(see illustration)**. Note which way round the rotors fit and how the driveshaft pin locates in the slots in the inner rotor.

8 Clean all the components in solvent **(see illustration)**.

9 Inspect the pump body and rotors for scoring and wear **(see illustration)**. If any damage, scoring or uneven or excessive wear is evident, renew the pump (individual components are not available).

10 Fit the outer rotor into the pump body. Fit the drive pin into the shaft, then slide the shaft into the inner rotor, locating the drive pin ends

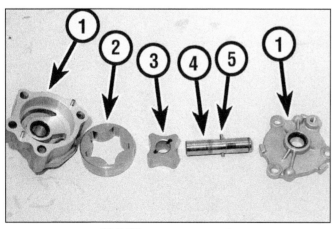

20.8 Oil pump components

1 Housing   2 Outer rotor   3 Inner rotor   4 Shaft   5 Drive pin

20.9 Look for scoring and wear, such as on this outer rotor

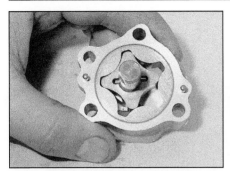

20.10a Assembled oil pump

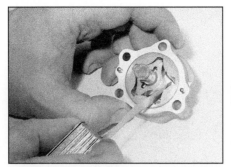

20.10b Measuring inner rotor tip-to-outer rotor tip clearance

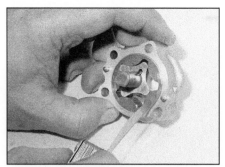

20.11 Measuring outer rotor-to-body clearance

in the slots in the rotor, then fit the inner rotor into the outer rotor **(see illustration)**. Measure the clearance between the inner rotor tip and the outer rotor with a feeler gauge and compare it to the maximum clearance listed in the specifications at the beginning of the Chapter **(see illustration)**. If the clearance measured is greater than the maximum listed, renew the pump.

11 Measure the clearance between the outer rotor and the pump body with a feeler gauge and compare it to the maximum clearance listed in the specifications at the beginning of the Chapter **(see illustration)**. If the clearance measured is greater than the maximum listed, renew the pump.

12 On 1996-on TDM models and all TRX models, lay a straight-edge across the rotors and

the pump body and, using a feeler gauge, measure the rotor end-float (the gap between the rotors and the straight-edge **(see illustration)**. If the clearance measured is greater than the maximum listed, renew the pump. No specifications are given for other models.

13 Check the nylon pump driven gears for wear or damage, and renew them if necessary. Damage to the steel drive gear is unlikely, but if found will necessitate crankshaft renewal.

14 If the pump is good, make sure all the components are clean, then lubricate them with new engine oil. Assemble the housing, making sure the pins locate correctly, and tighten the assembly screw to the torque setting specified at the beginning of the Chapter, not forgetting the cam chain guide on

the feed pump **(see illustration 20.7b and a)**.

15 Rotate the pump shaft by hand and check that the rotors turn smoothly and freely. If not, renew the pump.

Installation

16 Install the pump using a new gasket, not forgetting the locating dowel for the scavenge pump, if removed, and tighten the screws to the torque setting specified at the beginning of the Chapter **(see illustrations)**.

17 Locate the pump driven gear onto its shaft, aligning the flat in the gear with that on the shaft, and secure it using a new circlip **(see illustrations 20.5b and a)**. Align the open end of the circlip with the flat on the shaft **(see illustration)**.

18 If removed, install the oil passage collar

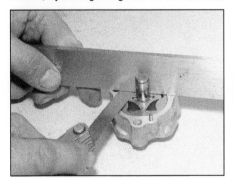

20.12 Measuring rotor end-float

20.16a Fit the gasket, on the scavenge pump locating it onto the dowel (arrowed)

20.16b Install the pump . . .

20.16c . . . and tighten its screws to the specified torque

20.17 Align the open ends of the circlips with the flats on the shafts

20.18 Fit a new O-ring around the collar

20.19a Make sure the gasket fits onto the dowels (arrowed) . . .

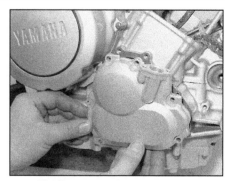

20.19b . . . then install the cover

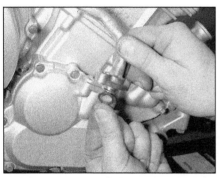

20.20a Use a new O-ring on the oil pipe union . . .

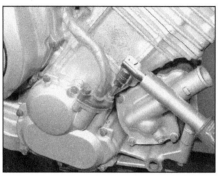

20.20b . . . and tighten its bolts to the specified torque

into the orifice in the scavenge pump, then fit a new O-ring **(see illustration)**.

19 If removed, fit the oil pump cover dowels into the crankcase, then install the cover using a new gasket, making sure it locates correctly onto the dowels **(see illustration)**. Tighten the cover bolts evenly in a criss-cross sequence to the specified torque setting **(see illustration)**.

20 Fit the oil pipe onto the cover using a new O-ring and tighten the bolts to the specified torque setting **(see illustrations)**.

21 On XTZ models, install the exhaust system (see Chapter 4) and the engine bashplate (see Chapter 8).

22 Fill the engine with the specified quantity and type of new engine oil (see Chapter 1).

21 Oil tank – removal and installation (1996-on TDM models and all TRX models)

Note: *To remove the oil tank, the engine must be removed from the frame.*

Removal

1 Remove the engine from the frame (see Section 5).

2 Unscrew the banjo bolts securing the oil pipe to the left-hand side of the oil tank and to the cylinder head, and the pipe bracket bolt, and remove the pipe. Discard the banjo bolt sealing washers as new ones must be used.

3 Unscrew the two bolts securing the oil pipe to the right-hand side of the oil tank and detach the pipe. Discard the O-ring as a new one must be used.

4 Slacken the clamp securing the oil pipe (from the rear of the oil tank) in the oil hose and detach the pipe from the hose. Unscrew the two bolts securing the pipe to the oil tank and withdraw the pipe. Discard the O-ring as a new one must be used.

5 Unscrew the bolts securing the top of the oil tank, noting which fits where as they are of different lengths, and noting the clip secured by the bolt on the right-hand side **(see illustration)**. Lift off the top of the tank, being prepared to catch any residue oil. Discard the gasket as a new one must be used. Note the

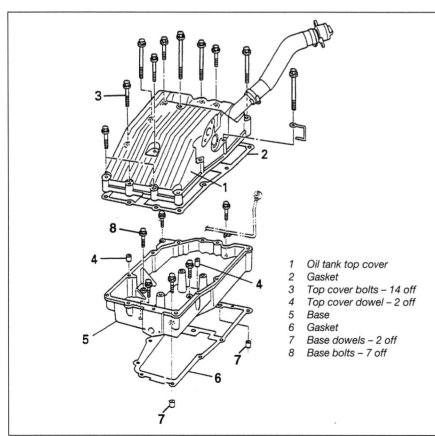

1 Oil tank top cover
2 Gasket
3 Top cover bolts – 14 off
4 Top cover dowel – 2 off
5 Base
6 Gasket
7 Base dowels – 2 off
8 Base bolts – 7 off

21.5 Oil tank (1996-on TDM and all TRX models)

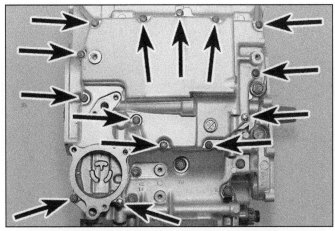

22.3 Unscrew the bolts (arrowed) and remove the sump

22.4a Remove the screws (arrowed) . . .

positions of the two dowels and remove them if they are loose.

6 Unscrew the bolts securing the base of the oil tank to the crankcase and lift off the base. Discard the gasket as a new one must be used. Note the positions of the two dowels and remove them if they are loose.

Installation

7 Installation is the reverse of removal, noting the following points:
a) Clean the oil tank in solvent and dry it using compressed air, if available.
b) Make sure the dowels are correctly located.
c) Use new gaskets.

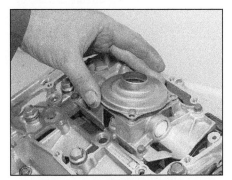

22.4b . . . and lift off the cover . . .

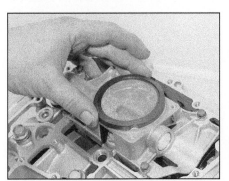

22.4c . . . and the strainer

d) Tighten the oil tank base and top bolts to the torque setting specified at the beginning of the Chapter.
e) Use new sealing washers on each side of the oil pipe banjo unions and tighten the banjo bolts to the specified torque setting.
f) Use new O-rings on the oil pipe unions and tighten the bolts to the specified torque setting.

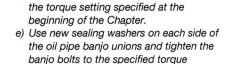

22 Oil sump, oil strainer and pressure relief valve – removal, inspection and installation

Note: The oil sump, strainer and pressure relief valve can be removed with the engine in the frame. If the engine has been removed, ignore the steps which don't apply.

Removal

1 On 1991 to 1995 TDM models and XTZ models, remove the engine bashplate (see Chapter 8). On TDM and TRX models remove the exhaust system (see Chapter 4).
2 Drain the engine oil and remove the oil filter (see Chapter 1).
3 Unscrew the sump bolts, slackening them evenly in a criss-cross sequence to prevent distortion, and remove the sump (see

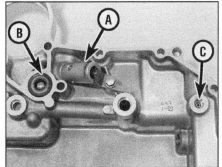

22.5 Pressure relief valve (A), bypass valve (B), oil nozzle (C)

illustration). Discard the gasket as a new one must be used. Note the positions of the dowels and remove them if they are loose.

4 Remove the screws securing the oil strainer cover and remove the cover and the strainer (see illustrations).

5 Remove the bolt securing the pressure relief valve holder and remove the holder (see illustration). Withdraw the valve and discard the O-ring as a new one must be used.

Inspection

6 Remove all traces of gasket from the sump and crankcase mating surfaces, and clean the inside of the sump with solvent.
7 Clean the oil strainer in solvent and remove any debris caught in its mesh. Inspect the strainer for any signs of wear or damage and renew it if necessary.
8 Push the relief valve plunger into the valve body and check that it moves smoothly and freely against the spring pressure. If not, renew the relief valve – individual components are not available. Similarly check that the bypass valve ball can be pushed into its bore and is not stuck (see illustration 22.5). Also check that the oil nozzle is securely screwed into its bore and has not worked loose.
9 Renew the O-rings around the oil passage collars in the crankcase (see illustration). Note their different sizes.

22.9 The O-rings (arrowed) should be renewed

22.12 Fit the new gasket, making sure the dowels (arrowed) are in place . . .

22.13 . . . then fit the sump

Installation

10 Fit a new O-ring onto the relief valve and smear it with clean oil, then push the valve into its socket in the crankcase. Fit the holder, then apply a suitable non-permanent thread locking compound to the bolt and tighten it to the torque setting specified at the beginning of the Chapter **(see illustration 22.5)**.

11 Install the oil strainer and its cover **(see illustrations 22.4c, b and a)**. Apply a suitable non-permanent thread locking compound to the cover screws and tighten them to the torque setting specified at the beginning of the Chapter.

12 If removed, fit the sump dowels into the crankcase. Lay a new gasket onto the sump (if the engine is in the frame) or onto the crankcase (if the engine has been removed and is positioned upside down on the work surface) **(see illustration)**. Make sure the holes in the gasket align correctly with the bolt holes.

13 Position the sump onto the crankcase, then apply a suitable non-permanent thread locking compound to the bolts and install them finger-tight **(see illustration)**. Tighten the bolts evenly in a criss-cross pattern to the specified torque setting.

14 Install the oil filter and cover and fill the engine with the correct type and quantity of oil (see Chapter 1).

15 On TDM and TRX models install the exhaust system (see Chapter 4). On 1991 to 1995 TDM models and XTZ models, install the

engine bashplate (see Chapter 8). Start the engine and check that there are no oil leaks around the sump and oil filter cover.

23 Balancer shafts – removal, inspection and installation

Note: *On 1991 to 1995 TDM models and XTZ models, the balancer shafts can be removed with the engine in the frame. If the engine has been removed, ignore the steps which do not apply. On 1996-on TDM models and all TRX models, the engine must be removed from the frame.*

Removal

1 On 1991 to 1995 TDM models and XTZ models, remove the seat, side covers and engine bashplate (see Chapter 8), the fuel tank and exhaust system (see Chapter 4), the starter clutch and idle/reduction gear (see Section 18), and the oil sump (see Section 22).

2 On 1996-on TDM models and TRX models, remove the oil tank (see Section 21), the starter clutch and idle/reduction gear (see Section 18), and the oil sump (see Section 22).

3 On 1992 to 1995 TDM models, unscrew the bolts securing the mudflap/engine top cover and remove the cover, feeding the earth cable through as you do **(see illustration)**.

4 On 1991 to 1995 TDM models and XTZ models, unscrew the oil pipe banjo bolts and the bracket bolt securing the oil pipe to the cylinder head and the crankcase top cover and remove the pipe **(see illustration)**. Discard the sealing washers as new ones must be used. Working evenly in a criss-cross pattern, unscrew the bolts securing the cover to the top of the crankcase and remove the cover **(see illustration)**. Note the position of the earth cable and cable guide(s) and of the bolt with the copper sealing washer. Discard the gasket as a new one must be used. Note the positions of the dowels and remove them if they are loose.

5 Unscrew the bolts securing the oil strainer holder and remove the holder **(see illustration)**. Remove the O-ring from the oil passage collar in the crankcase **(see illustration)**; a new O-ring is required for reassembly.

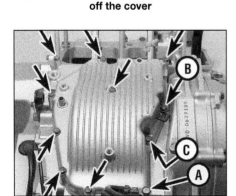

23.3 Remove the screws (arrowed) and lift off the cover

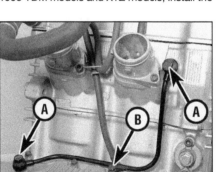
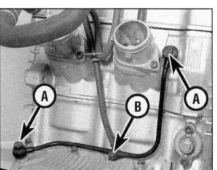

23.4a Unscrew the banjo bolts (A) and the bracket bolt (B) and remove the pipe

23.4b Unscrew the bolts (arrowed) and remove the cover, noting the earth cable (A), cable guide (B) and copper washer (C)

23.5a Unscrew the bolts (arrowed) and remove the holder

23.5b The O-ring (arrowed) should be renewed

23.6 Each retainer plate is secured by a Torx screw (arrowed)

23.7a Unscrew the bolts (arrowed) and remove the holder . . .

23.7b . . . then withdraw the shaft and lift out the rear weight

6 Unscrew the Torx bolt securing each balancer shaft retainer plate and remove the plates, noting how they fit **(see illustration)**.

7 Unscrew the bolts securing the rear balancer shaft holder and remove the holder **(see illustration)**. Remove the dowels if they are loose. Support the rear balancer shaft weight, then withdraw the shaft from the left-hand side of the crankcase and lift the weight out of the top **(see illustration)**. Discard the shaft O-ring as a new one must be used. Keep the weight and shaft together as a matched pair, and do not confuse them with the front weight and shaft.

8 Unscrew the bolts securing the front balancer shaft holder and remove the holder **(see illustration)**. Remove the dowels if they are loose. Support the front balancer shaft weight, then withdraw the shaft from the left-hand side of the crankcase and remove the weight from the bottom **(see illustration)**.

Inspection

9 Check the weights for cracked, chipped and worn teeth on the driven gears and renew the weight if any are found. The drive gears on the crankshaft should also be checked. Check the condition of the needle bearings in the bore of the weight. If they are worn, the weight must be renewed as the bearings are not listed as being available separately, though it is worth checking with a Yamaha dealer or bearing specialist.

10 Check the shafts are straight by rolling them on a flat surface such as a piece of glass. Also check the bearing surfaces for scuffing and wear.

Installation

11 Turn the crankshaft until the Woodruff key slot (for the alternator rotor) on the left-hand end aligns with the triangular mark on the crankcase **(see illustration)**. The best way to turn the engine with the alternator rotor removed is to engage a gear and use the front sprocket nut. If the engine is still in the frame, the rear wheel can be used. Turn the sprocket in an anti-clockwise direction only and remove the spark plugs (see Chapter 1) to release the compression in the engine,

23.8a Unscrew the bolts (arrowed) and remove the holder . . .

23.8b . . . then withdraw the shaft and lift out the front weight

making it much easier to turn and to prevent the nut from undoing.

12 Apply clean engine oil to the front balancer shaft. Position the front balancer weight in the engine, aligning the punch mark on the larger gear with the mark on the crankcase, then slide the shaft in from the left-hand side until it is fully home **(see illustration and 23.8b)**. Check that the marks on both the crankshaft and the balancer shaft are still correctly aligned. If removed, fit the balancer holder dowels, then install the holder and tighten its bolts to the torque setting specified at the beginning of the Chapter **(see illustration)**.

13 Fit a new O-ring onto the rear balancer shaft and smear it with lithium-based grease

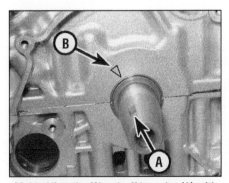

23.11 Align the Woodruff key slot (A) with the triangular mark (B)

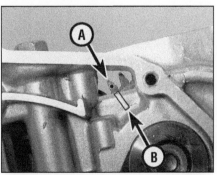

23.12a Align the punch mark on the gear (A) with the mark on the crankcase (B)

23.12b Fit the holder onto the dowels

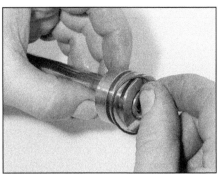

23.13a Fit a new O-ring into the narrow groove

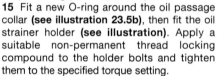

23.13b Align the punch mark on the gear (A) with the mark on the crankcase (B)

23.13c Fit the holder onto the dowels

(see illustration). Apply clean engine oil to the shaft. Position the rear balancer weight in the engine, aligning the punch mark on the larger gear with the mark on the crankcase, then slide the shaft in from the left-hand side until it is fully home (see illustration and 23.7b). Check that the marks on both the crankshaft and the balancer shaft are still correctly aligned. If removed, fit the balancer holder dowels, then install the holder and tighten its bolts to the torque setting specified at the beginning of the Chapter (see illustration).

14 Fit the shaft retainer plates with the counter-sink for the screw heads on the outside, then apply a suitable non-permanent thread locking compound to the Torx screw threads and tighten them to the specified torque setting (see illustration).

15 Fit a new O-ring around the oil passage collar (see illustration 23.5b), then fit the oil strainer holder (see illustration). Apply a suitable non-permanent thread locking compound to the holder bolts and tighten them to the specified torque setting.

16 On 1991 to 1995 TDM models and XTZ models, if removed, install the crankcase top cover dowels. Fit the cover using a new gasket, then tighten the bolts evenly in a criss-cross pattern to the specified torque, not forgetting the earth cable and cable guide(s) and making sure the bolt with the copper washer is positioned at the rear on the right-hand side (see illustrations). Install the oil pipe using new sealing washers on each side of the unions and tighten the banjo bolts and the bracket bolt to the specified torque settings (see illustration).

17 Install all remaining components or assemblies in a reverse of the removal procedure (see Steps 3, 2 and 1).

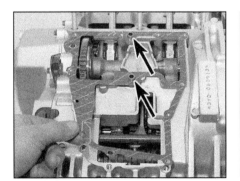

23.14 Fit each retainer plate into its slot in the shaft end

23.15 Install the strainer holder

23.16a Fit the new gasket onto the dowels (arrowed) . . .

23.16b . . . then install the cover

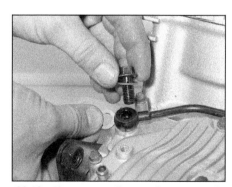

23.16c Use new sealing washers on each side of the union

24.2 Draw the cam chain out of the engine

24.4a Note how the front guide locates in the cylinder head (arrow) . . .

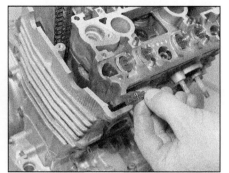

24.4b . . . and lift it out

24 Cam chain and guides –
removal, inspection and installation

Removal

Cam chain

1 Remove the valve cover (see Section 7), the cam chain tensioner (see Section 9), the cam chain top guide and the camshaft sprockets (see Section 8), and the oil pumps (see Section 20).
2 Feed the cam chain down through the tunnel and draw it out of the oil pump housing **(see illustration)**.

Chain guides

3 The cam chain top guide can be unbolted from the cylinder head after the valve cover has been removed (see Section 7) **(see illustration 8.4)**.
4 The cam chain front guide can be lifted from the cylinder head after the cam chain tensioner (see Section 9) and the exhaust camshaft sprocket have been removed (see Section 8) **(see illustrations)**. Note which way up and round the guide fits and how it locates.
5 The cam chain rear guide is secured by a pivot pin, which is located behind one of the 6 mm crankcase bolts. Remove the cam chain tensioner (see Section 9), the inlet camshaft sprocket (see Section 8) and the oil pump

cover (see Section 20). Unscrew the bolt **(see illustration)**. As the pivot pin is set deep, its centre is threaded to accept a 5 mm bolt. Thread the bolt into the pin, then draw out the bolt with the pin attached and lift the guide out of the top of the tunnel **(see illustrations)**.

Inspection

Cam chain

6 Check the chain for binding, kinks and any obvious damage and renew it if necessary. Check the camshaft sprocket teeth for wear and renew the cam chain and sprockets as a set if necessary (see Chapter 8).

Chain guides

7 Check the guides for excessive wear, deep grooves, cracking and other obvious damage, and renew them if necessary. Check the condition of the pivot hardware on the rear guide and renew any components that are damaged or deteriorated.

Installation

8 Installation of the chain and guides is the reverse of removal, noting the following:
a) Apply engine oil to the faces of the guides, to the rear guide pivot pin, and to the chain.
b) Use a piece of bent wire to hook up the cam chain and draw it up the tunnel.
c) Tighten the 6 mm crankcase bolt for the rear guide to the torque setting specified at the beginning of the Chapter.

25 Crankcase halves –
separation and reassembly

Note: To separate the crankcase halves, the engine must be removed from the frame.

Separation

1 To access the connecting rods, crankshaft, bearings, transmission shafts and the selector drum and forks, the crankcase must be split into two parts.
2 To enable the crankcases to be separated, the engine must be removed from the frame (see Section 5). Before the crankcases can be separated the following components must be removed:
a) Valve cover (Section 7).
b) Cylinder head (Section 10).
c) Cylinder block (Section 13).
d) Pistons (Section 14).
e) Clutch (Section 16).
f) Starter clutch and idle/reduction gear (Section 18).
g) Gearchange mechanism external components (Section 19).
h) Oil pumps (Section 20).
i) Cam chain and guides (Section 24).
j) Oil tank (1996-on TDM models and all TRX models) (Section 21).
k) Oil sump (Section 22).
l) Balancer shafts (Section 23).
m) Water pump (Chapter 3).
n) Starter motor (if required) (Chapter 9).

24.5a Unscrew the crankcase bolt (arrowed) . . .

24.5b . . . then thread a 5 mm bolt into the head of the pivot pin . . .

24.5c . . . then withdraw the pin and lift out the guide

25.3 Unscrew the bolts (arrowed) and remove the plate

3 Unscrew the bolts securing the transmission output shaft retainer plate to the left-hand side of the crankcase and remove the plate **(see illustration)**.
4 Unscrew the 6 mm and 8 mm upper crankcase bolts **(see illustrations)**. Unscrew the bolts evenly, a little at a time in a reverse of the numerical sequence until they are finger-tight, then remove them. The number of each bolt is cast into the crankcase. Note the copper washers fitted with some of the bolts. **Note:** *As each bolt is removed, store it in its relative position, with its washer where applicable, in a cardboard template of the crankcase halves. This will ensure all bolts are installed in the correct location on reassembly.*

5 Turn the engine upside down so that it rests on the cylinder head studs.
6 Unscrew the 6 mm lower crankcase bolts, the 8 mm bolts, and the 10 mm bolts **(see illustrations 25.4a and b)**. Unscrew the bolts evenly, a little at a time in a reverse of the numerical sequence until they are finger-tight, then remove them. The number of each bolt is cast into the crankcase. Note the copper washers fitted with some of the bolts, and also the cable guide. **Note:** *As each bolt is removed, store it in its relative position, with its washer and cable guide where applicable, in a cardboard template of the crankcase halves. This will ensure all bolts are installed in the correct location on reassembly.*

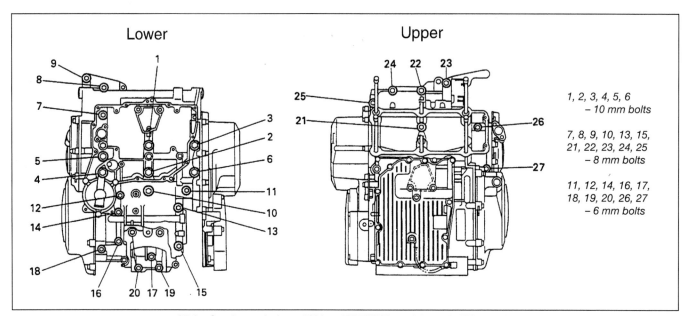

25.4a Crankcase bolts – 1991 to 1995 TDM models and XTZ models

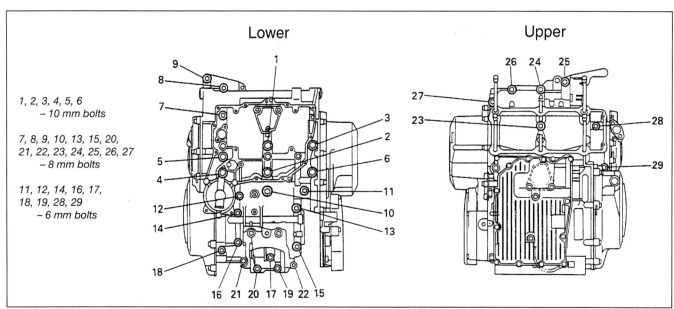

25.4b Crankcase bolts – 1996-on TDM models and TRX models

25.8 Remove the dowel (arrowed) if it is loose

25.11 Use a new output shaft oil seal if required

7 Carefully lift the lower crankcase half off the upper half, using a soft-faced hammer to tap around the joint to initially separate the halves if necessary **(see illustration 25.15)**. **Note:** *If the halves do not separate easily, make sure all fasteners have been removed. Do not try and separate the halves by levering against the crankcase mating surfaces as they are easily scored and will leak oil. Tap around the joint faces with a soft-faced mallet.*

8 Remove the locating dowel from the crankcase if it is loose (it could be in either crankcase half) **(see illustration)**.

9 Refer to Sections 26 to 32 for the removal and installation of the components housed within the crankcases.

Reassembly

10 Remove all traces of sealant from the crankcase mating surfaces.

11 Ensure that all components and their bearings are in place in the upper and lower crankcase halves. If the transmission shafts have not been removed, check the condition of the output shaft oil seal on the left-hand

end of the shaft and renew it if it is damaged or deteriorated **(see illustration)**.

12 Generously lubricate the crankshaft and transmission shafts, particularly around the bearings, with clean engine oil, then use a rag soaked in high flash-point solvent to wipe over the mating surfaces of both crankcase halves to remove all traces of oil.

13 If removed, install the locating dowel in the upper crankcase half **(see illustration 25.8)**.

14 Apply a small amount of suitable sealant (such as Yamaha Bond 1215) to the outer mating surface of one crankcase half **(see illustration)**.

Caution: Do not apply an excessive amount of sealant as it will ooze out when the case halves are assembled and may obstruct oil passages. Do not apply the sealant on or too close (within 2 to 3 mm) to any of the bearing inserts or surfaces.

15 Check again that all components are in position, particularly that the bearing shells are still correctly located in the lower crankcase half. Carefully install the lower crankcase half down onto the upper

crankcase half, making sure the dowel locates correctly into the lower crankcase half **(see illustration)**.

16 Check that the lower crankcase half is correctly seated. **Note:** *The crankcase halves should fit together without being forced. If the casings are not correctly seated, remove the lower crankcase half and investigate the problem. Do not attempt to pull them together using the crankcase bolts as the casing will crack and be ruined.*

17 Clean the threads of the 10 mm lower crankcase bolts and apply molybdenum disulphide oil (a 50/50 mixture of molybdenum disulphide grease and new engine oil) to their threads. Insert them with their washers in their original locations. Clean the threads of the 8 mm and 6 mm lower crankcase bolts and apply new engine oil to their threads. Insert them (with their washers where fitted, and not forgetting the cable guide) in their original locations. Secure all bolts finger-tight at first, then tighten them evenly and a little at a time in the correct numerical sequence to the torque settings specified at the beginning of the Chapter **(see illustrations 25.4a or b)**.

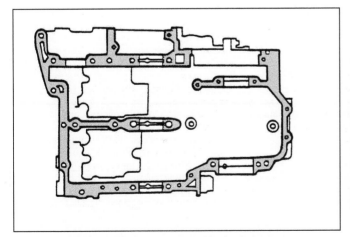

25.14 Apply the sealant to the shaded areas

25.15 Fit the lower half onto the upper half, making sure it locates onto the dowel (arrowed)

25.20 Install the retainer plate

18 Turn the engine over. Clean the threads of the 8 and 6 mm upper crankcase bolts and apply new engine oil to their threads. Insert them (with their washers where fitted) in their original locations. Secure all bolts finger-tight at first, then tighten them evenly and a little at a time in the correct numerical sequence to the torque settings specified at the beginning of the Chapter **(see illustrations 25.4a or b)**.

19 With all crankcase fasteners tightened, check that the crankshaft and transmission shafts rotate smoothly and easily. Check that the transmission shafts rotate freely and independently in neutral, then rotate the selector drum by hand and select each gear in turn whilst rotating the input shaft. Check that all gears can be selected and that the shafts rotate freely in every gear. If there are any signs of undue stiffness, tight or rough spots, or of any other problem, the fault must be rectified before proceeding further.

20 Install the transmission output shaft retainer plate onto the left-hand side of the crankcase **(see illustration)**. Apply a suitable non-permanent thread locking compound to the threads of the bolts and tighten them to the specified torque setting.

21 Install all other removed assemblies in the reverse of the sequence given in Step 2.

26 Crankcase halves – inspection and servicing

1 After the crankcases have been separated, remove the crankshaft, connecting rods, transmission shafts, selector drum and forks, water pump drive gear, and neutral switch, referring to the relevant Sections of this Chapter, and to Chapter 3 for the water pump and Chapter 9 for the neutral switch. Also remove the oil passage collars and their O-rings **(see illustration 22.9)**. Discard the O-rings as new ones must be used.

2 The crankcases should be cleaned thoroughly with new solvent and dried with compressed air. All oil passages should be blown out with compressed air. Also check that the oil nozzles are securely screwed into their bores and have not worked loose.

3 All traces of old gasket sealant should be removed from the mating surfaces. Minor damage to the surfaces can be cleaned up with a fine sharpening stone or grindstone. *Caution: Be very careful not to nick or gouge the crankcase mating surfaces or oil leaks will result. Check both crankcase halves very carefully for cracks and other damage.*

4 Small cracks or holes in aluminium castings may be repaired with an epoxy resin adhesive as a temporary measure. Permanent repairs can only be effected by argon-arc welding, and only a specialist in this process is in a position to advise on the economy or practical aspect of such a repair. If any damage is found that can't be repaired, renew the crankcase halves as a set.

5 Damaged threads can be economically reclaimed by using a diamond section wire insert, of the Heli-Coil type, which is easily fitted after drilling and re-tapping the affected thread.

6 Sheared studs or screws can usually be removed with screw extractors, which consist of a tapered, left thread screw of very hard steel. These are inserted into a pre-drilled hole in the stud, and usually succeed in dislodging the most stubborn stud or screw.

 HAYNES HINT *Refer to Tools and Workshop Tips for details of installing a thread insert and using screw extractors.*

7 Install all components and assemblies, referring to the relevant Sections of this Chapter and to Chapters 3 and 9, before reassembling the crankcase halves. Do not forget to install the oil passage collars using new O-rings.

27 Main and connecting rod bearings – general information

1 Even though main and connecting rod bearings are generally renewed during the engine overhaul, the old bearings should be retained for close examination as they may reveal valuable information about the condition of the engine.

2 Bearing failure occurs mainly because of lack of lubrication, the presence of dirt or other foreign particles, overloading the engine and/or corrosion. Regardless of the cause of bearing failure, it must be corrected before the engine is reassembled to prevent it from happening again.

3 When examining the connecting rod bearings, remove them from the connecting rods and caps and lay them out on a clean surface in the same general position as their location on the crankshaft journals. This will enable you to match any noted bearing problems with the corresponding crankshaft journal.

4 Dirt and other foreign particles get into the engine in a variety of ways. It may be left in the engine during assembly or it may pass through filters or breathers. It may get into the oil and from there into the bearings. Metal chips from machining operations and normal engine wear are often present. Abrasives are sometimes left in engine components after reconditioning operations, especially when parts are not thoroughly cleaned using the proper cleaning methods. Whatever the source, these foreign objects often end up imbedded in the soft bearing material and are easily recognised. Large particles will not imbed in the bearing and will score or gouge the bearing and journal. The best prevention for this cause of bearing failure is to clean all parts thoroughly and keep everything spotlessly clean during engine reassembly. Frequent and regular oil and filter changes are also recommended.

5 Lack of lubrication or lubrication breakdown has a number of interrelated causes. Excessive heat (which thins the oil), overloading (which squeezes the oil from the bearing face) and oil leakage or throw off (from excessive bearing clearances, worn oil pumps or high engine speeds) all contribute to lubrication breakdown. Blocked oil passages will also starve a bearing and destroy it. When lack of lubrication is the cause of bearing failure, the bearing material is wiped or extruded from the steel backing of the bearing. Temperatures may increase to the point where the steel backing and the journal turn blue from overheating.

 HAYNES HINT *Refer to Tools and Workshop Tips for bearing fault finding.*

6 Riding habits can have a definite effect on bearing life. Full throttle low speed operation, or labouring the engine, puts very high loads on bearings, which tend to squeeze out the oil film. These loads cause the bearings to flex, which produces fine cracks in the bearing face (fatigue failure). Eventually the bearing material will loosen in pieces and tear away from the steel backing. Short trip riding leads to corrosion of bearings, as insufficient engine heat is produced to drive off the condensed water and corrosive gases produced. These products collect in the engine oil, forming acid and sludge. As the oil is carried to the engine bearings, the acid attacks and corrodes the bearing material.

7 Incorrect bearing installation during engine assembly will lead to bearing failure as well. Tight fitting bearings which leave insufficient bearing oil clearances result in oil starvation. Dirt or foreign particles trapped behind a bearing insert result in high spots on the bearing which lead to failure.

8 To avoid bearing problems, clean all parts thoroughly before reassembly, double check all bearing clearance measurements and lubricate the new bearings with clean engine oil during installation.

28.2 Measure the connecting rod side clearance using a feeler gauge

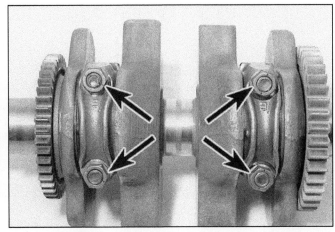

28.4 Unscrew the nuts (arrowed) and remove the connecting rods

28 Connecting rods – removal, inspection and installation

Note: *To remove the connecting rods the engine must be removed from the frame and the crankcases separated.*

Removal

1 Remove the engine from the frame (see Section 5) and separate the crankcase halves (see Section 25).
2 Before removing the rods from the crankshaft, measure the side clearance on each rod with a feeler gauge **(see illustration)**. If the clearance between any rod is greater than the service limit listed in this Chapter's Specifications, replace that rod with a new one.
3 Using paint or a felt marker pen, mark the relevant cylinder identity on each connecting rod and cap. Mark across the cap-to-connecting rod join and note the Y mark on each connecting rod which must face to the left-hand side of the engine to ensure that the cap and rod are fitted the correct way around on reassembly. Note that the number etched

across the rod and cap indicates rod size grade, not cylinder number.
4 Unscrew the big-end cap nuts and separate the cap from the crankpin **(see illustration)**. Do not remove the bolts from the connecting rods. Immediately install the relevant bearing shells (if removed), bearing cap, and nuts on each piston/connecting rod assembly so that they are all kept together as a matched set to ensure correct installation.

Inspection

5 Check the connecting rods for cracks and other obvious damage.
6 Apply clean engine oil to the piston pin, insert it into the connecting rod small-end and check for any freeplay between the two **(see illustration)**. Measure the pin external and compare the result to the specifications at the beginning of the Chapter **(see illustration)**. If the piston pin is worn below the service limit it should be renewed.
7 Refer to Section 27 and examine the connecting rod bearing shells. If they are scored, badly scuffed or appear to have seized, new shells must be installed. Always renew the shells in the connecting rods as a set. If they are badly damaged, check the corresponding crankpin. Evidence of extreme

heat, such as discoloration, indicates that lubrication failure has occurred. Be sure to thoroughly check the oil pump and pressure relief valve as well as all oil holes and passages before reassembling the engine.
8 Have the rods checked for twist and bend by a Yamaha dealer or engineer if you are in doubt about their straightness.

Oil clearance check

9 Whether new bearing shells are being fitted or the original ones are being re-used, the connecting rod bearing oil clearance should be checked prior to reassembly.
10 Clean the backs of the bearing shells and the bearing locations in both the connecting rod and cap.
11 Press the bearing shells into their locations, ensuring that the tab on each shell engages the notch in the connecting rod/cap **(see illustration)**. Make sure the bearings are fitted in the correct locations and take care not to touch any shell's bearing surface with your fingers.
12 Cut a length of the appropriate size Plastigauge (it should be slightly shorter than the width of the crankpin). Place a strand of Plastigauge on the (cleaned) crankpin journal.
13 Apply molybdenum disulphide grease to

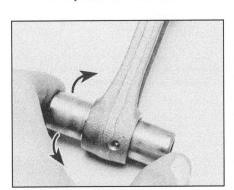

28.6a Slip the piston pin into the rod's small-end and rock it back and forth to check for looseness

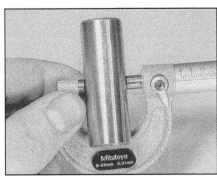

28.6b Measure the external diameter of the pin

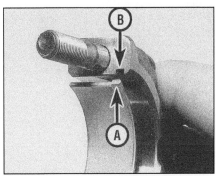

28.11 Make sure the tab (A) locates in the notch (B)

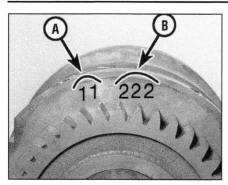

28.21a Big-end journal size numbers (A), main journal size numbers (B)

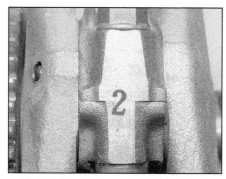

28.21b Connecting rod size number is marked across the cap and rod join

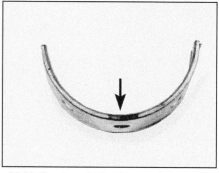

28.22 Bearing shell colour code location

the bolt shanks and threads and to the seats of the nuts. Install the (clean) connecting rod, shells and cap. Make sure the cap is fitted the correct way around so the previously made markings align, and that the rod is facing the right way (see Step 3). Tighten the nuts finger-tight, making sure the connecting rod does not rotate on the crankshaft.

14 Tighten the bearing cap nuts evenly, in two or three stages, to the initial torque setting specified at the beginning of the Chapter, making sure the connecting rod does not rotate on the crankshaft. Now tighten each nut in turn and in one continuous movement to the final torque setting specified. If the tightening is interrupted between the initial and final torque settings, slacken the nuts and begin the procedure again.

15 Slacken the cap nuts and remove the connecting rod, again taking great care not to rotate the rod or crankshaft.

16 Compare the width of the crushed Plastigauge on the crankpin to the scale printed on the Plastigauge envelope to obtain the connecting rod bearing oil clearance **(see illustration 29.20)**. Compare the reading to the specifications at the beginning of the Chapter.

17 On completion carefully scrape away all traces of the Plastigauge material from the crankpin and bearing shells using a fingernail or other object which is unlikely to score the shells.

18 If the clearance is within the range listed in this Chapter's Specifications and the bearings are in perfect condition, they can be reused. If the clearance is beyond the service limit, renew the shells (see Steps 21 and 22). Check the oil clearance once again (the new shells may be thick enough to bring bearing clearance within the specified range). Always renew the shells in both connecting rods at the same time.

19 If the clearance is still greater than the service limit listed in this Chapter's Specifications, the crankpin is worn and the crankshaft should be renewed.

20 Repeat the bearing selection procedure for other connecting rod.

Bearing shell selection

21 New bearing shells for the big-end bearings are supplied on a selected fit basis. Code numbers stamped on various components are used to identify the correct parts. The crankshaft journal size numbers are stamped on the outside of the crankshaft web on the right-hand end **(see illustration)**. The block of two numbers are for the big-end bearing journals (the block of three numbers are for the main bearing journals). The left-hand number is for the left-hand (No. 1 cylinder) journal. The connecting rod numbers are marked in ink on the flat face of the connecting rod and cap **(see illustration)**.

22 A range of bearing shells is available. To select the correct bearing for a particular connecting rod, subtract the big-end bearing journal number (stamped on the crank web) from the connecting rod number (marked on the rod). Compare the bearing number calculated with the table below to find the colour coding of the new bearing required. The bearing shell colour code is marked on the side of the shell **(see illustration)**.

Number	Colour
1	Blue
2	Black
3	Brown
4	Green

Installation

23 Clean the backs of the bearing shells and the bearing locations in both the connecting rod and cap.

24 Press the bearing shells into their locations, making sure the tab on each shell locates in the notch in the connecting rod/cap **(see illustration 28.11)**. Make sure the bearings are fitted in their correct locations and take care not to touch any shell's bearing surface with your fingers. Lubricate the shells with clean engine oil.

25 Apply molybdenum disulphide grease to the bolt shanks and threads and to the seats of the nuts. Assemble the connecting rod and cap on the crankpin. Make sure the cap is

fitted the correct way around so the previously made markings align, and that the rod is facing the right way (see Step 3). Tighten the nuts finger-tight, making sure the connecting rod does not rotate on the crankshaft. Check again to make sure all components have been returned to their original locations using the marks made on disassembly.

26 Tighten the bearing cap nuts evenly, in two or three stages, to the initial torque setting specified at the beginning of the Chapter, making sure the connecting rod does not rotate on the crankshaft. Now tighten each nut in turn and in one continuous movement to the final torque setting specified. If the tightening is interrupted between the initial and final torque settings, slacken the nuts and begin the procedure again.

27 Check that the rods rotate smoothly and freely on the crankpin. If there are any signs of roughness or tightness, remove the rods and re-check the bearing clearance. Sometimes tapping the bottom of the connecting rod cap will relieve tightness, but if in doubt, recheck the clearances.

28 Reassemble the crankcase halves (see Section 25).

29 Crankshaft and main bearings – removal, inspection and installation

Note: *To remove the crankshaft the engine must be removed from the frame and the crankcase halves separated.*

Removal

1 Remove the engine from the frame (see Section 5) and separate the crankcase halves (see Section 25).

2 Separate the connecting rods from the crankshaft (see Section 28). **Note:** *If no work is to be carried out on the crankshaft or connecting rod assemblies, there is no need to separate them.*

3 Lift the crankshaft out of the upper

29.3 Carefully lift the crankshaft out of the crankcase

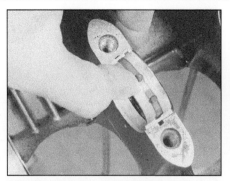

29.4 To remove a main bearing shell, push it sideways and lift it out

29.5 Check the condition of the gear and sprocket teeth

crankcase half, taking care not to dislodge the main bearing shells **(see illustration)**.

4 The main bearing shells can be removed from the crankcase halves by pushing their centres to the side, then lifting them out **(see illustration)**. Keep the shells in order.

Inspection

5 Clean the crankshaft with solvent, using a rifle-cleaning brush to scrub out the oil passages. If available, blow the crank dry with compressed air, and also blow through the oil passages. Check the drive gears for wear or damage **(see illustration)**. If any of the gear teeth are excessively worn, chipped or broken, the crankshaft must be renewed. If wear or damage is found, check the driven gears on the balancer shafts, oil pumps, water pump and clutch housing.

6 Refer to Section 27 and examine the main bearing shells. If they are scored, badly scuffed or appear to have been seized, new bearings must be installed. Always renew the main bearings as a set. If they are badly damaged, check the corresponding crankshaft journals. Evidence of extreme heat, such as discoloration, indicates that lubrication failure has occurred. Be sure to thoroughly check the oil pump and pressure relief valve as well as all oil holes and passages before reassembling the engine.

7 Give the crankshaft journals a close visual examination, paying particular attention where damaged bearings have been discovered. If the journals are scored or pitted in any way a new crankshaft will be required. Note that undersizes are not available, precluding the option of re-grinding the crankshaft.

8 Place the crankshaft on V-blocks and check the runout at the main bearing journals using a dial gauge **(see illustration)**. Compare the reading to the maximum specified at the beginning of the Chapter. If the runout exceeds the limit, the crankshaft must be renewed.

Oil clearance check

9 Whether new bearing shells are being fitted or the original ones are being re-used, the main bearing oil clearance should be checked before the engine is reassembled. Main

bearing oil clearance is measured with a product known as Plastigauge.

10 Clean the backs of the bearing shells and the bearing housings in both crankcase halves.

11 Press the bearing shells into their cut-outs, ensuring that the tab on each shell engages in the notch in the crankcase **(see illustration)**. Make sure the bearings are fitted in the correct locations and take care not to touch any shell's bearing surface with your fingers.

12 Ensure the shells and crankshaft are clean and dry. Lay the crankshaft in position in the upper crankcase.

13 Cut several lengths of the appropriate size Plastigauge (they should be slightly shorter than the width of the crankshaft journals).

Place a strand of Plastigauge on each (cleaned) journal **(see illustration)**. Make sure the crankshaft is not rotated.

14 If removed, install the locating dowel in the upper crankcase half **(see illustration 25.8)**. Carefully install the lower crankcase half on to the upper half, making sure the dowel locates correctly into the lower crankcase half **(see illustration 25.15)**. Check that the lower crankcase half is correctly seated. **Note:** *Do not tighten the crankcase bolts if the casing is not correctly seated.*

15 Clean the threads of the 10 mm lower crankcase bolts and apply molybdenum disulphide oil (a 50/50 mixture of molybdenum disulphide grease and new engine oil) to their threads. Insert them with their washers in their original locations. Clean the threads of the

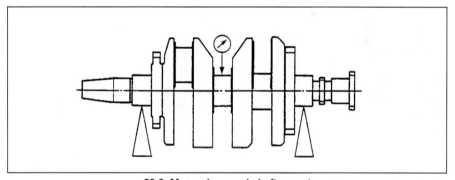

29.8 Measuring crankshaft runout

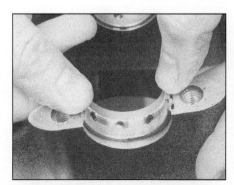

29.11 Make sure the tab on the shell locates in the notch in the rod

29.13 Lay a strip of Plastigauge on each journal parallel to the crankshaft centreline

29.20 Measure the width of the crushed Plastigauge (be sure to use the correct scale – metric and imperial are included)

8 and 6 mm lower crankcase bolts and apply new engine oil to their threads. Insert them (with their washers where fitted) in their original locations. Secure all bolts finger-tight at first, then tighten them evenly and a little at a time in the correct numerical sequence to the torque settings specified at the beginning of the Chapter **(see illustrations 25.4a or b)**. Make sure that the crankshaft is not rotated as the bolts are tightened.

16 Turn the engine over. Clean the threads of the 8 and 6 mm upper crankcase bolts and apply new engine oil to their threads. Insert them (with their washers where fitted) in their original locations. Secure all bolts finger-tight at first, then tighten them evenly and a little at a time in the correct numerical sequence to the torque settings specified at the beginning of the Chapter **(see illustrations 25.4a or b)**. Make sure that the crankshaft is not rotated as the bolts are tightened.

17 Unscrew the 6 mm and 8 mm upper crankcase bolts evenly, a little at a time in a **reverse** of the numerical sequence until they are finger-tight, then remove them **(see illustrations 25.4a or b)**. The number of each bolt is cast into the crankcase. Note the copper washers fitted with some of the bolts. **Note:** *As each bolt is removed, store it in its relative position, with its washer where applicable, in a cardboard template of the*

crankcase halves. This will ensure all bolts are installed in the correct location on reassembly.
18 Turn the engine upside down so that it rests on the cylinder head studs.
19 Unscrew the 6 mm lower crankcase bolts, the 8 mm bolts, and the 10 mm bolts evenly, a little at a time in a **reverse** of the numerical sequence until they are finger-tight, then remove them **(see illustrations 25.4a or b)**. The number of each bolt is cast into the crankcase. Carefully lift off the lower crankcase half, making sure the Plastigauge is not disturbed.
20 Compare the width of the crushed Plastigauge on each crankshaft journal to the scale printed on the Plastigauge envelope to obtain the main bearing oil clearance **(see illustration)**. Compare the reading to the specifications at the beginning of the Chapter.
21 On completion carefully scrape away all traces of the Plastigauge material from the crankshaft journal and bearing shells; use a fingernail or other object which is unlikely to score them.
22 If the oil clearance falls into the specified range, new bearing shells are not required (provided they are in good condition). If the clearance is beyond the service limit, refer to the marks on the case and the marks on the crankshaft and select new bearing shells (see Steps 24 and 25). Install the new shells and check the oil clearance once again (the new shells may bring bearing clearance within the specified range). Always renew all of the main bearing shells at the same time.
23 If the clearance is still greater than the service limit listed in this Chapter's Specifications (even with new shells), the crankshaft journal is worn and the crankshaft should be renewed.

Main bearing shell selection

24 New bearing shells for the main bearings are supplied on a selected fit basis. Code numbers stamped on various components are used to identify the correct size bearings. The crankshaft journal size numbers are stamped on the outside of the crankshaft web on the

right-hand end **(see illustration 28.21a)**. The block of three numbers are for the main bearing journals (the block of two numbers are for the big-end bearing journals). The main bearing housing numbers are stamped into the upper crankcase half **(see illustration)**. Note that if there is only one number stamped into the crankcase, it means that all the journals are the same number.
25 A range of bearing shells is available. To select the correct bearing for a particular journal, subtract the main bearing journal number (stamped on the crank web) from the main bearing housing number (stamped on the crankcase). Compare the bearing number calculated with the table below to find the colour coding of the new bearings required. The bearing shell colour code is marked on the side of the shell **(see illustration 28.22)**.

Number	Colour
1	Blue
2	Black
3	Brown
4	Green
5	Yellow
6	Pink
7	Red

Installation

26 Clean the backs of the bearing shells and the bearing cut-outs in both crankcase halves. If new shells are being fitted, ensure that all traces of the protective grease are cleaned off using paraffin (kerosene). Wipe dry the shells and crankcase halves with a lint-free cloth. Make sure all the oil passages and holes are clear, and blow them through with compressed air if it is available.
27 Press the bearing shells into their locations. Make sure the tab on each shell engages in the notch in the casing **(see illustration 29.11)**. Make sure the bearings are fitted in the correct locations and take care not to touch any shell's bearing surface with your fingers. Lubricate each shell with clean engine oil **(see illustration)**.
28 Lower the crankshaft into position in the

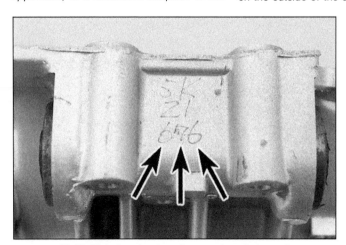

29.24 Main bearing housing numbers (arrowed)

29.27 Generously lubricate all the bearing shells

30.2 Lift out the output shaft

30.4a Draw out the shaft once the retainer screws have been removed

upper crankcase, making sure all bearings remain in place **(see illustration 29.3)**.
29 Fit the connecting rods onto the crankshaft (see Section 28).
30 Reassemble the crankcase halves (see Section 25).

30 Transmission shafts and bearings – removal and installation

Note: *To remove the transmission shafts the engine must be removed from the frame and the crankcase halves separated.*

Removal

1 Remove the engine from the frame (see Section 5) and separate the crankcase halves (see Section 25).
2 Lift the output shaft out of the casing, noting how the selector forks locate in the grooves **(see illustration)**. If it is stuck, use a soft-faced hammer and gently tap on the ends of the shaft to free it. Remove the bearing half-ring retainer from the right-hand end of the output shaft and note how the locating pin on each bearing fits into the cutouts in the crankcase **(see illustration 30.11)**. If the half-ring retainer is not in the slot in the crankcase, remove it from the slot in the bearing.
3 Remove the selector forks (see Section 32).
4 Remove the three Torx screws securing the input shaft bearing retainer on the right-hand end of the shaft **(see illustration 30.7c)**. Draw the shaft out of the crankcase from the right-hand side **(see illustration)**. If it is stuck, thread a 6 mm bolt into the centre of the blanking plug on the left-hand end of the shaft and remove the plug by pulling on the bolt **(see illustration)**. Discard the plug O-ring as a new one must be used. Once the plug is removed, tap on the end of the shaft using a soft-faced mallet to free it from the crankcase.
5 If necessary, the input shaft and output shaft can be disassembled and inspected for wear or damage (see Section 31).

6 Referring to *Tools and Workshop Tips* (Section 5) in the Reference Section, check the bearings on the transmission shafts or in the bearing housings in the crankcase. Renew the bearings if necessary. Also check the condition of the output shaft oil seal and renew it if it is worn or damaged **(see illustration 25.11)**.

Installation

7 Slide the input shaft into the crankcase, aligning the four holes in the bearing retainer with those in the crankcase **(see illustration and 30.4b)**. Use the screws, a long bolt or a

30.4b Thread a suitable bolt into the plug and pull it out

30.7b Tap the shaft into place as shown

rod as a guide to align the holes, as once the retainer is in the housing it will be difficult to turn. Use a hammer and block of wood to drive the shaft fully home **(see illustration)**. Apply a suitable non-permanent thread locking compound to the Torx screws and tighten them to the torque setting specified at the beginning of the Chapter. **Note:** *It is advisable to renew the Torx screws because the originals are likely to have been damaged by previous staking.* Using a suitable punch, stake the screws against the retainer **(see illustration)**. If it was removed, fit the blanking plug with a new O-ring and press it home **(see illustrations)**.

30.7a Note how the holes must align (arrow)

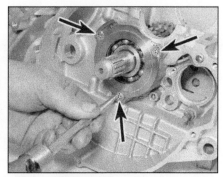

30.7c Install the Torx screws (arrowed) and stake them in place

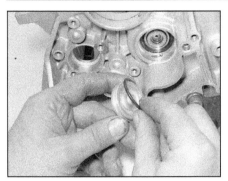

30.7d Fit a new O-ring onto the plug . . .

30.7e . . . and press it into place

30.9 Fit the half-ring retainer into the slot

8 Install the selector forks (see Section 32).
9 Install the bearing half-ring retainer for the right-hand end of the output shaft into its slot in the upper crankcase half **(see illustration)**.
10 If it has not been removed, slide the output shaft oil seal off the left-hand end of the shaft **(see illustration 25.11)**; the seal must be renewed. Lubricate the shaft and new seal with clean oil and slide it onto the shaft. Smear the seal rim with oil.
11 Lower the output shaft into position in the crankcase half **(see illustration 30.2)**, making sure the selector fork guide pins are engaged with their selector drum groove and the forks themselves fit into the grooves in the pinions, and the slot in the right-hand bearing engages correctly with the bearing half-ring retainer, the circlip on the left-hand bearing fits into its slot, and the bearing locating pins fit into the cutouts in the crankcase **(see illustration)**.
12 Make sure both transmission shafts are correctly seated and their related pinions are correctly engaged.
Caution: If the bearing half-ring retainer, circlip and locating pins are not correctly engaged, the crankcase halves will not seat correctly.
13 Position the gears in the neutral position and check the shafts are free to rotate easily and independently (ie the input shaft can turn whilst the output shaft is held stationary) before proceeding further.
14 Reassemble the crankcase halves (see Section 25).

31 Transmission shafts –
disassembly, inspection and reassembly

1 Remove the transmission shafts from the casing (see Section 30). Always disassemble the transmission shafts separately to avoid mixing up the components.

Input shaft disassembly

> **HAYNES HiNT** *When disassembling the transmission shafts, place the parts on a long rod or thread a wire through them to keep them in order and facing the proper direction.*

2 Remove the 2nd gear pinion from the left-hand end of the shaft using a puller, referring to *Tools and Workshop Tips (*Section 5) in the Reference Section if required **(see illustration)**. If a legged puller is being used, it will be easier to set it up with the legs behind the 5th gear pinion, and draw the 2nd and 5th pinions off together. **Note:** *In our experience an hydraulic press was needed to remove the 2nd gear pinion as it was so tight on the shaft. Take the shaft to a properly equipped workshop if necessary.*
3 Slide the 5th gear pinion off the shaft **(see illustration 31.17d)**.
4 To remove the 5th gear pinion bush, set up a puller behind the 3rd gear pinion and use

that to draw the bush off **(see illustration)**. Remove the thrust washer and the 3rd gear pinion **(see illustration 31.17a and 31.16)**.
5 Remove the circlip securing the 4th gear pinion, then slide the splined washer and the pinion off the shaft **(see illustrations 31.15c, b and a)**. The 4th gear pinion bush is a press fit. Do not remove it unless it needs to be renewed. Remove it using a puller.
6 The 1st gear pinion is integral with the shaft.

Input shaft inspection

7 Wash all of the components in clean solvent and dry them off.
8 Check the gear teeth for cracking, chipping, pitting and other obvious wear or damage. Any pinion that is damaged as such must be renewed.
9 Inspect the dogs and the dog holes in the gears for cracks, chips, and excessive wear especially in the form of rounded edges. Make sure mating gears engage properly. Renew the paired gears as a set if necessary.
10 Check for signs of scoring or bluing on the pinions, bushes and shaft. This could be caused by overheating due to inadequate lubrication. Check that all the oil holes and passages are clear. Renew any damaged pinions or bushes.
11 Check that each mobile pinion moves freely on the shaft or bush but without undue freeplay.
12 The shaft is unlikely to sustain damage unless the engine has seized, placing an

30.11 Make sure that each pin (arrowed) locates in its cutout

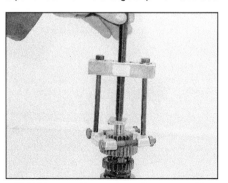

31.2 Use a puller or press to remove the 2nd gear pinion

31.4 Draw off the bush using a puller behind the 3rd gear pinion

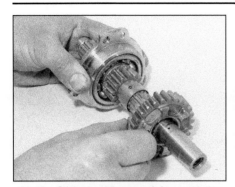

31.15a Slide the 4th gear pinion onto the bush . . .

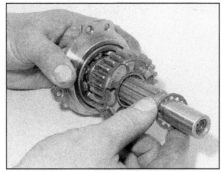

31.15b . . . then slide on the splined washer . . . .

31.15c . . . and secure them with the circlip

unusually high loading on the transmission, or the machine has covered a very high mileage. Check the surface of the shaft, especially where a pinion turns on it, and renew the shaft if it has scored or picked up, or if there are any cracks. Damage of any kind can only be cured by renewal. Check the shaft runout using V-blocks and a dial gauge and renew the shaft if the runout exceeds the limit specified at the beginning of the Chapter.

13 Check the washers and circlips and renew any that are bent or appear weakened or worn. It is a good policy to renew all circlips and washers as a matter of course during a gearshaft overhaul.

Input shaft reassembly

14 During reassembly, apply engine oil to the mating surfaces of the shaft, pinions and bushes. When installing the circlips, do not expand their ends any further than is necessary. Install the stamped circlips so that their chamfered side faces the pinion it secures and the sharp edged sides faces the direction of thrust load (see 'correct fitting of a stamped circlip illustration' in *Tools and Workshop Tips* in the Reference section).

15 If removed, drive or press the 4th gear pinion bush onto the shaft, aligning the oil hole in the bush with the hole in the shaft. Slide the 4th gear pinion, with the pinion dog holes facing away from the integral 1st gear onto the bush **(see illustration)**. Slide the splined washer onto the shaft, then fit the circlip, making sure that it locates

correctly in the groove in the shaft **(see illustrations)**.

16 Slide the 3rd gear pinion onto the shaft with the selector fork groove facing the 4th gear pinion **(see illustration)**.

17 Slide the thrust washer onto the shaft, then drive or press the 5th gear pinion bush into place, aligning the oil hole in the bush with the hole in the shaft **(see illustrations)**. Slide the 5th gear pinion onto the bush **(see illustration)**.

18 Press the 2nd gear pinion onto the left-hand end of the shaft using a press or tubular drift, referring to *Tools and Workshop Tips* (Section 5) in the Reference Section if required **(see illustration)**. Set the pinion so that the distance between the outside edge of the 2nd gear pinion and the outside edge of

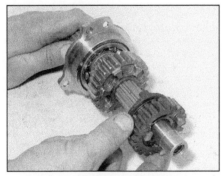

31.16 Slide the 3rd gear pinion onto the shaft, making sure it is the correct way round

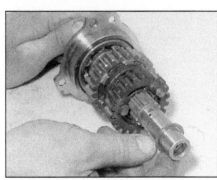

31.17a Slide on the thrust washer . . .

31.17b . . . then fit the bush . . .

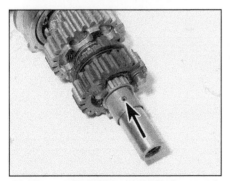

31.17c . . . aligning the oil holes (arrowed)

31.17d Install the 5th gear pinion over the bush

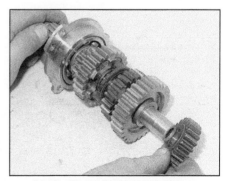

31.18a Fit the 2nd gear pinion . . .

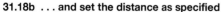

31.18b . . . and set the distance as specified

31.19 The assembled input shaft should be as shown

the 1st gear pinion (which is integral with the shaft) is 116.6 mm to 116.8 mm **(see illustration)**.

19 Check that all components have been correctly installed **(see illustration)**.

Output shaft disassembly

1991 to 1994 TDM models and all XTZ models

20 Remove the caged ball bearing from the right-hand end of the shaft **(see illustration 31.41)**.

21 Slide the 1st gear pinion and the 4th gear pinion off the right-hand end of the shaft **(see illustrations 34.40b and a)**.

22 Remove the circlip securing the 3rd gear pinion, then slide the splined washer, the 3rd gear pinion and its splined bush, followed by the 5th gear pinion off the shaft **(see illustrations 31.39d, c, b and a, and 31.37)**.

23 This leaves the 2nd gear pinion, its bush and the bearing on the left-hand end of the shaft; these components are not available individually – refer to a Yamaha dealer if they need renewing.

1995-on TDM models and all TRX models

24 Remove the caged ball bearing from the right-hand end of the shaft **(see illustration 31.41)**.

25 Slide the thrust washer, the 1st gear pinion and the 4th gear pinion off the right-hand end of the shaft **(see illustrations 31.40c, b and a)**.

26 Remove the circlip securing the 3rd gear pinion, then slide the splined washer, the 3rd gear pinion and its splined bush off the shaft **(see illustrations 31.39d, c, b and a)**

27 Slide the lockwasher and the splined washer off the shaft, noting how they fit together, then slide the 5th gear pinion off the shaft **(see illustrations 31.38c, b and a, and 31.37)**.

28 This leaves the 2nd gear pinion, its bush and the bearing on the left-hand end of the shaft; these components are not available

individually – refer to a Yamaha dealer if they need renewing.

Output shaft inspection

29 Refer to Steps 7 to 13 above.

Output shaft reassembly

1991 to 1994 TDM models and XTZ models

30 During reassembly, apply engine oil to the mating surfaces of the shaft, pinions and bushes. When installing the circlips, do not expand their ends any further than is necessary. Install the stamped circlips so that their chamfered side faces the pinion it secures and the sharp edged sides faces the direction of thrust load (see 'correct fitting of a stamped circlip illustration' in *Tools and Workshop Tips* in the Reference section).

31 Slide the 5th gear pinion onto the right-hand end of the shaft, with its dogs facing the 2nd gear pinion (integral with the shaft) **(see illustration 31.37)**.

32 Slide the 3rd gear pinion splined bush onto the shaft, followed by the 3rd gear pinion, and the splined washer, and secure them with the circlip, making sure it locates correctly in its groove in the shaft **(see illustrations 31.39a, b, c and d)**.

31.37 Slide the 5th gear pinion onto the shaft, making sure it is the correct way round

33 Slide the 4th gear pinion onto the shaft, with its selector fork groove facing the 3rd gear pinion, followed by the 1st gear pinion **(see illustrations 31.40a and b)**.

34 Fit the caged ball bearing onto the right-hand end of the shaft **(see illustration 31.41)**.

35 Check that all components have been correctly installed.

1995-on TDM models and TRX models

36 During reassembly, apply engine oil to the mating surfaces of the shaft, pinions and bushes. When installing the circlips, do not expand their ends any further than is necessary. Install the stamped circlips so that their chamfered side faces the pinion it secures and the sharp edged sides faces the direction of thrust load (see 'correct fitting of a stamped circlip illustration' in *Tools and Workshop Tips* in the Reference section).

37 Slide the 5th gear pinion onto the right-hand end of the shaft, with its dogs facing the 2nd gear pinion (integral with the shaft) **(see illustration)**.

38 Slide the slotted splined washer onto the shaft and locate it in its groove, then turn it in the groove so that the splines on the washer locate between the splines of the shaft and secure the washer in the groove **(see illustrations)**. Slide the lockwasher onto the

31.38a Slide the slotted splined washer on . . .

31.38b . . . and align it as shown . . .

31.38c . . . then slide the lockwasher on, fitting the tabs into the slots

31.39a Slide on the splined bush . . .

shaft, so that the tabs on the lockwasher face the left-hand end of the shaft and locate into the slots in the outer rim of the splined washer **(see illustration)**.

39 Slide the 3rd gear pinion splined bush onto the shaft, followed by the 3rd gear pinion, and the splined washer, and secure them with the circlip, making sure it locates correctly in its groove in the shaft **(see illustrations)**.

40 Slide the 4th gear pinion onto the shaft, with its selector fork groove facing the 3rd gear pinion, followed by the 1st gear pinion, and the thrust washer **(see illustrations)**.

41 Fit the caged ball bearing onto the right-hand end of the shaft **(see illustration)**.

42 Check that all components have been correctly installed.

31.39b . . . the 3rd gear pinion . . .

31.39c . . . and the splined washer . . .

32 Selector drum and forks –
removal, inspection and installation

Note: *To remove the selector drum and forks the engine must be removed from the frame and the crankcase halves separated.*

Removal

1 Remove the engine (see Section 5) and separate the crankcase halves (see Section 25). The selector drum and forks are located in the upper crankcase half.

31.39d . . . and secure them with the circlip

31.40a Slide on the 4th gear pinion, making sure it is the correct way round . . .

31.40b . . . followed by the 1st gear pinion . . .

31.40c . . . the thrust washer . . .

31.41 . . . and the bearing

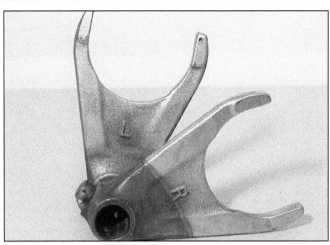

32.4 Note the letter on each fork denoting its position

32.12 Slide the drum into the casing

2 Remove the transmission output shaft (see Section 30, Step 2).

3 If not already done when removing the gearchange mechanism (external components), remove the selector drum retainer plate and the stopper arm return spring, noting how the plate locates against the flats on the selector fork shaft ends (see Section 19).

4 Before removing the selector forks, note that each fork is lettered for identification. The right-hand fork has an 'R', the centre fork a 'C', and the left-hand fork an 'L' **(see illustration)**. These letters face the right-hand side of the engine. If no letters are visible, mark them yourself using a felt pen.

5 Support the selector forks and withdraw the shafts from the casing, then remove the forks **(see illustrations 32.13b and a)**. Once removed from the case, slide the forks back onto their shafts in their correct order and way round. On 1991 to 1995 TDM models and XTZ models, note the spring fitted on the outside of the left-hand fork.

6 Withdraw the selector drum from the right-hand side of the casing **(see illustration 32.12)**.

Inspection

7 Inspect the selector forks for any signs of wear or damage, especially around the fork ends where they engage with the groove in the pinion. Check that each fork fits correctly in its pinion groove. Check closely to see if the forks are bent. If the forks are in any way damaged they must be renewed.

8 Check that the forks fit correctly on their shaft. They should move freely with a light fit but no appreciable freeplay. Check that the fork shaft holes in the casing are not worn or damaged.

9 The selector fork shaft can be checked for trueness by rolling it along a flat surface. A bent shaft will cause difficulty in selecting gears and make the gearchange action heavy. Renew the shaft if it is bent.

10 Inspect the selector drum grooves and selector fork guide pins for signs of wear or damage. If either component shows signs of wear or damage the selector(s) and drum must be renewed.

11 Check that the selector drum bearing rotates freely and has no sign of freeplay between it and the casing. Renew the bearing

if necessary (see *Tools and Workshop Tips* (Section 5) in the Reference Section). Also check that the neutral switch contact plunger in the other end of the drum is free to move in and out under spring pressure. If required, remove the screw securing the contact plate and remove the plunger and spring for inspection or renewal (see Chapter 9).

Installation

12 Slide the selector drum into position in the crankcase and position it so that the neutral contact is against the neutral switch **(see illustration)**.

13 Refer to Step 4 for the correct location of each fork **(see illustration 32.4)**. Lubricate the selector fork shafts with clean engine oil and slide them into the crankcase, with the cut end of the upper (single fork) shaft facing the right-hand side, and the spring (where fitted) in the lower shaft end facing the left-hand side. Slide each shaft through its fork(s) and into its bore, locating the guide pin on the end of each fork into its groove in the drum as you do **(see illustrations)**.

14 Locate the stopper arm spring, then install the selector drum retainer plate, making sure

32.13a Fit the centre fork (C) into the groove in the input shaft pinion and locate the guide pin in its groove in the drum, then slide in the shaft

32.13b Slide the shaft into the casing and through each fork in turn – note the spring (arrowed)

it locates correctly against the flat in the end of the fork shaft (see Section 19).
15 Install the transmission output shaft (see Section 30, Step 11).
16 Reassemble the crankcase halves (see Section 25).

33 Initial start-up after overhaul

1 Make sure the engine oil level and coolant level are correct (see *Daily (pre-ride) checks*).
2 Make sure there is fuel in the tank, then turn the fuel tap to the ON or RES position as required, and set the choke on.
3 As there isn't an oil pressure warning light fitted, an oil pressure check must be carried out. Follow the procedure in Chapter 1, Section 32.
4 If the oil pressure test is satisfactory, allow the engine to run at a moderately fast idle until

it reaches operating temperature and check that there are no oil and coolant leaks. Stop the engine.
5 Check carefully that the transmission and controls, especially the brakes, function properly before road testing the machine. Refer to Section 34 for the recommended running-in procedure.
6 Upon completion of the road test, and after the engine has cooled down completely, recheck the valve clearances (see Chapter 1) and check the engine oil and coolant levels (see *Daily (pre-ride) checks*).

34 Recommended running-in procedure

1 Treat the machine gently for the first few miles to make sure oil has circulated throughout the engine and any new parts installed have started to seat.

2 Even greater care is necessary if the engine has been rebored or a new crankshaft has been installed. In the case of a rebore, the bike will have to be run in as when new. This means greater use of the transmission and a restraining hand on the throttle until at least 600 miles (1000 km) have been covered. There's no point in keeping to any set speed limit – the main idea is to keep from labouring the engine and to gradually increase performance up to the 600 mile (1000 km) mark. These recommendations can be lessened to an extent when only a new crankshaft is installed. Experience is the best guide, since it's easy to tell when an engine is running freely. The accompanying table indicates maximum engine speed limitations, which Yamaha provide for new motorcycles, can be used as a guide.
3 If a lubrication failure is suspected, stop the engine immediately and try to find the cause. If an engine is run without oil, even for a short period of time, severe damage will occur.

1991 to 1995 TDM models and all XTZ models

Up to 100 miles (150 km)	4000 rpm max	Vary throttle position/speed. Do not use full throttle. Stop the engine and let it cool for 5 to 10 minutes after every hour of operation.
100 to 300 miles (150 to 500 km)	5000 rpm max	Vary throttle position/speed. Do not use full throttle
300 to 600 miles (500 to 1000 km)	6000 rpm max	Vary throttle position/speed. Use full throttle for short bursts
Over 600 miles (1000 km)	8000 rpm max	Do not exceed tachometer red line

1996-on TDM models and all TRX models

Up to 100 miles (150 km)	5000 rpm max	Vary throttle position/speed. Do not use full throttle. Stop the engine and let it cool for 5 to 10 minutes after every hour of operation.
100 to 300 miles (150 to 500 km)	6000 rpm max	Vary throttle position/speed. Do not use full throttle
300 to 600 miles (500 to 1000 km)	7000 rpm max	Vary throttle position/speed. Use full throttle for short bursts
Over 600 miles (1000 km)	8000 rpm max	Do not exceed tachometer red line

Notes

Chapter 3
Cooling system

Contents

Degrees of difficulty

| Easy, suitable for novice with little experience | | Fairly easy, suitable for beginner with some experience | | Fairly difficult, suitable for competent DIY mechanic | | Difficult, suitable for experienced DIY mechanic | | Very difficult, suitable for expert DIY or professional |  |

Specifications

Coolant
Mixture type and capacity . . . . see Chapter 1

Radiator
Cap valve opening pressure . . . . 11 to 15 psi (0.75 to 1.05 Bar)

Fan switch
Cooling fan cut-in temperature . . . . 102 to 108°C
Cooling fan cut-out temperature . . . . 98°C

Coolant temperature sensor
Resistance – 1991 to 1995 TDM models and all XTZ models
   @ 50°C . . . . 154 ohms
   @ 80°C . . . . 47 to 53 ohms
   @ 100°C . . . . 26 to 29 ohms
   @ 120°C . . . . 16 ohms
Resistance – 1996-on TDM models and all TRX models
   @ 80°C . . . . 47 to 53 ohms
   @ 100°C . . . . 26 to 30 ohms

Thermostat
Opening temperature . . . . 80 to 84°C
Valve lift . . . . 8 mm (min) @ 95°C

Torque settings
Cooling fan switch . . . . 28 Nm
Coolant temperature sensor
   1991 to 1995 TDM models and all XTZ models . . . . 13 Nm
   1996-on TDM models and all TRX models . . . . 15 Nm
Thermostat cover bolts . . . . 10 Nm
Thermostat mounting bolt . . . . 10 Nm
Water pump bolts . . . . 10 Nm
Frame downtube bolts/nuts (XTZ models) . . . . 32 Nm

1 General information

The cooling system uses a water/antifreeze coolant to carry away excess energy in the form of heat. The cylinders are surrounded by a water jacket from which the heated coolant is circulated by thermo-syphonic action in conjunction with a water pump, driven by the front balancer shaft. The hot coolant passes upwards to the thermostat and through to the radiator. The coolant then flows across the radiator core, where it is cooled by the passing air, to the water pump and back to the engine where the cycle is repeated.

A thermostat is fitted in the system to prevent the coolant flowing through the radiator when the engine is cold, therefore accelerating the speed at which the engine reaches normal operating temperature. A coolant temperature sensor mounted in the thermostat housing transmits to the temperature gauge on the instrument panel. A thermostatically-controlled cooling fan is also fitted to aid cooling in extreme conditions. The fan switch is mounted in the thermostat housing.

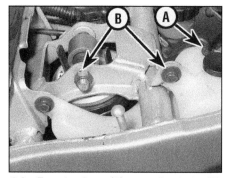

3.2a Breather hose (A), mounting bolts (B) – TDM models

The complete cooling system is partially sealed and pressurised, the pressure being controlled by a valve contained in the spring-loaded radiator cap. By pressurising the coolant the boiling point is raised, preventing premature boiling in adverse conditions. The overflow pipe from the system is connected to a reservoir into which excess coolant is expelled under pressure. The discharged coolant automatically returns to the radiator when the engine cools.

⚠️ *Warning: Do not remove the pressure cap from the radiator when the engine is hot. Scalding hot coolant and steam may be blown out under pressure, which could cause serious injury. When the engine has cooled, place a thick rag, like a towel over the pressure cap; slowly rotate the cap anti-clockwise to the first stop. This procedure allows any residual pressure to escape. When the steam has stopped escaping, press down on the cap while turning it anti-clockwise and remove it. Do not allow antifreeze to come in contact with your skin or painted surfaces of the motorcycle. Rinse off any spills immediately with plenty of water. Antifreeze is highly toxic if ingested. Never leave antifreeze lying around in an open container or in puddles on the floor; children and pets are attracted by its sweet smell and may drink it. Check with the local authorities about disposing of used antifreeze. Many communities will have collection centres which will see that antifreeze is disposed of safely.*
Caution: At all times use the specified type of antifreeze, and always mix it with distilled water in the correct proportion. The antifreeze contains corrosion inhibitors which are essential to avoid damage to the cooling system. A lack of these inhibitors could lead to a build-up of corrosion which would block the coolant passages,

resulting in overheating and severe engine damage. Distilled water must be used as opposed to tap water to avoid a build-up of scale which would also block the passages.

2 Radiator pressure cap – check

1 If problems such as overheating or loss of coolant occur, check the entire system as described in Chapter 1. The radiator cap opening pressure should be checked by a Yamaha dealer with the special tester required to do the job. If the cap is defective, renew it.

3 Coolant reservoir – removal and installation

Removal

1 On TDM models, remove the seat (see Chapter 8). On TRX models, remove the seat and the side covers (see Chapter 8). On XTZ models remove the left-hand side cover (see Chapter 8).
2 Release the clamp securing the breather hose (coming out of the top of the reservoir) and detach the hose **(see illustrations)**.
3 Place a suitable container underneath the reservoir, then release the clamp securing the radiator overflow hose to the base of the reservoir. Detach the hose and allow the coolant to drain into the container.
4 Unscrew the reservoir mounting bolts or screws and remove the reservoir, noting how it fits **(see illustrations 3.2a, b and c)**.

Installation

5 Installation is the reverse of removal. Make sure the hoses are correctly installed and secured with their clamps. On completion refill the reservoir as described in Chapter 1.

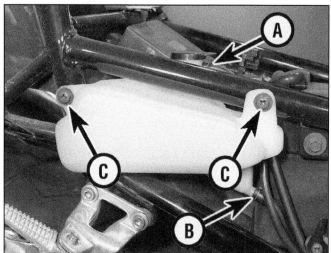

3.2b Breather hose (A), radiator overflow hose (B), mounting screws (C) – TRX models

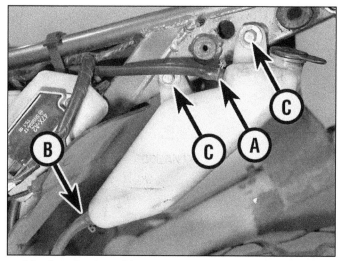

3.2c Breather hose (A), radiator overflow hose (B), mounting screws (C) – XTZ models

4.3a Fan motor wiring connector (arrowed) – TDM models

4.3b Fan motor wiring connector (arrowed) – XTZ models

4 Cooling fan and cooling fan switch – check and renewal

Cooling fan

Check

1 If the engine is overheating and the cooling fan isn't coming on, first check the fan circuit fuse (see Chapter 9) and then the fan switch as described in Steps 9 to 13 below.

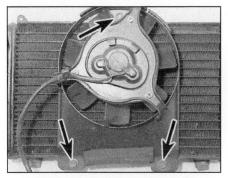

4.5 Fan assembly mounting bolts (arrowed)

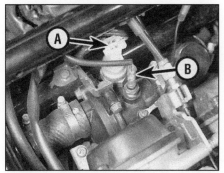

4.9b Fan switch wiring connector (A), temperature sender wiring connector (B) – TRX models

2 If the fan does not come on, (and the fan switch is good), the fault lies in either the cooling fan motor or the relevant wiring. Test all the wiring and connections as described in Chapter 9.

3 To test the cooling fan motor, trace the fan motor wiring and disconnect it at the connector (see illustrations). Remove the fuel tank and on TDM and TRX the air filter housing for best access. Using a 12 volt battery and two jumper wires, connect the battery leads to the fan wiring connector. Once connected the fan should operate. If it

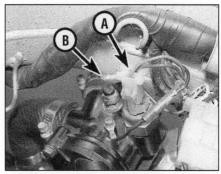

4.9a Fan switch wiring connector (A), temperature sender wiring connector (B) – TDM models

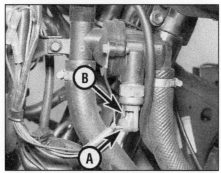

4.9c Fan switch wiring connector (A), temperature sender wiring connector (B) – XTZ models

does not, and the wiring is all good, then the fan is faulty.

Renewal

 Warning: The engine must be completely cool before carrying out this procedure.

4 Remove the radiator (see Section 7).
5 Unscrew the three bolts securing the fan shroud and fan assembly to the radiator (see illustration). On TDM and TRX models, unscrew the bolts on the front of the fan securing it to the shroud and remove the shroud. Separate the fan blade from the motor and renew the motor. On XTZ models, individual components are not available and the entire fan assembly must be renewed.
6 Installation is the reverse of removal.
7 Install the radiator (see Section 7).

Cooling fan switch

Check

8 If the engine is overheating and the cooling fan isn't coming on, first check the fan circuit fuse (see Chapter 9). If the fuse is blown, check the fan circuit for a short to earth (see the wiring diagrams at the end of this book).
9 If the fuse is good, on TDM and TRX models, remove the fuel tank and air filter housing (see Chapter 4). On XTZ models, remove the left-hand fairing side panel (see Chapter 8). Disconnect the wiring connector(s) from the fan switch, mounted in the thermostat housing (see illustrations). Using a jumper wire, connect between the terminals in the wiring connector(s). The fan should come on. If it does, the fan switch is defective and must be renewed. If it does not come on, the fan should be tested (see Step 3).
10 If the fan is on the whole time, disconnect the wiring connector. The fan should stop. If it does, the fan switch is defective and must be renewed. If it doesn't, check the wiring between the fan switch and the fan motor, and the fan itself.
11 If the fan works but is suspected of

cutting in at the wrong temperature, a more comprehensive test of the switch can be made as follows.

12 Remove the switch (see Steps 14 to 17). Fill a small heatproof container with coolant and place it on a stove. Connect the probes of an ohmmeter to the terminals of the switch, and using some wire or other support suspend the switch in the coolant so that just the sensing portion and switch body are submerged **(see illustration)**. Also place a thermometer capable of reading temperatures up to 110°C in the coolant so that its bulb is close to the switch. **Note:** *None of the components should be allowed to directly touch the container.*

13 Initially the ohmmeter reading should be very high indicating that the switch is open (OFF). Heat the coolant, stirring it gently.

 Warning: This must be done very carefully to avoid the risk of personal injury.

When the temperature reaches around 102 to 108°C the meter reading should drop to around zero ohms, indicating that the switch has closed (ON). Now turn the heat off. As the temperature falls below 98°C the meter reading should show infinite (very high) resistance, indicating that the switch has opened (OFF). If the meter readings obtained are different, or they are obtained at different temperatures, then the switch is faulty and must be renewed.

Removal and installation

 Warning: The engine must be completely cool before carrying out this procedure.

14 Drain the cooling system (see Chapter 1). **Note:** *The fan switch is positioned near the top of the cooling system so coolant draining can be avoided if care is taken to catch any coolant which escapes as the switch is removed.*

15 On TDM and TRX models, remove the fuel tank and air filter housing (see Chapter 4). On XTZ models, remove the left-hand fairing side panel (see Chapter 8). Disconnect the wiring

connector(s) from the fan switch, mounted in the thermostat housing **(see illustrations 4.9a, b and c)**. Unscrew the switch and withdraw it from the housing.

16 Apply a suitable thread locking and sealing compound to the switch threads, then install the switch and tighten it to the torque setting specified at the beginning of the Chapter. Take care not to overtighten the switch as the housing could be damaged.

17 Reconnect the switch wiring and refill or top up the cooling system (see Chapter 1).

5 Coolant temperature gauge/warning light and sender – check and renewal

 Warning: The engine must be completely cool before carrying out work on the temperature sender.

Coolant temperature gauge (XTZ, TRX and 1991-98 TDM models)

Check

1 The circuit consists of the sender mounted in the thermostat housing and the gauge assembly mounted in the instrument panel. If the system malfunctions check first that the battery is fully charged and that the fuses are all good. If they are, on TDM and TRX models, remove the fuel tank and air filter housing (see Chapter 4). On XTZ models, remove the left-hand fairing side panel (see Chapter 8).

2 Disconnect the wire from the sender and turn the ignition switch ON **(see illustrations 4.9a, b and c)**. The temperature gauge needle should be on the C on the gauge. Now earth the sender wire on the engine. The needle should swing immediately over to the H on the gauge. *Caution: Do not earth the wire for any longer than is necessary to take the reading, or the gauge may be damaged.*

If the needle moves as described above, the sender is proven defective and must be renewed.

3 If the needle movement is still faulty, or if it does not move at all, the fault lies in the wiring or the gauge itself. Check all the relevant wiring and wiring connectors (see Chapter 9). If all appears to be well, the gauge is defective and must be renewed.

Removal and installation

4 See Chapter 9, Section 16.

Coolant temperature warning light (1999 TDM models)

5 The circuit consists of the sender mounted in the thermostat housing and the coolant temperature warning light in the instrument panel. The warning light should illuminate briefly when the ignition is first turned on as a check of the warning light bulb; the light should then extinguish. If the bulb doesn't light, it is probably blown and should be renewed as described in Chapter 9. Less likely is a wiring fault, but referring to the wiring diagram at the end of this manual, check the coolant temperature warning light circuit wiring for continuity.

6 The bulb should illuminate if the engine coolant ever reaches too high a temperature. If you suspect that the bulb is failing to come on check the sender as described below.

Sender check (all models)

7 The sender is mounted in the thermostat housing. On TDM and TRX models, remove the fuel tank and air filter housing (see Chapter 4). On XTZ models, remove the left-hand fairing side panel (see Chapter 8). Drain the cooling system (see Chapter 1). **Note:** *The sender is positioned near the top of the cooling system so coolant draining can be avoided if care is taken to catch any coolant which escapes as the sender is removed.*

8 Disconnect the sender wiring connector **(see illustrations 4.9a, b and c)**. Using a continuity tester, check for continuity between the sender body and earth on the motorcycle's frame. There should be continuity. If there is no continuity, check that the thermostat mounting is secure, and where fitted, that the thermostat housing earth wire is securely connected.

9 Unscrew the sender and remove it from the thermostat housing (see below). Test the sender according to the appropriate sub-section.

1991 to 1995 TDM models and all XTZ models

10 Fill a small heatproof container with coolant mixture and place it on a stove. Using an ohmmeter, connect the positive (+ve) probe of the meter to the terminal on the sender, and the negative (-ve) probe to the tip of the sender. Using some wire or other support suspend the sender in the coolant so that it is submerged. Also place a thermometer capable of reading temperatures up to 120°C in the coolant so that its bulb is close to the sender **(see illustration)**. **Note:** *None of the components should be allowed to directly touch the container.*

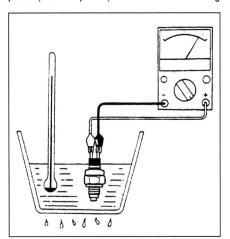

4.12 Fan switch testing set-up

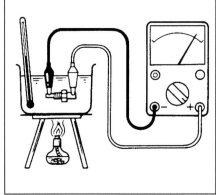

5.10 Temperature sender testing set-up – 1991 to 1995 TDM models and all XTZ models

11 Heat the coolant, stirring it gently. When the temperature reaches around 50°C the meter should read 154 ohms. When the temperature reaches around 80°C the meter should read between 47 and 53 ohms. When the temperature reaches around 100°C the meter should read between 26 and 29 ohms. When the temperature reaches around 120°C the meter should read 16 ohms. If the meter readings obtained are different, or they are obtained at different temperatures, then the sender is faulty and must be renewed.

1996-on TDM models and all TRX models

12 Fill a small heatproof container with water and place it on a stove. Using an ohmmeter, connect the positive (+ve) probe of the meter to the terminal on the sender, and the negative (-ve) probe to the body of the sender. Using some wire or other support suspend the sender in the water so that just the sensing portion and the threads are submerged. Also place a thermometer capable of reading temperatures up to 110°C in the water so that its bulb is close to the sender **(see illustration)**. **Note:** *None of the components should be allowed to directly touch the container.*

13 Heat the water, stirring it gently. When the temperature reaches around 80°C the meter should read 47 to 53 ohms. When the temperature reaches around 100°C the meter should read 26 to 30 ohms. If the meter readings obtained are different, or they are obtained at different temperatures, then the sender is faulty and must be renewed.

Sender removal and installation (all models)

14 Drain the cooling system (see Chapter 1). On TDM and TRX models, remove the fuel tank and air filter housing (see Chapter 4). On XTZ models, remove the left-hand fairing side panel (see Chapter 8).

15 Disconnect the sender wiring connector

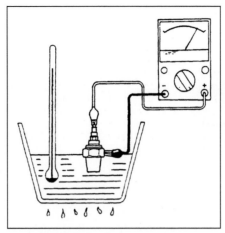

5.12 Temperature sender testing set-up – 1996-on TDM models and all TRX models

(see illustrations 4.9a, b and c). Unscrew the sender and remove it from the thermostat housing.

16 Apply a suitable thread locking and sealing compound to the sender threads, then install the sender and tighten it to the torque setting specified at the beginning of the Chapter. Take care not to overtighten the sender as the housing could be damaged.

17 Reconnect the sender wiring and top up the cooling system (see Chapter 1).

---

6 Thermostat housing and thermostat – removal, check and installation

Removal

Warning: The engine must be completely cool before carrying out this procedure.

1 The thermostat is automatic in operation and should give many years of service without requiring attention. In the event of a failure, the valve will probably jam open, in which

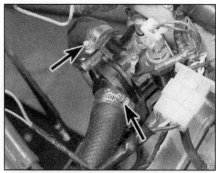

6.3 Slacken the clamp screws and pull off the hoses

case the engine will take much longer than normal to warm up. Conversely, if the valve jams shut, the coolant will be unable to circulate and the engine will overheat. Neither condition is acceptable, and the fault must be investigated promptly.

2 Drain the cooling system (see Chapter 1).

3 The thermostat is located in the thermostat housing. On TDM and TRX models, remove the fuel tank and air filter housing (see Chapter 4). On XTZ models, remove the left-hand fairing side panel (see Chapter 8). Slacken the clamps securing the hoses to the housing and detach the hoses, noting which fits where **(see illustration and 4.9b and c)**. On XTZ models, release the clamp securing the overflow hose to the filler neck and detach the hose.

4 Disconnect the fan switch and temperature sensor wiring connectors **(see illustrations 4.9a, b and c)**. Where fitted, also slacken the screw securing the earth lead and detach the lead.

5 Unscrew the bolt securing the thermostat housing and remove the housing, noting how it fits **(see illustration and 4.9b and c)**.

6 Unscrew the two bolts securing the cover and separate it from the housing **(see illustration)**. Withdraw the thermostat, noting

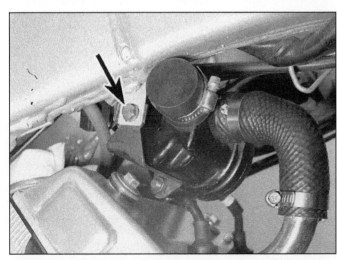

6.5 Thermostat housing mounting bolt (arrowed) – TDM models

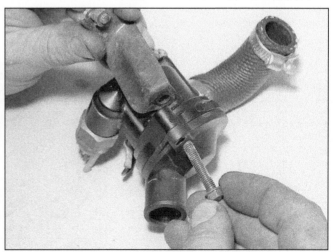

6.6a Unscrew the bolts and remove the cover . . .

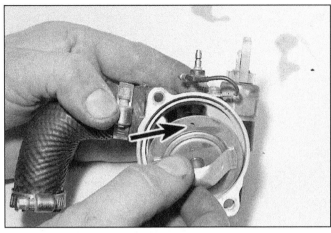

6.6b . . . and withdraw the thermostat

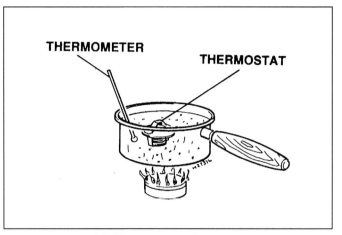

6.8 Thermostat testing set-up

how it fits **(see illustration)**. Discard the cover O-ring as a new one must be used.

Check

7 Examine the thermostat visually before carrying out the test. If it remains in the open position at room temperature, it should be renewed.

8 Suspend the thermostat by a piece of wire in a container of cold water. Place a thermometer in the water so that the bulb is close to the thermostat **(see illustration)**. Heat the water, noting the temperature when the thermostat opens, and compare the result

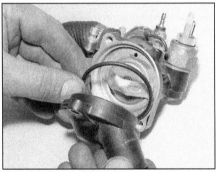

6.11 Fit the cover using a new O-ring

with the specifications given at the beginning of the Chapter. Also check the amount the valve opens after it has been heated at 95°C for a few minutes and compare the measurement to the specifications. If the readings obtained differ from those given, the thermostat is faulty and must be renewed.

9 In the event of thermostat failure, as an emergency measure only, it can be removed and the machine used without it. **Note:** *Take care when starting the engine from cold as it will take much longer than usual to warm up.* Ensure that a new unit is installed as soon as possible.

Installation

10 Fit the thermostat into the housing, making sure that it seats correctly and that the hole is at the top **(see illustration 6.6b)**.

11 Fit a new O-ring onto the cover, using a dab of grease to keep it in place if required **(see illustration)**. Fit the cover onto the housing, then install the two bolts and tighten them to the torque setting specified at the beginning of the Chapter **(see illustrations 6.6a)**.

12 Install the thermostat housing and tighten the bolt to the specified torque setting **(see illustrations 4.9b and c)**. Connect the hoses

and tighten the clamps securely. Also connect the wiring connectors, not forgetting the earth lead, where fitted.

13 Refill the cooling system (see Chapter 1).

7 Radiator – removal and installation

Removal

 Warning: The engine must be completely cool before carrying out this procedure.

1 Remove the fairing side panels on TDM and XTZ models, and the fairing on TRX models (see Chapter 8). Remove the fuel tank, and on TDM and TRX models, the air filter housing (see Chapter 4). Drain the cooling system (see Chapter 1).

2 Trace the fan motor wiring and disconnect it at the connector **(see illustrations 4.3a and b)**.

3 Slacken the clamps securing the radiator hoses and detach them from the radiator **(see illustrations)**.

4 Unscrew the bolts securing the radiator, noting the arrangement of the collars and rubber grommets, and carefully manoeuvre

7.3a Detach the upper . . .

7.3b . . . and lower radiator hoses (early TDM shown) . . .

7.3c . . . and on TDM and TRX models the overflow hose (arrowed)

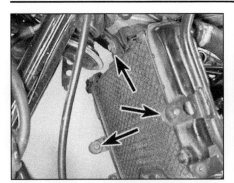

7.4a Radiator mounting bolts (arrowed) –
1991 to 1995 TDM models

7.4b Radiator mounting bolts (arrowed) –
1996-on TDM models and all TRX models
(TRX shown)

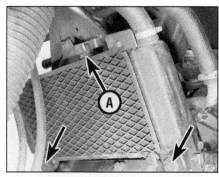

7.4c Radiator mounting bolts (arrowed) –
XTZ models. Note how the rubber damper
locates in the bracket (A)

the radiator away from the machine, noting how it fits **(see illustrations)**.

5 On TDM models, if required, unscrew the bolts securing the radiator stay to the frame and remove the stay.

6 If necessary, remove the cooling fan (see Section 4) from the radiator.

7 If required, remove the stone guard from the radiator. Check the stone guard and the radiator for signs of damage and clear any dirt or debris that might obstruct air flow and inhibit cooling. If the radiator fins are badly damaged or broken the radiator must be renewed. Also check the rubber mounting grommets, and renew them if necessary.

Installation

8 Installation is the reverse of removal, noting the following.

a) *Make sure the various collars and grommets are correctly installed with the mounting bolts.*

b) *Make sure that the fan wiring is correctly connected.*

c) *Ensure the coolant hoses are in good condition (see Chapter 1), and are securely retained by their clamps, using new ones if necessary.*

d) *On completion refill the cooling system as described in Chapter 1.*

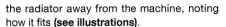

8 Water pump – check, removal, and installation

Check

1 The water pump is located on the right-hand side of the engine. Visually check the area around the pump for signs of leakage.

2 To prevent leakage of water from the cooling system into the lubrication system and vice versa, two seals are fitted on the pump shaft. On the underside of the pump body there is a drainage hole **(see illustration 8.12a)**. If either seal fails, this hole should allow the coolant or oil to escape and prevent the oil and coolant mixing.

3 If there is any leakage from the drainage hole, remove the pump and renew it – individual components (except O-rings and bolts) are not available.

Removal

4 Drain the coolant (see Chapter 1). Place a suitable container below the water pump to catch any residue as the water pump is removed. On XTZ models, remove the exhaust system (see Chapter 4). Also unscrew the bolts securing the right-hand frame downtube section and remove it.

5 Slacken the clamp securing the coolant hose to the pump cover and detach the hose **(see illustration)**.

6 Unscrew the bolts securing the pump to the crankcase **(see illustration)**. Carefully draw the pump from the crankcase, noting how it fits. It may be necessary to lever it out to overcome the O-rings on the pump body and on the joint pipe between the top of the pump housing and the union on the cylinder block.

Caution: A shim is fitted on the pump shaft between the circlip and the drive gear. The shim will probably stick to the gear, however great care must be taken as it is possible for the shim to slip down into the engine as the shaft is withdrawn from the gear.

Remove the O-ring from the rear of the pump body and from the joint pipe and discard them as new ones must be used. Note the position of each bolt as their lengths differ.

7 Unscrew the remaining bolts securing the pump cover and remove the cover **(see illustration 8.6)**. Discard the cover O-ring as a new one must be used.

8 Wiggle the water pump impeller back-and-forth and in-and-out. If there is excessive movement the pump must be renewed. Rotate the impeller and check that it turns smoothly and freely. Also check for corrosion or a build-up of scale in the pump body and clean or renew the pump as necessary.

9 To remove the pump drive gear, first remove the front balancer shaft (see Chapter 2). Slide the gear out of its bore in the crankcase and lift it out, noting how it fits **(see illustration)**.

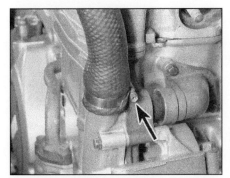

8.5 Slacken the clamp (arrowed) and
detach the hose

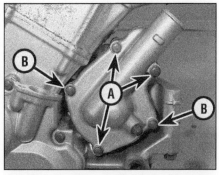

8.6 Water pump mounting bolts (A),
cover bolts (A) and (B)

8.9 Water pump drive gear (arrowed)

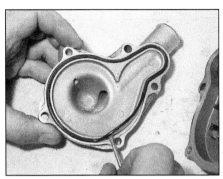

8.11a Fit the O-ring into the groove in the cover . . .

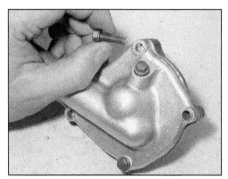

8.11b . . . then fit the cover and its two bolts

8.12a Fit a new O-ring onto the body . . .

Installation

10 If removed, slide the shouldered side of the pump drive gear into its bore in the crankcase **(see illustration 8.9)**. Install the front balancer shaft (see Chapter 2).

11 Install the new cover O-ring into its groove in the pump **(see illustration)**. Fit the cover and secure it with the two bolts **(see illustration)**.

12 Fit the new pump body O-ring and joint pipe O-ring **(see illustration)**. Apply some grease to the shim to stick it in place, then slide it onto the pump shaft **(see illustrations)**. Install the pump into the crankcase, making sure it locates correctly into the driven gear **(see illustration)**. Install the bolts and tighten them to the torque setting specified at the beginning of the Chapter **(see illustration 8.6)**. Make sure the different length bolts are in their correct locations.

13 Attach the coolant hose to the pump cover and secure it with its clamp **(see illustration 8.5)**.

14 On XTZ models, install the frame downtube and tighten its bolts to the specified torque setting (see Chapter 2).

Also install the exhaust system (see Chapter 4).

15 Refill the cooling system (see Chapter 1).

9 Coolant hoses – removal and installation

Removal

1 Before removing a hose, drain the coolant (see Chapter 1).

2 Use a screwdriver to slacken the larger-bore hose clamps, then slide them back along the hose and clear of the union spigot **(see illustrations 6.3, 7.3a and b)**. The smaller-bore hoses are secured by spring clamps which can be expanded by squeezing their ears together with pliers **(see illustration 7.3c)**.

Caution: The radiator unions are fragile. Do not use excessive force when attempting to remove the hoses.

3 If a hose proves stubborn, release it by rotating it on its union before working it off. If all else fails, cut the hose with a sharp knife then slit it at each union so that it can be peeled off in two pieces. Whilst this means replacing the hose, it is preferable to buying a new radiator.

4 The water pipe union on the front of the cylinder block can be removed by unscrewing the retaining bolts (see Chapter 2, Section 13). If it is removed, the O-rings must be renewed.

Installation

5 Slide the clamp onto the hose and then work it on to its respective union.

 HAYNES HiNT *If the hose is difficult to push on its union, it can be softened by soaking it in very hot water, or alternatively a little soapy water can be used as a lubricant.*

6 Rotate the hose on its union to settle it in position before sliding the clamp into place and tightening it securely.

7 If the water pipe union on the engine has been removed, fit new O-rings, then install the union and tighten the mounting bolts to the specified torque setting (see Chapter 2, Section 13).

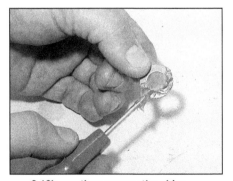

8.12b . . . then grease the shim . . .

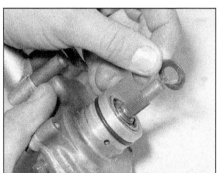

8.12c . . . and slide it onto the shaft

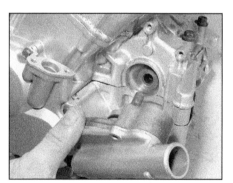

8.12d Install the pump, making sure it locates correctly into the drive gear

Chapter 4
Fuel and exhaust systems

Contents

Degrees of difficulty

| Easy, suitable for novice with little experience | | Fairly easy, suitable for beginner with some experience | | Fairly difficult, suitable for competent DIY mechanic | | Difficult, suitable for experienced DIY mechanic | | Very difficult, suitable for expert DIY or professional | |

Specifications

Fuel

Grade . . . . Unleaded, minimum 91 RON (Research Octane Number)
Fuel tank capacity (including reserve)
  1991 to 1995 TDM models . . . . 18.0 litres
  1996-on TDM models . . . . 20.0 litres
  TRX models . . . . 18.0 litres
  XTZ models . . . . 26.0 litres
Reserve
  1991 to 1995 TDM models . . . . 3.5 litres
  1996-on TDM models . . . . 3.1 litres
  TRX models . . . . 3.5 litres
  XTZ models . . . . 5.0 litres

Carburettors

Type
    1991 to 1998 TDM models, all TRX and XTZ models . . . .   Mikuni BDST38
    1999 TDM models . . . .   Mikuni BDSR38
ID mark
    1991 to 1995 TDM models 3VD 00
    1996 to 1998 TDM models 4TX 00
    1999 TDM models 4TX4
    TRX models 4UN 00
    XTZ models 3LD 00
Pilot screw setting (turns out)
    1991 to 1995 TDM models   3
    1996-on TDM models   2
    TRX models 2 1/2
    XTZ models   2
Fuel level (see text)
    1991 to 1995 TDM models . . . .   7.4 to 8.4 mm above float chamber line
    1996 to 1998 TDM models and TRX models . . . .   15.8 to 16.8 mm below MIKUNI mark
    1999 TDM models . . . .   3.4 to 4.4 mm below line
    XTZ models . . . .   5.1 to 6.1 mm above float chamber line
Idle speed . . . .   see Chapter 1

Carburettor jet sizes

Main jet
    1991 to 1995 TDM models   140
    1999 TDM models 147.5
    All other models 142.5
Main air jet
    1991 to 1995 TDM models   50
    1999 TDM models   65
    All other models   60
Jet needle
    1991 to 1995 TDM models 5G52-3
    1996 to 1998 TDM models and all TRX models 5E185-2/5
    1999 TDM models . . . .   1 - 6DJP17; 2 - 6CL1
    XTZ models 5C19-3
Needle jet
    1991 to 1995 TDM models and all XTZ models Y-4
    1996 to 1998 TDM models and all TRX models Y-2
    1999 TDM models . . . .   P-O
Pilot air jet
    XTZ models   60
    1999 TDM models 87.5
    All other models   70
Pilot jet
    1991 to 1995 TDM models 37.5
    1996 to 1998 TDM models and all TRX models   45
    1999 TDM models 17.5
    XTZ models 42.5
Starter jet
    XTZ models   70
    1999 TDM models 32.5
    All other models   75

Fuel level sender

Resistance
    Fuel tank full . . . .   4 to 10 ohms @ 20°C
    Fuel tank empty . . . .   90 to 100 ohms @ 20°C

Torque settings

Exhaust downpipe flange nuts . . . .   20 Nm
Exhaust clamp bolts . . . .   20 Nm
Silencer and collector box mounting bolts . . . .   24 Nm
Footrest bracket mounting bolts (XTZ models) . . . .   20 Nm

1 General information and precautions

General information

The fuel system consists of the fuel tank with internal filter, fuel tap, fuel pump, carburettors, fuel hoses and control cables.

On TDM models, a remote fuel tap is fitted for normal operation, while the filter is integral with the fuel outlet assembly from the tank. On TRX models, a vacuum-operated fuel tap with integral filter is mounted on the left-hand side of the fuel tank. On XTZ models, a fuel tap with integral filter is mounted on each side of the fuel tank.

Fuel is pumped to the carburettors by a vacuum-operated fuel pump on all TRX and XTZ models and 1991 to 1998 TDM models. The 1999 TDM model has an electrically-operated fuel pump.

The carburettors used on all models are CV types. There is a carburettor for each cylinder. For cold starting, a choke knob is connected to the carburettors by a cable. On 1991 to 1995 TDM models, the choke knob is mounted above the front sprocket cover; on 1996-on TDM models and XTZ models it is mounted on the handlebars; on TRX models it is mounted on the frame between the fuel tank and the fairing. On 1996-on TDM and TRX models the carburettors are warmed by the engine's coolant.

Air is drawn into the carburettors via an air filter which is housed under the fuel tank.

The exhaust system is a two-into-two design.

Many of the fuel system service procedures are considered routine maintenance items and for that reason are included in Chapter 1.

Precautions

⚠ *Warning: Petrol (gasoline) is extremely flammable, so take extra precautions when you work on any part of the fuel system. Don't smoke or allow open flames or bare light bulbs near the work area, and don't work in a garage where a natural gas-type appliance is present. If you spill any fuel on your skin, rinse it off immediately with soap and water. When you perform any kind of work on the fuel system, wear safety glasses and have a fire extinguisher suitable for a class B type fire (flammable liquids) on hand.*

Always perform service procedures in a well-ventilated area to prevent a build-up of fumes.

Never work in a building containing a gas appliance with a pilot light, or any other form of naked flame. Ensure that there are no naked light bulbs or any sources of flame or sparks nearby.

Do not smoke (or allow anyone else to smoke) while in the vicinity of petrol (gasoline) or of components containing it. Remember the possible presence of vapour from these sources and move well clear before smoking.

Check all electrical equipment belonging to the house, garage or workshop where work is being undertaken (see the Safety first! section of this manual). Remember that certain electrical appliances such as drills, cutters etc. create sparks in the normal course of operation and must not be used near petrol (gasoline) or any component containing it. Again, remember the possible presence of fumes before using electrical equipment.

Always mop up any spilt fuel and safely dispose of the rag used.

Any stored fuel that is drained off during servicing work must be kept in sealed containers that are suitable for holding petrol (gasoline), and clearly marked as such; the containers themselves should be kept in a safe place. Note that this last point applies equally to the fuel tank if it is removed from the machine; also remember to keep its filler cap closed at all times.

Read the Safety first! section of this manual carefully before starting work.

2 Fuel tank and fuel tap(s) – removal and installation

⚠ *Warning: Refer to the precautions given in Section 1 before starting work.*

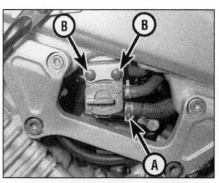

2.2 Detach the lower hose (A), then unscrew the bolts (B) and displace the tap

Fuel tank – TDM models

Removal

1 Make sure the fuel cap is secure and the fuel tap is in the OFF position. On 1991 to 1995 models, remove the seat, the fairing side panels and the fairing (see Chapter 8). On 1996-on models, remove the seat, the fairing side panels and the side trim panels (see Chapter 8).

2 On 1991 to 1995 models, release the clamp securing the lower hose (to the fuel pump) on the remote fuel tap and detach the hose, then unscrew the bolts securing the tap and displace it **(see illustration)**.

3 On 1996 to 1998 models, either proceed as described for the earlier models in Step 2, or close the tap on the fuel outlet assembly under the tank and detach the fuel hoses from the outlet, noting which fits where. Note that access may be restricted until the tank bolts have been removed and the tank can be raised at the rear.

4 On 1999 models, turn the fuel tap lever to the OFF position. Release the clamp securing the hose to the side of the fuel tap and detach the hose.

5 Unscrew the bolt securing the rear of the tank, then unscrew the bolt on each side at the front and release the trim panel from the lug **(see illustrations)**. Raise the tank at the rear and release the clamp securing the breather hose to its union and detach the hose **(see illustration)**. On 1991 to 1998

2.5a Unscrew the rear bolt (arrowed) . . .

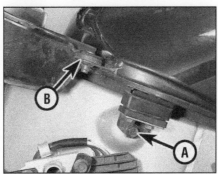

2.5b . . . and the bolt on each side (A), and release the trim from the lug (B)

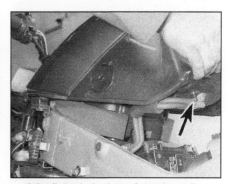

2.5c Detach the hose from the union (arrowed) and remove the tank

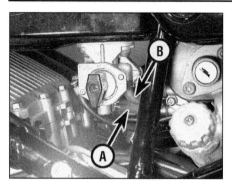

2.9a Detach the fuel hose (A), the vacuum hose (B) . . .

2.9b . . . and the breather hose (arrowed)

2.10a Remove the rear mounting bolt (arrowed) . . .

models, carefully lift the tank off the frame and remove it, bringing the remote fuel tap and hoses with it (where still attached), making sure the tap does not get snagged. On 1999 models, carefully lift the tank up to access the fuel level sender wiring; disconnect the wiring and remove the tank, making sure the tap does not get snagged.

6 Inspect the tank mounting rubbers for signs of damage or deterioration and renew them if necessary.

Installation

7 Installation is the reverse of removal, noting the following:
a) *Make sure the hoses are properly attached and secured by their clamps.*
b) *On 1996 to 1998 models, if the tap on the fuel outlet from the tank was turned OFF, do not forget to turn it back ON.*
c) *Don't forget to reconnect the fuel level sender wiring on 1999 TDM models.*
d) *Start the engine and check that there is no sign of fuel leakage, then shut if off.*

Fuel tank – TRX models

Removal

8 Make sure the fuel filler cap is secure and the fuel tap is in the ON or RES position. Remove the seat (see Chapter 8).

9 Release the clamps securing the fuel hose to the fuel pump and the vacuum hose to the fuel tap and detach the hoses **(see illustration)**. Also release the clamp securing

the breather hose to its union and detach the hose **(see illustration)**.

10 Unscrew the nut and withdraw bolt securing the rear of the tank, then unscrew the bolt on each side at the front **(see illustrations)**.

11 Carefully lift the tank off the frame and remove it.

12 Inspect the tank mounting rubbers for signs of damage or deterioration and renew them if necessary.

Installation

13 Installation is the reverse of removal, noting the following:
a) *Make sure the hoses are properly attached and secured by their clamps.*
b) *Start the engine and check that there is no sign of fuel leakage, then shut if off.*

Fuel tank – XTZ models

Removal

14 Make sure the fuel filler cap is secure and both fuel taps are in the OFF position. Remove the seat and the fairing side panels (see Chapter 8).

15 Release the clamp securing the fuel hose to each fuel tap and detach the hoses.

16 Unscrew the bolts securing the rear of the tank, then unscrew the bolt on each side at the front, and the top bracket-to-frame bolt **(see illustrations)**.

17 Carefully lift the tank off the frame and remove it.

18 Inspect the tank mounting rubbers for signs of damage or deterioration and renew them if necessary.

Installation

19 Installation is the reverse of removal, noting the following:
a) *Make sure the hoses are properly attached and secured by their clamps.*
b) *Start the engine and check that there is no sign of fuel leakage, then shut if off.*

Fuel tap(s)

Removal

Note: *The tap should not be removed unnecessarily from the tank to prevent the possibility of damaging the O-ring or the filter.*

20 Remove the fuel tank as described above.

21 On 1991 to 1995 TDM models, connect a drain hose to the fuel outlet union on the remote tap and insert its end in a container suitable and large enough for storing the petrol. Turn the fuel tap to the RES position and allow the tank to drain. When the tank has drained, turn the tap to the OFF position.

22 On 1996 to 1998 TDM models, if the remote tap is still attached, connect a drain hose to the fuel outlet union on the remote tap and insert its end in a container suitable and large enough for storing the petrol. Turn the fuel tap to the RES position and allow the tank to drain. If the remote tap was left in situ, connect a drain hose to each union on the fuel outlet on the tank and insert their ends in a container suitable and

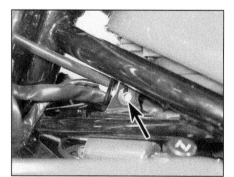

2.10b . . . and the front mounting bolt (arrowed) on each side

2.16a Remove the rear mounting bolts (arrowed) . . .

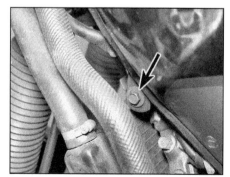

2.16b . . . and the front mounting bolt (arrowed) on each side

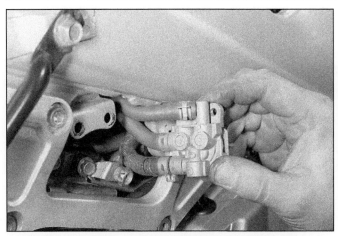

2.26 Note which hose fits where before detaching them

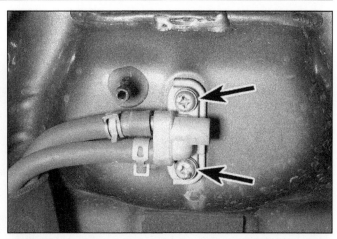

2.27a Fuel outlet screws (arrowed) – 1991 to 1995 TDM models

large enough for storing the petrol. Turn the outlet tap to the ON position and allow the tank to drain. When the tank has drained, turn the tap to the OFF position.

23 On 1999 TDM models, connect a drain hose to the union on the fuel tap and insert its end in a container suitable and large enough for storing the petrol. Turn the tap ON and allow the tank to drain. When the tank has drained, turn the tap to the OFF position.

24 On TRX models, connect a drain hose to the fuel outlet union on the tap and insert its end in a container suitable and large enough for storing the petrol. Turn the fuel tap to the PRI position and allow the tank to drain. When the tank has drained, turn the tap back to the ON or RES position.

25 On XTZ models, connect a drain hose to the fuel outlet union on each tap and insert their ends in a container suitable and large enough for storing the petrol. Turn the fuel taps to the RES position and allow the tank to drain. When the tank has drained, turn the taps to the OFF position.

26 If the fuel tap has been leaking, tightening the assembly screws may help. Slacken all the

screws a little first, then tighten them evenly a little at a time to ensure the cover seats properly on the tap body. If leakage persists, the tap should be renewed, however nothing is lost by dismantling the tap for further inspection. Unscrew the screws and disassemble the tap, noting how the components fit. Inspect all components for wear or damage, and renew them as necessary, if available. If any of the components are worn or damaged beyond repair and are not available individually, a new tap must be fitted. On 1991 to 1998 TDM models, note which hose fits where on the remote tap **(see illustration)**.

27 Remove the screws securing the tap to the tank and withdraw the tap assembly **(see illustrations)**. Check the condition of the O-ring. If it is in good condition it can be re-used, though it is better to use a new one. If it is in any way deteriorated or damaged it must be renewed.

28 Clean the gauze filters to remove all traces of dirt and fuel sediment. Check the gauze for holes. If any are found, a new tap should be fitted as the filters are not available individually.

29 On TRX models, the fuel tap is automatic, operated by a vacuum created when the engine is turned over. If it is faulty, it can be disassembled and inspected. The most likely problem is a hole or split in the diaphragm. Before removing and dismantling the tap, check that the vacuum hose is securely attached at both ends, and that there are no splits or cracks in the hose. If in doubt, attach a spare hose to the vacuum union on the tap and apply a vacuum to the hose. If fuel does not flow through the tap (make sure it is turned to ON or RES), remove it and disassemble it to check the diaphragm (the best way is to hold it up to the light, which will show through any splits or holes). Some individual components are available for the tap, but if the diaphragm is split the whole tap will probably have to be renewed – check with your dealer.

Installation

30 Installation is the reverse of removal. Use a new O-ring on the tap if required, and tighten the bolts securely.

31 Install the fuel tank (see above).

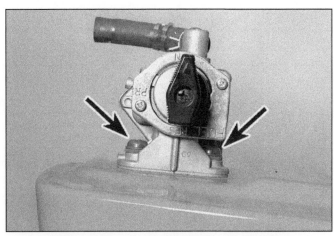

2.27b Fuel tap screws (arrowed) – TRX models

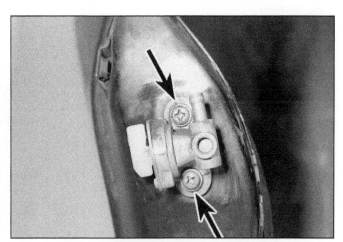

2.27c Fuel tap screws (arrowed) – XTZ models

3 Fuel tank – cleaning and repair

1 All repairs to the fuel tank should be carried out by a professional who has experience in this critical and potentially dangerous work. Even after cleaning and flushing of the fuel system, explosive fumes can remain and ignite during repair of the tank.

2 If the fuel tank is removed from the bike, it should not be placed in an area where sparks or open flames could ignite the fumes coming out of the tank. Be especially careful inside garages where a natural gas-type appliance is located, because the pilot light could cause an explosion.

4 Air filter housing – removal and installation

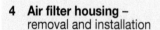

Removal

1 Remove the fuel tank (see Section 2).

2 Release the clamps securing the breather hose and the drain hose to the air filter housing and detach the hoses **(see illustration)**. Depending on your model, it may be easier to detach the drain hose once the housing has been lifted off the carburettors.

3 On TDM and XTZ models, unscrew the bolt securing the front of the housing to the frame **(see illustrations)**. On all models, slacken the clamp screws securing the housing to the carburettor intakes **(see illustration)**.

4 Lift the housing up off the carburettors and remove it, on TRX models noting how the peg at the front on the right locates in the grommet on the frame **(see illustration)**. On XTZ models, draw the intake ducts apart so that they clear the frame tube **(see illustration)**.

Installation

5 Installation is the reverse of removal. Check the condition of the various hoses and their clamps and renew them if necessary.

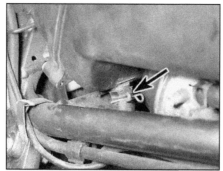

4.2 Drain hose (arrowed) – XTZ models

4.3b Air filter housing bolt (arrowed) – XTZ models

5 Idle fuel/air mixture adjustment – general information

1 Due to the increased emphasis on controlling exhaust emissions, certain governmental regulations have been formulated which directly affect the carburation of this machine. The pilot screws can be adjusted, but the use of an exhaust gas analyser and an auxiliary tachometer capable of accurately displaying changes of 50 rpm is the only certain way to adjust the idle fuel/air mixture and be sure the machine doesn't exceed the emissions regulations.

2 The pilot screws are set to their correct position by the manufacturer and should not

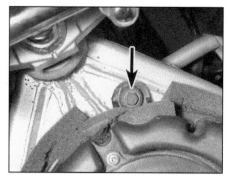

4.3a Air filter housing bolt (arrowed) – TDM models

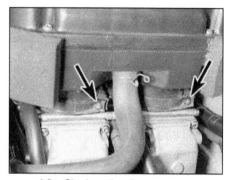

4.3c Slacken the clamp screws (arrowed) . . .

be adjusted or removed unless it is necessary to do so during a carburettor overhaul. If the screws are to be removed, record the pilot screw's current setting by turning the screw it in until it seats lightly, counting the number of turns necessary to achieve this, then fully unscrew it. On installation, the screw is simply backed out the number of turns you've recorded. Note that for some markets, the pilot screws are sealed with a plug to prevent tampering.

3 If the engine runs extremely rough at idle or continually stalls, and if a carburettor overhaul does not cure the problem, take the motorcycle to a Yamaha dealer equipped with an exhaust gas analyser. They will be able to properly adjust the idle fuel/air mixture to achieve a smooth idle and restore low speed performance.

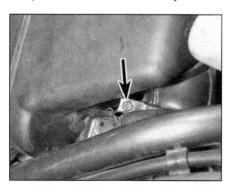

4.3d . . . which on XTZ models are accessed from each side (arrow)

4.4a On TRX models, note how the peg locates in the grommet

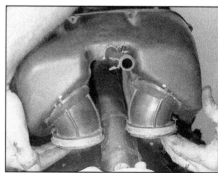

4.4b On XTZ models, draw the ducts apart to clear the frame

6 Carburettor overhaul – general information

1 Poor engine performance, hesitation, hard starting, stalling, flooding and backfiring are all signs that major carburettor maintenance may be required.

2 Keep in mind that many so-called carburettor problems are really not carburettor problems at all, but mechanical problems within the engine or ignition system malfunctions. Try to establish for certain that the carburettors are in need of maintenance before beginning a major overhaul.

3 Check the fuel tap and filter, the fuel and vacuum hoses, the intake manifold joint clamps, the air filter, the ignition system, the spark plugs, valve clearances and carburettor synchronisation before assuming that a carburettor overhaul is required.

4 Most carburettor problems are caused by dirt particles, varnish and other deposits which build up in and block the fuel and air passages, especially if the motorcycle has been laid up for a time. Also, in time, gaskets and O-rings shrink or deteriorate and cause fuel and air leaks which lead to poor performance.

5 When overhauling the carburettors, disassemble them completely and clean the parts thoroughly with a carburettor cleaning solvent and dry them with filtered, unlubricated compressed air. Blow through the fuel and air passages with compressed air to force out any dirt that may have been loosened but not removed by the solvent. Once the cleaning process is complete, reassemble the carburettor using new gaskets and O-rings.

6 Before disassembling the carburettors, make sure you have all necessary O-rings and other parts, some carburettor cleaner, a supply of clean rags, some means of blowing out the carburettor passages and a clean place to work. It is recommended that only one carburettor be overhauled at a time to avoid mixing up parts.

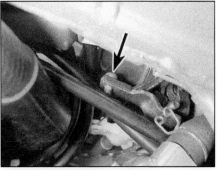

7.2a Slacken the clamp screw (arrowed) . . .

7.4a Idle speed adjuster bolt (arrowed) – TDM models

7 Carburettors – removal and installation

⚠️ **Warning: Refer to the precautions given in Section 1 before starting work.**

Removal

1 Remove the fuel tank and the air filter housing (see Sections 2 and 4).

2 Slacken the choke outer cable bracket screw and free the cable from the bracket on the front of the carburettors, then detach the inner cable nipple from the choke linkage lever **(see illustrations)**.

3 Detach the throttle cables from the carburettors (see Section 11, Steps 2 and 3).

7.2b . . . and detach the cable end from the lever

7.4b Idle speed adjuster bolt (arrowed) – TRX models

If access is too restricted, detach them after the carburettors have been lifted off the cylinder head intakes.

4 On TDM and TRX models, unscrew the bolt securing the idle speed adjuster and feed it through to the base of the carburettors **(see illustrations)**.

5 Release the clamp securing the drain hose to the bottom of each float chamber and detach the hoses **(see illustration)**. Also release the clamp securing the fuel supply hose to the carburettors and detach the hose **(see illustration)**; be careful to catch the small gauze filter fitted in the fuel supply hose union as the hose is detached (except 1999 TDM models).

6 On 1996-on TDM models and TRX models, disconnect the wiring connector from the throttle position sensor on the left-hand end of the carburettors **(see illustration)**. Also

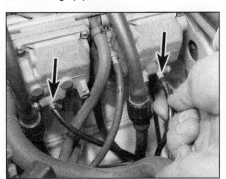

7.5a Detach the drain hoses (arrowed) . . .

7.5b . . . and the fuel hose

7.6 Disconnect the throttle position sensor wiring connector (arrowed)

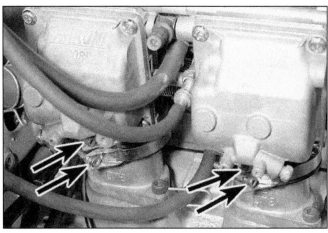

7.7a Slacken the upper or lower clamp screws as required (arrows) . . .

7.7b . . . and remove the carburettors

clamp the two warmer system coolant hoses to prevent loss of coolant and disconnect the hose from the side of each carburettor.

7 Fully slacken the clamps on the cylinder head intake rubbers, then ease the carburettors off the intakes and remove them **(see illustrations)**. To remove the carburettors with the rubbers, slacken the lower clamp bolts (which are more accessible). To leave the rubbers on the cylinder head, slacken the upper clamp bolts. **Note:** *Keep the carburettors level to prevent fuel spillage from the float chambers and the possibility of the piston diaphragms being damaged.*

Caution: Stuff clean rag into each cylinder head intake after removing the carburettors to prevent anything from falling in.

8 Place a suitable container below the float chambers, then slacken the drain screw on each chamber in turn and drain all the fuel from the carburettors **(see illustration)**. Tighten the drain screws securely once all the fuel has been drained.

9 If necessary, slacken the clamps securing the intake rubbers and remove them, noting which way up and round they fit.

Installation

10 Installation is the reverse of removal, noting the following.

a) *Check for cracks or splits in the cylinder head intake rubbers, and renew them if necessary.*

b) *Make sure the carburettors are fully engaged with the intake rubbers and the clamps are securely tightened.*

c) *Make sure all hoses are correctly routed and secured and not trapped or kinked.*

d) *Refer to Section 11 for installation of the throttle cables. Check the operation of the cables and adjust them as necessary (see Chapter 1).*

e) *Refer to Section 12 for details of choke cable reconnection.*

f) *Check idle speed and carburettor synchronisation and adjust as necessary (see Chapter 1).*

8 Carburettors – disassembly, cleaning and inspection

Warning: Refer to the precautions given in Section 1 before starting work.

1991 to 1998 TDM models, all TRX and XTZ models

Disassembly

1 Remove the carburettors from the machine as described in the previous Section. **Note:** *Do not separate the carburettors unless absolutely necessary; each carburettor can be dismantled sufficiently for all normal cleaning and adjustments while in place on the mounting brackets. Dismantle the carburettors separately to avoid interchanging parts.*

2 Unscrew and remove the top cover retaining screws **(see illustration)**. Lift off the cover and remove the spring from inside the piston, noting the spring seat fitted in the

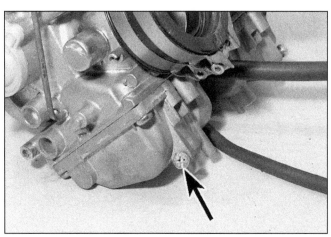

7.8 Float chamber drain screw (arrowed)

8.2 Remove the screws (arrowed) and lift off the cover

8.3 Remove the air passage O-ring

8.4 Lift out the diaphragm/piston assembly

bottom of the spring **(see illustrations 10.12b and a)**.

3 Remove the air passage O-ring and discard it as a new one should be used **(see illustration)**.

4 Carefully peel the diaphragm away from its sealing groove in the carburettor and withdraw the diaphragm and piston assembly **(see illustration)**.

Caution: Do not use a sharp instrument to displace the diaphragm as it is easily damaged.

5 Push the jet needle up from the bottom of the piston and withdraw it from the top, along

with the washer **(see illustration)**. If the E-clip is removed from the needle, note which notch it is fitted into.

6 Remove the screws securing the float chamber to the base of the carburettor and remove the float chamber, noting how it fits **(see illustration)**. Remove the rubber gasket and discard it as a new one must be used.

7 Carefully prise the float assembly out of the carburettor body, noting how it fits **(see illustration)**. Remove the O-ring and discard it as a new one must be used. If required, withdraw the float pivot pin and remove the float and needle valve, then unhook the

needle valve from the tab on the float, noting how it fits **(see illustration)**.

8 Unscrew and remove the starter jet, then remove the main jet holder, noting how it fits **(see illustration)**. Remove the main jet – it is a push fit. Discard the O-ring as a new one should be used.

9 Unscrew and remove the pilot jet **(see illustration 8.8)**.

10 Unscrew the bolt securing the jet housing and remove the collar **(see illustration)**. Remove the jet housing and discard its rubber gasket as a new one should be used. Push on the needle jet and withdraw the piston guide

8.5 Remove the jet needle and its washer

8.6 Remove the screws (arrowed) and lift off the float chamber

8.7a Carefully prise out the float assembly

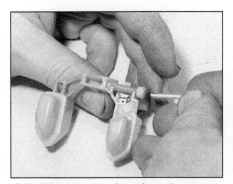

8.7b Withdraw the pivot pin and separate the float, needle valve and seat

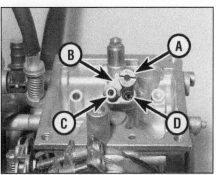

8.8 Starter jet (A), main jet holder (B), main jet (C), pilot jet (D)

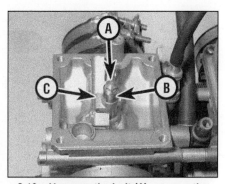

8.10a Unscrew the bolt (A), remove the collar (B), and lift off the jet housing (C)

8.10b Push on the needle jet . . .

8.10c . . . and withdraw the piston guide and jet from the top

and needle jet from the top of the carburettor **(see illustrations)**. Note which way round the guide fits into the carburettor body. Discard the O-ring on the bottom of the guide as a new one must be used. If required, push the needle jet up from the bottom and remove it from the guide, noting which way round it fits **(see illustration)**.

11 The pilot screw can be removed from the carburettor, but note that its setting will be disturbed (see *Haynes Hint*). Unscrew and remove the pilot screw along with its spring, washer and O-ring **(see illustration)**. Discard the O-ring as a new one must be used.

12 Push out the rubber clips securing the choke linkage bar to the carburettors, then remove the choke linkage bar, noting how it fits **(see illustration)**. Compress the clip ends

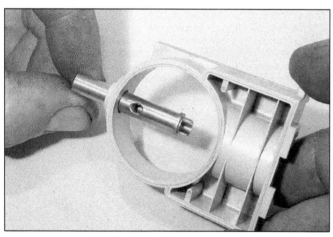

8.10d Push the jet out of the guide

8.11 Pilot screw (arrowed)

8.12a Push out the clips and remove the linkage bar

8.12b Compress the clips . . .

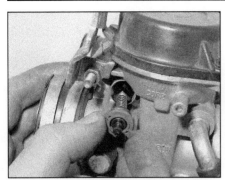

8.12c . . . and withdraw the plunger

8.13a Remove the screws (arrowed) . . .

8.13b . . . and remove the cover, spring and diaphragm

> **HAYNES HiNT** *To record the pilot screw's current setting, turn the screw it in until it seats lightly, counting the number of turns necessary to achieve this, then fully unscrew it. On installation, the screw is simply backed out the number of turns you've recorded.*

securing the choke plunger to the carburettor body and withdraw the plunger, noting how it fits **(see illustrations)**.

13 Remove the cut-off diaphragm cover screws and lift off the cover, noting that there is a spring fitted behind it **(see illustration)**. Remove the spring and carefully remove the diaphragm, noting how it fits **(see illustration)**.

14 On 1996-98 TDM models and TRX models a throttle position sensor is mounted on the outside of the left-hand carburettor. Do not remove the sensor from the carburettor unless it is known to be faulty and is being renewed. Refer to Chapter 5 for check and adjustment of the sensor.

Cleaning

Caution: Use only a petroleum-based solvent for carburettor cleaning. Don't use caustic cleaners.

15 Submerge the metal components in the solvent for approximately thirty minutes (or longer, if the directions recommend it).

16 After the carburettor has soaked long enough for the cleaner to loosen and dissolve most of the varnish and other deposits, use a nylon-bristled brush to remove the stubborn deposits. Rinse it again, then dry it with compressed air.

17 Use a jet of compressed air to blow out all of the fuel and air passages in the main and upper body.

Caution: Never clean the jets or passages with a piece of wire or a drill bit, as they will be enlarged, causing the fuel and air metering rates to be upset.

Inspection

18 Check the operation of the choke plunger. If it doesn't move smoothly, inspect the needle on the end of the choke plunger, the spring and the plunger linkage bar **(see illustration)**. Renew any component that is worn, damaged or bent.

19 If removed from the carburettor, check the tapered portion of the pilot screw and the spring and O-ring for wear or damage **(see illustration)**. Renew them if necessary.

20 Check the carburettor body, float chamber and top cover for cracks, distorted sealing surfaces and other damage. If any defects are found, renew the faulty component, although renewal of the entire carburettor will probably be necessary (check with a Yamaha dealer on the availability of separate components).

21 Check the piston diaphragm and cut-off diaphragm for splits, holes and general deterioration. Holding them up to a light will help to reveal problems of this nature.

22 Insert the piston guide and piston in the carburettor body and check that the piston moves up-and-down smoothly. Check the surface of the piston for wear. If it's worn excessively or doesn't move smoothly in the guide, renew the components as necessary.

23 Check the jet needle for straightness by rolling it on a flat surface such as a piece of glass (having first removed the E-clip and washer, noting which notch the E-clip fits into). Renew it if it's bent or if the tip is worn.

24 Check the tip of the float needle valve and the valve seat. If either has grooves or scratches in it, or is in any way worn, they must be renewed as a set **(see illustration)**.

25 Operate the throttle shaft to make sure the throttle butterfly valve opens and closes smoothly. If it doesn't, cleaning the throttle linkage may help. Otherwise, renew the carburettor.

26 Check the floats for damage. This will usually be apparent by the presence of fuel inside one of the floats. If the floats are damaged, they must be renewed.

1999 TDM model
Disassembly

27 Remove the carburettors from the machine as described in the previous Section. **Note:** *Do not separate the carburettors unless absolutely necessary; each carburettor can be dismantled sufficiently for all normal cleaning and adjustments while in place on the mounting brackets. Dismantle the carburettors separately to avoid interchanging parts.*

8.18 Inspect the choke plunger for wear

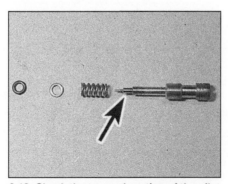

8.19 Check the tapered portion of the pilot screw (arrowed) for wear

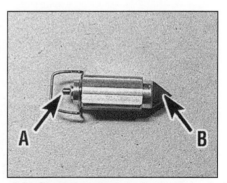

8.24 Check the valve's spring loaded rod (A) and tip (B) for wear or damage

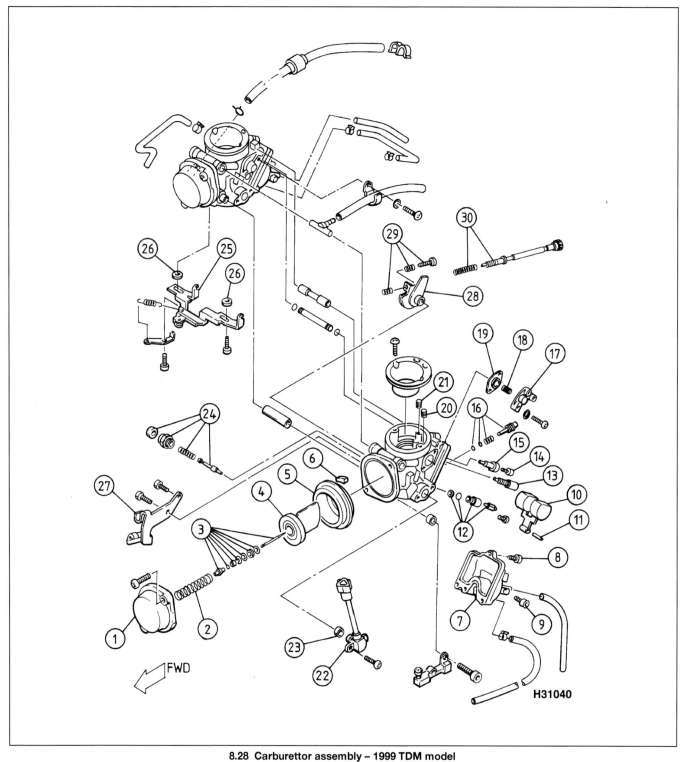

8.28 Carburettor assembly – 1999 TDM model

1 Top cover	9 Drain screw	17 Cut-off valve cover	25 Choke linkage bar
2 Spring	10 Floats	18 Spring	26 Plastic washers
3 Jet needle assembly	11 Pivot pin	19 Diaphragm	27 Throttle cable bracket
4 Piston	12 Float needle valve and seat	20 Main air jet	28 Throttle cam
5 Diaphragm	13 Pilot jet	21 Main air jet	29 Synchronising screw and
6 Cap	14 Main jet	22 Throttle position sensor	springs
7 Float chamber	15 Main jet holder	23 Seal	30 Idle adjusting screw
8 Screw – 3 off	16 Pilot screw assembly	24 Choke plunger assembly	

28 Unscrew and remove the top cover retaining screws **(see illustration)**. Lift off the cover and remove the spring from inside the piston.

29 Withdraw the piston assembly and diaphragm. Push the jet needle up from the bottom of the piston and withdraw it from the top, noting the exact order of the components at the top of the jet needle. If the E-clip is removed from the needle, note which notch it is fitted into.

Caution: Do not use a sharp instrument to displace the diaphragm as it is easily damaged.

30 Remove the screws securing the float chamber to the base of the carburettor and remove the float chamber complete with its rubber gasket. Withdraw the float pivot pin and remove the float and needle valve, then unhook the needle valve from the tab on the float, noting how it fits.

31 Unscrew and remove the pilot jet, the main jet and the main jet holder.

32 The pilot screw can be removed from the carburettor, but note that its setting will be disturbed (see **Haynes Hint**). Unscrew and remove the pilot screw along with its spring, washer and O-ring. Discard the O-ring as a new one must be used.

HAYNES HiNT *To record the pilot screw's current setting, turn the screw it in until it seats lightly, counting the number of turns necessary to achieve this, then fully unscrew it. On installation, the screw is simply backed out the number of turns you've recorded.*

33 Remove the two screws which retain the choke linkage bar to the carburettors and remove the bar noting the two plastic washers. Disengage the linkage bar hooks from the ends of the choke plungers. To remove the choke plunger, peel off the rubber cap then unscrew the retaining nut to allow the spring and plunger to be withdrawn.

34 Remove the cut-off diaphragm cover screws and lift off the cover, noting that there is a spring fitted behind it. Remove the spring and carefully remove the diaphragm, noting how it fits.

35 Do not disturb the throttle position sensor

on the left-hand carburettor unless absolutely necessary. Refer to Chapter 5 for check and adjustment of the sensor.

Cleaning and Inspection

36 Refer to Steps 15 to 26 of this Section, noting that there is no piston guide in this carburettor.

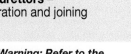

9 Carburettors –
separation and joining

⚠ *Warning: Refer to the precautions given in Section 1 before proceeding*

1991 to 1998 TDM models, all TRX and XTZ models

Separation

1 The carburettors do not need to be separated for normal overhaul. If you need to separate them (to renew a carburettor body, for example), refer to the following procedure.

2 Remove the carburettors from the machine (see Section 7). Mark the body of each carburettor with its cylinder location to ensure that it is positioned correctly on reassembly.

3 Make a note of how the throttle return springs, linkage assembly and carburettor synchronisation springs are arranged to ensure that they are fitted correctly on reassembly **(see illustration)**. Also note the arrangement of the various hoses, unions,

joint pieces and collar, and of the cable brackets **(see illustrations)**.

4 Push out the clips securing the choke linkage bar to the carburettors, then remove the choke linkage bar from the plungers, noting how it fits **(see illustrations 8.12a, 10.2a and b)**.

5 Unscrew the nuts from the through-bolts securing the carburettors together and withdraw the bolts **(see illustrations)**. Remove the spacing collars, noting how the choke cable lever fits on the top one **(see illustration 10.2b)**.

6 Carefully separate the carburettors. Retrieve the synchronisation springs and note the fitting of the fuel hose T-piece and its seals, and the vent hose T-piece as they are separated. On 1996-on TDM and TRX models note that the warmer system coolant hose between the carburettors must be detached at one end.

Joining

7 Assembly is the reverse of the disassembly procedure, noting the following.

a) *Make sure the fuel hose T-piece and seals and the air vent hose T-piece are correctly and securely inserted into the carburettors.*

b) *Install the synchronisation spring after the carburettors are joined together. Make sure it is correctly and squarely seated.*

c) *Check the operation of both the choke and throttle linkages ensuring that both operate smoothly and return quickly under spring pressure before installing the carburettors on the machine.*

d) *Install the carburettors (see Section 7) and check carburettor synchronisation and idle speed (see Chapter 1).*

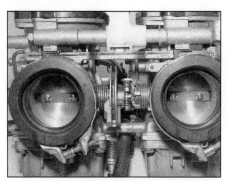
9.3a Throttle linkage assembly

9.3b Note how the various joint pieces fit . . .

9.3c . . . and the cable bracket

9.5a Unscrew the nuts (arrowed) . . .

9.5b . . . and withdraw the bolts (arrowed)

1999 TDM model

Separation

8 The carburettors do not need to be separated for normal overhaul. If you need to separate them (to renew a carburettor body, for example), refer to the following procedure and illustration 8.28.

9 Remove the carburettors from the machine (see Section 7). Mark the body of each carburettor with its cylinder location to ensure that it is positioned correctly on reassembly.

10 Make a note of how the throttle return springs, linkage assembly and carburettor synchronisation springs are arranged to ensure that they are fitted correctly on reassembly. Also note the arrangement of the various hoses, unions, joint pieces and collar, and of the cable brackets.

11 Remove the two screws which retain the choke linkage bar to the carburettors and remove the bar noting the two plastic washers. Disengage the linkage bar hooks from the ends of the choke plungers.

12 Carefully separate the carburettors. Retrieve the synchronisation springs and note the fitting of the fuel and vent hose T-pieces and unions as they are separated. Note that the warmer system coolant hose between the carburettors must be detached at one end.

Joining

13 Assembly is the reverse of the disassembly procedure, noting the following.

a) Make sure the fuel and vent hose T-pieces, unions and O-rings are all correctly located as the two carburettors are pushed back together.

b) Install the synchronisation spring after the carburettors are joined together. Make sure it is correctly and squarely seated.

c) Install the choke linkage bar making sure that its hooks engage the ends of the choke plungers. Position the plastic washers between the linkage bar and carburettor bodies and tighten the screws securely.

d) Check the operation of both the choke and throttle linkages ensuring that both operate smoothly and return quickly under spring pressure before installing the carburettors on the machine.

e) Install the carburettors (see Section 7) and check carburettor synchronisation and idle speed (see Chapter 1).

10 Carburettors – reassembly and fuel level check

> **Warning: Refer to the precautions given in Section 1 before proceeding**

1991 to 1998 TDM models, all TRX and XTZ models

Reassembly

Note: When reassembling the carburettors, be sure to use new O-rings and seals at all joints. Do not overtighten the carburettor jets and screws as they are easily damaged.

1 Install the cut-off diaphragm, then locate the spring in its centre, fit the cover onto the spring and secure it with the screws (**see illustrations 8.13b and a**).

2 Install the choke plunger into the carburettor body, making sure the clips locate correctly in their holes (**see illustration 8.12c**). Fit the choke linkage bar onto the plungers, making sure the slots in the arms locate correctly behind the nipple on the end of each choke plunger, and that the central tab locates into the slot in the base of the choke cable lever (**see illustrations**). Secure the linkage bar in place with the clips, making sure their ends locate over the ends of the slide guide (**see illustration 8.12a**).

3 Install the pilot screw (if removed) along with its spring, washer and O-ring, turning it in until it seats lightly (**see illustration 8.11**). Now, turn the screw out the number of turns previously recorded, or as specified at the beginning of the Chapter.

4 Fit the jet needle into the piston guide, making sure it is the correct way round (**see illustration 8.10d**). Fit a new O-ring onto the base of the guide (**see illustration**). Install the guide assembly into the carburettor body, making sure it is the right way round and properly seated (**see illustration 8.10c**).

5 Fit a new gasket onto the jet housing, then locate the housing over the needle jet and onto the carburettor (**see illustrations**). Fit the collar and secure the housing with the bolt (**see illustration**).

10.2a Make sure the slots locate correctly behind each choke plunger nipple . . .

10.2b . . . and that the tab fits into the slot in the choke cable lever

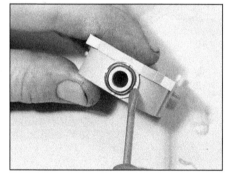

10.4 Fit a new O-ring into the groove in the base of the guide

10.5a Fit a new O-ring onto the housing . . .

10.5b . . . then fit the housing . . .

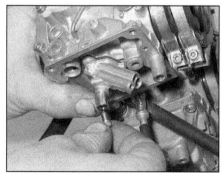

10.5c . . . and secure it with the collar and bolt

10.6 Install the pilot jet . . .

10.7a . . . and the main jet, using a new O-ring . . .

10.7b . . . then fit the main jet holder and the starter jet

6 Install the pilot jet **(see illustration)**.

7 Fit a new O-ring onto the main jet and push it into its bore, making sure it is correctly seated **(see illustration)**. Fit the main jet holder and secure it by screwing in the starter jet **(see illustration)**.

8 If separated, fit the float needle valve into its seat, then fit the tab on the float into the hook on the top of the valve and install the pivot pin **(see illustrations)**. Fit a new O-ring to the base of the float assembly, then carefully press the assembly into the carburettor body, making sure the tab locates in its cut-out **(see illustration 8.7a)**.

9 Fit a new gasket onto the float chamber, making sure it is seated properly in its groove, then install the chamber on the carburettor

and tighten its screws securely **(see illustrations)**.

10 Install the jet needle with its washer into the diaphragm assembly **(see illustration 8.5)**.

11 Insert the diaphragm assembly into the piston guide and lightly push the piston down, ensuring the needle is correctly aligned with the needle jet **(see illustration 8.4)**. Press the diaphragm outer edge into its groove, making sure it is correctly seated. Check the diaphragm is not creased, and that the piston moves smoothly up and down in the guide.

12 Fit a new O-ring onto the air passage **(see illustration 8.3)**. Install the spring into the diaphragm assembly with the spring seat in the bottom, then fit the top cover onto the

carburettor, locating the peg into the top of the spring, and tighten its screws securely **(see illustrations)**.

13 Install the carburettors (see Section 7), but if the fuel level is to be checked do not yet install the air filter housing or fuel tank.

1999 TDM model

Note: *When reassembling the carburettors, be sure to use new O-rings and seals at all joints. Do not overtighten the carburettor jets and screws as they are easily damaged.*

14 Install the cut-off diaphragm, then locate the spring in its centre, fit the cover onto the spring and secure it with the screws.

15 Install the choke plunger into the carburettor body, followed by the spring.

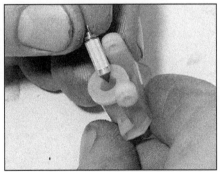

10.8a Fit the needle valve into the seat . . .

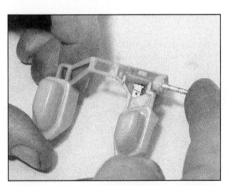

10.8b . . . then locate the float and slide in the pin

10.9a Fit a new gasket into the groove . . .

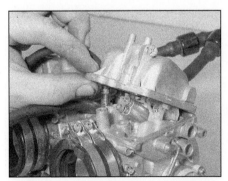

10.9b . . . and install the float chamber

10.12a Insert the spring . . .

10.12b . . . then locate the peg in the top of the spring and fit the cover

Screw the retaining nut into place and fit the rubber cap over its end. Install the choke linkage bar making sure that its hooks engage the ends of the choke plungers. Position plastic washers between the linkage bar and carburettor bodies and tighten the screws securely.

16 Install the pilot screw (if removed) along with its spring, washer and O-ring, turning it in until it seats lightly. Now, turn the screw out the number of turns previously recorded, or as specified at the beginning of the Chapter.

17 Install the pilot jet, main jet holder and main jet.

18 Attach the float needle valve to the float, then slip the needle valve into its seat in the carburettor. Secure the float with the pivot pin.

19 Make sure that the float chamber sealing ring is seated properly in its groove, then install the chamber on the carburettor and tighten its screws securely.

20 Install the jet needle assembly into the diaphragm. Insert the piston/diaphragm into the carburettor taking care that the jet needle isn't damaged. Press the diaphragm outer edge into its groove, making sure it is correctly seated. Check the diaphragm is not creased, and that the piston moves smoothly up and down in the carburettor.

21 Install the spring into the diaphragm assembly, then fit the top cover onto the carburettor and tighten its screws securely.

22 Install the carburettors (see Section 7), but if the fuel level is to be checked do not yet install the air filter housing or fuel tank.

Fuel level check – all models

Note: *Checking the fuel level requires the use of some form or calibrated gauge with the correct size hoses to fit the drain hose union*

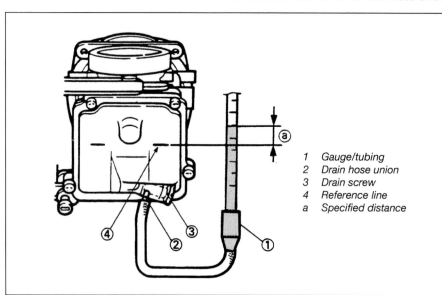

1 Gauge/tubing
2 Drain hose union
3 Drain screw
4 Reference line
a Specified distance

10.25a Measuring fuel level – 1991 to 1995 TDM models and XTZ models

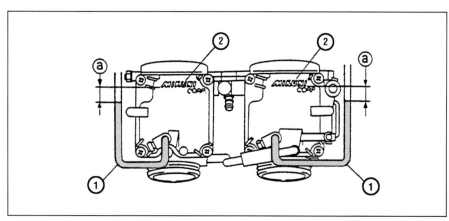

10.25b Measuring fuel level – 1996 to 1998 TDM models and all TRX models

1 Gauge/tubing
2 Reference mark
a Specified distance

on the carburettor float chamber. If you don't have the equipment or the skill to carry out this task it is advised that you take the bike to a Yamaha dealer for the fuel level check and adjustment.

 Warning: Be particularly careful if connecting up an auxiliary fuel supply or when connecting the level gauge that there are no fuel leaks. Fuel leakage poses a serious fire risk.

23 When checking the fuel level the motorcycle must be on level ground and supported on an auxiliary stand so that it is upright. Remove the seat (see Chapter 8) and the fuel tank (see Section 2 of this Chapter).

24 Arrange a temporary fuel supply, either by using a small temporary tank or by using an extra long fuel pipe to the now remote fuel tank. Alternatively, position the tank on a suitable base on the motorcycle, taking care not to scratch any paintwork, and making sure that the tank is safely and securely supported. Connect the fuel line to the carburettors. On TRX models turn the fuel tap to the PRI position. On all other models turn the fuel tap(s) to the ON or RES positions, then run the engine for a minute or two to ensure that the float chambers are full, then stop the engine.

25 Yamaha provide a fuel level gauge (part No, 90890-01312), or alternatively a suitable length of clear plastic tubing can be used. Pull the drain hose off its union on the float chamber **(see illustration 7.5a)**, then attach the gauge or tubing to the drain hose union and position its open end vertically alongside the carburettor body. Slacken the drain screw and allow the fuel to flow into the tube **(see illustration 7.8)**; don't move the position of the gauge at all during the check. The level at which the fuel stabilises in the tube indicates the level of the fuel inside the float chamber. Measure the distance from the fuel level to the reference point on the carburettor **(see illustrations)**. Compare your reading to the Specifications at the beginning of the Chapter to see if the fuel level is correct. If you accidentally raise or lower the gauge during the check, start the fuel level check again.

26 Repeat the fuel level check on the other carburettor. It is important that the fuel level is equal in each carburettor and that it corresponds to the manufacturer's specification.

27 If the fuel level in either carburettor is incorrect, drain the fuel from the float chamber, then referring to Section 8 detach the fuel float chamber from the carburettor and remove the float assembly. An incorrect fuel level can be due to wear of the float valve and its seat in the carburettor, dirt trapped between the valve and seat, or simply an incorrect float height. If the float valve and its seat are unworn and clean, adjust the float height by very carefully bending the metal

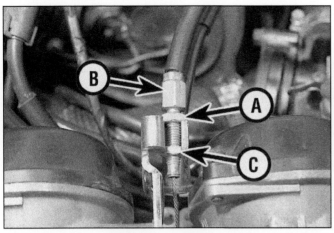

11.3a Slacken the locknut (A), then thread the adjuster (B) out of the captive nut (C) . . .

11.3b . . . until the accelerator cable is free of the bracket

tang of the float; only make a small adjustment and then refit the float and its chamber and recheck the fuel level.

28 When checking and adjustment are complete, reconnect the drain hoses to the float chambers and make sure the drain screws are secure. Install the fuel tank as described in Section 2.

11 Throttle cables –
removal and installation

 Warning: Refer to the precautions given in Section 1 before proceeding.

Removal

1 Remove the fuel tank and the air filter housing (see Sections 2 and 4). Whilst it is possible to detach the throttle cables with the carburettors in situ, there is a limited amount of space to work in and it can be tricky. If

required, displace the carburettors to improve access (see Section 7).

2 Mark each cable according to its location.

3 Slacken the accelerator cable adjuster locknut, then unscrew the adjuster so that it threads out of the captive nut, until it is clear of the small lug on the bracket **(see illustration)**. Slip the adjuster out of the bracket and detach the cable nipple from the carburettors **(see**

illustration)**. Pull the decelerator cable out of its holder and slide the inner cable through the slot in the holder, then detach the inner cable nipple from the carburettors **(see illustrations)**. Withdraw the cables from the machine noting the correct routing of each cable.

4 Pull the rubber boot back off the throttle housing on the handlebar **(see illustrations)**. Remove the throttle housing screws and

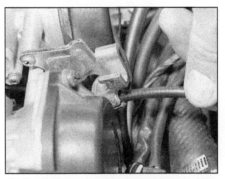

11.3c Pull the decelerator cable out of its seat . . .

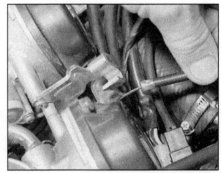

11.3d . . . and slip the inner cable out through the slot . . .

11.3e . . . and detach the cable end from the carburettor (arrowed)

11.4a Pull the boot back off the housing (TDM shown) . . .

11.4b . . . on TRX and XTZ models, the housing is the other way up

11.4c Throttle housing screws (arrowed)

11.4d Detach the cable elbows from the housing, noting how they fit . . .

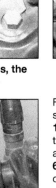

11.4e . . . and free the cable ends from the throttle pulley

separate the halves (see illustration). Displace the cable elbows from the housing, noting how they fit, and detach the cable nipples from the pulley (see illustrations). Mark each cable to ensure it is connected correctly on installation.

Installation

5 Lubricate the cable nipples with multi-purpose grease and install them into the throttle pulley at the handlebar (see illustration 11.4e). The accelerator cable nipple fits into the front socket on the pulley on TDM models, where the sockets are on the top, and into the rear socket on TRX and XTZ models where the assembly is upside down.

Fit the cable elbows into the housing, making sure they locate correctly (see illustration 11.4d). Join the housing halves, making sure the pin locates in the hole in the handlebar, and tighten the screws (see illustrations).
6 Feed the cables through to the carburettors, making sure they are correctly routed. The cables must not interfere with any other component and should not be kinked or bent sharply.
7 Lubricate the decelerator cable nipple with multi-purpose grease and fit it into the lower socket on the carburettor throttle cam (see illustration 11.3e). Slip the inner cable through the slot in the holder and locate the outer cable into the holder (see illustrations 11.3d and c). Lubricate the accelerator cable nipple with multi-purpose grease and fit it into the upper socket on the carburettor throttle cam. Fit the accelerator cable adjuster into the upper bracket, then locate the captive nut against the lug so that it is held, and thread the adjuster into the nut until the specified amount of cable freeplay is obtained (see Chapter 1) (see illustrations 11.3b and a). Tighten the locknut against the bracket.
8 Operate the throttle to check that it opens and closes freely.
9 Check and adjust the throttle cable freeplay (see Chapter 1). Turn the handlebars back and forth to make sure the cable doesn't cause the steering to bind.

10 Install the carburettors (if displaced), the air filter housing and the fuel tank (see Sections 7, 4 and 2).
11 Start the engine and check that the idle speed does not rise as the handlebars are turned. If it does, the throttle cables are routed incorrectly. Correct the problem before riding the motorcycle.

12 Choke cable – removal and installation

Removal

1 Remove the fuel tank and the air filter housing (see Sections 2 and 4).
2 Slacken the choke outer cable bracket screw and free the cable from the bracket on the front of the carburettors, then detach the inner cable nipple from the choke linkage lever (see illustrations 7.2a and b).
3 On TRX, XTZ and 1991 to 1998 TDM models, unscrew the nut securing the choke knob in its bracket and withdraw the cable through the bracket, feeding the nut off the end, and noting its routing. On 1999 TDM models, refer to Chapter 9, Section 20 and remove the two screws which retain the left-hand handlebar switch halves; free the choke lever from the switch and disconnect the cable.

11.5a Make sure the pin (arrowed) in the housing locates in the hole in the handlebar . . .

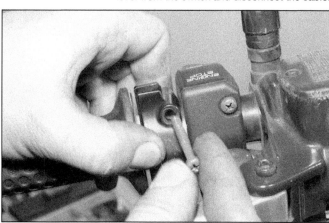

11.5b . . . then install the screws

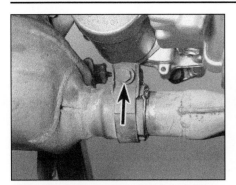

13.1a Slacken the clamp bolt (arrowed) . . .

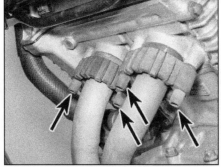

13.1b . . . then unscrew the downpipe nuts
(arrowed) . . .

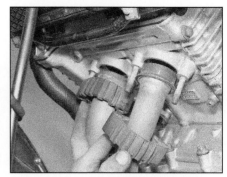

13.1c . . . and remove the pipes

Installation

4 Feed the cable through the bracket and slip the nut over the end, then feed the cable to the carburettors, making sure it is correctly routed. The cable must not interfere with any other component and should not be kinked or bent sharply. Fit the choke knob in its bracket and tighten the nut to secure it.

5 Lubricate the cable nipple with multi-purpose grease and attach it to the choke linkage lever on the carburettor **(see illustration 7.2b)**. Fit the outer cable into its bracket, making sure there is a small amount of freeplay in the inner cable, and tighten the screw **(see illustration 7.2a)**.

6 Check the operation of the choke cable (see Chapter 1).

7 Install the air filter housing and the fuel tank (see Sections 4 and 2).

13 Exhaust system –
removal and installation

Warning: If the engine has been running the exhaust system will be very hot. Allow the system to cool before carrying out any work.

Removal – TDM models

1 To remove the downpipe section, slacken the clamp bolt securing the downpipes in the

collector box, then unscrew the downpipe flange retaining nuts from the cylinder head and remove the downpipes **(see illustrations)**. Remove the gasket from each port in the cylinder head and discard them as new ones must be fitted.

2 To remove the collector box/silencer assembly, first remove the outer front sprocket cover to provide access to the collector box mounting bolt **(see illustration)**. Slacken the clamp bolt securing the downpipes in the collector box **(see illustration 13.1a)**, then unscrew the collector box mounting bolt **(see illustration)**. Now unscrew the silencer mounting bolts and draw the assembly back off the downpipes **(see illustration)**.

3 To remove the complete system as one

assembly, first remove the outer front sprocket cover to provide access to the collector box mounting bolt, then unscrew the mounting bolt **(see illustrations 13.2a and b)**. Unscrew the downpipe flange retaining nuts from the cylinder head **(see illustration 13.1b)**, then unscrew the silencer mounting bolts and manoeuvre the system off the machine **(see illustration 13.2c)**. Remove the gasket from each port in the cylinder head and discard them as new ones must be fitted.

Removal - TRX models

4 To remove the downpipe section, slacken the clamp bolt securing each downpipe in its silencer, then unscrew the bolt securing the downpipe assembly to the underside of the engine **(see illustrations)**. Unscrew the

13.2a Unscrew the bolts (arrowed) and
remove the cover . . .

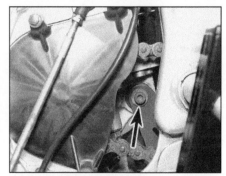

13.2b . . . then unscrew the collector box
bolt (arrowed) . . .

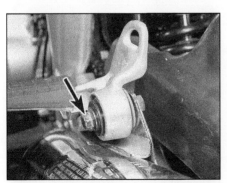

13.2c . . . and each silencer mounting bolt
(arrowed)

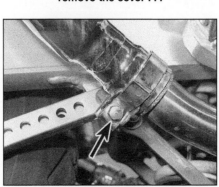

13.4a Slacken each clamp bolt
(arrowed) . . .

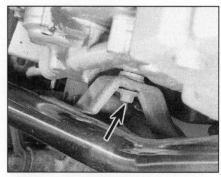

13.4b . . . and remove the mounting bolt
(arrowed)

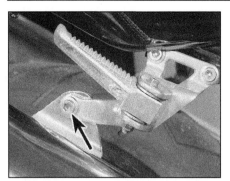

13.5 Silencer mounting bolt (arrowed)

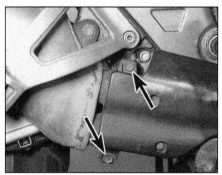

13.7 Slacken the clamp bolts (arrowed)

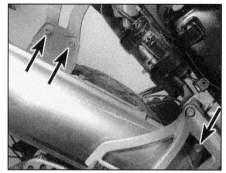

13.8 Silencer mounting bolts (arrowed)

13.10a Always use new port gaskets . . .

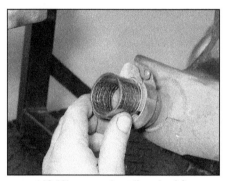

13.10b . . . and sealing ring(s)

downpipe flange retaining nuts from the cylinder head and remove the downpipes **(see illustrations 13.1b and c)**. Remove the gasket from each port in the cylinder head and discard them as new ones must be fitted.

5 To remove the silencers, slacken the clamp bolt securing the downpipe in its silencer **(see illustration 13.4a)**, then unscrew the silencer mounting bolt and draw the silencer back off the downpipe **(see illustration)**.

6 To remove the complete system, unscrew the bolt securing the downpipe assembly to the underside of the engine **(see illustration 13.4b)**, then unscrew the downpipe flange retaining nuts from the cylinder head and the silencer mounting bolts and manoeuvre the system off the machine **(see illustrations 13.1b and 13.5)**. Remove the gasket from

each port in the cylinder head and discard them as new ones must be fitted.

Removal - XTZ models

7 To remove the downpipe section, slacken the clamp bolt securing each downpipe in its silencer **(see illustration)**, then unscrew the downpipe flange retaining nuts from the cylinder head and remove the downpipes **(see illustrations 13.1b and c)**. Remove the gasket from each port in the cylinder head and discard them as new ones must be fitted.

8 To remove the silencer, slacken the clamp bolts securing the downpipes in the silencer **(see illustration 13.7)**, then unscrew the silencer mounting bolts and draw the silencer back off the downpipe **(see illustration)**.

9 To remove the complete system, first unscrew the bolts securing the right-hand

passenger footrest bracket and remove the bracket. Unscrew the downpipe flange retaining nuts from the cylinder head and the silencer mounting bolts and manoeuvre the system off the machine **(see illustrations 13.1b and 13.8)**. Remove the gasket from each port in the cylinder head and discard them as new ones must be fitted.

Installation – all models

10 Installation is the reverse of removal, noting the following:

a) Use new gaskets in each cylinder head port **(see illustration)**.

b) Use new sealing ring(s) between the downpipes and silencer or collector box, if separated **(see illustration)**.

c) Apply some copper grease to the clamp bolts to prevent them from seizing up.

d) Leave all fasteners loose until the entire system has been installed, making alignment of the various sections easier. Tighten the silencer mountings last.

e) Tighten the system mounting bolts and nuts to the torque settings specified at the beginning of the Chapter.

f) On XTZ models, tighten the right-hand footrest bracket bolts to the specified torque setting.

g) Run the engine and check the system for leaks.

---

14 Fuel pump – check and renewal (TRX, XTZ and 1991 to 1998 TDM models)

⚠️ **Warning: Refer to the precautions given in Section 1 before proceeding.**

Note: A vacuum type fuel pump is fitted to all TRX and XTZ models and 1991 to 1998 TDM models.

Check

1 On TDM models remove the seat and on XTZ models remove the left-hand side cover (see Chapter 8). On TDM models, the fuel pump is mounted under the fuel tank bracket **(see illustration)**. On TRX models, the fuel pump is mounted under the back of the fuel tank **(see illustration)** – remove the fuel tank

14.1a Fuel pump (arrowed) – TDM models (1991 to 1995 type shown)

14.1b Fuel pump (arrowed) – TRX models

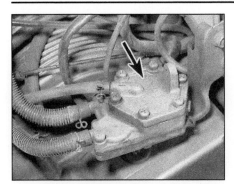

**14.1c Fuel pump (arrowed) –
XTZ models**

for improved access. On XTZ models, the fuel pump is mounted above the front sprocket cover **(see illustration)**.

2 To check whether the pump is operating, release the clamp securing the fuel supply hose to the carburettor and detach the hose **(see illustration 7.5b)**; taken note of the filter in the hose union and remove it for safekeeping. Place the open end of this hose in a container suitable for storing petrol.

3 Turn the engine over on the starter motor and check to see whether fuel flows from the hose into the container. If fuel flows, the pump is working correctly. When reconnecting the fuel hose to the carburettor don't forget to insert the filter into the union.

4 If no fuel flows, first check that this is not due to a blocked filter or fuel hose, or due to a split in the small-bore hose from the vacuum cover of the fuel pump. Check all the hoses for splits, cracks and kinks, and check that they are securely connected on each end by a good clamp. If all the hoses are good, renew the pump. It is possible to disassemble the pump for cleaning or inspection – holding the diaphragm up to the light will reveal any splits or holes – but no individual components are available for it.

Removal and installation

5 On TDM models remove the seat and on XTZ models remove the left-hand side cover (see Chapter 8). On TDM models, the fuel pump is mounted under the fuel tank bracket **(see illustration 14.1a)**. On TRX models, the fuel pump is mounted under the back of the fuel tank **(see illustration 14.1b)**; remove the fuel tank for access. On XTZ models, the fuel pump is mounted above the front sprocket cover **(see illustration 14.1c)**.

6 Make sure the fuel taps are turned OFF on TDM and XTZ models, and to ON or RES on TRX models. Release the clamps securing the various hoses to the pump and detach them from the pump, noting which fits where, and being prepared to catch any residue fuel in a suitable container.

7 Unscrew the nuts or bolts securing the pump and remove the pump, noting which way up it fits.

8 Install the new pump, making sure the hoses are correctly attached and secured by a

strong clamp. If the old ones are weakened or deformed, use new ones. There should be arrows cast into the pump at the fuel inlet and outlet unions denoting the direction of fuel flow. Attach the hose from the fuel tap to the union with the arrow pointing into the pump. Attach the hose to the carburettors to the union with the arrow pointing out of the pump. Attach the small-bore vacuum hose to the remaining union.

15 Fuel pump – check and renewal (1999 TDM models)

Check

1 The fuel pump circuit consists of the pump, the pump relay (housed in the relay unit), the igniter, the engine kill switch, the ignition switch, fuses, battery and associated wiring.

2 With the engine kill switch in the RUN position, the fuel pump should start and run for about five seconds after the ignition is switched ON. It should shut off once the carburettor float chambers are full, then run again once the engine is started. If the pump does not operate, first check that the main or ignition circuit fuse is not blown, and make sure that the battery is fully charged. If the fuses and battery are in good order, check the fuel pump circuit in a logical order as described below; be prepared to remove bodywork to access some of the components or wire connectors.

3 To check the ignition switch, first disconnect the battery negative lead, then trace the wiring from the ignition switch to its block connector. Separate the connector and using a continuity tester or ohmmeter, check for continuity between the red wire terminal and brown/blue wire terminal on the switch side of the connector with switch key rotated to the ON position. If continuity is indicated the switch is good, whereas no continuity (infinite resistance) indicates an open-circuit inside the switch. Join the connector halves.

4 To check the engine kill switch, trace the wiring from the right handlebar switch and disconnect the block connector. Separate the connector and using a continuity tester or ohmmeter, check for continuity between the red/wire and red/black wire terminals on the switch side of the connector with the kill switch in the RUN position. If continuity is indicated the switch is good, whereas no continuity (infinite resistance) indicates an open-circuit inside the switch. Join the connector halves.

5 Locate the starter circuit cut-off relay (see Chapter 9), disconnect its connector and move the relay unit to the bench for testing of the fuel pump relay. Using jumper wires connect the positive terminal of a 12 volt battery to the red/black wire terminal and the battery negative terminal to the blue/red wire terminal (see wiring diagram at the end of this

manual). Now connect an ohmmeter or continuity tester between the red/black wire terminal and blue/black wire terminal. Continuity should be shown. No continuity indicates a faulty fuel pump relay, and thus a new relay unit will be required. Install the relay on the motorcycle when testing is complete.

6 The fuel pump can be checked for correct operation by disconnecting its output hose (the hose between the pump and carburettor) and directing the hose end into a container suitable for the storage of fuel. Trace the 2-pin wire connection from the fuel pump and disconnect it. Using jumper wires and a 12 volt battery, connect the battery positive terminal to the black/blue wire terminal on the pump side of the connector and the battery negative terminal to the black wire terminal on the pump side of the connector **(see illustration)**. If the fuel pump is good it will be heard to operate and fuel will flow out of the hose. If the pump does not operate as described, it is faulty and must be renewed.

7 As a further check of the fuel pump, connect a multimeter set to the ohms scale between the two wire terminals on the pump side of its 2-pin wire connector. A reading of 4 to 10 ohms should be indicated.

8 If all the above components function correctly, yet the pump doesn't operate in circuit, the igniter unit is probably at fault. There are no test specifications for the igniter unit so it can only be tested by substitution of a known good igniter. Note that fuel pump failure could be due to a wire breakage between any of the components in the fuel pump circuit; check each wire and connector block for continuity before condemning the igniter.

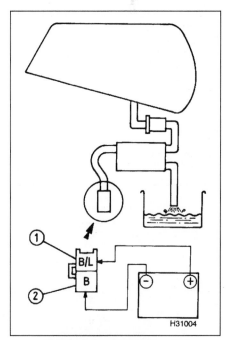

15.6 Fuel pump operation test

1 B/L (black/blue) wire terminal
2 B (black) wire terminal

9 When testing is complete, reconnect the battery negative lead.

Removal and installation

10 Remove the fuel tank (see Section 2). Detach the fuel hose from the carburettors or pump.
11 Trace the wiring from the fuel pump to the 2-pin connector and disconnect it.

12 Take note of the fuel inlet hose (from the tank and filter) and outlet line (to the carburettors) locations on the end of the fuel pump so that the hoses can be returned to their correct locations on installation **(see illustration)**. Place a rag under the fuel hose connections and squeeze the clamp ears together to allow the clamp to be drawn away from the union – the fuel inlet hose can be left

in place and the pump removed with the fuel filter if desired. Gently ease the fuel pump out of its clamp.
13 Installation is a reverse of the removal procedure. Make sure that you connect the fuel hoses the correct way around and check that there are no fuel leaks.

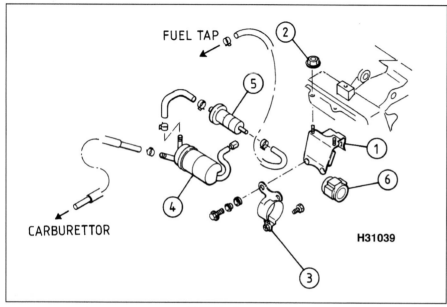

FUEL TAP

CARBURETTOR

H31039

15.12 Fuel pump

1	Mounting bracket	3	Clamp	5	Fuel filter
2	Nut – 2 off	4	Fuel pump	6	Filter rubber mounting

16 Carburettor warmer system – 1996-on TDM and TRX models

1 The carburettors are warmed by the engine's coolant passing through the body of the right-hand carburettor, then via a short link hose to the left-hand carburettor. A small-bore hose carries coolant from a take-off stub on the coolant pipe which locates in the valve cover on the engine right-hand side to the carburettors. From the body of the left-hand carburettor, the coolant is returned to the cooling system via a small-bore hose to a union at the base of the thermostat housing on TRX and 1991 to 1998 TDM models, and to a union next to the top hose connection on the radiator left-hand side on 1999 TDM models.
2 If you need to disconnect the coolant hoses there is no need to drain the cooling system. Use hose clamps (see *Tools and Workshop Tips* in the Reference section) to pinch the hoses whilst they are detached from their unions on the carburettors.

Chapter 5
Ignition system

Contents

Degrees of difficulty

| Easy, suitable for novice with little experience | | Fairly easy, suitable for beginner with some experience | | Fairly difficult, suitable for competent DIY mechanic | | Difficult, suitable for experienced DIY mechanic | | Very difficult, suitable for expert DIY or professional | |

Specifications

General information
Cylinder numbering
  Left 1
  Right 2
Spark plugs . . . . see Chapter 1

Ignition timing
At idle . . . . 10° BTDC
Full advance
  1991 to 1995 TDM models . . . . 42° BTDC @ 5000 rpm
  XTZ models . . . . 43° BTDC @ 6000 rpm
  1996-on TDM models and TRX models . . . . not available

Pick-up coil
Resistance
  1991 to 1995 TDM models and XTZ models . . . . 184 to 276 ohms @ 20°C
  1996-on TDM models and TRX models . . . . 192 to 288 ohms @ 20°C

Ignition HT coils
Primary winding resistance
  1991 to 1995 TDM models and all XTZ models . . . . 2.38 to 3.22 ohms @ 20°C
  1996-on TDM models and all TRX models . . . . 3.10 to 4.60 ohms @ 20°C
Secondary winding resistance (without plug cap)
  1991 to 1995 TDM models and all XTZ models . . . . 12.0 to 18.0 K-ohms @ 20°C
  1996-on TDM models and all TRX models . . . . 10.4 to 15.6 K-ohms @ 20°C
Spark plug cap resistance . . . . 10 K-ohms @ 20°C
Minimum spark gap (see Section 2) . . . . 6 mm

1 General information

All models are fitted with a fully transistorised electronic ignition system, which due to its lack of mechanical parts is totally maintenance free. The system comprises a rotor, pick-up coil, ignitor unit and ignition HT coil(s) (refer to the wiring diagrams at the end of Chapter 9 for details). All TRX models and 1996-on TDM models are fitted with two HT coils, while all other models have one coil supplying both cylinders. The TRX models and 1996-on TDM models are also fitted with a throttle position sensor.

The ignition triggers, which are on the alternator rotor on the left-hand end of the crankshaft, magnetically operate the pick-up coil as the crankshaft rotates. The pick-up coil sends a signal to the ignitor unit which then supplies the ignition HT coil(s) with the power necessary to produce a spark at the plugs. The ignitor incorporates an electronic advance system controlled by signals generated by the ignition triggers and the pick-up coil.

The ignitor is linked to the clutch and sidestand cut-off switches. This safety circuit prevents the bike being started in gear unless the clutch lever is pulled in, and prevents the bike being ridden with the sidestand down.

Because of their nature, the individual ignition system components can be checked but not repaired. If ignition system troubles occur, and the faulty component can be isolated, the only cure for the problem is to renew the part. Keep in mind that most electrical parts, once purchased, cannot be returned. To avoid unnecessary expense, make very sure the faulty component has been positively identified before buying a new part.

Note that there is no provision for adjusting the ignition timing on these models.

2 Ignition system – check

 Warning: The energy levels in electronic systems can be very high. On no account should the ignition be switched on whilst the plugs or plug caps are being held. Shocks from the HT circuit can be most unpleasant. Secondly, it is vital that the engine is not turned over or run with either of the plug caps removed, and that the plugs are soundly earthed (grounded) when the system is checked for sparking. The ignition system components can be seriously damaged if the HT circuit becomes isolated.

1 As no means of adjustment is available, any failure of the system can be traced to failure of a system component or a simple wiring fault. Of the two possibilities, the latter is by far the most likely. In the event of failure, check the system in a logical fashion, as described below.

2 Disconnect the HT leads from the spark plugs. Connect each lead to a spare spark plug and lay each plug on the engine with the threads contacting the engine **(see illustration)**. If necessary, hold each spark plug with an insulated tool.

 Warning: Do not remove the spark plugs from the engine to perform this check – atomised fuel being pumped out of an open spark plug hole could ignite, causing severe injury!

3 Having observed the above precautions, check that the kill switch is in the RUN position and the transmission is in neutral, then turn the ignition switch ON and turn the engine over on the starter motor. If the system is in good condition a regular, fat blue spark should be evident at each plug electrode. If the spark appears thin or yellowish, or is non-

existent, further investigation will be necessary. Before proceeding further, turn the ignition OFF.

4 The ignition system must be able to produce a spark which is capable of jumping a particular size gap. A healthy system should produce a spark capable of jumping at least 6 mm. A simple testing tool can be made to test the minimum gap across which the spark will jump (see **Tool Tip**) or alternatively it is possible to buy an ignition spark gap tester tool and some of these tools are adjustable to alter the spark gap.

A simple spark gap testing tool can be made from a block of wood, a large alligator clip and two nails, one of which is fashioned so that a spark plug cap or bare HT lead end can be connected to its end. Make sure the gap between the two nail ends is the same as specified.

5 Connect one of the spark plug HT leads to the protruding electrode on the test tool, and clip the tool to a good earth (ground) on the engine or frame **(see illustration)**. Check that the kill switch is in the RUN position, turn the ignition switch ON and turn the engine over on the starter motor. If the system is in good condition a regular, fat blue spark should be seen to jump the gap between the nail ends. On 1996-on TDM models and TRX models,

2.2 Earth the spark plug and operate the starter – bright blue sparks should be visible

2.5 Connect the tester as shown – when the starter is operated sparks should jump between the nails

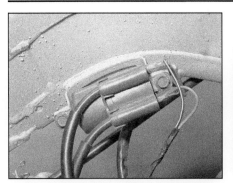

3.4a Ignition coil – 1991 to 1995 TDM models

3.4b Ignition coil – TRX models

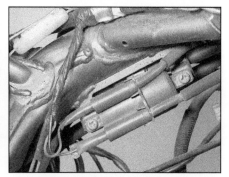

3.4c Ignition coil – XTZ models

repeat the test for the other coil. If the test results are good the entire ignition system can be considered good. If the spark appears thin or yellowish, or is non-existent, further investigation will be necessary.

6 Ignition faults can be divided into two categories, namely those where the ignition system has failed completely, and those which are due to a partial failure. The likely faults are listed below, starting with the most probable source of failure. Work through the list systematically, referring to the subsequent sections for full details of the necessary checks and tests. **Note:** *Before checking the following items ensure that the battery is fully charged and that all fuses are in good condition.*

a) *Loose, corroded or damaged wiring connections, broken or shorted wiring*

between any of the component parts of the ignition system (see Chapter 9).
b) *Faulty HT lead or spark plug cap, faulty spark plug, dirty, worn or corroded plug electrodes, or incorrect gap between electrodes.*
c) *Faulty ignition (main) switch or engine kill switch (see Chapter 9).*
d) *Faulty neutral, clutch or sidestand switch, and on XTZ models, diode (see Chapter 9).*
e) *Faulty pick-up coil or damaged rotor triggers.*
f) *Faulty ignition HT coil(s).*
g) *Faulty ignitor unit.*

7 If the above checks don't reveal the cause of the problem, have the ignition system tested by a Yamaha dealer equipped with diagnostic testing equipment.

3 Ignition HT coils – check, removal and installation

Check

1 The ignition HT coil(s) can be checked visually (for cracks and other damage) and the primary and secondary coil resistance can be measured with a multimeter. If the coil is undamaged, and if the resistance readings are as specified at the beginning of the Chapter, it is probably capable of proper operation, although note that sometimes a fault is only evident when the coil is under load and the engine running at high speed.

2 Remove the left-hand side cover (XTZ models) or the seat (all other models) (see Chapter 8).

3 Disconnect the battery negative (-ve) lead.

4 On TDM and TRX models, the coil(s) is/are mounted on the inside of the frame behind the steering head – remove the fuel tank and the air filter housing for access (see Chapter 4) **(see illustrations)**. On XTZ models, the coil is mounted underneath the rear of the fuel tank – remove the tank for access (see Chapter 4) **(see illustration)**.

5 Disconnect the primary circuit electrical connectors from the coil and the HT leads from the spark plugs. Mark the locations of all wires and leads before disconnecting them.

6 Set the meter to the ohms x 1 scale and measure the resistance between the primary circuit terminals on the coil **(see illustration)**. This will give a resistance reading of the primary windings of the coil and should be consistent with the value given in the Specifications at the beginning of the Chapter.

7 To check the condition of the secondary windings, unscrew the spark plug caps from the HT leads and set the meter to the K ohm scale. On 1991 to 1995 TDM models and XTZ models, connect one meter probe to one HT lead end and the other probe to the other HT lead end **(see illustration)**. On 1996-on TDM models and TRX models, connect the positive (+ve) meter probe to the HT lead end and the negative (-ve) probe to the red/black wire

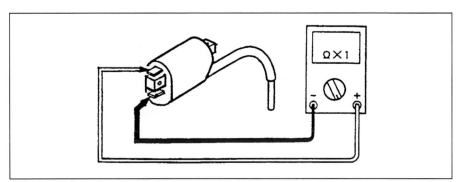

3.6 To test the coil primary resistance, connect the multimeter leads between the primary circuit terminals on the coil

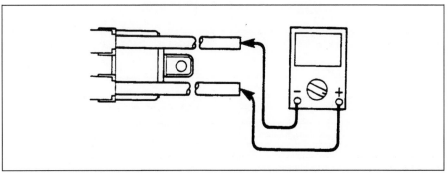

3.7a Coil secondary resistance test – 1991 to 1995 TDM and all XTZ models

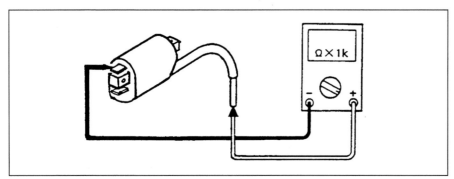

3.7b Coil secondary resistance test – 1996-on TDM and all TRX models

3.8 Measure the resistance of the spark plug cap

primary circuit terminal **(see illustration)**. If the reading obtained is not within the range shown in the Specifications, it is likely that the coil is defective.

8 If the reading is as specified, measure the resistance of the spark plug cap by connecting the meter probes between the HT lead socket in the cap and the spark plug contact in the cap **(see illustration)**. If the reading obtained is not as specified, renew the spark plug caps.

9 Should any of the above checks not produce the expected result, have your findings confirmed by a Yamaha dealer. If the coil is confirmed to be faulty, it must be renewed; the coil is a sealed unit and cannot therefore be repaired.

Removal

10 Remove the left-hand side cover (XTZ models) or the seat (all other models) (see Chapter 8). Disconnect the battery negative (-ve) lead.

11 On TDM and TRX models, the coil/s is/are mounted on the inside of the frame behind the steering head – remove the fuel tank and the air filter housing for access (see Chapter 4) **(see illustrations 3.4a and b)**. On XTZ models, the coil is mounted underneath the rear of the fuel tank – remove the tank for access (see Chapter 4) **(see illustration 3.4c)**.

12 Disconnect the primary circuit electrical connectors from the coil and disconnect the HT lead(s) from the spark plug(s). Mark the

locations of all wires and leads before disconnecting them.

13 Unscrew the two bolts or screws securing each coil, noting any spacers, and on TRX models the earth wire secured by one of the screws, and remove the coils **(see illustrations 3.4a, b and c)**. Note the routing of the HT leads.

Installation

14 Installation is the reverse of removal. Make sure the wiring connectors and HT leads are securely connected.

4 Pick-up coil – check and replacement

Check

1 On TDM and TRX models remove the seat, and on XTZ models remove the left-hand side cover (see Chapter 8). Disconnect the battery negative (-ve) lead.

2 On TRX models, remove the side covers (see Chapter 8).

3 Trace the pick-up coil/alternator wiring from the top of the alternator cover and disconnect it at the connector with the white/green and white/red (early TDM models) or green/white and blue/yellow (all other models) wires **(see illustrations)**. Using a multimeter set to the ohms x 100 scale, measure the resistance between the terminals on the pick-up coil side of the connector.

4 Compare the reading obtained with that given in the Specifications at the beginning of this Chapter. The pick-up coil must be renewed if the reading obtained differs greatly from that given, particularly if the meter indicates a short circuit (no measurable resistance) or an open circuit (infinite, or very high resistance).

5 If the pick-up coil is thought to be faulty, first check that this is not due to a damaged or broken wire from the coil to the connector; pinched or broken wires can usually be repaired.

Replacement

6 The pick-up coil is wired integrally with the alternator stator, which means that the stator must be removed and renewed along with the coil if the coil is faulty. However it is worth checking with a Yamaha dealer to see if the coil can be obtained separately and wired into the loom to avoid the extra expense of paying for a stator as well.

7 Refer to Chapter 9 for details of alternator stator/pick-up coil assembly removal.

5 Ignitor unit – check, removal and installation

Check

1 If the tests shown in the preceding or following Sections have failed to isolate the

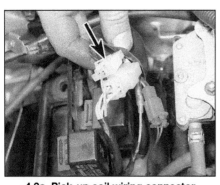

4.3a Pick-up coil wiring connector (arrowed) – TDM models

4.3b Pick-up coil wiring connector (arrowed) – TRX models

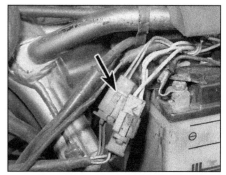

4.3c Pick-up coil wiring connector (arrowed) – XTZ models

5.3a Ignitor unit – TDM and TRX models

5.3b Ignitor unit – XTZ models

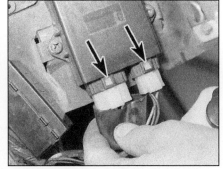

5.4 Disconnect the wiring connectors (arrowed)

cause of an ignition fault, it is possible that the ignitor unit itself is faulty. No test details are available with which the unit can be tested on home workshop equipment. Take the machine to a Yamaha dealer for testing.

Removal

2 On TDM and TRX models remove the seat, and on XTZ models remove the left-hand side cover and right-hand fairing side panel (see Chapter 8). Disconnect the battery negative (-ve) lead.
3 On TDM and TRX models the ignitor is mounted under the seat, and on XTZ models it is mounted in the fairing **(see illustrations)**.
4 Disconnect the wiring connectors from the ignitor unit **(see illustration)**.
5 Remove the screws securing the ignitor unit and remove the unit.

Installation

6 Installation is the reverse of removal. Make sure the wiring connectors are correctly and securely connected.

---

6 Ignition timing – general information and check

General information

1 Since no provision exists for adjusting the ignition timing and since no component is subject to mechanical wear, there is no need for regular checks; only if investigating a fault such as a loss of power or a misfire, should the ignition timing be checked.
2 The ignition timing is checked dynamically (engine running) using a stroboscopic lamp. The inexpensive neon lamps should be adequate in theory, but in practice may produce a pulse of such low intensity that the timing mark remains indistinct. If possible, one of the more precise xenon tube lamps should be used, powered by an external source of the appropriate voltage. **Note:** *Do not use the machine's own battery as an incorrect reading may result from stray impulses within the machine's electrical system.*

Check

3 Warm the engine up to normal operating temperature then stop it.
4 Unscrew the timing inspection plug from the alternator cover **(see illustration)**. Discard the cover O-ring as a new one must be used.
5 The timing mark on the alternator rotor which indicates the firing point at idle speed for the no. 1 cylinder is a 'I I' mark. The static timing mark with which this should align is the notch in the threads for the inspection plug on the alternator cover **(see illustration)**.
6 Connect the timing light to the no. 1 cylinder HT lead as described in the manufacturer's instructions.

> **HAYNES HINT** *The timing marks can be highlighted with white paint to make them more visible under the stroboscope light.*

7 Start the engine and aim the light at the static timing mark.
8 With the machine idling at the specified speed, the static timing mark should lie between the two vertical lines 'I I'.
9 Slowly increase the engine speed whilst observing the 'I I' mark. The mark should move clockwise, increasing in relation to the engine speed until it reaches full advance (no identification mark).
10 As already stated, there is no means of adjustment of the ignition timing on these machines. If the ignition timing is incorrect, or suspected of being incorrect, one of the

6.4 Unscrew the timing inspection plug (arrowed)

ignition system components is at fault, and the system must be tested as described in the preceding Sections of this Chapter.
11 When the check is complete, install the timing inspection plug using a new O-ring and tighten it securely.

---

7 Throttle position sensor (1996-on TDM and TRX) – check, adjustment and replacement

1 The throttle position sensor is located on the side of the left-hand carburettor and is keyed to the end of the throttle operating shaft. The sensor provides the ignitor unit with information relating to throttle opening and the ignitor is thus able to set the ignition timing accordingly to produce the best running conditions and cleaner exhaust emissions. Not surprisingly it is essential that the throttle position sensor should be set up correctly. Do not tamper with the sensor's position unless it has been disturbed during carburettor overhaul or poor running problems have been experienced.
2 When the engine is running, the throttle position sensor performs its own self-diagnosis in the event of failure or faulty wiring. When this diagnosis occurs, the tachometer will be seen to display zero rpm for 3 seconds, then 3000 rpm for 2.5 seconds, then the actual engine speed for 3 seconds, whereupon it will repeat the cycle until the engine is switched off.

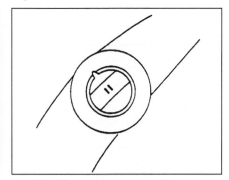

6.5 Ignition timing marks at idle speed

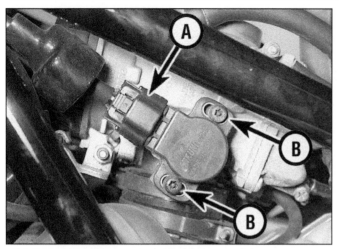

7.3 Throttle position sensor wiring connector (A) and mounting screws (B)

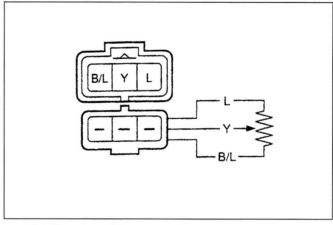

7.4 Throttle position sensor wiring connector terminals

B/L   Black and blue   L   Blue
Y   Yellow

Check

3 Remove the fuel tank and the air filter housing (see Chapter 4). The throttle sensor is mounted on the outside of the left-hand carburettor **(see illustration)**.

4 Make sure that the ignition is OFF, then disconnect the throttle sensor's wire connector. Using a multimeter set on the K-ohms range, measure the resistance between the blue and black/blue wire terminals on the throttle sensor half of the connector; 3.5 to 6.5 K-ohms should be shown **(see illustration)**. Now measure the resistance between the yellow and black/blue wire terminals on the same half of the connector; whilst rotating the throttle grip slowly the resistance should vary between 0 to 5 K-ohms ± 1.5 K-ohm. If either test does not produce the correct readings the throttle sensor should be renewed.

5 If the fault cannot be traced to the throttle sensor, check all three wires between the ignitor and throttle sensor for continuity. Check for continuity between one end to the other on each wire. If no continuity is indicated, this is probably due to a damaged or broken wire between the connectors; pinched or broken wires can usually be repaired. If the wiring and connectors are good, check the adjustment of the sensor as described below.

6 If the sensor is suspected of being faulty, take it to a Yamaha dealer for further testing. If it is confirmed to be faulty, it must be renewed; the sensor is a sealed unit and cannot therefore be repaired. If the sensor is good, have the ignitor checked by the dealer.

Adjustment

7 Before adjusting the sensor, check the idle speed and carburettor synchronisation (see Chapter 1).

8 Turn the ignition switch ON, then disconnect and reconnect the sensor wiring connector. This sets the ignitor unit to sensor adjustment mode.

9 Slacken the sensor mounting screws and rotate the sensor until the tachometer needle reads 4000 rpm. If the tachometer reads either 1000 rpm or 8000 rpm, the angle of the sensor is either too narrow or too wide. Adjust it as required until the reading is 4000 rpm, then tighten the screws.

10 To come out of the adjustment mode, start the engine or simply turn the ignition switch OFF.

Replacement

11 Remove the carburettors (see Chapter 4).

12 The throttle sensor is mounted on the outside of the left-hand carburettor **(see illustration 7.3)**. Disconnect the wiring connector, then unscrew the sensor mounting screws and remove the sensor, noting how it fits. Retrieve the seal from behind the sensor as it is withdrawn. On TRX models and 1991 to 1998 TDM models the sensor mounts on a plate which is itself secured to the carburettor body by two screws.

13 Install the sensor and lightly tighten the screws. After installing the carburettors follow the adjustment procedure above to set the correct sensor position.

Chapter 6
Frame, suspension and final drive

Contents

Degrees of difficulty

Easy, suitable for novice with little experience	Fairly easy, suitable for beginner with some experience	Fairly difficult, suitable for competent DIY mechanic	Difficult, suitable for experienced DIY mechanic	Very difficult, suitable for expert DIY or professional

Specifications

Front forks

Fork oil type
  1996-on TDM models . . . . Suspension oil 01
  All other models . . . . 10W fork oil
Fork oil capacity
  1991 to 1995 TDM models . . . . 395 cc
  1996-on TDM models . . . . 515 cc
  TRX models . . . . 483 cc
  XTZ models . . . . 669 cc
Fork oil level*
  1991 to 1995 TDM models . . . . 151 mm
  1996-on TDM models, TRX models and XTZ models . . . . 130 mm
Fork spring free length
  1991 to 1995 TDM models
    Standard . . . . 427 mm
    Service limit . . . . 406 mm
  1996-on TDM models
    Standard . . . . 505 mm
    Service limit . . . . 500 mm
  TRX models
    Standard . . . . 385 mm
    Service limit . . . . 381 mm
  XTZ models
    Standard . . . . 544.5 mm
    Service limit . . . . 517 mm
Fork tube runout limit . . . . 0.2 mm
*Oil level is measured from the top of the tube with the fork spring removed and the leg fully compressed.

Rear suspension

Shock absorber spring free length
   TDM models
      Main spring . . . . 144 mm
      Sub spring . . . . 69 mm
   TRX models . . . . 220.5 mm
   XTZ models . . . . 240 mm
Swingarm – XTZ models
   Side clearance . . . . 0.4 to 0.7 mm
   Bearing spacer length (right-hand) . . . . 90.95 to 91.10 mm
   Bearing spacer length (left-hand) . . . . 80.95 to 81.10 mm
   Washer thickness . . . . 1.9 to 2.0 mm

Final drive chain

Chain size
   TDM and TRX models 525
   XTZ model 520
No. of links
   TDM model 114
   TRX model 110
   XTZ model 112
Chain freeplay and lubricant . . . . see Chapter 1
Chain stretch limit (10-link length)
   1991 to 1995 TDM models . . . . 150 mm
   1996-on TDM models . . . . 159 mm
   TRX models . . . . 155 mm
   XTZ models . . . . 150 mm

Torque settings

Footrest bracket bolts – TDM and TRX models . . . . 30 Nm
Footrest bracket bolts – XTZ models
   Front . . . . 45 Nm
   Rear . . . . 20 Nm
Brake pedal pivot bolt – TRX models . . . . 35 Nm
Handlebar holder clamp bolts – TDM models . . . . 23 Nm
Handlebar holder clamp bolts – XTZ models . . . . 20 Nm
Handlebar retaining bolt – TRX models . . . . 23 Nm
Handlebar holder positioning bolt – TRX models . . . . 10 Nm
Handlebar holder clamp bolt – TRX models . . . . 17 Nm
Fork clamp bolts
   TDM and XTZ models . . . . 23 Nm
   TRX models
      Top yoke . . . . 23 Nm
      Bottom yoke . . . . 30 Nm
Fork top bolt
   TDM models . . . . 24 Nm
   TRX and XTZ models . . . . 23 Nm
Fork damper rod bolt – TDM and TRX models . . . . 30 Nm
Fork damper rod bolt – XTZ models . . . . 62 Nm
Steering stem nut
   1991 to 1995 TDM models . . . . 110 Nm
   1996-on TDM models . . . . 108 Nm
   TRX models . . . . 110 Nm
Steering stem bolt (XTZ models) . . . . 80 Nm
Rear shock absorber mounting bolt nuts – TDM models . . . . 64 Nm
Rear shock absorber mounting bolt nuts – TRX models . . . . 40 Nm
Rear shock absorber mounting bolt nuts – XTZ models . . . . 35 Nm
Suspension linkage bolt nuts – TRX models . . . . 48 Nm
Suspension linkage bolt nuts – XTZ models . . . . 59 Nm
Swingarm pivot bolt nut
   TDM and XTZ models . . . . 90 Nm
   TRX models . . . . 125 Nm
Rear brake torque arm nuts – TRX models . . . . 30 Nm
Front sprocket nut . . . . 70 Nm
Rear sprocket nuts
   TDM and TRX models . . . . 60 Nm
   XTZ models . . . . 55 Nm
Gearchange linkage arm pinch bolt . . . . 12 Nm
Outer sprocket cover bolts . . . . 5 Nm

3.1a Note how the spring end (arrowed) locates

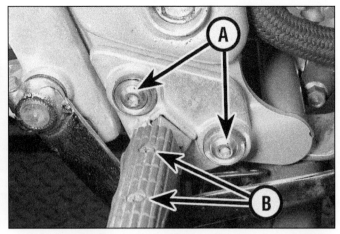

3.1b Footrest bracket bolts (A), footrest rubber screws (B)

1 General information

TDM models use a twin spar box-section aluminium frame which uses the engine as a stressed member.

TRX models use a trellis-type steel tube frame which uses the engine as a stressed member.

XTZ models use a cradle-type steel frame.

Front suspension is by a pair of oil-damped telescopic forks. On XTZ models, the forks have a conventional damper system, while TDM and TRX models have a cartridge damper. On TDM and TRX models the forks are adjustable for pre-load and rebound damping.

At the rear, an aluminium swingarm acts on a single shock absorber, on TRX and XTZ models via a three-way linkage. The shock absorber is adjustable for spring pre-load on all models, for rebound damping on TDM models, and for both rebound and compression damping on TRX models. On TRX models, the shock absorber has a remote reservoir.

The drive to the rear wheel is by chain.

2 Frame – inspection and repair

1 The frame should not require attention unless accident damage has occurred. In most cases, frame renewal is the only satisfactory remedy for such damage. A few frame specialists have the jigs and other equipment necessary for straightening the frame to the required standard of accuracy, but even then there is no simple way of assessing to what extent the frame may have been over stressed.

2 After the machine has accumulated a lot of miles, the frame should be examined closely

for signs of cracking or splitting at the welded joints. Loose engine mount bolts can cause ovaling or fracturing of the mounting tabs. Minor damage can often be repaired by welding, depending on the extent and nature of the damage. This is, however, a job for a frame specialist, especially where an aluminium frame is concerned.

3 Remember that a frame which is out of alignment will cause handling problems. If misalignment is suspected as the result of an accident, it will be necessary to strip the machine completely so the frame can be thoroughly checked.

3 Footrests, brake pedal and gearchange lever – removal and installation

Footrests

Removal – front footrests

1 On TDM models, remove the rubber cap from the back of the footrest bracket, then unscrew the nut and separate the footrest from the bracket, noting how the return spring end locates in the bracket (see illustration). For easier access to the nut, first unscrew the

two bolts securing the bracket and remove it (see illustration). The footrest rubber can be renewed by removing the two screws that secure it to the footrest.

2 On TRX models, unscrew the nut from the back of the footrest bracket and separate the peg from the bracket. The footrest rubber can be renewed by removing the two screws that secure it to the footrest. For easier access to the nut, first remove the brake pedal or gearchange lever (see below), then unscrew the bolts securing the footrest bracket and displace it.

3 On XTZ models, remove the split pin and washer (where fitted) from the bottom of the footrest pivot pin, then withdraw the pivot pin and remove the footrest (see illustration). Note the fitting of the return spring. The footrest rubber can be renewed by removing the two bolts that secure it to the peg.

Removal – rear footrests

4 On 1991 to 1995 TDM models, remove the split pin from the bottom of the footrest pivot pin, then withdraw the pivot pin and remove the footrest (see illustration). Note the fitting of the detent plate, ball and spring, and take care that they do not spring out when removing the footrest. Also note the collar for the pivot pin. The footrest rubber can be

3.3 Remove the split pin (A) and withdraw the pivot pin, noting how the spring ends locate (B)

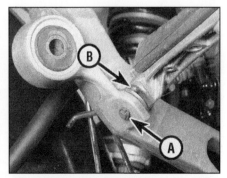

3.4 Remove the split pin (A) and withdraw the pivot pin, noting how the detent plate and ball fit (B)

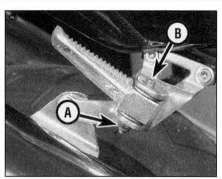

3.6 Unscrew the nut (A) and withdraw the bolt (B)

3.7 Remove the split pin (arrowed) and withdraw the pivot pin

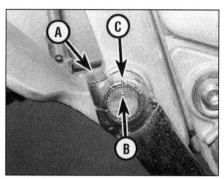

3.9a Remove the pinch bolt (A) and slide the pedal off the shaft. Note the alignment of the punch mark (B) with the notch (C)

renewed by removing the two screws that secure it to the footrest.

5 On 1996-on TDM models, unscrew the nut from the bottom of the footrest pivot bolt, then withdraw the bolt and remove the footrest. Note the fitting of the detent plates, ball and spring, and take care that they do not spring out when removing the footrest. Also note the collar for the pivot bolt. The footrest rubber can be renewed by removing the two screws that secure it to the footrest.

6 On TRX models, unscrew the nut from the bottom of the footrest pivot bolt, then withdraw the bolt and remove the footrest. Note the fitting of the detent plates, ball and spring, and take care that they do not spring out when removing the footrest (see illustration). Also note the collar for the pivot bolt.

7 On XTZ models, remove the split pin and washer (where fitted) from the bottom of the footrest pivot pin, then withdraw the pivot pin and remove the footrest (see illustration). The footrest rubber can be renewed by removing the washer and drawing the rubber off the footrest. If it is stuck fast, slit it with a sharp knife.

Installation

8 Installation is the reverse of removal. On TDM and TRX models, if removed, tighten the front footrest bracket bolts to the torque setting specified at the beginning of the chapter.

Brake pedal

Removal

9 On TDM models, note the alignment of the notch in the top of the pedal with the punch mark on the shaft, then unscrew and remove the pinchbolt and slide the arm off the shaft (see illustration). If required, unhook the brake pedal return spring and the brake light switch spring from the bracket on the inside of the pedal shaft, then remove the split pin from the clevis pin securing the master cylinder pushrod to the bracket (see illustration). Remove the clevis pin and separate the pushrod from the bracket, then draw the shaft assembly out of the frame.

10 On TRX models, unhook the brake pedal return spring and the brake light switch spring from the bracket on the pedal. Remove the split pin from the clevis pin securing the brake pedal to the master cylinder pushrod (see illustration). Remove the clevis pin and separate the pushrod from the pedal. Unscrew the pedal pivot bolt and remove the pedal. If required, remove the screw securing the spring bracket to the inside of the pedal and remove the bracket.

11 On XTZ models, unhook the brake pedal return spring and the brake light switch spring from the bracket on the pedal. Remove the split pin from the clevis pin securing the brake

pedal to the master cylinder pushrod. Remove the clevis pin and separate the pushrod from the pedal. Remove the split pin holding the pedal pivot in the frame and remove the pedal. Discard the split pin as a new one must be used.

Installation

12 Installation is the reverse of removal, noting the following:

a) Apply molybdenum disulphide grease to the brake pedal pivot, or on TDM models, the unsplined section of the shaft.

b) On TRX models, tighten the pedal pivot bolt securely.

c) Use a new split pin on the clevis pin securing the brake pedal to the master cylinder pushrod, and on XTZ models on the brake pedal pivot..

d) Check the operation of the rear brake light switch (see Chapter 1).

Gearchange lever

Removal

13 On TDM and XTZ models, unscrew the bolts securing the outer front sprocket cover and remove the cover (see illustration).

14 To remove the lever on its own, slacken the gearchange lever linkage rod locknuts, then unscrew the rod and separate it from the

3.9b Unhook the springs and separate the pushrod from the bracket (arrowed)

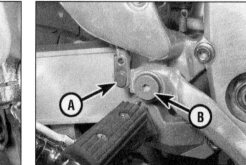

3.10 Unhook the springs at the back, then remove the clevis pin (A) and unscrew the pivot bolt (B)

3.13 Sprocket cover bolts (arrowed)

3.14a Slacken the locknuts (arrowed) and thread the rod out of the lever and arm

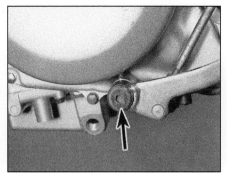

3.14b Unscrew the pivot bolt . . .

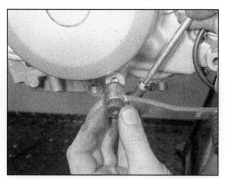

3.14c . . . and remove the lever, noting the washers

lever and the arm (the rod is reverse-threaded on one end and so will simultaneously unscrew from both lever and arm when turned in the one direction) **(see illustration)**. Note the how far the rod is threaded into the lever and arm as this determines the height of the lever relative to the footrest. Unscrew the pivot bolt and remove the lever, noting the arrangement of the washers **(see illustrations)**.

15 To remove the lever with the linkage rod and arm as an assembly, first note the alignment of the punch mark on the gearchange shaft with the slit in the linkage arm, then unscrew the linkage arm pinchbolt and slide the arm off the shaft **(see illustrations)**. Now unscrew the lever pivot bolt and remove the lever and linkage assembly, noting how it fits **(see illustrations 3.14b and c)**.

Installation

16 Installation is the reverse of removal, noting the following:

a) *Apply molybdenum disulphide oil to the gear lever pivot.*

b) *Align the punch mark on the shaft with the slit in the clamp as noted on removal (see illustrations 3.15a and b).*

c) *Tighten the gearchange lever pivot bolt securely.*

d) *Adjust the gear lever height as required by screwing the rod in or out of the lever and arm. Tighten the locknuts securely (see illustration 3.14a).*

3.15a Linkage arm/shaft alignment – TDM models

4 Sidestand –
removal and installation

1 Support the bike using an auxiliary stand.
2 On TDM and XTZ models, unhook the stand springs, then counter-hold the pivot bolt and unscrew the nut on the inside of the bracket **(see illustration)**. Withdraw the pivot bolt and remove the stand, noting how it locates against the sidestand switch plunger.
3 On TRX models, unhook the stand springs, then unscrew the retaining bolt **(see illustration)**. Slide the stand off its pivot, noting how it fits. If required, counter-hold the pivot piece and unscrew the nut

3.15b Linkage arm/shaft alignment – TRX models

securing it in the bracket, then withdraw the pivot.
4 On installation apply grease to the pivot and a suitable non-permanent thread locking compound to the bolt threads. Tighten the nut/bolt securely. Reconnect the sidestand spring and check that it holds the stand securely up when not in use – an accident is almost certain to occur if the stand extends while the machine is in motion.
5 Check the operation of the sidestand switch (see Chapter 1).

5 Handlebars and levers –
removal and installation

Handlebars

Removal

Note: *The handlebars can be displaced from the top yoke without having to remove any of the lever or switch assemblies. On TRX models, the handlebars can be removed from the handlebar holders which clamp around the top of the forks, leaving the holders in place.*
1 Displace the front brake master cylinder and reservoir (see Chapter 7). There is no need to disconnect the hydraulic hose. Keep the reservoir upright to prevent possible fluid leakage and make sure no strain is placed on the hydraulic hose(s).
2 Displace the throttle cable housing from the handlebars (see Chapter 4). There is no need

4.2 Sidestand pivot bolt (arrowed) – TDM models

4.3 Sidestand retaining bolt (arrowed) – TRX models

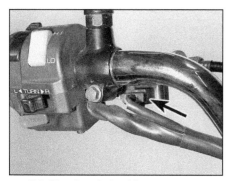

5.3 Clutch switch wiring connector (arrowed) – TDM models

5.5a On TDM models, remove the blanking caps

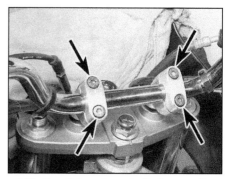

5.5b Handlebar clamp bolts (arrowed) – TDM models

to detach the cables from the carburettors.

3 Either remove the clutch lever (see below), or detach the clutch cable from the lever (see Chapter 2). Disconnect the clutch switch wiring connector (see Chapter 9) **(see illustration)**.

4 Displace the handlebar switches (see Chapter 9). There is no need to disconnect the wiring connectors.

5 On TDM models, lever out the handlebar holder clamp bolt blanking caps **(see illustration)**. On TDM and XTZ models, unscrew the handlebar holder clamp bolts and remove the handlebars, noting how the choke knob fits, where appropriate **(see illustrations)**.

6 On TRX models, to remove the handlebar

and leave the holder in place, remove the blanking cap from the inner end of the handlebar, then unscrew the retaining bolt and slide the bar out of the holder, noting how it locates **(see illustration)**.

7 On TRX models, to remove the handlebar and holder together, remove the blanking cap from the holder positioning bolt, then unscrew the bolt **(see illustration)**. Slacken the handlebar holder clamp bolt, then ease the handlebar holder up and off the fork.

Installation

8 Installation is the reverse of removal, noting the following.

a) On TDM models, align the mark on the front of the handlebars with the mating

surfaces of the holder **(see illustration)**. Make sure the handlebars are centrally positioned. Install the holder clamp with the arrow pointing up, then tighten the front clamp bolt first, followed by the rear bolt, to the torque setting specified at the beginning of the Chapter **(see illustrations)**.

b) On XTZ models, make sure the handlebars are centrally positioned. Install the holder clamp with the punch mark pointing forward, then tighten the front clamp bolt first, followed by the rear bolt, to the torque setting specified at the beginning of the Chapter.

c) On TRX models, if separated, make sure the flat on the inner end of the handlebar

5.5c Handlebar clamp bolts – XTZ models

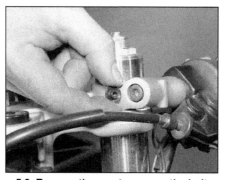

5.6 Remove the cap to access the bolt

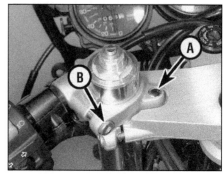

5.7 Remove the cap and unscrew the positioning bolt (A), then slacken the clamp bolt (B)

5.8a Align the mark (arrowed) with the clamp mating surfaces

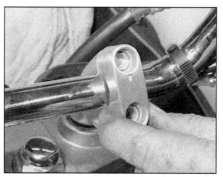

5.8b Fit the clamps with the arrow pointing up . . .

5.8c . . . and tighten the bolts as described to the specified torque

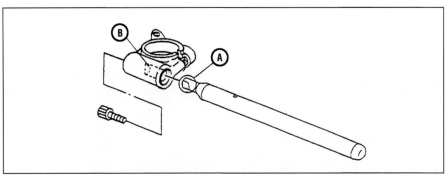

5.8d Ensure that the flat (A) aligns with the cut-out (B)

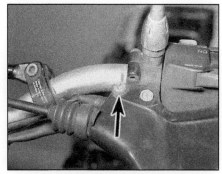

5.9 Handguard retaining screw – XTZ models

aligns correctly with the corresponding cut-out in the holder *(see illustration)*. Tighten the retaining bolts, positioning bolts and clamp bolts to the torque settings specified at the beginning of the Chapter. Tighten the positioning bolt before the clamp bolt.

d) *Refer to the relevant Chapters as directed for the installation of the handlebar mounted assemblies*

e) *Do not forget to reconnect the front brake light switch and clutch switch wiring connectors.*

Clutch lever

9 On XTZ models, remove the hand guard **(see illustration)**.

10 Slacken the clutch cable adjuster lockring and thread the adjuster fully into the bracket to provide maximum freeplay in the cable **(see illustration)**. Unscrew the lever pivot bolt locknut, then withdraw the pivot bolt and remove the lever, detaching the cable nipple via the slots in the adjuster and lockring. On TRX models, note the collar for the pivot bolt.

11 Installation is the reverse of removal. Apply grease to the pivot bolt shaft, or on TRX models to the collar, and the contact areas between the lever and its bracket, and to the clutch cable nipple. Adjust the clutch cable freeplay (see Chapter 1).

Front brake lever

12 On XTZ models, remove the hand guard **(see illustration 5.9)**.

13 On TDM models, remove the cap from the end of the master cylinder pushrod in the lever, then remove the E-clip, the nut, the spring and the plate **(see illustration)**.

14 Unscrew the lever pivot bolt locknut, then withdraw the pivot bolt and remove the lever **(see illustration)**.

15 Installation is the reverse of removal. Apply grease to the pivot bolt shaft and the contact areas between the lever and its bracket. On TDM models, locate the master cylinder pushrod through the pivot in the lever, and install the plate, the spring, the nut, the E-clip and the cap.

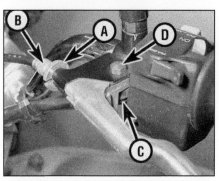

5.10 Slacken the lockring (A) and turn the adjuster (B) fully in, then unscrew the nut (C) and withdraw the pivot bolt (D) to free the lever

6 Forks – removal and installation

Removal

Caution: Although not strictly necessary, before removing the forks it is recommended that the fairing panels and/or fairing are removed (see Chapter 8). This will prevent accidental damage to the paintwork.

1 Remove the front wheel (see Chapter 7).

2 Remove the front mudguard (see Chapter 8).

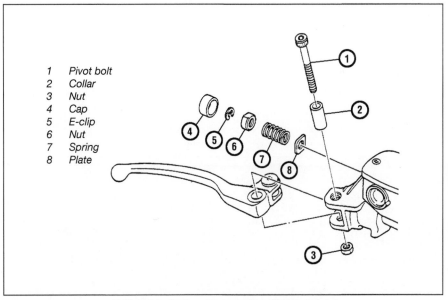

1 Pivot bolt
2 Collar
3 Nut
4 Cap
5 E-clip
6 Nut
7 Spring
8 Plate

5.13 Brake lever components – TDM models

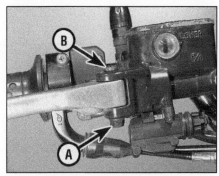

5.14 Unscrew the nut (A) and withdraw the bolt (B)

6.3 Brake hose clamp bolt (arrowed)

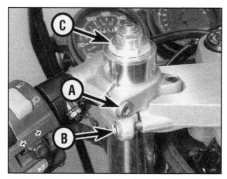

6.4 Handlebar holder clamp bolt (A), fork clamp bolt (B), fork top bolt (C)

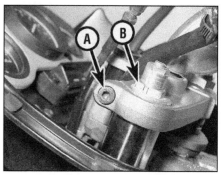

6.5 Slacken the fork clamp bolt (A), and if required the fork top bolt (B)

3 Unscrew the brake hose clamp bolt from each fork slider **(see illustration)**. If not already done, displace the front brake calipers (see Chapter 7). There is no need to disconnect the hydraulic hoses. Release the speedometer cable from any guides, and loosen any cable ties around the top of the fork tubes.
4 On TRX models, slacken the handlebar holder clamp bolts **(see illustration)**.
5 Slacken the fork clamp bolts in the top yoke

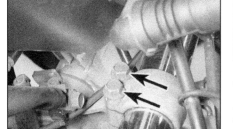

6.6a Slacken the bottom yoke fork clamp bolts (arrowed) . . .

(see illustration). If the forks are to be disassembled, or if the fork oil is being changed, it is advisable to slacken the fork top bolts at this stage.
6 Note the alignment or amount of protrusion of the tops of the fork tubes with the top yoke. Slacken but do not remove the fork clamp bolts in the bottom yoke, and remove the forks by twisting them and pulling them downwards **(see illustrations)**.

 HAYNES HINT *If the fork legs are seized in the yokes, spray the area with penetrating oil and allow time for it to soak in before trying again.*

Installation

7 Remove all traces of corrosion from the fork tubes and the yokes. Slide the forks up through the bottom yoke, then install the wiring ties where appropriate onto the forks **(see illustration 6.6b)**. Slide the forks up into the top yoke. Check that the amount of protrusion of the fork tube above the top yoke is as noted on removal and equal on both

sides. On TDM and XTZ models, the tops of the tubes should be flush with the top of the top yoke. On TRX models, the top of the fork tube should protrude 18.5 mm above the top of the handlebar holder.
8 Tighten the fork clamp bolts in the bottom yoke to the torque setting specified at the beginning of the Chapter **(see illustration 6.6a)**. If the fork legs have been dismantled or if the fork oil has been changed, the fork top bolts should now be tightened to the specified torque setting. Now tighten the fork clamp bolts in the top yoke, and on TRX models the handlebar holder clamp bolts, to the specified torque settings **(see illustration and 6.4)**.
9 Install the front wheel (see Chapter 7), the front mudguard (see Chapter 8), and the brake calipers (see Chapter 7). Fit the brake hose clamps onto the mudguard **(see illustration 6.3)**. On all models except the 1999 TDM, make sure the speedometer cable is routed through its guide(s). On 1999 TDM models make sure that the speedometer sensor lead is well secured by its ties.
10 Check the operation of the front forks and brakes before taking the machine out on the road.

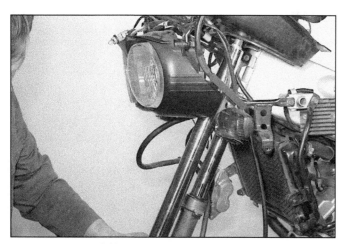

6.6b . . . and remove the forks

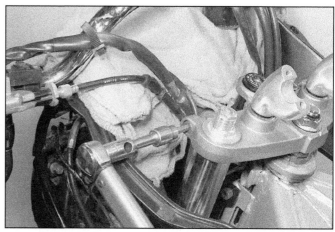

6.8 Tighten the various clamp bolts to their specified torque settings

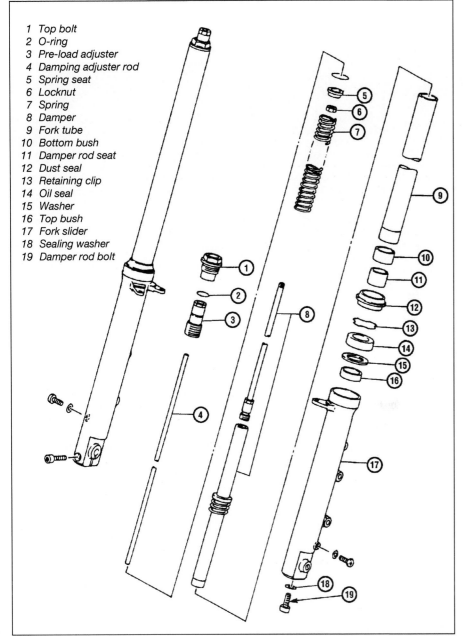

1 Top bolt
2 O-ring
3 Pre-load adjuster
4 Damping adjuster rod
5 Spring seat
6 Locknut
7 Spring
8 Damper
9 Fork tube
10 Bottom bush
11 Damper rod seat
12 Dust seal
13 Retaining clip
14 Oil seal
15 Washer
16 Top bush
17 Fork slider
18 Sealing washer
19 Damper rod bolt

7.1 Front fork components – 1991 to 1995 **TDM** models

7 Forks – disassembly, inspection and reassembly

1991 to 1995 TDM models
Disassembly
1 Always dismantle the fork legs separately to avoid interchanging parts and thus causing an accelerated rate of wear. Store all components in separate, clearly marked containers **(see illustration)**.
2 Before dismantling the fork, it is advised that the damper rod bolt be slackened at this stage. Compress the fork tube in the slider so that the spring exerts maximum pressure on the damper rod head, then have an assistant slacken the damper rod bolt in the base of the fork slider **(see illustration)**.
3 If the fork top bolt was not slackened with the fork in situ, carefully clamp the fork tube in a vice equipped with soft jaws, taking care not to overtighten or score its surface, and slacken the top bolt.
4 Unscrew the fork top bolt from the top of the fork tube **(see illustration)**. The bolt can remain threaded on the pre-load adjuster, but remove it by holding the adjuster and unscrewing it if required **(see illustration)**.
5 Carefully clamp the fork slider in a vice and slide the fork tube down into the slider a little way (wrap a rag around the top of the tube to minimise oil spillage) while, with the aid of an assistant if necessary, keeping the damper rod fully extended. Counter-hold the pre-load adjuster and thread the locknut to the base of its threads **(see illustration)**. Now counter-

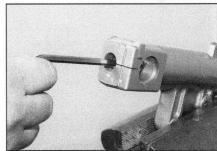

7.2 Slacken the damper rod Allen bolt

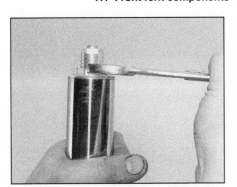

7.4a Unscrew the top bolt from the fork tube . . .

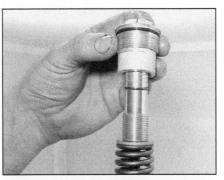

7.4b . . . and thread it off the adjuster if required

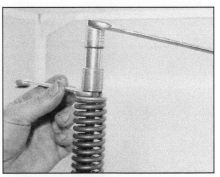

7.5 Remove the pre-load adjuster as described

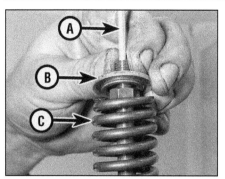

7.6 Withdraw the damping adjuster rod (A), then remove the spring seat (B) and withdraw the spring (C)

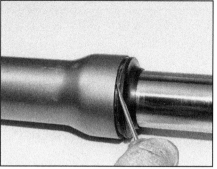

7.10 Prise out the dust seal using a flat-bladed screwdriver

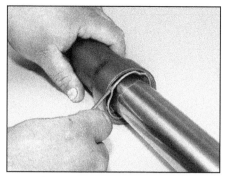

7.11 Prise out the retaining clip using a flat-bladed screwdriver

hold the locknut and thread the pre-load adjuster (with the top bolt if not removed) off the damper rod.

6 Remove the damping adjuster rod from the centre of the damper rod, then remove the spring seat and withdraw the spring from the tube, noting which way up it fits **(see illustration)**.

7 Invert the fork leg over a suitable container and pump the fork and the damper rod vigorously to expel as much fork oil as possible.

8 Remove the previously slackened damper rod bolt and its copper sealing washer from the bottom of the slider. Discard the sealing washer as a new one must be used on

reassembly. If the damper rod bolt was not slackened before dismantling the fork, use the Yamaha service tool (90890-01447) to prevent the damper rod from turning. This tool is passed down through the fork tube and engages the damper rod head; a similar tool can be easily made in the home workshop.

9 Invert the fork and withdraw the damper rod from inside the fork tube **(see illustration 7.20a)**.

10 Carefully prise out the dust seal from the top of the slider to gain access to the oil seal retaining clip **(see illustration)**. Discard the dust seal as a new one must be used.

11 Carefully remove the retaining clip, taking care not to scratch the surface of the tube **(see illustration)**.

12 To separate the tube from the slider it is necessary to displace the top bush and oil seal. The bottom bush should not pass through the top bush, and this can be used to good effect. Push the tube gently inwards until it stops against the damper rod seat. Take care not to do this forcibly or the seat may be damaged. Then pull the tube sharply outwards until the bottom bush strikes the top bush. Repeat this operation until the top bush and seal are tapped out of the slider **(see illustration)**.

13 With the tube removed, slide off the oil seal, washer and top bush, noting which way up they fit **(see illustration)**. Discard the oil seal as a new one must be used.

Caution: Do not remove the bottom bush from the tube unless it is to be renewed.

14 Tip the damper rod seat out of the slider, noting which way up it fits.

Inspection

15 Clean all parts in solvent and blow them dry with compressed air, if available. Check the fork tube for score marks, scratches, flaking of the chrome finish and excessive or abnormal wear. Look for dents in the tube and renew the tube in both forks if any are found. Check the fork seal seat for nicks, gouges and scratches. If damage is evident, leaks will occur. Also check the oil seal washer for damage or distortion and renew it if necessary.

16 Check the fork tube for runout (bending) using V-blocks and a dial gauge, or have it done by a dealer **(see illustration)**. Yamaha do not specify a runout limit, but if the tube is bent it should be renewed.

17 Check the spring for cracks and other damage. Measure the spring free length and compare the measurement to the specifications at the beginning of the Chapter. If it is defective or sagged below the service limit, renew the springs in both forks. Never renew only one spring. Also check the rebound spring on the damper.

18 Examine the working surfaces of the two bushes; if worn or scuffed they must be renewed. To remove the bottom bush from the fork tube, prise it apart at the slit using a flat-bladed screwdriver and slide it off **(see illustration)**. Make sure the new one seats properly.

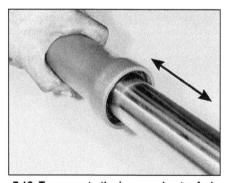

7.12 To separate the inner and outer fork tubes, pull them apart firmly several times – the slide-hammer effect will pull the tubes apart

7.13 The oil seal (1), washer (2), top bush (3) and bottom bush (4) will come out with the fork tube

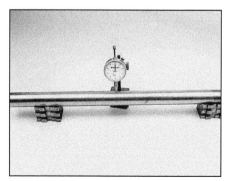

7.16 Check the fork tube for runout using V-blocks and a dial gauge

7.18 Prise off the bottom bush using a flat-bladed screwdriver

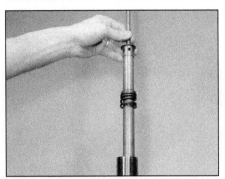
7.20a Slide the damper into the tube . . .

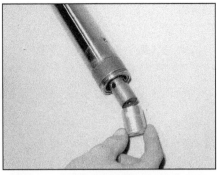
7.20b . . . and fit the seat onto its bottom end

7.21 Apply a thread locking compound to the damper rod bolt and use a new sealing washer

19 Check the damper rod assembly for damage and wear, and renew it if necessary. Holding the outside of the damper, pump the rod in and out of the damper. If the rod does not move smoothly in the damper it must be renewed.

Reassembly

20 Insert the damper rod into the fork tube and slide it into place so that it projects fully from the bottom of the tube, then install the seat on the bottom of the damper rod, making sure the projection in the base of the seat locates with the flat on the bottom of the damper **(see illustrations)**.

21 Oil the fork tube and bottom bush with the specified fork oil and insert the assembly into the slider. Fit a new copper sealing washer to the damper rod bolt and apply a few drops of a suitable non-permanent thread locking compound, then install the bolt into the bottom of the slider **(see illustration)**. Tighten the bolt to the specified torque setting. If the damper rod rotates inside the tube, wait until the fork is fully reassembled before tightening the bolt.

22 Push the fork tube fully into the slider, then oil the top bush and slide it down over the tube **(see illustration)**. Press the bush squarely into its recess in the slider as far as possible, then install the oil seal washer with its flat side facing up **(see illustration)**. Either use the Yamaha service tool or a

suitable piece of tubing to tap the bush fully into place; the tubing must be slightly larger in diameter than the fork tube and slightly smaller in diameter than the bush recess in the slider. Take care not to scratch the fork tube during this operation; it is best to make sure that the fork tube is pushed fully into the slider so that any accidental scratching is confined to the area above the oil seal.

23 When the bush is seated fully and squarely in its recess in the slider, (remove the washer to check, wipe the recess clean, then reinstall the washer), install the new oil seal. Smear the seal's lips with fork oil and slide it over the tube so that its markings face upwards and drive the seal into place as

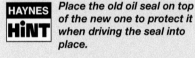
HAYNES HiNT *Place the old oil seal on top of the new one to protect it when driving the seal into place.*

described above until the retaining clip groove is visible above the seal **(see illustration)**.

24 Once the seal is correctly seated, fit the retaining clip, making sure it is correctly located in its groove **(see illustration)**.

25 Lubricate the lips of the new dust seal then slide it down the fork tube and press it into position **(see illustration)**.

26 Slowly pour in the specified quantity of the specified grade of fork oil and pump the fork and damper rod at least ten times each to

7.22a Install the top bush . . .

7.22b . . . followed by the washer

7.23 Make sure the oil seal is the correct way up

7.24 Install the retaining clip . . .

7.25 . . . followed by the dust seal

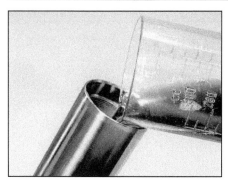

7.26a Pour the oil into the top of the tube

7.26b Measure the oil level with the fork held vertical

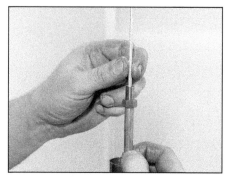

7.27a Insert the damping adjuster rod

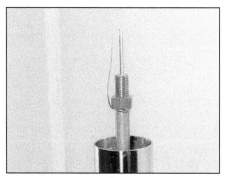

7.27b Tie a piece of wire around the base of the locknut to keep the damper rod extended . . .

7.27c . . . and install the spring

distribute it evenly **(see illustration)**; wait ten minutes then measure the oil level and adjust as necessary by adding or subtracting oil. Fully compress the fork tube and damper rod into the slider and measure the fork oil level from the top of the tube **(see illustration)**. Add or subtract fork oil until it is at the level specified at the beginning of the Chapter.

27 Fit the damping adjuster rod into the damper rod **(see illustration)**. It is advisable to tie a piece of wire around the locknut so that it can be used to hold the damper rod out when installing the spring – otherwise the rod

will settle down into the fork and will be inaccessible with the spring installed **(see illustration)**. Clamp the slider in a vice via the brake caliper mounting lugs, taking care not to overtighten and damage them. Pull the fork tube and damper rod out of the slider as far as possible then install the spring with its closer-wound coils at the top **(see illustration)**. Fit the spring seat, with its shouldered side fitting down into the top of the spring **(see illustration 7.6)**.

28 Fit a new O-ring onto the fork top bolt. Thread the pre-load adjuster (with the top bolt

if it wasn't removed) onto the damper rod as far as it will go, then counter-hold it and tighten the locknut securely against it **(see illustration and 7.5)**. If it was removed, thread the top bolt onto the pre-load adjuster **(see illustration 7.4b)**.

29 Withdraw the tube fully from the slider and carefully screw the top bolt into the fork tube making sure it is not cross-threaded **(see illustration)**. **Note:** *The top bolt can be tightened to the specified torque setting at this stage if the tube is held between the padded jaws of a vice, but do not risk distorting the tube by doing so. A better method is to tighten the top bolt when the fork leg has been installed and is securely held in the triple clamps.*

> **TOOL TiP** *Use a ratchet-type tool when installing the fork top bolt. This makes it unnecessary to remove the tool from the bolt whilst threading it in making it easier to maintain a downward pressure on the spring.*

If the damper rod Allen bolt requires tightening, clamp the fork slider between the padded jaws of a vice and have an assistant compress the tube into the slider so that

7.28 Thread the pre-load adjuster onto the damper rod and tighten the locknut against it

7.29 Thread the top bolt into the fork tube

maximum spring pressure is placed on the damper rod head – tighten the damper Allen bolt to the specified torque setting **(see illustration 7.2)**.

30 Install the forks (see Section 6). Set the spring pre-load adjuster as required (see Section 12).

1996-on TDM models and TRX models

Disassembly

31 Always dismantle the fork legs separately to avoid interchanging parts and thus causing an accelerated rate of wear. Store all components in separate, clearly marked containers **(see illustration)**.

32 Before dismantling the fork, it is advised that the damper rod bolt be slackened at this stage. Compress the fork tube in the slider so that the spring exerts maximum pressure on the damper rod head, then have an assistant slacken the damper rod bolt in the base of the fork slider **(see illustration 7.2)**.

33 If the fork top bolt was not slackened with the fork in situ, carefully clamp the fork tube in a vice equipped with soft jaws, taking care not to overtighten or score its surface, and slacken the top bolt **(see illustration 7.4)**.

34 The fork top bolt comes as an assembly with the pre-load adjuster and damping adjuster rod. Unscrew the fork top bolt from the top of the fork tube and lift it out until the damping adjuster rod is clear.

35 Slide the fork tube down into the slider. On TDM models withdraw the spring seat and spring from the tube. On TRX models withdraw the washer, spacer, spring seat and the spring from the tube. Note which way up the spring is fitted.

36 Invert the fork leg over a suitable container and pump the fork vigorously to expel as much fork oil as possible.

37 Remove the previously slackened damper rod bolt and its copper sealing washer from the bottom of the slider. Discard the sealing washer as a new one must be used on reassembly. If the damper rod bolt was not slackened before dismantling the fork, use the Yamaha service tool (TDM models – pt. nos. 90890-01465 and 90890-01326, TRX models – pt. nos. 90890-01388 and 90890-01326) to prevent the damper rod from turning. This tool is passed down through the fork tube and engages the damper rod head; a similar tool can be easily made in the home workshop.

38 Invert the fork and withdraw the damper rod from inside the fork tube **(see illustration)**. If required, slide the rebound spring off the damper rod.

39 Carefully prise out the dust seal from the top of the slider to gain access to the oil seal retaining clip **(see illustration 7.10)**. Discard the dust seal as a new one must be used.

40 Carefully remove the retaining clip, taking care not to scratch the surface of the tube **(see illustration 7.11)**.

41 To separate the tube from the slider it is

1 Top bolt and pre-load adjuster
2 O-ring
3 Washer – TRX only
4 Spacer – TRX only
5 Spring seat
6 Spring
7 Damper rod and rebound spring
8 Fork tube and bottom bush
9 Damper rod seat
10 Dust seal
11 Retaining clip
12 Oil seal
13 Washer
14 Top bush
15 Slider
16 Damper rod bolt and sealing washer

7.31 Front fork components – 1996-on TDM models and TRX models

necessary to displace the top bush and oil seal. The bottom bush should not pass through the top bush, and this can be used to good effect. Push the tube gently inwards until it stops against the damper rod seat. Take care not to do this forcibly or the seat may be damaged. Then pull the tube sharply outwards until the bottom bush strikes the top bush. Repeat this operation until the top bush and seal are tapped out of the slider **(see illustration 7.12)**.

42 With the tube removed, slide off the oil seal, washer and top bush, noting which way up they fit **(see illustration 7.13)**. Discard the oil seal as a new one must be used.

Caution: Do not remove the bottom bush from the tube unless it is to be renewed.

43 Tip the damper rod seat out of the slider, noting which way up it fits.

Inspection

44 Clean all parts in solvent and blow them dry with compressed air, if available. Check the fork tube for score marks, scratches, flaking of the chrome finish and excessive or abnormal wear. Look for dents in the tube and renew the tube in both forks if any are found.

Check the fork seal seat for nicks, gouges and scratches. If damage is evident, leaks will occur. Also check the oil seal washer for damage or distortion and renew it if necessary.

45 Check the fork tube for runout (bending) using V-blocks and a dial gauge, or have it done by a dealer **(see illustration 7.16)**. Yamaha do not specify a runout limit, but if the tube is bent it should be renewed.

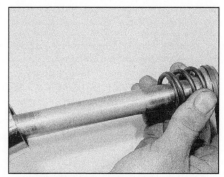

7.38 Withdraw the damper rod and rebound spring from the tube

46 Check the spring for cracks and other damage. Measure the spring free length and compare the measurement to the specifications at the beginning of the Chapter. If it is defective or sagged below the service limit, renew the springs in both forks. Never renew only one spring. Also check the rebound spring on the damper.

47 Examine the working surfaces of the two bushes; if worn or scuffed they must be renewed. To remove the bottom bush from the fork tube, prise it apart at the slit using a flat-bladed screwdriver and slide it off **(see illustration 7.18)**. Make sure the new one seats properly.

48 Check the damper rod for damage and wear, and renew it if necessary.

Reassembly

49 If removed, slide the rebound spring onto the damper rod. Insert the damper rod into the fork tube and slide it into place so that it projects fully from the bottom of the tube, then fit the seat onto the bottom of the damper rod **(see illustrations 7.38 and 7.20b)**.

50 Oil the fork tube and bottom bush with the specified fork oil and insert the assembly into the slider. Fit a new copper sealing washer to the damper rod bolt and apply a few drops of a suitable non-permanent thread locking compound, then install the bolt into the bottom of the slider **(see illustration 7.21)**. Tighten the bolt to the specified torque setting. If the damper rod rotates inside the tube, use the tool described in Step 37 to hold the damper rod.

51 Push the fork tube fully into the slider, then oil the top bush and slide it down over the tube **(see illustration 7.22a)**. Press the bush squarely into its recess in the slider as far as possible, then install the oil seal washer **(see illustration 7.22b)**. Either use the Yamaha service tool or a suitable piece of tubing to tap the bush fully into place; the tubing must be slightly larger in diameter than the fork tube and slightly smaller in diameter than the bush recess in the slider. Take care not to scratch the fork tube during this operation; it is best to make sure that the fork tube is pushed fully into the slider so that any accidental scratching is confined to the area above the oil seal.

52 When the bush is seated fully and squarely in its recess in the slider, (remove the washer to check, wipe the recess clean, then reinstall the washer), install the new oil seal. Smear the seal's lips with lithium-based grease and slide it over the tube so that its markings face upwards and drive the seal into place as described above until the retaining clip groove is visible above the seal **(see illustration 7.23)**.

 HAYNES HiNT *Place the old oil seal on top of the new one to protect it when driving the seal into place.*

53 Once the seal is correctly seated, fit the retaining clip, making sure it is correctly located in its groove **(see illustration 7.24)**.

54 Lubricate the lips of the new dust seal then slide it down the fork tube and press it into position **(see illustration 7.25)**.

55 Slowly pour in the specified quantity of the specified grade of fork oil and pump the fork at least ten times to distribute it evenly **(see illustration 7.26a)**; the oil level should also be measured and adjustment made by adding or subtracting oil. Fully compress the fork tube into the slider and measure the fork oil level from the top of the tube **(see illustration 7.26b)**. Add or subtract fork oil until it is at the level specified at the beginning of the Chapter.

56 Clamp the slider upright in a soft-jawed vice using the brake caliper mounting lugs, taking care not to overtighten and damage them. Pull the fork tube out of the slider as far as possible then install the spring and the spring seat. On TRX models fit the spacer and the washer.

57 Apply a smear of fork oil or grease to the new top bolt O-ring. Install the top bolt assembly, making sure the bottom of the damping adjuster rod locates correctly into the hole in the top of the damper rod, and thread the bolt into the top of the fork tube **(see illustration 7.29)**.

 Warning: It will be necessary to compress the spring by pressing it down using the top bolt to engage the threads of the top bolt with the fork tube. This is a potentially dangerous operation and should be performed with care, using an assistant if necessary. Wipe off any excess oil before starting to prevent the possibility of slipping.

Keep the fork tube fully extended whilst pressing on the spring. Screw the top bolt carefully into the fork tube making sure it is not cross-threaded. **Note:** *The top bolt can be tightened to the specified torque setting at this stage if the tube is held between the padded jaws of a vice, but do not risk distorting the tube by doing so. A better method is to tighten the top bolt when the fork has been installed in the bike and is securely held in the bottom yoke.*

58 Install the forks (see Section 6).

XTZ models

Disassembly

59 Always dismantle the fork legs separately to avoid interchanging parts and thus causing an accelerated rate of wear. Store all components in separate, clearly marked containers **(see illustration)**.

60 Slacken the clamps securing the fork gaiter and slide the gaiter off the top of the fork.

61 Before dismantling the fork, it is advised that the damper rod bolt be slackened at this stage. Compress the fork tube in the slider so that the spring exerts maximum pressure on the damper rod head, then have an assistant slacken the damper rod bolt in the base of the fork slider **(see illustration 7.2)**. If an assistant is not available, clamp the brake caliper mounting lugs in a soft-jawed vice to support the fork.

62 If the fork top bolt was not slackened with the fork in situ, carefully clamp the fork tube in a vice equipped with soft jaws, taking care not to overtighten or score its surface, and slacken the top bolt.

63 Unscrew the fork top bolt from the top of the fork tube.

 Warning: The fork spring is pressing on the fork top bolt (via the spacer) with considerable pressure. Unscrew the bolt very carefully, keeping a downward pressure on it and release it slowly as it is likely to spring clear. It is advisable to wear some form of eye and face protection when carrying out this operation.

64 Slide the fork tube down into the slider and withdraw the spacer, spring seat and the spring from the tube. Note which way up the spring is fitted.

65 Invert the fork leg over a suitable container and pump the fork vigorously to expel as much fork oil as possible.

66 Remove the previously slackened damper rod bolt and its copper sealing washer from the bottom of the slider. Discard the sealing washer as a new one must be used on reassembly. If the damper rod bolt was not slackened before dismantling the fork, use the Yamaha service tool (pt. nos. 90890-01326 and 90890-01327) to prevent the damper rod from turning. This tool is passed down

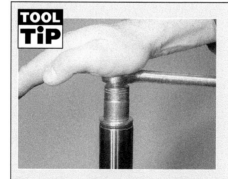
TOOL TiP

Use a ratchet-type tool when installing the fork top bolt. This makes it unnecessary to remove the tool from the bolt whilst threading it in making it easier to maintain a downward pressure on the spring.

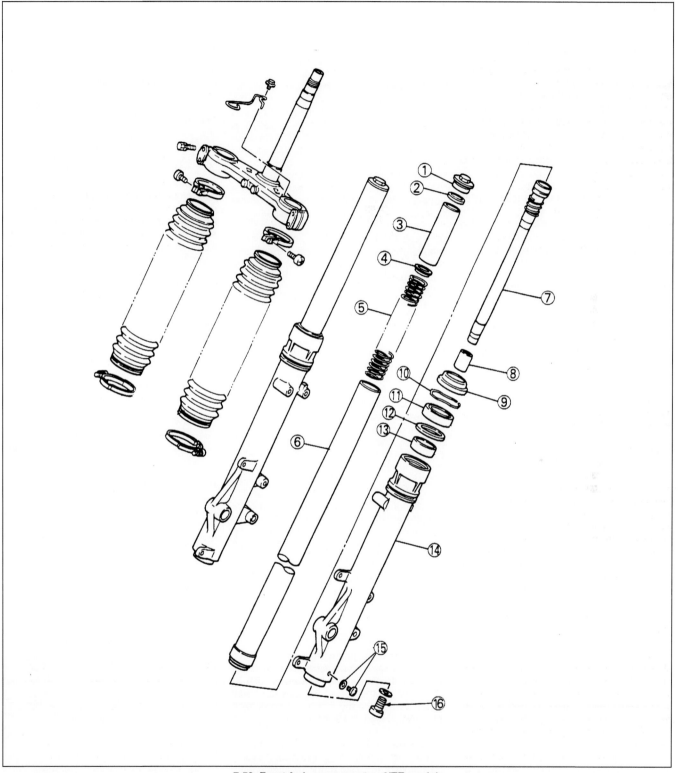

7.59 Front fork components – XTZ models

1 Top bolt
2 O-ring
3 Spacer
4 Spring seat
5 Spring
6 Fork tube and bottom bush

7 Damper rod and rebound spring
8 Damper rod seat
9 Dust seal
10 Retaining clip
11 Oil seal
12 Washer

13 Top bush
14 Slider
15 Oil drain screw and sealing washer –
    1989-94 models
16 Damper rod bolt and sealing washer

through the fork tube and engages the damper rod head; a similar tool can be easily made in the home workshop..

67 Invert the fork and withdraw the damper rod from inside the fork tube **(see illustration 7.38)**. If required, slide the rebound spring off the damper rod.

68 Carefully prise out the dust seal from the top of the slider to gain access to the oil seal retaining clip **(see illustration 7.10)**. Discard the dust seal as a new one must be used.

69 Carefully remove the retaining clip, taking care not to scratch the surface of the tube **(see illustration 7.11)**.

70 To separate the tube from the slider it is necessary to displace the top bush and oil seal. The bottom bush should not pass through the top bush, and this can be used to good effect. Push the tube gently inwards until it stops against the damper rod seat. Take care not to do this forcibly or the seat may be damaged. Then pull the tube sharply outwards until the bottom bush strikes the top bush. Repeat this operation until the top bush and seal are tapped out of the slider **(see illustration 7.12)**.

71 With the tube removed, slide off the oil seal, washer and top bush, noting which way up they fit **(see illustration 7.13)**. Discard the oil seal as a new one must be used.

Caution: Do not remove the bottom bush from the tube unless it is to be renewed.

72 Tip the damper rod seat out of the slider, noting which way up it fits.

Inspection

73 Clean all parts in solvent and blow them dry with compressed air, if available. Check the fork tube for score marks, scratches, flaking of the chrome finish and excessive or abnormal wear. Look for dents in the tube and renew the tube in both forks if any are found. Check the fork seal seat for nicks, gouges and scratches. If damage is evident, leaks will occur. Also check the oil seal washer for damage or distortion and renew it if necessary.

74 Check the fork tube for runout (bending) using V-blocks and a dial gauge, or have it done by a dealer **(see illustration 7.16)**. Yamaha do not specify a runout limit, but if the tube is bent it should be renewed.

75 Check the spring for cracks and other damage. Measure the spring free length and compare the measurement to the specifications at the beginning of the Chapter. If it is defective or sagged below the service limit, renew the springs in both forks. Never renew only one spring. Also check the rebound spring.

76 Examine the working surfaces of the two bushes; if worn or scuffed they must be renewed. To remove the bottom bush from the fork tube, prise it apart at the slit using a flat-bladed screwdriver and slide it off **(see illustration 7.18)**. Make sure the new one seats properly.

77 Check the damper rod for damage and wear, and renew it if necessary.

Reassembly

78 If removed, slide the rebound spring onto the rod. Insert the damper rod into the fork tube and slide it into place so that it projects fully from the bottom of the tube, then fit the seat onto the bottom of the damper rod **(see illustration 7.38 and 7.20b)**.

79 Oil the fork tube and bottom bush with the specified fork oil and insert the assembly into the slider. Fit a new copper sealing washer to the damper rod bolt and apply a few drops of a suitable non-permanent thread locking compound, then install the bolt into the bottom of the slider **(see illustration 7.21)**. Tighten the bolt to the specified torque setting. If the damper rod rotates inside the tube, use the tool described in Step 66 to hold the damper rod.

80 Push the fork tube fully into the slider, then oil the top bush and slide it down over the tube **(see illustration 7.22a)**. Press the bush squarely into its recess in the slider as far as possible, then install the oil seal washer **(see illustration 7.22b)**. Either use the Yamaha service tool or a suitable piece of tubing to tap the bush fully into place; the tubing must be slightly larger in diameter than the fork tube and slightly smaller in diameter than the bush recess in the slider. Take care not to scratch the fork tube during this operation; it is best to make sure that the fork tube is pushed fully into the slider so that any accidental scratching is confined to the area above the oil seal.

81 When the bush is seated fully and squarely in its recess in the slider, (remove the washer to check, wipe the recess clean, then reinstall the washer), install the new oil seal. Smear the seal's lips with lithium-base grease and slide it over the tube so that its markings face upwards and drive the seal into place as described above until the retaining clip groove is visible above the seal **(see illustration 7.23)**.

 Place the old oil seal on top of the new one to protect it when driving the seal into place.

82 Once the seal is correctly seated, fit the retaining clip, making sure it is correctly located in its groove **(see illustration 7.24)**.

83 Lubricate the lips of the new dust seal then slide it down the fork tube and press it into position **(see illustration 7.25)**.

84 Slowly pour in the specified quantity of the specified grade of fork oil and pump the fork at least ten times to distribute it evenly **(see illustration 7.26a)**; the oil level should also be measured and adjustment made by adding or subtracting oil. Fully compress the fork tube into the slider and measure the fork oil level from the top of the tube **(see illustration 7.26b)**. Add or subtract fork oil until it is at the level specified at the beginning of the Chapter.

85 Clamp the slider in a soft-jawed vice using the brake caliper mounting lugs, taking care not to overtighten and damage them. Pull the fork tube out of the slider as far as possible then install the spring, the spring seat, with its shouldered side fitting down into the top of the spring, and the spacer.

86 Apply a smear of grease to the new top bolt O-ring and thread the bolt into the top of the fork tube.

 Warning: It will be necessary to compress the spring by pressing it down using the top bolt to engage the threads of the top bolt with the fork tube. This is a potentially dangerous operation and should be performed with care, using an assistant if necessary. Wipe off any excess oil before starting to prevent the possibility of slipping. Keep the fork tube fully extended whilst pressing on the spring. Screw the top bolt carefully into the fork tube making sure it is not cross-threaded. Note: *The top bolt can be tightened to the specified torque setting at this stage if the tube is held between the padded jaws of a vice, but do not risk distorting the tube by doing so (see **Tool Tip**). A better method is to tighten the top bolt when the fork has been installed in the bike and is securely held in the bottom yoke.*

87 Install the forks (see Section 6).

8 Steering stem – removal and installation

Removal

1 Remove the front forks (see Section 6).

2 On TDM models, displace the handlebars from the top yoke (see Section 5), then disconnect the horn wiring connectors and unscrew the bolts securing the front brake hose/horn bracket to the bottom yoke **(see illustration)**. On 1996-on models, unscrew the bolts securing the choke knob and the cable guide to the top yoke.

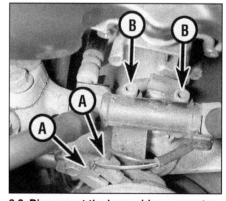

8.2 Disconnect the horn wiring connectors (A), then unscrew the bolts (B) and displace the brake hose union/horn assembly

8.3 Disconnect the horn wiring connectors, then unscrew the bolts (arrowed) and displace the brake hose/horn assembly

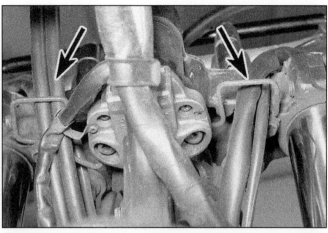

8.4a Free the cable and wiring from the guides (arrowed) on the top yoke . . .

3 On TRX models, disconnect the horn wiring connectors and unscrew the bolts securing the front brake hose/horn bracket to the bottom yoke **(see illustration)**.

4 On XTZ models, displace the handlebars from the top yoke (see Section 5). Slip the cables and wiring out of the guides on the top yoke, and unscrew the bolts securing the front brake hose and the cable guide to the bottom yoke **(see illustrations)**.

5 Unscrew the steering stem nut or bolt and remove it along with its washer, where fitted **(see illustration)**. Lift the top yoke off the steering stem and place it aside, making sure no strain is placed on the ignition switch wiring **(see illustration)**. On TRX models the yoke should be supported so that the master cylinder reservoir remains upright and so that no strain is placed on the hydraulic hoses.

6 On TDM and TRX models, remove the tabbed lockwasher, noting how it fits, then unscrew and remove the locknut using either a C-spanner, a peg spanner or a drift located in one of the notches **(see illustration)**. Remove the washer.

7 Supporting the bottom yoke, unscrew the adjuster nut using either a C-spanner, a peg-spanner or a drift located in one of the notches, then remove the adjuster nut and the bearing cover from the steering stem.

8 Gently lower the bottom yoke and steering stem out of the frame.

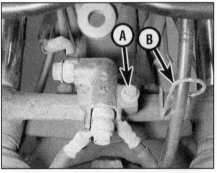

8.4b . . . and displace the brake hose union (A) and guide (B) from the bottom yoke by unscrewing the bolts

9 Remove the upper bearing from the top of the steering head. Remove all traces of old grease from the bearings and races and check them for wear or damage as described in Section 9. **Note:** *Do not attempt to remove the outer races from the frame or the lower bearing from the steering stem unless they are to be renewed.*

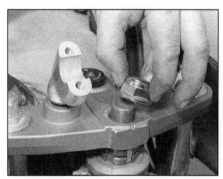

8.5a Unscrew the steering stem nut or bolt . . .

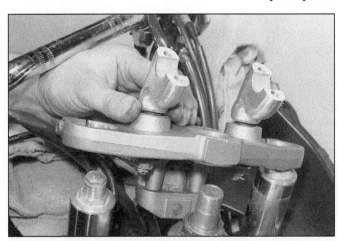

8.5b . . . and lift off the top yoke

8.6 Remove the lockwasher, then unscrew the locknut (arrowed)

8.12 Align the adjuster nut and locknut so that the lockwasher tabs fit into the notches in both

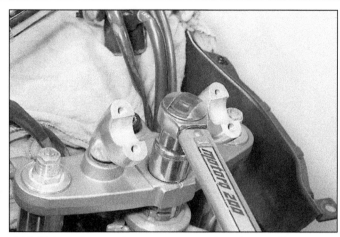

8.13 Tighten the steering stem nut or bolt to the specified torque

Installation

10 Smear a liberal quantity of lithium-based grease on the bearing races in the frame. Also work some grease well into both the upper and lower bearings.

11 Carefully lift the steering stem/bottom yoke up through the steering head. Fit the upper bearing into the top of the steering head, then install the bearing cover. Thread the adjuster nut onto the steering stem and adjust the bearings as described in Chapter 1.

12 On TDM and TRX models, install the washer and the locknut. On 1991 to 1995 TDM models the tapered side of the locknut must face down. Tighten the locknut finger-tight, then tighten it further until its notches align with those in the adjuster nut. If necessary, counter-hold the adjuster nut and tighten the locknut using a C-spanner or drift until the notches align, but make sure the adjuster nut does not turn as well. Install the tabbed lockwasher so that the tabs fit into the notches in both the locknut and adjuster nut **(see illustration)**.

13 Fit the top yoke onto the steering stem **(see illustration 8.5b)**, then install the washer (where fitted) and steering stem nut or bolt and tighten it finger-tight **(see illustration 8.5a)**. Temporarily install one of the forks to

align the top and bottom yokes, and secure it by tightening the bottom yoke clamp bolt only. Now tighten the steering stem nut or bolt to the torque settings specified at the beginning of the Chapter **(see illustration)**.

14 Install the remaining components in a reverse of the removal procedure.

15 Carry out a check of the steering head bearing freeplay as described in Chapter 1, and if necessary re-adjust.

9 Steering head bearings – inspection and replacement

Inspection

1 Remove the steering stem (see Section 8).

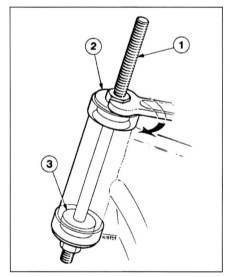

9.6 Drawbolt arrangement for fitting steering stem bearing outer races

1   Long bolt or threaded bar
2   Thick washer
3   Guide for lower race

2 Remove all traces of old grease from the bearings and races and check them for wear or damage.

3 The outer races should be polished and free from indentations. Inspect the bearing rollers for signs of wear, damage or discoloration, and examine the bearing roller retainer cage for signs of cracks or splits. Spin the bearings by hand. They should spin freely and smoothly. If there are any signs of wear on any of the above components both upper and lower bearing assemblies must be renewed as a set. Only remove the races if they need to be renewed – do not re-use them once they have been removed.

Replacement

4 The outer races are an interference fit in the steering head and can be tapped from position with a suitable drift **(see illustration)**. Tap firmly and evenly around each race to ensure that it is driven out squarely. It may prove advantageous to curve the end of the drift slightly to improve access.

5 Alternatively, the races can be removed using a slide-hammer type bearing extractor; these can often be hired from tool shops.

6 The new outer races can be pressed into the head using a drawbolt arrangement **(see illustration)**, or by using a large diameter tubular drift which bears only on the outer edge of the race. Ensure that the drawbolt washer or drift (as applicable) bears only on the outer edge of the race and does not contact the working surface. Alternatively, have the races installed by a Yamaha dealer equipped with the bearing race installing tools.

> **HAYNES HiNT** *Installation of new bearing outer races is made much easier if the races are left overnight in the freezer. This causes them to contract slightly making them a looser fit. Alternatively, use a freeze spray.*

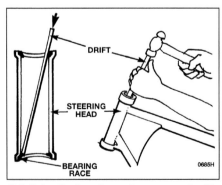

9.4 Drive the bearing outer races out with a drift as shown

9.7a Remove the lower bearing and grease seal only if they are being renewed

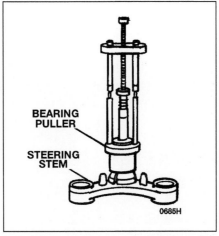

9.7b It is best to remove the lower bearing using a puller

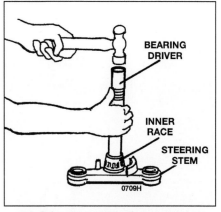

9.8 Drive the new bearing on using a suitable bearing driver or a length of pipe that bears only against the inner race and not against the rollers or cage

7 The lower bearing should only be removed if a new one is being fitted **(see illustration)**. To remove the lower bearing from the steering stem, use two screwdrivers placed on opposite sides of the race to work it free. If the bearing is firmly in place it will be necessary to use a bearing puller **(see illustration)**, or in extreme circumstances to split the bearing's inner section using an angle grinder. Take the steering stem to a Yamaha dealer if required. Check the condition of the dust seal that fits under the lower bearing and renew it if it is worn, damaged or deteriorated.

8 Fit the new lower bearing onto the steering stem. A length of tubing with an internal diameter slightly larger than the steering stem will be needed to tap the new bearing into position **(see illustration)**. Ensure that the drift bears only on the inner edge of the bearing and does not contact the rollers.

9 Install the steering stem (see Section 8).

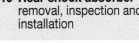

10 Rear shock absorber – removal, inspection and installation

⚠️ *Warning: Do not attempt to disassemble this shock absorber. It is nitrogen-charged under high pressure. Improper disassembly could result in serious injury. Instead, take the shock to a Yamaha dealer or suspension specialist with the proper equipment to do the job.*

Removal

TDM models

1 Place the machine on an auxiliary stand. Position a support under the rear wheel so that it does not drop when the shock absorber is removed, but also making sure that the weight of the machine is off the rear suspension so that the shock is not compressed.

2 Remove the seat (see Chapter 8).

3 Unscrew the nut and withdraw the bolt

securing the bottom of the shock absorber to the swingarm **(see illustrations)**.

4 Unscrew the nut on the shock absorber upper mounting bolt **(see illustration)**. Support the shock absorber and withdraw the upper mounting bolt, then manoeuvre the shock down and out of the bottom of the machine **(see illustration)**.

TRX and XTZ models

5 Place the machine on an auxiliary stand. Position a support under the rear wheel so

10.3a Unscrew the nut (arrowed) . . .

10.4a Unscrew the nut (arrowed) . . .

that it does not drop when the shock absorber is removed, but also making sure that the weight of the machine is off the rear suspension so that the shock is not compressed.

6 Remove the seat (see Chapter 8). If required for improved clearance, also remove the exhaust system (see Chapter 4). On XTZ models, remove the fuel tank (see Chapter 4), and where fitted, remove the rubber boot from around the shock absorber lower mounting.

7 Unscrew the nut and withdraw the bolt

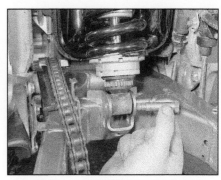

10.3b . . . and withdraw the bolt

10.4b . . . then support the shock and withdraw the bolt

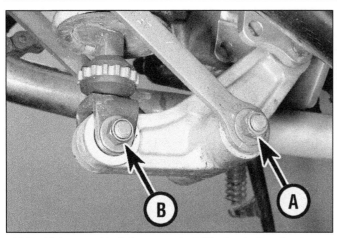

10.7a Linkage rod to linkage arm bolt (A), shock absorber lower mounting bolt (B) – TRX models

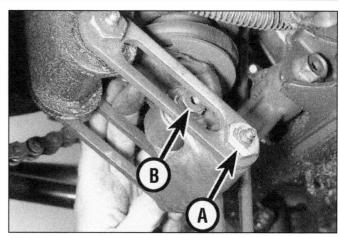

10.7b Linkage rod to linkage arm bolt (A), shock absorber lower mounting bolt (B) – XTZ models

securing the linkage rods to the linkage arm (see illustrations). Unscrew the nut and withdraw the bolt securing the bottom of the shock absorber to the suspension linkage arm. Swing the linkage rods rearwards and the linkage arm down.

8 On TRX models, slacken the clamp screw securing the reservoir to its holder and free the hose from its clip on the frame (see illustrations). Slip the reservoir out and feed it through to the shock absorber.

9 Unscrew the nut on the shock absorber upper mounting bolt (see illustrations).

10 Support the shock absorber and withdraw

the upper mounting bolt, then manoeuvre the shock down and out of the bottom of the machine, on TRX models feeding the reservoir through as you do.

Inspection

11 Inspect the shock absorber for obvious physical damage and the coil spring for looseness, cracks or signs of fatigue.

12 Inspect the damper rod for signs of bending, pitting and oil leakage (see illustration).

13 Inspect the pivot hardware at the top and bottom of the shock for wear or damage.

Installation

14 Installation is the reverse of removal. Apply molybdenum disulphide grease to the shock absorber and linkage rod pivot points. Install the bolts and nuts finger-tight only until all components are in position, then tighten the nuts to the torque settings specified at the beginning of the Chapter.

11 Rear suspension linkage (TRX and XTZ models) – removal, inspection and installation

Removal

1 Place the machine on an auxiliary stand. Position a support under the rear wheel so that it does not drop when the shock absorber lower mounting bolt is removed, but also making sure that the weight of the machine is off the rear suspension so that the shock is not compressed.

2 Remove the seat (see Chapter 8). If required for improved clearance, also remove the exhaust system (see Chapter 4). On XTZ models, where fitted, remove the rubber boot from around the shock absorber lower mounting.

10.8a Slacken the clamp screw (arrowed) and free the reservoir . . .

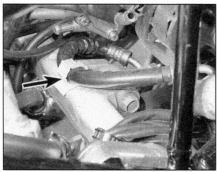

10.8b . . . and release the hose from its clip (arrowed)

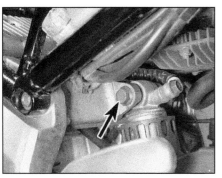

10.9a Shock absorber upper mounting bolt (arrowed) – TRX models

10.9b Shock absorber upper mounting bolt (arrowed) – XTZ models

10.12 Look for cracks, pitting and oil leakage on the damper rod (arrowed)

3 Unscrew the nuts and withdraw the bolts securing the shock absorber and the linkage rods to the linkage arm **(see illustrations)**. Note which bolts fit where.

4 Unscrew the nut and withdraw the bolt securing the linkage rods to the swingarm and remove the rods.

5 Unscrew the nut and withdraw bolt securing the linkage arm to the frame and remove the linkage arm, noting which way round it fits.

Inspection

6 Withdraw the inner sleeves and lever out the grease seals from the linkage arm and swingarm, noting their different sizes **(see illustrations)**. Thoroughly clean all

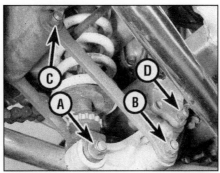

11.3a Shock absorber to linkage arm bolt (A), linkage rod to linkage arm bolt (B), linkage rod to swingarm bolt (C), linkage arm to frame bolt (D) – TRX models

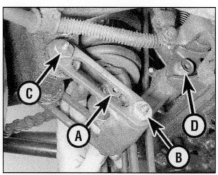

11.3b Shock absorber to linkage arm bolt (A), linkage rod to linkage arm bolt (B), linkage rod to swingarm bolt (C), linkage arm to frame bolt (D) – XTZ models

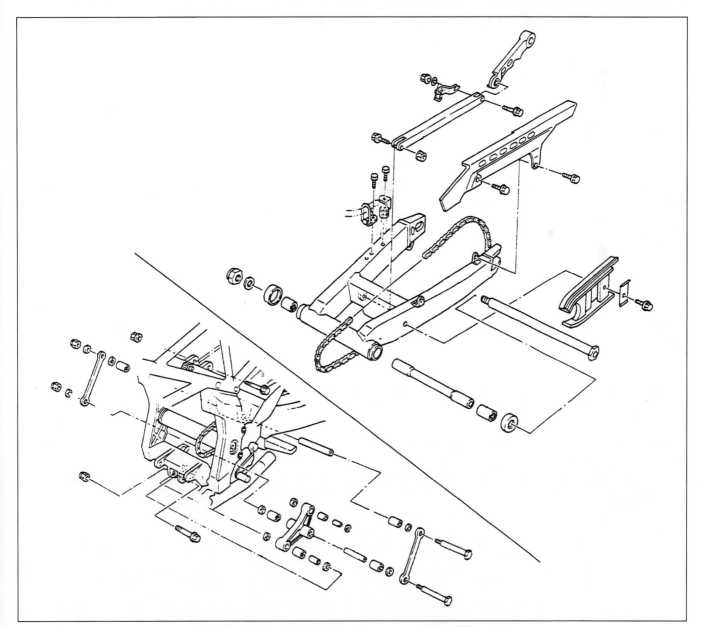

11.6a Suspension linkage and swingarm assembly – TRX models

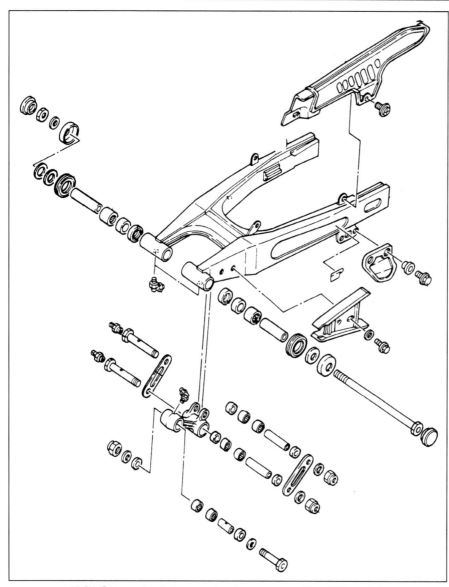

11.6b Suspension linkage and swingarm assembly – XTZ models

components, removing all traces of dirt, corrosion and grease. On XTZ models make sure that the grease nipple passages in the linkage arm and pivot bolts are clear.

7 Inspect all components closely, looking for obvious signs of wear such as heavy scoring, or for damage such as cracks or distortion.

8 Check the condition of the needle roller bearings in the linkage arm and swingarm.

9 Worn bearings can be drifted out of their bores, but note that removal will destroy them; new components should be obtained before work commences. The new ones should be pressed or drawn into their bores rather than driven into position. In the absence of a press, a suitable drawbolt arrangement can be made up as described below.

10 Obtain a long bolt or a length of threaded rod from a local engineering works or some other supplier. The bolt or rod should be about one inch longer than the combined width of the linkage piece and one bearing. Also required are suitable nuts and two large and robust washers having a larger outside diameter than the bearing housing. In the case of the threaded rod, fit one nut to one end of the rod and stake it in place for convenience.

11 Fit one of the washers over the bolt or rod so that it rests against the head or staked nut, then pass the assembly through the relevant bore. Over the projecting end place the bearing, which should be greased to ease installation, followed by the remaining washer and nut.

12 Holding the bearing to ensure that it is kept square, slowly tighten the nut so that the bearing is drawn into its bore.

13 Once it is fully home, remove the drawbolt arrangement and, if necessary, repeat the procedure to fit the other bearings.

14 Lubricate the needle roller bearings and the spacers with molybdenum disulphide grease (TRX models) or lithium-based grease (XTZ models) and install the inner sleeves.

15 Check the condition of the grease seals and renew them if they are damaged or deteriorated. Press the seals squarely into place.

Installation

16 Installation is the reverse of removal. Apply molybdenum disulphide grease (TRX models) or lithium-based grease (XTZ models) to the pivot points. Install the bolts and nuts finger-tight only until all components are in position, then tighten the nuts to the torque settings specified at the beginning of the Chapter.

12 Suspension – adjustments

Front forks

1 On XTZ models, the front forks are not adjustable.

2 On TDM and TRX models, spring pre-load is adjusted using a suitable spanner on the adjuster flats on the top of the forks **(see illustration)**. The amount of pre-load is indicated by lines on the adjuster. There are five lines on TDM models and eight on TRX models. The standard position is with the fifth (1991 to 1995 TDM models), third (1996-on TDM models) or sixth (TRX models) line just visible above the top bolt hex. Turn the adjuster clockwise to increase pre-load and anti-clockwise to decrease it. Always make sure both adjusters are set equally.

3 On TDM models, rebound damping is adjusted using a screwdriver in the slot in the adjuster protruding from the pre-load adjuster **(see illustration 12.2)**. The amount of damping is indicated by the number of clicks when turned anti-clockwise from the fully screwed-in position. There are six positions on 1991 to 1995 TDM models, and five on 1996-on TDM models. The standard position is four clicks out. Turn the adjuster clockwise

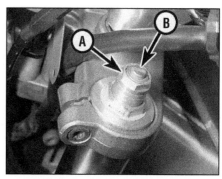

12.2 Spring pre-load adjuster (A), rebound damping adjuster (B) – TDM and TRX models

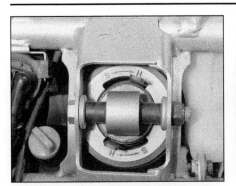

12.6a The basic SOFT/HARD pre-load adjuster is on the top of the shock absorber

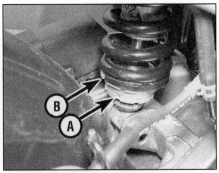

12.6b For finer pre-load adjustment, slacken the locknut (A) and turn the adjuster as required and according to the settings specified . . .

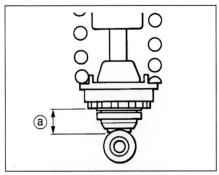

12.6c Fine adjustment settings – 1991 to 1995 TDM models

Standard length, a = 24 mm
Maximum length, a = 29 mm
Minimum length, a = 22 mm

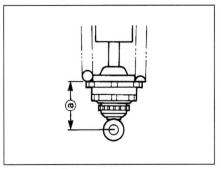

12.6d Fine adjustment settings – 1996-on TDM models

Standard length, a = 61 mm
Maximum length, a = 63 mm
Minimum length, a = 59 mm

to increase damping and anti-clockwise to decrease it. To establish the current setting, turn the adjuster in (clockwise) until it stops, counting the number of clicks, then reset it as required by turning it out. Always make sure both adjusters are set equally.

4 On TRX models, rebound damping is adjusted using a screwdriver in the slot in the adjuster protruding from the pre-load adjuster **(see illustration 12.2)**. The amount of damping is indicated by the number of clicks when turned clockwise. There are four positions. The standard position is the second click. If the adjuster is turned clockwise from the fourth click, there will be a half-turn with no clicks, then the adjuster resets itself to the first click. Always make sure both adjusters are set equally.

Rear shock absorber

5 On all models the rear shock absorber is adjustable for spring pre-load, on TDM and TRX models it is also adjustable for rebound damping, and on TRX models for compression damping.

6 On TDM models, basic pre-load adjustment is made by turning the adjuster on the top of the shock absorber **(see illustration)**. Remove the seat for access (see Chapter 8). There are two settings, soft and hard. The adjuster can be turned manually, though a

tool is provided in the toolkit if required. Align the handles of the adjuster with the S or H as required. Finer pre-load adjustments can be made by slackening the locknut on the base of the shock absorber, then turning the adjuster nut clockwise (as you look up at it from the bottom) to increase pre-load or anti-clockwise to decrease it **(see illustration)**. Refer to the diagrams for the standard, maximum and minimum settings **(see illustrations)**. Tighten the locknut securely after adjustment.

Caution: On TDM and TRX models, do not turn the pre-load adjuster beyond the maximum or minimum settings as shown in the relevant diagram.

7 On TRX models, pre-load adjustment is made using a suitable C-spanner (one is provided in the toolkit) to turn the spring seat on the top of the shock absorber **(see illustration)**. There are seven positions. Position 1 is the softest setting, position 3 is the standard, position 7 is the hardest. Align the setting required with the adjustment stopper. To increase the pre-load, turn the spring seat clockwise. To decrease the pre-load, turn the spring seat anti-clockwise.

8 On TDM and TRX models, rebound damping adjustment is made by turning the toothed adjuster wheel on the bottom of the shock absorber **(see illustrations)**. Turn the

adjuster clockwise (as you look up at it from the bottom) to increase damping and anti-clockwise to decrease it. To establish the current setting, turn the adjuster in (clockwise) until it stops, counting the number of clicks, then reset it as required by turning it out. There are twenty positions. The standard position is ten clicks out on TDM models and eight clicks out on TRX models.

9 On TRX models, compression damping adjustment is made by turning the adjuster on

12.7 Pre-load adjuster – TRX models

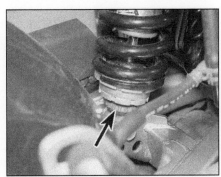

12.8a Rebound damping adjuster – TDM models

12.8b Rebound damping adjuster – TRX models

12.9 Compression damping adjuster – TRX models

the shock absorber reservoir **(see illustration)**. Turn the adjuster clockwise to increase damping and anti-clockwise to decrease it. To establish the current setting, turn the adjuster in (clockwise) until it stops, counting the number of clicks, then reset it as required by turning it out. There are twenty positions. The standard position is ten clicks out.

10 On XTZ models, pre-load adjustment is made by slackening the locknut on the base of the shock absorber, then turning the adjuster nut clockwise (as you look up at it from the bottom) to increase pre-load and anti-clockwise to decrease it **(see illustration)**. Refer to the diagram for the standard, maximum and minimum settings **(see illustration)**. Tighten the locknut securely after adjustment.

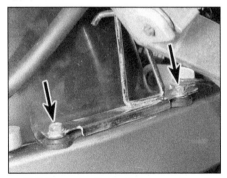

13.3 Unscrew the bolts (arrowed) and detach the hose guide

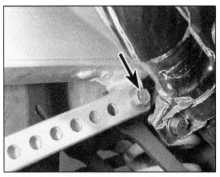

13.4b Detach the torque arm by removing the bolt (arrowed)

12.10a Slacken the locknut (A) and turn the adjuster (B) as required . . .

13 Swingarm – removal and installation

Removal

1 Remove the rear wheel (see Chapter 7).
2 On XTZ models, the swingarm side clearance should be measured prior to removal. Push the swingarm to one side of the frame, then slip a feeler gauge between the frame and the swingarm on the side from which the swingarm was pushed and measure the clearance. If it is greater than specified, refer to Section 14.
3 On TDM models, unscrew the bolt which secures the caliper bracket to the swingarm and remove the bracket (see Chapter 7,

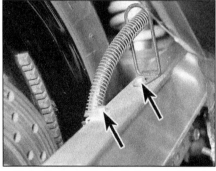

13.4a Unscrew the bolts (arrowed) and detach the hose guides

13.5 Unscrew the bolts (arrowed) and detach the hose

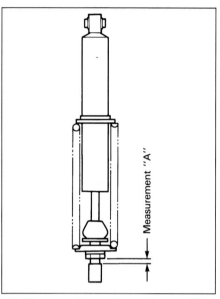

12.10b . . . and according to the specified settings

Standard length, A = 5.4 mm
Minimum length, A = 5.4 mm
Maximum length, A = 15.4 mm

Section 12, Step 2). Unscrew the bolts securing the hose guide to the swingarm, noting how they also secure the rear mudguard **(see illustration)**.
4 On TRX models, unscrew the bolt securing each brake hose guide to the swingarm **(see illustration)**. Remove the split pin from the bolt securing the brake torque arm to the swingarm, then unscrew the nut, withdraw the bolt and detach the arm **(see illustration)**.
5 On XTZ models, unscrew the bolt securing each brake hose guide to the underside of the swingarm **(see illustration)**. Disconnect the brake hose from the rear caliper (see Chapter 7) and remove the caliper. Feed the hose through its guide on the inside of the swingarm and support it with its end upright.
6 Unscrew the bolts securing the chain guard to the swingarm and remove the guard, on TDM models along with the rear mudguard, noting how they fit **(see illustration)**.

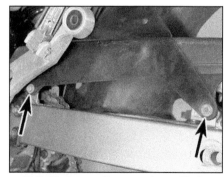

13.6 Chainguard/rear mudguard bolts (arrowed) – TDM shown

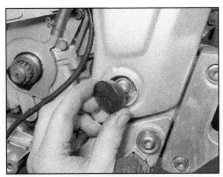

13.9a Remove the blanking caps if fitted . . .

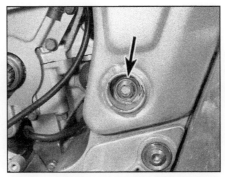

13.9b . . . then unscrew the swingarm nut (arrowed) – TDM shown

13.10 Withdraw the pivot bolt and remove the swingarm – TDM shown

7 On TDM models, unscrew the nut and withdraw the bolt securing the bottom of the shock absorber to the swingarm **(see illustrations 10.3a and b)**.

8 On TRX and XTZ models, remove the rear shock absorber (see Section 10). If required, remove the linkage rods from the swingarm (see Section 11).

9 Where fitted, remove the blanking cap from each end of the swingarm pivot **(see illustration)**. Unscrew the nut on the end of the swingarm pivot bolt and remove the washer, where fitted **(see illustration)**.

10 Support the swingarm, then withdraw the pivot bolt and remove the swingarm **(see illustration)**. Knock the pivot bolt through using a drift if required.

11 Remove the chain slider from the front of the swingarm if necessary, noting how it fits **(see illustration)**. If it is badly worn or damaged, it should be renewed.

12 Inspect all components for wear or damage as described in Section 14.

Installation

13 If removed, install the chain slider and tighten its bolt(s) securely **(see illustration 13.11)**.

14 Remove the cap and washer (where fitted) from each side of the swingarm, and withdraw the bearing spacer(s) **(see illustrations)**. Lubricate the seals (XTZ models) and bearings with molybdenum disulphide grease (TRX models) or lithium-based grease (XTZ models). Also grease the collar(s) and swingarm pivot. Re-install the washers and caps.

15 Offer up the swingarm, and have an assistant hold it in place **(see illustration)**. Make sure the drive chain is looped over the front of the swingarm. Slide the pivot bolt through the swingarm **(see illustration 13.10)**, on TDM models making sure the flats on the head of the pivot bolt locate correctly with the flats in the frame **(see illustration)**. Install the

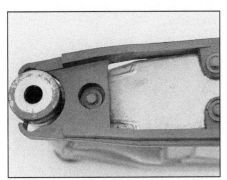

13.11 Remove the chain slider if required

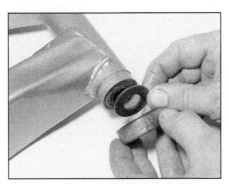

13.14a Remove the cap and washer (where fitted) . . .

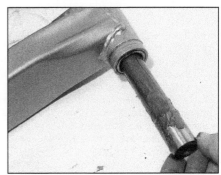

13.14b . . . then withdraw the collar . . .

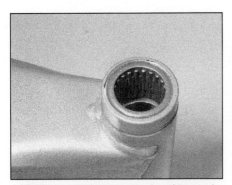

13.14c . . . and grease the bearings and other components as described

13.15a Do not forget to loop the chain over the swingarm

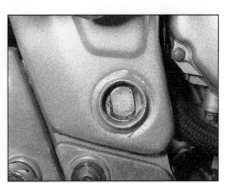

13.15b On TDM models, make sure the bolt head flats locate correctly

13.15c Fit the nut (with its washer, where fitted) . . .

13.15d . . . and tighten it to the specified torque

13.17a On TDM models, locate the chainguard as shown . . .

nut with its washer, where fitted and tighten the nut to the torque setting specified at the beginning of the Chapter (see illustrations). On TRX and XTZ models it may be necessary to counter-hold the bolt head to prevent it from turning. Where removed, fit the blanking caps (see illustration 13.9a).

16 Install the rear shock absorber (see Section 10) and on TRX and XTZ models the suspension linkage rods, if removed (see Section 11).

17 Install the chainguard, along with the rear fender on TDM models, making sure it locates correctly over the lugs on the swingarm (see illustrations).

18 On TDM models, fit the caliper bracket onto the swingarm and loosely install the bolt (see illustration). Fit the brake hose guide onto the swingarm (see illustration 13.3).

19 On TRX models, fit the brake torque arm onto the swingarm, then install the bolt and tighten the nut to the specified torque setting (see illustration 13.4b). Fit a new split pin onto the bolt. Fit the brake hose guides onto the swingarm (see illustration 13.4a).

20 On XTZ models, feed the brake hose through its guide on the inside of the swingarm and install it onto the caliper (see Chapter 7); note that the rear brake hydraulic system will require topping up and bleeding of air. Fit the brake hose guides onto the underside of the swingarm (see illustration 13.5).

21 Install the rear wheel (see Chapter 7), not

forgetting to tighten the caliper bracket bolt on TDM models.

22 Check and adjust the drive chain slack (see Chapter 1). Check the operation of the rear suspension before taking the machine on the road.

14 Swingarm – inspection and bearing replacement

Inspection

1 Thoroughly clean all components, removing all traces of dirt, corrosion and grease (see illustrations 11.6a and b).

2 Inspect all components closely, looking for obvious signs of wear such as heavy scoring, and cracks or distortion due to accident damage. Any damaged or worn component must be renewed.

3 Check the swingarm pivot bolt for straightness by rolling it on a flat surface such as a piece of plate glass (first wipe off all old grease and remove any corrosion using fine emery cloth). If the equipment is available, place the axle in V-blocks and measure the runout using a dial gauge. Yamaha do not specify a maximum runout limit but if it is obviously bent it must be renewed.

Bearing replacement – TDM and TRX models

4 Remove the cap and washer (where fitted)

from each side of the swingarm (see illustration 13.14a).

5 Withdraw the bearing spacer (see illustration 13.14b) and clean all old grease off the spacer and the two needle roller bearings in the swingarm. If the bearings do not run smoothly and freely they must be renewed (see illustration 13.14c). Refer to Tools and Workshop Tips (Section 5) in the Reference section for details of using a drawbolt tool or bearing extractor with slide-hammer attachment to remove the bearings and install new ones.

6 Lubricate the bearings and the spacer with molybdenum disulphide grease. Install the caps and washers (where fitted) on the swingarm ends

Bearing replacement – XTZ models

7 Remove the cap and washer (and any shims, where fitted) from each side of the swingarm (see illustration 13.14a). Lever out the grease seal on each side of each swingarm pivot.

8 Withdraw the bearing spacers, noting their different length (see illustration 13.14b). Clean all old grease off the spacers, the two needle roller bearings and the two plain bushes in the swingarm. Examine the bearings and the bushes; if the bearings do not run smoothly and freely and the bushes are scored or worn they must all be renewed. Refer to Tools and Workshop Tips (Section 5)

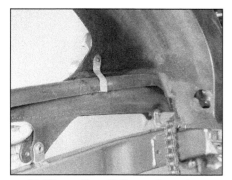

13.17b . . . then fit the mudguard . . .

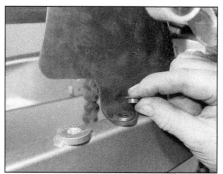

13.17c . . . not forgetting the collars

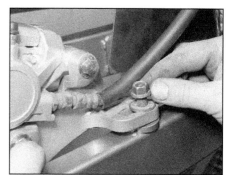

13.18 Locate the caliper bracket and loosely install the bolt

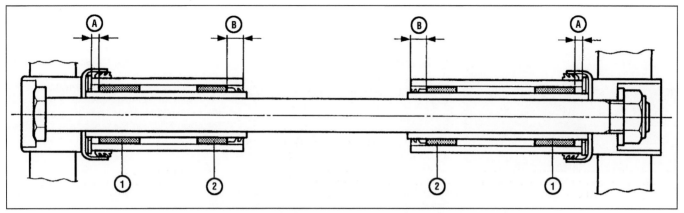

14.8 Swingarm bearing (1) and bush (2) installed depth

A   4 mm   B   8 mm

in the Reference section for details of using a drawbolt tool or bearing extractor with slide-hammer attachment to remove the bearings and bushes and install new ones. When installing the new components note that they must be positioned to a specific depth in the swingarm housings **(see illustration)**.

9 Measure the length of each bearing spacer and the thickness of each washer and compare them to the specifications, renewing any component that is worn. **Note:** *Worn components will increase swingarm sideplay.*

10 Although it is possible to measure the swingarm sideplay with all components assembled on the bike it is preferably to calculate sideplay by direct measurement of the individual components. Done this way, you will be able to install any shims required as the swingarm is refitted. You will need a vernier gauge to do this accurately. Measure the width of the swingarm mounting boss on the engine and call this dimension A. Record the lengths of the two spacers measured in Step 9 as dimensions B and C. Now measure the overall length of the swingarm (from the outside of one bearing housing to the outside of the other) and record this as dimension D. Record the thicknesses of the two washers (added together) measured in Step 9 and record this as dimension E. Compute swingarm sideplay by subtracting the swingarm width and washer thicknesses from the boss width and spacer lengths, thus:

Sideplay = (A + B + C) – (D + E)

If the sideplay is within the limit of 0.4 to 0.7 mm no shims are required. If sideplay exceeds 0.7 mm, fit one or two shims as required to bring sideplay within the specified limit. Shims are available in 0.3 mm thicknesses. The shims should be fitted between the cap and washer; if two shims are required fit one on each side, whereas if only one shim is required fit this on the right-hand side.

11 Press the grease seals into their locations in each side of the swingarm bearing housings, renewing them if they are damaged or deteriorated.

12 Lubricate the bearings, bushes and spacers with lithium-based grease. Do not forget to install the bearing spacer between the bearings in the swingarm. Install the washers, shims (where fitted) and caps on the outer ends of the swingarm.

15 Drive chain – removal, cleaning and installation

Endless type chain

Note: *An endless chain has no riveted (soft) link – all links and pins are the same. The chain fitted as original equipment and supplied as a spare part from Yamaha dealers is of the endless type.*

 Warning: NEVER install a drive chain which uses a clip-type master (split) link.

Removal

1 Remove the swingarm (see Section 13). Note that if the front sprocket is being removed, the sprocket nut should be slackened before removing the swingarm, so that the rear brake can be used so stop the sprocket turning (see Section 16).

15.2b Linkage arm/shaft alignment – TDM models

2 On TDM and XTZ models, unscrew the bolts securing the outer front sprocket cover and remove the cover **(see illustration)**. Unscrew the gearchange lever linkage arm pinchbolt and remove the arm from the shaft, noting the alignment of the punch mark with the slit in the clamp **(see illustration)**. If no mark is visible, make your own before removing the arm so that it can be correctly aligned with the shaft on installation. Unscrew the bolts securing the inner sprocket cover, on TDM models noting the clip secured by the top rear bolt, and remove the cover **(see illustration)**.

3 On TRX models, unscrew the gearchange

15.2a Unscrew the bolts (arrowed) and remove the cover

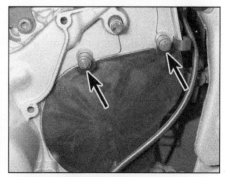

15.2c Unscrew the bolts (arrowed) and remove the inner cover

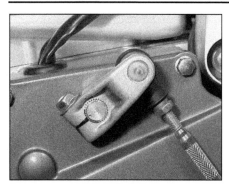

15.3 Linkage arm/shaft alignment – TRX models

lever linkage arm pinchbolt and remove the arm from the shaft, noting the alignment of the punch mark with the slit in the clamp **(see illustration)**. If no mark is visible, make your own before removing the arm so that it can be correctly aligned with the shaft on installation. Unscrew the bolts securing the outer front sprocket cover and remove the cover, then unscrew the bolts securing the inner sprocket cover, noting the clip secured by the top rear bolt, and remove the cover.

4 Slip the chain off the front sprocket and remove it from the bike.

Cleaning and wear check

5 Soak the chain in paraffin (kerosene) for approximately five or six minutes.
Caution: Don't use gasoline (petrol), solvent or other cleaning fluids. Don't use high-pressure water. Remove the chain, wipe it off, then blow dry it with compressed air immediately. The entire process shouldn't take longer than ten minutes – if it does, the O-rings in the chain rollers could be damaged.

6 Once the chain has been cleaned and dried, check it for wear by measuring a 10-link length with the chain taught; anchor one end of the chain and hold the other end tensioned whilst the measurement is taken **(see illustration)**. Compare the result the wear limits at the beginning of this Chapter. Note that chains do not wear evenly, so take measurements at various points in the chain's run.

Installation

7 Installation is the reverse of removal. On completion adjust and lubricate the chain

following the procedures described in Chapter 1.

Riveted link type chain

Removal

Note: *The riveted (soft) link can be identified by its identification markings on the side plate and usually slightly different colour. Also the staked ends of the link's two pins look as if they have been deeply centre-punched, instead of peened over as with all other pins.*

8 Locate the joining link in a suitable position to work on by rotating the back wheel; midway between the sprockets is ideal.

9 Slacken the drive chain as described in Chapter 1.

10 Split the chain at the joining link using an approved chain breaker tool intended for motorcycle use. There are a number of types available for motorcycle use and it is important to follow carefully the instructions supplied with the tool – see *Tools and Workshop Tips* in the Reference section for a typical example. Remove the chain from the bike, noting its routing through the swingarm.

Cleaning and wear check

11 See Steps 5 and 6.

Installation

 Warning: NEVER install a drive chain which uses a clip-type master (split) link. If you do not have access to a chain riveting tool, have the chain fitted by a Yamaha dealer.

12 Remove the engine sprocket cover as described in Steps 2 or 3, as applicable.

13 Thread the chain into position, making sure that it takes the correct route around the swingarm and sprockets and leave the two ends in a convenient place to work on. Obtain a new soft link – never attempt to reuse an old link.

14 Install the new soft link complete with an O-ring on each of its pins through the chain ends from the inside of the chain. Install an O-ring over the pin ends and fit the side plate with its identification marks facing out; use chain tool to press the side plate into position.

15 Stake the new link pins using the chain riveting tool, following carefully the instructions of both the chain manufacturer and the tool manufacturer. Refer to *Tools and Workshop Tips* in the Reference section for

chain riveting details using a typical commercially available tool.

16 After riveting, check the soft link pin ends for any signs of cracking. If there is any evidence of cracking, the soft link, O-rings and side plate must be removed and the procedure repeated with a new soft link.

17 Install the sprocket cover in a reverse of the removal procedure. Adjust and lubricate the chain following the procedures described in Chapter 1.

16 Sprockets –
check and replacement

Check

1 On TDM and XTZ models, unscrew the bolts securing the outer front sprocket cover and remove the cover **(see illustration 15.2a)**. Unscrew the gearchange lever linkage arm pinchbolt and remove the arm from the shaft, noting the alignment of the punch mark with the slit in the clamp **(see illustration 15.2b)**. If no mark is visible, make your own before removing the arm so that it can be correctly aligned with the shaft on installation. Unscrew the bolts securing the inner sprocket cover, on TDM models noting the clip secured by the top rear bolt, and remove the cover **(see illustration 15.2c)**.

2 On TRX models, unscrew the gearchange lever linkage arm pinchbolt and remove the arm from the shaft, noting the alignment of the punch mark with the slit in the clamp **(see illustration 15.3)**. If no mark is visible, make your own before removing the arm so that it can be correctly aligned with the shaft on installation. Unscrew the bolts securing the outer front sprocket cover and remove the cover, then unscrew the bolts securing the inner sprocket cover, noting the clip secured by the top rear bolt, and remove the cover.

3 Check the wear pattern on both sprockets **(see illustration 1.7 in Chapter 1)**. If the sprocket teeth are worn excessively, renew the chain and both sprockets as a set. Whenever the sprockets are inspected, the drive chain should be inspected also (see Chapter 1). If you are renewing the chain, renew the sprockets as well.

4 Adjust and lubricate the chain following the procedures described in Chapter 1.
Caution: Use only the recommended lubricant.

Replacement

Front sprocket

5 On TDM and XTZ models, unscrew the bolts securing the outer front sprocket cover and remove the cover **(see illustration 15.2a)**. Unscrew the gearchange lever linkage arm pinchbolt and remove the arm from the shaft, noting the alignment of the punch mark with the slit in the clamp **(see illustration 15.2b)**. If

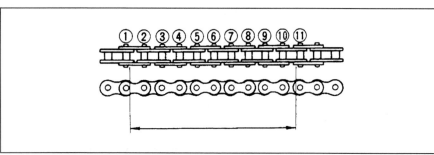

15.6 Check the amount of stretch by measuring a 10-link length as shown

16.7 Bend back the lockwasher tab(s) (arrowed), then unscrew the nut

16.8 Slide the sprocket off the shaft and remove it

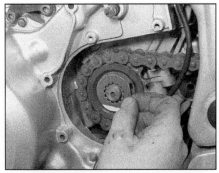

16.10a Fit a new lockwasher . . .

16.10b . . . make sure the nut is the correct way round . . .

16.10c . . . and tighten it to the specified torque

16.10d Bend the tabs up against the nut

no mark is visible, make your own before removing the arm so that it can be correctly aligned with the shaft on installation. Unscrew the bolts securing the inner sprocket cover, on TDM models noting the clip secured by the top rear bolt, and remove the cover **(see illustration 15.2c)**.

6 On TRX models, unscrew the gearchange lever linkage arm pinchbolt and remove the arm from the shaft, noting the alignment of the punch mark with the slit in the clamp **(see illustration 15.3)**. If no mark is visible, make your own before removing the arm so that it can be correctly aligned with the shaft on installation. Unscrew the bolts securing the outer front sprocket cover and remove the cover, then unscrew the bolts securing the inner sprocket cover, noting the clip secured by the top rear bolt, and remove the cover.

7 Bend down the tab(s) on the sprocket nut lockwasher **(see illustration)**. Have an assistant apply the rear brake, then unscrew the nut and remove the washer. Refer to Chapter 1 and adjust the chain so that it is fully slack.

8 Slide the sprocket and chain off the shaft and slip the sprocket out of the chain **(see illustration)**. If there is not enough slack on the chain to remove the sprocket, disengage the chain from the rear wheel.

9 Engage the new sprocket with the chain and slide it on the shaft **(see illustration 16.8)**. Take up the slack in the chain (see Chapter 1).

10 Slide on a new lockwasher, then fit the nut with its recessed side facing in and tighten it to the torque setting specified at the beginning of the Chapter, using the method employed on removal to prevent the sprocket from turning **(see illustrations)**. Bend up one of the pre-formed tabs of the lockwasher against the nut flats **(see illustration)**.

11 On TDM and XTZ models, install the inner sprocket cover, on TDM models not forgetting the clip secured by the top rear bolt, and tighten the bolts securely **(see illustration 15.2c)**. Align the split in the gearchange linkage arm clamp with the punch mark on the shaft, then fit the arm on the shaft and tighten the pinchbolt to the specified torque setting **(see illustration 15.2b)**. Install the outer sprocket cover and tighten its bolts to the specified torque **(see illustration 15.2a)**.

12 On TRX models, install the inner sprocket cover, not forgetting the clip secured by the top rear bolt, and tighten the bolts securely. Install the outer sprocket cover and tighten its bolts to the specified torque. Align the split in the gearchange linkage arm clamp with the punch mark on the shaft, then fit the arm on the shaft and tighten the pinchbolt to the specified torque setting **(see illustration 15.3)**.

Rear sprocket

13 Remove the rear wheel (see Chapter 7).

14 On XTZ models, bend back the locking tabs on the sprocket nut lockplates.

15 Unscrew the nuts securing the sprocket to the hub assembly **(see illustration)**. Remove the sprocket, noting which way round it fits.

16 Install the sprocket onto the hub with the stamped mark facing out. On XTZ models, install the lockplates, noting that new ones should be used. Tighten the nuts evenly and in a criss-cross sequence to the torque setting specified at the beginning of the Chapter. On XTZ models, bend the tabs of the lockplates up against the nut flats.

17 Install the rear wheel (see Chapter 7).

16.15 Unscrew the nuts (arrowed) and remove the sprocket

17.2 Lift the sprocket coupling out of the wheel . . .

17.3 . . . and remove the rubber dampers

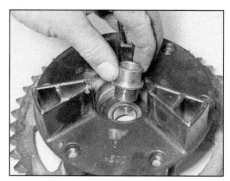

17.5 Fit the spacer into the bearing if it was removed

17 Rear sprocket coupling/rubber dampers – check and replacement

1 Remove the rear wheel (see Chapter 7).
Caution: Do not lay the wheel down on the disc as it could become warped. Lay the wheel on wooden blocks so that the disc is off the ground.

2 Lift the sprocket coupling out of the wheel leaving the rubber dampers in position in the wheel **(see illustration)**. Note the spacer inside the coupling – it should be a tight fit but remove it if it is likely to drop out. Check the coupling for cracks or any obvious signs of damage. Also check the sprocket studs for wear or damage.
3 Lift the rubber damper segments from the wheel and check them for cracks, hardening and general deterioration **(see illustration)**. Renew the rubber dampers as a set if necessary.
4 Checking and replacement procedures for the sprocket coupling bearing are described in Chapter 7.
5 Installation is the reverse of removal. Make sure the spacer is still correctly installed in the coupling, or install it if it was removed **(see illustration)**.
6 Install the rear wheel (see Chapter 7).

Chapter 7
Brakes, wheels and tyres

Contents

Degrees of difficulty

Easy, suitable for novice with little experience		Fairly easy, suitable for beginner with some experience		Fairly difficult, suitable for competent DIY mechanic		Difficult, suitable for experienced DIY mechanic		Very difficult, suitable for expert DIY or professional	

Specifications

Brakes

Brake fluid type . . . . DOT 4
Brake pad friction material wear limit
    TDM and TRX models . . . . 0.5 mm
    XTZ models . . . . 1.5 mm
Front caliper bore ID
    1991 to 1995 TDM models . . . . 45.40 mm
    1996-on TDM models
        Upper bore . . . . 33.96 mm
        Lower bore . . . . 30.23 mm
    TRX models . . . . 32.10 mm
    XTZ models . . . . 27.00 mm
Front disc thickness
    Standard . . . . 4.0 mm
    Service limit . . . . 3.5 mm
Front disc maximum runout . . . . 0.2 mm
Front master cylinder bore ID
    TDM and TRX models . . . . 15.8 mm
    XTZ models . . . . 14.0 mm
Rear caliper bore ID
    TDM and TRX models . . . . 42.8 mm
    XTZ models . . . . 27.0 mm
Rear disc minimum thickness
    Standard . . . . 5.0 mm
    Service limit . . . . 4.5 mm
Rear disc maximum runout . . . . 0.15 mm
Rear master cylinder bore ID . . . . 14.0 mm

Wheels

Wheel runout (max)
  Axial (side-to-side)
    TDM and XTZ models .... 0.5 mm
    TRX models .... 2.0 mm
  Radial (out-of-round)
    TDM and XTZ models .... 1.0 mm
    TRX models .... 2.0 mm

Tyres

Tyre pressures .... see *Daily (pre-ride)* checks
Tyre sizes*
  1991 to 1995 TDM models
    Front .... 110/80-18 58H, tubeless
    Rear .... 150/70-17 69H, tubeless
  1996-on TDM models
    Front .... 110/80-ZR18, tubeless
    Rear .... 150/70-ZR17, tubeless
  TRX models
    Front .... 120/60-ZR17, tubeless
    Rear .... 160/60-ZR17, tubeless
  XTZ models
    Front .... 90/90-21 54H, tubed
    Rear .... 140/80-17 69H, tubed
*Refer to the owners handbook or the tyre information label on the swingarm for approved tyre brands.

Torque settings

Brake pad retaining pins – XTZ models .... 18 Nm
Brake caliper mounting bolts
  1991 to 1995 TDM models .... 35 Nm
  1996-on TDM models and TRX models .... 40 Nm
  XTZ models .... 35 Nm
Brake hose banjo bolts
  1991 to 1995 TDM models .... 26 Nm
  1996-on TDM models and TRX models .... 30 Nm
  XTZ models .... 25 Nm
Brake disc bolts
  TDM models and XTZ models .... 20 Nm
  TRX models .... 23 Nm
Front brake master cylinder clamp bolts
  TDM models .... 9 Nm
  TRX and XTZ models .... 10 Nm
Rear brake master cylinder bolts
  TDM and TRX models .... 23 Nm
  XTZ models .... 20 Nm
Brake caliper bleed valves .... 6 Nm
Front wheel axle
  TDM models .... 58 Nm
  TRX models .... 65 Nm
Front wheel axle clamp bolt
  TDM models .... 19 Nm
  TRX models .... 20 Nm
Front wheel axle nut – XTZ models .... 110 Nm

1 General information

TDM and TRX models are fitted with cast alloy wheels designed for tubeless tyres only. XTZ models are fitted with spoked wheels designed for tubed tyres only. Both front and rear brakes are hydraulically operated disc brakes.

On TDM and TRX models, the front brakes are twin opposed-piston calipers, and the rear brake is a single opposed piston caliper. On XTZ models, both front and rear brakes are twin piston sliding calipers.

 Warning: Disc brake components rarely require disassembly. Do not disassemble components unless absolutely necessary. If a hydraulic brake line is loosened, the entire system must be disassembled, drained, cleaned and then properly filled and bled upon reassembly. Do not use solvents on internal brake components. Solvents will cause the seals to swell and distort. Use only clean brake fluid or denatured alcohol for cleaning. Use care when working with brake fluid as it can injure your eyes and it will damage painted surfaces and plastic parts.

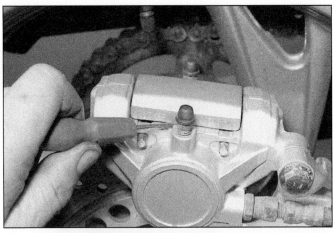

2.1a Remove the pad cover . . .

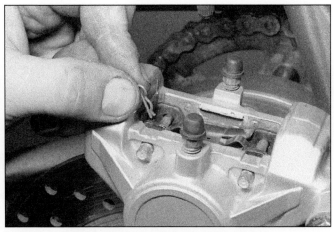

2.1b . . . then remove the retaining clips . . .

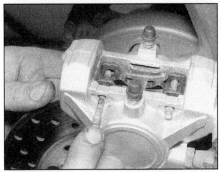

2.1c . . . and withdraw the pad pins

2.1d Remove the pad spring . . .

2.1e . . . and lift out the pads

2 Brake pads – replacement

⚠ **Warning: The dust created by the brake system may contain asbestos, which is harmful to** *your health. Never blow it out with compressed air and don't inhale any of it. An approved filtering mask should be worn when working on the brakes.*

1 On TDM and TRX models, where fitted, remove the pad cover from the top of the caliper **(see illustration)**. Remove the pad pin retaining clips, then withdraw the pad pins from the caliper, noting how they locate against the pad spring **(see illustrations)**. Remove the spring, noting how it fits, then lift out the pads **(see illustrations)**. Where fitted, remove the shims from the back of the pads, noting how they fit.

2 On XTZ models, slacken the pad retaining pins, then unscrew the caliper mounting bolts and slide the caliper off the disc **(see illustrations)**. Unscrew the pad retaining pins

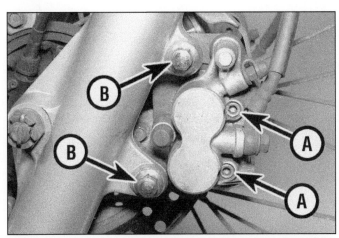

2.2a Slacken the pad retaining pins (A), then unscrew the caliper mounting bolts (B) . . .

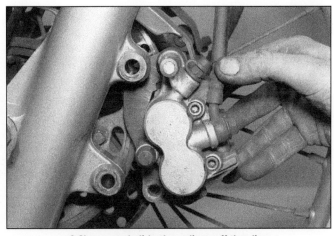

2.2b . . . and slide the caliper off the disc

2.2c Remove the pad pins . . .

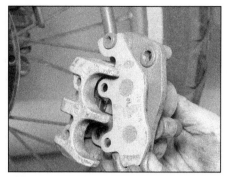

2.2d . . . and lift out the pads, noting how they fit

2.2e Slide the bracket out of the caliper

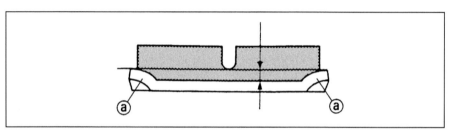

2.3a Pad wear indicator tangs (a) and minimum friction material limit (arrowed) – TDM and TRX

and withdraw them (see illustration). Remove the inner pad, noting how it locates against the guide pin on the caliper bracket, then remove the outer pad, noting how it sits in the caliper bracket (see illustration). Where fitted, remove the shims from the back of the pads, noting how they fit. Separate the bracket from the caliper, noting how it fits (see illustration). Remove the pad spring if required, noting how it fits (see illustration 2.11a).

3 Inspect the surface of each pad for contamination and check that the friction material has not worn level with or beyond the wear indicator tangs or groove (see Chapter 1) (see illustrations). Yamaha also specify a minimum friction material thickness (see Specifications) which should correspond with the tang height or groove depth on genuine Yamaha pads. It is strongly advised that the pads are renewed well before the wear indicators or minimum amount of friction material is reached. The pads should also be renewed if they are fouled with oil or grease, or heavily scored or damaged by dirt and debris; it is not possible to degrease the friction material. Always renew both pads in the caliper and renew the pads in each front caliper at the same time.

4 If the pads are in good condition clean them carefully, using a fine wire brush which is completely free of oil and grease to remove all traces of road dirt and corrosion. Using a pointed instrument, clean out the grooves in the friction material and dig out any embedded particles of foreign matter. Any areas of glazing may be removed using emery cloth.

5 Check the condition of the brake disc(s) (see Section 4).

6 Remove all traces of corrosion from the pad pins. Inspect the pins for signs of damage and renew them if necessary.

7 On XTZ models, clean the old grease off the caliper slider pins on the bracket and check the rubber boots in the caliper (see illustration 2.2e). If they are damaged or deteriorated, they should be renewed.

8 Push the pistons as far back into the caliper as possible using hand pressure or a piece of wood as leverage. Due to the increased friction material thickness of new pads, it may be necessary to remove the master cylinder reservoir cover and diaphragm and siphon out some fluid.

9 Where removed, fit the shims onto the back of the pads, making sure the arrow points in the direction of normal disc rotation (see illustration). The following step is necessary on UK models, and anywhere else where salt is used on the roads, to ensure that the pads move freely in the calipers. Apply a thin film of Duckhams Copper 10 or equivalent to the

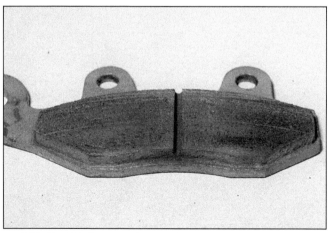

2.3b Pad friction material showing wear limit groove – XTZ models

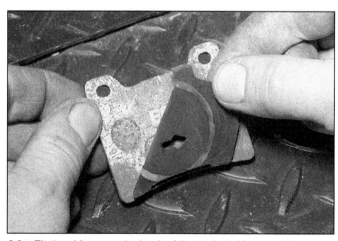

2.9a Fit the shim onto the back of the pad, making sure the arrow points in the direction of normal disc rotation

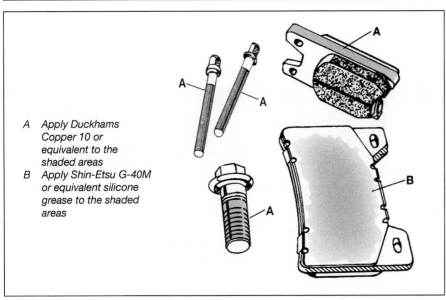

A   Apply Duckhams
    Copper 10 or
    equivalent to the
    shaded areas
B   Apply Shin-Etsu G-40M
    or equivalent silicone
    grease to the shaded
    areas

2.9b Special lubricants are required in the UK (and recommended anywhere salt is used on the roads) to prevent corrosion

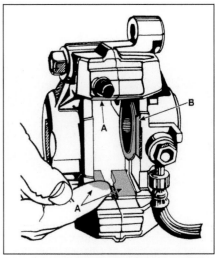

2.9c Apply the recommended lubricants to the pad friction areas inside the caliper and to the exposed portion of the caliper pistons

A   Duckhams Copper 10
B   Shin-Etsu G-40M or equivalent silicone grease

following areas before installing the pads (see illustrations):

a) To the edges of the metal backing on the brake pads.
b) To the pad retaining pins.
c) To the areas of the caliper where the pads rub.
d) To the threads of the caliper mounting bolts.
e) To the surfaces of the slider pins on XTZ models.

Caution: Don't use too much Copper 10 and make sure it doesn't contact the brake discs or the pad friction surfaces.

Apply a thin film of Shin-Etsu G-40M or equivalent silicone grease to the following:

f) Exposed areas of the caliper pistons

g) The areas of the pad backing plates that contact the pistons.

10 On TDM and TRX models, insert the pads into the caliper so that the friction material faces the disc (see illustration 2.1e). Fit the pad spring onto the pads, making sure the arrow (where present) or the longer outer tabs point in the direction of normal disc rotation (see illustration 2.1d). Install the pad pins, making sure they pass through the hole in each pad and locate correctly onto the pad spring, then fit the retaining clips (see illustrations 2.1c and b). Where fitted, install the caliper cover (see illustration).

11 On XTZ models, if removed, fit the pad spring into the caliper, making sure the larger tabs point to the outside of the caliper (see illustration). Apply the specified grease (see Step 9) to the slider pins on the bracket and slide the bracket into the caliper (see

2.10 Clip the cover onto the caliper, making sure it is secure

illustration 2.2e). Fit the outer pad, making sure it locates correctly (see illustration),

2.11a Install the pad spring as shown

2.11b Locate the outer pad into the caliper as shown

2.11c Slide the caliper onto the disc . . .

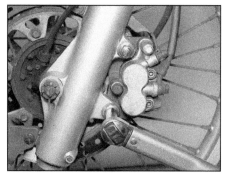

2.11d . . . and tighten the mounting bolts . . .

2.11e . . . and the pad pins to the specified torque

then fit the inner pad, locating the cutout against the guide **(see illustration 2.2d)**. Install the pad pins, making sure they pass through the hole in each pad, and tighten them finger-tight **(see illustration 2.2c)**. Install the brake caliper and tighten its bolts to the torque setting specified at the beginning of the Chapter, then tighten the pad retaining pins to the specified torque **(see illustrations)**.

12 Top up the master cylinder reservoir if necessary (see *Daily (pre-ride) checks*), and refit the reservoir cover and diaphragm.

3.1 Unscrew the bolts (arrowed) and remove the shield

13 Operate the brake lever several times to bring the pads into contact with the disc. Check the operation of the brake before riding the motorcycle.

3 Brake calipers – removal, overhaul and installation

⚠️ *Warning: If a caliper indicates the need for an overhaul (usually due to leaking fluid or sticky operation), all old brake fluid should be flushed from the system. Also, the dust created by the brake system may contain asbestos, which is harmful to your health. Never blow it out with compressed air and don't inhale any of it. An approved filtering mask should be worn when working on the brakes. Do not, under any circumstances, use petroleum-based solvents to clean brake parts. Use clean brake fluid only on the internal parts. Brake cleaner or denatured alcohol can be used on external parts.*

Removal

1 On XTZ models, if removing the rear brake caliper, unscrew the bolts securing the rear

caliper shield and remove the shield **(see illustration)**. If the brake pads are being removed from the calipers, slacken the pad retaining pins now **(see illustration 2.2a)**.

2 If the calipers are just being displaced and not completely removed or overhauled, do not disconnect the brake hose. If the calipers are being overhauled, unscrew the brake hose banjo bolt **(see illustration)**. Note the alignment of the hose on the caliper and separate the hose from the caliper. On the rear caliper on TDM models, counter-hold the hose nut and unscrew the locknut and separate the hose from the hose joint in the caliper **(see illustration)**. Plug the hose end or wrap a plastic bag tightly around it to minimise fluid loss and prevent dirt entering the system. Discard the banjo bolt sealing washers as new ones must be used on installation. **Note:** *If you are planning to overhaul the caliper and don't have a source of compressed air to blow out the pistons, just loosen the banjo bolt at this stage and retighten it lightly. The bike's hydraulic system can then be used to force the pistons out of the body once the pads have been removed. Disconnect the hose once the pistons have been sufficiently displaced.*

3 Unscrew the caliper mounting bolts, and

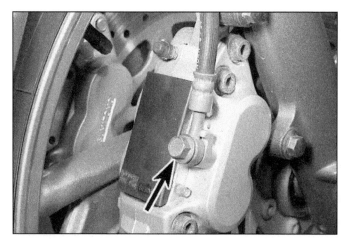

3.2a Unscrew the brake hose banjo bolt (arrowed), noting its alignment

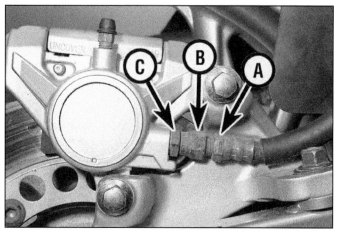

3.2b Counter-hold the hose nut (A) and unscrew the locknut (B) from the hose joint (C)

3.3a Unscrew the caliper mounting bolts (arrowed) . . .

3.3b . . . and slide the caliper off the disc

slide the caliper off the disc (see illustrations).

4 If the calipers are being overhauled, remove the brake pads (see Section 2). If the calipers are just being displaced, the pads can be left in place.

Overhaul

5 Clean the exterior of the caliper with brake system cleaner or denatured alcohol. On XTZ models, if not already done, separate the caliper bracket from the caliper, noting how it fits (see illustration 2.2e).

6 Displace the pistons as far as possible from the caliper body, either by pumping them out by operating the front brake lever or rear brake pedal (as applicable), or by forcing them out using compressed air. If the compressed air method is used, place a wad of rag between the pistons and the caliper to act as a cushion, then use compressed air directed into the fluid inlet to force the pistons out of the body. Use only low pressure to ease the pistons out and make sure the pistons are displaced at the same time. If the air pressure is too high and the pistons are forced out, the caliper and/or pistons may be damaged. On opposed piston calipers there is not enough room to remove the pistons from both sides at the same time, so block one side in their

bores using a piece of wood and displace the opposite side first, then remove the seals (see below), reinstall the removed pistons and block them using the wood while removing the other side. Now remove the wood and the first pistons, which can now be easily removed. Mark each piston head and caliper body with a felt marker to ensure that the pistons can be matched to their original bores on reassembly.

 Warning: Never place your fingers in front of the pistons in an attempt to catch or protect them when applying compressed air, as serious injury could result.
Caution: On TDM and TRX models, do not attempt to remove the caliper body bolts and separate the caliper halves.

7 Using a wooden or plastic tool, remove the dust seals from the caliper bores (see illustration). Discard them as new ones must be used on installation. If a metal tool is being used, take great care not to damage the caliper bores.

8 Remove and discard the piston seals in the same way.

9 Clean the pistons and bores with clean brake fluid. If compressed air is available, use it to dry the parts thoroughly (make sure it's filtered and unlubricated).

Caution: Do not, under any circumstances, use a petroleum-based solvent to clean brake parts.

10 Inspect the caliper bores and pistons for signs of corrosion, nicks and burrs and loss of plating. If surface defects are present, the caliper assembly must be renewed. If the caliper is in bad shape the master cylinder should also be checked.

11 Lubricate the new piston seals with clean brake fluid and install them in their grooves in the caliper bores. Note that on some models different sizes of bore and piston are used (see Specifications), and care must therefore be taken to ensure that the correct size seals are fitted to the correct bores. The same applies when fitting the new dust seals and pistons.

12 Lubricate the new dust seals with clean brake fluid and install them in their grooves in the caliper bores.

13 Lubricate the pistons with clean brake fluid and install them closed-end first into the caliper bores. Using your thumbs, push the pistons all the way in, making sure they enter the bore squarely.

Installation

14 Install the brake pads (see Section 2).

15 Install the caliper on the brake disc making sure the pads sit squarely either side of the disc (see illustration 3.3b).

16 Install the caliper mounting bolts, and tighten them to the torque setting specified at the beginning of the Chapter (see illustration). On XTZ models, if the pads were removed, now tighten the pad retaining pins to the specified torque (see illustration 2.2a).

17 If removed, connect the brake hose to the caliper, using new sealing washers on each side of the banjo fittings (see illustration 7.4). Align the hose as noted on removal (see illustration 3.2a). Tighten the banjo bolt to the torque setting specified at the beginning of the Chapter. On the rear caliper on TDM models, fit the hose against the hose joint and tighten the locknut onto the hose, counter-

3.7 Use a plastic or wooden tool (such as a pencil) to remove the seals

3.16 Tighten the caliper mounting bolts to the specified torque

4.2 Set up a dial gauge with the probe contacting the brake disc, then rotate the wheel to check for runout

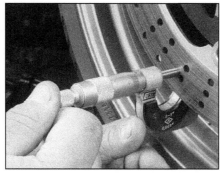

4.3 Using a micrometer to measure disc thickness

4.5 Unscrew the bolts (arrowed) and remove the disc – TDM rear disc shown

holding the hose nut to prevent the hose twisting **(see illustration 3.2b)**. Do not overtighten the locknut. Top up the master cylinder reservoir with DOT 4 brake fluid (see *Daily (pre-ride) checks*) and bleed the hydraulic system as described in Section 8.

18 On XTZ models, install the rear brake caliper shield.

19 Check for leaks and thoroughly test the operation of the brake before riding the motorcycle.

4 Brake discs – inspection, removal and installation

Inspection

1 Visually inspect the surface of the disc for score marks and other damage. Light scratches are normal after use and won't affect brake operation, but deep grooves and heavy score marks will reduce braking efficiency and accelerate pad wear. If a disc is badly grooved it must be machined or renewed.

2 To check disc runout, position the bike on an auxiliary stand and support it so that the wheel is raised off the ground. On XTZ models, remove the front disc covers **(see illustration 11.5)**. Mount a dial gauge on a fork slider or on the swingarm, with the plunger on the gauge touching the surface of the disc about 10 mm (1/2 in) from the outer edge **(see illustration)**. Rotate the wheel and watch the gauge needle, comparing the reading with the limit listed in the Specifications at the beginning of the Chapter. If the runout is greater than the service limit, check the wheel bearings for play (see Chapter 1). If the bearings are worn, renew them (see Section 13) and repeat this check. If the disc runout is still excessive, it will have to be renewed, although machining by an engineer may be possible.

3 The disc must not be machined or allowed to wear down to a thickness less than the service limit as listed in this Chapter's Specifications. The thickness of the disc can be checked with a micrometer **(see**

illustration). If the thickness of the disc is less than the service limit, it must be renewed.

Removal

4 Remove the wheel (see Section 11 (front) or 12 (rear)).
Caution: Do not lay the wheel down and allow it to rest on the disc or sprocket – they could become warped. Set the wheel on wood blocks so the disc doesn't support the weight of the wheel.

5 Mark the relationship of the disc to the wheel, so it can be installed in the same position. Unscrew the disc retaining bolts, loosening them a little at a time in a criss-cross pattern to avoid distorting the disc, then remove the disc from the wheel **(see illustration)**.

Installation

6 Install the disc on the wheel, making sure the marked side is on the outside. Align the previously applied matchmarks (if you're reinstalling the original disc).

7 Apply a suitable non-permanent thread locking compound to the disc bolts, then install the bolts and tighten them in a criss-cross pattern evenly and progressively to the torque setting specified at the beginning of the Chapter. Clean off all grease from the brake disc(s) using acetone or brake system cleaner. If a new brake disc has been installed, remove any protective coating from its working surfaces.

8 Install the wheel (see Section 11 or 12).

9 Operate the brake lever or pedal several times to bring the pads into contact with the

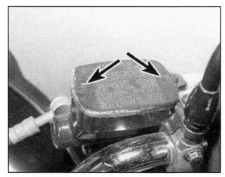

5.3a On TDM and XTZ models, slacken the reservoir cover screws (arrowed)

disc. Check the operation of the brakes carefully before riding the bike.

5 Front brake master cylinder – removal, overhaul and installation

1 If the master cylinder is leaking fluid, or if the lever does not produce a firm feel when the brake is applied, and bleeding the brakes does not help (see Section 8), and the hydraulic hoses are all in good condition, then master cylinder overhaul is recommended.

2 Before disassembling the master cylinder, read through the entire procedure and make sure that you obtain a new piston/seal kit. Also, you will need some new DOT 4 brake fluid, some clean rags and internal circlip pliers. **Note:** *To prevent damage to the paint from spilled brake fluid, always cover the fuel tank when working on the master cylinder.*
Caution: Disassembly, overhaul and reassembly of the brake master cylinder must be done in a spotlessly clean work area to avoid contamination and possible failure of the brake hydraulic system components.

Removal

3 On XTZ models, remove the hand guard. On TDM and XTZ models, loosen, but do not remove, the screws holding the reservoir cover in place **(see illustration)**. On TRX models, remove the reservoir cap clamp and partially unscrew the cap **(see illustration)**.

5.3b On TRX models, remove the clamp (arrowed) and partially unscrew the cap

5.4a Brake switch wiring connector
(arrowed) – TDM models

5.4b Brake switch wiring connectors
(arrowed) – TRX models

5.6a Brake hose banjo bolt (arrowed) –
TDM models

5.6b Brake hose banjo bolt (arrowed) –
TRX models

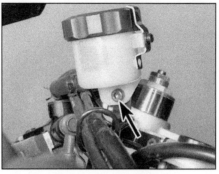

5.7a Reservoir mounting bolt . . .

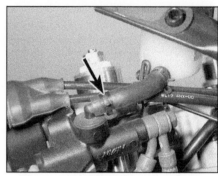

5.7b . . . and hose clamp – TRX models

4 On TDM and TRX models, disconnect the brake light switch wiring connector(s) **(see illustrations)**. On XTZ models, remove the switch from the brake lever bracket.

5 Remove the front brake lever (see Chapter 6). On TDM and XTZ models, remove the rear view mirror.

6 Unscrew the brake hose banjo bolt and separate the hose(s) from the master cylinder, noting the alignment **(see illustrations)**. Discard the sealing washers as they must be renewed. Wrap the end(s) of the hose(s) in a clean rag and suspend in an upright position or bend down carefully and place the open end(s) in a clean container. The objective is to prevent excessive loss of

brake fluid, fluid spills and system contamination.

7 On TRX models, unscrew the bolt securing the reservoir to the bracket, then release the clamp securing the reservoir hose to the union on the master cylinder **(see illustrations)**. Remove the reservoir cap and lift off the diaphragm plate and the rubber diaphragm. Drain the brake fluid from the reservoir into a suitable container, then detach the reservoir hose from its union on the master cylinder. Wipe any remaining fluid out of the reservoir with a clean rag.

8 Unscrew the master cylinder clamp bolts, then lift the master cylinder away from the handlebar **(see illustrations)**.

9 On TDM and XTZ models, remove the reservoir cover retaining screws and lift off the cover, the diaphragm plate and the rubber diaphragm. Drain the brake fluid from the reservoir into a suitable container. Wipe any remaining fluid out of the reservoir with a clean rag.

10 If required, on TDM and TRX models, remove the brake light switch (see Chapter 9).

Overhaul

11 On TDM models, thread the adjuster off the pushrod and remove the spring (where fitted), the nut and the plate.

12 Carefully remove the dust boot from the master cylinder **(see illustration)**.

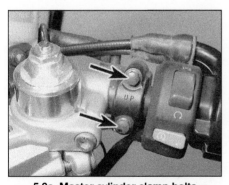

5.8a Master cylinder clamp bolts
(arrowed) – TRX models

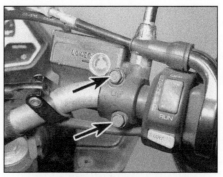

5.8b Master cylinder clamp bolts
(arrowed) – XTZ models

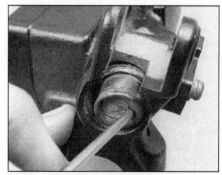

5.12 Remove the rubber boot from the end
of the master cylinder piston . . .

5.13a ... then depress the piston and remove the circlip using a pair of internal circlip pliers

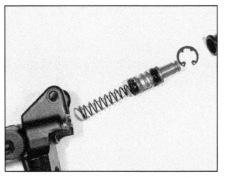

5.13b Lay out the internal parts as shown, even if new parts are being used, to avoid confusion on reassembly

5.24 Align the clamp mating surfaces with the punch mark on the handlebar (arrowed)

13 Using circlip pliers, remove the circlip and slide out the washer and pushrod (TDM models), the piston assembly and the spring, noting how they fit (see illustration). Lay the parts out in the proper order to prevent confusion during reassembly (see illustration).

14 On TRX models, remove the fluid reservoir hose union rubber cap, then remove the circlip and detach the union from the master cylinder. Discard the O-ring as a new one must be used. Inspect the reservoir hose for cracks or splits and renew if necessary.

15 Clean all parts with clean brake fluid. If compressed air is available, use it to dry the parts thoroughly (make sure it's filtered and unlubricated).

Caution: Do not, under any circumstances, use a petroleum-based solvent to clean brake parts.

16 Check the master cylinder bore for corrosion, scratches, nicks and score marks. If damage or wear is evident, the master cylinder must be renewed. If the master cylinder is in poor condition, then the calipers should be checked as well. Check that the fluid inlet and outlet ports in the master cylinder are clear.

17 The dust boot, circlip, piston, seal, primary cup and spring are only available as a kit. Use all of the new parts, regardless of the apparent condition of the old ones. If the seal and cup are not already on the piston, fit them according to the layout of the old piston assembly.

18 Install the spring in the master cylinder. On TDM models the spring's tapered end faces in, and on TRX and XTZ models its tapered end faces out.

19 Lubricate the piston, seal and cup with clean brake fluid. Install the assembly into the master cylinder, making sure it is the correct way round (see illustration 5.13b). Make sure the lips on the cup do not turn inside out when they are slipped into the bore. On TDM models slide in the pushrod with its washer. Depress the piston and install the new circlip, making sure that it locates in the master cylinder groove (see illustration 5.13a).

20 Install the rubber dust boot, making sure the lip is seated correctly in the groove (see illustration 5.12).

21 On TRX models, fit a new O-ring onto the reservoir hose union, then press the union into the master cylinder and secure it with the circlip. Fit the rubber cap over the circlip.

22 Inspect the reservoir cover rubber diaphragm and renew it if it is damaged or deteriorated.

Installation

23 If removed, on TDM and TRX models, install the brake light switch (see Chapter 9).

24 Attach the master cylinder to the handlebar and, where marked, fit the clamp with its UP mark facing up, aligning the top mating surfaces of the clamp with the punch mark on the handlebar (see illustration). Tighten first the upper bolt, then the lower bolt to the torque setting specified at the beginning of the Chapter (see illustrations 5.8a and b).

25 Connect the brake hose(s) to the master cylinder, using new sealing washers on each side of the union(s), and aligning the hose(s) as noted on removal (see illustrations 5.6a and b). Tighten the banjo bolt to the torque setting specified at the beginning of this Chapter.

26 Install the brake lever (see Chapter 6), and on TDM and XTZ models the rear view mirror.

27 On TRX models, mount the reservoir onto its bracket and tighten the bolt securely (see illustration 5.7a). Connect the reservoir hose to the union and secure it with the clamp (see illustration 5.7b).

28 On TDM and TRX models, connect the brake light switch wiring (see illustrations 5.4a and b). On XTZ models, fit the switch into the lever bracket.

29 Fill the fluid reservoir with new DOT 4 brake fluid as described in *Daily (pre-ride) checks*. Refer to Section 8 of this Chapter and bleed the air from the system.

30 Fit the rubber diaphragm, making sure it is correctly seated, the diaphragm plate and the cover or cap onto the master cylinder reservoir (see illustration 5.3a). On TRX models, fit the cap clamp (see illustration 5.3b).

31 Check the operation of the front brake before riding the motorcycle.

6 Rear brake master cylinder – removal, overhaul and installation

1 If the master cylinder is leaking fluid, or if the lever does not produce a firm feel when the brake is applied, and bleeding the brakes does not help (see Section 8), and the hydraulic hoses are all in good condition, then master cylinder overhaul is recommended.

2 Before disassembling the master cylinder, read through the entire procedure and make sure that you obtain a new piston/seal kit. Also, you will need some new DOT 4 brake fluid, some clean rags and internal circlip pliers. Note: *To prevent damage to the paint from spilled brake fluid, always cover the surrounding components when working on the master cylinder.*

Caution: Disassembly, overhaul and reassembly of the brake master cylinder must be done in a spotlessly clean work area to avoid contamination and possible failure of the brake hydraulic system components.

Removal

3 On TDM models, remove the seat, and on XTZ models remove the right-hand side cover (see Chapter 8).

4 Unscrew the bolt securing the master cylinder fluid reservoir to the frame, then remove the reservoir cap and pour the fluid into a container (see illustrations). Release

6.4a Master cylinder reservoir screw (arrowed) – TDM models

6.4b Master cylinder reservoir screw (arrowed) – TRX models

6.4c Master cylinder reservoir bolt (arrowed) – XTZ models

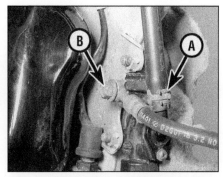

6.5a Reservoir hose clamp (A), brake hose banjo bolt (B) – TDM models

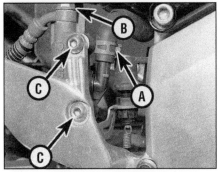

6.5b Reservoir hose clamp (A), brake hose banjo bolt (B), master cylinder mounting bolts (C) – TRX models

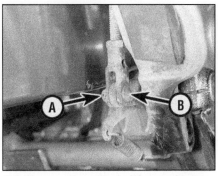

6.6 Remove the split pin (A) and withdraw the clevis pin (B)

6.7 Master cylinder mounting bolts (arrowed) – TDM shown

the clamp securing the reservoir hose to the union on the master cylinder and detach the hose **(see illustrations 6.5a and b)**.

5 Unscrew the brake hose banjo bolt and separate the brake hose from the master cylinder, noting its alignment **(see illustrations)**. Discard the two sealing washers as they must be renewed. Wrap the end of the hose in a clean rag and suspend the hose in an upright position or bend it down carefully and place the open end in a clean container. The objective is to prevent excessive loss of brake fluid, fluid spills and system contamination.

6 Remove the split pin and washer from the clevis pin securing the brake pedal to the master cylinder pushrod **(see illustration)**. Withdraw the clevis pin and separate the pedal from the pushrod. Discard the split pin as a new one must be used.

7 Unscrew the two bolts securing the master cylinder to the bracket and remove the master cylinder **(see illustration and 6.5b)**.

Overhaul

8 If required, mark the position of the clevis locknut on the pushrod, then slacken the locknut and thread the clevis and its base nut off the pushrod **(see illustration)**.

9 Dislodge the rubber dust boot from the base of the master cylinder to reveal the pushrod retaining circlip **(see illustrations)**.

10 Depress the pushrod and, using

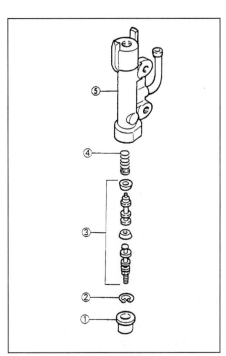

6.9a Master cylinder components

1 Rubber boot
2 Circlip
3 Piston/seal assembly
4 Spring
5 Master cylinder

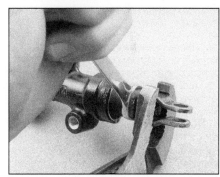

6.8 Hold the clevis and slacken the locknut

6.9b Remove the dust boot from the pushrod

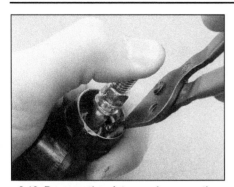

6.10 Depress the piston and remove the circlip from the cylinder

circlip pliers, remove the circlip **(see illustration)**. Slide out the piston assembly and spring. If they are difficult to remove, apply low pressure compressed air to the fluid outlet. Lay the parts out in the proper order to prevent confusion during reassembly.

11 Clean all of the parts with clean brake fluid.

Caution: Do not, under any circumstances, use a petroleum-based solvent to clean brake parts. If compressed air is available, use it to dry the parts thoroughly (make sure it's filtered and unlubricated).

12 Check the master cylinder bore for corrosion, scratches, nicks and score marks. If damage is evident, the master cylinder must be renewed. If the master cylinder is in poor condition, then the caliper should be checked as well.

13 Inspect the reservoir hose for cracks or splits and renew if necessary. If required, on TDM models remove the screw and on XTZ models the circlip securing the hose union to the master cylinder. On TRX models the union is a push fit. Pull the union from the master cylinder. Discard the O-ring or bush (TRX models) as a new one must be used.

14 The dust boot, circlip, piston, seal, primary cup and spring are only available as a kit. Use all of the new parts, regardless of the apparent condition of the old ones. If the seal and cup are not already on the piston, fit them according to the layout of the old piston assembly.

7.2 Flex the brake hoses and check for cracks, bulges and leaking fluid

15 Install the spring in the master cylinder so that its tapered end faces the piston.

16 Lubricate the piston, seal and cup with clean brake fluid. Install the assembly into the master cylinder, making sure it is the correct way round. Make sure the lips on the cup do not turn inside out when they are slipped into the bore.

17 Install and depress the pushrod, then fit a new circlip, making sure it is properly seated in the groove.

18 Install the rubber dust boot, making sure the lip is seated properly in the groove.

19 If removed, fit a new O-ring or bush (TRX models) to the fluid reservoir hose union, then push the union into the master cylinder and on TDM and XTZ models secure it with its screw or circlip.

Installation

20 If removed, install the clevis locknut, the clevis and the base nut onto the master cylinder pushrod end. Position the clevis as noted on removal, then tighten the clevis locknut securely **(see illustration 6.8)**.

21 Install the master cylinder onto the footrest bracket and tighten its mounting bolts to the torque setting specified at the beginning of the Chapter **(see illustration 6.5b and 6.7)**.

22 Align the brake pedal with the master cylinder pushrod clevis, then slide in the clevis pin and secure it using a new split pin, not forgetting the washer **(see illustration 6.6)**.

23 Connect the brake hose banjo bolt to the master cylinder, using a new sealing washer on each side of the banjo union. Ensure that the hose is positioned so that it butts against the lug and tighten the banjo bolt to the specified torque setting **(see illustrations 6.5a and b)**.

24 Secure the fluid reservoir to the frame with its retaining bolt **(see illustrations 6.4a, b and c)**. Ensure that the hose is correctly routed, then connect it to the union on the master cylinder and secure it with the clamp **(see illustration 6.5a and b)**. Check that the hose is secure and clamped at the reservoir end as well. If the clamps have weakened, use new ones.

25 Fill the fluid reservoir with new DOT 4

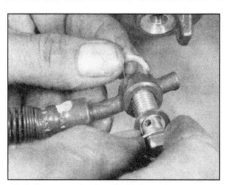

7.4 Remove the banjo bolt and separate the hose from the caliper; there is a sealing washer on each side of the fitting

brake fluid (see *Daily (pre-ride) checks*) and bleed the system following the procedure in Section 8.

26 On TDM models, install the seat, and on XTZ models install the right-hand side cover (see Chapter 8).

27 Check the operation of the brake carefully before riding the motorcycle.

---

7 Brake hoses, pipes and unions – inspection and replacement

Inspection

1 Brake hose and pipe condition should be checked regularly and the hoses renewed at the specified interval (see Chapter 1).

2 Twist and flex the rubber hoses while looking for cracks, bulges and seeping fluid **(see illustration)**. Check extra carefully around the areas where the hoses connect with the banjo fittings, as these are common areas for hose failure.

3 Inspect the metal brake pipe (1996-on models) and the banjo union fittings connected to the brake hoses. If the fittings are rusted, scratched or cracked, renew them.

Replacement

4 The brake hoses have banjo union fittings on each end, with the exception of the rear caliper hose on TDM models which has a joint piece. On 1996-on TDM models, the brake pipe splitting the front brake hose has flare nuts. Cover the surrounding area with plenty of rags and unscrew the banjo bolt or flare nut at each end of the hose or pipe, noting its alignment. On the rear caliper on TDM models, counter-hold the hose nut and unscrew the locknut and separate the hose from the hose joint in the caliper **(see illustration 3.2b)**. If required, unscrew the joint from the caliper. Free the hose or pipe from any clips or guides and remove it. Discard the sealing washers on the hose unions **(see illustration)**.

5 Position the new hose or pipe, making sure it isn't twisted or otherwise strained, and abut the tab on the hose union with the lug on the component casting, where present. Otherwise align the hose or pipe as noted on removal. Install the hose banjo bolts using new sealing washers on both sides of the unions. Tighten the banjo bolts to the torque settings specified at the beginning of this Chapter. Do not overtighten the brake pipe flare nuts. On the rear caliper on TDM models, if removed, thread the joint piece into the caliper using a new sealing washer and tighten securely **(see illustration 3.2b)**. Fit the hose against the hose joint and tighten the locknut onto the hose, counter-holding the hose nut to prevent the hose twisting. Do not overtighten the locknut. Make sure the hoses and pipes are correctly aligned and routed clear of all moving components.

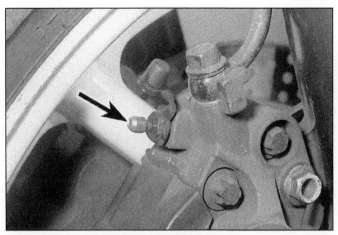

8.6a Brake caliper bleed valve

8.6b To bleed the brakes, you need a spanner, a short section of clear tubing, and a clear container half-filled with brake fluid

6 Flush the old brake fluid from the system, refill with new DOT 4 brake fluid (see *Daily (pre-ride) checks*) and bleed the air from the system (see Section 8). Check the operation of the brakes carefully before riding the motorcycle.

8 Brake system – bleeding

1 Bleeding the brakes is simply the process of removing all the air bubbles from the brake fluid reservoirs, the hoses and the brake calipers. Bleeding is necessary whenever a brake system hydraulic connection is loosened, when a component or hose is renewed, or when the master cylinder or caliper is overhauled. Leaks in the system may also allow air to enter, but leaking brake fluid will reveal their presence and warn you of the need for repair.
2 To bleed the brakes, you will need some new DOT 4 brake fluid, a length of clear vinyl or plastic tubing, a small container partially filled with clean brake fluid, some rags and a spanner to fit the brake caliper bleed valves.
3 Cover the fuel tank and other painted components to prevent damage in the event that brake fluid is spilled.
4 When bleeding the rear brake, on TDM models, remove the seat, and on XTZ models remove the right-hand side cover (see Chapter 8) for access to the fluid reservoir.
5 Remove the reservoir cover or cap, diaphragm plate (where fitted) and diaphragm and slowly pump the brake lever or pedal a few times, until no air bubbles can be seen floating up from the holes in the bottom of the reservoir. Doing this bleeds the air from the master cylinder end of the line. Loosely refit the reservoir cover.
6 Pull the dust cap off the bleed valve **(see illustration)**. Attach one end of the clear vinyl or plastic tubing to the bleed valve and

submerge the other end in the brake fluid in the container **(see illustration)**.
7 Remove the reservoir cover and check the fluid level. Do not allow the fluid level to drop below the lower mark during the bleeding process.
8 Carefully pump the brake lever or pedal three or four times and hold it in (front) or down (rear) while opening the caliper bleed valve. When the valve is opened, brake fluid will flow out of the caliper into the clear tubing and the lever will move toward the handlebar or the pedal will move down.
9 Retighten the bleed valve, then release the brake lever or pedal gradually. Repeat the process until no air bubbles are visible in the brake fluid leaving the caliper and the lever or pedal is firm when applied. On completion, disconnect the bleeding equipment, then tighten the bleed valve to the torque setting specified at the beginning of the chapter and install the dust cap.
10 On TDM and TRX models front brakes, go on to bleed air from the other brake caliper. On the rear brake of TDM and TRX models, go on to bleed air from the other side of the caliper (two bleed valves are fitted).
11 Install the diaphragm and cover assembly, wipe up any spilled brake fluid and check the entire system for leaks.

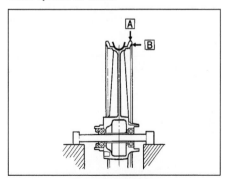

9.2 Check the wheel for radial (out-of-round) runout (A) and axial (side-to-side) runout (B)

 If it's not possible to produce a firm feel to the lever or pedal the fluid my be aerated. Let the brake fluid in the system stabilise for a few hours and then repeat the procedure when the tiny bubbles in the system have settled out.

9 Wheels – inspection and repair

1 In order to carry out a proper inspection of the wheels, it is necessary to support the bike upright so that the wheel being inspected is raised off the ground. Position the motorcycle on an auxiliary stand. Clean the wheels thoroughly to remove mud and dirt that may interfere with the inspection procedure or mask defects. Make a general check of the wheels (see Chapter 1) and tyres (see *Daily (pre-ride) checks*).
2 Attach a dial gauge to the fork slider or the swingarm and position its stem against the side of the rim. Spin the wheel slowly and check the axial (side-to-side) runout of the rim. In order to accurately check radial (out of round) runout with the dial gauge, the wheel would have to be removed from the machine, and the tyre from the wheel. With the axle clamped in a vice and the dial gauge positioned on the top of the rim, the wheel can be rotated to check the runout **(see illustration)**.
3 An easier, though slightly less accurate, method is to attach a stiff wire pointer to the fork slider or the swingarm and position the end a fraction of an inch from the wheel (where the wheel and tyre join). If the wheel is true, the distance from the pointer to the rim will be constant as the wheel is rotated. **Note:** *If wheel runout is excessive, check the wheel or hub bearings very carefully before replacing the wheel.*

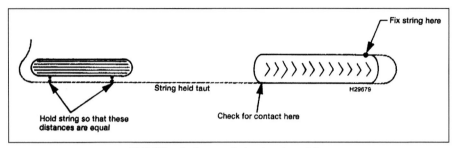

10.5 Wheel alignment check using string

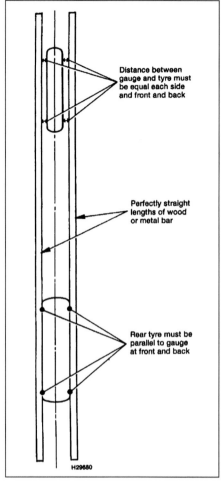

10.7 Wheel alignment check using a straight-edge

4 The wheels should also be visually inspected for cracks, flat spots on the rim and other damage. On cast alloy wheels, look very closely for dents in the area where the tyre bead contacts the rim. Dents in this area may prevent complete sealing of the tyre against the rim, which leads to deflation of the tyre over a period of time. If damage is evident, or if runout in either direction is excessive, the wheel will have to be renewed. Never attempt to repair a damaged cast alloy wheel.

5 On XTZ models, check for loose or broken spokes. Tapping the spokes with a screwdriver is the best guide to their tension. A loose spoke will make a dull flat note compared to a tight one. Loose spokes must be tightened by turning the nipple at the spoke end in an anti-clockwise direction. Always check for runout after altering the tension in any of the spokes. Small irregularities can be corrected by adjusting the spokes in the affected area, although a certain amount of practice is necessary to prevent over-correction. If the wheel runout continues to be excessive, take the wheel to a professional wheel builder for inspection and adjustment.

10 Wheels – alignment check

1 Misalignment of the wheels, which may be due to a cocked rear wheel or a bent frame or fork yokes, can cause strange and possibly serious handling problems. If the frame or yokes are at fault, repair by a frame specialist or replacement with new parts are the only alternatives.

2 To check the alignment you will need an assistant, a length of string or a perfectly straight piece of wood and a ruler. A plumb bob or other suitable weight will also be required.

3 In order to make a proper check of the wheels it is necessary to support the bike in an upright position, using an auxiliary stand. Measure the width of both tyres at their widest points. Subtract the smaller measurement from the larger measurement, then divide the difference by two. The result is the amount of offset that should exist between the front and rear tyres on both sides.

4 If a string is used, have your assistant hold one end of it about halfway between the floor and the rear axle, touching the rear sidewall of the tyre.

5 Run the other end of the string forward and pull it tight so that it is roughly parallel to the floor. Slowly bring the string into contact with the front sidewall of the rear tyre, then turn the front wheel until it is parallel with the string. Measure the distance from the front tyre sidewall to the string **(see illustration)**.

6 Repeat the procedure on the other side of the motorcycle. The distance from the front tyre sidewall to the string should be equal on both sides.

7 As was previously pointed out, a perfectly straight length of wood may be substituted for the string **(see illustration)**. The procedure is the same.

8 If the distance between the string and tyre is greater on one side, or if the rear wheel appears to be cocked, refer to Chapter 1, Section 1 and check that the chain adjuster markings coincide on each side of the swingarm.

9 If the front-to-back alignment is correct, the wheels still may be out of alignment vertically.

10 Using the plumb bob, or other suitable weight, and a length of string, check the rear wheel to make sure it is vertical. To do this, hold the string against the tyre upper sidewall and allow the weight to settle just off the floor. When the string touches both the upper and lower tyre sidewalls and is perfectly straight, the wheel is vertical. If it is not, place thin spacers under one leg of the auxiliary stand.

11 Once the rear wheel is vertical, check the front wheel in the same manner. If both wheels are not perfectly vertical, the frame and/or major suspension components are bent.

11 Front wheel – removal and installation

Removal

1 Position the motorcycle on an auxiliary stand and support it under the crankcase so that the front wheel is off the ground. Always make sure the motorcycle is properly supported.

2 Remove the brake caliper mounting bolts and slide the calipers off the discs (see Section 3). Support the calipers with a piece of wire or a bungee cord so that no strain is placed on the hydraulic hoses. There is no need to disconnect the hoses from the calipers. **Note:** *Do not operate the front brake lever with the calipers removed.*

3 On TRX, XTZ and 1991 to 1998 TDM models, unscrew the knurled ring securing the speedometer cable to the drive gear and detach the cable **(see illustration and 11.5)**.

11.3 Unscrew the ring (arrowed) and detach the cable

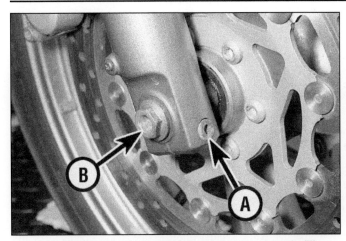

11.4 Slacken the clamp bolt (A) and unscrew the axle (B)

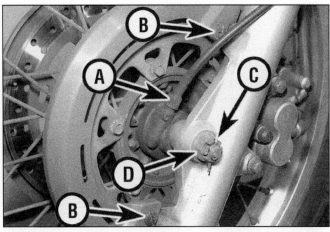

11.5 Speedometer cable (A), disc cover screws (B), split pin (C), axle nut (D)

On 1999 TDM models, trace the wiring from the speedometer drive gear up to its 3-pin connector and disconnect it, then free the wiring from the clips which retain it to the brake hose; alternatively, leave the wiring attached so that as the wheel is removed the drive gear is left joined to its lead.

4 On TDM and TRX models, slacken the axle clamp bolt on the bottom of the right-hand fork, then unscrew the axle **(see illustration)**.

5 On XTZ models, first remove the screws securing the disc covers and remove the covers **(see illustration)**. Remove the split pin from the end of the axle, then unscrew the axle nut and remove the washer. Counter-hold the axle head to prevent it turning if necessary. Discard the split pin as a new one should be used.

6 Support the wheel, then withdraw the axle from the right-hand side and carefully lower the wheel. Use a drift to drive out the axle if required.

7 Remove the spacer from the right-hand side of the wheel and the speedometer drive gear from the left-hand side, noting how they fit **(see illustrations)**.

Caution: Don't lay the wheel down and allow it to rest on a disc – the disc could become warped. Set the wheel on wood blocks so the disc doesn't support the weight of the wheel, or keep it upright.

8 Check the axle for straightness by rolling it on a flat surface such as a piece of plate glass (first wipe off all old grease and remove any corrosion using fine emery cloth). If the axle is bent, renew it.

9 Check the condition of the wheel bearings (see Section 13).

Installation

10 Apply lithium-based grease to the wheel spacer, the lips of the grease seals and to the to the speedometer drive gear. Fit the spacer into the right-hand side of the wheel and the drive gear into the left-hand side, making sure

the tabs locate in the slots **(see illustrations 11.7a and b)**.

11 Manoeuvre the wheel into position. Apply a thin coat of grease to the axle.

12 Lift the wheel into place between the fork sliders, making sure the spacer and drive gear remain in position, and that the slot in the drive gear locates over the tab on the inside of the fork **(see illustration)**. Slide the axle in from the right-hand side **(see illustration)**.

13 On TDM and TRX models, tighten the axle to the torque setting specified at the beginning of the Chapter **(see illustration)**.

11.7a Remove the spacer . . .

11.7b . . . and the speedometer drive gear housing

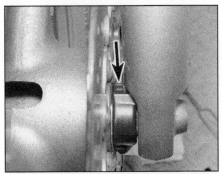

11.12a Locate the tab on the inside of the fork in the slot in the top of the housing . . .

11.12b . . . and insert the axle

11.13 Tighten the axle to the specified torque

Now tighten the axle clamp bolt on the bottom of the right-hand fork to the specified torque setting (see illustration 11.4).

14 On XTZ models, fit the washer and axle nut, then counter-hold the head of the axle and tighten the nut to the torque setting specified at the beginning of the Chapter. Fit a new split through the end of the axle (see illustration 11.5). Install the disc covers.

15 Install the brake calipers, making sure the pads sit squarely on either side of the discs (see Section 3). Tighten the caliper mounting bolts to the specified torque setting.

16 Fit the speedometer cable into the drive housing and tighten the knurled ring securely (see illustrations 11.3 and 11.5). On 1991 TDM models if the speedometer wiring was disconnected, remake the 3-pin connector and secure the wiring to the brake hose and the guide provided on the brake caliper lower mounting bolt; use the proper clips to the secure the wire to the brake hose and don't fasten them too tight otherwise the hose will be distorted.

17 Apply the front brake a few times to bring the pads back into contact with the discs. Move the motorcycle off the stand, apply the front brake and pump the front forks a few times to settle all components in position.

18 Check for correct operation of the front brake before riding the motorcycle.

12 Rear wheel –
removal and installation

Removal

1 Position the motorcycle on an auxiliary stand so that the wheel is off the ground. On XTZ models, unscrew the bolts securing the rear brake caliper shield and remove the cover (see illustration 3.1).

2 Remove the brake caliper mounting bolts and slide the caliper off the disc (see Section 3). Support the caliper with a piece of wire or a bungee cord so that no strain is placed on the hydraulic hose. There is no need to disconnect the hose from the caliper. Note: Do not operate the brake pedal with the calipers removed. On TDM models, slacken the caliper bracket bolt on the swingarm (see illustration).

3 Where fitted, remove the split pin from the axle nut on the end of the axle (see illustration). Unscrew the axle nut and remove the washer, and on TRX models the adjuster position marker (see illustration).

4 Support the wheel then withdraw the axle and lower the wheel to the ground (see illustration). On TRX models, retrieve the adjustment position marker. Note how the caliper bracket locates between the wheel and the swingarm.

5 Disengage the chain from the sprocket and remove the wheel from the swingarm (see illustration 12.10).
Caution: Do not lay the wheel down and allow it to rest on the disc or the sprocket – they could become warped. Set the wheel on wood blocks so the disc or the sprocket doesn't support the weight of the wheel. Do not operate the brake pedal with the wheel removed.

6 Check the axle for straightness by rolling it on a flat surface such as a piece of plate glass (first wipe off all old grease and remove any corrosion using fine emery cloth). If the axle is bent, renew it.

7 Remove the collar from each side of the wheel, noting which fits where (see illustrations). Check the condition of the grease seals and wheel bearings (see Section 13).

Installation

8 Apply a thin coat of lithium-based grease to the lips of each grease seal, and also to the collars and the axle. On TRX models, slide the right-hand adjustment position marker onto the axle, making sure it is the correct way round.

9 Install the short collar into the left-hand side of the wheel and the long shouldered collar into the right-hand side (see illustrations 12.7b and a). Manoeuvre the wheel so that it is in between the ends of the swingarm. Align

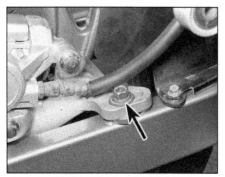

12.2 On TDM models, slacken the caliper bracket bolt (arrowed)

12.3a Rear axle nut and split pin – 1991 to 1995 TDM models

12.3b Rear axle nut (A) and position marker (B) – TRX models

12.4 Withdraw the axle and remove the wheel

12.7a Remove the collar from each side . . .

12.7b . . . noting which way round they fit

12.10 Manoeuvre the wheel into position and fit the chain onto the sprocket

12.11 On TRX models, make sure the axle head locates correctly in the adjustment marker

12.12 Where fitted, use a new split pin

the brake caliper bracket, on XTZ models locating it against the swingarm so that the lug on the swingarm fits into the slot in the bracket.

10 Engage the drive chain with the sprocket and lift the wheel into position **(see illustration)**. Make sure the collars and caliper bracket remain correctly in place.

11 Install the axle with its washer, or on TRX models with the adjustment marker **(see illustration 12.4)**. On 1991 to 1995 TDM models, the axle goes in from the left, while on all other models it goes in from the right. Make sure it passes through the chain adjusters and the caliper bracket. On TRX models, align the flats on the axle head with the adjustment marker **(see illustration)**. Check that

everything is correctly aligned, then fit the left-hand adjustment position marker (TRX models), the washer and the axle nut **(see illustration 12.3b)**. Tighten the nut lightly at this stage, on TDM and XTZ models counter-holding the axle head on the other side of the wheel.

12 Adjust the chain slack as described in Chapter 1. Now tighten the axle nut to the specified torque setting. On 1991 to 1995 TDM models and XTZ models, secure the nut using a new split pin **(see illustration)**. On TDM models, tighten the caliper bracket bolt to the specified torque setting **(see illustration 12.2)**.

13 Install the brake caliper, making sure the pads sit squarely on either side of the disc

(see Section 3). Tighten the caliper mounting bolts to the specified torque setting. On XTZ models, install the caliper shield **(see illustration 3.1)**.

14 Operate the brake pedal several times to bring the pads into contact with the disc. Check the operation of the rear brake carefully before riding the bike.

13 Wheel bearings – removal, inspection and installation

Front wheel bearings

Note: *Always renew the wheel bearings in pairs. Never renew the bearings individually. Avoid using a high pressure cleaner on the wheel bearing area.*

1 Remove the wheel (see Section 11).

2 Set the wheel on blocks so as not to allow the weight of the wheel to rest on the brake disc.

3 On 1991 to 1998 TDM and all TRX models, lever out the grease seal on each side of the wheel using a flat-bladed screwdriver, taking care not to damage the rim of the hub **(see illustration)**. Discard the seals if they are damaged or deteriorated. Lever out the retainer plate on the left-hand side of the wheel and remove the speedometer drive plate, noting how it fits **(see illustrations)**.

> **HAYNES HiNT** *Position a piece of wood against the wheel to prevent the screwdriver shaft damaging it when levering the grease seals out.*

4 On XTZ models, lever out the grease seal on the right-hand side of the wheel using a flat-bladed screwdriver, taking care not to damage the rim **(see illustration 13.3)**.

5 Using a metal rod (preferably a brass drift punch) inserted through the centre of the one bearing, tap evenly around the inner race of the other bearing to drive it from the hub **(see illustrations)**. The bearing spacer will also come out.

13.3a Lever out the grease seal . . .

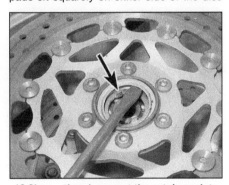

13.3b . . . then lever out the retainer plate and remove the drive plate (arrowed)

13.5a Knock out the bearings using a drift . . .

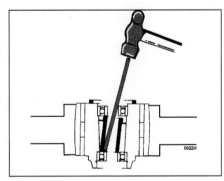

13.5b . . . locating it as shown

13.10 A socket can be used to drive in the bearing

13.12a Fit the drive plate as described . . .

13.12b . . . then fit the retainer plate

6 Lay the wheel on its other side so that the remaining bearing faces down. Drive the bearing out of the wheel using the same technique as above.

7 If the bearings are of the unsealed type or are only sealed on one side, clean them with a high flash-point solvent (one which won't leave any residue) and blow them dry with compressed air (don't let the bearings spin as you dry them). Apply a few drops of oil to the bearing. **Note:** *If the bearing is sealed on both sides don't attempt to clean it.*

 Refer to Tools and Workshop Tips (Section 5) for more information about bearings.

8 Hold the outer race of the bearing and rotate the inner race – if the bearing doesn't turn smoothly, has rough spots or is noisy, renew it.

9 If the bearing is good and can be re-used, wash it in solvent once again and dry it, then pack the bearing with lithium-based grease.

10 Thoroughly clean the hub area of the wheel. Install the right-hand bearing into its recess in the hub, with the marked or sealed side facing outwards. Using the old bearing (if new ones are being fitted), a bearing driver or a socket large enough to contact the outer race of the bearing, drive it in until it's completely seated **(see illustration)**.

11 Turn the wheel over and install the bearing spacer. Drive the left-hand bearing into place as described above.

12 On 1991 to 1998 TDM and all TRX models, fit the speedometer drive plate into the left-hand side of the wheel, with the drive tabs facing out and aligning the flat tabs with the cutouts in the hub **(see illustration)**. Press the retainer plate onto the drive plate **(see illustration)**.

13 Apply a smear of lithium-based grease to the lips of the seal(s), then press them into the wheel, using a seal or bearing driver or a suitable socket to drive it into place if necessary **(see illustration)**.

14 Clean off all grease from the brake discs using acetone or brake system cleaner then install the wheel (see Section 11).

Rear wheel bearings

15 Remove the rear wheel (see Section 12). Lift the sprocket coupling out of the wheel, noting how it fits **(see illustration)**.

16 Set the wheel on blocks so as not to allow the weight of the wheel to rest on the brake disc.

17 Lever out the grease seal on the right-hand side of the wheel using a flat-bladed screwdriver, taking care not to damage the rim of the hub **(see illustration)**. Discard the seal as a new one should be used.

18 Using a metal rod (preferably a brass drift punch) inserted through the centre of one bearing, tap evenly around the inner race of the other bearing to drive it from the hub **(see illustrations 13.5a and b)**. The bearing spacer will also come out.

19 Lay the wheel on its other side so that the remaining bearing faces down. Drive the bearing out of the wheel using the same technique as above.

20 Refer to Steps 7 to 9 above and check the bearings.

21 Thoroughly clean the hub area of the wheel. First install the right-hand bearing into its recess in the hub, with the marked or sealed side facing outwards. Using the old bearing (if new ones are being fitted), a bearing driver or a socket large enough to contact the outer race of the bearing, drive it in squarely until it's completely seated **(see illustration 13.10)**.

22 Turn the wheel over and install the bearing spacer. Drive the left-hand side bearing into place as described above.

23 Apply a smear of grease to the lips of the new grease seal, and press it into the right-hand side of the wheel, using a seal or bearing driver, a suitable socket or a flat piece of wood to drive it into place if necessary **(see illustration)**.

24 Clean off all grease from the brake disc

13.13 Press the grease seal into place

13.15 Lift the sprocket coupling out of the wheel

13.17 Lever out the grease seal

13.23 Where the seal sits flush with the rim, a piece of wood can be used as shown

13.26a Use a socket to drive out the spacer . . .

13.26b . . . noting how it fits

using acetone or brake system cleaner. Install the sprocket coupling assembly onto the wheel, then install the wheel (see Section 12).

Sprocket coupling bearing

25 Remove the rear wheel (see Section 12). Lift the sprocket coupling out of the wheel, noting how it fits **(see illustration 13.15)**.

26 Remove the spacer from the inside of the coupling bearing, using a suitable socket to drive it out if it is tight, noting which way round it fits **(see illustrations)**. Using a flat-bladed screwdriver, lever out the grease seal from the outside of the coupling **(see illustration)**.

27 Support the coupling on blocks of wood and drive the bearing out from the inside using a bearing driver or socket **(see illustration)**.

28 Refer to Steps 7 to 9 above and check the bearings.

29 Thoroughly clean the bearing recess then install the bearing into the recess in the coupling, with the marked or sealed side facing out. Using the old bearing (if new ones are being fitted), a bearing driver or a socket large enough to contact the outer race of the bearing, drive it in until it is completely seated **(see illustration 13.10)**.

30 Apply a smear of grease to the lips of the new seal, and press it into the coupling, using

13.26c Lever out the grease seal

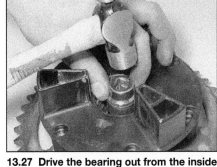

13.27 Drive the bearing out from the inside

a seal or bearing driver, a suitable socket or a flat piece of wood to drive it into place if necessary **(see illustration)**. Install the spacer into the inside of the coupling, making sure it is the correct way round **(see illustration 13.26b)**, and drive it into place if it is tight **(see illustration)**.

31 Check the sprocket coupling/rubber damper (see Chapter 6).

32 Clean off all grease from the brake disc using acetone or brake system cleaner. Fit the sprocket coupling into the wheel **(see illustration 13.15)**, then install the wheel (see Section 12).

14 Tyres – general information and fitting

General information

1 The wheels fitted on TDM and TRX models are designed to take tubeless tyres only. The wheels fitted on XTZ models are designed to take tubed tyres only. Tyre sizes are given in the Specifications at the beginning of this chapter.

2 Refer to the Daily (pre-ride) checks listed at

13.30a Fit the grease seal . . .

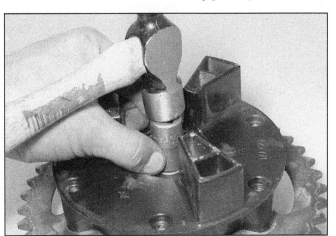

13.30b . . . and the spacer

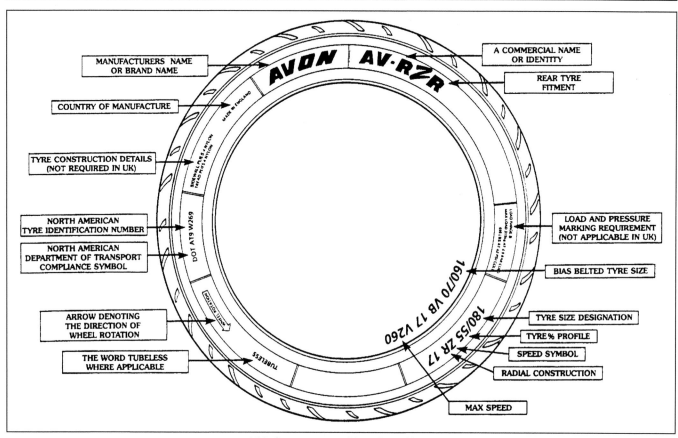

MANUFACTURERS NAME
OR BRAND NAME

A COMMERCIAL NAME
OR IDENTITY

REAR TYRE
FITMENT

COUNTRY OF MANUFACTURE

TYRE CONSTRUCTION DETAILS
(NOT REQUIRED IN UK)

NORTH AMERICAN
TYRE IDENTIFICATION NUMBER

NORTH AMERICAN
DEPARTMENT OF TRANSPORT
COMPLIANCE SYMBOL

LOAD AND PRESSURE
MARKING REQUIREMENT
(NOT APPLICABLE IN UK)

BIAS BELTED TYRE SIZE

TYRE SIZE DESIGNATION

ARROW DENOTING
THE DIRECTION OF
WHEEL ROTATION

TYRE % PROFILE

SPEED SYMBOL

RADIAL CONSTRUCTION

THE WORD TUBELESS
WHERE APPLICABLE

MAX SPEED

14.3 Common tyre sidewall markings

the beginning of this manual for tyre maintenance.

Fitting new tyres

3 When selecting new tyres, refer to the tyre information label on the swingarm and the tyre options listed in the owners handbook. Ensure that front and rear tyre types are compatible, the correct size and correct speed rating; if necessary seek advice from a Yamaha dealer or tyre fitting specialist **(see illustration)**.
4 It is recommended that tyres are fitted by a

motorcycle tyre specialist rather than attempted in the home workshop. This is particularly relevant in the case of tubeless tyres because the force required to break the seal between the wheel rim and tyre bead is substantial, and is usually beyond the capabilities of an individual working with normal tyre levers. Additionally, the specialist will be able to balance the wheels after tyre fitting.
5 Note that punctured tubeless tyres can in

some cases be repaired. Any such repairs must be carried out professionally by a motorcycle tyre fitting specialist and advice sought on reduced speed limits for repaired tyres.
6 A punctured tubed tyre is best repaired by fitting a new inner tube and of course removing the item which caused the puncture from the tyre tread. Inner tubes can be repaired using a kit, but the safest option is to renew the inner tube.

Chapter 8
Bodywork

Contents

Degrees of difficulty

Easy, suitable for novice with little experience	**Fairly easy,** suitable for beginner with some experience	**Fairly difficult,** suitable for competent DIY mechanic	**Difficult,** suitable for experienced DIY mechanic	**Very difficult,** suitable for expert DIY or professional

1 General information

This Chapter covers the procedures necessary to remove and install the body parts. Since many service and repair operations on these motorcycles require the removal of the body parts, the procedures are grouped here and referred to from other Chapters.

In the case of damage to the body parts, it is usually necessary to remove the broken component and renew it (or replace it with a used one from a breaker). Note that there are however some companies that specialise in 'plastic welding' and there are a number of bodywork repair kits now available for motorcycles.

When attempting to remove any body panel, first study it closely, noting any fasteners and associated fittings, to be sure of returning everything to its correct place on installation. In some cases the aid of an assistant will be required when removing panels, to help avoid the risk of damage to paintwork. Once the evident fasteners have been removed, try to withdraw the panel as described but DO NOT FORCE IT – if it will not release, check that all fasteners have been removed and try again. Where a panel engages another by means of tabs, be careful not to break the tab or its mating slot or to damage the paintwork. Remember that a few moments of patience at this stage will save you a lot of money in renewing broken fairing panels!

When installing a body panel, first study it closely, noting any fasteners and associated fittings removed with it, to be sure of returning everything to its correct place. Check that all fasteners are in good condition, including all trim nuts or clips and damping/rubber mounts;

any of these must be renewed if faulty before the panel is reassembled. Check also that all mounting brackets are straight and repair or renew them if necessary before attempting to install the panel. Where assistance was required to remove a panel, make sure your assistant is on hand to install it.

Tighten the fasteners securely, but be careful not to overtighten any of them or the panel may break (not always immediately) due to the uneven stress. Where quick-release fasteners are fitted, turn them 90° anti-clockwise to release them, and 90° clockwise to secure them.

> **HAYNES HiNT** *Note that a small amount of lubricant (liquid soap or similar) applied to mounting rubber grommets will assist pegs to engage without the need for undue pressure.*

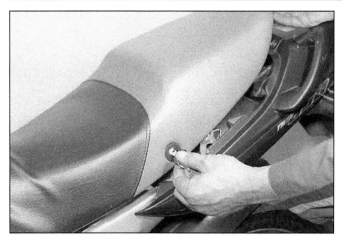

2.2 Turn the key to release the latch

2.3 Make sure the seat locates correctly against the tank – peg-type (arrowed)

2 Seat –
removal and installation

1991 to 1995 TDM models

1 Pull the sides of the seat away from the fuel tank to release the Velcro fastener or the pegs from the grommets.

2 Insert the ignition key into the seat lock located behind the rider's seat, and turn it clockwise to unlock the seat **(see illustration)**. Remove the seat, noting how it fits.

3 Installation is the reverse of removal. Make sure the tab at the front of the seat locates correctly under the tank bracket. Make sure the Velcro fastens or the pegs locate correctly in their rubber grommets **(see illustration)**. Push down on the rear of the seat to engage the latch.

1996-on TDM models

4 Insert the ignition key into the seat lock located behind the rider's seat, and turn it clockwise to unlock the seat. Remove the seat, noting how it fits.

5 Installation is the reverse of removal. Make sure the tabs at the front of the seat locate correctly under and on the back of the tank. Push down on the rear of the seat to engage the latch.

TRX models

6 Insert the ignition key into the seat lock located below the side cover on the left-hand side, and turn it clockwise to unlock the passenger seat **(see illustration)**. Remove the seat, noting how it fits.

7 Pull back the latch at the back of the rider's seat and remove the seat, noting how it fits **(see illustration)**.

8 Installation is the reverse of removal. Make sure the tabs at the front of the rider's seat locate correctly under the tank bracket, then push down on the back of the seat to engage the latch. Make sure the hooks on the front of the passenger seat locate correctly under the hooks, then push down on the rear of the seat to engage the latch.

XTZ models

9 Remove the side covers (see Section 3).

10 Unscrew the bolt securing each side of the seat and remove the seat, noting how it fits **(see illustration)**.

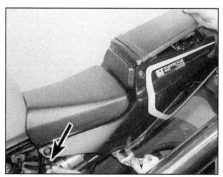

2.6 Turn the key in the lock (arrowed) and remove the passenger seat

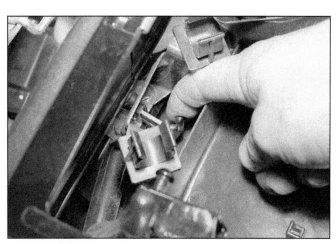

2.7 Pull back the latch to release the rider's seat

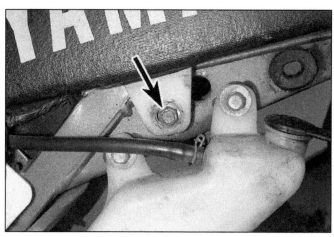

2.10 Unscrew the bolt on each side (arrow) and remove the seat

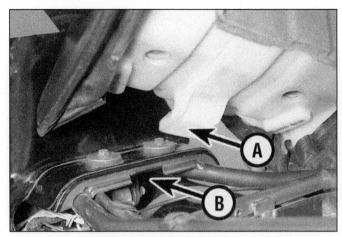

2.11 Locate the tab (A) under the bracket (B)

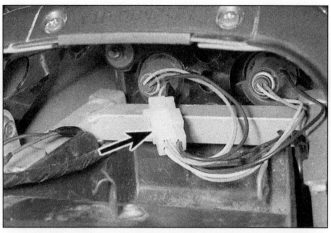

3.1 Disconnect the tail light wiring connector (arrowed)

11 Installation is the reverse of removal. Make sure the tab at the front of the seat locates correctly under the tank bracket, then tighten the bolts securely **(see illustration)**.

3 Side covers –
removal and installation

TDM models

1 Remove the seat (see Section 2). Disconnect the tail light wiring connector **(see illustration)**.
2 Unscrew the four bolts securing the side cover assembly to the frame **(see illustration)**. Carefully pull each side away from the frame at the front to release the clips from the grommets **(see illustration)**. Carefully lift one side up to clear the frame then remove the assembly along with the tail light **(see illustration)**.
3 Installation is the reverse of removal.

TRX models

4 Remove the seats (see Section 2).

5 Remove the six screws securing the side cover assembly **(see illustration)**. Carefully lift one side up to clear the frame then remove the assembly **(see illustration)**.
6 Installation is the reverse of removal.

XTZ models

7 Remove the screw securing the side cover **(see illustration)**. Carefully pull the cover away from the frame to release the pegs from the grommets, one at each end of the cover **(see illustration)**.
8 Installation is the reverse of removal.

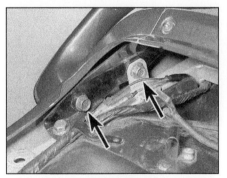

3.2a Unscrew the two bolts (arrowed) on each side . . .

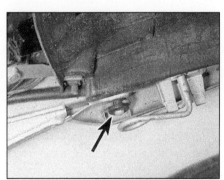

3.2b . . . then release each clip from its grommet (arrow) . . .

3.2c . . . and remove the side cover assembly

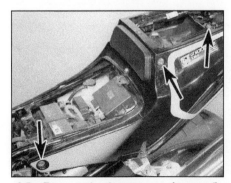

3.5a Remove the three screws (arrowed) on each side . . .

3.5b . . . and remove the side cover assembly

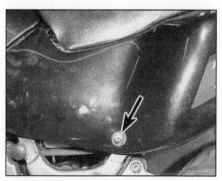

3.7a Remove the screw (arrowed) . . .

3.7b . . . then draw the cover away to release the pegs from the grommets (arrowed)

4.1a Remove the four screws (arrowed) . . .

4.1b . . . and remove the panel

4 Fairing side panels – removal and installation

1991 to 1995 TDM models

1 Remove the four screws securing the side panel and carefully manoeuvre the panel away, noting how it fits (see illustrations).

2 Installation is the reverse of removal.

1996-on TDM models

3 Remove the three screws securing the side panel, then carefully draw the panel away to release the peg from the grommet (see illustration).

4 If required, remove the single screw securing the side trim panel and remove the panel, noting how it locates onto the lug on the frame.

5 Installation is the reverse of removal.

XTZ models

6 Remove the seven screws securing the side cover (see illustration). Carefully release the slot at the bottom from the tab, then release the tabs at the top from the fairing and remove the panel (see illustrations).

7 Installation is the reverse of removal.

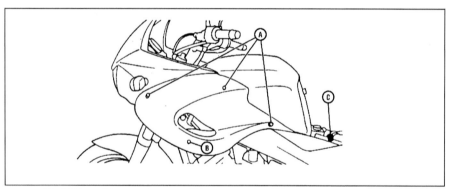

4.3 Fairing side panel screws (A), peg location (B) and trim panel screw (C)

4.6a Remove the screws (arrowed) . . .

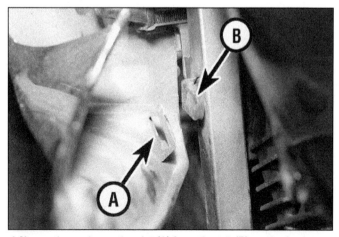

4.6b . . . then release the slot (A) from the tab (B) on the frame . . .

4.6c . . . and the tabs (arrowed) from the slots in the fairing

5.2a Remove the screws and bolts (arrowed) . . .

5.2b . . . then draw the fairing forward and remove the auxiliary light bulbholder . . .

5 Fairing –
removal and installation

1991 to 1995 TDM models

Removal

1 Remove the fairing side panels (see Section 4).
2 Remove the two screws and two bolts securing the fairing **(see illustration)** on each side. Carefully draw the fairing up and forward until the auxiliary light bulbholder becomes accessible, then remove it from the auxiliary light and remove the fairing **(see illustrations)**.

Installation

3 Installation is the reverse of removal. Make sure the wiring connector is correctly and securely connected.

1996-on TDM models

Removal

4 Remove the fairing side panels (see Section 4). Remove the three screws securing the instrument cluster cover and remove the cover and the foam damper **(see illustration)**.
5 Remove the screws securing the windshield and remove the windshield. Ease the rubber expanders out of the windshield mounting points in the fairing.

5.2c . . . and remove the fairing

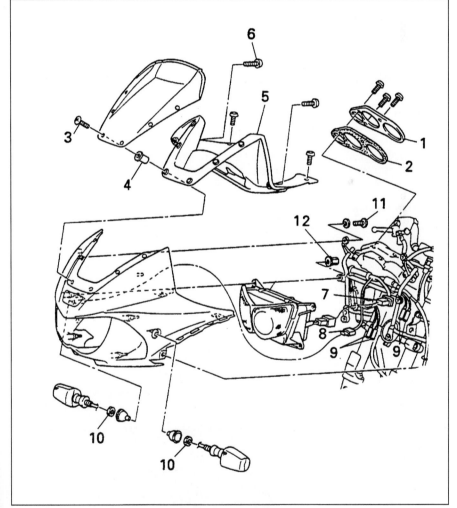

5.4 Fairing mountings

1 Instrument cluster cover	5 Cockpit trim panel	9 Turn signal connectors
2 Foam damper	6 Screw – 4 off	10 Turn signal retaining nuts
3 Windshield screw – 6 off	7 Headlight connector	11 Fairing mounting screw – 2 off
4 Rubber expander – 6 off	8 Auxiliary light connector	12 Fairing mounting nut – 4 off

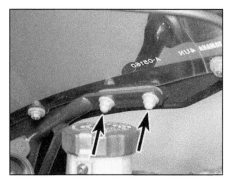

5.10a Unscrew the nuts (arrowed) . . .

5.10b . . . withdraw the screws and remove the mirrors . . .

5.10c . . . and the rubber pad

5.11a Disconnect the headlight wiring connector (arrowed) . . .

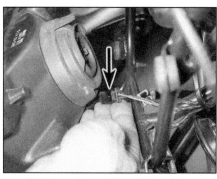

5.11b . . . the auxiliary light wiring connector (arrowed) . . .

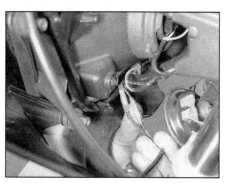

5.11c . . . and the turn signal wiring connectors

6 Remove the remaining screws securing the cockpit trim panel and remove the panel.
7 Reach inside the fairing and disconnect the headlight, auxiliary light and turn signal wiring connectors. Unscrew the nut which retains each turn signal to the fairing. Thread the nut off the wires and remove each turn signal assembly
8 Remove the two screws and the four nuts securing the fairing and headlight to the bracket. Carefully draw the fairing forward and remove it along with the headlight. If required, lift the headlight out of the fairing.

Installation

9 Installation is the reverse of removal. Make sure the wiring connectors are correctly and securely connected. Check that the headlight, auxiliary light and turn signals are all working.

TRX models

Removal

10 Unscrew the nuts securing the rear view mirrors to the fairing bracket and remove the mirrors along with the rubber pads **(see illustrations)**.
11 Disconnect the headlight, auxiliary light and turn signal wiring connectors **(see illustrations)**.
12 Remove the screw securing each side of the fairing and the four nuts securing the fairing and headlight to the bracket **(see illustration)**. Carefully draw the fairing forward and remove it along with the headlight. If required, lift the headlight out of the fairing.

Installation

13 Installation is the reverse of removal. Make sure the arrow on each rubber pad for the mirror is on the outside and pointing forward **(see illustration 5.10c)**. Make sure the wiring connectors are correctly and securely connected. Check that the headlight, auxiliary light and turn signals are all working.

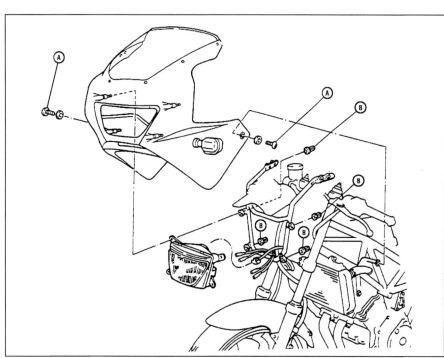

5.12 Fairing mounting screws (A) and nuts (B)

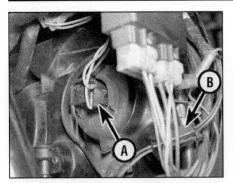

5.15 Disconnect the headlight wiring connector (A) and the auxiliary light wiring connector (B) for each light

5.16 The headlight comes away with the fairing

6.2a On TDM models, note how the mounting brackets fit

XTZ models

Removal

14 Remove the fairing side panels (see Section 4).
15 Disconnect the headlight wiring connectors and the auxiliary light wiring connectors **(see illustration)**.
16 Remove the three nuts securing the fairing and headlight to the bracket. Carefully draw the fairing forward and remove it along with the headlight **(see illustration)**. If required, lift the headlight out of the fairing.

Installation

17 Installation is the reverse of removal.

Make sure the wiring connectors are correctly and securely connected. Check that the headlights and auxiliary lights are all working.

6 Front mudguard – removal and installation

Removal

1 On 1991 to 1995 TDM models, unscrew the knurled ring securing the speedometer to the drive housing on the front wheel, then detach

the cable and draw it up through the guide on the mudguard.
2 Unscrew the four bolts securing the mudguard to the holder on each fork slider and remove the mudguard, noting how it fits **(see illustrations)**.

Installation

3 Installation is the reverse of removal.

7 Engine bashplate (1991–95 TDM and all XTZ) – removal and installation

Removal

1 On TDM models, remove the cap from the end of the through-bolt, then remove the split pin and washer and withdraw the bolt **(see illustration)**. Unscrew the two bolts on the bottom of the plate and remove the bashplate, noting how it fits.
2 On XTZ models unscrew the four bolts securing the bashplate to the frame and engine and remove the plate, noting how it fits **(see illustrations)**.

Installation

3 Installation is the reverse of removal.

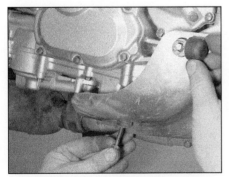

6.2b Mudguard mounting bolts (arrowed) – TRX models

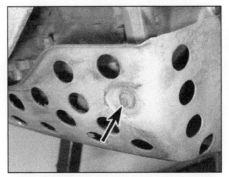

6.2c On XTZ models, the bolts (arrowed) are on the inside of the fork leg

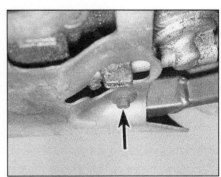

7.1 Engine bashplate mountings – TDM models

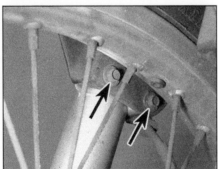

7.2a The bashplate is secured by a bolt (arrowed) on each side at the front . . .

7.2b . . and on each side underneath

Notes

Chapter 9
Electrical system

Contents

Degrees of difficulty

Easy, suitable for novice with little experience	**Fairly easy,** suitable for beginner with some experience	**Fairly difficult,** suitable for competent DIY mechanic	**Difficult,** suitable for experienced DIY mechanic	**Very difficult,** suitable for expert DIY or professional

Specifications

Battery

Capacity	
TDM and TRX models	12V, 10Ah
XTZ models	12V, 14Ah
Voltage – TDM and TRX models	
Fully charged	12.8V
Requires charging	below 12.5V
Specific gravity – XTZ models	
Fully charged	1.280
Requires charging	below 1.280
Charging time – TDM and TRX models	until fully charged (12.8V) (max 6.5 hrs for a flat battery)
Charging rate – XTZ models	0.4A for 10 hrs

Charging system

Current leakage limit	1mA (max)
Regulated voltage output (no load)	14.3 to 15.3V @ 5000 rpm
Alternator nominal output	
TDM and XTZ models	14V, 25A @ 5000 rpm
TRX models	14V, 23.5A @ 5000 rpm
Alternator stator coil resistance	
1991 to 1995 TDM models and XTZ models	0.20 to 0.30 ohms @ 20°C
1996-on TDM models	0.23 to 0.35 ohms @ 20°C
TRX models	0.22 to 0.32 ohms @ 20°C

Starter motor

Brush length

    Standard . . . . 12.5 mm

    Service limit (min) . . . . 5 mm

Commutator diameter

    Standard . . . . 28 mm

    Service limit (min) . . . . 27 mm

Mica depth . . . . 0.7 mm

Armature coil resistance . . . . 0.01 ohms @ 20ºC

Fuses

1991 to 1995 TDM models

    Main 30A

    Headlight 20A

    Signals 10A

    Ignition 10A

    Fan 10A

1996 to 1998 TDM models

    Main 30A

    Headlight 15A

    Signals 15A

    Ignition 7.5A

    Fan 7.5A

1999 TDM models

    Main 30A

    Headlight 15A

    Signals 15A

    Ignition 10A

    Auxiliary light and hazard 10A

    Fan 7.5A

    Back-up 5A

TRX models

    Main 30A

    Headlight 15A

    Signals 15A

    Ignition 7.5A

    Fan 7.5A

XTZ models

    Main 30A

    Fan 10A

Bulbs

Headlight

    1991 to 1995 TDM models . . . . 35/35W halogen x 2

    1996-on TDM models . . . . 55W halogen H3 x 2

    TRX models . . . . 60/55W halogen x 1

    XTZ models . . . . 35/35W halogen x 2

Auxiliary light

    TDM models . . . . 5.0W x 1

    TRX models . . . . 3.4W x 1

    XTZ models . . . . 3.4W x 2

Brake/tail light 21/5W

Turn signal lights 21W

Instrument and warning lights – TRX, XTZ and 1991 to 1998 TDM models

    Instrument lights 3.4W, 1.7W

    Turn signal indicator light 3.4W

    Neutral indicator light 3.4W

    High beam indicator light 3.4W

Instrument and warning lights – 1999 TDM models

    Instrument lights 2.0W

    Turn signal indicator light 1.4W

    Neutral indicator light 1.4W

    High beam indicator light 1.4W

    Coolant warning light 1.4W

    Fuel level warning light 2.0W

Torque settings

Transmission output shaft retainer plate bolts . . . . 10 Nm
Starter motor mounting bolts . . . . 10 Nm
Alternator rotor screws . . . . 7 Nm
Pick-up coil screws . . . . 4 Nm
Alternator rotor bolt . . . . 130 Nm

1 General information

All models have a 12-volt electrical system charged by a three-phase alternator with a separate regulator/rectifier.

The regulator maintains the charging system output within the specified range to prevent overcharging, and the rectifier converts the ac (alternating current) output of the alternator to dc (direct current) to power the lights and other components and to charge the battery. The alternator rotor is mounted on the left-hand end of the crankshaft.

The starter motor is mounted on the bottom of the engine. The starting system includes the motor, the battery, the relay and the various wires and switches. A safety cut-out circuit prevents the starter motor operating unless the transmission is in neutral or the clutch lever is pulled in and the sidestand is up

Note: *Keep in mind that electrical parts, once purchased, cannot be returned. To avoid unnecessary expense, make very sure the faulty component has been positively identified before buying a new part.*

2 Electrical system – fault finding

 Warning: To prevent the risk of short circuits, the ignition (main) switch must always be OFF and the battery negative (-ve) terminal should be disconnected before any of the bike's other electrical components are disturbed. Don't forget to reconnect the terminal securely once work is finished or if battery power is needed for circuit testing.

1 A typical electrical circuit consists of an electrical component, the switches, relays, etc. related to that component and the wiring and connectors that hook the component to both the battery and the frame. To aid in locating a problem in any electrical circuit, refer to the wiring diagrams at the end of this Chapter.
2 Before tackling any troublesome electrical circuit, first study the wiring diagram (see end of Chapter) thoroughly to get a complete picture of what makes up that individual circuit. Trouble spots, for instance, can often

be narrowed down by noting if other components related to that circuit are operating properly or not. If several components or circuits fail at one time, chances are the fault lies in the fuse or earth connection, as several circuits often are routed through the same fuse and earth connections.
3 Electrical problems often stem from simple causes, such as loose or corroded connections or a blown fuse. Prior to any electrical fault finding, always visually check the condition of the fuse, wires and connections in the problem circuit. Intermittent failures can be especially frustrating, since you can't always duplicate the failure when it's convenient to test. In such situations, a good practice is to clean all connections in the affected circuit, whether or not they appear to be good. All of the connections and wires should also be wiggled to check for looseness which can cause intermittent failure.
4 If testing instruments are going to be utilised, use the wiring diagram to plan where you will make the necessary connections in order to accurately pinpoint the trouble spot.
5 The basic tools needed for electrical fault finding include a battery and bulb test circuit, a continuity tester, a test light, and a jumper wire. A multimeter capable of reading volts, ohms and amps is also very useful as an alternative to the above, and is necessary for performing more extensive tests and checks.

 Refer to Fault Finding Equipment in the Reference section for details of how to use electrical test equipment.

3 Battery – removal, installation, inspection and maintenance

Caution: Be extremely careful when handling or working around the battery. The electrolyte is very caustic and an explosive gas (hydrogen) is given off when the battery is charging.

Removal and installation

1 Remove the seat(s) (see Chapter 8).
2 On 1991 to 1995 TDM models, TRX and XTZ models, unscrew the negative (-ve) terminal bolt first and disconnect the lead from the battery **(see illustration)**. Lift up the insulating cover to access the positive (+ve) terminal, then unscrew the bolt and disconnect the lead. Release the battery strap or holder, where fitted, and remove the battery from the bike **(see illustration)**.
3 On 1996-on TDM models, lift the insulating cover from the battery negative (-ve) lead terminal on the frame, then remove the terminal screw and detach the lead. Lift the insulating cover from the battery positive (+ve) lead terminal on the starter relay, then remove the terminal screw and detach the lead. Fit the insulating covers back over the lead ends and tape them in place to prevent the lead ends contacting each other and shorting the battery when it is being manoeuvred out of the frame. Remove the two screws securing the battery box, then manoeuvre the box around the right-hand side of the shock absorber and draw it out of the bike. If required, disconnect the leads from the battery, noting which fits where, and lift the battery out of its box.
4 On 1991 to 1995 TDM models, if required,

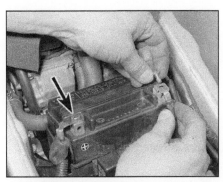
3.2a Detach the negative lead first, then the positive (arrowed) . . .

3.2b . . . and remove the battery

3.4a Unscrew the bolt (arrowed) on each side . . .

3.4b . . . and lift out the box

unscrew the two bolts securing the battery box and lift out the box (see illustrations).

5 On installation, clean the battery terminals and lead ends with a wire brush or knife and emery paper. Reconnect the leads, connecting the positive (+ve) terminal first.

 HAYNES HiNT *Battery corrosion can be kept to a minimum by applying a layer of petroleum jelly to the terminals after the cables have been connected.*

6 Install the seat(s) (see Chapter 8).

Inspection and maintenance

7 The battery fitted to XTZ models is of the conventional lead/acid type, requiring regular checks of the electrolyte level, as described in Chapter 1, in addition to those detailed below.
8 The battery fitted to TDM and TRX models is of the maintenance free (sealed) type, therefore requiring no specific maintenance. However, the following checks should still be regularly performed.
9 Check the battery terminals and leads for tightness and corrosion. If corrosion is evident, unscrew the terminal screws and disconnect the leads from the battery, disconnecting the negative (-ve) terminal first, and clean the terminals and lead ends with a wire brush or knife and emery paper. Reconnect the leads, connecting the negative (-ve) terminal last, and apply a thin coat of petroleum jelly to the connections to slow further corrosion.
10 The battery case should be kept clean to prevent current leakage, which can discharge the battery over a period of time (especially when it sits unused). Wash the outside of the case with a solution of baking soda and water. Rinse the battery thoroughly, then dry it.
11 Look for cracks in the case and renew the battery if any are found. If acid has been spilled on the frame or battery box, neutralise it with a baking soda and water solution, dry it

thoroughly, then touch up any damaged paint.
12 If the motorcycle sits unused for long periods of time, disconnect the cables from the battery terminals, negative (-ve) terminal first. Refer to Section 4 and charge the battery once every month to six weeks.
13 The condition of the battery can be assessed by measuring the voltage present at the battery terminals. Connect the voltmeter positive (+ve) probe to the battery positive (+ve) terminal, and the negative (-ve) probe to the battery negative (-ve) terminal. When fully charged there should be more than 12.5 volts present. If the voltage falls below 12.5 volts the battery must be removed, disconnecting the negative (-ve) terminal first, and recharged as described in Section 4.
14 On XTZ models, if available, an hydrometer should be used to measure the specific gravity of the electrolyte. Remove the battery and its cell caps, then measure each cell in turn. If the reading is below the level specified, the battery should be recharged.

 HAYNES HiNT *Refer to 'Fault Finding Equipment' in the Reference section for more information on battery voltage and specific gravity checks.*

4 Battery – charging

Caution: Be extremely careful when handling or working around the battery. The electrolyte is very caustic and an explosive gas (hydrogen) is given off when the battery is charging.
1 Remove the battery (see Section 3). Connect the charger to the battery, making sure that the positive (+ve) lead on the charger is connected to the positive (+ve) terminal on the battery, and the negative (-ve) lead is connected to the negative (-ve) terminal.

2 If the battery is fully discharged, Yamaha recommend that the battery should be charged for a maximum of 6.5 hours (TDM and TRX models) or at a maximum rate of 0.4 amps for 10 hours (XTZ models). If the battery was partially charged, the battery should be charged until the voltage across the terminals reaches 12.8 V, or on XTZ models until the specific gravity is at its correct reading (see above). Exceeding this can cause the battery to overheat, buckling the plates and rendering it useless. Few owners will have access to an expensive current controlled charger, so if a normal domestic charger is used check that after a possible initial peak, the charge rate falls to a safe level (see illustration). If the battery becomes hot during charging stop. Further charging will cause damage. Note: *In emergencies the battery can be charged at a higher rate of around 3.0 amps for a period of 1 hour. However, this is not recommended and the low amp charge is by far the safer method of charging the battery.*
3 If the recharged battery discharges rapidly if left disconnected it is likely that an internal short caused by physical damage or sulphation has occurred. A new battery will be required. A sound item will tend to lose its charge at about 1% per day.

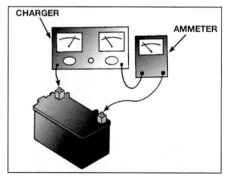

4.2 If the charger doesn't have ammeter built in, connect one in series as shown. DO NOT connect the ammeter between the battery terminals or it will be ruined

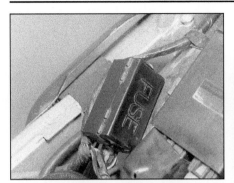

5.1a Fusebox – TDM models

5.1b Fusebox – TRX models

5.1c Cooling fan fuse – XTZ models

4 Install the battery (see Section 3).
5 If the motorcycle sits unused for long periods of time, charge the battery once every month to six weeks and leave it disconnected.

5 Fuses – check and renewal

1 The electrical system is protected by fuses of different ratings. On TDM and TRX models, the fuses are housed in the fusebox, which is located under the seat **(see illustrations)**, although on 1996-on TDM and all TRX models the main fuse is located on the starter relay (see Section 27). On XTZ models, the main fuse is housed in the battery bracket on the front of the battery, while the cooling fan fuse is fitted in line with the wiring for the fan **(see illustration)**.
2 To access the fuses on TDM and TRX models, remove the seat (see Chapter 8) and unclip the fusebox lid **(see illustration)**. On XTZ models, remove the left-hand side cover to access the main fuse (see Chapter 8), and the fuel tank to access the cooling fan fuse (see Chapter 4).
3 The fuses can be removed and checked visually. If you can't pull the fuse out with your fingertips, use a pair of suitable pliers. TDM and TRX models use flat-blade type fuses and the XTZ model uses glass cartridge type fuses. A blown fuse is easily identified by a break in the element **(see illustration)**. Each

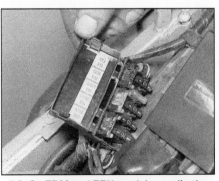

5.2 On TDM and TRX models, unclip the fusebox lid to access the fuses

fuse is clearly marked with its rating and must only be replaced by a fuse of the correct rating. A spare fuse of each rating is housed in the fusebox on TDM and TRX models, and a spare main fuse in the battery bracket on XTZ models. If a spare fuse is used, always renew it so that a spare of each rating is carried on the bike at all times.

⚠️ **Warning: Never put in a fuse of a higher rating or bridge the terminals with any other substitute, however temporary it may be. Serious damage may be done to the circuit, or a fire may start.**

4 If a fuse blows, be sure to check the wiring circuit very carefully for evidence of a short-circuit. Look for bare wires and chafed, melted or burned insulation. If the fuse is renewed before the cause is located, the new fuse will blow immediately.
5 Occasionally a fuse will blow or cause an open-circuit for no obvious reason. Corrosion of the fuse ends and fusebox terminals may occur and cause poor fuse contact. If this happens, remove the corrosion with a wire brush or emery paper, then spray the fuse end and terminals with electrical contact cleaner.

6 Lighting system – check

1 The battery provides power for operation of the headlight, tail light, brake light, turn

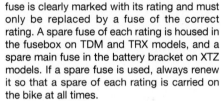

5.3 A blown fuse can be identified by a break in its element – flat-blade type fuse

signals and instrument cluster lights. If none of the lights operate, always check battery voltage before proceeding. Low battery voltage indicates either a faulty battery or a defective charging system. Refer to Section 3 for battery checks and Sections 30 and 31 for charging system tests. Also, check the condition of the fuses. When checking for a blown filament in a bulb, it is advisable to back up a visual check with a continuity test of the filament as it is not always apparent that a bulb has blown. When testing for continuity, remember that on tail light and turn signal bulbs it is often the metal body of the bulb which is the earth.

Headlight

2 If the headlight fails to work, first check the fuse with the key ON (see Section 5), and then the bulb (see Section 7). If they are both good, use jumper wires to connect the bulb directly to the battery terminals. If the light comes on, the problem lies in the wiring or one of the switches in the circuit. Refer to Section 19 for the switch testing procedures, and also the wiring diagrams at the end of this Chapter.
3 On 1996 to 1998 TDM models, a diode is fitted in the headlight circuit (see *Wiring Diagrams* at the end of the Chapter). To test the diode, disconnect it from the harness. Using an ohmmeter or continuity tester, connect the positive (+ve) probe to the female terminal of the diode and the negative (-ve) probe to the male terminal. The diode should show continuity. Now reverse the probes. The diode should show no continuity. If it doesn't behave as stated, renew the diode. The diode is located on the left-hand side of the headlight assembly.

Tail light

4 If the tail light fails to work, check the bulbs and the bulb terminals first (see Section 9), then the fuse, then check for battery voltage at the blue/red (TDM and XTZ models), or blue (TRX models) terminal on the supply side of the tail light wiring connector. If voltage is present, check the earth circuit for an open or poor connection.
5 If no voltage is indicated, check the wiring between the tail light and the ignition switch,

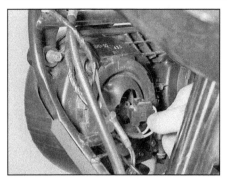

7.2a Disconnect the wiring connector . . .

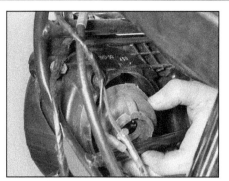

7.2b . . . and remove the dust cover

then check the switch. Also check the lighting switch.

Brake light

6 If the brake light fails to work, check the bulbs and the bulb terminals first (see Section 9), then the fuse, then check for battery voltage at the yellow (TDM and TRX models) or green/yellow (XTZ models) terminal on the supply side of the tail light wiring connector, with the brake lever pulled in or the pedal depressed. If voltage is present, check the earth circuit for an open or poor connection.

7 If no voltage is indicated, check the brake light switches, then the wiring between the tail light and the switches.

8 See Section 14 for brake switch check and Section 9 for tail light bulb renewal.

Instrument and warning lights

9 See Section 17 for instrument and warning light bulb renewal.

Turn signal lights

10 See Section 11 for turn signal circuit check.

7 Headlight bulb and auxiliary light bulb – renewal

Note: *The headlight bulb is of the quartz-halogen type. Do not touch the bulb glass as skin acids will shorten the bulb's service life. If the bulb is accidentally touched, it*

should be wiped carefully when cold with a rag soaked in methylated spirit and dried before fitting.

> **Warning: Allow the bulb time to cool before removing it if the headlight has just been on.**

Headlight

1 For best access to the headlight bulb(s), remove the fairing on TDM models and the relevant fairing side panel on XTZ models (see Chapter 8).

2 Disconnect the relevant wiring connector from the back of the headlight assembly and remove the rubber dust cover, noting how it fits **(see illustrations)**.

3 Release the bulb retaining ring or clip, noting how it fits, then remove the bulb **(see illustrations)**.

4 Fit the new bulb, bearing in mind the information in the **Note** above. Make sure the tabs on the bulb fit correctly in the slots in the bulb housing, and secure it in position with the retaining ring or clip.

5 Install the dust cover, making sure it is correctly seated and with the TOP mark at the top, and connect the wiring connector.

6 Check the operation of the headlight.

> **HAYNES HINT** *Always use a paper towel or dry cloth when handling new bulbs to prevent injury if the bulb should break and to increase bulb life.*

Auxiliary light

7 On TDM models, remove the screws securing the auxiliary light lens and remove the lens **(see illustration)**. Carefully pull the bulb out of its holder and install the new one, then refit the lens **(see illustration)**. Do not overtighten the screws as the lens could crack.

8 On XTZ models, for best access remove the relevant fairing side panel (see Chapter 8). On TRX and XTZ models, release the bulbholder from its socket in the base of the headlight, then press the bulb in and twist it anti-

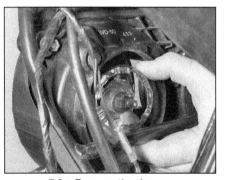

7.3a Remove the ring . . .

7.3b . . . or release the clip . . .

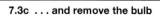

7.3c . . . and remove the bulb

7.7a Remove the screws (arrowed) and the lens . . .

7.7b . . . and pull out the bulb

7.8 Pull the bulbholder out of the base of the headlight

8.2a Removing the headlight – TRX models

8.2b Removing the headlight – XTZ models

clockwise to release it from the holder **(see illustration)**. Install the new bulb in the bulbholder, then install the bulbholder in the headlight. Make sure the rubber cover is correctly seated.

9 Check the operation of the auxiliary light.

8 Headlight assembly – removal and installation

Removal

1 Remove the fairing (see Chapter 8).
2 On 1996-on TDM models, TRX and XTZ models, lift the headlight out of the fairing **(see illustration)**.
3 On 1991 to 1995 TDM models, disconnect the headlight wiring connectors **(see illustration 7.2a)**, then unscrew the three nuts securing the headlight assembly to the bracket and draw the assembly forward and off the bracket **(see illustrations)**.
4 On 1991 to 1995 TDM models and XTZ models, the headlight can be disassembled and the lights renewed individually if required.

Installation

5 Installation is the reverse of removal. Make sure all the wiring is correctly connected and secured. Check the operation of the headlight

8.3a Unscrew the nut on each side (A), and the central nut on the bottom (B) . . .

and auxiliary light. Check the headlight aim (see Chapter 1).

9 Brake/tail light bulb – renewal

1 On TDM models, remove the seat (see Chapter 8). On TRX models, remove the passenger seat, though best access is obtained by removing the side covers as well (see Chapter 8). On XTZ models open the storage compartment cover behind the seat and remove the cover **(see illustration)**.
2 Turn the bulbholder anti-clockwise and

8.3b . . . and remove the headlight assembly

withdraw it from the tail light **(see illustration)**.
3 Push the bulb into the holder and twist it anti-clockwise to remove it **(see illustration)**. Check the socket terminals for corrosion and clean them if necessary. Line up the pins of the new bulb with the slots in the socket, then push the bulb in and turn it clockwise until it locks into place. **Note:** *The pins on the bulb are offset so it can only be installed one way. It is a good idea to use a paper towel or dry cloth when handling the new bulb to prevent injury if the bulb should break and to increase bulb life.*
4 Install the bulbholder into the tail light and turn it clockwise to secure it.

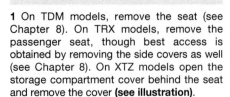

9.1 On XTZ models, remove the storage cover to access the bulbs

9.2 Release the bulbholder . . .

9.3 . . . and remove the bulb

10.2a Tail light wiring connector (arrowed) – TRX models

10.2b Tail light wiring connector (arrowed) – XTZ models

10 Tail light assembly – removal and installation

Removal

1 On TDM and TRX models remove the side covers (see Chapter 8). On XTZ models open the storage compartment cover behind the seat and remove the cover (see illustration 9.1).

2 On TRX and XTZ models, disconnect the tail light wiring connector (see illustrations).

3 Unscrew the nuts securing the tail light assembly to either the side cover assembly (TDM models) or the frame (TRX and XTZ models) and carefully remove it noting how it

fits (see illustrations). If required, turn the bulbholders anti-clockwise and withdraw them from the tail light.

Installation

4 Installation is the reverse of removal. Check the operation of the tail light and the brake light.

11 Turn signal circuit – check

Flasher relay

1 The battery provides power for operation of the turn signal lights, so if they do not operate,

always check the battery voltage first. Low battery voltage indicates either a faulty battery or a defective charging system. Refer to Section 3 for battery checks and Sections 30 and 31 for charging system tests. Also, check the fuse (except XTZ models) (see Section 5) and the switch (see Section 19).

2 Most turn signal problems are the result of a burned out bulb or corroded socket. This is especially true when the turn signals function properly in one direction, but fail to flash in the other direction. Check the bulbs and the sockets (see Section 12).

3 The relay is mounted under the seat on TDM and TRX models, and behind the fairing on XTZ models (see illustrations). Remove the seat or fairing for access (see Chapter 8). If the bulbs and sockets are good, check for voltage at the turn signal relay brown wire (brown/red on 1997-on UK models) with the ignition ON. If no voltage is present, using the appropriate wiring diagram at the end of this Chapter check the wiring between the relay and the ignition (main) switch. On 1999 TDM models, if there's no voltage check the hazard relay as described below.

4 If voltage was present, check for voltage at the relay brown/white wire with the ignition ON. If no voltage is present, renew the relay. If voltage is present, check the wiring between the relay, turn signal switch and turn signal lights for continuity. Turn the ignition OFF when the check is complete.

Hazard relay (1999 TDM models)

5 If there's no voltage at the flasher relay brown/red wire (see Step 3) check for voltage at the hazard relay brown wires with the ignition ON. If no voltage is shown check the signal fuse and the wiring between the fuse and hazard relay for a break or bad connection.

6 Also check for voltage at the hazard relay blue/red wire with the ignition ON; if no voltage is shown check the hazard fuse and the wiring between the hazard fuse and hazard relay. Finally check the brown/red wire from the hazard relay to the flasher relay for a break or bad connection. If the fault still exists, renew the hazard relay.

10.3a Tail light assembly nuts (arrowed) – TDM models

10.3b Tail light assembly nuts (arrowed) – XTZ models

11.3a Turn signal relay (arrowed) – TDM models

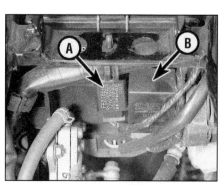

11.3b Turn signal relay (A), starter circuit cut-off relay (B) – TRX models

11.3c Turn signal relay (arrowed) – XTZ models

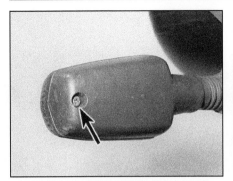

12.1a Turn signal lens screw (arrowed) – TDM models

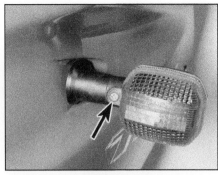

12.1b Turn signal lens screw (arrowed) – TRX models

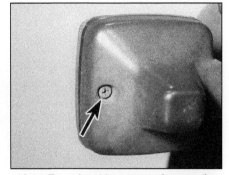

12.1c Turn signal lens screw (arrowed) – XTZ models

12 Turn signal bulbs – renewal

1 Remove the screw securing the turn signal lens and remove the lens, noting how it fits **(see illustrations)**.
2 Push the bulb into the holder and twist it anti-clockwise to remove it **(see illustration)**. Check the socket terminals for corrosion and clean them if necessary. Line up the pins of the new bulb with the slots in the socket, then push the bulb in and turn it clockwise until it locks into place.
3 Fit the lens onto the holder. Do not overtighten the screw as the lens or threads could be damaged.

12.1d Remove the screw and detach the lens . . .

12.2 . . . and remove the bulb

13 Turn signal assemblies – removal and installation

Removal

1 Disconnect the turn signal wiring connectors. On the front turn signals, they are on the inside of the fairing **(see illustrations)**. On TDM models remove the fairing, and on XTZ models the fairing side panel(s) for best access (see Chapter 8). On the rear turn signals, remove the seat (see Chapter 8) **(see illustrations)**.

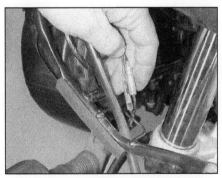

13.1a Front turn signal wiring connectors – TDM models

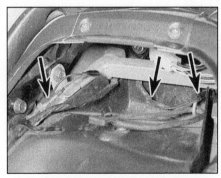

13.1b Rear turn signal wiring connectors (arrowed) – TDM models

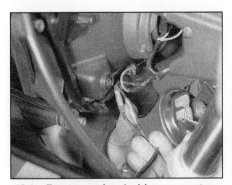

13.1c Front turn signal wiring connectors – TRX models

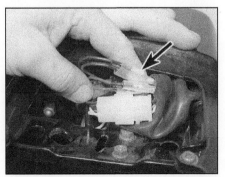

13.1d Rear turn signal wiring connectors – TRX models

13.1e Front turn signal wiring connectors – XTZ models

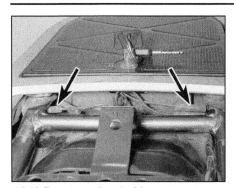

13.1f Rear turn signal wiring connectors –
XTZ models

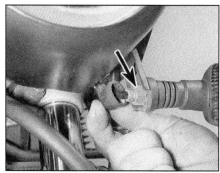

13.2a Front turn signal mounting nut
(arrowed) – TDM models

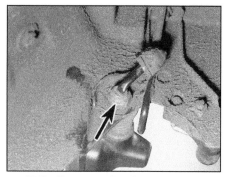

13.2b Rear turn signal mounting nut
(arrowed) – XTZ models

2 On TDM and XTZ models, pull back the rubber boot and unscrew the nut securing the turn signal **(see illustration)**. Remove the assembly, taking care not to snag the wiring.

3 On TRX models, remove the screw or nut securing the assembly to either the inside of the fairing or rear mudguard **(see illustration)**. Remove the mounting plate, noting how it fits, and withdraw the turn signal, taking care not to snag the wiring.

Installation

4 Installation is the reverse of removal. Check the operation of the turn signals.

14 Brake light switches –
check and replacement

Circuit check

1 Before checking any electrical circuit, check the bulbs (see Section 9) and fuses (see Section 5).

2 On XTZ models, remove the fuel tank to access the front brake switch wiring connector (see Chapter 4). On all models, remove the seat to access the rear brake switch connector (see Chapter 8).

3 Using a multimeter or test light connected to a good earth, check for voltage at the brake light switch brown or black/red

13.3 Front turn signal mounting screw and
plate – TRX models

wire (as applicable) connector with the ignition ON (connector halves remain joined). If there's no voltage present, check the wire between the switch and the ignition switch (see the *wiring diagrams* at the end of this Chapter).

4 If voltage is available, touch the probe of the test light to the other terminal of the switch, then pull the brake lever in or depress the brake pedal. If no reading is obtained or the test light doesn't light up, renew the switch.

5 If a reading is obtained or the test light does light up, check the wiring between the switch and the brake light bulb (see the *wiring diagrams* at the end of this Chapter).

14.7a Front brake switch wiring connector
(arrowed) – TDM models

Switch replacement

Front brake lever switch

6 The switch is mounted on the underside of the brake lever bracket on TDM and TRX models, and is a push-fit into the bracket on XTZ models. On XTZ models remove the fuel tank to access the wiring connector.

7 Disconnect the wiring connector(s), then either remove the screws and detach the switch or withdraw the switch from the bracket, according to model **(see illustrations)**. On XTZ models, free the wiring from any clips or ties.

8 Installation is the reverse of removal. The switch isn't adjustable.

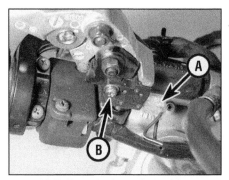

14.7b Front brake switch wiring
connectors (A), mounting screw (B) –
TRX models

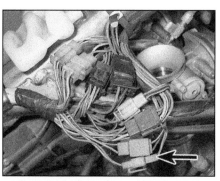

14.7c Front brake switch wiring connector
(arrowed) – XTZ models

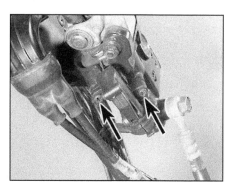

14.7d Front brake switch screws
(arrowed) – TDM models

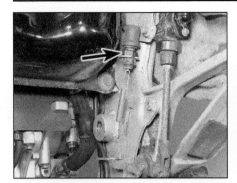

14.9a Rear brake light switch (arrowed) – TDM models

14.9b Rear brake light switch (arrowed) – TRX models

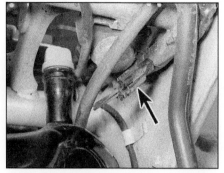

14.9c Rear brake switch wiring connector (arrowed) – TDM models

Rear brake pedal switch

9 The switch is mounted on the inside of the right-hand footrest bracket **(see illustrations)**. Remove the seat for access to the connector (see Chapter 8). Trace the wiring from the switch and disconnect it at the connector **(see illustration)**. Free the wiring from any clips or ties.

10 Detach the lower end of the switch spring from the brake pedal, then unscrew and remove the switch.

11 Installation is the reverse of removal. Make sure the brake light is activated just before the rear brake pedal takes effect. If adjustment is necessary, hold the switch and turn the adjusting ring on the switch body until the brake light is activated when required.

---

15 Instrument cluster and speedometer cable – removal and installation

Instrument cluster

Removal

1 Remove the fairing (see Chapter 8). On TRX models, remove the fuel tank and air filter housing for best access to the wiring connectors (see Chapter 4). On XTZ models, release the clips on the instrument cluster surround from the grommets on the cluster and remove the surround **(see illustration)**. On TRX models, remove the screws securing the trim cover to free the wiring loom **(see illustration)**.

2 On all except 1999 TDM models, unscrew the knurled ring securing the speedometer cable to the back of the speedometer and detach the cable **(see illustration 15.6a)**.

3 Disconnect the instrument cluster wiring connector(s) **(see illustrations)**.

4 Unscrew the nuts securing the instrument cluster to the bracket and lift the cluster off, noting how it fits **(see illustrations)**.

15.1a Release the clips from the grommets and remove the surround

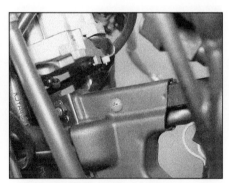

15.1b On TRX models, remove the trim that houses the wiring loom

15.3a Instrument cluster wiring connectors – TDM models

15.3b On TRX models, the wiring connectors are located behind the steering head

15.3c Instrument cluster wiring connector (arrowed) – XTZ models

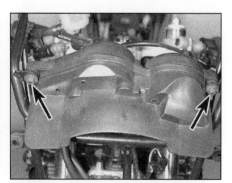

15.4a Unscrew the nuts (arrowed) . . .

15.4b . . . and remove the cluster (TRX shown)

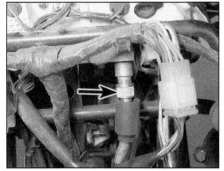

15.6a Unscrew the ring (arrowed) (XTZ shown) . . .

15.6b . . . and detach the cable (TDM shown)

Installation

5 Installation is the reverse of removal. Make sure that the speedometer cable and wiring connectors are correctly routed and secured.

Speedometer cable (TRX, XTZ and 1991 to 1998 TDM models)

Removal

6 Remove the fairing (see Chapter 8). Unscrew the knurled ring securing the speedometer cable to the back of the speedometer and detach the cable **(see illustration)**. On TRX models, access is restricted due to the surround, so if required, displace the instrument cluster **(see illustrations 15.4a and b)**, then remove the screw securing the surround and remove the surround **(see illustration 16.2)**.
7 Unscrew the knurled ring securing the lower end of the cable to the drive housing on the front wheel and detach the cable **(see illustrations)**.
8 Withdraw the cable, releasing it from its guides, and remove it from the bike, noting its correct routing.

Installation

9 Route the cable up through its guides to the back of the instrument cluster.

10 Connect the cable upper end to the speedometer and tighten the retaining ring securely **(see illustrations 15.6b and a)**.
11 Connect the cable lower end to the drive housing and tighten the retaining ring securely **(see illustrations 15.7b and a)**.
12 Check that the cable doesn't restrict steering movement or interfere with any other components.

---

16 Instruments – check, replacement and bulbs

Speedometer

Check (TRX, XTZ and 1991 to 1998 TDM models)

1 Special instruments are required to properly check the operation of this meter. If it is believed to be faulty, take the motorcycle to a Yamaha dealer for assessment. Check that the fault is not due to a broken cable.

Check (1999 TDM models)

2 The electronic speedometer is supplied with wheel speed information by a sensor on

the front wheel. To test the sensor, disconnect its 3-pin connector and make the following test on the sensor side of the connector. Set a multimeter to the 0 to 20 volts DC scale and connect its positive (+ve) probe to the white wire terminal and its negative (-ve) probe to the black wire terminal. Now connect a fully charged 12V battery: positive lead to the red wire terminal and negative lead to the black wire terminal. Position the bike on an auxiliary stand and support it under the crankcase so that the front wheel is off the ground. Slowly rotate the front wheel and note the reading on the meter. If the sensor is operating correctly, it should read 5V four times per wheel revolution.
3 If the speed sensor doesn't produce the correct reading it must be renewed. If the reading is correct, the fault must lie in the speedometer or the wiring between the sensor and speedometer.
4 If the electronic clock/odometer is faulty note that it is only available as part of the speedometer and tachometer assembly.

Replacement – all models

5 Remove the instrument cluster (see Section 15). On TRX models, remove the screw

15.7a Unscrew the ring (arrowed) . . .

15.7b . . . and detach the cable

16.5 Remove the screw and detach the surround

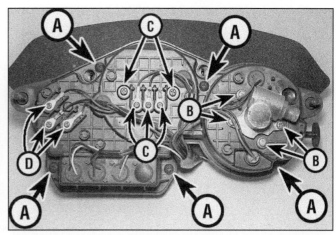

16.6a Casing screws (A), speedometer screws (B), tachometer screws (C), temperature gauge screws (D) – 1991 to 1998 TDM models

securing the surround and remove the surround **(see illustration)**.

6 On TRX, XTZ and 1991 to 1998 TDM models, remove the casing screws from the back of the cluster and lift off the front cover assembly **(see illustrations)**. On 1999 TDM models, remove the seven screws from the base of the cluster and separate the upper and lower covers from the instrument assembly; note that the speedometer and tachometer are only available as a unit with their housing – remove the fuel gauge and transfer it to the new assembly.

7 On 1991 to 1998 TDM and all TRX models, remove the two screws securing the speedometer gearbox and lift off the box.

8 Remove the two screws securing the speedometer to the casing. Carefully withdraw the speedometer from the front.

9 Installation is the reverse of removal.

Tachometer
Check

10 Special instruments are required to properly check the operation of this meter. If it

is believed to be faulty, take the motorcycle to a Yamaha dealer for assessment.

Replacement

11 Remove the instrument cluster (see Section 15). On TRX models, remove the screw securing the surround and remove the surround **(see illustration 16.5)**.

12 On TRX, XTZ and 1991 to 1998 TDM models, remove the casing screws from the back of the cluster and lift off the front cover assembly **(see illustrations 16.6a, b or c)**. On 1999 TDM models, remove the seven screws from the base of the cluster and separate the upper and lower covers from the instrument assembly; note that the speedometer and tachometer are only available as a unit with their housing – remove the fuel gauge and transfer it to the new assembly.

13 Remove the screws securing the three tachometer wires and detach the wires, noting which fits where.

14 Remove the two screws securing the tachometer to the casing. Carefully withdraw the tachometer from the front.

15 Installation is the reverse of removal.

Make sure the wiring is correctly connected. As you look at the back of the cluster, the brown wire is for the left-hand terminal, the black for the middle terminal, and the grey for the right-hand terminal.

Coolant temperature gauge (TRX, XTZ and 1991 to 1998 TDM models)

Check

16 See Chapter 3.

Replacement

17 Remove the instrument cluster (see Section 15). On TRX models, remove the screw securing the surround and remove the surround **(see illustration 16.5)**.

18 Remove the casing screws from the back of the cluster and lift off the front cover assembly **(see illustrations 16.6a, b or c)**.

19 Remove the screws securing the three temperature gauge wires and detach the wires, noting which fits where.

20 Carefully withdraw the temperature gauge from the front.

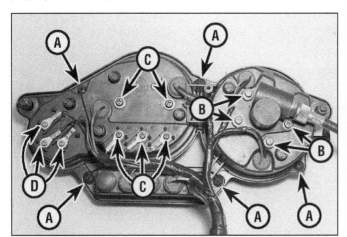

16.6b Casing screws (A), speedometer screws (B), tachometer screws (C), temperature gauge screws (D) – TRX models

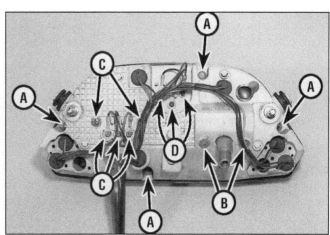

16.6c Casing screws (A), speedometer screws (B), tachometer screws (C), temperature gauge screws (D) – XTZ models

16.26a Pull out the bulbholder . . .

16.26b . . . and remove the bulb

poor wire connection or break in any of the circuit wiring. Check that the fuel level warning light bulb has not blown.

Replacement

5 Refer to Section 16 for renewal of the fuel gauge and warning light bulb.

6 To access the sender unit, first remove the fuel tank as described in Chapter 4 and drain all fuel from the tank into a suitable container.

7 Remove the four bolts which retain the sender unit to the base of the tank. Withdraw the sender unit very carefully so that its float and arm and not bent. Check that the float is not punctured and that the arm moves smoothly.

8 When installing the sender unit, always use a new gasket between the sender and tank and make sure that the washers are in place on the four retaining bolts.

> ⚠️ **Warning: Petrol is extremely flammable, so take extra precautions when you work on any part of the fuel system.** *Don't smoke or allow open flames or bare light bulbs near the work area, and don't work in a garage where a natural gas-type appliance is present. If you spill any fuel on your skin, rinse it off immediately with soap and water. When you perform any kind of work on the fuel system, wear safety glasses and have a fire extinguisher suitable for a class B type fire (flammable liquids) on hand.*

21 Installation is the reverse of removal. Make sure the wiring is correctly connected. As you look at the back of the cluster, the green/red wire is for the left-hand terminal, the black for the middle terminal, and the brown for the right-hand terminal.

Fuel gauge (1999 TDM models)

Check

22 See Section 17.

Replacement

23 Remove the instrument cluster (see Section 15). Remove the seven screws from the base of the cluster and separate the upper and lower covers from the instrument assembly. The fuel gauge is retained by three screws.

24 Installation is the reverse of removal.

Bulb renewal

25 Remove the fairing (see Chapter 8). The bulbs are accessible with the instrument cluster in place, but access is quite restricted. If it is too restricted, unscrew the nuts securing the instrument cluster and displace it as required to improve access (see Section 15).

26 Gently pull the bulbholder out of the instrument casing, then pull the bulb out of the bulbholder **(see illustrations)**. If the socket contacts are dirty or corroded, scrape them clean and spray with electrical contact cleaner before a new bulb is installed. Carefully push the new bulb into the holder and push the holder into the casing.

27 Install the fairing (see Chapter 8).

---

17 Fuel gauge and sender unit – check and replacement (1999 TDM models)

Check

1 If the fuel gauge fails to operate or the warning light doesn't come on when the fuel level falls to a low level, the fuel sender unit in the tank may be at fault. Remove the fuel sender unit from the tank as described below.

2 Reconnect the sender wiring, then turn the ignition ON and manually raise its float. With the float fully raised the gauge needle should swing over to the F on the gauge. Now lower the float and check that the needle swings over to the E on the gauge. Turn the ignition OFF when the check is complete. If the gauge does not operate as described it should be renewed.

3 Make the following test with the sender unit disconnected from the bike and on the bench. Using a multimeter set to the ohms x 1 range, connect the meter's positive probe to the green/red wire terminal of the wire connector and its negative probe to the black wire terminal of the connector. With the float in the down position, 90 to 100 ohms should be indicated on the meter. Raise the float up to its highest position and check the meter reading – 4 to 10 ohms should now be indicated. If the sender unit does not produce the correct readings it must be renewed.

4 Before renewing the fuel gauge or the sender unit, check that the fault is not due to a

---

18 Ignition (main) switch – check, removal and installation

> ⚠️ **Warning: To prevent the risk of short circuits, disconnect the battery negative (-ve) lead before making any ignition (main) switch checks.**

Check

1 On TDM models, remove the fairing. On TRX models remove the air filter housing, and on XTZ models remove the fuel tank (see Chapter 4). Trace the ignition (main) switch wiring back from the base of the switch and disconnect it at the connector **(see illustrations and 15.3b)**.

2 Using an ohmmeter or a continuity tester, check the continuity of the connector terminal pairs (see the *wiring diagrams* at the end of this Chapter). Continuity should exist between the terminals connected by a solid line on the diagram when the switch is in the indicated position.

3 If the switch fails any of the tests, renew it.

Removal

4 On TDM models, remove the fairing. On TRX models remove the air filter housing, and on XTZ models remove the fuel tank (see Chapter 4). Trace the ignition (main) switch

18.1a Ignition switch wiring connector – TDM models

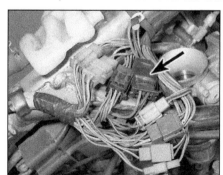

18.1b Ignition switch wiring connector (arrowed) – XTZ models

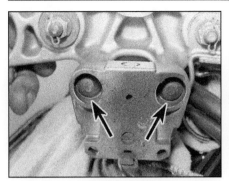

18.8 Ignition switch bolts (arrowed)

19.3 Handlebar switch wiring connectors – TDM models

wiring back from the base of the switch and disconnect it at the connector **(see illustrations 18.1a and b and 15.3b)**. Draw the wiring through to the switch, freeing it from any clips or ties and noting its routing.

5 On 1996-on TDM models, unscrew the bolts securing the choke knob and the cable guide to the top yoke. On TRX models, unscrew the bolt securing the master cylinder reservoir to the top yoke. On XTZ models, unscrew the bolt securing the cable guide to the top yoke.

6 Displace the handlebars from the top yoke (see Chapter 6).

7 Slacken the fork clamp bolts in the top yoke. Unscrew the steering stem nut or bolt and remove it along with its washer, where fitted. Lift the top yoke off the steering stem and remove it.

8 Two shear-head bolts mount the ignition switch to the underside of the top yoke **(see illustration)**. The heads of the bolts must be drilled off before the switch can be removed. Mount the yoke in a vice equipped with soft jaws and padded out with rags and drill off the heads. Remove the bolts and withdraw the switch from the top yoke.

Installation

9 Installation is the reverse of removal. Tighten the new bolts until the heads shear

off. Make sure the wiring connector is securely connected and correctly routed.

19 Handlebar switches – check

1 Generally speaking, the switches are reliable and trouble-free. Most troubles, when they do occur, are caused by dirty or corroded contacts, but wear and breakage of internal parts is a possibility that should not be overlooked. If breakage does occur, the entire switch and related wiring harness will have to be renewed, as individual parts are not available.

2 The switches can be checked for continuity using an ohmmeter or a continuity test light. Always disconnect the battery negative (-ve) cable, which will prevent the possibility of a short circuit, before making the checks.

3 On TDM models, remove the fairing (see Chapter 8). On TRX models remove the air filter housing, and on XTZ models remove the fuel tank (see Chapter 4). Trace the wiring harness of the switch in question back to its connector and disconnect it **(see illustration and 18.1b and 15.3b)**.

4 Check for continuity between the terminals of the switch harness with the switch in the various positions (ie switch off – no continuity,

switch on – continuity) – see the *wiring diagrams* at the end of this Chapter.

5 If the continuity check indicates a problem exists, refer to Section 20, remove the switch and spray the switch contacts with electrical contact cleaner. If they are accessible, the contacts can be scraped clean with a knife or polished with crocus cloth. If switch components are damaged or broken, it will be obvious when the switch is disassembled.

20 Handlebar switches – removal and installation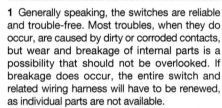

Removal

1 If the switch is to be removed from the bike, rather than just displaced from the handlebar, trace the wiring harness of the switch in question back to its connector(s) and disconnect it/them. On TDM models, remove the fairing (see Chapter 8). On TRX models remove the air filter housing, and on XTZ models remove the fuel tank (see Chapter 4). Trace the wiring harness of the switch in question back to its connector and disconnect it **(see illustrations 19.3, 18.1b and 15.3b)**. Work back along the harness, freeing it from all the relevant clips and ties, whilst noting its correct routing.

2 On TDM and TRX models, disconnect the wiring connector(s) from the brake light switch (if removing the right-hand switch) or the clutch switch (if removing the left-hand switch) **(see illustrations 14.7a and b, or 23.2a)**.

3 Unscrew the handlebar switch screws and free the switch from the handlebar by separating the halves **(see illustrations)**.

Installation

4 Installation is the reverse of removal. Make sure the locating pin in the switch housing locates in the hole in the handlebar and on 1999 TDM models ensure that the choke lever locates correctly.

20.3a Right-hand switch housing screws (arrowed) – TDM models

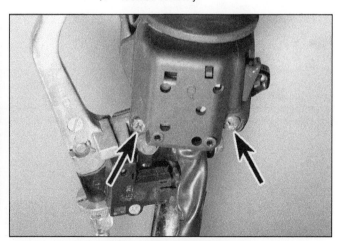

20.3b Left-hand switch housing screws (arrowed) – TDM models

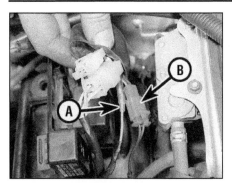

21.2a Neutral switch wiring connector (A), sidestand switch wiring connector (B) – TDM models

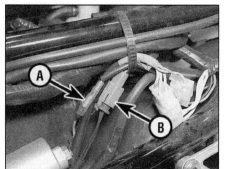

21.2b Neutral switch wiring connector (A), sidestand switch wiring connector (B) – TRX models

21.2c Neutral switch wiring connector (arrowed) – XTZ models

21 Neutral switch – check, removal and installation

Check

1 Before checking the electrical circuit, check the bulb (see Section 16) and fuse (see Section 5).
2 The switch is located in the left-hand side of the transmission casing above the front sprocket. To access the wiring connector, on TDM models remove the seat, on TRX models remove the side covers, and on XTZ models remove the left-hand side cover (see Chapter 8). Trace the single light blue wire from the top of the alternator cover and disconnect it at

21.8 Unscrew the bolts (arrowed) and remove the plate

the connector **(see illustrations)**. Make sure the transmission is in neutral.
3 With the connector disconnected and the ignition switched ON, the neutral light should be out. If not, the wire between the connector and instrument cluster must be earthed at some point.
4 Check for continuity between the wire terminal on the switch side of the wiring connector and the crankcase. With the transmission in neutral, there should be continuity. With the transmission in gear, there should be no continuity. If the tests prove otherwise, then the switch is faulty.
5 If the continuity tests prove the switch is good, check for voltage at the terminal on the wiring loom side of the wiring connector using a test light with the ignition ON. If there's no voltage present, check the wire between the connector, the instrument cluster and fusebox (see the *wiring diagrams* at the end of this Chapter). Turn the ignition OFF.

Removal

6 Make sure the transmission is in neutral. The switch is located in the left-hand side of the transmission casing above the front sprocket. To access the wiring connector, on TDM models remove the seat, on TRX models remove the side covers, and on XTZ models remove the left-hand side cover (see Chapter 8). Trace the single light blue wire from the top of the alternator cover and disconnect it at the connector **(see illustrations 21.2a, b and c)**.

7 Remove the alternator cover (see Section 32).
8 Unscrew the bolts securing the transmission output shaft retainer plate to the left-hand side of the crankcase and remove the plate **(see illustration)**.
9 Pull the wiring grommet from its cutout in the crankcase **(see illustration)**.
10 Remove the screws securing the switch and detach it from the casing **(see illustration)**. Discard the O-ring as a new one must be used.

Installation

11 Fit a new O-ring onto the switch **(see illustration)**, then install the switch and tighten its screws securely **(see illustration 21.9)**.
12 Press the wiring grommet into its cutout in the crankcase **(see illustration 21.9)**.
13 Install the transmission output shaft retainer plate onto the left-hand side of the crankcase **(see illustration 21.8)**. Apply a suitable non-permanent thread locking compound to the threads of the bolts and tighten them to the specified torque setting.
14 Connect the wiring connector **(see illustrations 21.2a, b and c)**. Check the operation of the neutral light.
15 Install the alternator cover (see Section 8).
16 On TDM models install the seat, on TRX models install the side covers, and on XTZ models install the left-hand side cover (see Chapter 8).

21.9 Detach the wiring grommet and remove the screws (arrowed) . . .

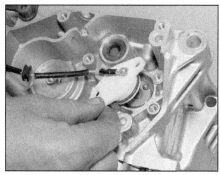

21.10 . . . and remove the switch

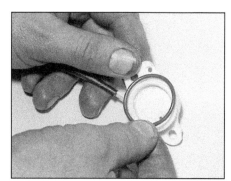

21.11 Fit a new O-ring onto the switch

22 Sidestand switch –
check and replacement

Check

1 The sidestand switch is mounted on the sidestand. The switch is part of the safety cut-out circuit which only allows the starter motor to operate if the transmission is in neutral or the clutch lever is pulled in and the sidestand is up. Before checking the electrical circuit, check the fuse (see Section 5).
2 To access the wiring connector, on TDM models remove the seat, on TRX models remove the side covers, and on XTZ models remove the left-hand side cover (see Chapter 8). Trace the wiring back from the switch and disconnect it at the connector **(see illustration and 21.2a and b)**.
3 Check the operation of the switch using an ohmmeter or continuity test light. Connect the meter probes to the terminals on the switch side of the connector. With the sidestand up there should be continuity (zero resistance) between the terminals, and with the stand down there should be no continuity (infinite resistance).
4 If the switch does not perform as expected, it is defective and must be renewed.
5 If the switch is good, check the wiring between the various components in the starter safety circuit (see the *wiring diagrams* at the end of this book).

Replacement

6 The sidestand switch is mounted on the sidestand. To access the wiring connector, on TDM models remove the seat, on TRX models remove the side covers, and on XTZ models remove the left-hand side cover (see Chapter 8). Trace the wiring back from the switch to its connector and disconnect it **(see illustrations 21.2a and b and 22.2)**. Work back along the switch wiring, freeing it from any relevant retaining clips and ties, noting its correct routing.
7 Unscrew the switch bolts or screws and remove the switch from the stand, noting how it fits **(see illustration)**.

22.2 Sidestand switch wiring connector – XTZ models

8 Fit the new switch onto the sidestand, making sure the plunger locates correctly, and tighten the bolts or screws securely.
9 Make sure the wiring is correctly routed up to the connector and retained by all the necessary clips and ties.
10 Reconnect the wiring connector and check the operation of the sidestand switch.
11 On TDM models install the seat, on TRX models install the side covers, and on XTZ models install the left-hand side cover (see Chapter 8).

23 Clutch switch –
check and replacement

Check

1 The clutch switch is mounted on the underside of the clutch lever bracket on TDM and TRX models, and is a push-fit into the bracket on the XTZ models. The switch is part of the safety circuit which prevents or stops the engine running if the transmission is in gear whilst the sidestand is down, and prevents the engine from starting if the transmission is in gear unless the sidestand is up and the clutch lever is pulled in. The switch isn't adjustable.
2 On XTZ models, to access the switch wiring connector, remove the fuel tank (see Chapter 4). To check the switch, disconnect the wiring connector(s) **(see illustrations)**. Connect the probes of an ohmmeter or a continuity test

22.7 Sidestand switch screws (arrowed) – TDM shown

light to the two switch terminals. With the clutch lever pulled in, continuity should be indicated. With the clutch lever out, no continuity (infinite resistance) should be indicated.
3 If the switch is good, check the other components in the starter circuit as described in the relevant sections of this Chapter. If all components are good, check the wiring between the various components (see the *wiring diagrams* at the end of this book).

Replacement

4 The clutch switch is mounted on the underside of the clutch lever bracket on TDM and TRX models, and is a push-fit into the bracket on XTZ models. On XTZ models, to access the switch wiring connector, remove the fuel tank (see Chapter 4).
5 Disconnect the wiring connector(s) **(see illustrations 23.2a and b)**, then either remove the screw(s) and detach the switch or withdraw the switch from the bracket, according to model **(see illustration)**.
6 Installation is the reverse of removal.

24 Diode (XTZ models) –
check and replacement

Check

1 The diode is a small block that plugs into the main wiring harness (see *Wiring Diagrams* at the end of the Chapter). Remove the seat

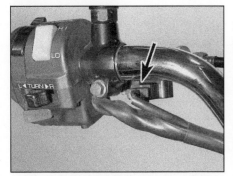

23.2a Clutch switch wiring connector (arrowed) – TDM models

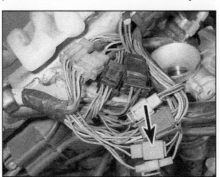

23.2b Clutch switch wiring connector (arrowed) – XTZ models

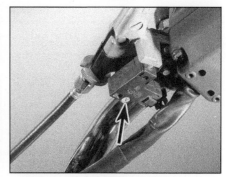

23.5 Clutch switch screw (arrowed) – TDM models

and fuel tank for access (see Chapters 8 and 4). The diode is part of the safety circuit which prevents or stops the engine running if the transmission is in gear whilst the sidestand is down, and prevents the engine from starting if the transmission is in gear unless the sidestand is up and the clutch lever is pulled in.

2 Disconnect the diode from the harness. The diode is situated on the left-hand side of the frame in the area where the fuel tank and side cover meet.

3 Using an ohmmeter or continuity tester, connect the positive (+ve) probe to one terminal of the diode and the negative (-ve) probe to the other terminal. Now reverse the probes. The diode should show continuity in one direction and no continuity in the other direction. If it doesn't behave as stated, renew the diode.

4 If the diode is good, check the other components in the starter circuit as described in the relevant sections of this Chapter. If all components are good, check the wiring between the various components (see the *wiring diagrams* at the end of this book).

Replacement

5 The diode is a small block that plugs into the main wiring harness on the left-hand side of the frame in the area where the fuel tank and side cover meet. Remove the seat and fuel tank for access (see Chapters 8 and 4). Disconnect the diode from the harness and connect the new one.

25.2a Starter circuit cut-off relay (arrowed) – TDM models

25.2b Starter circuit cut-off relay (arrowed) – XTZ models

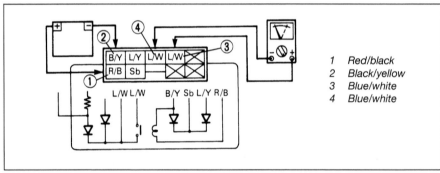

25.3a Starter circuit cut-off relay test set-up – 1991 to 1995 TDM models

1 Red/black
2 Black/yellow
3 Blue/white
4 Blue/white

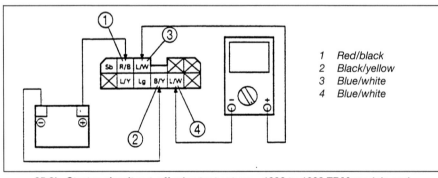

25.3b Starter circuit cut-off relay test set-up – 1996 to 1998 TDM models and TRX models

1 Red/black
2 Black/yellow
3 Blue/white
4 Blue/white

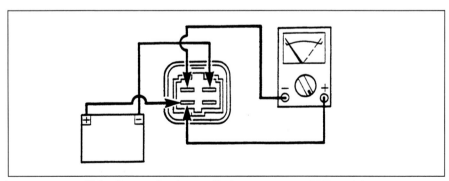

25.3c Starter circuit cut-off relay test set-up – XTZ models

25 Starter circuit cut-off relay – check and replacement

Check

1 The starter circuit cut-off relay is part of the safety circuit which prevents or stops the engine running if the transmission is in gear whilst the sidestand is down, and prevents the engine from starting if the transmission is in gear unless the sidestand is up and the clutch lever is pulled in.

2 If the starter circuit is faulty, first check the fuse (see Section 5). The starter cut-off relay is located under the seat on all except 1996-on TDM models, where it is behind the fairing. Remove the seat or fairing for access (see Chapter 8). Disconnect the relay wiring connector and remove the relay **(see illustrations and 11.3b)**.

3 Set a multimeter to the ohms x 1 scale and connect it across the relay's terminals as shown, according to your model **(see illustrations)**. Using a fully-charged 12 volt battery and two insulated jumper wires, connect the battery to the relay's terminals as shown, according to your model. At this point the multimeter should show zero ohms (continuity). If this is the case the relay is proved good. If the relay indicates no continuity (infinite resistance) across its terminals, it is faulty and must be renewed. **Note:** *No test details are available for the 1999 TDM model – the relay can only be checked by the substitution of a new relay.*

4 If the relay is good, check the other components in the starter circuit as described in the relevant sections of this Chapter. If all components are good, check the wiring between the various components (see the *wiring diagrams* at the end of this book).

Replacement

5 The starter cut-off relay is located under the seat on all except 1996-on TDM models, where it is behind the fairing. Remove the seat or fairing for access (see Chapter 8). Disconnect the relay wiring connector and remove the relay **(see illustrations 25.2a and b, and 11.3b)**.

6 Installation is the reverse of removal.

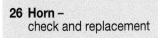

26 Horn –
check and replacement

Check

1 If the horn, doesn't work, first check the fuse (see Section 5) and the battery (see Section 3).

2 The horn is mounted behind the fairing side panels or the fairing, depending on model. On TDM and TRX models, remove the fairing, and on XTZ models remove the left-hand fairing side panel (see Chapter 8).

3 Unplug the wiring connectors from the horn **(see illustrations)**. Using two jumper wires, apply battery voltage directly to the terminals on the horn. If the horn sounds, check the switch (see Section 19) and the wiring between the switch and the horn (see the *wiring diagrams* at the end of this Chapter).

4 If the horn doesn't sound, renew it.

Replacement

5 The horn is mounted behind the fairing side panels or the fairing, depending on model. On TDM and TRX models, remove the fairing, and on XTZ models remove the left-hand fairing side panel (see Chapter 8).

6 Unplug the wiring connectors from the horn, then unscrew the bolt(s) securing the horn and remove it from the bike **(see illustrations 26.3a, b, c and d)**.

7 Install the horn and securely tighten the bolt(s). Connect the wiring connectors to the horn.

27 Starter relay –
check and replacement

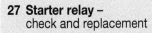

Check

1 If the starter circuit is faulty, first check the fuse (see Section 5).

2 The starter relay is located under the seat. Remove the seat for access (see Chapter 8). Lift the rubber terminal cover and unscrew the bolt securing the starter motor lead **(see illustration)**; position the lead away from the relay terminal. With the ignition switch ON, the engine kill switch in the RUN position, the transmission in

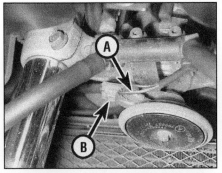
26.3a Horn wiring connectors (A) and mounting bolt (B) – TDM models

26.3c . . . and mounting bolt (B) – TRX models

neutral and the clutch pulled in, press the starter switch. The relay should be heard to click.

3 If the relay doesn't click, switch off the ignition and remove the relay as described below; test it as follows.

4 This test is made with the relay removed from the bike and on the bench. Set a multimeter to the ohms x 1 scale and connect it across the relay's starter motor and battery lead terminals. Using a fully-charged 12 volt battery and two insulated jumper wires, connect the jumper leads as follows according to the model being worked on:

1991 to 95 TDM	Battery positive lead to the red wire terminal of the relay, negative lead to the blue/white terminal
1996-on TDM	Battery positive lead to the red/white wire terminal of the relay, negative lead to the blue/white terminal
TRX	Battery positive lead to the blue/white wire terminal of the relay, negative lead to the red terminal
XTZ	Battery positive lead to the blue/white wire terminal of the relay, negative lead to the red/white terminal

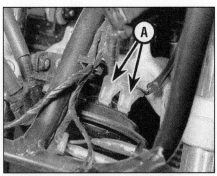
26.3b Horn wiring connectors (A) . . .

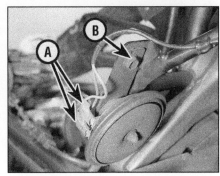
26.3d Horn wiring connectors (A) and mounting bolt (B) – XTZ models

At this point the relay should be heard to click and the multimeter read 0 ohms (continuity). If this is the case the relay is proved good. If the relay does not click when battery voltage is applied and indicates no continuity (infinite resistance) across its terminals, it is faulty and must be renewed.

5 If the relay is good, check the other components in the starter circuit as described in the relevant sections of this Chapter. If all components are good, check the wiring between the various components (see the *wiring diagrams* at the end of this book).

Replacement

6 Remove the seat (see Chapter 8).

7 Disconnect the relay wiring connector, and unscrew the two nuts securing the starter motor and battery leads to the relay and

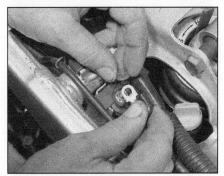
27.2 Detach the starter motor lead from the relay

27.7 Pull back the covers to access the terminal nuts

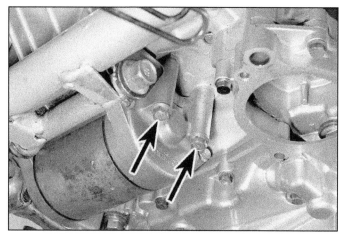

28.4a Unscrew the bolts (arrowed) . . .

detach the leads **(see illustration)**. Remove the relay with its rubber sleeve from its mounting lug on the frame.

8 Installation is the reverse of removal. Make sure the terminal nuts are securely tightened. Connect the negative (-ve) lead last when reconnecting the battery.

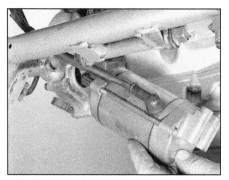

28.4b . . . and remove the starter motor

28 Starter motor – removal and installation

Removal

1 Remove the seat (see Chapter 8). Disconnect the battery negative (-ve) lead.

2 The starter motor is mounted underneath the engine.

3 Peel back the rubber terminal cover and remove the nut securing the starter lead to the starter relay **(see illustration 27.2)**. Detach the lead and feed it through to the starter motor.

4 Unscrew the two bolts securing the starter motor to the crankcase **(see illustration)**. Slide the starter motor out from the crankcase and remove it from the machine **(see illustration)**.

5 Remove the O-ring on the end of the starter

motor and discard it as a new one must be used.

Installation

6 Install a new O-ring on the end of the starter motor and ensure it is seated in its groove **(see illustration)**. Apply a smear of engine oil to the O-ring to aid installation.

7 Manoeuvre the motor into position and slide it into the crankcase **(see illustration 28.4b)**. Ensure that the starter motor teeth mesh correctly with those of the starter idle/reduction gear. Install the mounting bolts and tighten them to the torque setting specified at the beginning of the Chapter **(see illustration)**.

8 Connect the starter lead to the starter relay and secure it with the nut **(see illustration 27.2)**. Make sure the rubber cover is correctly seated over the terminal.

9 Connect the battery negative (-ve) lead and install the seat (see Chapter 8).

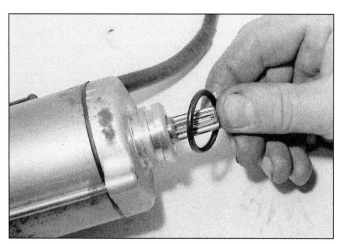

28.6 Fit a new O-ring into the groove

28.7 Install the bolts and tighten them to the specified torque

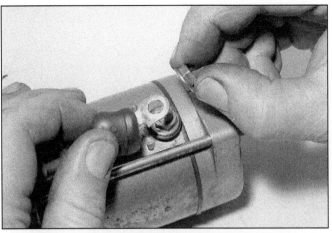

29.1 Unscrew the terminal nut and detach the lead

29.2 Note the alignment marks (arrowed), or make your own

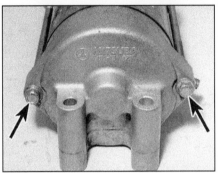

29.3 Unscrew the long bolts (arrowed)

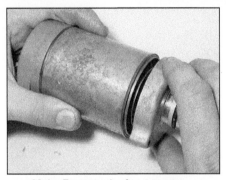

29.4a Remove the front cover . . .

29.4b . . . and slide off the shims

29 Starter motor – disassembly, inspection and reassembly

Disassembly

1 Remove the starter motor (see Section 28). Pull back the rubber terminal cover, then unscrew the nut and detach the lead from the terminal bolt **(see illustration)**.

2 Note the alignment marks between the main housing and the front and rear covers, or make your own if they aren't clear **(see illustration)**.

3 Unscrew the two long bolts and withdraw them from the starter motor **(see illustration)**.

4 Wrap some insulating tape around the teeth on the end of the starter motor shaft – this will protect the oil seal from damage as the front cover is removed. Remove the front cover from the motor **(see illustration)**. Remove the cover O-ring from the main housing and discard it as a new one must be used.

Remove the shims from the front end of the armature shaft or the inside of the front cover, noting their correct fitted locations **(see illustration)**. Also remove the tabbed thrust washer from the front cover **(see illustration 29.20b)**.

5 Remove the rear cover from the motor **(see illustration)**. Remove the cover O-ring from the main housing and discard it as a new one must be used. Remove the shims from the rear end of the armature shaft or from inside the rear cover **(see illustration)**.

29.5a Remove the rear cover . . .

29.5b . . . and slide off the shims

29.6 Withdraw the armature

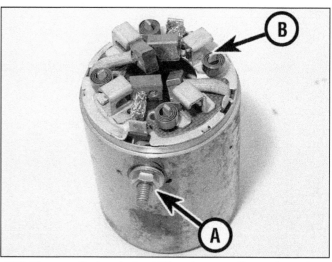

29.7 Unscrew the terminal nut (A) and remove the washers, then lift out the brushplate (B)

6 Withdraw the armature from the main housing **(see illustration)**.

7 Noting the correct fitted location of each component, unscrew the terminal nut and remove it along with its washer and the insulating washers **(see illustration)**. Withdraw the brushplate assembly and

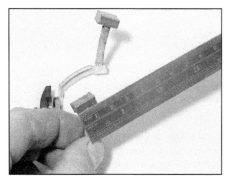

29.8 Measure the length of each brush

terminal bolt from the main housing. Remove the brushplate seat **(see illustration 29.15a)**.

Inspection

8 The parts of the starter motor that are most likely to require attention are the brushes. Measure the length of the brushes and compare the results to the brush length listed in this Chapter's Specifications **(see illustration)**. If any of the brushes are worn beyond the service limit, renew the brush assembly. If the brushes are not worn excessively, nor cracked, chipped, or otherwise damaged, they may be re-used.

9 Inspect the commutator bars on the armature for scoring, scratches and discoloration. The commutator can be cleaned and polished with crocus cloth, but do not use sandpaper or emery paper. After cleaning, wipe away any residue with a cloth soaked in electrical system cleaner or denatured alcohol. Measure the diameter of

the commutator and compare it to the specifications. If it has worn below the wear limit, renew the starter motor. Measure the depth of the insulating Mica below the surface of the commutator bars. If the Mica is less than the depth specified, scrape it away until the specified depth is reached.

10 Using an ohmmeter or a continuity test light, check for continuity between the commutator bars **(see illustration)**. Continuity should exist between each bar and all of the others. Also, check for continuity between the commutator bars and the armature shaft **(see illustration)**. There should be no continuity (infinite resistance) between the commutator and the shaft. If the checks indicate otherwise, the armature is defective.

11 Check for continuity between the terminal bolt and the housing (when assembled). There should be no continuity (infinite resistance).

12 Check the front end of the armature shaft for worn, cracked, chipped and broken teeth.

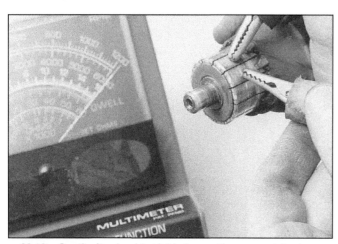

29.10a Continuity should exist between the commutator bars

29.10b There should be no continuity between the commutator bars and the armature shaft

29.15a Fit the brushplate seat

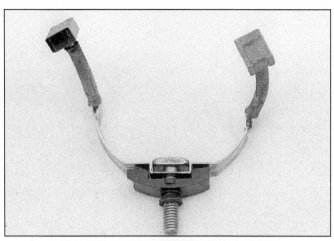

29.15b Make sure the insulators are in place . . .

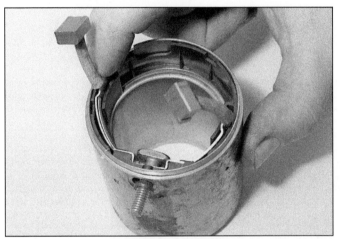

29.15c . . . then install the terminal bolt assembly into the housing and brushplate seat . . .

29.15d . . . and fit the washers and nut

If the shaft is damaged or worn, renew the armature.

13 Inspect the end covers for signs of cracks or wear. Inspect the magnets in the main housing and the housing itself for cracks.

14 Inspect the insulating washers and front cover oil seal for signs of damage and renew them if necessary.

Reassembly

15 Fit the brushplate seat into the main housing **(see illustration)**. Ensure that the inner rubber insulator and O-ring are in place on the terminal bolt, then insert the bolt through the main housing and locate the arms into the brushplate seat **(see illustrations)**. Fit the insulating washers over the terminal, then fit the standard washer and the nut **(see illustration)**.

16 Fit the brushplate assembly onto the main housing, locating the terminal bolt brush wires in the cutouts and making sure the tab on the plate locates in the cutout in the housing **(see illustration)**.

17 Fit each brush into its holder and press it back against the spring, then lock it in that position by inserting a strip of plastic (such as the cut-off end of a cable tie) between the spring end and the holder, preventing the spring from pushing the brush back out **(see illustration)**. This provides the clearance necessary for the armature to be installed

without becoming entangled with the exposed brush ends.

18 Insert the armature into the main housing, noting that it will be forcibly drawn in by the attraction of the magnets **(see illustration 29.6)**. Remove the strips securing the brushes. Check that each brush is securely pressed against the commutator

29.16 Fit the brushplate, locating the tab in the notch (A) the brush wires in the cutouts (B)

29.17 Lock the brushes into their holders as described and shown

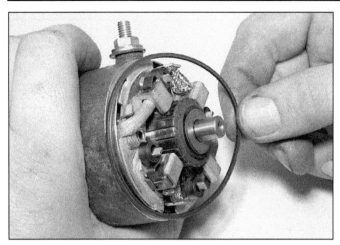

29.19 Fit a new O-ring onto the rear of the housing

29.20a Fit a new O-ring onto the front of the housing . . .

by its spring and is free to move easily in its holder.
19 Slide the shims onto the end of the armature **(see illustration 29.5b)**, then fit a new rear cover O-ring **(see illustration)**. Fit the rear cover onto the housing, aligning the marks noted or made earlier **(see illustration 29.5a)**.
20 Slide the shims onto the front of the armature **(see illustration 29.4b)**, then fit a new front cover O-ring **(see illustration)**. Apply a smear of grease to the lips of the front cover oil seal. Fit the tabbed washer onto the cover **(see illustration)**, making sure the tabs locate correctly, then install the cover, aligning the marks made on removal **(see illustration 29.4a)**. Remove the protective tape from the shaft end.
21 Check the alignment marks made on removal are correctly aligned, then install the long bolts and tighten them securely **(see illustration)**.
22 Fit the starter motor lead onto the terminal bolt, then secure it with the nut and cover it with the rubber boot **(see illustration 29.1)**.
23 Install the starter motor (see Section 28).

30 Charging system testing – general information and precautions

1 If the performance of the charging system is suspect, the system as a whole should be checked first, followed by testing of the individual components. **Note:** *Before beginning the checks, make sure the battery is fully charged and that all system connections are clean and tight.*
2 Checking the output of the charging system and the performance of the various components within the charging system requires the use of a multimeter (with voltage, current and resistance checking facilities).
3 When making the checks, follow the procedures carefully to prevent incorrect connections or short circuits, as irreparable damage to electrical system components may result if short circuits occur.
4 If a multimeter is not available, the job of checking the charging system should be left to a Yamaha dealer.

31 Charging system – leakage and output test

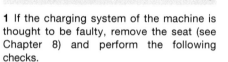

1 If the charging system of the machine is thought to be faulty, remove the seat (see Chapter 8) and perform the following checks.

Leakage test

Caution: Always connect an ammeter in series, never in parallel with the battery, otherwise it will be damaged. Do not turn the ignition ON or operate the starter motor when the ammeter is connected – a sudden surge in current will blow the meter's fuse.
2 Turn the ignition switch OFF and disconnect the lead from the battery negative (-ve) terminal.
3 Set the multimeter to the Amps function and connect its negative (-ve) probe to the battery negative (-ve) terminal, and positive (+ve) probe to the disconnected negative (-ve) lead **(see**

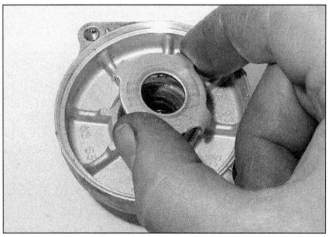

29.20b . . . and fit the tabbed washer into the cover

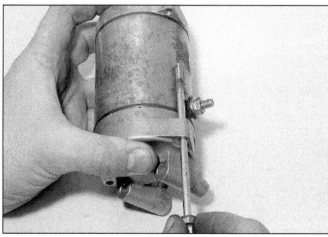

29.21 Install and tighten the long bolts

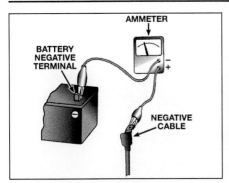

31.3 Checking the charging system leakage rate – connect the ammeter as shown

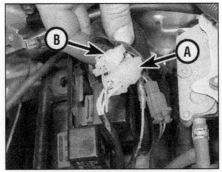

32.2a Alternator wiring connector (A), pick-up coil wiring connector (B) – TDM models

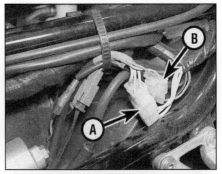

32.2b Alternator wiring connector (A), pick-up coil wiring connector (B) – TRX models

illustration). Always set the meter to a high amps range initially and then bring it down to the mA (milli Amps) range; if there is a high current flow in the circuit it may blow the meter's fuse.

4 If the current leakage indicated exceeds the amount specified at the beginning of the Chapter, there is probably a short circuit in the wiring. Disconnect the meter and connect the negative (-ve) lead to the battery, tightening it securely,

5 If leakage is indicated, use the wiring diagrams at the end of this book to systematically disconnect individual electrical components and repeat the test until the source is identified.

Output test

6 Start the engine and warm it up to normal operating temperature. Remove the seat (see Chapter 8).

7 To check the regulated voltage output, allow the engine to idle and connect a multimeter set to the 0 to 20 volts DC scale (voltmeter) between the terminals of the battery (meter positive (+ve) lead to battery positive terminal, meter negative (-ve) lead to battery negative terminal). Slowly increase the engine speed to 5000 rpm and note the reading obtained. The regulated voltage should be as specified at the beginning of the Chapter. If the voltage is outside these limits, check the alternator and the regulator (see Sections 32 and 33).

 HAYNES HiNT *Clues to a faulty regulator are constantly blowing bulbs, with brightness varying considerably with engine speed, and battery overheating.*

 32 Alternator – check, removal and installation

Check

1 To access the wiring connectors, on TDM models remove the seat, on TRX models remove the side covers, and on XTZ models remove the left-hand side cover (see Chapter 8).

2 Trace the wiring back from the top of the alternator cover on the left-hand side of the engine and disconnect it at the white connector containing the three white wires **(see illustrations)**.

3 Using a multimeter set to the ohms x 1 (ohmmeter) scale measure the resistance between each of the white wires on the alternator side of the connector, taking a total of three readings, then check for continuity between each terminal and earth. If the stator coil windings are in good condition the three readings should be within the range shown in the Specifications at the start of this Chapter

and there should be no continuity (infinite resistance) between any of the terminals and earth. If not, the alternator stator coil assembly is at fault and should be renewed. **Note:** *Before condemning the stator coils, check the fault is not due to damaged wiring between the connector and coils.*

Removal

4 To access the wiring connectors, on TDM models remove the seat, on TRX models remove the side covers, and on XTZ models remove the left-hand side cover (see Chapter 8).

5 Trace the alternator/pick-up coil wiring back from the top of the alternator cover on the left-hand side of the engine and disconnect it at the two white connectors **(see illustrations 32.2a, b and c)**. Free the wiring from any clips or guides and feed it through to the alternator cover.

6 On TDM and XTZ models, unscrew the bolts securing the outer front sprocket cover and remove the cover **(see illustration)**. Unscrew the gearchange lever linkage arm pinchbolt and remove the arm from the shaft, noting the alignment of the punch mark with the slit in the clamp **(see illustration)**. If no mark is visible, make your own before removing the arm so that it can be correctly aligned with the shaft on installation. Unscrew the bolts securing the inner sprocket cover, on TDM models noting the clip secured by the

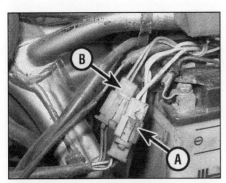

32.2c Alternator wiring connector (A), pick-up coil wiring connector (B) – XTZ models

32.6a Unscrew the bolts (arrowed) and remove the cover

32.6b Gearchange arm/shaft alignment – TDM models

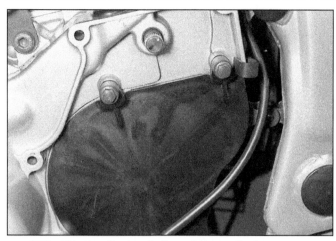

32.6c Unscrew the two bolts and remove the inner cover

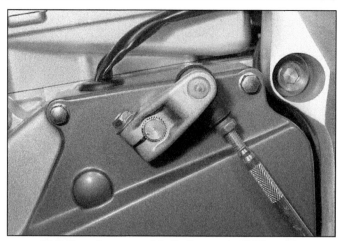

32.7 Gearchange arm/shaft alignment – TRX models

top rear bolt, and remove the cover **(see illustration)**.

7 On TRX models, unscrew the gearchange lever linkage arm pinchbolt and remove the arm from the shaft, noting the alignment of the punch mark with the slit in the clamp **(see illustration)**. If no mark is visible, make your own before removing the arm so that it can be correctly aligned with the shaft on installation.

Unscrew the bolts securing the outer front sprocket cover and remove the cover, then unscrew the bolts securing the inner sprocket cover, noting the clip secured by the top rear bolt, and remove the cover.

8 Working in a criss-cross pattern, unscrew the bolts securing the alternator cover and remove the cover **(see illustration)**. Discard the gasket as a new one must be used. Note

the position of the dowels and remove them if loose.

9 Withdraw the shaft from the starter idle/reduction gear and remove the gear, noting how it fits **(see illustration)**.

10 To remove the rotor bolt it is necessary to stop the rotor from turning. If a rotor holding strap or tool is not available, and if the engine is still in the fame, place the transmission in gear and have an assistant apply the rear brake, then unscrew the bolt **(see illustration)**.

11 To remove the rotor from the shaft it is necessary to use a rotor puller. Yamaha provide a special tool (Pt. Nos. 90890-01362 and 90890-01382, or alternatively a similar tool can be set up as shown, using the threaded holes in the rotor **(see illustration)**. After the rotor has been removed, remove the Woodruff key from the slot in the crankshaft for safekeeping if loose **(see illustration 32.14a)**.

12 To remove the stator from the cover, remove the three screws securing the stator, and the two screws securing the pick-up coil,

32.8 Unscrew the bolts (arrowed) and remove the cover

32.9 Withdraw the shaft (arrowed) and remove the gear

32.10 Unscrew the rotor bolt (arrowed)

32.11 Drawing the rotor off the shaft using a puller

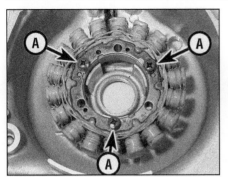

32.12a Remove the rotor screws (A) . . .

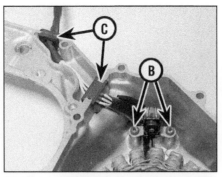

32.12b . . . and the pick-up coil screws (B), and free the wiring grommets (C)

32.14a If removed, fit the Woodruff key into its slot . . .

then remove the assembly, noting how the rubber wiring grommets fit **(see illustrations)**.

Installation

13 Install the stator and the pick-up coil in the cover, aligning the rubber wiring grommets with the grooves **(see illustrations 32.12a and b)**. Apply a suitable non-permanent thread locking compound to the stator and pick-up coil screw threads, then install the screws and tighten them to the torque settings specified at the beginning of the Chapter. Apply a suitable sealant to the wiring grommets, then press them into the cut-outs in the cover.

14 Clean the tapered end of the crankshaft and the corresponding mating surface on the inside of the rotor with a suitable solvent. Fit the Woodruff key into its slot in the crankshaft **(see illustration)**. Make sure that no metal objects have attached themselves to the magnet on the inside of the rotor, then install the rotor onto the shaft, making sure the slot is correctly aligned with the key **(see illustration)**.

15 Install the rotor bolt with its washer and tighten it to the torque setting specified at the beginning of the Chapter, using the method employed on removal to prevent the rotor from turning **(see illustrations)**.

16 Lubricate the starter idle/reduction gear shaft with clean engine oil. Install the

32.14b . . . then slide on the rotor, aligning the slot (arrowed) with the key

idle/reduction gear, making sure it engages correctly with both the starter motor pinion and the starter clutch pinion, and insert the shaft **(see illustration 32.9)**.

17 Install the alternator cover using a new gasket, making sure it locates onto the dowels, and tighten the cover bolts evenly in a criss-cross pattern to the specified torque setting **(see illustrations)**. Connect the alternator and pick-up coil wiring connectors, making sure they are correctly routed and secured by any clips or ties **(see illustrations 32.2a, b and c)**.

18 On TDM and XTZ models, install the inner sprocket cover, on TDM models not forgetting the clip secured by the top rear bolt, and tighten the bolts securely **(see illustration**

32.15a Install the bolt . . .

32.6c). Align the split in the gearchange linkage arm clamp with the punch mark on the shaft, then fit the arm on the shaft and tighten the pinchbolt to the specified torque setting **(see illustration 32.6b)**. Install the outer sprocket cover and tighten its bolts to the specified torque **(see illustration 32.6a)**.

19 On TRX models, install the inner sprocket cover, not forgetting the clip secured by the top rear bolt, and tighten the bolts securely. Install the outer sprocket cover and tighten its bolts to the specified torque. Align the split in the gearchange linkage arm clamp with the punch mark on the shaft, then fit the arm on the shaft and tighten the pinchbolt to the specified torque setting **(see illustration 32.7)**.

32.15b . . . and tighten it to the specified torque

32.17a Locate the gasket onto the dowels (arrowed) . . .

32.17b . . . then install the cover

33 Regulator/rectifier – check and replacement

Check

1 Yamaha provide no test specifications for the regulator/rectifier. If it is suspected of being faulty, first check all other components and wiring in the charging circuit, referring to the relevant Sections in this Chapter and to the wiring diagrams at the end.

2 If all other components and the wiring are good, then the regulator/rectifier could be faulty. Remove the unit (see below) and take it to a Yamaha dealer for testing. Alternatively, substitute the suspect unit with a known good one and see if the fault is cured.

Replacement

3 On 1991 to 1995 TDM models, the regulator/rectifier is mounted on the outside of the left-hand frame beam **(see illustration)**. On 1996-on TDM models, it is mounted behind the fairing. Remove the fairing for access (see Chapter 8). On 1991 to 1995

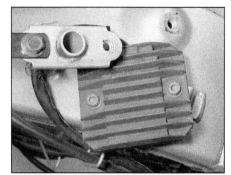

33.3a Regulator/rectifier – 1991 to 1995 TDM models

models, remove the air filter housing for access to the wiring connector (see Chapter 4) **(see illustration)**.

4 On TRX models, the regulator/rectifier is mounted to the underside of the rear mudguard near the top of the shock absorber **(see illustration)**. Remove the rider's seat to access its wiring connector (see Chapter 8) **(see illustration)**.

33.3b Regulator/rectifier wiring connector – 1991 to 1995 TDM models

5 On XTZ models, the regulator/rectifier is mounted behind the left-hand side cover **(see illustration)**. Remove the cover for access (see Chapter 8).

6 Disconnect the wiring connector.

7 Unscrew the two bolts or nuts securing the regulator/rectifier and remove it.

8 Install the new unit and tighten its bolts or nuts securely. Connect the wiring connector.

33.4a Regulator/rectifier – TRX models

33.4b Regulator/rectifier wiring connector – TRX models

33.5 Regulator/rectifier – XTZ models

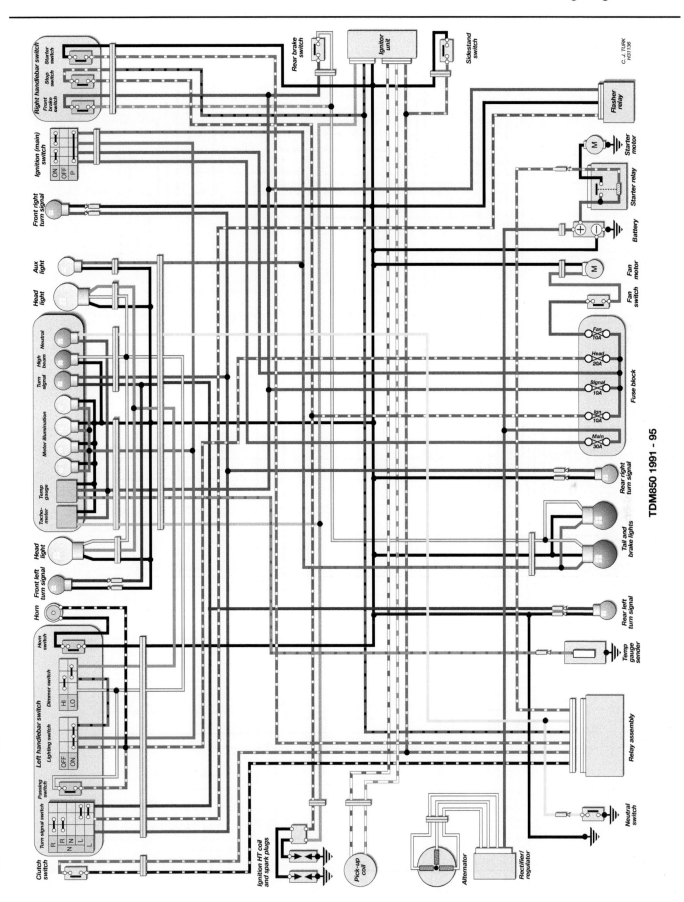

TDM850 1991 - 95

C. J. TURK
H31136

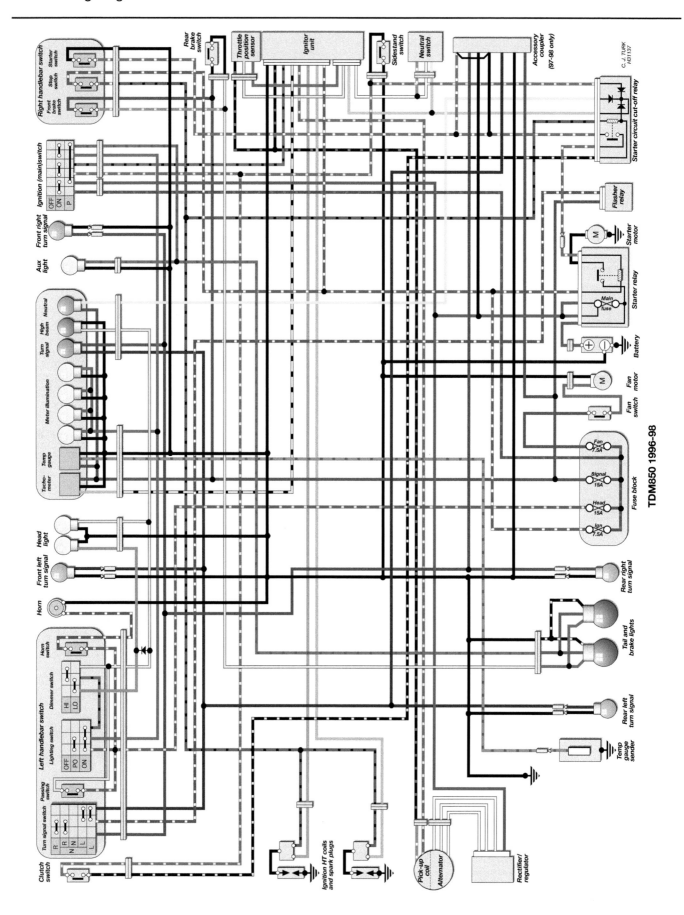

TDM850 1996-98

C. J. TURK
H31137

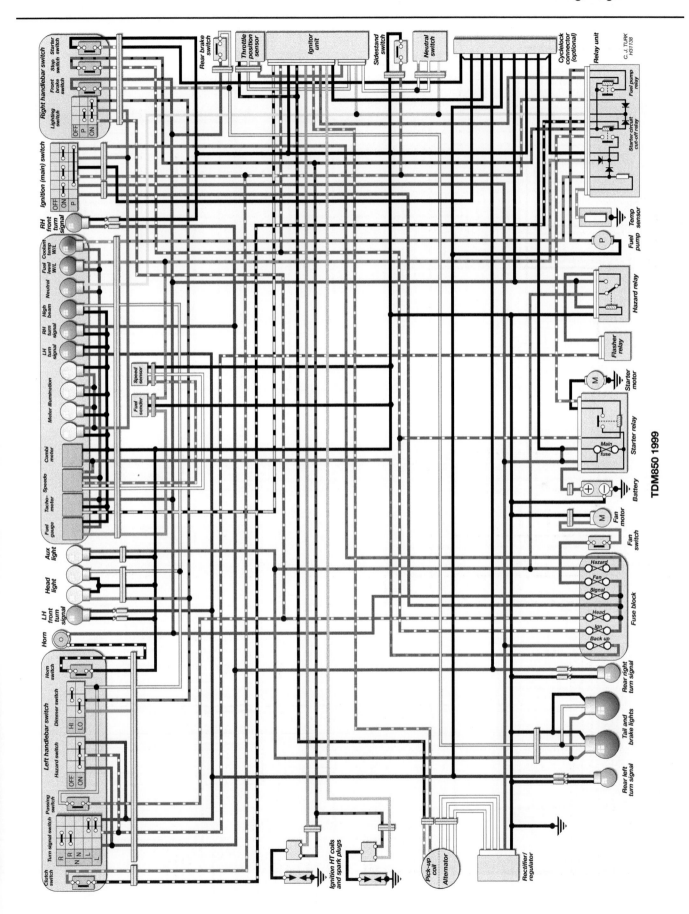

TDM850 1999

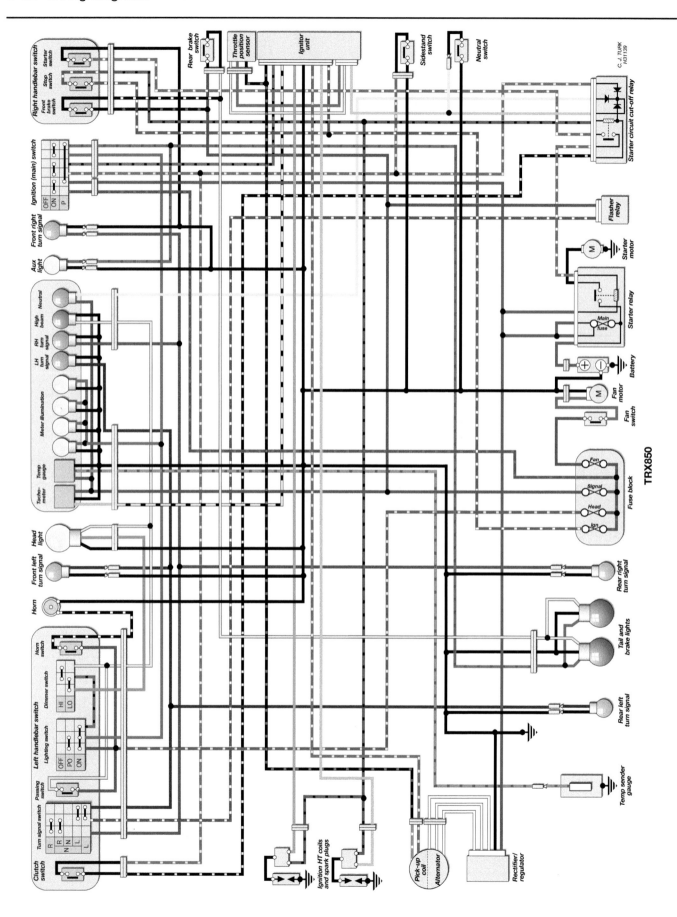

TRX850

C.J. TURK
H31139

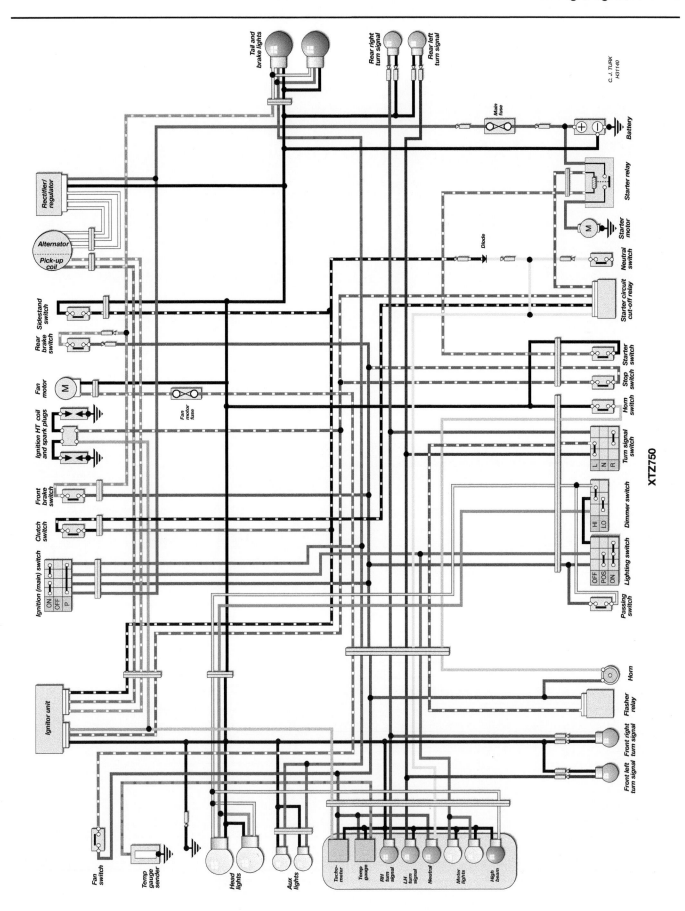

XTZ750

Notes

Dimensions and weights

1991 to 1995 TDM models
Overall length . . . . .2175 mm
Overall width . . . . .780 mm
Overall height . . . . .1260 mm
Seat height . . . . .795 mm
Wheelbase . . . . .1475 mm
Ground clearance . . . . .160 mm
Weight (with fuel and oil) . . . . .230 kg

1996-on TDM models
Overall length . . . . .2165 mm
Overall width . . . . .790 mm
Overall height . . . . .1285 mm
Seat height . . . . .805 mm
Wheelbase . . . . .1475 mm
Ground clearance . . . . .165 mm
Weight (with fuel and oil) . . . . .229 kg (232 kg 1999 model)

TRX models
Overall length . . . . .2070 mm
Overall width . . . . .700 mm
Overall height . . . . .1155 mm
Seat height . . . . .795 mm
Wheelbase . . . . .1435 mm
Ground clearance . . . . .140 mm
Weight (with fuel and oil) . . . . .209 kg

XTZ models
Overall length . . . . .2285 mm
Overall width . . . . .815 mm
Overall height . . . . .1355 mm
Seat height . . . . .865 mm
Wheelbase . . . . .1505 mm
Ground clearance . . . . .240 mm
Weight (with fuel and oil) . . . . .226 kg

Buying tools

A toolkit is a fundamental requirement for servicing and repairing a motorcycle. Although there will be an initial expense in building up enough tools for servicing, this will soon be offset by the savings made by doing the job yourself. As experience and confidence grow, additional tools can be added to enable the repair and overhaul of the motorcycle. Many of the specialist tools are expensive and not often used so it may be preferable to hire them, or for a group of friends or motorcycle club to join in the purchase.

As a rule, it is better to buy more expensive, good quality tools. Cheaper tools are likely to wear out faster and need to be renewed more often, nullifying the original saving.

> ⚠ **Warning: To avoid the risk of a poor quality tool breaking in use, causing injury or damage to the component being worked on, always aim to purchase tools which meet the relevant national safety standards.**

The following lists of tools do not represent the manufacturer's service tools, but serve as a guide to help the owner decide which tools are needed for this level of work. In addition, items such as an electric drill, hacksaw, files, soldering iron and a workbench equipped with a vice, may be needed. Although not classed as tools, a selection of bolts, screws, nuts, washers and pieces of tubing always come in useful.

For more information about tools, refer to the Haynes *Motorcycle Workshop Practice TechBook* (Bk. No. 3470).

Manufacturer's service tools

Inevitably certain tasks require the use of a service tool. Where possible an alternative tool or method of approach is recommended, but sometimes there is no option if personal injury or damage to the component is to be avoided. Where required, service tools are referred to in the relevant procedure.

Service tools can usually only be purchased from a motorcycle dealer and are identified by a part number. Some of the commonly-used tools, such as rotor pullers, are available in aftermarket form from mail-order motorcycle tool and accessory suppliers.

Maintenance and minor repair tools

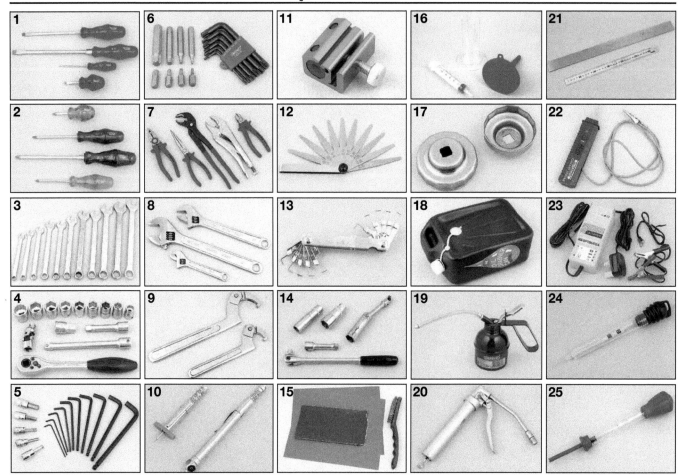

1 *Set of flat-bladed screwdrivers*
2 *Set of Phillips head screwdrivers*
3 *Combination open-end and ring spanners*
4 *Socket set (3/8 inch or 1/2 inch drive)*
5 *Set of Allen keys or bits*

6 *Set of Torx keys or bits*
7 *Pliers, cutters and self-locking grips (Mole grips)*
8 *Adjustable spanners*
9 *C-spanners*
10 *Tread depth gauge and tyre pressure gauge*

11 *Cable oiler clamp*
12 *Feeler gauges*
13 *Spark plug gap measuring tool*
14 *Spark plug spanner or deep plug sockets*
15 *Wire brush and emery paper*

16 *Calibrated syringe, measuring vessel and funnel*
17 *Oil filter adapters*
18 *Oil drainer can or tray*
19 *Pump type oil can*
20 *Grease gun*

21 *Straight-edge and steel rule*
22 *Continuity tester*
23 *Battery charger*
24 *Hydrometer (for battery specific gravity check)*
25 *Anti-freeze tester (for liquid-cooled engines)*

Repair and overhaul tools

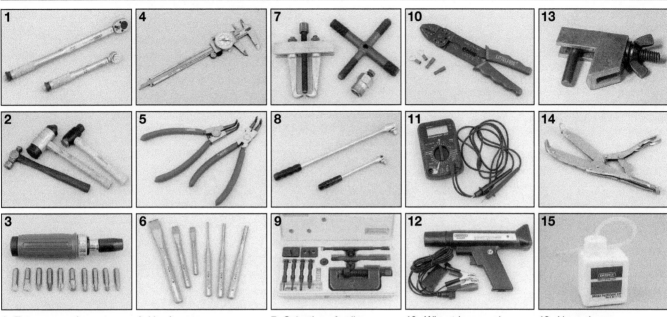

1 Torque wrench
  (small and mid-ranges)
2 Conventional, plastic or
  soft-faced hammers
3 Impact driver set

4 Vernier gauge
5 Circlip pliers (internal and
  external, or combination)
6 Set of cold chisels
  and punches

7 Selection of pullers
8 Breaker bars
9 Chain breaking/
  riveting tool set

10 Wire stripper and
   crimper tool
11 Multimeter (measures
   amps, volts and ohms)
12 Stroboscope (for
   dynamic timing checks)

13 Hose clamp
   (wingnut type shown)
14 Clutch holding tool
15 One-man brake/clutch
   bleeder kit

Specialist tools

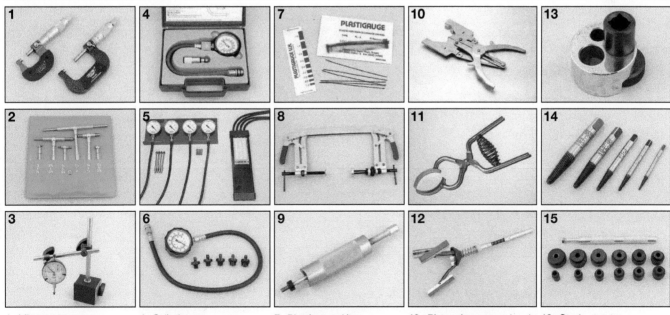

1 Micrometers
  (external type)
2 Telescoping gauges
3 Dial gauge

4 Cylinder
  compression gauge
5 Vacuum gauges (left) or
  manometer (right)
6 Oil pressure gauge

7 Plastigauge kit
8 Valve spring compressor
  (4-stroke engines)
9 Piston pin drawbolt tool

10 Piston ring removal and
   installation tool
11 Piston ring clamp
12 Cylinder bore hone
   (stone type shown)

13 Stud extractor
14 Screw extractor set
15 Bearing driver set

1 Workshop equipment and facilities

The workbench

● Work is made much easier by raising the bike up on a ramp - components are much more accessible if raised to waist level. The hydraulic or pneumatic types seen in the dealer's workshop are a sound investment if you undertake a lot of repairs or overhauls **(see illustration 1.1)**.

1.1 Hydraulic motorcycle ramp

● If raised off ground level, the bike must be supported on the ramp to avoid it falling. Most ramps incorporate a front wheel locating clamp which can be adjusted to suit different diameter wheels. When tightening the clamp, take care not to mark the wheel rim or damage the tyre - use wood blocks on each side to prevent this.
● Secure the bike to the ramp using tie-downs **(see illustration 1.2)**. If the bike has only a sidestand, and hence leans at a dangerous angle when raised, support the bike on an auxiliary stand.

1.2 Tie-downs are used around the passenger footrests to secure the bike

● Auxiliary (paddock) stands are widely available from mail order companies or motorcycle dealers and attach either to the wheel axle or swingarm pivot **(see illustration 1.3)**. If the motorcycle has a centrestand, you can support it under the crankcase to prevent it toppling whilst either wheel is removed **(see illustration 1.4)**.

1.3 This auxiliary stand attaches to the swingarm pivot

1.4 Always use a block of wood between the engine and jack head when supporting the engine in this way

Fumes and fire

● Refer to the Safety first! page at the beginning of the manual for full details. Make sure your workshop is equipped with a fire extinguisher suitable for fuel-related fires (Class B fire - flammable liquids) - it is not sufficient to have a water-filled extinguisher.
● Always ensure adequate ventilation is available. Unless an exhaust gas extraction system is available for use, ensure that the engine is run outside of the workshop.
● If working on the fuel system, make sure the workshop is ventilated to avoid a build-up of fumes. This applies equally to fume build-up when charging a battery. Do not smoke or allow anyone else to smoke in the workshop.

Fluids

● If you need to drain fuel from the tank, store it in an approved container marked as suitable for the storage of petrol (gasoline) **(see illustration 1.5)**. Do not store fuel in glass jars or bottles.

1.5 Use an approved can only for storing petrol (gasoline)

● Use proprietary engine degreasers or solvents which have a high flash-point, such as paraffin (kerosene), for cleaning off oil, grease and dirt - never use petrol (gasoline) for cleaning. Wear rubber gloves when handling solvent and engine degreaser. The fumes from certain solvents can be dangerous - always work in a well-ventilated area.

Dust, eye and hand protection

● Protect your lungs from inhalation of dust particles by wearing a filtering mask over the nose and mouth. Many frictional materials still contain asbestos which is dangerous to your health. Protect your eyes from spouts of liquid and sprung components by wearing a pair of protective goggles **(see illustration 1.6)**.

1.6 A fire extinguisher, goggles, mask and protective gloves should be at hand in the workshop

● Protect your hands from contact with solvents, fuel and oils by wearing rubber gloves. Alternatively apply a barrier cream to your hands before starting work. If handling hot components or fluids, wear suitable gloves to protect your hands from scalding and burns.

What to do with old fluids

● Old cleaning solvent, fuel, coolant and oils should not be poured down domestic drains or onto the ground. Package the fluid up in old oil containers, label it accordingly, and take it to a garage or disposal facility. Contact your local authority for location of such sites or ring the oil care hotline.

OIL CARE
FOLLOW THE CODE
OIL BANK LINE
0800 66 33 66

Note: It is antisocial and illegal to dump oil down the drain. To find the location of your local oil recycling bank, call this number free.

In the USA, note that any oil supplier must accept used oil for recycling.

2 Fasteners -
screws, bolts and nuts

Fastener types and applications

Bolts and screws

● Fastener head types are either of hexagonal, Torx or splined design, with internal and external versions of each type **(see illustrations 2.1 and 2.2)**; splined head fasteners are not in common use on motorcycles. The conventional slotted or Phillips head design is used for certain screws. Bolt or screw length is always measured from the underside of the head to the end of the item **(see illustration 2.11)**.

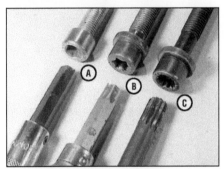

2.1 Internal hexagon/Allen (A), Torx (B) and splined (C) fasteners, with corresponding bits

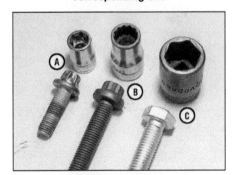

2.2 External Torx (A), splined (B) and hexagon (C) fasteners, with corresponding sockets

● Certain fasteners on the motorcycle have a tensile marking on their heads, the higher the marking the stronger the fastener. High tensile fasteners generally carry a 10 or higher marking. Never replace a high tensile fastener with one of a lower tensile strength.

Washers **(see illustration 2.3)**

● Plain washers are used between a fastener head and a component to prevent damage to the component or to spread the load when torque is applied. Plain washers can also be used as spacers or shims in certain assemblies. Copper or aluminium plain washers are often used as sealing washers on drain plugs.

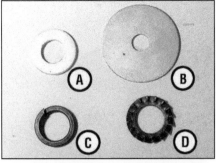

2.3 Plain washer (A), penny washer (B), spring washer (C) and serrated washer (D)

● The split-ring spring washer works by applying axial tension between the fastener head and component. If flattened, it is fatigued and must be renewed. If a plain (flat) washer is used on the fastener, position the spring washer between the fastener and the plain washer.

● Serrated star type washers dig into the fastener and component faces, preventing loosening. They are often used on electrical earth (ground) connections to the frame.

● Cone type washers (sometimes called Belleville) are conical and when tightened apply axial tension between the fastener head and component. They must be installed with the dished side against the component and often carry an OUTSIDE marking on their outer face. If flattened, they are fatigued and must be renewed.

● Tab washers are used to lock plain nuts or bolts on a shaft. A portion of the tab washer is bent up hard against one flat of the nut or bolt to prevent it loosening. Due to the tab washer being deformed in use, a new tab washer should be used every time it is disturbed.

● Wave washers are used to take up endfloat on a shaft. They provide light springing and prevent excessive side-to-side play of a component. Can be found on rocker arm shafts.

Nuts and split pins

● Conventional plain nuts are usually six-sided **(see illustration 2.4)**. They are sized by thread diameter and pitch. High tensile nuts carry a number on one end to denote their tensile strength.

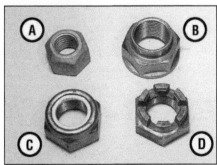

2.4 Plain nut (A), shouldered locknut (B), nylon insert nut (C) and castellated nut (D)

● Self-locking nuts either have a nylon insert, or two spring metal tabs, or a shoulder which is staked into a groove in the shaft - their advantage over conventional plain nuts is a resistance to loosening due to vibration. The nylon insert type can be used a number of times, but must be renewed when the friction of the nylon insert is reduced, ie when the nut spins freely on the shaft. The spring tab type can be reused unless the tabs are damaged. The shouldered type must be renewed every time it is disturbed.

● Split pins (cotter pins) are used to lock a castellated nut to a shaft or to prevent slackening of a plain nut. Common applications are wheel axles and brake torque arms. Because the split pin arms are deformed to lock around the nut a new split pin must always be used on installation - always fit the correct size split pin which will fit snugly in the shaft hole. Make sure the split pin arms are correctly located around the nut **(see illustrations 2.5 and 2.6)**.

2.5 Bend split pin (cotter pin) arms as shown (arrows) to secure a castellated nut

2.6 Bend split pin (cotter pin) arms as shown to secure a plain nut

Caution: If the castellated nut slots do not align with the shaft hole after tightening to the torque setting, tighten the nut until the next slot aligns with the hole - never slacken the nut to align its slot.

● R-pins (shaped like the letter R), or slip pins as they are sometimes called, are sprung and can be reused if they are otherwise in good condition. Always install R-pins with their closed end facing forwards **(see illustration 2.7)**.

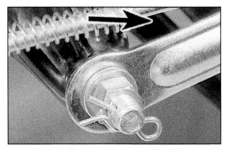

2.7 Correct fitting of R-pin. Arrow indicates forward direction

Circlips (see illustration 2.8)

● Circlips (sometimes called snap-rings) are used to retain components on a shaft or in a housing and have corresponding external or internal ears to permit removal. Parallel-sided (machined) circlips can be installed either way round in their groove, whereas stamped circlips (which have a chamfered edge on one face) must be installed with the chamfer facing away from the direction of thrust load **(see illustration 2.9)**.

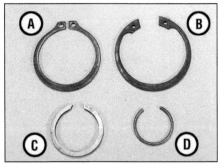

2.8 External stamped circlip (A), internal stamped circlip (B), machined circlip (C) and wire circlip (D)

● Always use circlip pliers to remove and install circlips; expand or compress them just enough to remove them. After installation, rotate the circlip in its groove to ensure it is securely seated. If installing a circlip on a splined shaft, always align its opening with a shaft channel to ensure the circlip ends are well supported and unlikely to catch **(see illustration 2.10)**.

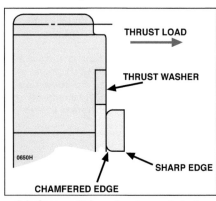

THRUST LOAD

THRUST WASHER

SHARP EDGE

CHAMFERED EDGE

0650H

2.9 Correct fitting of a stamped circlip

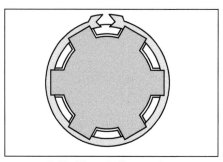

2.10 Align circlip opening with shaft channel

● Circlips can wear due to the thrust of components and become loose in their grooves, with the subsequent danger of becoming dislodged in operation. For this reason, renewal is advised every time a circlip is disturbed.
● Wire circlips are commonly used as piston pin retaining clips. If a removal tang is provided, long-nosed pliers can be used to dislodge them, otherwise careful use of a small flat-bladed screwdriver is necessary. Wire circlips should be renewed every time they are disturbed.

Thread diameter and pitch

● Diameter of a male thread (screw, bolt or stud) is the outside diameter of the threaded portion **(see illustration 2.11)**. Most motorcycle manufacturers use the ISO (International Standards Organisation) metric system expressed in millimetres, eg M6 refers to a 6 mm diameter thread. Sizing is the same for nuts, except that the thread diameter is measured across the valleys of the nut.
● Pitch is the distance between the peaks of the thread **(see illustration 2.11)**. It is expressed in millimetres, thus a common bolt size may be expressed as 6.0 x 1.0 mm (6 mm thread diameter and 1 mm pitch). Generally pitch increases in proportion to thread diameter, although there are always exceptions.
● Thread diameter and pitch are related for conventional fastener applications and the accompanying table can be used as a guide. Additionally, the AF (Across Flats), spanner or socket size dimension of the bolt or nut **(see illustration 2.11)** is linked to thread and pitch specification. Thread pitch can be measured with a thread gauge **(see illustration 2.12)**.

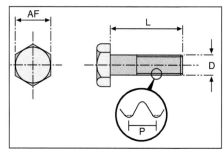

AF

L

D

P

2.11 Fastener length (L), thread diameter (D), thread pitch (P) and head size (AF)

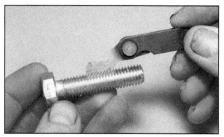

2.12 Using a thread gauge to measure pitch

AF size	Thread diameter x pitch (mm)
8 mm	M5 x 0.8
8 mm	M6 x 1.0
10 mm	M6 x 1.0
12 mm	M8 x 1.25
14 mm	M10 x 1.25
17 mm	M12 x 1.25

● The threads of most fasteners are of the right-hand type, ie they are turned clockwise to tighten and anti-clockwise to loosen. The reverse situation applies to left-hand thread fasteners, which are turned anti-clockwise to tighten and clockwise to loosen. Left-hand threads are used where rotation of a component might loosen a conventional right-hand thread fastener.

Seized fasteners

● Corrosion of external fasteners due to water or reaction between two dissimilar metals can occur over a period of time. It will build up sooner in wet conditions or in countries where salt is used on the roads during the winter. If a fastener is severely corroded it is likely that normal methods of removal will fail and result in its head being ruined. When you attempt removal, the fastener thread should be heard to crack free and unscrew easily - if it doesn't, stop there before damaging something.
● A smart tap on the head of the fastener will often succeed in breaking free corrosion which has occurred in the threads **(see illustration 2.13)**.
● An aerosol penetrating fluid (such as WD-40) applied the night beforehand may work its way down into the thread and ease removal. Depending on the location, you may be able to make up a Plasticine well around the fastener head and fill it with penetrating fluid.

2.13 A sharp tap on the head of a fastener will often break free a corroded thread

● If you are working on an engine internal component, corrosion will most likely not be a problem due to the well lubricated environment. However, components can be very tight and an impact driver is a useful tool in freeing them **(see illustration 2.14)**.

**2.14 Using an impact driver
to free a fastener**

● Where corrosion has occurred between dissimilar metals (eg steel and aluminium alloy), the application of heat to the fastener head will create a disproportionate expansion rate between the two metals and break the seizure caused by the corrosion. Whether heat can be applied depends on the location of the fastener - any surrounding components likely to be damaged must first be removed **(see illustration 2.15)**. Heat can be applied using a paint stripper heat gun or clothes iron, or by immersing the component in boiling water - wear protective gloves to prevent scalding or burns to the hands.

2.15 Using heat to free a seized fastener

● As a last resort, it is possible to use a hammer and cold chisel to work the fastener head unscrewed **(see illustration 2.16)**. This will damage the fastener, but more importantly extreme care must be taken not to damage the surrounding component.

Caution: Remember that the component being secured is generally of more value than the bolt, nut or screw - when the fastener is freed, do not unscrew it with force, instead work the fastener back and forth when resistance is felt to prevent thread damage.

**2.16 Using a hammer and chisel
to free a seized fastener**

Broken fasteners and damaged heads

● If the shank of a broken bolt or screw is accessible you can grip it with self-locking grips. The knurled wheel type stud extractor tool or self-gripping stud puller tool is particularly useful for removing the long studs which screw into the cylinder mouth surface of the crankcase or bolts and screws from which the head has broken off **(see illustration 2.17)**. Studs can also be removed by locking two nuts together on the threaded end of the stud and using a spanner on the lower nut **(see illustration 2.18)**.

**2.17 Using a stud extractor tool to remove
a broken crankcase stud**

**2.18 Two nuts can be locked together to
unscrew a stud from a component**

● A bolt or screw which has broken off below or level with the casing must be extracted using a screw extractor set. Centre punch the fastener to centralise the drill bit, then drill a hole in the fastener **(see illustration 2.19)**. Select a drill bit which is approximately half to three-quarters the

**2.19 When using a screw extractor,
first drill a hole in the fastener . . .**

diameter of the fastener and drill to a depth which will accommodate the extractor. Use the largest size extractor possible, but avoid leaving too small a wall thickness otherwise the extractor will merely force the fastener walls outwards wedging it in the casing thread.

● If a spiral type extractor is used, thread it anti-clockwise into the fastener. As it is screwed in, it will grip the fastener and unscrew it from the casing **(see illustration 2.20)**.

**2.20 . . . then thread the extractor
anti-clockwise into the fastener**

● If a taper type extractor is used, tap it into the fastener so that it is firmly wedged in place. Unscrew the extractor (anti-clockwise) to draw the fastener out.

⚠️ *Warning: Stud extractors are very hard and may break off in the fastener if care is not taken - ask an engineer about spark erosion if this happens.*

● Alternatively, the broken bolt/screw can be drilled out and the hole retapped for an oversize bolt/screw or a diamond-section thread insert. It is essential that the drilling is carried out squarely and to the correct depth, otherwise the casing may be ruined - if in doubt, entrust the work to an engineer.

● Bolts and nuts with rounded corners cause the correct size spanner or socket to slip when force is applied. Of the types of spanner/socket available always use a six-point type rather than an eight or twelve-point type - better grip

2.21 Comparison of surface drive ring spanner (left) with 12-point type (right)

is obtained. Surface drive spanners grip the middle of the hex flats, rather than the corners, and are thus good in cases of damaged heads **(see illustration 2.21)**.

● Slotted-head or Phillips-head screws are often damaged by the use of the wrong size screwdriver. Allen-head and Torx-head screws are much less likely to sustain damage. If enough of the screw head is exposed you can use a hacksaw to cut a slot in its head and then use a conventional flat-bladed screwdriver to remove it. Alternatively use a hammer and cold chisel to tap the head of the fastener around to slacken it. Always replace damaged fasteners with new ones, preferably Torx or Allen-head type.

HAYNES HiNT

A dab of valve grinding compound between the screw head and screw-driver tip will often give a good grip.

Thread repair

● Threads (particularly those in aluminium alloy components) can be damaged by overtightening, being assembled with dirt in the threads, or from a component working loose and vibrating. Eventually the thread will fail completely, and it will be impossible to tighten the fastener.

● If a thread is damaged or clogged with old locking compound it can be renovated with a thread repair tool (thread chaser) **(see illustrations 2.22 and 2.23)**; special thread

2.22 A thread repair tool being used to correct an internal thread

2.23 A thread repair tool being used to correct an external thread

chasers are available for spark plug hole threads. The tool will not cut a new thread, but clean and true the original thread. Make sure that you use the correct diameter and pitch tool. Similarly, external threads can be cleaned up with a die or a thread restorer file **(see illustration 2.24)**.

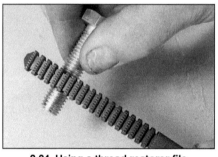

2.24 Using a thread restorer file

● It is possible to drill out the old thread and retap the component to the next thread size. This will work where there is enough surrounding material and a new bolt or screw can be obtained. Sometimes, however, this is not possible - such as where the bolt/screw passes through another component which must also be suitably modified, also in cases where a spark plug or oil drain plug cannot be obtained in a larger diameter thread size.

● The diamond-section thread insert (often known by its popular trade name of Heli-Coil) is a simple and effective method of renewing the thread and retaining the original size. A kit can be purchased which contains the tap, insert and installing tool **(see illustration 2.25)**. Drill out the damaged thread with the size drill specified **(see illustration 2.26)**. Carefully retap the thread **(see illustration 2.27)**. Install the

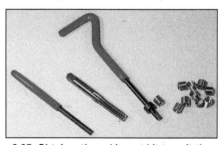

2.25 Obtain a thread insert kit to suit the thread diameter and pitch required

2.26 To install a thread insert, first drill out the original thread . . .

2.27 . . . tap a new thread . . .

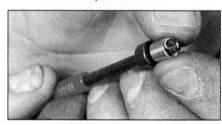

2.28 . . . fit insert on the installing tool . . .

2.29 . . . and thread into the component . . .

2.30 . . . break off the tang when complete

insert on the installing tool and thread it slowly into place using a light downward pressure **(see illustrations 2.28 and 2.29)**. When positioned between a 1/4 and 1/2 turn below the surface withdraw the installing tool and use the break-off tool to press down on the tang, breaking it off **(see illustration 2.30)**.

● There are epoxy thread repair kits on the market which can rebuild stripped internal threads, although this repair should not be used on high load-bearing components.

Thread locking and sealing compounds

● Locking compounds are used in locations where the fastener is prone to loosening due to vibration or on important safety-related items which might cause loss of control of the motorcycle if they fail. It is also used where important fasteners cannot be secured by other means such as lockwashers or split pins.

● Before applying locking compound, make sure that the threads (internal and external) are clean and dry with all old compound removed. Select a compound to suit the component being secured - a non-permanent general locking and sealing type is suitable for most applications, but a high strength type is needed for permanent fixing of studs in castings. Apply a drop or two of the compound to the first few threads of the fastener, then thread it into place and tighten to the specified torque. Do not apply excessive thread locking compound otherwise the thread may be damaged on subsequent removal.

● Certain fasteners are impregnated with a dry film type coating of locking compound on their threads. Always renew this type of fastener if disturbed.

● Anti-seize compounds, such as copper-based greases, can be applied to protect threads from seizure due to extreme heat and corrosion. A common instance is spark plug threads and exhaust system fasteners.

3 Measuring tools and gauges

Feeler gauges

● Feeler gauges (or blades) are used for measuring small gaps and clearances **(see illustration 3.1)**. They can also be used to measure endfloat (sideplay) of a component on a shaft where access is not possible with a dial gauge.

● Feeler gauge sets should be treated with care and not bent or damaged. They are etched with their size on one face. Keep them clean and very lightly oiled to prevent corrosion build-up.

3.1 Feeler gauges are used for measuring small gaps and clearances - thickness is marked on one face of gauge

● When measuring a clearance, select a gauge which is a light sliding fit between the two components. You may need to use two gauges together to measure the clearance accurately.

Micrometers

● A micrometer is a precision tool capable of measuring to 0.01 or 0.001 of a millimetre. It should always be stored in its case and not in the general toolbox. It must be kept clean and never dropped, otherwise its frame or measuring anvils could be distorted resulting in inaccurate readings.

● External micrometers are used for measuring outside diameters of components and have many more applications than internal micrometers. Micrometers are available in different size ranges, eg 0 to 25 mm, 25 to 50 mm, and upwards in 25 mm steps; some large micrometers have interchangeable anvils to allow a range of measurements to be taken. Generally the largest precision measurement you are likely to take on a motorcycle is the piston diameter.

● Internal micrometers (or bore micrometers) are used for measuring inside diameters, such as valve guides and cylinder bores. Telescoping gauges and small hole gauges are used in conjunction with an external micrometer, whereas the more expensive internal micrometers have their own measuring device.

External micrometer

Note: *The conventional analogue type instrument is described. Although much easier to read, digital micrometers are considerably more expensive.*

● Always check the calibration of the micrometer before use. With the anvils closed (0 to 25 mm type) or set over a test gauge (for

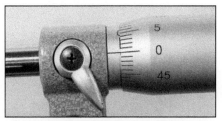

3.2 Check micrometer calibration before use

the larger types) the scale should read zero **(see illustration 3.2)**; make sure that the anvils (and test piece) are clean first. Any discrepancy can be adjusted by referring to the instructions supplied with the tool. Remember that the micrometer is a precision measuring tool - don't force the anvils closed, use the ratchet (4) on the end of the micrometer to close it. In this way, a measured force is always applied.

● To use, first make sure that the item being measured is clean. Place the anvil of the micrometer (1) against the item and use the thimble (2) to bring the spindle (3) lightly into contact with the other side of the item **(see illustration 3.3)**. Don't tighten the thimble down because this will damage the micrometer - instead use the ratchet (4) on the end of the micrometer. The ratchet mechanism applies a measured force preventing damage to the instrument.

● The micrometer is read by referring to the linear scale on the sleeve and the annular scale on the thimble. Read off the sleeve first to obtain the base measurement, then add the fine measurement from the thimble to obtain the overall reading. The linear scale on the sleeve represents the measuring range of the micrometer (eg 0 to 25 mm). The annular scale

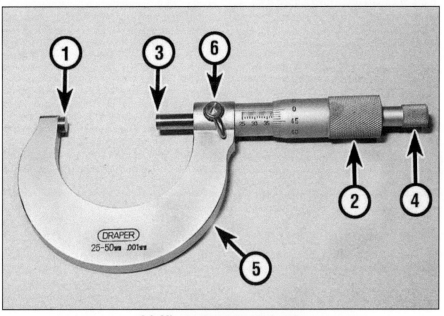

3.3 Micrometer component parts

1	Anvil	3	Spindle
2	Thimble	4	Ratchet

5	Frame
6	Locking lever

on the thimble will be in graduations of 0.01 mm (or as marked on the frame) - one full revolution of the thimble will move 0.5 mm on the linear scale. Take the reading where the datum line on the sleeve intersects the thimble's scale. Always position the eye directly above the scale otherwise an inaccurate reading will result.

In the example shown the item measures 2.95 mm **(see illustration 3.4)**:

Linear scale	2.00 mm
Linear scale	0.50 mm
Annular scale	0.45 mm
Total figure	**2.95 mm**

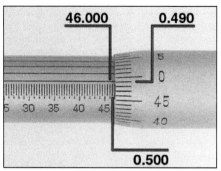

3.5 Micrometer reading of 46.99 mm on linear and annular scales . . .

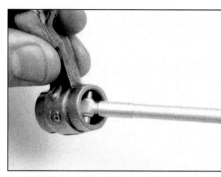

3.7 Expand the telescoping gauge in the bore, lock its position . . .

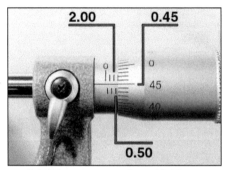

3.4 Micrometer reading of 2.95 mm

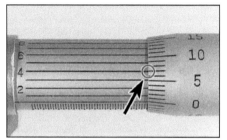

3.6 . . . and 0.004 mm on vernier scale

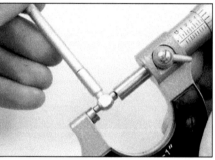

3.8 . . . then measure the gauge with a micrometer

Most micrometers have a locking lever (6) on the frame to hold the setting in place, allowing the item to be removed from the micrometer.
● Some micrometers have a vernier scale on their sleeve, providing an even finer measurement to be taken, in 0.001 increments of a millimetre. Take the sleeve and thimble measurement as described above, then check which graduation on the vernier scale aligns with that of the annular scale on the thimble **Note:** *The eye must be perpendicular to the scale when taking the vernier reading - if necessary rotate the body of the micrometer to ensure this.* Multiply the vernier scale figure by 0.001 and add it to the base and fine measurement figures.

In the example shown the item measures 46.994 mm **(see illustrations 3.5 and 3.6)**:

Linear scale (base)	46.000 mm
Linear scale (base)	00.500 mm
Annular scale (fine)	00.490 mm
Vernier scale	00.004 mm
Total figure	**46.994 mm**

Internal micrometer

● Internal micrometers are available for measuring bore diameters, but are expensive and unlikely to be available for home use. It is suggested that a set of telescoping gauges and small hole gauges, both of which must be used with an external micrometer, will suffice for taking internal measurements on a motorcycle.
● Telescoping gauges can be used to measure internal diameters of components. Select a gauge with the correct size range, make sure its ends are clean and insert it into the bore. Expand the gauge, then lock its position and withdraw it from the bore **(see illustration 3.7)**. Measure across the gauge ends with a micrometer **(see illustration 3.8)**.
● Very small diameter bores (such as valve guides) are measured with a small hole gauge. Once adjusted to a slip-fit inside the component, its position is locked and the gauge withdrawn for measurement with a micrometer **(see illustrations 3.9 and 3.10)**.

Vernier caliper

Note: *The conventional linear and dial gauge type instruments are described. Digital types are easier to read, but are far more expensive.*
● The vernier caliper does not provide the precision of a micrometer, but is versatile in being able to measure internal and external diameters. Some types also incorporate a depth gauge. It is ideal for measuring clutch plate friction material and spring free lengths.
● To use the conventional linear scale vernier, slacken off the vernier clamp screws (1) and set its jaws over (2), or inside (3), the item to be measured **(see illustration 3.11)**. Slide the jaw into contact, using the thumb-wheel (4) for fine movement of the sliding scale (5) then tighten the clamp screws (1). Read off the main scale (6) where the zero on the sliding scale (5) intersects it, taking the whole number to the left of the zero; this provides the base measurement. View along the sliding scale and select the division which

3.9 Expand the small hole gauge in the bore, lock its position . . .

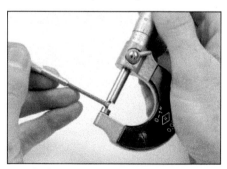

3.10 . . . then measure the gauge with a micrometer

lines up exactly with any of the divisions on the main scale, noting that the divisions usually represents 0.02 of a millimetre. Add this fine measurement to the base measurement to obtain the total reading.

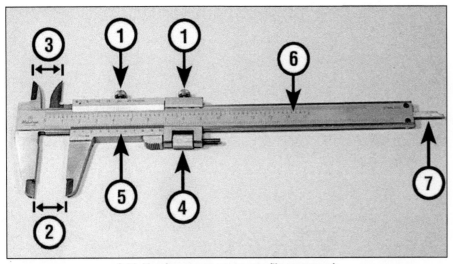

3.11 Vernier component parts (linear gauge)

1 Clamp screws   3 Internal jaws   5 Sliding scale   7 Depth gauge
2 External jaws   4 Thumbwheel   6 Main scale

In the example shown the item measures 55.92 mm **(see illustration 3.12)**:

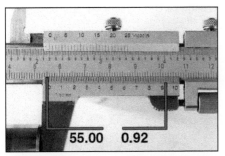

3.12 Vernier gauge reading of 55.92 mm

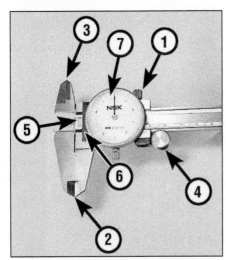

3.13 Vernier component parts (dial gauge)

1 Clamp screw   5 Main scale
2 External jaws   6 Sliding scale
3 Internal jaws   7 Dial gauge
4 Thumbwheel

Base measurement	55.00 mm
Fine measurement	00.92 mm
Total figure	**55.92 mm**

● Some vernier calipers are equipped with a dial gauge for fine measurement. Before use, check that the jaws are clean, then close them fully and check that the dial gauge reads zero. If necessary adjust the gauge ring accordingly. Slacken the vernier clamp screw (1) and set its jaws over (2), or inside (3), the item to be measured **(see illustration 3.13)**. Slide the jaws into contact, using the thumbwheel (4) for fine movement. Read off the main scale (5) where the edge of the sliding scale (6) intersects it, taking the whole number to the left of the zero; this provides the base measurement. Read off the needle position on the dial gauge (7) scale to provide the fine measurement; each division represents 0.05 of a millimetre. Add this fine measurement to the base measurement to obtain the total reading.

In the example shown the item measures 55.95 mm **(see illustration 3.14)**:

Base measurement	55.00 mm
Fine measurement	00.95 mm
Total figure	**55.95 mm**

3.14 Vernier gauge reading of 55.95 mm

Plastigauge

● Plastigauge is a plastic material which can be compressed between two surfaces to measure the oil clearance between them. The width of the compressed Plastigauge is measured against a calibrated scale to determine the clearance.

● Common uses of Plastigauge are for measuring the clearance between crankshaft journal and main bearing inserts, between crankshaft journal and big-end bearing inserts, and between camshaft and bearing surfaces. The following example describes big-end oil clearance measurement.

● Handle the Plastigauge material carefully to prevent distortion. Using a sharp knife, cut a length which corresponds with the width of the bearing being measured and place it carefully across the journal so that it is parallel with the shaft **(see illustration 3.15)**. Carefully install both bearing shells and the connecting rod. Without rotating the rod on the journal tighten its bolts or nuts (as applicable) to the specified torque. The connecting rod and bearings are then disassembled and the crushed Plastigauge examined.

3.15 Plastigauge placed across shaft journal

● Using the scale provided in the Plastigauge kit, measure the width of the material to determine the oil clearance **(see illustration 3.16)**. Always remove all traces of Plastigauge after use using your fingernails.

Caution: Arriving at the correct clearance demands that the assembly is torqued correctly, according to the settings and sequence (where applicable) provided by the motorcycle manufacturer.

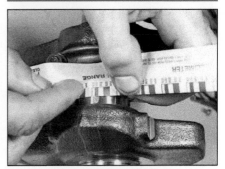

3.16 Measuring the width of the crushed Plastigauge

Dial gauge or DTI (Dial Test Indicator)

● A dial gauge can be used to accurately measure small amounts of movement. Typical uses are measuring shaft runout or shaft endfloat (sideplay) and setting piston position for ignition timing on two-strokes. A dial gauge set usually comes with a range of different probes and adapters and mounting equipment.

● The gauge needle must point to zero when at rest. Rotate the ring around its periphery to zero the gauge.

● Check that the gauge is capable of reading the extent of movement in the work. Most gauges have a small dial set in the face which records whole millimetres of movement as well as the fine scale around the face periphery which is calibrated in 0.01 mm divisions. Read off the small dial first to obtain the base measurement, then add the measurement from the fine scale to obtain the total reading.

In the example shown the gauge reads 1.48 mm **(see illustration 3.17)**:

Base measurement	1.00 mm
Fine measurement	0.48 mm
Total figure	**1.48 mm**

3.17 Dial gauge reading of 1.48 mm

● If measuring shaft runout, the shaft must be supported in vee-blocks and the gauge mounted on a stand perpendicular to the shaft. Rest the tip of the gauge against the centre of the shaft and rotate the shaft slowly whilst watching the gauge reading **(see illustration 3.18)**. Take several measurements along the length of the shaft and record the

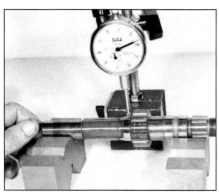

3.18 Using a dial gauge to measure shaft runout

maximum gauge reading as the amount of runout in the shaft. **Note:** *The reading obtained will be total runout at that point - some manufacturers specify that the runout figure is halved to compare with their specified runout limit.*

● Endfloat (sideplay) measurement requires that the gauge is mounted securely to the surrounding component with its probe touching the end of the shaft. Using hand pressure, push and pull on the shaft noting the maximum endfloat recorded on the gauge **(see illustration 3.19)**.

3.19 Using a dial gauge to measure shaft endfloat

● A dial gauge with suitable adapters can be used to determine piston position BTDC on two-stroke engines for the purposes of ignition timing. The gauge, adapter and suitable length probe are installed in the place of the spark plug and the gauge zeroed at TDC. If the piston position is specified as 1.14 mm BTDC, rotate the engine back to 2.00 mm BTDC, then slowly forwards to 1.14 mm BTDC.

Cylinder compression gauges

● A compression gauge is used for measuring cylinder compression. Either the rubber-cone type or the threaded adapter type can be used. The latter is preferred to ensure a perfect seal against the cylinder head. A 0 to 300 psi (0 to 20 Bar) type gauge (for petrol/gasoline engines) will be suitable for motorcycles.

● The spark plug is removed and the gauge either held hard against the cylinder head (cone type) or the gauge adapter screwed into the cylinder head (threaded type) **(see illustration 3.20)**. Cylinder compression is measured with the engine turning over, but not running - carry out the compression test as described in

3.20 Using a rubber-cone type cylinder compression gauge

Fault Finding Equipment. The gauge will hold the reading until manually released.

Oil pressure gauge

● An oil pressure gauge is used for measuring engine oil pressure. Most gauges come with a set of adapters to fit the thread of the take-off point **(see illustration 3.21)**. If the take-off point specified by the motorcycle manufacturer is an external oil pipe union, make sure that the specified replacement union is used to prevent oil starvation.

3.21 Oil pressure gauge and take-off point adapter (arrow)

● Oil pressure is measured with the engine running (at a specific rpm) and often the manufacturer will specify pressure limits for a cold and hot engine.

Straight-edge and surface plate

● If checking the gasket face of a component for warpage, place a steel rule or precision straight-edge across the gasket face and measure any gap between the straight-edge and component with feeler gauges **(see illustration 3.22)**. Check diagonally across the component and between mounting holes **(see illustration 3.23)**.

3.22 Use a straight-edge and feeler gauges to check for warpage

3.23 Check for warpage in these directions

● Checking individual components for warpage, such as clutch plain (metal) plates, requires a perfectly flat plate or piece or plate glass and feeler gauges.

4 Torque and leverage

What is torque?

● Torque describes the twisting force about a shaft. The amount of torque applied is determined by the distance from the centre of the shaft to the end of the lever and the amount of force being applied to the end of the lever; distance multiplied by force equals torque.

● The manufacturer applies a measured torque to a bolt or nut to ensure that it will not slacken in use and to hold two components securely together without movement in the joint. The actual torque setting depends on the thread size, bolt or nut material and the composition of the components being held.

● Too little torque may cause the fastener to loosen due to vibration, whereas too much torque will distort the joint faces of the component or cause the fastener to shear off. Always stick to the specified torque setting.

Using a torque wrench

● Check the calibration of the torque wrench and make sure it has a suitable range for the job. Torque wrenches are available in Nm (Newton-metres), kgf m (kilograms-force metre), lbf ft (pounds-feet), lbf in (inch-pounds). Do not confuse lbf ft with lbf in.

● Adjust the tool to the desired torque on the scale (see illustration 4.1). If your torque wrench is not calibrated in the units specified, carefully convert the figure (see Conversion Factors). A manufacturer sometimes gives a torque setting as a range (8 to 10 Nm) rather than a single figure - in this case set the tool midway between the two settings. The same torque may be expressed as 9 Nm ± 1 Nm. Some torque wrenches have a method of locking the setting so that it isn't inadvertently altered during use.

4.1 Set the torque wrench index mark to the setting required, in this case 12 Nm

● Install the bolts/nuts in their correct location and secure them lightly. Their threads must be clean and free of any old locking compound. Unless specified the threads and flange should be dry - oiled threads are necessary in certain circumstances and the manufacturer will take this into account in the specified torque figure. Similarly, the manufacturer may also specify the application of thread-locking compound.

● Tighten the fasteners in the specified sequence until the torque wrench clicks, indicating that the torque setting has been reached. Apply the torque again to double-check the setting. Where different thread diameter fasteners secure the component, as a rule tighten the larger diameter ones first.

● When the torque wrench has been finished with, release the lock (where applicable) and fully back off its setting to zero - do not leave the torque wrench tensioned. Also, do not use a torque wrench for slackening a fastener.

Angle-tightening

● Manufacturers often specify a figure in degrees for final tightening of a fastener. This usually follows tightening to a specific torque setting.

● A degree disc can be set and attached to the socket (see illustration 4.2) or a protractor can be used to mark the angle of movement on the bolt/nut head and the surrounding casting (see illustration 4.3).

4.2 Angle tightening can be accomplished with a torque-angle gauge . . .

4.3 . . . or by marking the angle on the surrounding component

Loosening sequences

● Where more than one bolt/nut secures a component, loosen each fastener evenly a little at a time. In this way, not all the stress of the joint is held by one fastener and the components are not likely to distort.

● If a tightening sequence is provided, work in the REVERSE of this, but if not, work from the outside in, in a criss-cross sequence (see illustration 4.4).

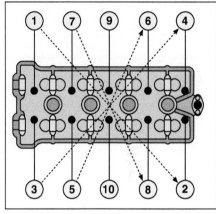

4.4 When slackening, work from the outside inwards

Tightening sequences

● If a component is held by more than one fastener it is important that the retaining bolts/nuts are tightened evenly to prevent uneven stress build-up and distortion of sealing faces. This is especially important on high-compression joints such as the cylinder head.

● A sequence is usually provided by the manufacturer, either in a diagram or actually marked in the casting. If not, always start in the centre and work outwards in a criss-cross pattern (see illustration 4.5). Start off by securing all bolts/nuts finger-tight, then set the torque wrench and tighten each fastener by a small amount in sequence until the final torque is reached. By following this practice,

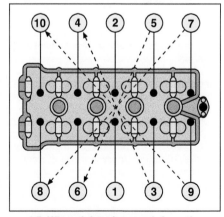

4.5 When tightening, work from the inside outwards

the joint will be held evenly and will not be distorted. Important joints, such as the cylinder head and big-end fasteners often have two- or three-stage torque settings.

Applying leverage

● Use tools at the correct angle. Position a socket wrench or spanner on the bolt/nut so that you pull it towards you when loosening. If this can't be done, push the spanner without curling your fingers around it **(see illustration 4.6)** - the spanner may slip or the fastener loosen suddenly, resulting in your fingers being crushed against a component.

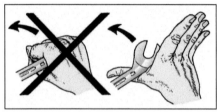

4.6 If you can't pull on the spanner to loosen a fastener, push with your hand open

● Additional leverage is gained by extending the length of the lever. The best way to do this is to use a breaker bar instead of the regular length tool, or to slip a length of tubing over the end of the spanner or socket wrench.
● If additional leverage will not work, the fastener head is either damaged or firmly corroded in place (see *Fasteners*).

5 Bearings

Bearing removal and installation

Drivers and sockets

● Before removing a bearing, always inspect the casing to see which way it must be driven out - some casings will have retaining plates or a cast step. Also check for any identifying markings on the bearing and if installed to a certain depth, measure this at this stage. Some roller bearings are sealed on one side - take note of the original fitted position.
● Bearings can be driven out of a casing using a bearing driver tool (with the correct size head) or a socket of the correct diameter. Select the driver head or socket so that it contacts the outer race of the bearing, not the balls/rollers or inner race. Always support the casing around the bearing housing with wood blocks, otherwise there is a risk of fracture. The bearing is driven out with a few blows on the driver or socket from a heavy mallet. Unless access is severely restricted (as with wheel bearings), a pin-punch is not recommended unless it is moved around the bearing to keep it square in its housing.

● The same equipment can be used to install bearings. Make sure the bearing housing is supported on wood blocks and line up the bearing in its housing. Fit the bearing as noted on removal - generally they are installed with their marked side facing outwards. Tap the bearing squarely into its housing using a driver or socket which bears only on the bearing's outer race - contact with the bearing balls/rollers or inner race will destroy it **(see illustrations 5.1 and 5.2)**.
● Check that the bearing inner race and balls/rollers rotate freely.

5.1 Using a bearing driver against the bearing's outer race

5.2 Using a large socket against the bearing's outer race

Pullers and slide-hammers

● Where a bearing is pressed on a shaft a puller will be required to extract it **(see illustration 5.3)**. Make sure that the puller clamp or legs fit securely behind the bearing and are unlikely to slip out. If pulling a bearing

5.3 This bearing puller clamps behind the bearing and pressure is applied to the shaft end to draw the bearing off

off a gear shaft for example, you may have to locate the puller behind a gear pinion if there is no access to the race and draw the gear pinion off the shaft as well **(see illustration 5.4)**.

> **Caution: Ensure that the puller's centre bolt locates securely against the end of the shaft and will not slip when pressure is applied. Also ensure that puller does not damage the shaft end.**

5.4 Where no access is available to the rear of the bearing, it is sometimes possible to draw off the adjacent component

● Operate the puller so that its centre bolt exerts pressure on the shaft end and draws the bearing off the shaft.
● When installing the bearing on the shaft, tap only on the bearing's inner race - contact with the balls/rollers or outer race with destroy the bearing. Use a socket or length of tubing as a drift which fits over the shaft end **(see illustration 5.5)**.

5.5 When installing a bearing on a shaft use a piece of tubing which bears only on the bearing's inner race

● Where a bearing locates in a blind hole in a casing, it cannot be driven or pulled out as described above. A slide-hammer with knife-edged bearing puller attachment will be required. The puller attachment passes through the bearing and when tightened expands to fit firmly behind the bearing **(see illustration 5.6)**. By operating the slide-hammer part of the tool the bearing is jarred out of its housing **(see illustration 5.7)**.
● It is possible, if the bearing is of reasonable weight, for it to drop out of its housing if the casing is heated as described opposite. If this

5.6 Expand the bearing puller so that it locks behind the bearing . . .

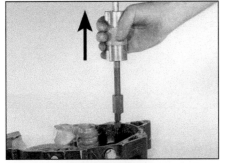

5.7 . . . attach the slide hammer to the bearing puller

method is attempted, first prepare a work surface which will enable the casing to be tapped face down to help dislodge the bearing - a wood surface is ideal since it will not damage the casing's gasket surface. Wearing protective gloves, tap the heated casing several times against the work surface to dislodge the bearing under its own weight **(see illustration 5.8)**.

5.8 Tapping a casing face down on wood blocks can often dislodge a bearing

● Bearings can be installed in blind holes using the driver or socket method described above.

Drawbolts

● Where a bearing or bush is set in the eye of a component, such as a suspension linkage arm or connecting rod small-end, removal by drift may damage the component. Furthermore, a rubber bushing in a shock absorber eye cannot successfully be driven out of position. If access is available to a engineering press, the task is straightforward. If not, a drawbolt can be fabricated to extract the bearing or bush.

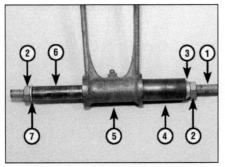

5.9 Drawbolt component parts assembled on a suspension arm

1 Bolt or length of threaded bar
2 Nuts
3 Washer (external diameter greater than tubing internal diameter)
4 Tubing (internal diameter sufficient to accommodate bearing)
5 Suspension arm with bearing
6 Tubing (external diameter slightly smaller than bearing)
7 Washer (external diameter slightly smaller than bearing)

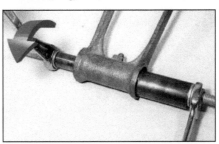

5.10 Drawing the bearing out of the suspension arm

● To extract the bearing/bush you will need a long bolt with nut (or piece of threaded bar with two nuts), a piece of tubing which has an internal diameter larger than the bearing/bush, another piece of tubing which has an external diameter slightly smaller than the bearing/ bush, and a selection of washers **(see illustrations 5.9 and 5.10)**. Note that the pieces of tubing must be of the same length, or longer, than the bearing/bush.
● The same kit (without the pieces of tubing) can be used to draw the new bearing/bush back into place **(see illustration 5.11)**.

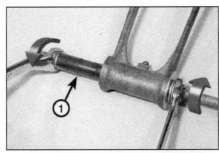

5.11 Installing a new bearing (1) in the suspension arm

Temperature change

● If the bearing's outer race is a tight fit in the casing, the aluminium casing can be heated to release its grip on the bearing. Aluminium will expand at a greater rate than the steel bearing outer race. There are several ways to do this, but avoid any localised extreme heat (such as a blow torch) - aluminium alloy has a low melting point.
● Approved methods of heating a casing are using a domestic oven (heated to 100°C) or immersing the casing in boiling water **(see illustration 5.12)**. Low temperature range localised heat sources such as a paint stripper heat gun or clothes iron can also be used **(see illustration 5.13)**. Alternatively, soak a rag in boiling water, wring it out and wrap it around the bearing housing.

> ⚠ **Warning: All of these methods require care in use to prevent scalding and burns to the hands. Wear protective gloves when handling hot components.**

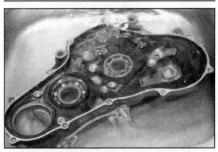

5.12 A casing can be immersed in a sink of boiling water to aid bearing removal

5.13 Using a localised heat source to aid bearing removal

● If heating the whole casing note that plastic components, such as the neutral switch, may suffer - remove them beforehand.
● After heating, remove the bearing as described above. You may find that the expansion is sufficient for the bearing to fall out of the casing under its own weight or with a light tap on the driver or socket.
● If necessary, the casing can be heated to aid bearing installation, and this is sometimes the recommended procedure if the motorcycle manufacturer has designed the housing and bearing fit with this intention.

● Installation of bearings can be eased by placing them in a freezer the night before installation. The steel bearing will contract slightly, allowing easy insertion in its housing. This is often useful when installing steering head outer races in the frame.

Bearing types and markings

● Plain shell bearings, ball bearings, needle roller bearings and tapered roller bearings will all be found on motorcycles (see illustrations 5.14 and 5.15). The ball and roller types are usually caged between an inner and outer race, but uncaged variations may be found.

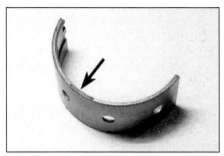

5.14 Shell bearings are either plain or grooved. They are usually identified by colour code (arrow)

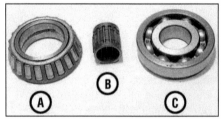

5.15 Tapered roller bearing (A), needle roller bearing (B) and ball journal bearing (C)

● Shell bearings (often called inserts) are usually found at the crankshaft main and connecting rod big-end where they are good at coping with high loads. They are made of a phosphor-bronze material and are impregnated with self-lubricating properties.

● Ball bearings and needle roller bearings consist of a steel inner and outer race with the balls or rollers between the races. They require constant lubrication by oil or grease and are good at coping with axial loads. Taper roller bearings consist of rollers set in a tapered cage set on the inner race; the outer race is separate. They are good at coping with axial loads and prevent movement along the shaft - a typical application is in the steering head.

● Bearing manufacturers produce bearings to ISO size standards and stamp one face of the bearing to indicate its internal and external diameter, load capacity and type (see illustration 5.16).

● Metal bushes are usually of phosphor-bronze material. Rubber bushes are used in suspension mounting eyes. Fibre bushes have also been used in suspension pivots.

5.16 Typical bearing marking

Bearing fault finding

● If a bearing outer race has spun in its housing, the housing material will be damaged. You can use a bearing locking compound to bond the outer race in place if damage is not too severe.

● Shell bearings will fail due to damage of their working surface, as a result of lack of lubrication, corrosion or abrasive particles in the oil (see illustration 5.17). Small particles of dirt in the oil may embed in the bearing material whereas larger particles will score the bearing and shaft journal. If a number of short journeys are made, insufficient heat will be generated to drive off condensation which has built up on the bearings.

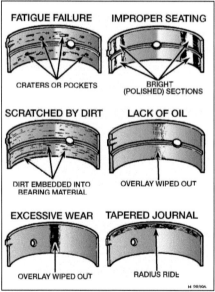

5.17 Typical bearing failures

● Ball and roller bearings will fail due to lack of lubrication or damage to the balls or rollers. Tapered-roller bearings can be damaged by overloading them. Unless the bearing is sealed on both sides, wash it in paraffin (kerosene) to remove all old grease then allow it to dry. Make a visual inspection looking to dented balls or rollers, damaged cages and worn or pitted races (see illustration 5.18).

● A ball bearing can be checked for wear by listening to it when spun. Apply a film of light oil to the bearing and hold it close to the ear - hold the outer race with one hand and spin the inner

5.18 Example of ball journal bearing with damaged balls and cages

5.19 Hold outer race and listen to inner race when spun

race with the other hand (see illustration 5.19). The bearing should be almost silent when spun; if it grates or rattles it is worn.

6 Oil seals

Oil seal removal and installation

● Oil seals should be renewed every time a component is dismantled. This is because the seal lips will become set to the sealing surface and will not necessarily reseal.

● Oil seals can be prised out of position using a large flat-bladed screwdriver (see illustration 6.1). In the case of crankcase seals, check first that the seal is not lipped on the inside, preventing its removal with the crankcases joined.

6.1 Prise out oil seals with a large flat-bladed screwdriver

● New seals are usually installed with their marked face (containing the seal reference code) outwards and the spring side towards the fluid being retained. In certain cases, such as a two-stroke engine crankshaft seal, a double lipped seal may be used due to there being fluid or gas on each side of the joint.

● Use a bearing driver or socket which bears only on the outer hard edge of the seal to install it in the casing - tapping on the inner edge will damage the sealing lip.

Oil seal types and markings

● Oil seals are usually of the single-lipped type. Double-lipped seals are found where a liquid or gas is on both sides of the joint.

● Oil seals can harden and lose their sealing ability if the motorcycle has been in storage for a long period - renewal is the only solution.

● Oil seal manufacturers also conform to the ISO markings for seal size - these are moulded into the outer face of the seal (see illustration 6.2).

6.2 These oil seal markings indicate inside diameter, outside diameter and seal thickness

7 Gaskets and sealants

Types of gasket and sealant

● Gaskets are used to seal the mating surfaces between components and keep lubricants, fluids, vacuum or pressure contained within the assembly. Aluminium gaskets are sometimes found at the cylinder joints, but most gaskets are paper-based. If the mating surfaces of the components being joined are undamaged the gasket can be installed dry, although a dab of sealant or grease will be useful to hold it in place during assembly.

● RTV (Room Temperature Vulcanising) silicone rubber sealants cure when exposed to moisture in the atmosphere. These sealants are good at filling pits or irregular gasket faces, but will tend to be forced out of the joint under very high torque. They can be used to replace a paper gasket, but first make sure that the width of the paper gasket is not essential to the shimming of internal components. RTV sealants should not be used on components containing petrol (gasoline).

● Non-hardening, semi-hardening and hard setting liquid gasket compounds can be used with a gasket or between a metal-to-metal joint. Select the sealant to suit the application: universal non-hardening sealant can be used on virtually all joints; semi-hardening on joint faces which are rough or damaged; hard setting sealant on joints which require a permanent bond and are subjected to high temperature and pressure. **Note:** *Check first if the paper gasket has a bead of sealant*

impregnated in its surface before applying additional sealant.

● When choosing a sealant, make sure it is suitable for the application, particularly if being applied in a high-temperature area or in the vicinity of fuel. Certain manufacturers produce sealants in either clear, silver or black colours to match the finish of the engine. This has a particular application on motorcycles where much of the engine is exposed.

● Do not over-apply sealant. That which is squeezed out on the outside of the joint can be wiped off, whereas an excess of sealant on the inside can break off and clog oilways.

Breaking a sealed joint

● Age, heat, pressure and the use of hard setting sealant can cause two components to stick together so tightly that they are difficult to separate using finger pressure alone. Do not resort to using levers unless there is a pry point provided for this purpose (see illustration 7.1) or else the gasket surfaces will be damaged.

● Use a soft-faced hammer (see illustration 7.2) or a wood block and conventional hammer to strike the component near the mating surface. Avoid hammering against cast extremities since they may break off. If this method fails, try using a wood wedge between the two components.

> **Caution: If the joint will not separate, double-check that you have removed all the fasteners.**

7.1 If a pry point is provided, apply gently pressure with a flat-bladed screwdriver

7.2 Tap around the joint with a soft-faced mallet if necessary - don't strike cooling fins

Removal of old gasket and sealant

● Paper gaskets will most likely come away complete, leaving only a few traces stuck on

Most components have one or two hollow locating dowels between the two gasket faces. If a dowel cannot be removed, do not resort to gripping it with pliers - it will almost certainly be distorted. Install a close-fitting socket or Phillips screwdriver into the dowel and then grip the outer edge of the dowel to free it.

the sealing faces of the components. It is imperative that all traces are removed to ensure correct sealing of the new gasket.

● Very carefully scrape all traces of gasket away making sure that the sealing surfaces are not gouged or scored by the scraper (see illustrations 7.3, 7.4 and 7.5). Stubborn deposits can be removed by spraying with an aerosol gasket remover. Final preparation of

7.3 Paper gaskets can be scraped off with a gasket scraper tool . . .

7.4 . . . a knife blade . . .

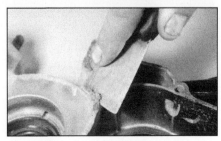

7.5 . . . or a household scraper

7.6 Fine abrasive paper is wrapped around a flat file to clean up the gasket face

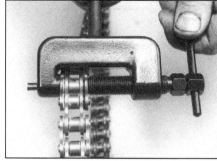

8.1 Tighten the chain breaker to push the pin out of the link . . .

8.4 Insert the new soft link, with O-rings, through the chain ends . . .

7.7 A kitchen scourer can be used on stubborn deposits

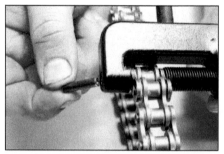

8.2 . . . withdraw the pin, remove the tool . . .

8.5 . . . install the O-rings over the pin ends . . .

the gasket surface can be made with very fine abrasive paper or a plastic kitchen scourer **(see illustrations 7.6 and 7.7).**

● Old sealant can be scraped or peeled off components, depending on the type originally used. Note that gasket removal compounds are available to avoid scraping the components clean; make sure the gasket remover suits the type of sealant used.

8 Chains

Breaking and joining final drive chains

● Drive chains for all but small bikes are continuous and do not have a clip-type connecting link. The chain must be broken using a chain breaker tool and the new chain securely riveted together using a new soft rivet-type link. Never use a clip-type connecting link instead of a rivet-type link, except in an emergency. Various chain breaking and riveting tools are available, either as separate tools or combined as illustrated in the accompanying photographs - read the instructions supplied with the tool carefully.

> ⚠ **Warning: The need to rivet the new link pins correctly cannot be overstressed - loss of control of the motorcycle is very likely to result if the chain breaks in use.**

● Rotate the chain and look for the soft link. The soft link pins look like they have been

8.3 . . . and separate the chain link

deeply centre-punched instead of peened over like all the other pins **(see illustration 8.9)** and its sideplate may be a different colour. Position the soft link midway between the sprockets and assemble the chain breaker tool over one of the soft link pins **(see illustration 8.1).** Operate the tool to push the pin out through the chain **(see illustration 8.2).** On an O-ring chain, remove the O-rings **(see illustration 8.3).** Carry out the same procedure on the other soft link pin.

> **Caution: Certain soft link pins (particularly on the larger chains) may require their ends to be filed or ground off before they can be pressed out using the tool.**

● Check that you have the correct size and strength (standard or heavy duty) new soft link - do not reuse the old link. Look for the size marking on the chain sideplates **(see illustration 8.10).**

● Position the chain ends so that they are engaged over the rear sprocket. On an O-ring

8.6 . . . followed by the sideplate

chain, install a new O-ring over each pin of the link and insert the link through the two chain ends **(see illustration 8.4).** Install a new O-ring over the end of each pin, followed by the sideplate (with the chain manufacturer's marking facing outwards) **(see illustrations 8.5 and 8.6).** On an unsealed chain, insert the link through the two chain ends, then install the sideplate with the chain manufacturer's marking facing outwards.

● Note that it may not be possible to install the sideplate using finger pressure alone. If using a joining tool, assemble it so that the plates of the tool clamp the link and press the sideplate over the pins **(see illustration 8.7).** Otherwise, use two small sockets placed over

8.7 Push the sideplate into position using a clamp

8.8 Assemble the chain riveting tool over one pin at a time and tighten it fully

8.9 Pin end correctly riveted (A), pin end unriveted (B)

the rivet ends and two pieces of the wood between a G-clamp. Operate the clamp to press the sideplate over the pins.

● Assemble the joining tool over one pin (following the maker's instructions) and tighten the tool down to spread the pin end securely **(see illustrations 8.8 and 8.9)**. Do the same on the other pin.

 Warning: Check that the pin ends are secure and that there is no danger of the sideplate coming loose. If the pin ends are cracked the soft link must be renewed.

Final drive chain sizing

● Chains are sized using a three digit number, followed by a suffix to denote the chain type **(see illustration 8.10)**. Chain type is either standard or heavy duty (thicker sideplates), and also unsealed or O-ring/X-ring type.

● The first digit of the number relates to the pitch of the chain, ie the distance from the centre of one pin to the centre of the next pin **(see illustration 8.11)**. Pitch is expressed in eighths of an inch, as follows:

8.10 Typical chain size and type marking

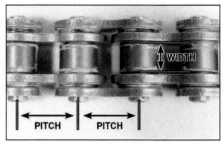

8.11 Chain dimensions

Sizes commencing with a 4 (eg 428) have a pitch of 1/2 inch (12.7 mm)
Sizes commencing with a 5 (eg 520) have a pitch of 5/8 inch (15.9 mm)
Sizes commencing with a 6 (eg 630) have a pitch of 3/4 inch (19.1 mm)

● The second and third digits of the chain size relate to the width of the rollers, again in imperial units, eg the 525 shown has 5/16 inch (7.94 mm) rollers **(see illustration 8.11)**.

9 Hoses

Clamping to prevent flow

● Small-bore flexible hoses can be clamped to prevent fluid flow whilst a component is worked on. Whichever method is used, ensure that the hose material is not permanently distorted or damaged by the clamp.

a) A brake hose clamp available from auto accessory shops **(see illustration 9.1)**.
b) A wingnut type hose clamp **(see illustration 9.2)**.

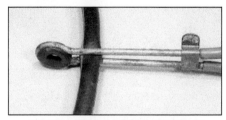

9.1 Hoses can be clamped with an automotive brake hose clamp . . .

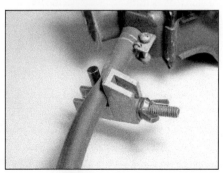

9.2 . . . a wingnut type hose clamp . . .

c) Two sockets placed each side of the hose and held with straight-jawed self-locking grips **(see illustration 9.3)**.
d) Thick card each side of the hose held between straight-jawed self-locking grips **(see illustration 9.4)**.

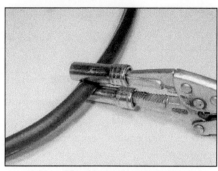

9.3 . . . two sockets and a pair of self-locking grips . . .

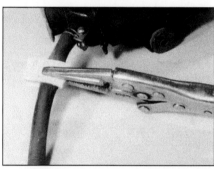

9.4 . . . or thick card and self-locking grips

Freeing and fitting hoses

● Always make sure the hose clamp is moved well clear of the hose end. Grip the hose with your hand and rotate it whilst pulling it off the union. If the hose has hardened due to age and will not move, slit it with a sharp knife and peel its ends off the union **(see illustration 9.5)**.

● Resist the temptation to use grease or soap on the unions to aid installation; although it helps the hose slip over the union it will equally aid the escape of fluid from the joint. It is preferable to soften the hose ends in hot water and wet the inside surface of the hose with water or a fluid which will evaporate.

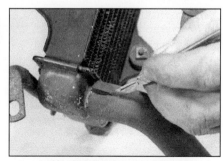

9.5 Cutting a coolant hose free with a sharp knife

Conversion Factors

Length (distance)
Inches (in)	x 25.4	= Millimetres (mm)	x 0.0394 =	Inches (in)
Feet (ft)	x 0.305	= Metres (m)	x 3.281 =	Feet (ft)
Miles	x 1.609	= Kilometres (km)	x 0.621 =	Miles

Volume (capacity)
Cubic inches (cu in; in³)	x 16.387	= Cubic centimetres (cc; cm³)	x 0.061 =	Cubic inches (cu in; in³)
Imperial pints (Imp pt)	x 0.568	= Litres (l)	x 1.76 =	Imperial pints (Imp pt)
Imperial quarts (Imp qt)	x 1.137	= Litres (l)	x 0.88 =	Imperial quarts (Imp qt)
Imperial quarts (Imp qt)	x 1.201	= US quarts (US qt)	x 0.833 =	Imperial quarts (Imp qt)
US quarts (US qt)	x 0.946	= Litres (l)	x 1.057 =	US quarts (US qt)
Imperial gallons (Imp gal)	x 4.546	= Litres (l)	x 0.22 =	Imperial gallons (Imp gal)
Imperial gallons (Imp gal)	x 1.201	= US gallons (US gal)	x 0.833 =	Imperial gallons (Imp gal)
US gallons (US gal)	x 3.785	= Litres (l)	x 0.264 =	US gallons (US gal)

Mass (weight)
Ounces (oz)	x 28.35	= Grams (g)	x 0.035 =	Ounces (oz)
Pounds (lb)	x 0.454	= Kilograms (kg)	x 2.205 =	Pounds (lb)

Force
Ounces-force (ozf; oz)	x 0.278	= Newtons (N)	x 3.6 =	Ounces-force (ozf; oz)
Pounds-force (lbf; lb)	x 4.448	= Newtons (N)	x 0.225 =	Pounds-force (lbf; lb)
Newtons (N)	x 0.1	= Kilograms-force (kgf; kg)	x 9.81 =	Newtons (N)

Pressure
Pounds-force per square inch (psi; lbf/in²; lb/in²)	x 0.070	= Kilograms-force per square centimetre (kgf/cm²; kg/cm²)	x 14.223 =	Pounds-force per square inch (psi; lbf/in²; lb/in²)
Pounds-force per square inch (psi; lbf/in²; lb/in²)	x 0.068	= Atmospheres (atm)	x 14.696 =	Pounds-force per square inch (psi; lbf/in²; lb/in²)
Pounds-force per square inch (psi; lbf/in²; lb/in²)	x 0.069	= Bars	x 14.5 =	Pounds-force per square inch (psi; lbf/in²; lb/in²)
Pounds-force per square inch (psi; lbf/in²; lb/in²)	x 6.895	= Kilopascals (kPa)	x 0.145 =	Pounds-force per square inch (psi; lbf/in²; lb/in²)
Kilopascals (kPa)	x 0.01	= Kilograms-force per square centimetre (kgf/cm²; kg/cm²)	x 98.1 =	Kilopascals (kPa)
Millibar (mbar)	x 100	= Pascals (Pa)	x 0.01 =	Millibar (mbar)
Millibar (mbar)	x 0.0145	= Pounds-force per square inch (psi; lbf/in²; lb/in²)	x 68.947 =	Millibar (mbar)
Millibar (mbar)	x 0.75	= Millimetres of mercury (mmHg)	x 1.333 =	Millibar (mbar)
Millibar (mbar)	x 0.401	= Inches of water (inH₂O)	x 2.491 =	Millibar (mbar)
Millimetres of mercury (mmHg)	x 0.535	= Inches of water (inH₂O)	x 1.868 =	Millimetres of mercury (mmHg)
Inches of water (inH₂O)	x 0.036	= Pounds-force per square inch (psi; lbf/in²; lb/in²)	x 27.68 =	Inches of water (inH₂O)

Torque (moment of force)
Pounds-force inches (lbf in; lb in)	x 1.152	= Kilograms-force centimetre (kgf cm; kg cm)	x 0.868 =	Pounds-force inches (lbf in; lb in)
Pounds-force inches (lbf in; lb in)	x 0.113	= Newton metres (Nm)	x 8.85 =	Pounds-force inches (lbf in; lb in)
Pounds-force inches (lbf in; lb in)	x 0.083	= Pounds-force feet (lbf ft; lb ft)	x 12 =	Pounds-force inches (lbf in; lb in)
Pounds-force feet (lbf ft; lb ft)	x 0.138	= Kilograms-force metres (kgf m; kg m)	x 7.233 =	Pounds-force feet (lbf ft; lb ft)
Pounds-force feet (lbf ft; lb ft)	x 1.356	= Newton metres (Nm)	x 0.738 =	Pounds-force feet (lbf ft; lb ft)
Newton metres (Nm)	x 0.102	= Kilograms-force metres (kgf m; kg m)	x 9.804 =	Newton metres (Nm)

Power
Horsepower (hp)	x 745.7	= Watts (W)	x 0.0013 =	Horsepower (hp)

Velocity (speed)
Miles per hour (miles/hr; mph)	x 1.609	= Kilometres per hour (km/hr; kph)	x 0.621 =	Miles per hour (miles/hr; mph)

Fuel consumption*
Miles per gallon (mpg)	x 0.354	= Kilometres per litre (km/l)	x 2.825 =	Miles per gallon (mpg)

Temperature
Degrees Fahrenheit = (°C x 1.8) + 32   Degrees Celsius (Degrees Centigrade; °C) = (°F - 32) x 0.56

It is common practice to convert from miles per gallon (mpg) to litres/100 kilometres (l/100km), where mpg x l/100 km = 282

A number of chemicals and lubricants are available for use in motorcycle maintenance and repair. They include a wide variety of products ranging from cleaning solvents and degreasers to lubricants and protective sprays for rubber, plastic and vinyl.

● **Contact point/spark plug cleaner** is a solvent used to clean oily film and dirt from points, grime from electrical connectors and oil deposits from spark plugs. It is oil free and leaves no residue. It can also be used to remove gum and varnish from carburettor jets and other orifices.

● **Carburettor cleaner** is similar to contact point/spark plug cleaner but it usually has a stronger solvent and may leave a slight oily reside. It is not recommended for cleaning electrical components or connections.

● **Brake system cleaner** is used to remove grease or brake fluid from brake system components (where clean surfaces are absolutely necessary and petroleum-based solvents cannot be used); it also leaves no residue.

● **Silicone-based lubricants** are used to protect rubber parts such as hoses and grommets, and are used as lubricants for hinges and locks.

● **Multi-purpose grease** is an all purpose lubricant used wherever grease is more practical than a liquid lubricant such as oil. Some multi-purpose grease is coloured white and specially formulated to be more resistant to water than ordinary grease.

● **Gear oil** (sometimes called gear lube) is a specially designed oil used in transmissions and final drive units, as well as other areas where high friction, high temperature lubrication is required. It is available in a number of viscosities (weights) for various applications.

● **Motor oil**, of course, is the lubricant specially formulated for use in the engine. It normally contains a wide variety of additives to prevent corrosion and reduce foaming and wear. Motor oil comes in various weights (viscosity ratings) of from 5 to 80. The recommended weight of the oil depends on the seasonal temperature and the demands on the engine. Light oil is used in cold climates and under light load conditions; heavy oil is used in hot climates and where high loads are encountered. Multi-viscosity oils are designed to have characteristics of both light and heavy oils and are available in a number of weights from 5W-20 to 20W-50.

● **Petrol additives** perform several functions, depending on their chemical makeup. They usually contain solvents that help dissolve gum and varnish that build up on carburettor and inlet parts. They also serve to break down carbon deposits that form on the inside surfaces of the combustion chambers. Some additives contain upper cylinder lubricants for valves and piston rings.

● **Brake and clutch fluid** is a specially formulated hydraulic fluid that can withstand the heat and pressure encountered in brake/clutch systems. Care must be taken that this fluid does not come in contact with painted surfaces or plastics. An opened container should always be resealed to prevent contamination by water or dirt.

● **Chain lubricants** are formulated especially for use on motorcycle final drive chains. A good chain lube should adhere well and have good penetrating qualities to be effective as a lubricant inside the chain and on the side plates, pins and rollers. Most chain lubes are either the foaming type or quick drying type and are usually marketed as sprays. Take care to use a lubricant marked as being suitable for O-ring chains.

● **Degreasers** are heavy duty solvents used to remove grease and grime that may accumulate on engine and frame components. They can be sprayed or brushed on and, depending on the type are rinsed with either water or solvent.

● **Solvents** are used alone or in combination with degreasers to clean parts and assemblies during repair and overhaul. The home mechanic should use only solvents that are non-flammable and that do not produce irritating fumes.

● **Gasket sealing compounds** may be used in conjunction with gaskets, to improve their sealing capabilities, or alone, to seal metal-to-metal joints. Many gasket sealers can withstand extreme heat, some are impervious to petrol and lubricants, while others are capable of filling and sealing large cavities. Depending on the intended use, gasket sealers either dry hard or stay relatively soft and pliable. They are usually applied by hand, with a brush, or are sprayed on the gasket sealing surfaces.

● **Thread locking compound** is an adhesive locking compound that prevents threaded fasteners from loosening because of vibration. It is available in a variety of types for different applications.

● **Moisture dispersants** are usually sprays that can be used to dry out electrical components such as the fuse block and wiring connectors. Some types can also be used as treatment for rubber and as a lubricant for hinges, cables and locks.

● **Waxes and polishes** are used to help protect painted and plated surfaces from the weather. Different types of paint may require the use of different types of wax polish. Some polishes utilise a chemical or abrasive cleaner to help remove the top layer of oxidised (dull) paint on older vehicles. In recent years many non-wax polishes (that contain a wide variety of chemicals such as polymers and silicones) have been introduced. These non-wax polishes are usually easier to apply and last longer than conventional waxes and polishes.

About the MOT Test

In the UK, all vehicles more than three years old are subject to an annual test to ensure that they meet minimum safety requirements. A current test certificate must be issued before a machine can be used on public roads, and is required before a road fund licence can be issued. Riding without a current test certificate will also invalidate your insurance.

For most owners, the MOT test is an annual cause for anxiety, and this is largely due to owners not being sure what needs to be checked prior to submitting the motorcycle for testing. The simple answer is that a fully roadworthy motorcycle will have no difficulty in passing the test.

This is a guide to getting your motorcycle through the MOT test. Obviously it will not be possible to examine the motorcycle to the same standard as the professional MOT

tester, particularly in view of the equipment required for some of the checks. However, working through the following procedures will enable you to identify any problem areas before submitting the motorcycle for the test.

It has only been possible to summarise the test requirements here, based on the regulations in force at the time of printing. Test standards are becoming increasingly stringent, although there are some exemptions for older vehicles. More information about the MOT test can be obtained from the TSO publications, *How Safe is your Motorcycle* and *The MOT Inspection Manual for Motorcycle Testing*.

Many of the checks require that one of the wheels is raised off the ground. If the motorcycle doesn't have a centre stand, note that an auxiliary stand will be required. Additionally, the help of an assistant may prove useful.

Certain exceptions apply to machines under 50 cc, machines without a lighting system, and Classic bikes - if in doubt about any of the requirements listed below seek confirmation from an MOT tester prior to submitting the motorcycle for the test.

Check that the frame number is clearly visible.

> **HAYNES HiNT** *If a component is in borderline condition, the tester has discretion in deciding whether to pass or fail it. If the motorcycle presented is clean and evidently well cared for, the tester may be more inclined to pass a borderline component than if the motorcycle is scruffy and apparently neglected.*

Electrical System

Lights, turn signals, horn and reflector

✔ With the ignition on, check the operation of the following electrical components. **Note:** *The electrical components on certain small-capacity machines are powered by the generator, requiring that the engine is run for this check.*

a) *Headlight and tail light. Check that both illuminate in the low and high beam switch positions.*
b) *Position lights. Check that the front position (or sidelight) and tail light illuminate in this switch position.*
c) *Turn signals. Check that all flash at the correct rate, and that the warning light(s) function correctly. Check that the turn signal switch works correctly.*
d) *Hazard warning system (where fitted). Check that all four turn signals flash in this switch position.*
e) *Brake stop light. Check that the light comes on when the front and rear brakes are independently applied. Models first used on or after 1st April 1986 must have a brake light switch on each brake.*
f) *Horn. Check that the sound is continuous and of reasonable volume.*

✔ Check that there is a red reflector on the rear of the machine, either mounted separately or as part of the tail light lens.
✔ Check the condition of the headlight, tail light and turn signal lenses.

Headlight beam height

✔ The MOT tester will perform a headlight beam height check using specialised beam setting equipment **(see illustration 1)**. This equipment will not be available to the home mechanic, but if you suspect that the headlight is incorrectly set or may have been maladjusted in the past, you can perform a rough test as follows.
✔ Position the bike in a straight line facing a brick wall. The bike must be off its stand, upright and with a rider seated. Measure the height from the ground to the centre of the headlight and mark a horizontal line on the wall at this height. Position the motorcycle 3.8 metres from the wall and draw a vertical

Headlight beam height checking equipment

line up the wall central to the centreline of the motorcycle. Switch to dipped beam and check that the beam pattern falls slightly lower than the horizontal line and to the left of the vertical line **(see illustration 2)**.

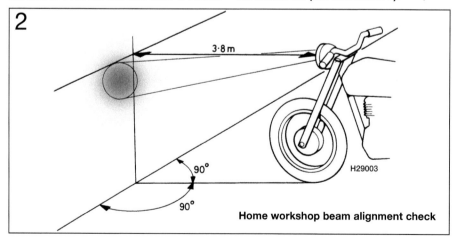

Home workshop beam alignment check

Exhaust System and Final Drive

Exhaust

✔ Check that the exhaust mountings are secure and that the system does not foul any of the rear suspension components.
✔ Start the motorcycle. When the revs are increased, check that the exhaust is neither holed nor leaking from any of its joints. On a linked system, check that the collector box is not leaking due to corrosion.

✔ Note that the exhaust decibel level ("loudness" of the exhaust) is assessed at the discretion of the tester. If the motorcycle was first used on or after 1st January 1985 the silencer must carry the BSAU 193 stamp, or a marking relating to its make and model, or be of OE (original equipment) manufacture. If the silencer is marked NOT FOR ROAD USE, RACING USE ONLY or similar, it will fail the MOT.

Final drive

✔ On chain or belt drive machines, check that the chain/belt is in good condition and does not have excessive slack. Also check that the sprocket is securely mounted on the rear wheel hub. Check that the chain/belt guard is in place.
✔ On shaft drive bikes, check for oil leaking from the drive unit and fouling the rear tyre.

Steering and Suspension

Steering

✔ With the front wheel raised off the ground, rotate the steering from lock to lock. The handlebar or switches must not contact the fuel tank or be close enough to trap the rider's hand. Problems can be caused by damaged lock stops on the lower yoke and frame, or by the fitting of non-standard handlebars.
✔ When performing the lock to lock check, also ensure that the steering moves freely without drag or notchiness. Steering movement can be impaired by poorly routed cables, or by overtight head bearings or worn bearings. The tester will perform a check of the steering head bearing lower race by mounting the front wheel on a surface plate, then performing a lock to

lock check with the weight of the machine on the lower bearing (see illustration 3).
✔ Grasp the fork sliders (lower legs) and attempt to push and pull on the forks (see

Front wheel mounted on a surface plate for steering head bearing lower race check

illustration 4). Any play in the steering head bearings will be felt. Note that in extreme cases, wear of the front fork bushes can be misinterpreted for head bearing play.
✔ Check that the handlebars are securely mounted.
✔ Check that the handlebar grip rubbers are secure. They should by bonded to the bar left end and to the throttle cable pulley on the right end.

Front suspension

✔ With the motorcycle off the stand, hold the front brake on and pump the front forks up and down (see illustration 5). Check that they are adequately damped.

Checking the steering head bearings for freeplay

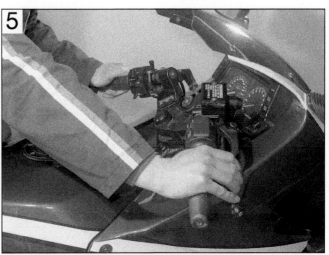

Hold the front brake on and pump the front forks up and down to check operation

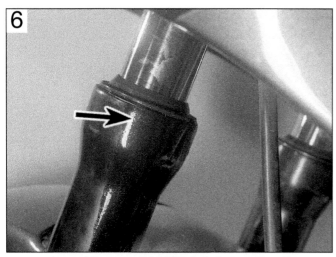

Inspect the area around the fork dust seal for oil leakage (arrow)

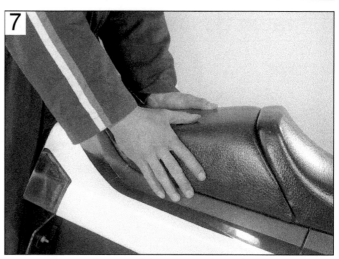

Bounce the rear of the motorcycle to check rear suspension operation

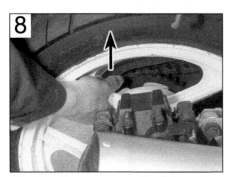

Checking for rear suspension linkage play

✔ Inspect the area above and around the front fork oil seals **(see illustration 6)**. There should be no sign of oil on the fork tube (stanchion) nor leaking down the slider (lower leg). On models so equipped, check that there is no oil leaking from the anti-dive units.

✔ On models with swingarm front suspension, check that there is no freeplay in the linkage when moved from side to side.

Rear suspension

✔ With the motorcycle off the stand and an assistant supporting the motorcycle by its handlebars, bounce the rear suspension **(see illustration 7)**. Check that the suspension components do not foul on any of the cycle parts and check that the shock absorber(s) provide adequate damping.

✔ Visually inspect the shock absorber(s) and check that there is no sign of oil leakage from its damper. This is somewhat restricted on certain single shock models due to the location of the shock absorber.

✔ With the rear wheel raised off the ground, grasp the wheel at the highest point and attempt to pull it up **(see illustration 8)**. Any play in the swingarm pivot or suspension linkage bearings will be felt as movement. **Note:** *Do not confuse play with actual suspension movement.* Failure to lubricate suspension linkage bearings can lead to bearing failure **(see illustration 9)**.

✔ With the rear wheel raised off the ground, grasp the swingarm ends and attempt to move the swingarm from side to side and forwards and backwards - any play indicates wear of the swingarm pivot bearings **(see illustration 10)**.

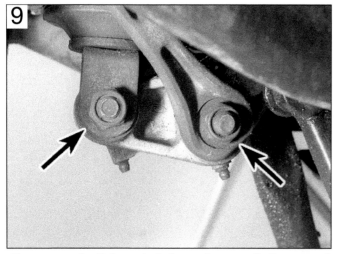

Worn suspension linkage pivots (arrows) are usually the cause of play in the rear suspension

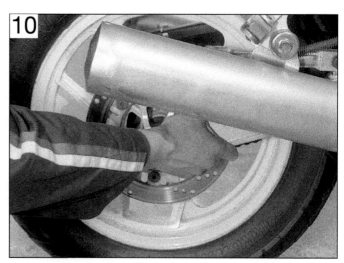

Grasp the swingarm at the ends to check for play in its pivot bearings

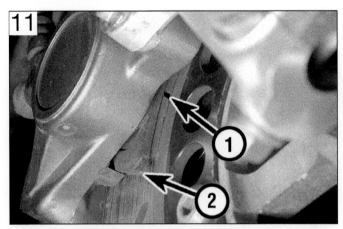

Brake pad wear can usually be viewed without removing the caliper. Most pads have wear indicator grooves (1) and some also have indicator tangs (2)

On drum brakes, check the angle of the operating lever with the brake fully applied. Most drum brakes have a wear indicator pointer and scale.

Brakes, Wheels and Tyres

Brakes

✔ With the wheel raised off the ground, apply the brake then free it off, and check that the wheel is about to revolve freely without brake drag.

✔ On disc brakes, examine the disc itself. Check that it is securely mounted and not cracked.

✔ On disc brakes, view the pad material through the caliper mouth and check that the pads are not worn down beyond the limit **(see illustration 11)**.

✔ On drum brakes, check that when the brake is applied the angle between the operating lever and cable or rod is not too great **(see illustration 12)**. Check also that the operating lever doesn't foul any other components.

✔ On disc brakes, examine the flexible hoses from top to bottom. Have an assistant hold the brake on so that the fluid in the hose is under pressure, and check that there is no sign of fluid leakage, bulges or cracking. If there are any metal brake pipes or unions, check that these are free from corrosion and damage. Where a brake-linked anti-dive system is fitted, check the hoses to the anti-dive in a similar manner.

✔ Check that the rear brake torque arm is secure and that its fasteners are secured by self-locking nuts or castellated nuts with split-pins or R-pins **(see illustration 13)**.

✔ On models with ABS, check that the self-check warning light in the instrument panel works.

✔ The MOT tester will perform a test of the motorcycle's braking efficiency based on a calculation of rider and motorcycle weight. Although this cannot be carried out at home, you can at least ensure that the braking systems are properly maintained. For hydraulic disc brakes, check the fluid level, lever/pedal feel (bleed of air if its spongy) and pad material. For drum brakes, check adjustment, cable or rod operation and shoe lining thickness.

Wheels and tyres

✔ Check the wheel condition. Cast wheels should be free from cracks and if of the built-up design, all fasteners should be secure. Spoked wheels should be checked for broken, corroded, loose or bent spokes.

✔ With the wheel raised off the ground, spin the wheel and visually check that the tyre and wheel run true. Check that the tyre does not foul the suspension or mudguards.

✔ With the wheel raised off the ground, grasp the wheel and attempt to move it about the axle (spindle) **(see illustration 14)**. Any play felt here indicates wheel bearing failure.

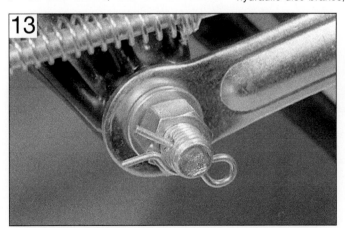

Brake torque arm must be properly secured at both ends

Check for wheel bearing play by trying to move the wheel about the axle (spindle)

Checking the tyre tread depth

Tyre direction of rotation arrow can be found on tyre sidewall

Castellated type wheel axle (spindle) nut must be secured by a split pin or R-pin

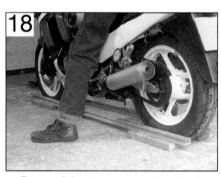

Two straightedges are used to check wheel alignment

✔ Check the tyre tread depth, tread condition and sidewall condition **(see illustration 15)**.
✔ Check the tyre type. Front and rear tyre types must be compatible and be suitable for road use. Tyres marked NOT FOR ROAD USE, COMPETITION USE ONLY or similar, will fail the MOT.

✔ If the tyre sidewall carries a direction of rotation arrow, this must be pointing in the direction of normal wheel rotation **(see illustration 16)**.
✔ Check that the wheel axle (spindle) nuts (where applicable) are properly secured. A self-locking nut or castellated nut with a split-pin or R-pin can be used **(see illustration 17)**.
✔ Wheel alignment is checked with the motorcycle off the stand and a rider seated. With the front wheel pointing straight ahead, two perfectly straight lengths of metal or wood and placed against the sidewalls of both tyres **(see illustration 18)**. The gap each side of the front tyre must be equidistant on both sides. Incorrect wheel alignment may be due to a cocked rear wheel (often as the result of poor chain adjustment) or in extreme cases, a bent frame.

General checks and condition

✔ Check the security of all major fasteners, bodypanels, seat, fairings (where fitted) and mudguards.

✔ Check that the rider and pillion footrests, handlebar levers and brake pedal are securely mounted.

✔ Check for corrosion on the frame or any load-bearing components. If severe, this may affect the structure, particularly under stress.

Sidecars

A motorcycle fitted with a sidecar requires additional checks relating to the stability of the machine and security of attachment and swivel joints, plus specific wheel alignment (toe-in) requirements. Additionally, tyre and lighting requirements differ from conventional motorcycle use. Owners are advised to check MOT test requirements with an official test centre.

Preparing for storage

Before you start

If repairs or an overhaul is needed, see that this is carried out now rather than left until you want to ride the bike again.

Give the bike a good wash and scrub all dirt from its underside. Make sure the bike dries completely before preparing for storage.

Engine

● Remove the spark plug(s) and lubricate the cylinder bores with approximately a teaspoon of motor oil using a spout-type oil can **(see illustration 1)**. Reinstall the spark plug(s). Crank the engine over a couple of times to coat the piston rings and bores with oil. If the bike has a kickstart, use this to turn the engine over. If not, flick the kill switch to the OFF position and crank the engine over on the starter **(see illustration 2)**. If the nature of the ignition system prevents the starter operating with the kill switch in the OFF position,

remove the spark plugs and fit them back in their caps; ensure that the plugs are earthed (grounded) against the cylinder head when the starter is operated **(see illustration 3)**.

⚠️ **Warning: It is important that the plugs are earthed (grounded) away from the spark plug holes otherwise there is a risk of atomised fuel from the cylinders igniting.**

HAYNES HiNT *On a single cylinder four-stroke engine, you can seal the combustion chamber completely by positioning the piston at TDC on the compression stroke.*

● Drain the carburettor(s) otherwise there is a risk of jets becoming blocked by gum deposits from the fuel **(see illustration 4)**.

● If the bike is going into long-term storage, consider adding a fuel stabiliser to the fuel in the tank. If the tank is drained completely, corrosion of its internal surfaces may occur if left unprotected for a long period. The tank can be treated with a rust preventative especially for this purpose. Alternatively, remove the tank and pour half a litre of motor oil into it, install the filler cap and shake the tank to coat its internals with oil before draining off the excess. The same effect can also be achieved by spraying WD40 or a similar water-dispersant around the inside of the tank via its flexible nozzle.

● Make sure the cooling system contains the correct mix of antifreeze. Antifreeze also contains important corrosion inhibitors.

● The air intakes and exhaust can be sealed off by covering or plugging the openings. Ensure that you do not seal in any condensation; run the engine until it is hot,

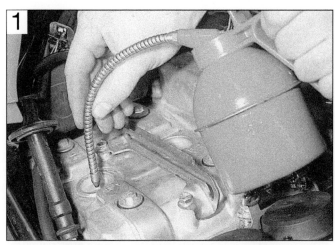

Squirt a drop of motor oil into each cylinder

Flick the kill switch to OFF . . .

. . . and ensure that the metal bodies of the plugs (arrows) are earthed against the cylinder head

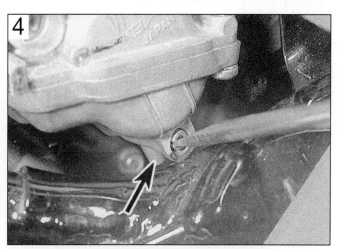

Connect a hose to the carburettor float chamber drain stub (arrow) and unscrew the drain screw

Exhausts can be sealed off with a plastic bag

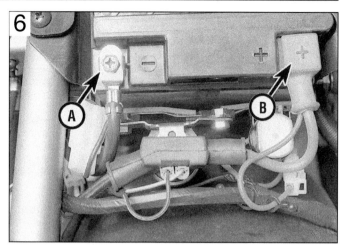

Disconnect the negative lead (A) first, followed by the positive lead (B)

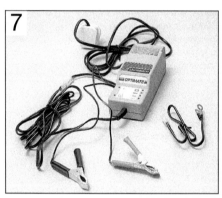

Use a suitable battery charger - this kit also assess battery condition

then switch off and allow to cool. Tape a piece of thick plastic over the silencer end(s) **(see illustration 5)**. Note that some advocate pouring a tablespoon of motor oil into the silencer(s) before sealing them off.

Battery

● Remove it from the bike - in extreme cases of cold the battery may freeze and crack its case **(see illustration 6)**.

● Check the electrolyte level and top up if necessary (conventional refillable batteries). Clean the terminals.
● Store the battery off the motorcycle and away from any sources of fire. Position a wooden block under the battery if it is to sit on the ground.
● Give the battery a trickle charge for a few hours every month **(see illustration 7)**.

Tyres

● Place the bike on its centrestand or an auxiliary stand which will support the motorcycle in an upright position. Position wood blocks under the tyres to keep them off the ground and to provide insulation from damp. If the bike is being put into long-term storage, ideally both tyres should be off the ground; not only will this protect the tyres, but will also ensure that no load is placed on the steering head or wheel bearings.
● Deflate each tyre by 5 to 10 psi, no more or the beads may unseat from the rim, making subsequent inflation difficult on tubeless tyres.

Pivots and controls

● Lubricate all lever, pedal, stand and

footrest pivot points. If grease nipples are fitted to the rear suspension components, apply lubricant to the pivots.
● Lubricate all control cables.

Cycle components

● Apply a wax protectant to all painted and plastic components. Wipe off any excess, but don't polish to a shine. Where fitted, clean the screen with soap and water.
● Coat metal parts with Vaseline (petroleum jelly). When applying this to the fork tubes, do not compress the forks otherwise the seals will rot from contact with the Vaseline.
● Apply a vinyl cleaner to the seat.

Storage conditions

● Aim to store the bike in a shed or garage which does not leak and is free from damp.
● Drape an old blanket or bedspread over the bike to protect it from dust and direct contact with sunlight (which will fade paint). This also hides the bike from prying eyes. Beware of tight-fitting plastic covers which may allow condensation to form and settle on the bike.

Getting back on the road

Engine and transmission

● Change the oil and replace the oil filter. If this was done prior to storage, check that the oil hasn't emulsified - a thick whitish substance which occurs through condensation.
● Remove the spark plugs. Using a spout-type oil can, squirt a few drops of oil into the cylinder(s). This will provide initial lubrication as the piston rings and bores comes back into contact. Service the spark plugs, or fit new ones, and install them in the engine.

● Check that the clutch isn't stuck on. The plates can stick together if left standing for some time, preventing clutch operation. Engage a gear and try rocking the bike back and forth with the clutch lever held against the handlebar. If this doesn't work on cable-operated clutches, hold the clutch lever back against the handlebar with a strong elastic band or cable tie for a couple of hours **(see illustration 8)**.
● If the air intakes or silencer end(s) were blocked off, remove the bung or cover used.
● If the fuel tank was coated with a rust

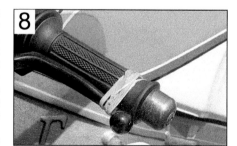

Hold clutch lever back against the handlebar with elastic bands or a cable tie

preventative, oil or a stabiliser added to the fuel, drain and flush the tank and dispose of the fuel sensibly. If no action was taken with the fuel tank prior to storage, it is advised that the old fuel is disposed of since it will go off over a period of time. Refill the fuel tank with fresh fuel.

Frame and running gear

● Oil all pivot points and cables.
● Check the tyre pressures. They will definitely need inflating if pressures were reduced for storage.
● Lubricate the final drive chain (where applicable).
● Remove any protective coating applied to the fork tubes (stanchions) since this may well destroy the fork seals. If the fork tubes weren't protected and have picked up rust spots, remove them with very fine abrasive paper and refinish with metal polish.
● Check that both brakes operate correctly. Apply each brake hard and check that it's not possible to move the motorcycle forwards, then check that the brake frees off again once released. Brake caliper pistons can stick due to corrosion around the piston head, or on the sliding caliper types, due to corrosion of the slider pins. If the brake doesn't free after repeated operation, take the caliper off for examination. Similarly drum brakes can stick

due to a seized operating cam, cable or rod linkage.
● If the motorcycle has been in long-term storage, renew the brake fluid and clutch fluid (where applicable).
● Depending on where the bike has been stored, the wiring, cables and hoses may have been nibbled by rodents. Make a visual check and investigate disturbed wiring loom tape.

Battery

● If the battery has been previously removal and given top up charges it can simply be reconnected. Remember to connect the positive cable first and the negative cable last.
● On conventional refillable batteries, if the battery has not received any attention, remove it from the motorcycle and check its electrolyte level. Top up if necessary then charge the battery. If the battery fails to hold a charge and a visual checks show heavy white sulphation of the plates, the battery is probably defective and must be renewed. This is particularly likely if the battery is old. Confirm battery condition with a specific gravity check.
● On sealed (MF) batteries, if the battery has not received any attention, remove it from the motorcycle and charge it according to the information on the battery case - if the battery fails to hold a charge it must be renewed.

Starting procedure

● If a kickstart is fitted, turn the engine over a couple of times with the ignition OFF to distribute oil around the engine. If no kickstart is fitted, flick the engine kill switch OFF and the ignition ON and crank the engine over a couple of times to work oil around the upper cylinder components. If the nature of the ignition system is such that the starter won't work with the kill switch OFF, remove the spark plugs, fit them back into their caps and earth (ground) their bodies on the cylinder head. Reinstall the spark plugs afterwards.
● Switch the kill switch to RUN, operate the choke and start the engine. If the engine won't start don't continue cranking the engine - not only will this flatten the battery, but the starter motor will overheat. Switch the ignition off and try again later. If the engine refuses to start, go through the fault finding procedures in this manual. **Note:** *If the bike has been in storage for a long time, old fuel or a carburettor blockage may be the problem. Gum deposits in carburettors can block jets - if a carburettor cleaner doesn't prove successful the carburettors must be dismantled for cleaning.*

● Once the engine has started, check that the lights, turn signals and horn work properly.

● Treat the bike gently for the first ride and check all fluid levels on completion. Settle the bike back into the maintenance schedule.

This Section provides an easy reference-guide to the more common faults that are likely to afflict your machine. Obviously, the opportunities are almost limitless for faults to occur as a result of obscure failures, and to try and cover all eventualities would require a book. Indeed, a number have been written on the subject.

Successful troubleshooting is not a mysterious 'black art' but the application of a bit of knowledge combined with a systematic and logical approach to the problem. Approach any troubleshooting by first accurately identifying the symptom and then checking through the list of possible causes, starting with the simplest or most obvious and progressing in stages to the most complex.

Take nothing for granted, but above all apply liberal quantities of common sense.

The main symptom of a fault is given in the text as a major heading below which are listed the various systems or areas which may contain the fault. Details of each possible cause for a fault and the remedial action to be taken are given, in brief, in the paragraphs below each heading. Further information should be sought in the relevant Chapter.

1 Engine doesn't start or is difficult to start

☐ Starter motor doesn't rotate
☐ Starter motor rotates but engine does not turn over
☐ Starter works but engine won't turn over (seized)
☐ No fuel flow
☐ Engine flooded
☐ No spark or weak spark
☐ Compression low
☐ Stalls after starting
☐ Rough idle

2 Poor running at low speed

☐ Spark weak
☐ Fuel/air mixture incorrect
☐ Compression low
☐ Poor acceleration

3 Poor running or no power at high speed

☐ Firing incorrect
☐ Fuel/air mixture incorrect
☐ Compression low
☐ Knocking or pinging
☐ Miscellaneous causes

4 Overheating

☐ Engine overheats
☐ Firing incorrect
☐ Fuel/air mixture incorrect
☐ Compression too high
☐ Engine load excessive
☐ Lubrication inadequate
☐ Miscellaneous causes

5 Clutch problems

☐ Clutch slipping
☐ Clutch not disengaging completely

6 Gearchanging problems

☐ Doesn't go into gear, or lever doesn't return
☐ Jumps out of gear
☐ Overshifts

7 Abnormal engine noise

☐ Knocking or pinging
☐ Piston slap or rattling
☐ Valve noise
☐ Other noise

8 Abnormal driveline noise

☐ Clutch noise
☐ Transmission noise
☐ Final drive noise

9 Abnormal frame and suspension noise

☐ Front end noise
☐ Shock absorber noise
☐ Brake noise

10 Oil pressure low

☐ Engine lubrication system

11 Excessive exhaust smoke

☐ White smoke
☐ Black smoke
☐ Brown smoke

12 Poor handling or stability

☐ Handlebar hard to turn
☐ Handlebar shakes or vibrates excessively
☐ Handlebar pulls to one side
☐ Poor shock absorbing qualities

13 Braking problems

☐ Brakes are spongy, don't hold
☐ Brake lever or pedal pulsates
☐ Brakes drag

14 Electrical problems

☐ Battery dead or weak
☐ Battery overcharged

1 Engine doesn't start or is difficult to start

Starter motor doesn't rotate

- ☐ Engine kill switch OFF.
- ☐ Fuse blown. Check main fuse (Chapter 9).
- ☐ Battery voltage low. Check and recharge battery (Chapter 9).
- ☐ Starter motor defective. Make sure the wiring to the starter is secure. Make sure the starter relay clicks when the start button is pushed. If the relay clicks, then the fault is in the wiring or motor.
- ☐ Starter relay faulty. Check it according to the procedure in Chapter 9.
- ☐ Starter switch not contacting. The contacts could be wet, corroded or dirty. Disassemble and clean the switch (Chapter 9).
- ☐ Wiring open or shorted. Check all wiring connections and harnesses to make sure that they are dry, tight and not corroded. Also check for broken or frayed wires that can cause a short to earth (see wiring diagram, Chapter 9).
- ☐ Ignition (main) switch defective. Check the switch according to the procedure in Chapter 9. Renew the switch if it is defective.
- ☐ Engine kill switch defective. Check for wet, dirty or corroded contacts. Clean or renew the switch as necessary (Chapter 9).
- ☐ Faulty neutral, side stand or clutch switch. Check the wiring to each switch and the switch itself according to the procedures in Chapter 9.
- ☐ Faulty starter safety cut-out relay (see Chapter 9).

Starter motor rotates but engine does not turn over

- ☐ Starter motor clutch defective. Inspect and repair or renew (Chapter 2).
- ☐ Damaged idler or starter gears. Inspect and renew the damaged parts (Chapter 2).

Starter works but engine won't turn over (seized)

- ☐ Seized engine caused by one or more internally damaged components. Failure due to wear, abuse or lack of lubrication. Damage can include seized valves, followers, camshafts, pistons, crankshaft, connecting rod bearings, or transmission gears or bearings. Refer to Chapter 2 for engine disassembly.

No fuel flow

- ☐ No fuel in tank.
- ☐ Fuel tank breather hose obstructed.
- ☐ Fuel tap filter or in-line filter clogged. Remove the tap and clean it and the filter (Chapters 4 and 1).
- ☐ Fuel tap vacuum hose split or diaphragm holed (TRX models). Check the hose.
- ☐ Fuel pump failure (Chapter 4).
- ☐ Fuel line clogged or on early models fuel filter at carburettor union clogged. Pull the fuel line loose and carefully blow through it.
- ☐ Float needle valve clogged. For all of the valves to be clogged, either a very bad batch of fuel with an unusual additive has been used, or some other foreign material has entered the tank. Many times after a machine has been stored for many months without running, the fuel turns to a varnish-like liquid and forms deposits on the inlet needle valves and jets. The carburettors should be removed and overhauled if draining the float chambers doesn't solve the problem.

Engine flooded

- ☐ Float height too high. Check as described in Chapter 4.
- ☐ Float needle valve worn or stuck open. A piece of dirt, rust or other debris can cause the valve to seat improperly, causing excess fuel to be admitted to the float chamber. In this case, the float chamber should be cleaned and the needle valve and seat inspected. If the needle and seat are worn, then the leaking will persist and the parts should be renewed (Chapter 4).

- ☐ Starting technique incorrect. Under normal circumstances (ie, if all the carburettor functions are sound) the machine should start with little or no throttle. When the engine is cold, the choke should be operated and the engine started without opening the throttle. When the engine is at operating temperature, only a very slight amount of throttle should be necessary.

No spark or weak spark

- ☐ Ignition switch OFF.
- ☐ Engine kill switch turned to the OFF position.
- ☐ Battery voltage low. Check and recharge the battery as necessary (Chapter 9).
- ☐ Spark plugs dirty, defective or worn out. Locate reason for fouled plugs using spark plug condition chart at the end of this manual and follow the plug maintenance procedures (Chapter 1).
- ☐ Spark plug caps or secondary (HT) wiring faulty. Check condition. Renew either or both components if cracks or deterioration are evident (Chapter 5).
- ☐ Spark plug caps not making good contact. Make sure that the plug caps fit snugly over the plug ends.
- ☐ Ignitor unit defective. Check the unit (Chapter 5).
- ☐ Pick-up coil defective. Check the unit (Chapter 5).
- ☐ Ignition HT coil(s) defective. Check the coil(s) (Chapter 5).
- ☐ Ignition or kill switch shorted. This is usually caused by water, corrosion, damage or excessive wear. The switches can be disassembled and cleaned with electrical contact cleaner. If cleaning does not help, renew the switches (Chapter 9).
- ☐ Wiring shorted or broken between:
  - a) Ignition (main) switch and engine kill switch (or blown fuse)
  - b) Ignitor unit and engine kill switch
  - c) Ignitor unit and ignition HT coil(s)
  - d) Ignition HT coil(s) and spark plugs
  - e) Ignitor unit and pick-up coil
- ☐ Make sure that all wiring connections are clean, dry and tight. Look for chafed and broken wires (Chapters 5 and 9).

Compression low

- ☐ Spark plugs loose. Remove the plugs and inspect their threads. Reinstall and tighten to the specified torque (Chapter 1).
- ☐ Cylinder head not sufficiently tightened down. If the cylinder head is suspected of being loose, then there's a chance that the gasket or head is damaged if the problem has persisted for any length of time. The head bolts/nuts should be tightened to the proper torque in the correct sequence (Chapter 2).
- ☐ Improper valve clearance. This means that the valve is not closing completely and compression pressure is leaking past the valve. Check and adjust the valve clearances (Chapter 1).
- ☐ Cylinder and/or piston worn. Excessive wear will cause compression pressure to leak past the rings. This is usually accompanied by worn rings as well. A top-end overhaul is necessary (Chapter 2).
- ☐ Piston rings worn, weak, broken, or sticking. Broken or sticking piston rings usually indicate a lubrication or carburation problem that causes excess carbon deposits or seizures to form on the pistons and rings. Top-end overhaul is necessary (Chapter 2).
- ☐ Piston ring-to-groove clearance excessive. This is caused by excessive wear of the piston ring lands. Piston renewal is necessary (Chapter 2).
- ☐ Cylinder head gasket damaged. If the head is allowed to become loose, or if excessive carbon build-up on the piston crown and combustion chamber causes extremely high compression, the head gasket may leak. Retorquing the head is not always sufficient to restore the seal, so gasket renewal is necessary (Chapter 2).
- ☐ Cylinder head warped. This is caused by overheating or improperly tightened head bolts/nuts. Machine shop resurfacing or head renewal is necessary (Chapter 2).

1 Engine doesn't start or is difficult to start (continued)

☐ Valve spring broken or weak. Caused by component failure or wear; the springs must be renewed (Chapter 2).

☐ Valve not seating properly. This is caused by a bent valve (from over-revving or improper valve adjustment), burned valve or seat (improper carburation) or an accumulation of carbon deposits on the seat (from carburation or lubrication problems). The valves must be cleaned and/or renewed and the seats serviced if possible (Chapter 2).

Stalls after starting

☐ Improper choke action. Make sure the choke linkage shaft is getting a full stroke and staying in the out position (Chapter 4).

☐ Ignition malfunction (Chapter 5).

☐ Carburettor malfunction (Chapter 4).

☐ Fuel contaminated. The fuel can be contaminated with either dirt or water, or can change chemically if the machine is allowed to sit for several months or more. Drain the tank and float chambers (Chapter 4).

☐ Intake air leak. Check for loose carburettor-to-intake manifold connections, loose or missing vacuum gauge adapter screws or hoses, or loose carburettor tops (Chapter 4).

☐ Engine idle speed incorrect. Turn idle adjusting screw until the engine idles at the specified rpm (Chapter 1).

Rough idle

☐ Ignition malfunction (Chapter 5).

☐ Idle speed incorrect (Chapter 1).

☐ Carburettors not synchronised. Adjust carburettors with vacuum gauge or manometer set as described in Chapter 1.

☐ Carburettor malfunction (Chapter 4).

☐ Fuel contaminated. The fuel can be contaminated with either dirt or water, or can change chemically if the machine is allowed to sit for several months or more. Drain the tank and float chambers (Chapter 4).

☐ Intake air leak. Check for loose carburettor-to-intake manifold connections, loose or missing vacuum gauge adapter screws or hoses, or loose carburettor tops (Chapter 4).

☐ Air filter clogged. Renew the air filter element (Chapter 1).

2 Poor running at low speeds

Spark weak

☐ Battery voltage low. Check and recharge battery (Chapter 9).

☐ Spark plugs fouled, defective or worn out. Refer to Chapter 1 for spark plug maintenance.

☐ Spark plug cap or HT wiring defective. Refer to Chapters 1 and 5 for details on the ignition system.

☐ Spark plug caps not making contact. Make sure they are securely pushed on to the plugs.

☐ Incorrect spark plugs. Wrong type, heat range or cap configuration. Check and install correct plugs listed in Chapter 1.

☐ Ignitor unit defective (Chapter 5).

☐ Pick-up coil defective (Chapter 5).

☐ Ignition HT coil(s) defective (Chapter 5).

Fuel/air mixture incorrect

☐ Pilot screws out of adjustment (Chapter 4).

☐ Pilot jet or air passage clogged. Remove and overhaul the carburettors (Chapter 4).

☐ Air bleed holes clogged. Remove carburettor and blow out all passages (Chapter 4).

☐ Air filter clogged, poorly sealed or missing (Chapter 1).

☐ Air filter housing poorly sealed. Look for cracks, holes or loose clamps and renew or repair defective parts.

☐ Fuel level too high or too low. Check the level (Chapter 4).

☐ Fuel tank breather hose obstructed.

☐ Carburettor intake manifolds loose. Check for cracks, breaks, tears or loose clamps. Renew the rubber intake manifold joints if split or perished.

Compression low

☐ Spark plugs loose. Remove the plugs and inspect their threads. Reinstall and tighten to the specified torque (Chapter 1).

☐ Cylinder head not sufficiently tightened down. If the cylinder head is suspected of being loose, then there's a chance that the gasket and head are damaged if the problem has persisted for any length of time. The head bolts/nuts should be tightened to the proper torque in the correct sequence (Chapter 2).

☐ Improper valve clearance. This means that the valve is not closing completely and compression pressure is leaking past the valve. Check and adjust the valve clearances (Chapter 1).

☐ Cylinder and/or piston worn. Excessive wear will cause compression pressure to leak past the rings. This is usually accompanied by worn rings as well. A top end overhaul is necessary (Chapter 2).

☐ Piston rings worn, weak, broken, or sticking. Broken or sticking piston rings usually indicate a lubrication or carburation problem that causes excess carbon deposits or seizures to form on the pistons and rings. Top-end overhaul is necessary (Chapter 2).

☐ Piston ring-to-groove clearance excessive. This is caused by excessive wear of the piston ring lands. Piston renewal is necessary (Chapter 2).

☐ Cylinder head gasket damaged. If the head is allowed to become loose, or if excessive carbon build-up on the piston crown and combustion chamber causes extremely high compression, the head gasket may leak. Retorquing the head is not always sufficient to restore the seal, so gasket renewal is necessary (Chapter 2).

☐ Cylinder head warped. This is caused by overheating or improperly tightened head bolts/nuts. Machine shop resurfacing or head renewal is necessary (Chapter 2).

☐ Valve spring broken or weak. Caused by component failure or wear; the springs must be renewed (Chapter 2).

☐ Valve not seating properly. This is caused by a bent valve (from over-revving or improper valve adjustment), burned valve or seat (improper carburation) or an accumulation of carbon deposits on the seat (from carburation, lubrication problems). The valves must be cleaned and/or renewed and the seats serviced if possible (Chapter 2).

Poor acceleration

☐ Carburettors leaking or dirty. Overhaul the carburettors (Chapter 4).

☐ Timing not advancing. The pick-up coil or the ignitor unit may be defective. If so, they must be renewed, as they can't be repaired.

☐ Carburettors not synchronised. Adjust them with a vacuum gauge set or manometer (Chapter 1).

☐ Engine oil viscosity too high. Using a heavier oil than that recommended in Chapter 1 can damage the oil pump or lubrication system and cause drag on the engine.

☐ Brakes dragging. Usually caused by debris which has entered the brake piston seals, or from a warped disc or bent axle. Repair as necessary (Chapter 7).

☐ Fuel pump flow rate insufficient. Check the pump (Chapter 4).

3 Poor running or no power at high speed

Firing incorrect

☐ Air filter restricted. Clean or renew filter (Chapter 1).
☐ Spark plugs fouled, defective or worn out. See Chapter 1 for spark plug maintenance.
☐ Spark plug caps or HT wiring defective. See Chapters 1 and 5 for details of the ignition system.
☐ Spark plug caps not in good contact (Chapter 5).
☐ Incorrect spark plugs. Wrong type, heat range or cap configuration. Check and install correct plugs listed in Chapter 1.
☐ Ignitor unit defective (Chapter 5).
☐ Ignition coil(s) defective (Chapter 5).

Fuel/air mixture incorrect

☐ Main jet clogged. Dirt, water or other contaminants can clog the main jets. Clean the fuel tap filter, the in-line filter, the float chamber area, and the jets and carburettor orifices (Chapter 4).
☐ Main jet wrong size. The standard jetting is for sea level atmospheric pressure and oxygen content.
☐ Air bleed holes clogged. Remove and overhaul carburettors (Chapter 4).
☐ Air filter clogged, poorly sealed, or missing (Chapter 1).
☐ Air filter housing poorly sealed. Look for cracks, holes or loose clamps, and renew or repair defective parts.
☐ Fuel level too high or too low. Check the level (Chapter 4).
☐ Fuel tank breather hose obstructed.
☐ Carburettor intake manifolds loose. Check for cracks, breaks, tears or loose clamps. Renew the rubber intake manifolds if they are split or perished (Chapter 4).

Compression low

☐ Spark plugs loose. Remove the plugs and inspect their threads. Reinstall and tighten to the specified torque (Chapter 1).
☐ Cylinder head not sufficiently tightened down. If the cylinder head is suspected of being loose, then there's a chance that the gasket and head are damaged if the problem has persisted for any length of time. The head bolts/nuts should be tightened to the proper torque in the correct sequence (Chapter 2).
☐ Improper valve clearance. This means that the valve is not closing completely and compression pressure is leaking past the valve. Check and adjust the valve clearances (Chapter 1).
☐ Cylinder and/or piston worn. Excessive wear will cause compression pressure to leak past the rings. This is usually accompanied by worn rings as well. A top-end overhaul is necessary (Chapter 2).
☐ Piston rings worn, weak, broken, or sticking. Broken or sticking piston rings usually indicate a lubrication or carburation problem that causes excess carbon deposits or seizures to form on the pistons and rings. Top-end overhaul is necessary (Chapter 2).
☐ Piston ring-to-groove clearance excessive. This is caused by excessive wear of the piston ring lands. Piston renewal is necessary (Chapter 2).

☐ Cylinder head gasket damaged. If the head is allowed to become loose, or if excessive carbon build-up on the piston crown and combustion chamber causes extremely high compression, the head gasket may leak. Retorquing the head is not always sufficient to restore the seal, so gasket renewal is necessary (Chapter 2).
☐ Cylinder head warped. This is caused by overheating or improperly tightened head bolts/nuts. Machine shop resurfacing or head renewal is necessary (Chapter 2).
☐ Valve spring broken or weak. Caused by component failure or wear; the springs must be renewed (Chapter 2).
☐ Valve not seating properly. This is caused by a bent valve (from over-revving or improper valve adjustment), burned valve or seat (improper carburation) or an accumulation of carbon deposits on the seat (from carburation or lubrication problems). The valves must be cleaned and/or renewed and the seats serviced if possible (Chapter 2).

Knocking or pinging

☐ Carbon build-up in combustion chamber. Use of a fuel additive that will dissolve the adhesive bonding the carbon particles to the crown and chamber is the easiest way to remove the build-up. Otherwise, the cylinder head will have to be removed and decarbonised (Chapter 2).
☐ Incorrect or poor quality fuel. Old or improper grades of fuel can cause detonation. This causes the piston to rattle, thus the knocking or pinking sound. Drain old fuel and always use the recommended fuel grade.
☐ Spark plug heat range incorrect. Uncontrolled detonation indicates the plug heat range is too hot. The plug in effect becomes a glow plug, raising cylinder temperatures. Install the proper heat range plug (Chapter 1).
☐ Improper air/fuel mixture. This will cause the cylinders to run hot, which leads to detonation. Clogged jets or an air leak can cause this imbalance. See Chapter 4.

Miscellaneous causes

☐ Throttle valve doesn't open fully. Adjust the throttle grip freeplay (Chapter 1).
☐ Clutch slipping. May be caused by loose or worn clutch components. Refer to Chapter 2 for clutch overhaul procedures.
☐ Timing not advancing.
☐ Engine oil viscosity too high. Using a heavier oil than the one recommended in Chapter 1 can damage the oil pump or lubrication system and cause drag on the engine.
☐ Brakes dragging. Usually caused by debris which has entered the brake piston seals, or from a warped disc or bent axle. Repair as necessary.
☐ Fuel pump flow rate insufficient. Check the pump (Chapter 4).

4 Overheating

Engine overheats

- ☐ Coolant level low. Check and add coolant (Chapter 1).
- ☐ Leak in cooling system. Check cooling system hoses and radiator for leaks and other damage. Repair or renew parts as necessary (Chapter 3).
- ☐ Thermostat sticking open or closed. Check and renew as described in Chapter 3.
- ☐ Faulty radiator cap. Remove the cap and have it pressure tested.
- ☐ Coolant passages clogged. Have the entire system drained and flushed, then refill with fresh coolant.
- ☐ Water pump defective. Remove the pump and check the components (Chapter 3).
- ☐ Clogged radiator fins. Clean them by blowing compressed air through the fins from the backside.
- ☐ Cooling fan or fan switch fault (Chapter 3).

Firing incorrect

- ☐ Spark plugs fouled, defective or worn out. See Chapter 1 for spark plug maintenance.
- ☐ Incorrect spark plugs.
- ☐ Ignitor unit defective (Chapter 5).
- ☐ Faulty ignition HT coil(s) (Chapter 5).

Fuel/air mixture incorrect

- ☐ Main jet clogged. Dirt, water and other contaminants can clog the main jets. Clean the fuel tap filter, the fuel pump in-line filter (where fitted), the float chamber area and the jets and carburettor orifices (Chapter 4).
- ☐ Main jet wrong size. The standard jetting is for sea level atmospheric pressure and oxygen content.
- ☐ Air filter clogged, poorly sealed or missing (Chapter 1).
- ☐ Air filter housing poorly sealed. Look for cracks, holes or loose clamps and renew or repair.
- ☐ Fuel level too low. Check the level (Chapter 4).
- ☐ Fuel tank breather hose obstructed.
- ☐ Carburettor intake manifolds loose. Check for cracks, breaks, tears or loose clamps. Renew the rubber intake manifold joints if split or perished.

Compression too high

- ☐ Carbon build-up in combustion chamber. Use of a fuel additive that will dissolve the adhesive bonding the carbon particles to the piston crown and chamber is the easiest way to remove the build-up. Otherwise, the cylinder head will have to be removed and decarbonised (Chapter 2).
- ☐ Improperly machined head surface or installation of incorrect gasket during engine assembly.

Engine load excessive

- ☐ Clutch slipping. Can be caused by damaged, loose or worn clutch components. Refer to Chapter 2 for overhaul procedures.
- ☐ Engine oil level too high. The addition of too much oil will cause pressurisation of the crankcase and inefficient engine operation. Check Specifications and drain to proper level (Chapter 1).
- ☐ Engine oil viscosity too high. Using a heavier oil than the one recommended in Chapter 1 can damage the oil pump or lubrication system as well as cause drag on the engine.
- ☐ Brakes dragging. Usually caused by debris which has entered the brake piston seals, or from a warped disc or bent axle. Repair as necessary.

Lubrication inadequate

- ☐ Engine oil level too low. Friction caused by intermittent lack of lubrication or from oil that is overworked can cause overheating. The oil provides a definite cooling function in the engine. Check the oil level (Chapter 1).
- ☐ Poor quality engine oil or incorrect viscosity or type. Oil is rated not only according to viscosity but also according to type. Some oils are not rated high enough for use in this engine. Check the Specifications section and change to the correct oil (Chapter 1).

Miscellaneous causes

- ☐ Modification to exhaust system. Most aftermarket exhaust systems cause the engine to run leaner, which make them run hotter. When installing an aftermarket exhaust system, always rejet the carburettors.

5 Clutch problems

Clutch slipping

- ☐ Insufficient clutch cable freeplay. Check and adjust (Chapter 1).
- ☐ Friction plates worn or warped. Overhaul the clutch assembly (Chapter 2).
- ☐ Plain plates warped (Chapter 2).
- ☐ Clutch springs broken or weak. Old or heat-damaged (from slipping clutch) springs should be renewed (Chapter 2).
- ☐ Clutch release mechanism defective. Renew any defective parts (Chapter 2).
- ☐ Clutch centre or housing unevenly worn. This causes improper engagement of the plates. Renew the damaged or worn parts (Chapter 2).

Clutch not disengaging completely

- ☐ Excessive clutch cable freeplay. Check and adjust (Chapter 1).
- ☐ Clutch plates warped or damaged. This will cause clutch drag, which in turn will cause the machine to creep. Overhaul the clutch assembly (Chapter 2).
- ☐ Clutch spring tension uneven. Usually caused by a sagged or broken spring. Check and renew the springs as a set (Chapter 2).
- ☐ Engine oil deteriorated. Old, thin, worn out oil will not provide proper lubrication for the plates, causing the clutch to drag. Renew the oil and filter (Chapter 1).
- ☐ Engine oil viscosity too high. Using a heavier oil than recommended in Chapter 1 can cause the plates to stick together, putting a drag on the engine. Change to the correct weight oil (Chapter 1).
- ☐ Clutch housing guide seized on mainshaft. Lack of lubrication, severe wear or damage can cause the guide to seize on the shaft. Overhaul of the clutch, and perhaps transmission, may be necessary to repair the damage (Chapter 2).
- ☐ Clutch release mechanism defective. Overhaul the clutch cover components (Chapter 2).
- ☐ Loose clutch centre nut. Causes housing and centre misalignment putting a drag on the engine. Engagement adjustment continually varies. Overhaul the clutch assembly (Chapter 2).

6 Gearchanging problems

Doesn't go into gear or lever doesn't return

☐ Clutch not disengaging. See above.
☐ Selector fork(s) bent or seized. Often caused by dropping the machine or from lack of lubrication. Overhaul the transmission (Chapter 2).
☐ Gear(s) stuck on shaft. Most often caused by a lack of lubrication or excessive wear in transmission bearings and bushings. Overhaul the transmission (Chapter 2).
☐ Selector drum binding. Caused by lubrication failure or excessive wear. Renew the drum and bearing (Chapter 2).
☐ Gearchange lever return spring weak or broken (Chapter 2).
☐ Gearchange lever broken. Splines stripped out of lever or shaft, caused by allowing the lever to get loose or from dropping the machine. Renew necessary parts (Chapter 2).
☐ Gearchange mechanism stopper arm broken or worn. Full engagement and rotary movement of shift drum results. Renew the arm (Chapter 2).
☐ Stopper arm spring broken. Allows arm to float, causing sporadic shift operation. Renew spring (Chapter 2).

Jumps out of gear

☐ Selector fork(s) worn. Overhaul the transmission (Chapter 2).
☐ Gear groove(s) worn. Overhaul the transmission (Chapter 2).
☐ Gear dogs or dog slots worn or damaged. The gears should be inspected and renewed. No attempt should be made to service the worn parts.

Overshifts

☐ Stopper arm spring weak or broken (Chapter 2).
☐ Gearchange shaft return spring post broken or distorted (Chapter 2).

7 Abnormal engine noise

Knocking or pinking

☐ Carbon build-up in combustion chamber. Use of a fuel additive that will dissolve the adhesive bonding the carbon particles to the piston crown and chamber is the easiest way to remove the build-up. Otherwise, the cylinder head will have to be removed and decarbonised (Chapter 2).
☐ Incorrect or poor quality fuel. Old or improper fuel can cause detonation. This causes the pistons to rattle, thus the knocking or pinking sound. Drain the old fuel and always use the recommended grade fuel (Chapter 4).
☐ Spark plug heat range incorrect. Uncontrolled detonation indicates that the plug heat range is too hot. The plug in effect becomes a glow plug, raising cylinder temperatures. Install the proper heat range plug (Chapter 1).
☐ Improper air/fuel mixture. This will cause the cylinders to run hot and lead to detonation. Clogged jets or an air leak can cause this imbalance. See Chapter 4.

Piston slap or rattling

☐ Cylinder-to-piston clearance excessive. Caused by improper assembly. Inspect and overhaul top-end parts (Chapter 2).
☐ Connecting rod bent. Caused by over-revving, trying to start a badly flooded engine or from ingesting a foreign object into the combustion chamber. Renew the damaged parts (Chapter 2).
☐ Piston pin or piston pin bore worn or seized from wear or lack of lubrication. Renew damaged parts (Chapter 2).
☐ Piston ring(s) worn, broken or sticking. Overhaul the top-end (Chapter 2).
☐ Piston seizure damage. Usually from lack of lubrication or overheating. Renew the pistons and bore the cylinders, as necessary (Chapter 2).

☐ Connecting rod upper or lower end clearance excessive. Caused by excessive wear or lack of lubrication. Renew worn parts.

Valve noise

☐ Incorrect valve clearances. Adjust the clearances by referring to Chapter 1.
☐ Valve spring broken or weak. Check and renew weak valve springs (Chapter 2).
☐ Camshaft or cylinder head worn or damaged. Lack of lubrication at high rpm is usually the cause of damage. Insufficient oil or failure to change the oil at the recommended intervals are the chief causes. Since there are no replaceable bearings in the head, the head itself will have to be renewed if there is excessive wear or damage (Chapter 2).

Other noise

☐ Cylinder head gasket leaking.
☐ Exhaust pipe leaking at cylinder head connection. Caused by improper fit of pipe(s) or loose exhaust flange. All exhaust fasteners should be tightened evenly and carefully. Failure to do this will lead to a leak.
☐ Crankshaft runout excessive. Caused by a bent crankshaft (from over-revving) or damage from an upper cylinder component failure. Can also be attributed to dropping the machine on either of the crankshaft ends.
☐ Engine mounting bolts loose. Tighten all engine mount bolts (Chapter 2).
☐ Crankshaft bearings worn (Chapter 2).
☐ Balancer shaft bearings worn (Chapter 2).
☐ Camshaft drive gear assembly defective. Renew according to the procedure in Chapter 2.

8 Abnormal driveline noise

Clutch noise

☐ Clutch outer drum/friction plate clearance excessive (Chapter 2).
☐ Loose or damaged clutch pressure plate and/or bolts (Chapter 2).

Transmission noise

☐ Bearings worn. Also includes the possibility that the shafts are worn. Overhaul the transmission (Chapter 2).
☐ Gears worn or chipped (Chapter 2).
☐ Metal chips jammed in gear teeth. Probably pieces from a broken clutch, gear or shift mechanism that were picked up by the gears. This will cause early bearing failure (Chapter 2).

☐ Engine oil level too low. Causes a howl from transmission. Also affects engine power and clutch operation (Chapter 1).

Final drive noise

☐ Chain not adjusted properly (Chapter 1).
☐ Front or rear sprocket loose. Tighten fasteners (Chapter 6).
☐ Sprockets worn. Renew sprockets (Chapter 6).
☐ Rear sprocket warped. Renew sprockets (Chapter 6).
☐ Loose or worn rear wheel or sprocket coupling bearings. Check and renew as needed (Chapter 7).

9 Abnormal frame and suspension noise

Front end noise

☐ Low fluid level or improper viscosity oil in forks. This can sound like spurting and is usually accompanied by irregular fork action (Chapter 6).

☐ Spring weak or broken. Makes a clicking or scraping sound. Fork oil, when drained, will have a lot of metal particles in it (Chapter 6).

☐ Steering head bearings loose or damaged. Clicks when braking. Check and adjust or renew as necessary (Chapters 1 and 6).

☐ Fork yokes loose. Make sure all clamp pinch bolts are tightened to the specified torque (Chapter 6).

☐ Fork tube bent. Good possibility if machine has been dropped. Renew both tubes (Chapter 6).

☐ Front axle bolt or axle clamp bolts loose. Tighten them to the specified torque (Chapter 7).

☐ Loose or worn wheel bearings. Check and renew as needed (Chapter 7).

Shock absorber noise

☐ Fluid level incorrect. Indicates a leak caused by defective seal. Shock will be covered with oil. Renew shock or seek advice on repair from a Yamaha dealer (Chapter 6).

☐ Defective shock absorber with internal damage. This is in the body of the shock and can't be remedied. The shock must be renewed (Chapter 6).

☐ Bent or damaged shock body. Renew the shock (Chapter 6).

☐ Loose or worn suspension linkage components (TRX and XTZ models). Check and renew as necessary (Chapter 6).

Brake noise

☐ Squeal caused by pad shim not installed or positioned correctly (where fitted) (Chapter 7).

☐ Squeal caused by dust on brake pads. Usually found in combination with glazed pads. Clean using brake cleaning solvent (Chapter 7).

☐ Contamination of brake pads. Oil, brake fluid or dirt causing brake to chatter or squeal. Clean or renew pads (Chapter 7).

☐ Pads glazed. Caused by excessive heat from prolonged use or from contamination. Do not use sandpaper, emery cloth, carborundum cloth or any other abrasive to roughen the pad surfaces as abrasives will stay in the pad material and damage the disc. A very fine flat file can be used, but pad renewal is suggested as a cure (Chapter 7).

☐ Disc warped. Can cause a chattering, clicking or intermittent squeal. Usually accompanied by a pulsating lever or pedal and uneven braking. Renew the disc (Chapter 7).

☐ Loose or worn wheel bearings. Check and renew as needed (Chapter 7).

10 Oil pressure low

Engine lubrication system

☐ Engine oil level low. Inspect for leak or other problem causing low oil level and add recommended oil (Chapter 1).

☐ Engine oil viscosity too low. Very old, thin oil or an improper weight of oil used in the engine. Change to correct oil (Chapter 1).

☐ Engine oil pump(s) defective, blocked oil strainer gauze or failed relief valve. Carry out oil pressure check (Chapter 1).

☐ Camshaft or journals worn. Excessive wear causing drop in oil pressure. Renew cam and/or cylinder head. Abnormal wear could be caused by oil starvation at high rpm from low oil level or improper weight or type of oil (Chapters 1 and 2).

☐ Crankshaft and/or bearings worn. Same problems as above. Check and renew crankshaft and/or bearings (Chapter 2).

11 Excessive exhaust smoke

White smoke

☐ Piston oil ring worn. The ring may be broken or damaged, causing oil from the crankcase to be pulled past the piston into the combustion chamber. Renew the rings (Chapter 2).

☐ Cylinders worn, cracked, or scored. Caused by overheating or oil starvation. The cylinders will have to be rebored and new pistons installed.

☐ Valve oil seal damaged or worn. Renew oil seals (Chapter 2).

☐ Valve guide worn. Perform a complete valve job (Chapter 2).

☐ Engine oil level too high, which causes the oil to be forced past the rings. Drain oil to the proper level (Chapter 1).

☐ Head gasket broken between oil return and cylinder. Causes oil to be pulled into the combustion chamber. Renew the head gasket and check the head for warpage (Chapter 2).

☐ Abnormal crankcase pressurisation, which forces oil past the rings. Clogged breather is usually the cause.

Black smoke

☐ Air filter clogged. Clean or renew the element (Chapter 1).

☐ Main jet too large or loose. Compare the jet size to the Specifications (Chapter 4).

☐ Choke cable or linkage shaft stuck, causing fuel to be pulled through choke circuit (Chapter 4).

☐ Fuel level too high. Check and adjust the fuel level as necessary (Chapter 4).

☐ Float needle valve held off needle seat. Clean the float chambers and fuel line and renew the needles and seats if necessary (Chapter 4).

Brown smoke

☐ Main jet too small or clogged. Lean condition caused by wrong size main jet or by a restricted orifice. Clean float chambers and jets and compare jet size to Specifications (Chapter 4).

☐ Fuel flow insufficient - float needle valve stuck closed due to chemical reaction with old fuel; fuel level incorrect; restricted fuel line; faulty fuel pump (Chapter 4).

☐ Carburettor intake manifold clamps loose (Chapter 4).

☐ Air filter poorly sealed or not installed (Chapter 1).

12 Poor handling or stability

Handlebar hard to turn

- [ ] Steering head bearing adjuster nut too tight. Check adjustment as described in Chapter 1.
- [ ] Bearings damaged. Roughness can be felt as the bars are turned from side-to-side. Renew bearings and races (Chapter 6).
- [ ] Races dented or worn. Denting results from wear in only one position (eg, straight ahead), from a collision or hitting a pothole or from dropping the machine. Renew races and bearings (Chapter 6).
- [ ] Steering stem lubrication inadequate. Causes are grease getting hard from age or being washed out by high pressure car washes. Disassemble steering head and repack bearings (Chapter 6).
- [ ] Steering stem bent. Caused by a collision, hitting a pothole or by dropping the machine. Renew damaged part. Don't try to straighten the steering stem (Chapter 6).
- [ ] Front tyre air pressure too low (Chapter 1).

Handlebar shakes or vibrates excessively

- [ ] Tyres worn or out of balance (Chapter 7).
- [ ] Swingarm bearings worn. Renew worn bearings (Chapter 6).
- [ ] Wheel rim(s) warped or damaged. Inspect wheels for runout (Chapter 7).
- [ ] Wheel bearings worn. Worn front or rear wheel bearings can cause poor tracking. Worn front bearings will cause wobble (Chapter 7).
- [ ] Handlebar clamp bolts loose (Chapter 6).
- [ ] Fork yoke bolts loose. Tighten them to the specified torque (Chapter 6).
- [ ] Engine mounting bolts loose. Will cause excessive vibration with increased engine rpm (Chapter 2).

Handlebar pulls to one side

- [ ] Frame bent. Definitely suspect this if the machine has been dropped. May or may not be accompanied by cracking near the bend. Renew the frame (Chapter 6).
- [ ] Wheels out of alignment. Caused by improper location of axle spacers or from bent steering stem or frame (Chapter 6).
- [ ] Swingarm bent or twisted. Caused by age (metal fatigue) or impact damage. Renew the arm (Chapter 6).
- [ ] Steering stem bent. Caused by impact damage or by dropping the motorcycle. Renew the steering stem (Chapter 6).
- [ ] Fork tube bent. Disassemble the forks and renew the damaged parts (Chapter 6).
- [ ] Fork oil level uneven. Check and add or drain as necessary (Chapter 6).

Poor shock absorbing qualities

- [ ] Too hard:
  - a) *Fork oil level excessive (Chapter 6).*
  - b) *Fork oil viscosity too high. Use a lighter oil (see the Specifications in Chapter 6).*
  - c) *Fork tube bent. Causes a harsh, sticking feeling (Chapter 6).*
  - d) *Fork internal damage (Chapter 6).*
  - e) *Shock shaft or body bent or damaged (Chapter 6).*
  - f) *Shock internal damage.*
  - g) *Tyre pressure too high (Chapter 1).*
- [ ] Too soft:
  - a) *Fork or shock oil insufficient and/or leaking (Chapter 6).*
  - b) *Fork oil level too low (Chapter 6).*
  - c) *Fork oil viscosity too light (Chapter 6).*
  - d) *Fork springs weak or broken (Chapter 6).*
  - e) *Shock internal damage or leakage (Chapter 6).*

13 Braking problems

Brakes are spongy, don't hold

- [ ] Air in brake line. Caused by inattention to master cylinder fluid level or by leakage. Locate problem and bleed brakes (Chapter 7).
- [ ] Pads or disc worn (Chapters 1 and 7).
- [ ] Brake fluid leak. See paragraph 1.
- [ ] Contaminated pads. Caused by contamination with oil, grease, brake fluid, etc. Clean or renew pads. Clean disc thoroughly with brake cleaner (Chapter 7).
- [ ] Brake fluid deteriorated. Fluid is old or contaminated. Drain system, replenish with new fluid and bleed the system (Chapter 7).
- [ ] Master cylinder internal parts worn or damaged causing fluid to bypass (Chapter 7).
- [ ] Master cylinder bore scratched by foreign material or broken spring. Repair or renew master cylinder (Chapter 7).
- [ ] Disc warped. Renew disc (Chapter 7).

Brake lever or pedal pulsates

- [ ] Disc warped. Renew disc (Chapter 7).
- [ ] Axle bent. Renew axle (Chapter 7).

- [ ] Brake caliper bolts loose (Chapter 7).
- [ ] Brake caliper sliders damaged or sticking (XTZ model), causing caliper to bind. Lubricate the sliders or renew them if they are corroded or bent (Chapter 7).
- [ ] Wheel warped or otherwise damaged (Chapter 7).
- [ ] Wheel bearings damaged or worn (Chapter 7).

Brakes drag

- [ ] Master cylinder piston seized. Caused by wear or damage to piston or cylinder bore (Chapter 7).
- [ ] Lever balky or stuck. Check pivot and lubricate (Chapter 7).
- [ ] Brake caliper binds. Caused by inadequate lubrication (all models) or damage to caliper sliders (XTZ model) (Chapter 7).
- [ ] Brake caliper piston seized in bore. Caused by wear or ingestion of dirt past deteriorated seal (Chapter 7).
- [ ] Brake pad damaged. Pad material separated from backing plate. Usually caused by faulty manufacturing process or from contact with chemicals. Renew pads (Chapter 7).
- [ ] Pads improperly installed (Chapter 7).

14 Electrical problems

Battery dead or weak

☐ Battery faulty. Caused by sulphated plates which are shorted through sedimentation. Also, broken battery terminal making only occasional contact (Chapter 9).

☐ Battery cables making poor contact (Chapter 9).

☐ Load excessive. Caused by addition of high wattage lights or other electrical accessories.

☐ Ignition (main) switch defective. Switch either earths internally or fails to shut off system. Renew the switch (Chapter 9).

☐ Regulator/rectifier defective (Chapter 9).

☐ Alternator stator coil open or shorted (Chapter 9).

☐ Wiring faulty. Wiring earthed or connections loose in ignition, charging or lighting circuits (Chapter 9).

Battery overcharged

☐ Regulator/rectifier defective. Overcharging is noticed when battery gets excessively warm (Chapter 9).

☐ Battery defective. Renew battery (Chapter 9).

☐ Battery amperage too low, wrong type or size. Install manufacturer's specified amp-hour battery to handle charging load (Chapter 9).

Checking engine compression

● Low compression will result in exhaust smoke, heavy oil consumption, poor starting and poor performance. A compression test will provide useful information about an engine's condition and if performed regularly, can give warning of trouble before any other symptoms become apparent.

● A compression gauge will be required, along with an adapter to suit the spark plug hole thread size. Note that the screw-in type gauge/adapter set up is preferable to the rubber cone type.

● Before carrying out the test, first check the valve clearances as described in Chapter 1.

1 Run the engine until it reaches normal operating temperature, then stop it and remove the spark plug(s), taking care not to scald your hands on the hot components.

2 Install the gauge adapter and compression gauge in No. 1 cylinder spark plug hole **(see illustration 1)**.

Screw the compression gauge adapter into the spark plug hole, then screw the gauge into the adapter

3 On kickstart-equipped motorcycles, make sure the ignition switch is OFF, then open the throttle fully and kick the engine over a couple of times until the gauge reading stabilises.

4 On motorcycles with electric start only, the procedure will differ depending on the nature of the ignition system. Flick the engine kill switch (engine stop switch) to OFF and turn the ignition switch ON; open the throttle fully and crank the engine over on the starter motor for a couple of revolutions until the gauge reading stabilises. If the starter will not operate with the kill switch OFF, turn the ignition switch OFF and refer to the next paragraph.

5 Install the spark plugs back into their suppressor caps and arrange the plug electrodes so that their metal bodies are earthed (grounded) against the cylinder head; this is essential to prevent damage to the ignition system as the engine is spun over **(see illustration 2)**. Position the plugs well

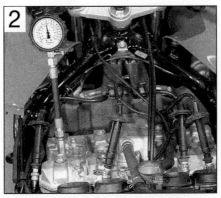

All spark plugs must be earthed (grounded) against the cylinder head

away from the plug holes otherwise there is a risk of atomised fuel escaping from the combustion chambers and igniting. As a safety precaution, cover the top of the valve cover with rag. Now turn the ignition switch ON and kill switch ON, open the throttle fully and crank the engine over on the starter motor for a couple of revolutions until the gauge reading stabilises.

6 After one or two revolutions the pressure should build up to a maximum figure and then stabilise. Take a note of this reading and on multi-cylinder engines repeat the test on the remaining cylinders.

7 The correct pressures are given in Chapter 2 Specifications. If the results fall within the specified range and on multi-cylinder engines all are relatively equal, the engine is in good condition. If there is a marked difference between the readings, or if the readings are lower than specified, inspection of the top-end components will be required.

8 Low compression pressure may be due to worn cylinder bores, pistons or rings, failure of the cylinder head gasket, worn valve seals, or poor valve seating.

9 To distinguish between cylinder/piston wear and valve leakage, pour a small quantity of oil into the bore to temporarily seal the piston rings, then repeat the compression tests **(see illustration 3)**. If the readings show

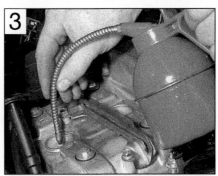

Bores can be temporarily sealed with a squirt of motor oil

a noticeable increase in pressure this confirms that the cylinder bore, piston, or rings are worn. If, however, no change is indicated, the cylinder head gasket or valves should be examined.

10 High compression pressure indicates excessive carbon build-up in the combustion chamber and on the piston crown. If this is the case the cylinder head should be removed and the deposits removed. Note that excessive carbon build-up is less likely with the used on modern fuels.

Checking battery open-circuit voltage

 Warning: The gases produced by the battery are explosive - never smoke or create any sparks in the vicinity of the battery. Never allow the electrolyte to contact your skin or clothing - if it does, wash it off and seek immediate medical attention.

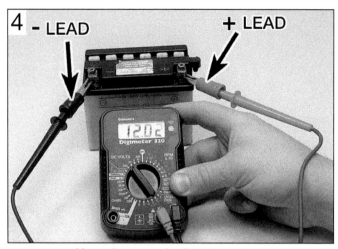

Measuring open-circuit battery voltage

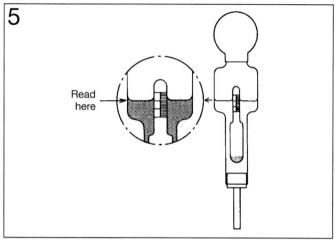

Float-type hydrometer for measuring battery specific gravity

● Before any electrical fault is investigated the battery should be checked.

● You'll need a dc voltmeter or multimeter to check battery voltage. Check that the leads are inserted in the correct terminals on the meter, red lead to positive (+ve), black lead to negative (-ve). Incorrect connections can damage the meter.

● A sound fully-charged 12 volt battery should produce between 12.3 and 12.6 volts across its terminals (12.8 volts for a maintenance-free battery). On machines with a 6 volt battery, voltage should be between 6.1 and 6.3 volts.

1 Set a multimeter to the 0 to 20 volts dc range and connect its probes across the battery terminals. Connect the meter's positive (+ve) probe, usually red, to the battery positive (+ve) terminal, followed by the meter's negative (-ve) probe, usually black, to the battery negative terminal (-ve) **(see illustration 4)**.

2 If battery voltage is low (below 10 volts on a 12 volt battery or below 4 volts on a six volt battery), charge the battery and test the voltage again. If the battery repeatedly goes flat, investigate the motorcycle's charging system.

Checking battery specific gravity (SG)

⚠️ *Warning: The gases produced by the battery are explosive - never smoke or create any sparks in the vicinity of the battery. Never allow the electrolyte to contact your skin or clothing - if it does, wash it off and seek immediate medical attention.*

● The specific gravity check gives an indication of a battery's state of charge.

● A hydrometer is used for measuring specific gravity. Make sure you purchase one which has a small enough hose to insert in the aperture of a motorcycle battery.

● Specific gravity is simply a measure of the electrolyte's density compared with that of water. Water has an SG of 1.000 and fully-charged battery electrolyte is about 26% heavier, at 1.260.

● Specific gravity checks are not possible on maintenance-free batteries. Testing the open-circuit voltage is the only means of determining their state of charge.

1 To measure SG, remove the battery from the motorcycle and remove the first cell cap. Draw

Digital multimeter can be used for all electrical tests

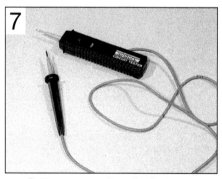

Battery-powered continuity tester

some electrolyte into the hydrometer and note the reading **(see illustration 5)**. Return the electrolyte to the cell and install the cap.

2 The reading should be in the region of 1.260 to 1.280. If SG is below 1.200 the battery needs charging. Note that SG will vary with temperature; it should be measured at 20°C (68°F). Add 0.007 to the reading for every 10°C above 20°C, and subtract 0.007 from the reading for every 10°C below 20°C. Add 0.004 to the reading for every 10°F above 68°F, and subtract 0.004 from the reading for every 10°F below 68°F.

3 When the check is complete, rinse the hydrometer thoroughly with clean water.

Checking for continuity

● The term continuity describes the uninterrupted flow of electricity through an electrical circuit. A continuity check will determine whether an **open-circuit** situation exists.

● Continuity can be checked with an ohmmeter, multimeter, continuity tester or battery and bulb test circuit **(see illustrations 6, 7 and 8)**.

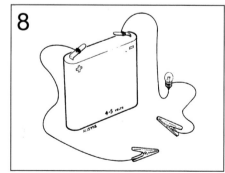

Battery and bulb test circuit

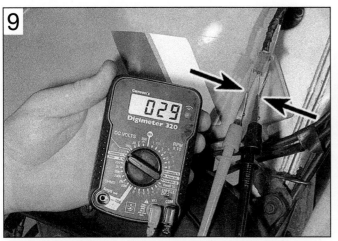

Continuity check of front brake light switch using a meter - note split pins used to access connector terminals

Continuity check of rear brake light switch using a continuity tester

● All of these instruments are self-powered by a battery, therefore the checks are made with the ignition OFF.

● As a safety precaution, always disconnect the battery negative (-ve) lead before making checks, particularly if ignition switch checks are being made.

● If using a meter, select the appropriate ohms scale and check that the meter reads infinity (∞). Touch the meter probes together and check that meter reads zero; where necessary adjust the meter so that it reads zero.

● After using a meter, always switch it OFF to conserve its battery.

Switch checks

1 If a switch is at fault, trace its wiring up to the wiring connectors. Separate the wire connectors and inspect them for security and condition. A build-up of dirt or corrosion here will most likely be the cause of the problem - clean up and apply a water dispersant such as WD40.

2 If using a test meter, set the meter to the ohms x 10 scale and connect its probes across the wires from the switch **(see illustration 9)**. Simple ON/OFF type switches, such as brake light switches, only have two

wires whereas combination switches, like the ignition switch, have many internal links. Study the wiring diagram to ensure that you are connecting across the correct pair of wires. Continuity (low or no measurable resistance - 0 ohms) should be indicated with the switch ON and no continuity (high resistance) with it OFF.

3 Note that the polarity of the test probes doesn't matter for continuity checks, although care should be taken to follow specific test procedures if a diode or solid-state component is being checked.

4 A continuity tester or battery and bulb circuit can be used in the same way. Connect its probes as described above **(see illustration 10)**. The light should come on to indicate continuity in the ON switch position, but should extinguish in the OFF position.

Wiring checks

● Many electrical faults are caused by damaged wiring, often due to incorrect routing or chaffing on frame components.

● Loose, wet or corroded wire connectors can also be the cause of electrical problems, especially in exposed locations.

1 A continuity check can be made on a single length of wire by disconnecting it at each end

and connecting a meter or continuity tester across both ends of the wire **(see illustration 11)**.

2 Continuity (low or no resistance - 0 ohms) should be indicated if the wire is good. If no continuity (high resistance) is shown, suspect a broken wire.

Checking for voltage

● A voltage check can determine whether current is reaching a component.

● Voltage can be checked with a dc voltmeter, multimeter set on the dc volts scale, test light or buzzer **(see illustrations 12 and 13)**. A meter has the advantage of being able to measure actual voltage.

● When using a meter, check that its leads are inserted in the correct terminals on the meter, red to positive (+ve), black to negative (-ve). Incorrect connections can damage the meter.

● A voltmeter (or multimeter set to the dc volts scale) should always be connected in parallel (across the load). Connecting it in series will destroy the meter.

● Voltage checks are made with the ignition ON.

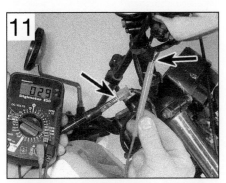

Continuity check of front brake light switch sub-harness

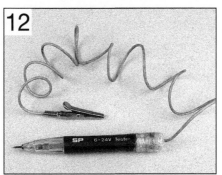

A simple test light can be used for voltage checks

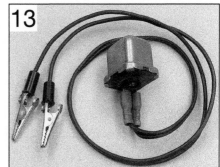

A buzzer is useful for voltage checks

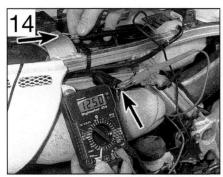

Checking for voltage at the rear brake light power supply wire using a meter . . .

1 First identify the relevant wiring circuit by referring to the wiring diagram at the end of this manual. If other electrical components share the same power supply (ie are fed from the same fuse), take note whether they are working correctly - this is useful information in deciding where to start checking the circuit.
2 If using a meter, check first that the meter leads are plugged into the correct terminals on the meter (see above). Set the meter to the dc volts function, at a range suitable for the battery voltage. Connect the meter red probe (+ve) to the power supply wire and the black probe to a good metal earth (ground) on the motorcycle's frame or directly to the battery negative (-ve) terminal (see illustration 14). Battery voltage should be shown on the meter

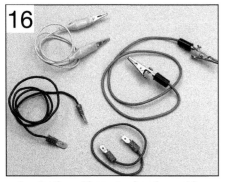

A selection of jumper wires for making earth (ground) checks

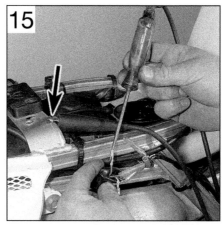

. . . or a test light - note the earth connection to the frame (arrow)

with the ignition switched ON.
3 If using a test light or buzzer, connect its positive (+ve) probe to the power supply terminal and its negative (-ve) probe to a good earth (ground) on the motorcycle's frame or directly to the battery negative (-ve) terminal (see illustration 15). With the ignition ON, the test light should illuminate or the buzzer sound.
4 If no voltage is indicated, work back towards the fuse continuing to check for voltage. When you reach a point where there is voltage, you know the problem lies between that point and your last check point.

Checking the earth (ground)

● Earth connections are made either directly to the engine or frame (such as sensors, neutral switch etc. which only have a positive feed) or by a separate wire into the earth circuit of the wiring harness. Alternatively a short earth wire is sometimes run directly from the component to the motorcycle's frame.
● Corrosion is often the cause of a poor earth connection.
● If total failure is experienced, check the security of the main earth lead from the

negative (-ve) terminal of the battery and also the main earth (ground) point on the wiring harness. If corroded, dismantle the connection and clean all surfaces back to bare metal.
1 To check the earth on a component, use an insulated jumper wire to temporarily bypass its earth connection (see illustration 16). Connect one end of the jumper wire between the earth terminal or metal body of the component and the other end to the motorcycle's frame.
2 If the circuit works with the jumper wire installed, the original earth circuit is faulty. Check the wiring for open-circuits or poor connections. Clean up direct earth connections, removing all traces of corrosion and remake the joint. Apply petroleum jelly to the joint to prevent future corrosion.

Tracing a short-circuit

● A short-circuit occurs where current shorts to earth (ground) bypassing the circuit components. This usually results in a blown fuse.

● A short-circuit is most likely to occur where the insulation has worn through due to wiring chafing on a component, allowing a direct path to earth (ground) on the frame.

1 Remove any bodypanels necessary to access the circuit wiring.
2 Check that all electrical switches in the circuit are OFF, then remove the circuit fuse and connect a test light, buzzer or voltmeter (set to the dc scale) across the fuse terminals. No voltage should be shown.
3 Move the wiring from side to side whilst observing the test light or meter. When the test light comes on, buzzer sounds or meter shows voltage, you have found the cause of the short. It will usually shown up as damaged or burned insulation.
4 Note that the same test can be performed on each component in the circuit, even the switch.

A

ABS (Anti-lock braking system) A system, usually electronically controlled, that senses incipient wheel lockup during braking and relieves hydraulic pressure at wheel which is about to skid.

Aftermarket Components suitable for the motorcycle, but not produced by the motorcycle manufacturer.

Allen key A hexagonal wrench which fits into a recessed hexagonal hole.

Alternating current (ac) Current produced by an alternator. Requires converting to direct current by a rectifier for charging purposes.

Alternator Converts mechanical energy from the engine into electrical energy to charge the battery and power the electrical system.

Ampere (amp) A unit of measurement for the flow of electrical current. Current = Volts ÷ Ohms.

Ampere-hour (Ah) Measure of battery capacity.

Angle-tightening A torque expressed in degrees. Often follows a conventional tightening torque for cylinder head or main bearing fasteners **(see illustration)**.

Angle-tightening cylinder head bolts

Antifreeze A substance (usually ethylene glycol) mixed with water, and added to the cooling system, to prevent freezing of the coolant in winter. Antifreeze also contains chemicals to inhibit corrosion and the formation of rust and other deposits that would tend to clog the radiator and coolant passages and reduce cooling efficiency.

Anti-dive System attached to the fork lower leg (slider) to prevent fork dive when braking hard.

Anti-seize compound A coating that reduces the risk of seizing on fasteners that are subjected to high temperatures, such as exhaust clamp bolts and nuts.

API American Petroleum Institute. A quality standard for 4-stroke motor oils.

Asbestos A natural fibrous mineral with great heat resistance, commonly used in the composition of brake friction materials. Asbestos is a health hazard and the dust created by brake systems should never be inhaled or ingested.

ATF Automatic Transmission Fluid. Often used in front forks.

ATU Automatic Timing Unit. Mechanical device for advancing the ignition timing on early engines.

ATV All Terrain Vehicle. Often called a Quad.

Axial play Side-to-side movement.

Axle A shaft on which a wheel revolves. Also known as a spindle.

B

Backlash The amount of movement between meshed components when one component is held still. Usually applies to gear teeth.

Ball bearing A bearing consisting of a hardened inner and outer race with hardened steel balls between the two races.

Bearings Used between two working surfaces to prevent wear of the components and a build-up of heat. Four types of bearing are commonly used on motorcycles: plain shell bearings, ball bearings, tapered roller bearings and needle roller bearings.

Bevel gears Used to turn the drive through 90º. Typical applications are shaft final drive and camshaft drive **(see illustration)**.

Bevel gears are used to turn the drive through 90°

BHP Brake Horsepower. The British measurement for engine power output. Power output is now usually expressed in kilowatts (kW).

Bias-belted tyre Similar construction to radial tyre, but with outer belt running at an angle to the wheel rim.

Big-end bearing The bearing in the end of the connecting rod that's attached to the crankshaft.

Bleeding The process of removing air from an hydraulic system via a bleed nipple or bleed screw.

Bottom-end A description of an engine's crankcase components and all components contained there-in.

BTDC Before Top Dead Centre in terms of piston position. Ignition timing is often expressed in terms of degrees or millimetres BTDC.

Bush A cylindrical metal or rubber component used between two moving parts.

Burr Rough edge left on a component after machining or as a result of excessive wear.

C

Cam chain The chain which takes drive from the crankshaft to the camshaft(s).

Canister The main component in an evaporative emission control system (California market only); contains activated charcoal granules to trap vapours from the fuel system rather than allowing them to vent to the atmosphere.

Castellated Resembling the parapets along the top of a castle wall. For example, a castellated wheel axle or spindle nut.

Catalytic converter A device in the exhaust system of some machines which converts certain pollutants in the exhaust gases into less harmful substances.

Charging system Description of the components which charge the battery, ie the alternator, rectifer and regulator.

Circlip A ring-shaped clip used to prevent endwise movement of cylindrical parts and shafts. An internal circlip is installed in a groove in a housing; an external circlip fits into a groove on the outside of a cylindrical piece such as a shaft. Also known as a snap-ring.

Clearance The amount of space between two parts. For example, between a piston and a cylinder, between a bearing and a journal, etc.

Coil spring A spiral of elastic steel found in various sizes throughout a vehicle, for example as a springing medium in the suspension and in the valve train.

Compression Reduction in volume, and increase in pressure and temperature, of a gas, caused by squeezing it into a smaller space.

Compression damping Controls the speed the suspension compresses when hitting a bump.

Compression ratio The relationship between cylinder volume when the piston is at top dead centre and cylinder volume when the piston is at bottom dead centre.

Continuity The uninterrupted path in the flow of electricity. Little or no measurable resistance.

Continuity tester Self-powered bleeper or test light which indicates continuity.

Cp Candlepower. Bulb rating commonly found on US motorcycles.

Crossply tyre Tyre plies arranged in a criss-cross pattern. Usually four or six plies used, hence 4PR or 6PR in tyre size codes.

Cush drive Rubber damper segments fitted between the rear wheel and final drive sprocket to absorb transmission shocks **(see illustration)**.

Cush drive rubbers dampen out transmission shocks

D

Degree disc Calibrated disc for measuring piston position. Expressed in degrees.

Dial gauge Clock-type gauge with adapters for measuring runout and piston position. Expressed in mm or inches.

Diaphragm The rubber membrane in a master cylinder or carburettor which seals the upper chamber.

Diaphragm spring A single sprung plate often used in clutches.

Direct current (dc) Current produced by a dc generator.

Decarbonisation The process of removing carbon deposits - typically from the combustion chamber, valves and exhaust port/system.

Detonation Destructive and damaging explosion of fuel/air mixture in combustion chamber instead of controlled burning.

Diode An electrical valve which only allows current to flow in one direction. Commonly used in rectifiers and starter interlock systems.

Disc valve (or rotary valve) A induction system used on some two-stroke engines.

Double-overhead camshaft (DOHC) An engine that uses two overhead camshafts, one for the intake valves and one for the exhaust valves.

Drivebelt A toothed belt used to transmit drive to the rear wheel on some motorcycles. A drivebelt has also been used to drive the camshafts. Drivebelts are usually made of Kevlar.

Driveshaft Any shaft used to transmit motion. Commonly used when referring to the final driveshaft on shaft drive motorcycles.

E

Earth return The return path of an electrical circuit, utilising the motorcycle's frame.

ECU (Electronic Control Unit) A computer which controls (for instance) an ignition system, or an anti-lock braking system.

EGO Exhaust Gas Oxygen sensor. Sometimes called a Lambda sensor.

Electrolyte The fluid in a lead-acid battery.

EMS (Engine Management System) A computer controlled system which manages the fuel injection and the ignition systems in an integrated fashion.

Endfloat The amount of lengthways movement between two parts. As applied to a crankshaft, the distance that the crankshaft can move side-to-side in the crankcase.

Endless chain A chain having no joining link. Common use for cam chains and final drive chains.

EP (Extreme Pressure) Oil type used in locations where high loads are applied, such as between gear teeth.

Evaporative emission control system Describes a charcoal filled canister which stores fuel vapours from the tank rather than allowing them to vent to the atmosphere. Usually only fitted to California models and referred to as an EVAP system.

Expansion chamber Section of two-stroke engine exhaust system so designed to improve engine efficiency and boost power.

F

Feeler blade or gauge A thin strip or blade of hardened steel, ground to an exact thickness, used to check or measure clearances between parts.

Final drive Description of the drive from the transmission to the rear wheel. Usually by chain or shaft, but sometimes by belt.

Firing order The order in which the engine cylinders fire, or deliver their power strokes, beginning with the number one cylinder.

Flooding Term used to describe a high fuel level in the carburettor float chambers, leading to fuel overflow. Also refers to excess fuel in the combustion chamber due to incorrect starting technique.

Free length The no-load state of a component when measured. Clutch, valve and fork spring lengths are measured at rest, without any preload.

Freeplay The amount of travel before any action takes place. The looseness in a linkage, or an assembly of parts, between the initial application of force and actual movement. For example, the distance the rear brake pedal moves before the rear brake is actuated.

Fuel injection The fuel/air mixture is metered electronically and directed into the engine intake ports (indirect injection) or into the cylinders (direct injection). Sensors supply information on engine speed and conditions.

Fuel/air mixture The charge of fuel and air going into the engine. See **Stoichiometric ratio**.

Fuse An electrical device which protects a circuit against accidental overload. The typical fuse contains a soft piece of metal which is calibrated to melt at a predetermined current flow (expressed as amps) and break the circuit.

G

Gap The distance the spark must travel in jumping from the centre electrode to the side electrode in a spark plug. Also refers to the distance between the ignition rotor and the pickup coil in an electronic ignition system.

Gasket Any thin, soft material - usually cork, cardboard, asbestos or soft metal - installed between two metal surfaces to ensure a good seal. For instance, the cylinder head gasket seals the joint between the block and the cylinder head.

Gauge An instrument panel display used to monitor engine conditions. A gauge with a movable pointer on a dial or a fixed scale is an analogue gauge. A gauge with a numerical readout is called a digital gauge.

Gear ratios The drive ratio of a pair of gears in a gearbox, calculated on their number of teeth.

Glaze-busting see **Honing**

Grinding Process for renovating the valve face and valve seat contact area in the cylinder head.

Gudgeon pin The shaft which connects the connecting rod small-end with the piston. Often called a piston pin or wrist pin.

H

Helical gears Gear teeth are slightly curved and produce less gear noise that straight-cut gears. Often used for primary drives.

Installing a Helicoil thread insert in a cylinder head

Helicoil A thread insert repair system. Commonly used as a repair for stripped spark plug threads **(see illustration)**.

Honing A process used to break down the glaze on a cylinder bore (also called glaze-busting). Can also be carried out to roughen a rebored cylinder to aid ring bedding-in.

HT (High Tension) Description of the electrical circuit from the secondary winding of the ignition coil to the spark plug.

Hydraulic A liquid filled system used to transmit pressure from one component to another. Common uses on motorcycles are brakes and clutches.

Hydrometer An instrument for measuring the specific gravity of a lead-acid battery.

Hygroscopic Water absorbing. In motorcycle applications, braking efficiency will be reduced if DOT 3 or 4 hydraulic fluid absorbs water from the air - care must be taken to keep new brake fluid in tightly sealed containers.

I

lbf ft Pounds-force feet. An imperial unit of torque. Sometimes written as ft-lbs.

lbf in Pound-force inch. An imperial unit of torque, applied to components where a very low torque is required. Sometimes written as in-lbs.

IC Abbreviation for Integrated Circuit.

Ignition advance Means of increasing the timing of the spark at higher engine speeds. Done by mechanical means (ATU) on early engines or electronically by the ignition control unit on later engines.

Ignition timing The moment at which the spark plug fires, expressed in the number of crankshaft degrees before the piston reaches the top of its stroke, or in the number of millimetres before the piston reaches the top of its stroke.

Infinity (∞) Description of an open-circuit electrical state, where no continuity exists.

Inverted forks (upside down forks) The sliders or lower legs are held in the yokes and the fork tubes or stanchions are connected to the wheel axle (spindle). Less unsprung weight and stiffer construction than conventional forks.

J

JASO Quality standard for 2-stroke oils.

Joule The unit of electrical energy.

Journal The bearing surface of a shaft.

K

Kickstart Mechanical means of turning the engine over for starting purposes. Only usually fitted to mopeds, small capacity motorcycles and off-road motorcycles.

Kill switch Handebar-mounted switch for emergency ignition cut-out. Cuts the ignition circuit on all models, and additionally prevent starter motor operation on others.

km Symbol for kilometre.

kmh Abbreviation for kilometres per hour.

L

Lambda (λ) sensor A sensor fitted in the exhaust system to measure the exhaust gas oxygen content (excess air factor).

Lapping see **Grinding**.
LCD Abbreviation for Liquid Crystal Display.
LED Abbreviation for Light Emitting Diode.
Liner A steel cylinder liner inserted in a aluminium alloy cylinder block.
Locknut A nut used to lock an adjustment nut, or other threaded component, in place.
Lockstops The lugs on the lower triple clamp (yoke) which abut those on the frame, preventing handlebar-to-fuel tank contact.
Lockwasher A form of washer designed to prevent an attaching nut from working loose.
LT Low Tension Description of the electrical circuit from the power supply to the primary winding of the ignition coil.

M

Main bearings The bearings between the crankshaft and crankcase.
Maintenance-free (MF) battery A sealed battery which cannot be topped up.
Manometer Mercury-filled calibrated tubes used to measure intake tract vacuum. Used to synchronise carburettors on multi-cylinder engines.
Micrometer A precision measuring instrument that measures component outside diameters **(see illustration)**.

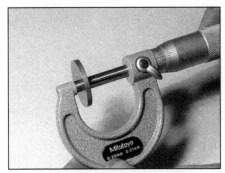

Tappet shims are measured with a micrometer

MON (Motor Octane Number) A measure of a fuel's resistance to knock.
Monograde oil An oil with a single viscosity, eg SAE80W.
Monoshock A single suspension unit linking the swingarm or suspension linkage to the frame.
mph Abbreviation for miles per hour.
Multigrade oil Having a wide viscosity range (eg 10W40). The W stands for Winter, thus the viscosity ranges from SAE10 when cold to SAE40 when hot.
Multimeter An electrical test instrument with the capability to measure voltage, current and resistance. Some meters also incorporate a continuity tester and buzzer.

N

Needle roller bearing Inner race of caged needle rollers and hardened outer race. Examples of uncaged needle rollers can be found on some engines. Commonly used in rear suspension applications and in two-stroke engines.
Nm Newton metres.
NOx Oxides of Nitrogen. A common toxic pollutant emitted by petrol engines at higher temperatures.

O

Octane The measure of a fuel's resistance to knock.
OE (Original Equipment) Relates to components fitted to a motorcycle as standard or replacement parts supplied by the motorcycle manufacturer.
Ohm The unit of electrical resistance. Ohms = Volts ÷ Current.
Ohmmeter An instrument for measuring electrical resistance.
Oil cooler System for diverting engine oil outside of the engine to a radiator for cooling purposes.
Oil injection A system of two-stroke engine lubrication where oil is pump-fed to the engine in accordance with throttle position.
Open-circuit An electrical condition where there is a break in the flow of electricity - no continuity (high resistance).
O-ring A type of sealing ring made of a special rubber-like material; in use, the O-ring is compressed into a groove to provide the sealing action.
Oversize (OS) Term used for piston and ring size options fitted to a rebored cylinder.
Overhead cam (sohc) engine An engine with single camshaft located on top of the cylinder head.
Overhead valve (ohv) engine An engine with the valves located in the cylinder head, but with the camshaft located in the engine block or crankcase.
Oxygen sensor A device installed in the exhaust system which senses the oxygen content in the exhaust and converts this information into an electric current. Also called a Lambda sensor.

P

Plastigauge A thin strip of plastic thread, available in different sizes, used for measuring clearances. For example, a strip of Plastigauge is laid across a bearing journal. The parts are assembled and dismantled; the width of the crushed strip indicates the clearance between journal and bearing.
Polarity Either negative or positive earth (ground), determined by which battery lead is connected to the frame (earth return). Modern motorcycles are usually negative earth.
Pre-ignition A situation where the fuel/air mixture ignites before the spark plug fires. Often due to a hot spot in the combustion chamber caused by carbon build-up. Engine has a tendency to 'run-on'.
Pre-load (suspension) The amount a spring is compressed when in the unloaded state. Preload can be applied by gas, spacer or mechanical adjuster.
Premix The method of engine lubrication on older two-stroke engines. Engine oil is mixed with the petrol in the fuel tank in a specific ratio. The fuel/oil mix is sometimes referred to as "petroil".
Primary drive Description of the drive from the crankshaft to the clutch. Usually by gear or chain.
PS Pfedestärke - a German interpretation of BHP.
PSI Pounds-force per square inch. Imperial measurement of tyre pressure and cylinder pressure measurement.
PTFE Polytetrafluoroethylene. A low friction substance.

Pulse secondary air injection system A process of promoting the burning of excess fuel present in the exhaust gases by routing fresh air into the exhaust ports.

Q

Quartz halogen bulb Tungsten filament surrounded by a halogen gas. Typically used for the headlight **(see illustration)**.

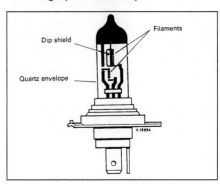

Quartz halogen headlight bulb construction

R

Rack-and-pinion A pinion gear on the end of a shaft that mates with a rack (think of a geared wheel opened up and laid flat). Sometimes used in clutch operating systems.
Radial play Up and down movement about a shaft.
Radial ply tyres Tyre plies run across the tyre (from bead to bead) and around the circumference of the tyre. Less resistant to tread distortion than other tyre types.
Radiator A liquid-to-air heat transfer device designed to reduce the temperature of the coolant in a liquid cooled engine.
Rake A feature of steering geometry - the angle of the steering head in relation to the vertical **(see illustration)**.

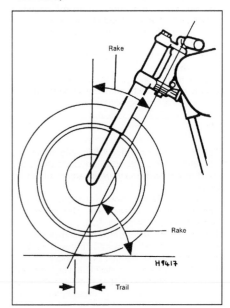

Steering geometry

Rebore Providing a new working surface to the cylinder bore by boring out the old surface. Necessitates the use of oversize piston and rings.

Rebound damping A means of controlling the oscillation of a suspension unit spring after it has been compressed. Resists the spring's natural tendency to bounce back after being compressed.

Rectifier Device for converting the ac output of an alternator into dc for battery charging.

Reed valve An induction system commonly used on two-stroke engines.

Regulator Device for maintaining the charging voltage from the generator or alternator within a specified range.

Relay A electrical device used to switch heavy current on and off by using a low current auxiliary circuit.

Resistance Measured in ohms. An electrical component's ability to pass electrical current.

RON (Research Octane Number) A measure of a fuel's resistance to knock.

rpm revolutions per minute.

Runout The amount of wobble (in-and-out movement) of a wheel or shaft as it's rotated. The amount a shaft rotates 'out-of-true'. The out-of-round condition of a rotating part.

S

SAE (Society of Automotive Engineers) A standard for the viscosity of a fluid.

Sealant A liquid or paste used to prevent leakage at a joint. Sometimes used in conjunction with a gasket.

Service limit Term for the point where a component is no longer useable and must be renewed.

Shaft drive A method of transmitting drive from the transmission to the rear wheel.

Shell bearings Plain bearings consisting of two shell halves. Most often used as big-end and main bearings in a four-stroke engine. Often called bearing inserts.

Shim Thin spacer, commonly used to adjust the clearance or relative positions between two parts. For example, shims inserted into or under tappets or followers to control valve clearances. Clearance is adjusted by changing the thickness of the shim.

Short-circuit An electrical condition where current shorts to earth (ground) bypassing the circuit components.

Skimming Process to correct warpage or repair a damaged surface, eg on brake discs or drums.

Slide-hammer A special puller that screws into or hooks onto a component such as a shaft or bearing; a heavy sliding handle on the shaft bottoms against the end of the shaft to knock the component free.

Small-end bearing The bearing in the upper end of the connecting rod at its joint with the gudgeon pin.

Spalling Damage to camshaft lobes or bearing journals shown as pitting of the working surface.

Specific gravity (SG) The state of charge of the electrolyte in a lead-acid battery. A measure of the electrolyte's density compared with water.

Straight-cut gears Common type gear used on gearbox shafts and for oil pump and water pump drives.

Stanchion The inner sliding part of the front forks, held by the yokes. Often called a fork tube.

Stoichiometric ratio The optimum chemical air/fuel ratio for a petrol engine, said to be 14.7 parts of air to 1 part of fuel.

Sulphuric acid The liquid (electrolyte) used in a lead-acid battery. Poisonous and extremely corrosive.

Surface grinding (lapping) Process to correct a warped gasket face, commonly used on cylinder heads.

T

Tapered-roller bearing Tapered inner race of caged needle rollers and separate tapered outer race. Examples of taper roller bearings can be found on steering heads.

Tappet A cylindrical component which transmits motion from the cam to the valve stem, either directly or via a pushrod and rocker arm. Also called a cam follower.

TCS Traction Control System. An electronically-controlled system which senses wheel spin and reduces engine speed accordingly.

TDC Top Dead Centre denotes that the piston is at its highest point in the cylinder.

Thread-locking compound Solution applied to fastener threads to prevent slackening. Select type to suit application.

Thrust washer A washer positioned between two moving components on a shaft. For example, between gear pinions on gearshaft.

Timing chain See Cam Chain.

Timing light Stroboscopic lamp for carrying out ignition timing checks with the engine running.

Top-end A description of an engine's cylinder block, head and valve gear components.

Torque Turning or twisting force about a shaft.

Torque setting A prescribed tightness specified by the motorcycle manufacturer to ensure that the bolt or nut is secured correctly. Undertightening can result in the bolt or nut coming loose or a surface not being sealed. Overtightening can result in stripped threads, distortion or damage to the component being retained.

Torx key A six-point wrench.

Tracer A stripe of a second colour applied to a wire insulator to distinguish that wire from another one with the same colour insulator. For example, Br/W is often used to denote a brown insulator with a white tracer.

Trail A feature of steering geometry. Distance from the steering head axis to the tyre's central contact point.

Triple clamps The cast components which extend from the steering head and support the fork stanchions or tubes. Often called fork yokes.

Turbocharger A centrifugal device, driven by exhaust gases, that pressurises the intake air. Normally used to increase the power output from a given engine displacement.

TWI Abbreviation for Tyre Wear Indicator. Indicates the location of the tread depth indicator bars on tyres.

U

Universal joint or U-joint (UJ) A double-pivoted connection for transmitting power from a driving to a driven shaft through an angle. Typically found in shaft drive assemblies.

Unsprung weight Anything not supported by the bike's suspension (ie the wheel, tyres, brakes, final drive and bottom (moving) part of the suspension).

V

Vacuum gauges Clock-type gauges for measuring intake tract vacuum. Used for carburettor synchronisation on multi-cylinder engines.

Valve A device through which the flow of liquid, gas or vacuum may be stopped, started or regulated by a moveable part that opens, shuts or partially obstructs one or more ports or passageways. The intake and exhaust valves in the cylinder head are of the poppet type.

Valve clearance The clearance between the valve tip (the end of the valve stem) and the rocker arm or tappet/follower. The valve clearance is measured when the valve is closed. The correct clearance is important - if too small the valve won't close fully and will burn out, whereas if too large noisy operation will result.

Valve lift The amount a valve is lifted off its seat by the camshaft lobe.

Valve timing The exact setting for the opening and closing of the valves in relation to piston position.

Vernier caliper A precision measuring instrument that measures inside and outside dimensions. Not quite as accurate as a micrometer, but more convenient.

VIN Vehicle Identification Number. Term for the bike's engine and frame numbers.

Viscosity The thickness of a liquid or its resistance to flow.

Volt A unit for expressing electrical "pressure" in a circuit. Volts = current x ohms.

W

Water pump A mechanically-driven device for moving coolant around the engine.

Watt A unit for expressing electrical power. Watts = volts x current.

Wear limit see **Service limit**

Wet liner A liquid-cooled engine design where the pistons run in liners which are directly surrounded by coolant **(see illustration)**.

Wet liner arrangement

Wheelbase Distance from the centre of the front wheel to the centre of the rear wheel.

Wiring harness or loom Describes the electrical wires running the length of the motorcycle and enclosed in tape or plastic sheathing. Wiring coming off the main harness is usually referred to as a sub harness.

Woodruff key A key of semi-circular or square section used to locate a gear to a shaft. Often used to locate the alternator rotor on the crankshaft.

Wrist pin Another name for gudgeon or piston pin.

Note: *References throughout this index are in the form - "Chapter number" • "page number"*

Preserving Our Motoring Heritage

> *The Model J Duesenberg Derham Tourster. Only eight of these magnificent cars were ever built – this is the only example to be found outside the United States of America*

Almost every car you've ever loved, loathed or desired is gathered under one roof at the Haynes Motor Museum. Over 300 immaculately presented cars and motorbikes represent every aspect of our motoring heritage, from elegant reminders of bygone days, such as the superb Model J Duesenberg to curiosities like the bug-eyed BMW Isetta. There are also many old friends and flames. Perhaps you remember the 1959 Ford Popular that you did your courting in? The magnificent 'Red Collection' is a spectacle of classic sports cars including AC, Alfa Romeo, Austin Healey, Ferrari, Lamborghini, Maserati, MG, Riley, Porsche and Triumph.

A Perfect Day Out

Each and every vehicle at the Haynes Motor Museum has played its part in the history and culture of Motoring. Today, they make a wonderful spectacle and a great day out for all the family. Bring the kids, bring Mum and Dad, but above all bring your camera to capture those golden memories for ever. You will also find an impressive array of motoring memorabilia, a comfortable 70 seat video cinema and one of the most extensive transport book shops in Britain. The Pit Stop Cafe serves everything from a cup of tea to wholesome, home-made meals or, if you prefer, you can enjoy the large picnic area nestled in the beautiful rural surroundings of Somerset.

> *John Haynes O.B.E., Founder and Chairman of the museum at the wheel of a Haynes Light 12.*

> *The 1936 490cc sohc-engined International Norton – well known for its racing success*

The Museum is situated on the A359 Yeovil to Frome road at Sparkford, just off the A303 in Somerset. It is about 40 miles south of Bristol, and 25 minutes drive from the M5 intersection at Taunton.
Open 9.30am - 5.30pm (10.00am - 4.00pm Winter) 7 days a week, *except Christmas Day, Boxing Day and New Years Day*
Special rates available for schools, coach parties and outings Charitable Trust No. 292048